Franchise Opportunities

HANDBOOK

A Complete Guide for People Who Want to Start Their Own Franchise

REVISED EDITION

by
LaVerne L. Ludden, Ed.D.

Park Avenue

Franchise Opportunities Handbook

A Complete Guide for People Who Want to Start Their Own Franchise
Revised Edition

© 1999, JIST Works, Inc.
Published by JIST Works, Inc.
720 North Park Avenue
Indianapolis, IN 46202-3490
Phone: 1-800-648-JIST   Fax: 1-800-JIST-FAX   E-mail: jistworks@aol.com
World Wide Web Address: http://www.jist.com

Interior Design by Debbie Berman

You can find additional JIST books and information on how to order them at the back of this book.

Library of Congress Cataloging-in-Publication Data

Ludden, LaVerne, 1949-   .
      Franchise opportunities handbook / by LaVerne Ludden. -- 2nd ed.
         p.   cm.
      "First edition was based on a directory of franchisors compiled by
the U.S. Department of Commerce"--Introd.
      Includes bibliographical references and index.
      1. Franchises (Retail trade)--United States--Handbooks, manuals,
etc.   2. Franchises (Retail trade)--United States--Directories.
   HF5429.235.U5L83   1998
   381'.13'02573--dc21   98-38529
                                                                 CIP

Printed in the United States of America.
02 01 00 99   9 8 7 6 5 4 3 2 1

ISBN 1-57112-091-2

Contents

Franchise Company Data (by Field)

APPENDIX A

Contact Information for the U.S. Small Business Administration 293

APPENDIX B

Directory of Small Business Development Centers 299

APPENDIX C

Service Corps of Retired Executives 357

APPENDIX D

Bibliography of Small Business Publications 375

APPENDIX E

Addresses of Additional Franchisors 379

Index of Franchising Participants

Introduction

This is the second edition of this book. The first edition was based on a directory of franchisors compiled by the U.S. Department of Commerce. This directory is no longer published by the government. However, the previous edition of this book was so popular that we decided to publish an updated version. As a result we initiated a survey to gather more current information about franchisors. The popularity of franchising is probably related to the enthusiasm shown by buyers and readers of this book.

Franchising is not only popular but also an important part of the United States economy. Just how important is illustrated by the following statistics compiled by the International Franchise Association, a non-profit trade association whose members are franchisors.

➤ Sales from franchisees in the United States are about $1 trillion a year.

➤ Franchise operations account for almost 50 percent of all retail sales.

➤ About 1 out of 12 businesses is a franchised operation—almost 600,000 businesses.

➤ Franchise establishments employ more than 8 million people.

➤ A franchised business has an average of 8 to 14 employees.

➤ A new franchise establishment is opened every 8 minutes of a business day.

➤ Studies have shown that 86 percent of franchise operations have the same owner five years after starting business and less than 3 percent failed over that same time.

These figures suggest why franchising is such a powerful economic force. What accounts for franchising's popularity? Perhaps this question can be answered by the results of a survey conducted by the Gallup Organization for the International Franchise Association. According to the poll, franchise owners had an average personal income of $124,290 in 1991, and 94 percent of the owners consider their operations to be successful. In addition, 75 percent of franchise owners indicated that their expectations for personal satisfaction in operating the franchise were met or exceeded.

Financial rewards and feelings of success experienced by franchise owners are attractive to potential business owners. People considering self-employment frequently regard a franchise as a practical option for starting a business. The purpose of this book is to help individuals who are thinking about buying a franchise make a wise decision. *Franchise Opportunities Handbook* is unique because of the resources it offers.

First and foremost, this book is a directory that lists more than 1,000 franchisors. However, it is far more than a directory. It provides valuable information about starting a business and selecting a franchise. You should find this guide to be a valuable reference in getting started on the road to self-employment.

Chapter 1 provides an introduction to self-employment. The chapter contains an assessment guide that helps you decide whether self-employment is an appropriate career choice. You also discover how to form your own business, write a business plan, finance the business, create a business team, and set up operations. This chapter can be a useful resource even if you decide not to buy a franchise but to create an original business instead.

Chapter 2 provides basic information about franchising. It defines terms commonly used, explains the reasons that businesses franchise their operations, and describes the advantages and disadvantages of starting a franchised business. An important feature is the information it provides for evaluating and selecting a franchise. It identifies the materials that franchisors are required to give you. This information is essential to evaluate the data from the many franchisors listed in the *Handbook*.

Chapter 3 comprises the main body of the book. This chapter is a directory that lists more than 1,000 franchises. Each franchise listed contains a description of the operation, contact information, number of franchises, time in business, date began franchising, equity capital needed, franchise fee, royalty fee, advertising co-op fee, financial assistance, managerial assistance, and training assistance. Since this information changes over time, it is important to verify the information when you first contact a franchisor. Please consider any difference in information to be legitimate and not due to a franchisor misleading you. In fact, a book this complex can have errors that are the result of honest mistakes made in its publication.

There are several appendixes containing a directory of resources that can be used by aspiring entrepreneurs. Appendix A lists all offices of the Small Business Administration (SBA). This is the branch of government that provides support, resources, loans, and other assistance to small business owners.

Appendix B contains a list of all Small Business Development Centers (SBDC). These organizations are funded by the SBA for the purpose of providing small business owners—or would-be owners—with technical assistance in the operation of their businesses. Appendix C includes a directory of Service Corps of Retired Executives (SCORE) offices. SCORE is a group of retired executives who volunteer their time to assist new and established entrepreneurs with business management and operational issues. Appendix D contains a bibliography of books available from the Small Business Administration. All of these resources can prove valuable to the reader in investigating the potential for buying and operating a franchise. You can keep up-to-date on information about all of these resources—plus discover other useful information—through the SBA Web site at www.sba.gov.

This book tries to take an open-mined view about franchise ownership. We think that you will find this book a helpful guide in identifying and choosing a franchise. Some readers may find that the greatest value of the book is the help it provides in the decision not to buy a franchise. The approach taken in this book is to help you make the decision that is most beneficial to you personally. We believe that for many, owning a franchise is the best business decision they can make, but for others, it is the worst decision. We have sought to provide sufficient information to help you make the best one possible. Good luck with your decision.

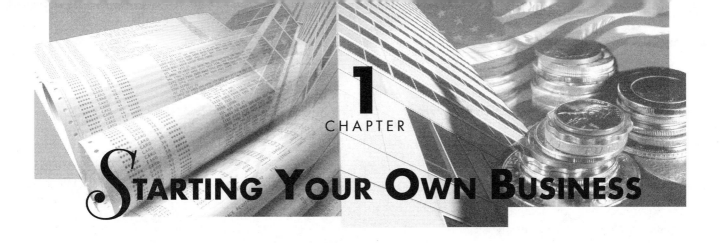

CHAPTER 1

STARTING YOUR OWN BUSINESS

An entrepreneur looks for an opportunity for financial growth and seeks to achieve certain business goals. Entrepreneurs use different styles and methods in choosing and establishing a business. Some entrepreneurs prefer to institute their own business from the ground floor. Others feel more comfortable buying a business started by someone else. Still others find that it is more suitable to purchase a franchise and follow a model successfully used by many other business people. There are basics that all entrepreneurs, regardless of style, need to know when starting a business. The purpose of this chapter is to provide this essential information. This chapter is based on the information found in the book *Mind Your Own Business: Getting Started as an Entrepreneur*[1]. For more detailed information about starting your own business, you should read this book.

In this chapter, you learn how to create and operate a successful new enterprise. The subjects include deciding whether to start a business, selecting the right legal structure for your business, preparing a business plan, financing your business, and choosing a business team. As you read this chapter, you will learn whether starting your own business or buying a franchise is more suitable for you.

Entrepreneurship as a Career

Nearly one million individuals start their own businesses every year. This section helps you answer the important question, "Should I go into business for myself?" Whether the answer is yes, no, or maybe, you will be better prepared to make an important career decision after reading this section.

People decide to start their own business for a variety of reasons. A person seldom has just one reason for starting a business. Typically several motivational factors are at work. Here are a few common reasons for starting a business.

Independence. Many people become self-employed because they believe self-employment will offer them independence and control over their own work. This is limited by constraints placed on you by customers, suppliers, employees, and others. But these constraints affect all businesses. As a self-employed individual, you have the freedom to make decisions about how these forces will affect the operation of your business.

Job satisfaction. Entrepreneurs gain a great deal of satisfaction from their jobs. They know that they are responsible for their own success and failure.

Financial achievement. Most people become self-employed for financial gain. This may be accomplished through a high-paying salary or by a major accumulation of wealth.

Career opportunity. Some people start their own business because they find it a desirable career opportunity. They perceive it as a high-status career that is enjoyable and challenging.

Myths about Small Business

A realistic assessment of your interest in self-employment requires that you examine four common myths about entrepreneurship. In this section each myth is explained, and you are asked to develop conclusions about the impact each might have on the business you start.

---

[1]LaVerne L. Ludden and Bonnie R. Maitlen, *Mind Your Own Business: Getting Started as an Entrepreneur*, Indianapolis, Indiana: JIST Works, Inc., 1994.

Myth #1: Entrepreneurs are born, not made.

Some people feel that they just aren't made to be entrepreneurs. Research on entrepreneurship has shown that experience and knowledge are far more critical to success than are personal characteristics. Your business knowledge and experience will contribute to your mastery of self-employment. You can increase your ability to have a successful small business by learning as much as you can about starting and managing small businesses.

Myth #2: The rate of small business failures is extremely high.

Most people have read statistics that indicate a high rate of failure among new enterprises. Rates as high as 80 percent of businesses failing within the first five years have been reported. A report released from the Department of Commerce indicates that fewer than 1 percent of all businesses were forced into bankruptcy during the period of 1972-1986. The number of new businesses that close within a five-year period may approach 50 percent, but the reasons for closure are not necessarily due to financial failures. The financial risk involved in starting a new business is therefore not as great as might be expected.

Myth #3: You need money to start your own business.

Adequate financing is important for your new business. One of the major reasons that new businesses fail is poor financial planning for business needs. However, a wide variety of methods exist for obtaining financial resources and controlling costs. Not all funds have to come from your own pocket. Also, many service-related businesses can be started with little investment.

Myth #4: Most small businesses fail because of uncontrollable factors.

A survey conducted by Minolta and reported in *USA Today* identified five major reasons for small business failure. These are (1) a lack of capital, (2) a lack of business knowledge, (3) poor management, (4) inadequate planning, and (5) inexperience. Such factors are controllable. To avoid potential problems that might affect your business, you must do adequate planning.

Why Self-Employment Is Easier Today

Self-employment today is easier than it has been in the past. This should be encouraging to those who are thinking about becoming entrepreneurs. Several reasons exist for this positive environment for self-employment, including resources that can help you start your business.

Capitalization. A number of sources currently exist for venture capital. Additionally, the home equity loan makes it possible for some individuals to invest in a small business opportunity using tax-deductible interest on their loans.

Lump-sum distributions. With a number of companies offering early retirement or the opportunity to sever employment, many individuals are given a severance package or pension benefit as a lump-sum distribution. This provides capital to invest in a business venture.

Computers and other electronic devices. Computers and other electronic devices, such as copiers, voice mail, and fax machines, make it easier for someone to conduct business. These computer and technical resources were unaffordable to small firms just a few short years ago.

Franchises. With the growing popularity of franchises, individuals can buy into an existing business without developing an original service or product. Some people prefer working with a tested idea instead of starting a business of their own.

State-wide programs for small business development. A number of state and national programs are designed to help small businesses. Some of these programs are described in the next section.

Help for Small Business Development

State economic development programs. Many state governments support small business development and have special programs to help small businesses. Those who make use of such resources will have a better chance of success in an adverse economy than those who do not. Check with your state Department of Commerce to see what programs are available in your geographic location. They can explain options such as training programs, incubator programs, and economic development incentives.

Small Business Administration. The federal government's Small Business Administration (SBA) has a variety of programs to assist small business owners. This includes special programs that provide management and technical assistance. In addition, loans and grants are available for qualified individuals. A list of SBA offices is contained in Appendix A.

Entrepreneurial Career Assessment

The *Entrepreneurial Career Assessment* Form is designed to introduce you to many of the characteristics of successful entrepreneurs. This self-evaluation can provide you with some guidance about the appropriateness of an entrepreneurial career for you. For the evaluation to be effective, you should respond to the questions in an honest and accurate manner.

Read the statements carefully, interpreting each one in the context of your personal experience. Determine how strongly you agree or disagree with the accuracy of the statement in describing yourself. Use the following scale to indicate your responses. Write the most appropriate number in the box before each statement.

Strongly Agree	5
	4
Somewhat Agree	3
	2
Strongly Disagree	1

____ 1. I am willing to work 50 hours or more per week regularly.

____ 2. My family will support my going into business.

____ 3. I am willing to accept both financial and career risks when necessary.

____ 4. I don't need all the fringe benefits provided by conventional employment.

____ 5. I would like to take full responsibility for the successes and failures of my business.

____ 6. I would experience more financial success by operating my own business.

____ 7. I feel a great deal of pride when I complete a project successfully.

____ 8. I have a high energy level that can be maintained over a long time.

____ 9. I enjoy controlling my own work assignments and making all decisions that affect my work.

____ 10. I believe that I am primarily responsible for my own successes and failures.

____ 11. I have a strong desire to achieve positive results even when they require a great deal of additional effort.

____ 12. I have a good understanding of how to manage a business.

____ 13. I can function in ambiguous situations.

____ 14. One or both of my parents were entrepreneurs.

____ 15. I believe that my abilities and skills are greater than those of most of my coworkers.

____ 16. People trust me and consider me honest and reliable.

____ 17. I always try to complete every project I start, regardless of obstacles and difficulties.

____ 18. I am willing to do something even when other people laugh or belittle me for doing it.

____ 19. I can make decisions quickly.

____ 20. I have a good network of friends, professionals, and business acquaintances.

____ **TOTAL**

Total the numbers you placed before the statements and enter the total in the space provided. Then refer to the following chart to determine a general assessment of your suitability for self-employment.

Score Assessment

80–100 — You have outstanding potential to be an entrepreneur.

60–79 — You have satisfactory potential to be an entrepreneur.

40–59 — Self-employment may not be an appropriate career for you.

0–39 — Probably you should avoid an entrepreneurial career.

Characteristics of an Entrepreneur

The following list describes some common characteristics of an entrepreneur. The number(s) after each characteristic indicates the related statement(s) in the assessment form you just used. This list interprets the form qualitatively and is based on research about entrepreneurs. Arriving at a conclusive portrait of a typical entrepreneur is very difficult. Therefore, you may score low on the assessment and still succeed as an entrepreneur.

Works hard (Statements 1 and 8). Self-employment requires a great deal of time and effort. The entrepreneur must perform a wide variety of time-consuming tasks. It is typical to put in 50- to 60-hour work weeks regularly.

Has family support (Statement 2). A successful entrepreneur needs family support. Stress caused by finances and time requirements can create disruptions in family relationships. The more positive support you receive from your family, the more you can concentrate on making the business a success.

Takes risks (Statement 3). Entrepreneurs are risk takers. They risk their careers, time, and money in order to make a success of their businesses. The entrepreneur typically sees a risk as a controllable situation. To be successful in self-

employment, you should feel comfortable taking reasonable risks.

Sacrifices employment benefits (Statement 4). Benefits that you will find missing as an entrepreneur include a regular paycheck, fringe benefits, a nice office, secretarial assistance, equipment, and other features of employment you have grown to expect. These are no longer available unless you pay for them yourself.

Is independent (Statements 5 and 9). Entrepreneurs like being independent and in control of situations. Although being independent may not be a major concern for you, it is certainly an aspect of self-employment that you need to feel comfortable with.

Wants financial success (Statement 6). A primary motivation most entrepreneurs have is the need to achieve financial success. The desire for financial success provides motivational drive for the self-employed person.

Is energetic (Statements 1 and 8). Self-employment requires long work hours. The entrepreneur must have a high energy level to respond to the job's demands. In fact, an entrepreneur will often be energized by the work that is demanded and finds an energy loss when "relaxing." You will need stamina that allows you to work 12 to 16 hours per day, 6 to 7 days per week, and 52 weeks per year. Expect long work hours especially when your business is getting started.

Has an internal locus of control (Statement 10). Successful entrepreneurs have an internal *locus of control,* or inner sense of responsibility, for the outcome of a venture. To be an entrepreneur, you should have a strong sense of being a "victor" who is responsible for your actions.

Has a need to achieve (Statements 7 and 11). Entrepreneurs have a strong need for achievement. They strive to excel and accomplish objectives that are quite high. If you want to become an entrepreneur, you should be willing to set high goals for yourself and enjoy striving to achieve those goals.

Has business experience (Statement 12). An entrepreneur should have extensive business experience to be successful. General management experience is beneficial because an entrepreneur must know something about all types of management.

Has a self-employed parent as a role model (Statement 14). Entrepreneurs are more likely to have a parent—particularly a father—who is self-employed. A parent's inspiration and knowledge about operating a business can contribute to an entrepreneur's success. If you have a parent who is self-employed, consider this a plus for your own success as an entrepreneur.

Has self-confidence (Statements 10, 15, and 18). An important characteristic of entrepreneurs is self-confidence. You need to believe in yourself. Your belief will help you overcome the problems that inevitably affect all self-employed persons at some point in their careers.

Has integrity (Statement 16). People often cite honesty and integrity as characteristics of entrepreneurs. Customers do not want to deal with business owners who are dishonest and unethical. You should feel positive about your ethical treatment of people and be committed to conducting your business with the utmost integrity.

Has determination (Statement 17). One of the most important characteristics of entrepreneurs is determination. This trait is closely related to self-confidence. The more you believe in yourself, the more likely you are to continue to struggle for success when faced with tremendous obstacles.

Adapts to change (Statements 13 and 19). A new business changes rapidly, so an entrepreneur must be able to adapt to change. The skills required for adaptation to change are the capacity to solve problems, the ability to make quick decisions, and the ability to learn from your experiences.

Has a good network of professionals (Statement 20). An entrepreneur has a good network of professionals. This network provides access to those who can be consulted for advice, information, and referrals. You should have an extensive network of professionals to whom you can turn for assistance.

Starting a Business

People often think of an entrepreneur as someone who has a new idea for a product or service and then creates a business to sell that new product or service. But being an entrepreneur doesn't always mean creating a new product or service. You can buy an existing business or purchase a franchise.

Starting Your Own Business

You might consider starting your own business if you have a new product or service or can add value to existing business concepts. Concepts for a new business may originate from your current employment or ideas refined from other people, hobbies, or spontaneously. Here is a list of advantages and disadvantages to starting your own business.

Advantages

➤ Starting your own business gives you more freedom in what you do and how you do it.

➤ Launching a new business avoids inheriting problems from a previous owner or facing restrictions from a franchisor.

➤ Starting your own business can usually be done with a smaller amount of capital.

➤ Owning the business you start and watching it grow can be very satisfying.

➤ Basing your own business on a new idea and a well-thought-out plan can be quite profitable.

Disadvantages

➤ It generally takes more time for a new business to become profitable.

➤ During the early stages of a new business, you may need to invest a great amount of time and money.

➤ A new business based on an innovative product or service may need additional capital during the start-up period to cover the time required to educate potential buyers about the new product or service.

➤ Starting a new business requires a number of business skills, such as time management, marketing, budgeting, goal setting, and sometimes specific technical skills.

Buying a Business

You might consider buying an existing business if you want to be a business owner but don't want to go through the pains of starting your own business. Some individuals may be uncertain of how to do this, or they lack (or think they lack) the creativity, talent, or special skills to start their own business. This option may be quite practical for someone leaving a large corporation, a person seeking semiretirement, and an owner of other businesses wanting to expand. There are a number of advantages and disadvantages to buying an existing business.

Advantages

➤ Purchasing a business usually takes much less time and effort than starting a business.

➤ An existing business already has a market and customer base.

➤ Such a business might have a staff and experts in place to work the plan.

➤ The business has a track record that can be reviewed and evaluated for future profitability.

➤ If the business is already profitable, it is possible to earn a profit from the beginning.

➤ If the established business is somewhat successful, the risk is considerably less.

➤ It is sometimes possible to get a real bargain by buying an existing business.

Disadvantages

➤ A business for sale may be on the market for internal problems known to the experienced seller, but not easily perceived by an inexperienced buyer.

➤ Even after you have done your homework to find out if an existing business has the right

potential, there are no guarantees that the business will continue to be profitable.

➤ You buy the bad as well as the good about an existing business. It might not be structured the way you would like it to be and have workforce problems, a poor location, or accounts receivable that are high and largely uncollectible.

➤ Most small businesses are successful because of the talent and skills of their owners. You have no way of knowing how the business will be affected by the owner's departure.

➤ The inventory may have book value but be worthless.

➤ Buying an existing business might be more expensive than starting one of your own.

Buying a Franchise

To become self-employed, you might consider buying a franchise. A *franchise* is a product or idea that can be purchased from another person or company along with the expertise to start and operate the business. The buyer of a franchise is called a *franchisee,* and the seller is called a *franchisor.* Consider the following advantages and disadvantages to buying a franchise.

Advantages

➤ A franchise product or service has already been developed and field-tested.

➤ A franchise often has instant name recognition.

➤ The franchisor provides assistance in starting the franchise business.

➤ The franchisor can often assist the franchisee in obtaining financing for the new business.

➤ The franchisor can often provide support through consultants and trainers.

➤ Other franchisees can offer advice, feedback on their experience, and practical suggestions.

➤ A franchise business can get high-volume purchase prices for products.

Disadvantages

➤ You will pay a substantial fee for the franchise.

➤ As a business owner, you give up a great deal of control when you operate a franchise.

➤ You usually have to maintain the business in accordance with standards set by the franchisor, and this can cost extra money.

➤ The franchisor might terminate your franchise if you don't abide by standards, or might be able to buy back the franchise from you whenever the franchisor wants.

➤ You are dependent on the success of the franchisor. Some franchisees develop an extremely strong business, but when their franchisor goes out of business, they find it difficult or sometimes impossible to continue operation.

Legal Forms of Organization

When you start a new business, you must determine its legal status. Each state has specific legal requirements you must meet to conduct business in the state. You will need to research what these requirements are for your state. You can get this information from the Secretary of State, a local attorney, certified public accountant, or government organizations that consult with small businesses.

Legal Status of an Organization

To do business, an organization must have one of four basic types of legal status: sole proprietorship, partnership, limited partnership, or corporation. There are legal and tax issues to consider for each entity. These will be explained in this section.

Sole proprietorship. A sole proprietorship is the simplest legal status for a business and its taxes. When you start a sole proprietorship, you don't need to create a new entity or shift assets. You merely segregate a portion of your assets and dedicate them for business use. You also may be required to file a notice of "Doing Business As" (DBA) with a state or local agency.

Partnership. According to the IRS, a partnership may be a syndicate, group, pool, joint venture, or some other unincorporated organization that carries on a venture, business, or financial operation. The intentions of a partnership are joint ownership, mutual contribution of capital and services, shared control of the business, and a sharing of profits and losses.

Limited partnership. Two or more persons can form a limited partnership. Typically a certificate for a limited partnership must be filed with the Secretary of State or some other state agency. A limited partnership has one or more general partners, who are involved in the daily management of the business, and at least one limited partner, who is involved as an investor.

Corporation. A corporation is a business entity created under state law. The corporation must have associates and a purpose for carrying on business. The corporation issues shares of stock to investors. Stock provides the legal arrangement for stipulating how profits are divided. Corporations must follow specific state laws for corporations and file annual reports.

Subchapter S corporation. A Subchapter S Corporation (commonly called an "S Corporation") is a corporation that files for IRS status as an S Corporation. In this type of corporation, all income is taxed through the shareholders rather than the corporation.

Selecting a Legal Structure

You will need to choose the best legal status for your new business. In making this determination, you should consider the following questions:

1. What are your personal skills and preferences?

2. What kind of organization will your business be?

3. What taxes will you need to pay?

Personal Skills and Preferences

Your skills and preferences may influence your selection of a legal structure for your business. You

may sense that they are more suitable for one type of legal structure than another.

To operate a sole proprietorship, a person must have general management skills. You need to feel comfortable in the areas of marketing, sales, accounting, finance, human resource management, customer service, facility management, inventory control, and so on. Because a sole proprietor manages the entire operation, the person needs this broad range of expertise.

A partnership is more suitable when you need others with specialized skills you don't have. If you find partners with skills that complement your own skills, you will create a stronger business.

A corporation requires someone who works well in a team environment. You and other working members of the corporation will have to function as an effective work team.

Organizational Considerations

To determine the best structure for your business, you should consider the following organizational considerations.

Personal liability. Persons who start a business are often interested in how they can insulate their personal assets from the operation of the business. Corporate shareholders are usually not liable for the corporation's debts or liabilities, making this one of the least risky options. Statutes in many states provide that if a judgment is made against one member of a partnership, the assets of the sued partner can be tapped, but the assets of partners who have not been sued cannot be accessed. However, one partner may obligate another without the other's approval. A sole proprietorship is not a separate legal entity, and both an entrepreneur's and a spouse's assets can be at risk.

Separate legal entity. A second important consideration is whether the organization will be a legal entity apart from the individual owners. A corporation is a separate legal entity and may sue or be sued, hold and receive property, and enter into contracts in its own name. Partnerships can entangle personal and business matters and assets. A sole proprietorship is not a separate legal entity.

Formality of business conduct. A third point to consider is how formal you want the management of the operation to be. A corporation is managed through a board of directors. The directors must be elected by the corporation shareholders. The corporation must follow articles of incorporation and bylaws, hold regular meetings of its shareholders and directors, and keep accurate records and minutes of all proceedings. Management and control of the limited partnership are placed in the hands of the general partners. A partnership is like a sole proprietorship to the extent that there are few formal restrictions on how the business is managed. The partners, however, must comply with any partnership agreement they establish. A sole proprietorship does not have to follow formalized procedures in its operation. The proprietor is free to make his or her own decisions and choose the businesses and locations in which he or she wants to operate.

Continuity of existence. A fourth consideration is how the business will continue if one of the principals of the business leaves the organization or dies. A corporation is a separate entity. Therefore, it continues to exist regardless of the resignation or death of a principal. The withdrawal or death of a partner may cause a limited partnership to cease and does cause a partnership to cease. If a sole proprietor dies, the business is terminated.

Transferability of interests. A fifth consideration is whether business interests can be transferred or sold. The corporation is the most flexible business form for transferring interests, because the property can be divided into any desired number of shares. Unless there is a different stipulation in an agreement, a general partner in a limited partnership—or a partner in a partnership—may transfer partnership interests and grant the rights to the transferee only with the consent of all other partners. A sole proprietor has complete freedom to sell or transfer any portion of his or her business assets. Legally, however, there is no business to sell because it doesn't exist without the proprietor.

Expense of organization. A sixth consideration is the amount of time and money you want to invest in forming a new business. Setting up a corporation can become expensive with the various required fees and start-up costs. Other possible expenses include fees to set up the formal structure, annual franchise taxes, costs to do business in other states, fees for preparing an annual tax return, and costs for reports required by the state. A limited partnership must follow statutory formalities, and compliance will incur certain expenses like filing fees and possible legal expenses. A general partnership can usually be organized with little formality or expense. A proprietorship usually has little or no expense.

Sources of operating capital. A seventh consideration is capital. You need to identify your capital needs, your resources, and potential sources of capital. If you can provide all of the capital needed to start the business successfully, you can select whatever legal structure meets your other needs and preferences. If, however, your financial resources are limited, you will need to consider your options for getting capital from other sources. The corporation is the most flexible structure to obtain operating capital. A corporation can issue common or preferred stock and issue bonds to raise capital. A limited partnership can increase capital resources by using resources from all of the general partners and from limited partners who provide capital but do not manage the partnership. A partnership can only access capital available from the partners. A sole proprietorship is usually limited to individual funds in combination with loans from various sources.

Tax considerations. You need to consider taxes before you determine your best form of business organization. The income earned by a corporation is taxed at a corporate rate rather than individual rate. The corporation's payment of corporate taxes and the shareholders' payment of individual taxes on dividends amount to double taxation. You can avoid double taxation by filing for Subchapter S status with the IRS. A certified public accountant (CPA) can advise how a tax is calculated for a Subchapter S corporation. Federal income tax is paid by the partners at individual tax rates. For tax purposes, the income a sole proprietorship earns is added to any other taxable income of the individual.

More than 70 percent of all businesses in the United States are sole proprietorships. This makes the sole proprietorship the most popular legal structure. Partnerships account for 10 percent, and corporations for a little over 19 percent of all businesses. Corporations, however, generate 90 percent of all American business revenues. This suggests that a corporation is the most successful form of legal structure because it provides the greatest opportunity for growth.

Writing a Business Plan

A business plan is a document that contains planning information about all aspects of a new enterprise. This section describes why and how to develop a business plan. You also learn the basics of a business plan and its main parts.

Goals of a Business Plan

New business owners tend to act with little thought about the need for planning. A reason is that planning can be hard and tedious work that produces no immediate response. A new venture needs a business plan for three basic reasons.

1. **Evaluate success.** Developing an entrepreneurial idea can generate much excitement and enthusiasm. With these emotions, you can overlook potential difficulties in starting a business. Creating a business plan forces you to look past the enthusiasm and examine carefully the business venture you are considering.

2. **Provide direction.** A business plan provides a blueprint for managing your new business. You can refer to the plan when you face critical decisions. This type of thoughtful management will help you be more effective in managing the growth of a new business.

3. **Obtain financing.** A business plan is an absolute requirement for getting outside financing for your business. Bankers, investors, government agencies, and venture

capitalists expect to see a business plan before they will consider providing financial resources for your business.

Why Entrepreneurs Don't Plan

Knowing why entrepreneurs don't take time to develop a business plan or keep it updated might help you avoid failing into a similar pattern.

Lack of time. The hectic pace often found in a new business distracts a person from planning. This is one of the reasons for developing a business plan before you start a business.

Procrastination. Many business owners put off planning. To avoid this, make planning a priority and establish a schedule for periodic reviews. Then stick to the schedule.

Lack of expertise. A business plan can be a difficult document to create and may require broad expertise in management. A local Small Business Development Center or Small Business Institute—found at many colleges and universities—can help you develop a business plan.

Lack of trust. Many entrepreneurs believe that they have a unique idea that must be kept secret for success. A nondisclosure agreement—written by an attorney—can help avoid the theft of an idea by someone for their own use. Ask any person reviewing your plan to sign a nondisclosure agreement.

Skepticism about value. Many business owners are skeptical about the value of planning. However, research indicates that this is one of the major reasons new businesses fail. The relationship between planning and success should provide some motivation to write a business plan.

Format for a Business Plan

No standard format exists for a business plan. A number of formats are available, and the Small Business Administration has a booklet that shows one suggested format. There are ten sections that you should consider putting in a business plan.

Executive summary. An executive summary provides an overview of a business plan. It should be informative and entice the reader to go further into the document. Avoid making the summary more than five pages.

Mission statement, goals, objectives, and strategies. Strategic planning principles should guide your business plan. It should include statements about four issues commonly associated with strategic planning: mission, goals, objectives, and strategies. The mission statement is a one-paragraph description of the reason or purpose for your business. A *goal* is a one-sentence statement of what you intend to accomplish during a three- to five-year span. Limit yourself to no more than seven of the most important goals for your business. An *objective* is a one-sentence statement about a specific benchmark you intend to achieve with your business in the fulfillment of a goal. Each goal should contain three to five objectives. A *strategy* is a one-sentence statement that indicates how to achieve an objective. Each objective may have several strategies.

Marketing plan. When you develop the marketing section of your business plan, you should consider three issues: the industry, the market, and marketing strategy. In the industry analysis include its history, future trends, and how your business will fit into the industry. Analyze the market by describing potential customers for your product, reasons for buying your product or service, the geographic area of your market, and the market's size. Finally, you should consider market strategies, such as product price, sales management advertising, and credit policies.

Design and development plan. A product or service that requires design and development needs a plan for these tasks. Describe the status of the product or service. Indicate problems that could occur during the design or development stage. Discuss how these difficulties might impede design or development and increase costs. Focus on the degree of risk involved during this. The budget should include detailed costs for the design and development phase.

Operations or manufacturing plan. This section of the plan shows how your business format will be implemented and operated. If your venture includes the manufacturing of a product, develop a manufacturing plan. This plan describes the facility needs, preferred plant location, space requirements, manufacturing process to be used, equipment requirements, and labor requirements.

If your business provides a service, you need to describe the service and how it is delivered. Your description should include the type of facility needed, methods that will be used to provide the service, equipment requirements, preferred location for the business, and labor force requirements.

Principal parties. The business plan should describe the principal parties involved in the business venture. This includes the experience, skills, and technical expertise of the management team. Provide a summary on each key individual. (You may use a resume for this purpose.) Describe the organizational structure of your business.

Work plan and schedule. Include a benchmark for each of the key activities described in the plan. Provide a general time line for the start-up of your business. Specify a time frame for the completion of each benchmark and indicate who will be responsible for completing it.

Potential problems and risks. A valuable exercise is to anticipate problems you may have during the startup of your business. You should identify potential risks and possible problem areas. In your discussion, explain how you might resolve these problems or risks. Investors want to know that you have anticipated such problems and are prepared to deal with them as they occur.

Benefits to the community. Discuss how your business will benefit the community in which you are living or working. Investors want to see how your business will especially benefit them or their community. This is particularly important if you seek government loans, grants, or tax deferments. Describe the potential economic or quality-of-life benefits you foresee.

Financial plan. The financial section is one of the most important parts of a business plan. The reason is that many businesses fail because of unrealistic financial projections. Make certain that the data you gather for this section of your business plan is both accurate and realistic. Investors especially want to know how you plan to finance your new business and how realistic your projections are. The financial plan should cover a three- to five-year period. Include a detailed operating budget, profit and loss forecast, cash flow projections, and balance sheets for start-up, first year, and end of the forecast period. Many lending institutions will suggest specific formats for a financial plan.

A business plan is a key planning and financing instrument for a new business venture. The purpose of the plan is to generate information for the sake of developing the plan. The Small Business Administration has some excellent materials on how to develop a business plan. In your early research, find examples of business plans.

Financing Your Business

When you start a business, the most critical factor is the initial capitalization. A business plan is an important tool for financing your new business successfully. A plan helps you determine the financial needs of the business during its first few years of operation. You can thus avoid failure due to insufficient finances. Furthermore, the sources you approach to finance a business usually require a business plan. In this section, you find out about the sources of funds available to begin a business.

Personal Resources

Many personal resources are usually available to start a business. Relying on such resources is sometimes called *bootstrap financing*. A simple list includes the following sources:

1. Savings

2. Life insurance cash values

3. Investments

4. Home mortgages

5. Relatives and friends

6. Contract from former employer

7. Initial contracts with new customers

8. Credit from vendors

Equity Capital

Another method for raising the necessary finances for your business is to give investors equity in the business in return for their cash investment. This approach increases the amount of money available to a new business. Most banks will back a strong group of investors more than a single individual. Disadvantages to this approach are a loss of control, increased legal requirements, less personal profit, and pressure to perform from shareholders.

Methods for Raising Equity Capital

There are many ways to raise capital through investors. It is advisable to retain the services of an attorney when you use any of these methods. Consider the following issues as you evaluate which method to use:

➤ You can increase the amount of potential investment by offering shares to more people.

➤ The more equity purchased by shareholders results in less personal profit and control.

➤ Seeking investors from other states is complicated by increased laws and regulations at both the state and federal levels.

Intrastate stock sale. The sale of stocks in just one state limits the complexity of legal requirements. Stock sales require management to disclose information sufficient for investors to make informed decisions. Both private placement of stock and public offerings may take place in intrastate transactions.

Private placement. A private stock placement is usually limited to no more than 35 purchasers. This placement is regulated by state and federal laws. The number of investors limits the availability of funds through this type of offering.

Public offering. For a public offering, a company must demonstrate that it can provide investors with a good return on investment. It also requires an underwriter that will help in selling the stock. When the stock is sold to the public, the owners have no control over who invests in the business.

Venture capital. A venture capital firm consists of individuals who invest funds in new or rapidly growing businesses. Because new ventures contain a high degree of risk, a venture capital firm expects a high rate of compensation—sometimes as much as 50 percent ownership or return on investment.

Small Business Investment Corporations (SBICs). An SBIC is a venture capital firm licensed by the Small Business Administration. The SBIC must raise private money and can then use it to borrow additional funds from the SBA.

State and local governments. Some states and local governments invest in new businesses. Typically these promote specific types of business—for example, high tech businesses, labor-intensive businesses, or businesses that will locate in economically depressed areas.

Obtaining Loans

Most lending institutions grant loans to a new business for specific purposes. In this section, you will read about the types of loans that may be obtained from a lending institution.

Secured loans. Lending institutions are likely to give a loan for the four purposes described here, because the loan can be secured by the company's assets.

1. **Equipment purchase.** Obtaining equipment for an office, a store, or a manufacturing operation is often possible because the lending institution can place a lien against the equipment.

2. **Inventory.** A lending institution sometimes provides the credit necessary to purchase inventory. When used by retailers, this credit is called *floor planning*. In essence, the

lending institution owns the inventory. As items are sold, the loan is repaid. This type of loan is usually a short-term loan.

3. **Buildings.** A bank might be willing to provide a loan for a building that it could secure with a mortgage. This type of loan would probably be for a long term (20+ years).

4. **Accounts receivable**. The receivable accounts of a business can often be used to get a loan. The lending institution speculates that most accounts will be paid and the business will be able to repay the loan.

Lending institution line of credit. A loan known as a line of credit establishes the maximum amount of money that may be borrowed from the lending institution. The borrower draws on the line of credit only as the money is needed.

Small Business Administration guaranteed loan programs. These programs provide guarantees to banks that lend to approved small businesses. The guarantees provide coverage of from 70 percent to 90 percent of a loan, depending on the amount. You can find out about these programs by contacting a local banker who works with or through the SBA. The SBA sponsors several additional programs to assist small businesses. Contact a local SBA office for information about these programs.

Federal Farmers Home Administration. To promote economic development of small businesses in rural areas, the FHA provides loan guarantees of up to 90 percent of the value of a loan.

State and local government programs. Many state and local governments have loan programs. These often are designed to promote specific government goals and policies.

Lenders' Criteria for Business Loans

Lending institutions are usually conservative in their decisions. They expect a business to demonstrate a high probability that it will repay a loan. The following points are normally considered by lending institutions.

Business concept (business plan). Your business plan should display a well-planned approach to business.

Collateral. The lender might secure the loan by holding a lien against buildings, equipment, inventory, or other assets.

Down payment. The lender might require a down payment on the loan that must come from you and other principals in the business.

Credit record. A new business does not have a credit record. Therefore, a lender often considers the credit history of the principals and may secure a loan through a lien on your personal assets.

Management ability. In deciding whether to grant you a loan, a lender will examine your management ability. This is evident in your work experience and business plan.

Considerations for a Financing Option

A decision about which financing option to use can be guided by the following considerations.

Availability. You might have a limited choice in financing options. The availability of capital from outside resources varies with the general health of the national economy, as well as that of your local area. Investors will be more likely to purchase stock when the economy is good. Government funds are usually more plentiful at the beginning and end of the government's fiscal year.

Repayment. A loan must be repaid with interest. You might be required to secure a loan with your personal assets, possibly taking on considerable financial risk. Shareholders do not have to be repaid.

Control. A lender will expect you to follow prudent management principles. Investors, however, will become more involved in decisions for the business. They will elect members to the board of directors and will serve as directors. An owner thus loses some control over the business when selling shares in it.

The Business Team

An entrepreneur benefits from building a team of key professionals who can help establish the business structure and operation. Every entrepreneur should seriously consider engaging an attorney, a certified public accountant, a banker, an insurance agent, and consultants as needed. These professionals can provide expertise and advice for the new business. It is shortsighted to avoid using these professionals because of the expense. As your business grows, you might pay far more monetarily and emotionally for mistakes which these professionals would have helped you avert.

Attorney

Initially, the attorney performs a critical function for your business by filing all the necessary legal documents and advising you on business licenses and zoning ordinances. The attorney thus helps you set up the legal foundation of your business. It is possible to find attorneys who will help you establish your business for a reasonable fee. You should expect legal assistance with the following matters.

Legal structure. An attorney will advise you on the best legal structure for your business. The attorney can prepare partnership agreements or incorporation papers. An attorney can also obtain stock certificates, a corporate seal, and a corporate record book, which are usually required by state law for a corporation.

Franchising and licensing. An attorney should review any type of licensing or franchise agreement that you sign. This helps protect you from problems you cannot foresee.

Patents, trademarks, and copyrights. The protection of intellectual property is a vital part of business law in a competitive society. An invention is protected by a *patent. A trademark* is a word, name, symbol, or device used by a business to differentiate itself or a product from the rest of the market. A *copyright* protects written property and computer software. The practice of patent, trademark, and copyright law is somewhat technical. You can file for trademarks and copyrights by yourself, but you may

want an attorney's assistance. Patents require much more technical knowledge, and you typically need the assistance of a patent attorney.

Contracts and agreements. Frequently, you will enter into business agreements with other organizations. Such arrangements need to be formalized with a contract or agreement, which should be prepared or reviewed by an attorney.

Federal and state reports. It is advisable to have your attorney prepare or review reports that you must make to federal and state governments that affect the legal status of your business.

General legal matters. During the operation of a business, many issues arise that have legal implications. For example, terminating an employee, having an employee sign a non-competition agreement, and complying with city ordinances are matters for which you will need legal advice.

Establishing a professional relationship with an attorney at the start of your business helps ensure that you are in compliance with all laws and regulations. The attorney will become familiar with your business and will be prepared to offer informed advice should a legal issue arise that requires an attorney's assistance.

Accountant

A certified public accountant (CPA) can provide important advice about the operation of your business. This member of your business team is particularly important if you need help with accounting or tax preparation. You will find that an accountant is useful for the following reasons.

Legal structure. A CPA can help you choose the type of legal structure that will be most beneficial from a tax perspective.

Government forms and filings. A CPA can help you comply with many government requirements—for example, filing for Subchapter S status, obtaining an employer identification number from the IRS, and completing government tax and financial reports.

Accounting procedures. A CPA can help you choose the method of bookkeeping most appropriate for your business. Many CPAs can recommend computer software programs that can maintain your financial records.

Tax preparation. A CPA can prepare the tax returns for your business. Tax regulations and tax court interpretations result in a complex system that requires an expert to keep abreast of changes.

Audits. A CPA can conduct an annual audit of your business if the volume of business is large in dollars. Publicly held corporations must obtain audits to disclose financial information to the shareholders. The audit protects business owners against misfeasance (unintentional violation of the law) or malfeasance (deliberate violation of the law) by employees who work with the finances for the business.

A CPA, therefore, can provide advice about a variety of financial matters, such as loans and the issuance of stock. It is useful to receive advice also on tax planning, mergers and acquisitions, financial strategies, and related matters.

Banker

Many new entrepreneurs mistakenly think that a banker is an antagonist whom they must overcome to get a loan. A banker, however, serves a vital role in the financing of the organization. This professional can help you maintain a healthy financial outlook for your business. You need a banker who perceives the banker's role as a consultant and advisor who will contribute to the success of the business.

Banking services. You should find a bank that provides the banking services you need for your business. These include checking accounts, loans, lease programs, credit cards, electronic fund transfers, and financial planning.

Financial advice. A banker can provide you with advice about starting your business and arranging financing. Usually, the banker will expect to see a business plan and will give you guidance on how to create and develop a plan if you don't have one.

Loans. A major service of a bank is the provision of business loans. Typical loans are for equipment and working capital. To help you meet your cash flow needs, seek a bank that is willing to provide a line of credit for your business.

Insurance Agent

A key element of any successful business is *risk management*. This refers to a plan for avoiding loss of business assets or earning capability. An insurance agent can show you how to manage your business risks by having several types of insurance.

Liability insurance. This insurance protects you from losses that might result from injuries to other people or their property. Depending on your type of business, liability insurance might include facilities insurance, product liability, vehicle insurance, officers and directors insurance, and professional liability.

Property insurance. Your business will need this type of insurance for protection against damage or theft to facilities, equipment, office furniture, and vehicles.

Earnings insurance. This insurance protects you from severe financial loss for which you are not responsible. Three types of insurance fall into this category: business interruption insurance, bad-debt insurance, and business owners life insurance.

Fidelity bonds. A fidelity bond protects your business against employee theft. Such a bond may be required by government or business to obtain contracts for work.

Workers' compensation. Many states require that a business with employees carry workers' compensation insurance. This insurance pays employees for losses due to accidents on the job

Health, life, and disability insurance. Business owners will typically need these insurance policies for protection against personal loss. You might also want to provide such insurance for employees if you want to remain competitive when recruiting employees.

A good insurance agent can advise you about which types of insurance are needed by your business. The agent can also recommend the coverage and deductible amounts that are most appropriate for your business.

Consultants

Consultants can often help a new business by providing expertise that an entrepreneur lacks. Some examples are described in the following paragraphs.

Business start-up. Some consultants specialize in starting new businesses. They can help you develop your business plan, get financing, and identify a location for the business.

Management. A business owner with technical expertise might need help from a consultant who can provide general management advice.

Human resources/Training. Personnel management is subject to many laws and technicalities. If you hire employees, you might need the services of a consultant who can advise you on the development and management of personnel systems and on employee training.

Technical expertise. You may need to hire a consultant who has technical expertise in the creation of a product or service that is integral to the operation of your company.

Consultants in the field. A valuable resource will be people who have gone into business for themselves and are working in the field or industry that interests you.

Selection of Your Business Team

Professionals who become part of your business team are important to the success of your business, but they can also have an adverse effect on your business. The following useful guidelines for choosing professionals for your business team are included to help you avoid adverse effects.

Time. The more time and effort that you expend in identifying professionals for your business team,

the greater will be the likelihood of getting the right people.

Develop a comprehensive list. Contact friends, relatives, and business acquaintances about professionals they have used. You also should contact local professional associations and ask for referrals to professionals who are familiar with entrepreneurial enterprises.

Interview the professionals. Contact the professionals directly. Interview more than one in each specialty before making your selection.

Check references. Talk to clients whom the professionals list as references. Seek a competent individual with whom you feel comfortable.

Care and attention. You need to be assured that the professional has the time and willingness to work with your business. A professional may be good, but a lack of attention will not help you solve business problems.

Character. The professional you select must be trustworthy, honest, and reliable. The professional must place the interests of your business above personal interests, or at least maintain a balance between them.

Charges or fees. You must consider the professional's fees for services, but this should not be the most important factor in making a choice.

Reflect on the following questions when making your final decision about which professional to use for your business.

1. How much experience with small businesses does the expert have?

2. Does the person appear enthusiastic about working with your business?

3. Did the professional offer advice you found useful?

4. Are the references from other clients positive?

5. Can you afford the fees the professional will charge?

6. Can the professional provide the services you might need as your business grows?

16

7. Will the person be able to grow with your business?

Assembling a competent, reliable, and enthusiastic business team is important for your new business. You should therefore select your business team carefully.

Beginning Operations

An obstacle facing every new business is the start-up phase. This includes all of the detailed activities involved in opening the business' doors to customers. Every new business needs a facility, equipment, supplies, and record keeping system. This section examines how to organize these parts of your business.

Establishing an Office

To choose a facility, you need to consider its location, the type of facility that is best for your business, and the purchase of office equipment and supplies.

Choosing a location. Most entrepreneurs start a business in close proximity to their home. There are other factors to consider when deciding where to locate a business. The following factors need to be considered.

Customers. A primary consideration is the location of your customers. Will they often come to your facility? If they will, you need to consider ease of access, parking, and visibility. Will you be manufacturing a product and shipping it to customers? If so, you need to consider ease of shipment. Will you frequently visit your customers' locations? If that is true, you should consider the selection of a site near most of your customers and good transportation facilities.

Workforce. A business that will require a significant number of employees should be located near a workforce with the skills needed and in sufficient number to fill your businesses needs. You will also want to consider locating near education resources that can provide continued training to keep the skills of your workforce current.

Preferences. Where would you enjoy working? You should consider your personal preferences as well as those of other principals in the business. You might prefer a location close to your home. You might want to move to a new part of the country. You might prefer a rural, urban, suburban, or metropolitan area.

Services. A business should be near the services and products that are necessary for its operation. Are there adequate utility supplies? Are there good telecommunication services available? Are there required suppliers nearby? Do you have access to support services, such as consultants, marketing firms, print shops, and temporary personnel agencies?

Costs. You must keep in mind the expenses for a particular location. What is the average pay and type of fringe benefits expected by the workforce in the area? What types of taxes must be paid? What are the costs of utilities? What will it cost to lease or buy a building? The costs for a location will affect the price of your product or service and the need for working capital.

Choosing a Facility

Once you have identified a location, you need to select the facility. First, determine the type of facility that will be most adequate for the business. Consider the following factors.

Number of employees needed. Try to project the number of employees needed for the next two to three years. This will help you determine the total amount of space, the number and size of rest rooms, the number of parking places, and the square footage of office or production space for each employee.

Customer access and service. There should be adequate parking space for customers. They should be able to access your building easily from the parking area. Drive-through services are important to many people who are busy. Likewise, your ability to deliver services to customers can be important.

Storage space. List all of the equipment, inventory, and supplies that will need to be stored. Deter-

mine the method for storage and how much space this will require.

Production space. Unless you have a great deal of experience in the type of production done by your business, you probably need an expert to help you calculate the production space required.

Office space. The amount and type of office space needed depends on the total number of employees who need office space, and the amount of privacy they require.

Shipment processing and distribution. If you plan to market products, you need adequate space for packaging them. You also need space to store products before they are shipped.

Utilities. You need access to utilities. These typically include water, electricity, and gas. Furthermore, you should be sure that the electrical wiring is adequate for all machinery and office equipment.

Type of Facility

You have three basic options when leasing or buying space for your business. The advantages and disadvantages of each are considered in the following paragraphs.

Working at home. Working at home is one inexpensive solution for a new business. American business is replete with legends of organizations that began in the owner's "garage." Its advantages are low cost, convenience, a relaxed environment, flexibility, and more family involvement. Disadvantages include distractions, a feeling of isolation, lower customer esteem, zoning limitations, and a merging of your social and business life.

Renting an office or suite. An alternative is to rent or lease a single office or an office suite. It is often possible to find an executive suite where a receptionist, secretarial staff, and specialized office equipment can be shared with other professionals. Some communities have business incubation centers that provide these facilities and services. The advantages to this approach are reasonable costs, association with other

professionals, improved image, business amenities, short-term commitment, and flexibility in office expansion. Its disadvantages are less control over facility, equipment, and personnel; reliance on a facility managed by someone else; the presence of competitors; and limited customer access.

Leasing or purchasing a building. Another alternative is to lease or purchase a building when several employees work in your business, when its operations are too large for an office environment, and when it is a retail business. Advantages include a high level of facility control, flexibility in remodeling and expansion, and better parking. The disadvantages are higher expenses, cost of furnishings, maintenance, and fulfilling the terms of the lease when you outgrow the facility.

Setting Up an Office

This section serves as a guide to purchasing the basic equipment and supplies commonly used in an efficient office.

Purchasing equipment. You will need equipment to outfit an office for your business. General equipment includes furniture, a phone system, a computer system, and various office machines.

1. **Furniture.** The amount and type of furniture you need depend on the need to impress customers and make them feel comfortable.

2. **Phone system.** Your phone system is one of your most important tools because it enables you to have good communication with customers. You would be well advised to hire a telecommunications consultant for one day to identify the most effective phone system for your business and to recommend the best vendors to supply and service the system.

3. **Computer system.** A computer system can help you make effective use of modern office tools. The software applications that you are likely to need are word processing, an electronic spreadsheet, a database, an

accounting program, communications, and a graphics presentation package.

4. **Copier.** A copier is essential to most businesses. You need to make copies of financial records, proposals to customers, letters, and many other kinds of documents.

5. **Fax.** A fax machine allows you to transmit images from one location to another. You must either have a dedicated phone line for the fax or buy a fax that senses when a fax message is incoming and switches from phone operation to fax operation. It is also possible to install a fax or modem/fax board in your computer.

6. **Dictation unit.** Having a portable dictation unit is helpful for making notes to yourself or for dictating documents. This unit is particularly useful if you do much traveling.

7. **Postage meter.** A business that mails a large volume of letters or packages through the U.S. Postal Service finds a postage meter quite useful. The cost of these units is reasonable.

Purchasing supplies. The best way to purchase office supplies is to get an office supply store catalog and go through it, making a list of the supplies you will need. You should consider also some special supplies.

1. **Printed materials.** You may want to have some special items printed. These should look attractive and project a professional image. Included in this category are letterheads, envelopes, business cards, invoices, shipping labels, and presentation folders.

2. **Time-appointment system.** An entrepreneur should manage time effectively. For this, you may need an appointment and time management system.

Keeping Records

An important task in starting a business is to develop a system for record keeping which will ensure that all important data is retained in a well-organized manner. Some legal requirements exist for record keeping, so you should make certain that you are aware of them. A personal computer provides inexpensive but highly effective ways to store, organize, and retrieve records. This section reviews items that you need to consider in record keeping.

Financial records. Many states require that a corporation use a double-entry bookkeeping system. If your business is a proprietorship or partnership, you should consult with an accountant to determine the best bookkeeping system for your needs. You should keep a general ledger, general journal, accounts receivable, accounts payable, payroll records, depreciation records, cash receipts, cash payments, inventory, sales, and payroll tax forms.

Personnel records. You must keep accurate and complete records about any employees you hire. Federal and state governments have many laws and regulations you must meet in the hiring, promotion, and termination of employees. The forms you should keep for each employee include application, proof of citizenship, I-9 form, withholding forms, copy of professional license, appraisals, and disciplinary actions.

Customer data. Customers are one of the most important assets your business possesses. You should retain information about your customers. If this information is complete and well organized, your business is more valuable to lenders and investors.

This section has indicated the types of records you should retain for your business. These records represent the minimum of record keeping for any organization. You are likely to find many other records useful, such as those about suppliers, professional contacts, advertisers, consultants, and competitors' products.

Summary

This chapter demonstrates the complexity of starting your own business. The chapter raises points that

help you consider whether self-employment is a feasible career for you. It may challenge you to start a new business venture, or it may result in a decision to remain an employee who has a steady paycheck. Those readers who have been encouraged to open a new business will want to read the next chapter.

By now you probably realize that starting a new business is more difficult and risky than you thought. A franchise offers you a proven business package that reduces risk and provides an established operation. Chapter 2 explains more about franchises. It also provides guidance on researching and selecting a franchise.

Buying a Franchise

A *franchise* is a license or agreement that permits a person to use the name, trademark, procedures, and products developed and owned by another business. The International Franchise Association, the major trade association in franchising, defines the term as "a continuing relationship in which the franchisor provides a licensed privilege to do business, plus assistance in organizing, training, merchandising, and management, in return for a consideration from the franchisee." In the United States, there are approximately 3,000 franchisors with almost 600,000 franchise operations. This method of owning and operating a business has proved to be very successful.

The purpose of this chapter is to help you understand how franchises operate. It concentrates on explaining the business format franchise—the most common form. There is also information to help you evaluate a franchise to determine both its viability and appropriateness.

Franchise Types

Franchises exists in many forms, but some are more common than others. There are four basic types of franchises used by business in the United States.

Product franchise. Manufacturers use the product franchise to govern how a retailer distributes a product. The manufacturer grants a store owner the authority to distribute goods by the manufacturer and allows the owner to use the name and trademark owned by the manufacturer. The store owner must pay a fee or purchase a minimum inventory of stock in return for these rights. Some tire stores are good examples of this type of franchise.

Manufacturing franchises. These types of franchises provide an organization the right to manufacture a product and sell it to the public, using the franchisor's name and trademark. This type of franchise is found most often in the food and beverage industry. Most bottlers of soft drinks receive a franchise from a company and must use its ingredients to produce, bottle, and distribute the soft drinks.

Business opportunity ventures. These ventures typically require that a business owner purchase and distribute products for one specific company. The company must provide customers or accounts to the business owner, and in return the business owner pays a fee or other consideration as compensation. Examples include vending machine routes and distributorships.

Business format franchises. This is the most popular form of franchising. In this approach, a company provides a business owner with a proven method for operating a business using the name and trademark of the company. The company will usually provide a significant amount of assistance to the business owner in starting and managing the company. The business owner pays a fee or royalty in return. Typically, a company also requires the owner to purchase supplies from the company.

Franchising Terms and Definitions

Several terms are commonly used in association with the concept of franchising. A person interested in purchasing a franchise should be familiar with these

terms. This section contains explanations for the most important of these terms.

Franchise—A legal agreement that allows one organization with a product, idea, name, or trademark to grant certain rights and information about operating a business to an independent business owner. In return, the business owner (franchisee) pays a fee and royalties to the franchisor.

Franchisor—A company that owns a product, service, trademark, or business format and provides this to a business owner in return for a fee and possibly other considerations. A franchisor often establishes the conditions under which a business owner operates but does not control the business or have financial ownership. McDonalds is an example of a franchisor.

Franchisee—A business owner who purchases a franchise from a franchisor and operates a business using the name, product, business format, and other items provided by the franchisor. For example, McDonalds—a franchisor—sells a franchise to a franchisee. This allows the franchisee to open and operate a McDonalds fast-food restaurant. Therefore, if you purchase a franchise, you become a franchisee.

Franchise fee—A one-time fee paid by the franchisee to the franchisor. The fee pays for the business concept, rights to use trademarks, management assistance, and other services from the franchisor. This fee gives the franchisee the right to open and operate a business using the franchisor's business ideas and products.

Royalty—A continual fee paid by the franchisee to the franchisor. The royalty is usually a percent of the gross revenue earned by the franchisee. You must pay this fee as long as you own the franchise.

Franchise trade rule—A law regulated by the Federal Trade Commission that places several legal requirements on franchisors. It requires that franchisors disclose all pertinent information to potential buyers of a franchise. These disclosures provide you with most information needed to make a wise purchasing decision.

Federal Trade Commission (FTC)—A commission authorized by the United States Congress to regulate the franchise business. The Federal Trade Commission oversees the implementation of the Franchise Trade Rule and monitors the activities of franchisors. You can register complaints about a franchisor with this agency. Contact the office of your local U.S. Representative or Senator for information about how to register a complaint with the FTC.

Disclosure statement—Sometimes called an offering circular, this is a document that provides information on 23 items required by the FTC. These items are described later in this chapter. The law requires that a franchisor provide a disclosure statement to you when you inquire about purchasing a franchise.

Trademark—A distinctive name or symbol used to distinguish a particular product or service from others. A trademark must be registered with the U.S. Patent and Trademark Office. It can be used exclusively by the owner, and no one else can use it without the owner's permission. Part of a franchise's value is the right to use a recognized trademark.

The Franchisor's Perspective

What motivates a business to offer a franchise? The answer to this question helps a potential franchisee become a more knowledgeable consumer. Understanding the franchisor's perspective can help you do a better job when selecting a franchise and negotiating its purchase.

More rapid expansion. A primary reason for a business to become a franchisor is the capability to expand more rapidly. A lack of capital and a dearth of skilled employees can slow business expansion. The franchisee provides both when opening a new outlet. A franchisor may assist you in obtaining financing for a new business, but you bear the liability for repayment of the funds. In addition, the franchisor evaluates you on your business experience and management skills. Thus, a franchise operation is a mutually beneficial proposition for both the franchisor and franchisee.

Higher motivation. When a business franchises its operations, it acquires a motivated group of managers. Each manager is an owner and has a high level of motivation for success. A manager also is more accountable for actions because the manager as an owner is totally responsible for business outcomes. This means you should ask the representative of the franchisor why the company wants you to purchase a franchise. If the only benefit you bring is money, then be cautious about the franchisor's operation.

Capital. There is another advantage to franchising a business. It allows a company to raise money without selling an interest in the business. The franchisor uses franchise fees for business expansion. Issuing stock often results in reduced control and less profits per shareholder. Loans are often given with certain provisions attached and cost a significant amount of money in the form of interest paid. The franchisor establishes the terms of a franchise agreement and retains control of the operation—but not day-to-day management of a franchisee.

While franchising is an alternative that has many positive benefits for a franchisor, there are also some disadvantages. It is useful to explore some of these drawbacks so you understand the reasons behind some policies of franchisors.

Image. The name and image of a company are at risk when it is sold to a franchisee. Thus, a franchisor often is quite particular about quality and standards that you are expected to meet. Franchisors usually designate very specific business practices that you must follow. The concern over image also helps explain why many franchisors reserve the right to buy back a franchise operation. You can take comfort in the fact that most franchisors want to see you succeed. A good franchisor provides the support necessary to help you achieve success.

Less profitability for franchisor. Another disadvantage to a franchisor is the sacrifice of profits. A company-owned outlet is often more profitable than a franchise. In addition, the company owns the outlet's assets. You should consider future motivations of a franchisor when purchasing a franchise. Will the franchisor try to buy back a business after you invest the time and energy to make the operation profitable? Look for a franchisor who views the success of a profitable operation as beneficial to both parties.

Potential competition. Franchising a business also has the liability of training potential competitors. You may learn how a business operates and then decide to replicate the operation under another name. This has happened to some franchisors, so it makes others cautious. A good franchisor will try to establish a positive relationship with franchisees to avoid this problem. The restrictions placed on franchisees are usually balanced by rewards in an attempt to retain their loyalty.

As you review a franchise agreement, keep in mind the franchisor's perspective. Look for an agreement that takes a balanced approach. A good franchisor is one who desires to create a relationship in which both parties are winners.

The Franchisee's Perspective

It is important to consider the costs and benefits from the franchisee's perspective before you consider the purchase of a franchise. This section examines both costs and advantages for you. The following benefits provide a good rationale for starting a business by purchasing a franchise.

Lower risks. Most business experts agree that a franchise operation has a lower risk of failure than an independent business. The statistics on this vary depending on the definition of failure. Whatever statistics are used, they consistently suggest that you are more likely to succeed with a franchise than with an independent business.

Established product or service. A franchisor offers you a product or service that has sold successfully. An independent business is based on both an untried idea and operation. Three factors can help predict the potential success of a franchise. The first is the number of franchises that are in operation. The second is how long the franchisor and its franchisees have been in operation. A third factor is the number of franchises that have failed, including those bought back by the franchisor.

Experience of franchisor. The experience of the franchisor's management team increases the potential for your success. This experience is often conveyed through formal instruction and on-the-job training.

Group purchasing power. It is often possible to obtain lower-cost goods and supplies through the franchisor. Lower costs result from the group purchasing power of all franchisees. To protect this benefit, most franchise agreements restrict you from purchasing goods and supplies through other sources.

Name recognition. Established franchisors can offer national or regional name recognition, but this may not be true with a new franchisor. However, one benefit of starting with a new franchisor is the potential to grow as its business and name recognition grow.

Efficiency in operation. Franchisors discover operating and management efficiencies that benefit new franchisees. Operational standards set in place by the franchisor also control quality and uniformity among its franchisees.

Management assistance. A franchisor provides management assistance to you. This includes accounting procedures, personnel management, facility management, and so on. Even if you have experience in these areas, you may lack the knowledge about how to apply them in a new business. The franchisor helps you overcome this lack of experience.

Business plan. Most franchisors help you develop a business plan. Many elements of the plan are standard operating procedures established by the franchisor. Other parts of the plan are customized to your personal needs.

Start-up assistance. The most difficult aspect of a new business is its start-up. Few experienced managers know about how to set up a new business, because they do it only a few times. However, a franchisor has a great deal of experience accumulated from helping its franchisees with start-up. This experience will help reduce mistakes that are costly in both money and time.

Marketing assistance. A franchisor typically offers several marketing advantages. The franchisor can prepare and pay for the development of professional advertising campaigns. Regional or national marketing done by the franchisor benefits all franchisees. In addition, the franchisor can provide advice about how to develop effective marketing programs for your local area. This benefit normally has a cost because many franchisors require franchisees to contribute a percent of their gross income—usually 1 percent to 5 percent—to a cooperative advertising fund.

Assistance in financing. The franchisor may help you find financing for a new franchise. A franchisor often makes arrangements with a lending institution to loan you money. Lending institutions find that such arrangements can be quite profitable and relatively safe because of the high success rate of franchise operations. You must still accept personal responsibility for the loan, but the franchisor's involvement usually increases the likelihood that a loan will be approved.

Proven system of operation. An attractive feature of most franchises is that each has a proven system of operation. The system has been developed and refined by the franchisor. A franchisor with many franchisees typically has a highly refined system based on the entire experience of all these operations.

The benefits of buying a franchise may explain why more than 600,000 franchise operations exist in the United States. However, there are almost 14 million independent businesses. The drawbacks to a franchise help explain this difference in numbers.

Payment of franchise fee. A major drawback to starting a franchise is the initial franchise fee. This can range from a few thousand to several hundred thousand dollars. There are two critical factors that can affect your decision about the cost of a franchise. One is whether you can afford the franchise fee. Another is whether you can expect a reasonable return on investment.

Ongoing royalty payments. Franchisors also typically require you to make periodic royalty payments throughout the lifetime of the franchise agreement. The payments are a percent of the

gross income from the business. Usually the royalty payment is less than 10 percent. Some franchisees, after they have had several years of experience and built a strong customer base, begin to resent the royalty payments. Franchisee success often results in a feeling that the business could continue without the assistance of the franchisor.

Conformity to standard operating procedures. It is important to understand that for most franchisors, there is just one way to do things, and that is *their way*. Success results from proven methods of operation, so the franchisor does not want any variations. You may become frustrated when you believe there is a better way to do things.

Inability to make changes readily. A franchisor may prohibit you from selling products or services other than those approved by the franchisor. These restrictions are difficult to follow when you believe that there is strong customer demand for a new or different product. For example, a frozen yogurt franchise owner may want to offer coffee to customers in the winter, but if this product isn't approved by the franchisor, it can't be done. There is often a method for making suggestions, but this can be cumbersome and time-consuming. You are subject to decisions made in the central office of the franchisor. As a franchisee, you must be willing to limit your independence as an entrepreneur.

Underfinanced, inexperienced, weak franchisor. It is important to realize that all franchisors are not equal. You may have more to offer the franchisor than the franchisor has to offer you. It is critical that you carefully check the credentials of the franchisor's management team and board of directors. However, do not ignore a franchisor just because the franchisor is new. Doing this may result in the loss of a great bargain. How many people wish they could have bought a McDonalds franchise when Ray Kroc first began selling it?

Duration of relationship. Most franchise agreements last for 10-15 years. There is typically no way to extricate yourself from a relationship with a franchisor other than to sell the business. Find out what restrictions exist on selling the franchise to another person. Also, determine what conditions must exist to force the franchisor to buy back the operation. Given the permanency of most franchise relationships, you need to ask yourself whether you want to be involved with the franchisor for the rest of your business career.

Dependent on franchisor's success. The success of a franchise is usually dependent on the franchisor's success. Some well-known franchisors have failed, such as Lums and Arthur Treacher's Fish & Chips. When this occurs, the franchisee usually fails. Carefully examine a franchisor's business plans and financial reports. This will help identify potential weaknesses. However, many problems occur when a franchisor is purchased by a larger corporation or when a new management team is brought in to run the business. When this occurs, the franchisees are unable to control the situation.

Personal Considerations

People who decide to purchase a franchise are typically happy with their decision. A Gallup poll found that almost 95 percent of franchisees considered themselves successful, and over 75 percent would buy the franchise again if they had to do it over. The growth rate for franchise operations often outpaces the economy. Thus, franchising can be an excellent choice. But is it the right choice for you?

As you review this section, you can assess both your interest in a franchise and financial ability to purchase one. You may find that there are many advantages for you to purchase a franchise. The reader who makes this discovery will find the next section quite useful. You will learn how to select a franchise.

Franchising is obviously a good choice for many business owners. However, you need to consider several personal issues when deciding whether franchising is the best option for you. Since you must live for many years with your decision to purchase a franchise, it is important that you are compatible with this form of business.

Franchise Compatibility Worksheet

The following questions will help you explore how well you might fit into a franchise operation. Check each statement that you agree with.

_____ I prefer to limit my risk as much as possible.

_____ I am willing to operate the business in exact accordance with the instructions of a franchisor.

_____ I am willing to forgo sales on new ideas and products because of franchisor restrictions.

_____ I am comfortable with sharing my success, including profits, with a franchisor.

_____ I enjoy being part of a well-known organization.

_____ I feel that I need the management experience and assistance that a franchisor can provide.

_____ I need assistance in developing a business plan.

_____ I do not feel comfortable with establishing a business from the ground floor up.

_____ My experience in marketing is limited, and a franchisor would help overcome this weakness.

_____ The help a franchisor provides in financing might make the difference in my ability to start a business.

_____ I am willing to pay a franchise fee to obtain a proven business operation.

_____ I feel comfortable establishing a long-term relationship with a franchisor.

_____ I am comfortable linking my success with the success of the franchisor.

_____ I enjoy selling products and services created by someone else, instead of creating my own.

_____ I am willing to purchase goods and services as directed from the franchisor.

Count the number of items that you have checked. Use the scores below to help you interpret the results.

0–5   Franchising is probably not a good alternative for you.

6–10   Franchising has some attraction, but you have some doubts that need to be carefully considered.

11–15   Franchising appears to be appealing and would probably fit your personal business needs.

EXERCISE I

Personal Financial Statement

ASSETS		LIABILITIES	
Cash on hand	$ _____	Accounts payable	$ _____
Savings account	_____	Loans payable	_____
Stocks or bonds	_____	Contracts payable	_____
Loans receivable	_____	Real estate loans	_____
Accounts receivable	_____	Taxes	_____
Real estate	_____	Other liabilities	_____
Life insurance	_____		_____
Automobiles	_____		_____
Other assets	_____		_____
TOTAL ASSETS	$ _____	TOTAL LIABILITIES $	_____
NET WORTH (ASSETS MINUS LIABILITIES)			$ _____

EXERCISE 2

Start-Up Costs Estimate

Franchise fee $_____

Building cost (new or
remodeling) $_____

Fixtures and equipment $_____

Installation of fixtures/
equipment $_____

Telephone system/installation $_____

Utility deposits $_____

Insurance $_____

Attorney, accountant, and
other professional fees $_____

Licenses, permits $_____

Supplies $_____

Initial inventory $_____

Advertising, promotions $_____

Signs $_____

Vehicles $_____

Other $_____

TOTAL START-UP COSTS $_____

EXERCISE 3

Monthly Expenses

Personal living expenses $_____

Employee wages $_____

Employee fringe benefits &
payroll taxes $_____

Building payment/rent $_____

Maintenance $_____

Utilities $_____

Insurance $_____

Advertising $_____

Supplies $_____

Postage/Shipping $_____

Transportation $_____

Inventory replacement $_____

Taxes $_____

Royalty payments $_____

Other $_____

TOTAL $_____

TOTAL × 3* $_____

*Multiplying by three provides an estimate of the operating capital that you will need. This would be enough money to operate for three months without having any income. Some experts recommend that you also plan on six to 12 months for personal living expenses. The reason for this is that it may take that long before you can withdraw any money from the business.

It is also important to determine your financial ability to invest in a franchise. This can be more important than your compatibility with franchising. Use the first exercise to evaluate your personal financial status. The second exercise helps determine the costs that are involved in starting a specific franchise operation. The third exercise assists in calculating the funds that you need for operating capital during the first three months of operation.

Selecting a Franchise

Franchising has been around since the Middle Ages but reached its economic apex in the 1970s in the United States. It has been enjoying a resurgence that started in the late 1980s. The success of franchising has attracted some inexperienced and occasionally fraudulent franchisors. In 1979 the federal government implemented a law to protect consumers from fraudulent franchisors—periodically this law is modified and expanded. However, the old Latin saying "caveat emptor," or "let the buyer beware," still applies to the purchase of a franchise.

A simple process to evaluate a franchise and protect your investment is described in this chapter. But the process is not foolproof, and misjudgments can still occur. However, following the process can help you avoid disastrous mistakes made by many other

people. The steps are explained to help you find a franchise that is a suitable match for you and has the potential for financial success.

Process for Selecting a Franchise

There are five steps you can follow to select a franchise with the most potential. The steps are presented in their logical sequence. However, you may find that it is possible to carry out more than one step at a time. These steps represent a process based on models frequently proposed in books and articles about franchises.

Step 1—Examine opportunities. There are thousands of franchises. In most types of businesses, you will find several franchise opportunities. For example, if you have an interest about a particular type of business, like a donut shop, you will find several such franchisors listed in this directory. There are other directories that you can use to expand your search along with some magazines that periodically publish lists of franchisors. It is wise to contact and compare all possible franchise choices. This gives you an opportunity to review the costs and benefits provided for each franchisor. You will probably want to narrow the possible alternatives to a final group—no greater than five in number. This group of finalists should represent those you want to consider more seriously. You need to complete the next four steps with each franchisor.

Step 2—Examine the franchise and franchisor. It is important to obtain thorough information from each franchisor about the franchise. In fact, the federal government and several states have laws stipulating the information that a franchisor must provide. The document containing this information is called a disclosure statement or may be referred to as a Uniform Franchise Offering Circular (UFOC). The following list contains the twenty-three items of information that must be supplied by a franchisor.

1. Information identifying the franchisor, its predecessors, and its affiliates and describing their business experience.

2. Information identifying and describing the business experience of each of the franchisor's officers, directors, and manage-

ment personnel responsible for franchise services, training, and other aspects of the franchise program. Each person's principal occupations and employers during the past five years must be included.

3. A description of the lawsuits in which the franchisor and its officers, directors, and management personnel have been involved.

4. Information about any previous bankruptcies in which the franchisor and its officers, directors, and management personnel have been involved.

5. Statement of the initial franchise fee, conditions under which it is refundable, and formula for calculating the fee if it is not uniform.

6. Statement of other fees that must be paid to the franchisor or its affiliates. This statement must explain the formula used to calculate the payments and any condition under which they might be refundable.

7. Information making clear the costs involved in the initial investment. This includes such items as real property, equipment, start-up inventory, deposits, utilities, licenses, and so on.

8. Information about any restrictions on the quality of goods and services used in the franchise and where they may be purchased, including restrictions requiring purchases from the franchisor or its affiliates.

9. A description of the principal obligations of the franchisee. There is a table of 25 items that the franchisee may be expected to comply with.

10. Information about any financing arrangements with the franchisor, its agents, or affiliates.

11. This item should explain the franchisor's obligations. This includes services that will be performed prior to opening, obligations during the operation of a franchise, method used to select a site for franchisee's operation, and the training program to be provided.

12. A description of any territorial protection that will be granted to the franchisees.

13. A description of the principal trademarks to be licensed to the franchisee.

14. A description of any patents or copyrights that are material or important to the franchise.

15. A description of the extent to which franchisees must personally participate in the operation of the franchise.

16. A description of restrictions on the goods or services franchisees are permitted to sell.

17. A description of the conditions under which the franchise may be repurchased or refused renewal by the franchisor, transferred to a third party by the franchisee, and terminated or modified by either party. Also, the method for resolving any disputes about these transactions needs to be explained.

18. A description of the involvement of any celebrities or public figures in the franchise and conditions of their involvement.

19. A complete statement of the basis for any earnings claims made to the franchisee, including the factual basis on which these claims are made. If there is not any such claim, this fact must be specifically stated.

20. Statistical information about the present number of franchises, the number of franchisees projected for the future, the number of franchises terminated, the number the franchisor has decided not to renew, and the number repurchased in the past.

21. The franchisor's balance sheets for the last two years, including the financial statements of any affiliated company.

22. Copies of all contracts that are a part of the franchise offering.

23. The UFOC's last page, which acknowledges receipt of the circular. You must sign this page and give it to the franchisor.

A franchisor may want to conduct a preliminary approval of your suitability as a franchisee before providing a UFOC. The law stipulates that the information must be provided before you sign a franchise agreement. Further, you must be given a chance to review this information without interference from the franchisor. The sooner you have this document, the sooner you can begin your screening process. Don't be reluctant to let a franchisor know you are reviewing this information and comparing it with competitors. Franchisors who are upset with this approach and unwilling to do business in this manner are probably not the kind of organization with which you want to be associated. A strong franchisor isn't afraid to compete directly with rivals.

Step 3—Analyze and evaluate the disclosure statement. Information contained in the disclosure statement provides a basis for thoroughly analyzing the potential for a franchise. However, it is also necessary to investigate the franchisor to ensure that all information is truthful and accurate. Note the following points about this step:

1. Points to consider about the franchisor.

    a) **Experience of the directors and management.** The experience of both management and directors can be critical to the franchisor's competence. These individuals should have sufficient experience that they can add significantly to your own business expertise. They should have special knowledge and understanding about the type of business operation that they are selling.

    b) **Number of franchises in operation.** The number of franchisees provides some measure of the stability and experience of the franchisor. It is possible that a new franchisor provides a great ground floor opportunity. However, your risk is reduced when you select a franchisor that has a large number of franchisees. Each franchisee provides the franchisor with added experience in starting and supporting new operations. This combined experience is highly beneficial in the success of your business.

c) **Number of franchises no longer in operation.** You need to determine the number of franchisees who have been closed or repurchased by the franchisor or gone out of business. This information can be even more important than the number of currently operating franchises. Franchisors will sometimes buy out or close unsuccessful franchisees in order to remove problems. It is important to know how many situations like this have occurred. The more franchisees that have experienced problems, the greater your risk becomes in purchasing a franchise.

d) **Years franchisor has been in operation.** The length of experience often indicates stability and a higher potential for franchises to succeed in the future. However, there are some good opportunities with younger franchisors. Do not let this factor alone discourage you from considering an association with a franchisor.

e) **Type and amount of training.** The type and amount of training the franchisor provides can prove critical to your success. The best training programs will include a combination of classroom training and on-the-job training. A few weeks of training can help you become highly effective.

f) **Type of management assistance provided.** There should be a large amount of assistance provided with the start-up of the business. This period of time is normally the most difficult and requires the greatest amount of assistance. However, continued assistance should be offered regularly and be available for unexpected crises.

g) **Financial stability.** The certified financial statement provided by the franchisor should indicate a financially healthy organization. Any questionable financial problem should alert you to be cautious about developing an association with the franchisor.

h) **Assistance in financing.** Determine what assistance the franchisor provides for financing your business. Does the financing include the franchise fee, equipment, building, supplies, and operating capital? A less reliable franchisor may not be able to obtain financing that offers the best terms for a franchisee. Be sure to examine carefully the interest rate and loan conditions and have them reviewed by an attorney or certified public accountant.

i) **Site location assistance.** An old expression about retail establishments states that there are three critical elements to business success. These are location, location, and location. While this is an exaggeration, it illustrates the importance of site location. An experienced franchisor should be able to provide sophisticated techniques for accomplishing this task.

j) **Planning and constructing a building.** Assistance in constructing a building can help you save a great deal of money. Find out whether there is any additional fee for this assistance.

k) **Reputation among franchisees.** The franchisor's customers are its franchisees. The best way to determine how you will be treated as a customer and franchisee is to talk with other franchisees. If possible, try to talk with some who are no longer in business. They can offer a unique insight into franchisor treatment and services. More is said about this later.

l) **Projected operating losses.** Determine how long a franchisee is expected to operate before revenue is sufficient to cover expenses. This provides data that you can use to calculate the amount of funds you need to raise in order to cover this deficit.

m) **Potential profits.** A critical element in deciding about a franchise is the amount of annual profits that you can expect.

Have a cost analysis done to determine whether the projected profit is enough to ensure a reasonable return on investment. You should ask other franchisees whether the profit they make each year is close to what the franchisor told them to expect. Project the length of time that it will take to recover your initial investment.

2. Points to consider about personal needs.

a) **Equity requirements.** The franchise fee and the capital investment requirements are the biggest obstacles for most potential franchisees. Use Exercise 1—presented earlier in this chapter—to calculate your net worth. Discuss this with a banker to determine an amount of money you can borrow. (There are other ways to raise capital, but a loan is perhaps the most common way of financing a franchise.) This information can be used to quickly eliminate those franchisors whose equity requirement is more than the amount of money you can finance.

b) **Interest and enthusiasm.** A franchisee needs to be excited and enthusiastic about a franchisor's product or service. There are several reasons for this. Your association with the franchisor is likely to last for many years. Another reason to be excited about the franchisor is that this can be sensed by customers and employees. Customers are more likely to patronize your business when they observe your enthusiasm. Employees work harder when they are inspired by your excitement.

c) **Business skills.** The franchise should be a good match with your business experience and skills. The more you know about the business operation, the higher your potential for success. This does not mean that you must have experience with the specific product or service. You should expect the franchisor to provide training and management assistance, but related skills and experience enhance these.

3. Points to consider about market viability.

a) **Community fit.** Many products and services can be successful in one area but may not work well in another. Customs, tastes, traditions, wealth, and other factors affect the success of a product or service in a community. Franchisors sometimes conduct a market survey to determine the franchise's viability for your community. However, you need to verify the accuracy of such a study. Less honest franchisors may attempt to modify the survey's outcome to use it as a selling point.

b) **Location availability.** The importance of location has already been noted. You need to consider how critical location is to this particular franchise. Next, it is necessary to determine whether a location suitable for the business exists within your community. If you have doubts about available sites, you should reconsider your investment in the franchise.

c) **Longevity of product.** Ask yourself whether the product or service is faddish. To protect your investment, the franchise should have long-term staying power. To do this, it is often necessary to look past your enthusiasm and be objective. Read what business magazines have to say about the product or service. Ask the advice of experienced business people. Talk with friends who would be typical of your future customers. These combined opinions can help you predict the product's longevity.

d) **Population stability.** Find out the population projections for the community in which you plan to place the franchise. Local city government, chamber of commerce, Small Business Development Corporation, economic devel-

ment commission, and other sources can help provide this information. The long-term growth of the population has a significant affect on the franchise's potential success.

e) **Competition.** Study the competition that competes directly against the franchise. Then study indirect competition. For example, a specialty coffee shop competes directly against other coffee shops but might indirectly compete against delis, gourmet shops, etc.

f) **Price.** The price for the product or service should be consistent with average incomes for people in your area. A high-price product may sell well in an area where income is high but might be a loser in an area with low-income households.

9) **Advertising.** Find out how much advertising the franchisor does locally, regionally, and nationally. This is very important when you consider the value of a franchise. A franchisor with a less expensive franchise and royalty fee may lower operating costs by limiting its advertising. This may hurt your franchise sales and business growth.

h) **Advertising campaign effectiveness.** The franchisor's marketing expertise is very important to your success. You should expect the franchisor's help in generating sales. A franchisor should offer effective advertising tools that include the creation of newspaper, radio, and television advertisements. These should be professionally prepared along with a marketing strategy that will maximize their use.

i) **Cooperative advertising.** Most franchisors require the franchisee to pay cooperative marketing fees. This is typically a percentage of revenues. It is important to understand how this money is used and how significant an impact it can have on your franchise.

Step 4—investigate the franchisor. It is important for you to investigate the franchisor thoroughly. You wouldn't want to become a partner with someone you didn't know or trust. Consider your relationship with the franchisor a partnership and check out the franchisor completely. There are three stages to this investigation. Beware of any franchisor who wants you to make a decision so quickly that you do not have time to go through the following investigative process.

1. Investigate the credibility and reliability of the franchisor.

   This is particularly critical with franchisors that have been in operation for a short time. Information from sources such as the Better Business Bureau and Dunn and Bradstreet can tell you a great deal about the franchisor. Try to find a person or company to run a credit check on the organization. If the franchisor is a smaller and less-well-known company, you may also want to conduct a background and credit check on the management and corporate officers.

   The disclosure statement must include information about lawsuits. If there are lawsuits pending against the franchisor, investigate these by contacting the attorney for the plaintiffs. Ask the attorney to explain anything he or she can about the lawsuit. Question the franchisor about what the attorney tells you. You should feel comfortable that the issues related to the lawsuit are not going to affect your franchise.

2. Talk with franchisees about their experience.

   The disclosure statement is required to provide a list of franchisees. Pick a group of franchisees at random to contact. Your conversation with franchisees can provide important information. Some questions to ask are these:

   a) Did the franchisor follow through on its promises?

   b) Does the franchisor provide good management assistance?

32

c) Does the franchisor provide good marketing and advertising programs?

d) What are the strengths of the franchisor? What are the weaknesses?

e) Do you consider your franchise to be a success? What has contributed the most to this success?

f) Did the franchisor make any mistakes during the start-up? How could the mistakes have been avoided?

g) Have there been management and operational mistakes? How could these have been avoided?

h) How strict is the franchisor about business being conducted exactly as described in operating manuals?

i) If you could do anything over again, what would it be?

j) Would you recommend that a person buy this franchise?

Carefully review the answers that you get. Are there consistent problems or concerns raised by the franchisees? A consistency indicates a pattern that increases the probability that the problem may be repeated with your franchise. Likewise, positive answers should encourage you to seriously consider entering into an agreement with the franchisor.

3. Seek the advice of professionals about the franchisor and franchise agreement.

Three professionals that you should definitely confer with are an attorney, an accountant, and a banker.

a) An attorney is needed to review the franchise agreement. This is your contract with the franchisor and provides the only written commitment and promises that exist. Anything that has been verbally promised should be in this agreement. The attorney and you should review the following terms in the agreement:

➤ How long is the contract in effect? It should be the same length promised in discussions with the franchisor.

➤ Does it provide an exclusive territory? If not, what protection is offered against other franchisees taking business away from you? Proliferation of franchisees can seriously erode your revenue. This is the reason that you need some protection.

➤ Are there restrictions on selling the franchise? The more limitations that exist, the more difficult it is for you to recover your money. Many franchisors offer to buy back the franchise, but there are often conditions placed on doing this. You need to have a clear understanding of what you must do in order to initiate the buy-back provision.

➤ What are the criteria you can use to cancel the contract? Likewise, what are the criteria the franchisor can use to cancel the contract? These criteria should be reasonable and provide a clear process for canceling the contract.

➤ Does the franchisor agree to buy back the franchise if the contract is canceled. This is absolutely necessary, or you risk losing all of your initial investment in the company. Furthermore, determine whether the franchisor promises to compensate you for the goodwill built during your operation of the franchise. Goodwill is a valuable asset and takes a significant investment of time and effort to accumulate.

➤ Are there any franchise requirements that you believe are unwise, illegal, or unethical? Sections of a contract that make you uncomfortable at the start of a business relationship may result in problems at a later date.

You will probably feel uncomfortable implementing a provision that you don't believe is right.

➤ Has the attorney identified any problems with the contract? There are a number of legal technicalities connected with most business contracts. An experienced attorney can advise you about these provisions.

b) An accountant should review two primary items for you. First, the accountant should examine the corporation's financial information that is provided in the disclosure statement. Second, the accountant should review the financial potential of the business. You should ask the accountant the following questions:

➤ Is the initial investment for the franchise fee, equipment, and building reasonable? The accountant may be familiar with fair market value for these things or should be able to obtain this information.

➤ Are the royalties and cooperative advertising rates reasonable? There are ratio tables that illustrate typical expenditures for certain categories of business. The tables can be used to indicate whether the rates being charged by the franchisor are within a normal range.

➤ What do you expect your financial situation to be during the first five years of operation? A form that is often used in a business plan is a financial pro forma. The financial pro forma is a five-year financial plan. The plan includes projections for income, expenses, cash flow, and profits. Review this plan with your accountant and determine the potential return on investment for the franchise.

➤ Is the investment a reasonable risk? All new businesses are risky.

However, you must balance out three key areas to determine the degree of personal risk. These include your personal assets, resources for financing the franchise, and the potential return on investment. You should be able to afford any loss to your personal assets. The financing should provide a monthly repayment schedule that is reasonable and affordable. Potential return on investment should directly correlate with the risk that is involved.

c) A banker should be contacted to review the franchise, the financial pro forma, and your personal financial statement. The banker can provide insight into the financing issues that will be involved. The banker needs to answer the following question:

➤ Would the bank consider giving you a loan to finance your business? While this question can be answered by your accountant from the standpoint of affordability and profitability, the banker's answers are given from a lender's viewpoint. When a bank turns you down for a loan, the loan officers have noted problems. Ask the loan officer to fully explain the reasons for not making the loan. This information allows you to evaluate for yourself whether these are serious problems that could impede the franchise's success.

➤ Do the loan officers feel that the franchisor is credible? The bank can take a higher risk when your personal assets are sufficient to underwrite the loan. This doesn't give you any assurance that they have made a positive assessment about the franchisor or the franchise agreement. Make sure that the loan officer provides a complete explanation about the loan review board's

evaluation of your potential for success. What strengths and weaknesses do they judge the franchisor to possess?

➤ What are the lending conditions? These conditions, including the interest rate, provide additional information that can be used to assess the viability of the franchise. More liberal conditions indicate a more positive evaluation of the franchise by the loan officers. Also, attractive conditions will increase your profit potential.

You should weigh the review and recommendations of all three professionals before you make your final decision about a franchise. These experts can provide important advice, and you should value their opinions.

Step 5—Make a decision. As with all decisions, this is usually easier said than done. This section contains dozens of questions that need to be investigated. Sometimes you discover positive facts about the franchise, and sometimes negative facts. It is possible that the positive or negative facts are so one-sided that it is simple to make a decision. However, it is more typical to find that the facts must be organized in a manner that facilitates the decision-making process.

A simple but effective decision-making approach is the T method. To follow this method, you make a T on a page. On the left side of the T, list all positive reasons for purchasing the franchise; and on the right side, all the negative reasons. Once the two lists are completed, assign each item a number to designate its importance. A simple scale of 1 for unimportant, 2 for somewhat important, and 3 for very important can be used. Total the numbers for both sides. The larger the numerical difference between these totals, the more sure you can be of your decision. Totals that are close will make it more difficult to decide. However, an investment of this importance should usually be one that makes you feel confident of success. After completing the T-method exercise, you should feel certain that your decision is correct. A decision to purchase a franchise should result in enthusiasm for the undertaking. Without dedication and enthusiasm, you may find it difficult to achieve success.

This exercise is just one of several that can help you make a decision about buying a franchise. As noted earlier, the entire decision-making process needs to include research about a franchisor. You can begin this research by using the directory in the following chapter to identify franchisors that interest you.

3 CHAPTER

DIRECTORY OF FRANCHISE OPPORTUNITIES

You can read about hundreds of franchises in this chapter. Franchises listed in the preceding edition of this book contained data that was collected by the U.S. Department of Commerce. Because of budget cutbacks, the Department decided not to continue the process of collecting data on franchises and publishing the *Handbook*. Therefore, we conducted a survey to update this edition of the book.

Source of Information

Franchisors were contacted by mail and requested to return a written survey by mail, fax, or e-mail. Franchisors that didn't respond were contacted by telephone, and information about them was modified to include more recent information. This process was completed during the first quarter of 1998. Additional information was collected from franchisors during this survey. For example, the advertising co-op fee and Web site information didn't appear in the preceding addition of the book.

Information about a franchise is recorded in the words of the franchise representative. This is done so that the words of a franchisor aren't distorted. Some minor editing was done to correct for grammatical errors. There are times when a franchisor may use terms or expressions that aren't entirely clear. In these cases we retained their words to avoid misinterpreting the information unintentionally. We suggest that you ask the franchise representative to clarify such items.

In some cases, a franchisor chose not to provide all information or update the information found in the preceding edition of the book. In these cases we included information that was supplied in the past. This means that some information may be slightly dated.

As you look through this book, you may find some franchisors missing that you expected to find. This is done purposely for one of the following reasons:

➤ Some franchisors requested not to be listed because they are not opening any new franchises. There are a variety of reasons for this. A franchisor may have grown so fast that it couldn't provide the support needed. Others have decided it would be better to expand through company-owned outlets. Still others have simply decided to discontinue expansion. There may be other reasons that weren't communicated to us during the survey.

➤ Some franchisors have a long list of approved applicants for a franchise. They have temporarily suspended applications for a franchise until the waiting list is shortened. They feel that being listed creates unnecessary work for both the franchisor and potential franchisees.

➤ A few franchisors are somewhat exclusive in their selection of applicants. They feel that being listed in any directory invites applications from many people who aren't suitable. They prefer to use methods other than notices in the mass media.

Discretion in Using Data

Information about franchises should be evaluated with discretion. You should consider the data to be a general guide. Here are some suggestions for using this information.

➤ The address, phone numbers, and Internet data have been carefully collected. This is so you can directly contact the franchisor to obtain the most

up-to-date information. The more time that passes from the date the survey was done, the greater likelihood that contact information can change.

➤ The description of a franchise remains relatively stable. A franchise concept is a core value and isn't likely to be changed significantly by a franchisor.

➤ Information about the number of franchises, company-operated units, and total units is the data most likely to be inaccurate. The reason is that the number of units in each category can change rapidly in a rather short time.

➤ The equity amount, franchise fee, royalty, and advertising co-op fee may also undergo change. Don't consider it unfair or misleading if you contact a franchisor and find out that these items have changed. The amounts listed in this directory do not represent any form of advertisement or guarantee by a franchisor. Rather than think of this data as being specific, think of it as a general approximation. For example, a franchise fee of $25,000 may actually be in a range from $20,000 to $30,000. This change may occur as a franchisor responds to market conditions.

➤ Financial, management, and training assistance is not likely to change significantly over time. Keep in mind that this information also attempts to condense in a few words some very complex activities. It is important to look to the franchisor for more detailed information on these subjects.

➤ Some franchisors are concerned that the information in a short summary isn't sufficiently able to convey the best features of their franchises. They are concerned that some people might not give serious consideration to their franchise because of a small amount of information. Many of these franchisors want to sell their franchise without any preconceived ideas in the customer's mind. You should contact a franchisor whenever you find the basic idea of a franchise interesting. Let them explain more about the franchise.

Interpreting the Information

Every franchise is described in a standard format that includes 12 items about a franchise and franchisor. Understanding how to interpret this information will help you use this handbook more effectively. As an example, an entry from the *Handbook* is shown below. Each item in the example is labeled with a number that corresponds with the explanation about the item. The explanations provide tips on how to best use the information contained in each item.

The information about each franchise is collected to help you research a potential business for you to buy. Below is some advice about how to use this information in the most advantageous manner.

1. **Contact Information.** This item includes the name of the franchiser and its address. It also includes telephone numbers. And in step with modern times, there is an e-mail address and Web site when available. If you are interested in a franchise, make contact with a company representative. Make it clear that you want some basic information about the franchise. The company representative may work with you directly or possibly have a sales representative contact you. Be prepared to ask some of the questions covered in chapter 2.

2. **Number of Franchises.** One important piece of information about a franchise is the number of franchisees that are in business. A franchiser with more franchises probably has a high level of experience and a good product that makes it attractive to other investors. Franchisors with fewer units may provide an opportunity to get in on the ground floor of a successful operation, but you should carefully investigate these franchisors.

   A franchisor's ownership of operating units can be an indicator of both positive and negative factors. The number of company-owned units provides information about two important questions to investigate. First, does the company own the units because the franchisees failed and the franchisor agreed to buy back the units? You can tell about the potential success of a franchise by asking this

Sample Entry

1 **The Krystal Company**
One Union Square, 10th Floor
Chattanooga, TN 37402
Web Site Address: www.krystalco.com
E-mail Address: kryfran@mindspring.com
Toll-Free Phone: (800) 458-5912
Phone: (423) 757-1535
Fax: (423) 757-5623
Contact: Franchise Development Manager

2 Number of Franchises: 97
Company-Owned Units: 249
Total Units: 346

3 **In Business Since:** 1932   **4** **Franchising Since:** 1989

5 **Description of Operation:** Krystal is a quick-service restaurant with a drive-thru window and inside seating. Menu includes breakfast and features the unique Krystal burger prepared on a grill with steamed onions for flavor. Open 24 hours offering full line of Krystal products.

6 **Equity Capital Needed:** $200,000

7 **Franchise Fee:** $32,500

8 **Royalty:** 4.5 percent of weekly gross

9 **Advertising Co-op Fee:** None

10 **Financial Assistance:** Not available.

11 **Management Assistance:** All the tools you need to successfully open and run your own Krystal restaurant are at your fingertips. With Krystal's tried-and-true operational systems, the processes to handle every task—from ordering supplies to preparing food—are already established. You get comprehensive management training and ongoing field support. Complete operations manuals for easy reference any time of day. An accessible and knowledgeable corporate management team to keep you updated on the latest food service innovations. You also benefit from broadcast and print advertising created to draw more customers to your restaurant and marketing materials and strategies created for you to use on a local level. Field support is provided through assistance by phone and through Franchise Field Consultants.

12 **Training Assistance:** We provide complete and comprehensive training for you and your key managers. In that way, you will be prepared for an efficient, productive Grand Opening and smooth operations thereafter. Your comprehensive training program includes three distinct phases. There is training at our Tennessee headquarters, when appropriate. Further training is provided at an operating certified Krystal training restaurant. Finally, there is training support at your location for a minimum of five days during your first month.

question. Second, were franchisees forced to sell units back to the company? This question can help you determine whether the franchiser might purposely use franchisees to start a business, wait until operations are successful, then purchase it back for their own financial gain. It is also important to ask franchisors that don't own any franchises why this is the case. They may become too removed from operations to relate to common problems encountered by franchisees. Inquire how they intend to overcome this issue.

3. **In Business Since.** This item tells you how long an organization has been in business. You can use this information, in combination with the number of franchisees, to evaluate the experience and stability of a franchisor. Many business experts feel that a business in operation for more than five years has a much higher chance of success. Look for experienced franchisors if you want to minimize your risk. Less-experienced franchisors present a higher risk but may offer a ground floor opportunity for what could become a booming franchise operation.

4. **Franchising Since.** It is interesting to note how long a span exists between the establishment of the business and the first franchise operation. A short time span probably indicates that the business started with the intent to develop franchise operations. On the positive side, the franchisor probably knows franchising and is interested in making this part of the business succeed. On the other side, the franchise operation may not be based on a mature and well-tested business model. You could be one of the "guinea pigs" that provides the franchiser with valuable information about how to operate a franchise.

A franchisor with a large time span between the establishment of the business and the beginning of franchising is probably a very experienced business operator. This type of franchisor has a great deal of operational experience that can be useful to you. However, be aware that this operator may give a higher priority to operating his or her own business units at the expense of support for franchisees. In addition, the owners may

know about operating a business unit but may not be proficient in managing a franchise operation. You may experience many frustrations because of such franchising inexperience.

5. **Description of Operation.** A brief description of the business concept is contained in this section. It provides information about the product or service and identifies some features that make the franchise unique. This is the most useful section for matching your business interests with franchise opportunities. Recognize that the limited space for the description means that you are reading an abbreviated explanation of the franchise concept. Therefore, you should consider further investigating those franchisors that appear to partially meet your interests. A more thorough examination of the franchisor may result in a better match with your business interests.

6. **Equity Capital Needed.** For most people, the money required to purchase a franchise and start operations is a critical element in identifying potential franchises. The stated equity capital typically represents an average that most franchisees spend to get their business started—it may even include initial operating costs needed prior to generating enough revenues to cover day-to-day expenses. You might be able to start a franchise for less, or it may cost more depending on factors such as location and construction. Consider it a "ballpark" estimate and don't immediately dismiss the possibility of getting the franchise without talking to the franchisor.

7. **Franchise Fee.** This is the amount of money that must be paid to the franchisor for the rights to operate a franchise. It normally pays for training and some managerial assistance. This money often cannot be recovered unlike equipment that can be sold. The franchise fee represents a significant part of the financial risk in purchasing a franchise. Check the conditions under which the fee may be recovered. For example, does the franchisor guarantee to buy back a failed franchise? Can the franchise be sold to another buyer? Under what conditions can the franchise be sold?

Carefully investigate whether the franchisor actually provides a concept and subsequent support system that warrants the fee it charges. A simple idea may be worth a great deal of money when the franchisor can provide a support system that has demonstrated the potential to help franchisees become successful. Conversely, a unique and exciting concept is worth little when there is insufficient support from the franchisor in implementing the business.

8. **Royalty.** This is an extremely important piece of information. It tells you how much the franchisor expects you to pay as an on-going cost of business. A franchisor typically expects the franchisee to pay the royalty on gross sales. This means that the franchisor gets paid regardless of the operation's profitability. A small royalty fee may indicate that little follow-up support is planned. A high royalty fee should ensure a significant amount of day-to-day support from the franchisor. Determine what you receive in return for the royalty. This assistance might include continued management assistance, advanced training, new marketing concepts, and continued product or service development.

9. **Advertising Co-op Fee.** Some franchisors require a cooperative advertising or marketing fee. This payment from franchisees is usually matched by the franchisor and is used for advertising campaigns. Information about how this fund works and how it will benefit you is important to discover. Determine what assurance you have that the money will be used for advertising. Most franchisors are small and must run local marketing campaigns rather than national ones. This is why a clear understanding about how the advertising strategy can benefit your franchise is important.

10. **Financial Assistance.** Financial assistance refers to the programs the franchisor provides to aid a franchisee in financing an operation.

This is an important consideration to investors who have a limited amount of capital or don't have enough money to finance all equity requirements. However, the franchisor may not be the only, or best, source of financing, so don't let the lack of such assistance deter you from further investigation.

11. **Managerial Assistance.** Managerial assistance should be available during all phases of your company's life span. A franchisor should view your success as an integral part of its success. The amount of assistance provided is one indicator of the franchisor's commitment to help your business succeed. Operation start-up is the most critical time for managerial assistance, but continued guidance is important to long-term growth of your company.

12. **Training Assistance.** An important service that a franchisor provides is training for the franchisee. You may want to be cautious in purchasing a franchise that provides a small amount of training. If the concept is so simple that you need little training, the franchisor's assistance to implement a new business may not be important enough to pay for. If the concept is more complex, you should expect a sufficient amount of training to gain the expertise needed to run a prosperous operation. The best training is a combination of classroom instruction and one-on-one training at the franchisor's facility, plus field training at your own place of business.

Use Data with Caution

Inclusion of a franchisor in this *Handbook* does not constitute an endorsement or recommendation, nor is the *Handbook* an exhaustive list of all franchisors. All reference books face the difficulty of being 100 percent accurate. It is possible that some inaccurate data has been inadvertently reported or compiled. Before making a decision, be sure to verify the data in this book by directly contacting the franchisor.

FRANCHISE COMPANY DATA

Art—Framing

Deck The Walls

100 Glenborough, 14th Floor
Houston, TX 77067
Web Address: www.deckthewalls.com
Toll-Free Phone: (800) 443-3325
Phone: (713) 874-3684
Fax: (713) 874-3668
Contact: Franchise Development Coordinator

Number of Franchises: 196
Company-Owned Units: 3
Total Units: 199

In Business Since: 1979 **Franchising Since:** 1980

Description of Operation: Art and customer framing retail stores located in regional malls.

Equity Capital Needed: $75,000

Franchise Fee: $35,000

Royalty: 6 percent

Advertising Co-op Fee:

Financial Assistance: SBA, through third party.

Management Assistance: Regional director offers complete assistance in all facets of business, including merchandising, employee relations, inventory control, selling, and so on.

Training Assistance: Two-week training class, plus in-store training.

Fastframe USA, Inc

1200 Lawrence Dr., #300
Newbury Park, CA 91320
Web Address: www.fastframe.com
E-mail Address: fastframe@ix.netcom.com
Toll-Free Phone: (888) 863-7263
Phone: (805) 498-4463
Fax: (805) 498-8983
Contact: Franchise Development

Number of Franchises: 159
Company-Owned Units: 0
Total Units: 160

In Business Since: 1986 **Franchising Since:** 1987

Description of Operation: Franchising of custom picture framing retail stores.

Equity Capital Needed: $150,000-$200,000

Franchise Fee: $19,500

Royalty: 7.5 percent

Advertising Co-op Fee: 3 percent

Financial Assistance: Start up cash $30,000-$50,000

Management Assistance: Assistance includes marketing, purchasing, operations and accounting.

Training Assistance: We provide two weeks of training at the corporate training center in retail management and custom framing techniques. One-week training in store.

Great Frame Up Systems

9335 Belmont Ave.
Franklin Park, IL 60131
Web Address: www.greatframup.com
Toll-Free Phone: (800) 553-7263
Phone: (847) 671-2530
Fax: (847) 671-2580
Contact: V.P. of Marketing & Franchise Sales

Number of Franchises: 125
Company-Owned Units: 0
Total Units: 125

In Business Since: 1971 **Franchising Since:** 1975

Description of Operation: Do-it-yourself and custom framing retail stores.

Equity Capital Needed: $140,000

Franchise Fee: $25,000

Royalty: 6 percent

Advertising Co-op Fee:

Financial Assistance: The franchisor will finance one-half of franchise fee to qualified veterans through VetFran program. No other financing is offered, but assistance in obtaining conventional financing is available.

Management Assistance: Besides manuals, monthly newsletters, workshops, advertising promotional material and an annual conference, our directors of business development call on each franchise five or six times per year, providing guidance and assistance in every aspect of their business. Toll-free numbers to our staff in Franklin Park, IL, are provided.

Training Assistance: An extensive 32-day training program in our Evanston, IL, training center. All aspects of business and framing are covered, as well as hands-on training in actual store situations. Workshops and toll-free phone to training center are provided for ongoing education.

Malibu Gallery

1919 S. 40th St., Ste. 202
Lincoln, NE 68506
Toll-Free Phone: (800) 865-2378
Phone: (402) 434-5620
Fax: (402) 434-5624
Contact: President

Number of Franchises: 3
Company-Owned Units: 4
Total Units: 7

In Business Since: 1986   **Franchising Since:** 1994

Description of Operation: Malibu Gallery offers high-quality custom framing and a customer-friendly, reasonably priced art gallery.

Equity Capital Needed: $100,000

Franchise Fee: $20,000

Royalty: 6 percent

Advertising Co-op Fee: 2 percent

Financial Assistance: Current financial review, support on a business plan, and third-party lending options provided.

Management Assistance: Complete training, software program, manuals, follow-up, and an 800 number are provided.

Training Assistance: One week at the home office and one week on-site.

Automobile—Body Repair

Altracolor System

P.O. Box 2124
Kenner, LA 70063
E-mail Address: altra@concentric.com
Toll-Free Phone: (800) 678-5220
Phone: (504) 454-7233
Fax: (504) 454-7233
Contact: Director of Franchise Development

Number of Franchises: 88
Company-Owned Units: 2
Total Units: 90

In Business Since: 1988   **Franchising Since:** 1991

Description of Operation: Mobile automotive paint repair and touch-up system.

Equity Capital Needed: $25,000-$40,000

Franchise Fee: $9,950

Royalty: $95 a week

Advertising Co-op Fee:

Financial Assistance: Cash required is $9,950, plus $1,750 training fee. $13,500 opening inventory may be financed by franchisor for 36 months at 12 percent interest.

Management Assistance: Orientation training includes guidance in purchasing and expense control. Field training includes opening of new accounts and organization counseling.

Training Assistance: Three days of in-house orientaion in New Orleans, LA, training center. One week in field includes setting up new accounts and technical advice.

Auto One Glass and Accessories

15965 Jeanette St.
Southfield, MI 48075
Toll-Free Phone:
Phone: (810) 557-2784
Fax: (810) 557-7931
Contact:

Number of Franchises: 40
Company-Owned Units: 0
Total Units: 40

In Business Since: 1988   **Franchising Since:** 1988

Description of Operation: Auto appearance and protective services.

Equity Capital Needed: $45,000-$90,000

Franchise Fee: $20,000

Royalty: 5 percent

Advertising Co-op Fee:

Financial Assistance: Indirect financing and leasing options are available.

Management Assistance:

Training Assistance: Yes

Cartex Limited

42816 Mound Rd.
Sterling Heights, MI 48314
Toll-Free Phone: (800) 421-7328
Phone: (810) 739-4330
Fax: (810) 739-4331
Contact: Chief Execuitve Officer

Number of Franchises: 71
Company-Owned Units: 3
Total Units: 74

In Business Since: 1980   **Franchising Since:** 1988

Description of Operation: Auto internal fabric repair, with national recognition, using the trademarked Fabrion system. This is a mobile business, servicing auto dealers, auction houses, and rental car agencies with the Fabrion repair system for cloth and velour auto interiors.

Equity Capital Needed: $18,500

Franchise Fee: $13,500-$19,500

Royalty: $160-$240. Not based on percentage of sales.

Advertising Co-op Fee:

Financial Assistance: No financial assistance is available.

Management Assistance: We will assist you in opening accounts and provide on-the-job training in franchisee's area. A support representative will visit whenever needed in your given area. The corporate office has a national recognition advertising campaign, with direct mail pieces going out every 60 days.

Training Assistance: Specific instructions on account billing and book records. Suggestions and contacts for employing contractors.

Collision Shop, The

15965 Jeanette St.
Southfield, MI 48075
Toll-Free Phone:
Phone: (810) 559-1415
Fax: (810) 557-7931
Contact:

Number of Franchises: 15
Company-Owned Units: 4
Total Units: 19

In Business Since: 1991　　**Franchising Since:** 1993

Description of Operation: Body and paint specialist.

Equity Capital Needed: $133,000

Franchise Fee: $35,000

Royalty: 6 percent

Advertising Co-op Fee:

Financial Assistance:

Management Assistance:

Training Assistance:

Dent Doctor

11301 W. Markham
Little Rock, AR 72211
Web Address: www.dentdoctorusa.com
E-mail Address: info@dentdoctorusa.com
Toll-Free Phone: (800) 946-3368
Phone: (501) 224-0500
Fax: (501) 224-0507
Contact: President

Number of Franchises: 26
Company-Owned Units: 3
Total Units: 29

In Business Since: 1986　　**Franchising Since:** 1990

Description of Operation: Succeed in PaintFree Dent Repair (PDR) with Dent Doctor®, the award-winning company that has pioneered quality (PDR) services in the

U.S. since 1986. You'll become an expert at removing dents and hail damage from vehicles using the proprietary Dent Doctor technology that requires no painting. You'll remove the dents in minutes, preserving the the original finish, and you'll save the customer up to 75 percent off the cost of repainting. The four-week, one-on-one training covers every aspect of operating your mobile and/or in-shop Dent Doctor franchise. Dent Doctor offers you a proven market-tested system of superior training, tools, and technology that you must have to succeed.

Equity Capital Needed: $40,000

Franchise Fee: $3,500 and up

Royalty: Varies

Advertising Co-op Fee:

Financial Assistance: Assistance in preparing SBA loan request.

Management Assistance: 1-800 toll-free consultation number and ongoing assistance in addition to manager training program and operations manual.

Training Assistance: Complete, comprehensive one-on-one, in-shop training divided into four one-week modules covering every aspect of PaintFree Dent Repair and the operation of the Dent Doctor franchise.

Dent Zone

1919 S. 40th St., Ste. 202
Lincoln, NE 68506
Toll-Free Phone: (800) 865-2378
Phone: (402) 434-5620
Fax: (402) 434-5624
Contact: President

Number of Franchises: 1
Company-Owned Units: 1
Total Units: 2

In Business Since: 1993　　**Franchising Since:** 1997

Description of Operation: Paintless Dent Removal (PDR) is a service that is poised for explosive growth. Dent Zone utilizes PDR methods to repair minor automotive dents and dings. This repair technique has gained acceptance by insurance companies, auto dealerships, and rental companies.

Equity Capital Needed: $50,000

Franchise Fee: $20,000

Royalty: 9 percent

Advertising Co-op Fee: 1 percent

Financial Assistance: Current financial review, support on a business plan, and third-party lending options available.

Management Assistance: Complete training, software program, manuals, follow-up, and an 800 number provided.

Training Assistance: Three to four weeks provided at the home office in Dallas, Texas.

DentPro

2837 Whipple Road
Union City, CA 94587
Web Address: www.dentpro.com
Toll-Free Phone: (800) 868-3368
Phone:
Fax: (510) 429-5099
Contact: Director of Franchise Sales

Number of Franchises: 15
Company-Owned Units: 0
Total Units: 15

In Business Since: 1991   **Franchising Since:** 1993

Description of Operation: DentPro specializes in removing dents and dings from vehicles without harming the paint. We offer a convenient and affordable way for people to repair and beautify their cars. The benefits to customers are enormous. Average repair time is minimized because DentPro is a mobile business. Repairs are made at the client's location. This significantly reduces costs over comparable body shop work and eliminates "down time." Specialized skills and techniques are used.

Equity Capital Needed: $35,000-$100,000

Franchise Fee: $25,000 and up

Royalty: 7 percent

Advertising Co-op Fee:

Financial Assistance: Financing is available.

Management Assistance: DentPro's ongoing support program keeps franchisees abreast of new technical advances as they develop and provides tips on how to operate your business more successfully. We have a 24-hour support line for technical and business assistance, a newsletter, special conferences and advanced training sessions to update your knowledge and benefit from networking with your colleagues.

Training Assistance: The key to your long-term success as a DentPro professional is the intensive training and apprenticeship you will receive. DentPro thoroughly trains new franchisees in the technical aspects of the business as well as in business management skills and finishing techniques that are exclusive to DentPro. The technical portion encompasses both dent removal skills and finishing techniques that are exclusive to DentPro. During the training, you will learn the ways of operating a successful dent repair business-advanced business systems, accounting, and so on.

FIXX Enterprises, DBA FIXX-A-DENT

4959 N. Buford Hwy., Ste. 6, P.O. Box 942
Norcross, GA 30071
Web Address: www.fixx-a-dent.com
E-mail Address: info@fixx-a-dent.com
Toll-Free Phone:
Phone: (770) 449-4878
Fax: (770) 448-8131
Contact: President

Number of Franchises: 3
Company-Owned Units: 3
Total Units: 6

In Business Since: 1992   **Franchising Since:** 1993

Description of Operation: The FIXX-A-DENT franchise owner sells automotive paintless dent removal services to various market segments. The combined FIXX-A-DENT technical and business support systems provide the franchise owner with an unparalleled edge over lesser training-only systems. Our six years of experience in this emerging industry takes the trial-and-error pain away from the franchisee and replaces it with proven methods and peace of mind. Our technical training systems enable the technician to push the edges of existing technology and extend the application of the process.

Equity Capital Needed: Approximately $70,000

Franchise Fee: $9,500

Royalty: 6 percent of gross sales

Advertising Co-op Fee:

Financial Assistance: None

Management Assistance: Two weeks of on-site, start-up assistance.

Training Assistance: Eight weeks of technical, sales, and business training.

MAACO Auto Painting and Bodyworks

381 Brooks Rd.
King of Prussia, PA 19406
Web Address: www.maaco.com
E-mail Address: franchise@maaco.com
Toll-Free Phone: (800) 296-2226
Phone: (610) 265-6606
Fax: (610) 337-6176
Contact: Administrative Assistant

Number of Franchises: 525
Company-Owned Units: 0
Total Units: 525

In Business Since: 1972   **Franchising Since:** 1972

Description of Operation: Since 1982, MAACO has been in the production auto paint and bodyworks industry. We have painted and repaired over 10 million automobiles. Our slogan, "Uh-oh, better get MAACO," has given MAACO national brand-name recognition.

Equity Capital Needed: $190,000 total investment, includes franchise fee.

Franchise Fee: $30,000

Royalty: 8 percent

Advertising Co-op Fee:

Financial Assistance: Third-party financal assistance is available to qualifed applicants.

Management Assistance: MAACO provides ongoing operational support, regional meetings, seminars, and conventions.

Training Assistance: We offer a comprehensive four-week training program, concentrating on the management, systems, and procedures of a MAACO center. Also, a center manager's training course is also available.

Miracle Auto Painting & Body Repair

3157 Corporate Pl.
Hayward, CA 94545
Toll-Free Phone:
Phone: (510) 887-2211
Fax:
Contact: Marketing Director

Number of Franchises: 32
Company-Owned Units: 5
Total Units: 37

In Business Since: 1953 **Franchising Since:** 1964

Description of Operation: Production auto painting and collision repair.

Equity Capital Needed: $150,000

Franchise Fee: $35,000

Royalty: 5 percent of gross sales

Advertising Co-op Fee: 5 percent of gross sales

Financial Assistance: Third-party referral

Management Assistance: Continuing assistance

Training Assistance: Four weeks of classroom tailored to needs. Two weeks training in the shop. Two weeks at opening of shop.

Novus Windshield Repair

10425 Hampshire Ave. S.
Minneapolis, MN 55438
Toll-Free Phone: (800) 328-1117
Phone: (612) 944-8000
Fax: (612) 944-2542
Contact: President

Number of Franchises: 887
Company-Owned Units: 1
Total Units: 888

In Business Since: 1972 **Franchising Since:** 1985

Description of Operation: NOVUS Windshield Repair is the #1 low-investement franchise in the United States. NOVUS franchisees offer customers a convenient, eco-nomical alternative to windshield replacement by repair-ing stone-damaged windshields with our patented process. NOVUS Windshield Repair is a high-potential, long-term, full-time franchise opportunity.

Equity Capital Needed: $21,000

Franchise Fee: $11,000

Royalty: 6 percent

Advertising Co-op Fee:

Financial Assistance: Not available.

Management Assistance: With our "Executive in the Field" program, you're sure to get your business off on the right foot. We offer national advertising programs and insurance programs. Our toll-free hot line allows you to order products 24 hours a day. One-on-one phone consultation is available with experienced support managers. Plus, you'll receive a monthly newsletter filled with information on technical procedures, sales tips, motivational profiles, and product news.

Training Assistance: NOVUS Windshield Repair gives you the ongoing training and support needed to guide you from your first day of training and throughout your career as a franchise owner. We offer complete technical and business training at our Minneapolis, MN, headquar-ters. We offer one-on-one consultation with our eight-day program and teach you how to offer a full-service windshield repair franchise.

Paint Shuttle, The

P.O. Box 478
Monee, IL 60449
Toll-Free Phone:
Phone: (708) 534-1419
Fax: (708) 534-9475
Contact: President

Number of Franchises: 26
Company-Owned Units: 2
Total Units: 28

In Business Since: 1988 **Franchising Since:** 1991

Description of Operation: Complete auto paint restoration process for the repair of stone chips, scratches, minor rust spots, molding, trim, and urethane bumpers. All of the latest products and equipment are included.

Equity Capital Needed: $50,000

Franchise Fee: $35,000

Royalty: 10 percent

Advertising Co-op Fee:

Financial Assistance: Financial assistance is available for qualified for franchisees.

Management Assistance: Ongoing support through telephone, pagers, manuals and periodic refresher courses of new products and applications.

Training Assistance: A two-week, extensive training program, consisting of all hands-on training by qualified Paint Shuttle technicians in the franchisee's geographical area. All accounts are acquired. All products and their uses are thoroughly gone over.

Superglass Windshield Repair

6090 McDonough Dr., Ste. O
Norcross, GA 30093
Toll-Free Phone:
Phone: (770) 409-1885
Fax: (770) 840-8182
Contact: President

Number of Franchises: 94
Company-Owned Units: 1
Total Units: 95

In Business Since: 1992   **Franchising Since:** 1993

Description of Operation: Mobile and fixed location repair of rock-damaged and cracked windshields for commercial fleets, auto dealerships, insurance companies, and individual motorists.

Equity Capital Needed: $9,500-$28,500

Franchise Fee: $5,617

Royalty: 3 percent

Advertising Co-op Fee:

Financial Assistance: Three to zero percent financing on entire franchise cost. Typical: $9,500 total price; $6,500 down payment; 24 payments of $138.43 after four-month grace period.

Management Assistance: Five days of on-site marketing assistance in the franchisee's exclusive territory. Ongoing telemarketing assistance for term of franchise agreement, monthly newsletters, annual convention, and national accounts.

Training Assistance: We provide five days in Atlanta, GA, for technical, marketing, and bookkeeping training. All manuals are provided. Five additional days of marketing assistance in franchisee's exclusive territory to establish regular commercial accounts.

Automobile—Maintenance & Repair

AAMCO Transmissions

One Presidential Blvd.
Bala Cynwyd, PA 19004
Web Address: www.aamco.com
Toll-Free Phone: (800) 223-8887
Phone: (610) 668-2900
Fax: (610) 617-9532
Contact: Vice President, Marketing & Franchise Development

Number of Franchises: 718
Company-Owned Units: 0
Total Units: 718

In Business Since: 1963   **Franchising Since:** 1963

Description of Operation: AAMCO is the world's largest chain of transmission specialists with 35 years of experience. Nationally recognized by 92 percent of the driving public, AAMCO is the undisputed industry leader. Transmission repair is a $2.5 billion business in the United States and is projected to be a $3.6 billion business by the year 2001. AAMCO continues to enjoy record-breaking success in the ever-expanding automotive aftermarket.

Equity Capital Needed: $150,000

Franchise Fee: $30,000

Royalty: 7 percent

Advertising Co-op Fee:

Financial Assistance: Assistance in acquiring financing is provided.

Management Assistance: Continued support is provided in Operations, Technical Services, Marketing, Advertising, and Customer Relations.

Training Assistance: AAMCO's proven business system is taught in a comprehensive four-week training course held at the corporate home office in suburban Philadelphia. Professional instruction comprises three weeks of classroom training and one week of field training.

All Tune and Lube

8334 Veterans Hwy.
Millersville, MD 21108
Web Address: www.alltune.com
Toll-Free Phone: (800) 935-8863
Phone: (410) 987-1011
Fax: (410) 987-3060
Contact: Vice President of Franchise Development

Number of Franchises: 229
Company-Owned Units: 0
Total Units: 229

In Business Since: 1985   **Franchising Since:** 1986

Description of Operation: Automotive servicing, "One stop" total car care, including tune-ups, brakes, exhaust, engine replacement, and more.

Equity Capital Needed: Approximately $119,000

Franchise Fee: $22,500

Royalty: 7 percent

Advertising Co-op Fee:

Financial Assistance: Yes.

Management Assistance: All Tune and Lube provides training manual, operations staff visits, toll-free telephone assistance, technical schools, newsletters, and more. Continuing support in all areas of franchise operations, including marketing, research, management, and administration.

Training Assistance: All Tune and Lube provides extensive training, consisting of two weeks of franchise business management, training at the corporate training facility, two weeks of in-center training, and one week of center management training and operational support.

American Brake Service

1 Battery March Park, # 105
Quincy, MA 02169
Toll-Free Phone: (800) 362-7005
Phone: (404) 262-7005
Fax:
Contact: President

Number of Franchises: 7
Company-Owned Units: 0
Total Units: 7

In Business Since: 1991   **Franchising Since:** 1991

Description of Operation: Automotive specialty brake service franchise, specializing in brakes, shocks, joints, and front suspension. We utilize existing or converted three to four bay facilities as well as build-to-suit locations and offer one hour or less brake service with a low price and lifetime guarantee.

Equity Capital Needed: $80,000-$140,000

Franchise Fee: $19,500

Royalty: 6 percent

Advertising Co-op Fee:

Financial Assistance: We assist each franchisee or master franchisee with preparation of his or her business plan and selection of lender.

Management Assistance: We assist the franchisee with preopening and postopening advertising, as well as supply him or her with approved creative materials. Further assistance is provided in preconstruction and postoperational support, ongoing technical assistance, and new programs.

Training Assistance: Two weeks of training at our corporate headquarters are required. These consists of one week of classroom and one week of technical store training. Ongoing training in various areas is also provided.

Atlas Transmission

4444 W. 147th St.
Midlothian, IL 60445
Toll-Free Phone: (800) 377-9247
Phone: (708) 389-5922
Fax: (708) 389-9882
Contact: Vice President of Franchise Development

Number of Franchises: 29
Company-Owned Units: 0
Total Units: 29

In Business Since: 1964   **Franchising Since:** 1982

Description of Operation: Transmission and drive-train service and repairs of trucks, cars, 4x4s and RVs. Foreign and domestic. Retail, wholesale, and fleet.

Equity Capital Needed: $100,000-$130,000

Franchise Fee: $27,500

Royalty: 7 percent

Advertising Co-op Fee:

Financial Assistance: Data not available.

Management Assistance: We provide operations, training, sales, owner's school, and ongoing assistance from operations, technical, legal, and accounting departments. Assistance with national accounts and vendors.

Training Assistance: We have a center manager's school for center training and owner's school. We also have an 800 number for operations and technical questions.

Auto Accents

6550 Pearl Rd.
Parma Heights, OH 44130
Web Address: www.autoaccents.com
Toll-Free Phone: (800) 567-3120
Phone: (216) 888-8886
Fax: (216) 888-4333
Contact: Franchise Director

Number of Franchises: 1
Company-Owned Units: 4
Total Units: 5

In Business Since: 1979   **Franchising Since:** 1991

Description of Operation: Auto accents is an automotive add-on center. We sell and install cellular phones, stereo systems, sun roofs, gold painting, alarms, running boards, and accessories for making driving more fun. Auto Accents was voted in Top 30 Autosound Retailer of the Year nationwide and Cellular One's Agent of the Year for Ohio.

Equity Capital Needed: $80,000-$120,000

Franchise Fee: $9,700

Royalty: 5 percent

Advertising Co-op Fee:

Financial Assistance: None

Management Assistance: Full training on all aspects of opening; hiring; dealing with landlords, municipalities, and paperwork; retaining and developing a good team, and all aspects of managing the business.

Training Assistance: Prior to opening, a full three weeks at headquarters is provided free to franchisee, and a full week after opening at franchisee's site. Franchisee will be regularly trained and updated on procedures and techniques.

Auto-Lab Diagnostic & Tune-Up Center

1346 W. Columbia Ave. Ste. 209
Battle Creek, MI 49015
Toll-Free Phone:
Phone: (616) 966-0500
Fax: (616) 966-0520
Contact:

Number of Franchises:
Company-Owned Units:
Total Units:

In Business Since: 1983   **Franchising Since:** 1989

Description of Operation: Engine performance, electrical system diagnostics, and repair, as well as general auto service.

Equity Capital Needed:

Franchise Fee: $19,500

Royalty: 6 percent

Advertising Co-op Fee:

Financial Assistance: Data not available.

Management Assistance: Data not available.

Training Assistance: Data not available.

Brake Shop, Inc., The

31900 Utica Rd., Ste. 202,
P.O. Box 370
Fraser, MI 48026
Toll-Free Phone: (800) 747-2113
Phone: (810) 415-2800
Fax:
Contact: Director of Franchise Devlopment

Number of Franchises: 75
Company-Owned Units: 3
Total Units: 78

In Business Since: 1987   **Franchising Since:** 1989

Description of Operation: The Brake Shop handles all automotive brake system repair needs. The Brake Shop, typically 1,500-4,000 square feet, is located in strip malls, automotive malls, or free-standing units. Prior automotive experience not needed.

Equity Capital Needed: $50,000-$80,000

Franchise Fee: $22,500

Royalty: 8 percent

Advertising Co-op Fee:

Financial Assistance: Equipment lease financing is available. The Brake Shop offers a special plan to veterans as a sponsor of Vetfran.

Management Assistance: Franchisees are given extensive training and support in the operations and marketing of the business. In addition to a comprehensive operations manual and marketing tool kit, the operations support team provides ongoing technical and sales seminars. A quarterly newsletter communicates new programs to the franchisees.

Training Assistance: The new fanchisee attends a two-week training session at the corporate training facility. Then, an operations manager provides two additional weeks of training on-site during the shop opening.

Brake World

300 N.W. 82nd Ave., Ste. 410
Ft. Lauderdale, FL 33324
Toll-Free Phone: (800) 392-7253
Phone: (954) 472-3333
Fax: (954) 452-9885
Contact: President

Number of Franchises: 21
Company-Owned Units: 1
Total Units: 22

In Business Since: 1972   **Franchising Since:** 1975

Description of Operation: Automotive and light truck brake and auto repairs.

Equity Capital Needed: $40,000-$45,000

Franchise Fee: $25,000

Royalty: 5 percent

Advertising Co-op Fee:

Financial Assistance: The franchisor may offer a financing arrangement to the franchisee for the initial franchise fee and/or for the purchase of the initial equipment, inventory, supplies, and other materials solely for the establishment of the franchise. This is offered as an accommodation to lessen the initial cash outlay of a franchisee.

Management Assistance: Data not available.

Training Assistance: Mandatory initial on-the-job training is provided for the franchisee by the franchisor at no charge. The training is led by a person designated by the franchisor at the franchisor's facilities in Miami, FL, or another site closer to the franchisee as designated by the franchisor. The franchisee will be responsible for travel, lodging, and living expenses. The franchisor presently does not offer any other refresher courses. Any personnel the franchisee wants to be trained can be trained for $50/day.

Budget Brake & Muffler

4940 Canada Way, #422
Burnaby, BC V5G 4K6
Web Address: www.budgetbrake.com
Toll-Free Phone:
Phone: (604) 294-6114
Fax: (604) 294-1648
Contact: President

Number of Franchises: 23
Company-Owned Units: 2
Total Units: 25

In Business Since: 1969   **Franchising Since:** 1972

Description of Operation: Retail automotive service repairs, specializing in brakes and exhaust.

Equity Capital Needed: $175,000

Franchise Fee: $25,000

Royalty: 4.5 percent

Advertising Co-op Fee:

Financial Assistance: Bank financing is available to approved franchisees. Normal cash requirements are 40 percent of new store operations.

Management Assistance: Assistance is available at all times. Support staff in-store operations, accounting, computer, and advertising are at head office.

Training Assistance: Average training takes 60 days. Two weeks of classroom and six weeks of in-store, hands-on training.

Car-X Muffler & Brake

8430 W. Bryn Mawr, Ste. 400
Chicago, IL 60631
Web Address: www.carx.com
E-mail Address: dmaltzma@speedy.com
Toll-Free Phone: (800) 359-2359
Phone: (773) 693-1000
Fax: (773) 693-0309
Contact: Franchice Development Manager

Number of Franchises: 119
Company-Owned Units: 53
Total Units: 172

In Business Since: 1971   **Franchising Since:** 1973

Description of Operation: Car-X Muffler & Brake is a midwest regional chain. We are beginning to expand beyond our midwestern development, opening prime new markets with opportunities for single and multiunit growth. We are retail automotive specialists providing service in brakes, exhaust, road handling, steering systems, and oil changes for all makes of cars and light trucks. Most of our franchisees have grown to become mutiunit shop owners.

Equity Capital Needed: $65,000 minimum

Franchise Fee: $18,500

Royalty: 5 percent of gross sales

Advertising Co-op Fee: 5-10 percent

Financial Assistance: Third-party financing for SBA-guaranteed loans to qualified applicants.

Management Assistance: We will initially train franchisee in all aspects of the shop's operation. Ongoing managerial assistance will be provided by telephone, personal shop visits, or vendor participation.

Training Assistance: We provide five weeks of training at our headquarters and shop, plus two weeks of training at the franchisee's shop. Ongoing training programs are available to franchisees and employees.

Champion Auto Stores

9353 Jefferson Highway
Maple Grove, MN 55369
Web Address: www.championauto.com
Toll-Free Phone: (800) 621-4227
Phone: (612) 391-6655
Fax: (612) 391-7540
Contact: Vice President, Franchise Development

Number of Franchises: 125
Company-Owned Units: 45
Total Units: 170

In Business Since: 1956   **Franchising Since:** 1961

Description of Operation: Retail sale of automotive parts, accessories, and tires.

Equity Capital Needed: $75,000-$100,000

Franchise Fee: $20,000

Royalty: 0 percent

Advertising Co-op Fee:

Financial Assistance: None

Management Assistance: The franchisor gives assistance in advertising, inventory control, purchasing, sales, merchandising, expense control, and employee management throughout the affiliation.

Training Assistance: Sales and management training with a minimum of 20 days is required by the franchisor.

Cottman Transmission Systems

240 New York Dr.
Fort Washington, PA 19034
Web Address: www.cottman.com
Toll-Free Phone: (888) 426-8862
Phone: (215) 643-5885
Fax: (215) 643-2519
Contact: Manager of Franchise Development

Number of Franchises: 203
Company-Owned Units: 2
Total Units: 205

In Business Since: 1962   **Franchising Since:** 1964

Description of Operation: Franchised repair centers, specializing in all types of transmission repair and related services. The company's mission is to promote dynamic growth through integrity, professionalism, and caring service.

Equity Capital Needed: $78,000-$114,000

Franchise Fee: $25,000

Royalty: 7.5 percent

Advertising Co-op Fee:

Financial Assistance: Licensed franchisees are provided with the assistance necessary to obtain financing.

Management Assistance: Cottman Transmission provides both initial and continual operational, sales, management, and technical support. Complete and professional advertising support services.

Training Assistance: Cottman Transmission provides a comprehensive, initial four weeks of training at the national support headquarters in Fort Washington, PA, as well as continual training at the franchisee's location.

Creative Colors International

5550 W. 175th Street
Tinley Park, IL 60477
E-mail Address: colors@franchise1.com
Toll-Free Phone: (800) 933-2656
Phone: (708) 614-7786
Fax: (708) 614-9685
Contact: President

Number of Franchises: 39
Company-Owned Units: 1
Total Units: 40

In Business Since: 1980   **Franchising Since:** 1991

Description of Operation: Mobile unit service business that repairs and restores leather, vinyl, plastics, fabric, carpeting, and many other upholstery-related items. Customers include automobile dealerships, furniture retailers and manufacturers, restaurants, hotels, airports, rental cars, buses, and many other markets. Explore all markets for tremendous growth potential.

Equity Capital Needed: $50,000 plus

Franchise Fee: $17,500

Royalty: 6 percent

Advertising Co-op Fee:

Financial Assistance: Finance initial start-up supplies up to $7,000

Management Assistance: Operations manuals and training manuals are provided. Field visits are conducted periodically. 800# is available for technical support. Monthly newsletter and yearly national seminars are also provided.

Training Assistance: Two weeks of training at headquarters that covers all hands-on repair and restoration techniques, advertising, sales, marketing, accounting, and bookkeeping. An additional one week of training in territory at grand opening to assist with obtaining new clients.

Dr. Nick's Transmissions

4444 W. 147th St.
Midlothian, IL 60445
Toll-Free Phone: (800) 377-9247
Phone: (708) 389-5922
Fax: (708) 389-9882
Contact: Vice President of Francise Development

Number of Franchises: 19
Company-Owned Units: 0
Total Units: 19

In Business Since: 1979   **Franchising Since:** 1979

Description of Operation: Transmission and drive-train service and repairs of trucks, cars, 4x4s, and RVs. Foreign and domestic. Retail, wholesale, and fleet.

Equity Capital Needed: $100,000-$130,000

Franchise Fee: $27,500

Royalty: 7 percent

Advertising Co-op Fee:

Financial Assistance: We provide referrals to third-party financing, based on only the prospect's credit.

Management Assistance: We provide operations; training, sales, owner's school, and ongoing assistance from operations, technical, legal, and accounting departments. Assistance with national accounts and vendors.

Training Assistance: We offer a center manager's school for center training and owner's school. We offer also an 800 number for operations and technical questions.

Dr. Vinyl & Associates, Ltd.

9501 E. 350 Hwy.
Raytown, MO 64133
Web Address: www.drvinyl.com
E-mail Address: drvinyl@drvinyl.com
Toll-Free Phone: (800) 531-6600
Phone: (816) 356-3312
Fax: (816) 356-9049
Contact: President

Number of Franchises: 116
Company-Owned Units: 3
Total Units: 119

In Business Since: 1972   **Franchising Since:** 1981

Description of Operation: Vinyl, leather, velour, fabric repair, and coloring. Auto windshield repair, dashboard, and hard plastic repair. Vinyl striping and protective molding to new and used car dealers.

Equity Capital Needed: $35,000-40,000

Franchise Fee: $19,500

Royalty: 4-7 percent

Advertising Co-op Fee: 1 percent

Financial Assistance: Up to $5,000 financing of initial franchise fee to qualified applicants. Also, assistance in preparation of business plan to obtain loans from third parties.

Management Assistance: Accounting package, comprehensive marketing plan, ongoing market and activity analysis, and assistance in evaluating potential employees.

Training Assistance: Two weeks of intensive classroom training. Two weeks of training in field in home territory.

Econo Lube n' Tune

4911 Birch St.
Newport Beach, CA 92660
Web Address: www.econolube.com
Toll-Free Phone: (800) 628-0253
Phone: (714) 852-6630
Fax: (714) 852-6688
Contact: Director

Number of Franchises: 130
Company-Owned Units: 65
Total Units: 195

In Business Since: 1977 **Franchising Since:** 1978

Description of Operation: Auto service, lube, tune, and brakes.

Equity Capital Needed: $60,000-$120,000

Franchise Fee: $29,500-$79,500

Royalty: 6 percent

Advertising Co-op Fee:

Financial Assistance: None

Management Assistance: Three-week training program. Ongoing support.

Training Assistance: One week of classroom training. One week of training in shop and one week of training in franchisee's shop.

Gas Tank Renu—USA

12727 Greenfield
Detroit, MI 48227
Web Address: www.gastankrenu.com
Toll-Free Phone: (800) 932-2766
Phone: (313) 837-6122
Fax: (313) 273-4759
Contact: Managing Partner

Number of Franchises: 57
Company-Owned Units: 0
Total Units: 57

In Business Since: 1986 **Franchising Since:** 1986

Description of Operation: Gas Tank Renu—USA has a patented process for the repair of fuel tanks for cars, trucks, boats, and industrial applications. It is well suited for the antique and auto collector marketplace.

Equity Capital Needed: $20,000-$30,000

Franchise Fee: $9,000

Royalty: 0 percent

Advertising Co-op Fee:

Financial Assistance: Data not available.

Management Assistance: Complete training for start-up on-site, site selection assistance, co-op advertising plan, site visits, newsletters, and conferences.

Training Assistance: Complete on-site training, usually two to three days.

Goodeal Discount Transmission

P.O. Box 50
National Park, NJ 08063
Toll-Free Phone:
Phone: (609) 665-5225
Fax: (609) 273-6913
Contact: President

Number of Franchises: 30
Company-Owned Units: 0
Total Units: 30

In Business Since: 1979 **Franchising Since:** 1984

Description of Operation: Transmission franchise.

Equity Capital Needed: $75,000

Franchise Fee: $22,500

Royalty: Flat fee.

Advertising Co-op Fee:

Financial Assistance: Equipment leasing to qualified operators.

Management Assistance: Ongoing training available throughout the term of the agreement.

Training Assistance: Ongoing training available throughout the term of the agreement.

Goodyear Tire Centers

1144 E. Market St.
Akron, OH 44316
Toll-Free Phone:
Phone: (330) 796-2738
Fax: (330) 796-1876
Contact: Manager of Franchising

Number of Franchises: 301
Company-Owned Units: 929
Total Units: 120

In Business Since: 1900 **Franchising Since:** 1968

Description of Operation: Retail tires and automotive services.

Equity Capital Needed: $75,000-$125,000

Franchise Fee: $15,000

Royalty: 3 percent

Advertising Co-op Fee:

Financial Assistance: Equipment leasing is available. Land, building, and financial support is available.

Management Assistance: An assigned dealer development counselor assists in franchise operation.

Training Assistance: Training includes 10 weeks of formal classroom and on-the-job training.

Guaranteed Tune Up, Inc.

89 Headquarters Plaza, North Tower, 14th Fl.
Morristown, NJ 07960
Toll-Free Phone: (800) 543-5829
Phone: (973) 539-7538
Fax: (973) 455-0447
Contact: Director of Marketing

Number of Franchises: 5
Company-Owned Units: 0
Total Units: 5

In Business Since: 1984   **Franchising Since:** 1984

Description of Operation: Automotive tune-up and automobile repair service business.

Equity Capital Needed: Approximatley $96,000

Franchise Fee: $15,000

Royalty: 6 percent

Advertising Co-op Fee:

Financial Assistance: We will assist in securing outside financing.

Management Assistance: Continual managerial assistance is provided in all phases of the operation to ensure the proper operation of the business.

Training Assistance: An intensive one-week training program is provided for shop managers, mechanics, or owners.

Kennedy Transmission

410 Gateway Blvd.
Burnsville, MN 55337
Toll-Free Phone:
Phone: (612) 894-7020
Fax: (612) 894-1849
Contact: President

Number of Franchises: 18
Company-Owned Units: 2
Total Units: 20

In Business Since: 1962   **Franchising Since:** 1977

Description of Operation: Retail repair and service of automatic and manual transmissions and other driveline components in automobiles and light trucks.

Equity Capital Needed: $85,000-$120,000

Franchise Fee: $17,500

Royalty: 6 percent

Advertising Co-op Fee:

Financial Assistance: No direct assistance. We can direct franchisee to sources of financing, and we can assist in SBA financing. We have a working relationship with a major bank with preferred SBA status.

Management Assistance: Assistance in all aspects of store setup, including hiring, office procedures, accounting, inventory management, goal setting, and tracking. Full set of written policies and procedures manuals. Limited group-buying agreements with critical vendors. Frequent store visits by franchise representatives.

Training Assistance: Three weeks of training included in initial franchise fee. Heavy sales emphasis—telephone skills, communicating repairs to customers, obtaining job approval, and arranging final vehicle delivery. Also, emphasis on shop workflow management.

Lee Myles Transmissions

140 Rt. 17 N.
Paramus, NJ 07652
Web Address: www.leemyles.com
Toll-Free Phone: (800) 533-6953
Phone: (201) 262-0555
Fax: (201) 262-5177
Contact: Marketing

Number of Franchises: 85
Company-Owned Units: 0
Total Units: 85

In Business Since: 1947   **Franchising Since:** 1964

Description of Operation: Automotive transmission service and repair.

Equity Capital Needed: $40,000-$60,000

Franchise Fee: $25,000

Royalty: 6 percent

Advertising Co-op Fee:

Financial Assistance: Some financing is available.

Management Assistance: Assistance includes in-class, on-site managment training on all Lee Myles policies and procedures, various technical training seminars, and the periodic on-site review and evaluation of center activities by home office professional personnel.

Training Assistance: Training includes an intensive two-week training period in our corporate office and in the franchisee's center, as well as special follow-up seminars on technical, sales, and marketing operations and business planning. One of the most valuable tools you will receive is the Lee Myles operations and owner's manual. In it, you will find explicit directions and methods on how to run your business. You will also receive ongoing in-center and operations support.

Lentz U.S.A. Service Center

1001 Riverview Dr.
Kalamazoo, MI 49001
Web Address: www.lentzusa.com
Toll-Free Phone: (800) 354-2131
Phone: (616) 342-2200
Fax: (616) 342-9461
Contact: Franchise Sales Director

Number of Franchises: 27
Company-Owned Units: 11
Total Units: 38

In Business Since: 1972   **Franchising Since:** 1989

Description of Operation: Automotive undercar repair facility. Lentz USA is a specialty shop concentrating on exhaust, brakes and suspension services. It is a middle to high-end service store with 10,000 associated warranty locations nationwide.

Equity Capital Needed: $36,00-$50,000

Franchise Fee: $20,000

Royalty: 7-0 percent

Advertising Co-op Fee:

Financial Assistance: The franchisor will assist signed franchisees with sources of financing. There are many alternatives available to those with a good credit rating. Although we do not finance our franchisees, we have many proven sources for our fanchisees.

Management Assistance: Our franchisees are trained initially for 80 hours of both classroom and hands-on training before grand opening. We have continuing support that includes site visits.

Training Assistance: Same as above.

Master Mechanic, Inc.

1989 Dundas St. E.
Mississauga, ON L4X 1M1
Toll-Free Phone:
Phone: (905) 629-3773
Fax: (905) 629-3864
Contact: President

Number of Franchises: 27
Company-Owned Units: 0
Total Units: 27

In Business Since: 1981   **Franchising Since:** 1986

Description of Operation: Full-service automotive repair garages to the retail market. Professional service for imported and domestic cars and vans. Specializing in general repairs, tune-ups, alignments, engine performance, and driveability.

Equity Capital Needed: $100,000 (Canadian)

Franchise Fee: $25,000 (Canadian)

Royalty: 6 percent

Advertising Co-op Fee:

Financial Assistance: Assistance with preparation of bank financing presentation. Franchisor will attend with franchisee to acquire bank and government-sponsored financing. Franchisee usually provided with "turnkey" operation.

Management Assistance: Training in existing locations, at head office, and with manufacturers of equipment and product. Operations manual. Monthly management meetings for all franchisees. On-site assistance by franchisor.

Training Assistance: Procedures and technical training are conducted on-site and at existing locations and head office. Management training courses provided by specialists in management and automotive servicing. Business training by franchisor accountants.

Meineke Discount Muffler Shops

128 S. Tryon St.; #900
Charlotte, NC 28202
Web Address: www.meineke.com
Toll-Free Phone: (800) 634-6353
Phone: (704) 377-8855
Fax: (704) 377-1490
Contact: Franchise Sales

Number of Franchises: 917
Company-Owned Units: 7
Total Units: 924

In Business Since: 1972   **Franchising Since:** 1972

Description of Operation: Meineke Discount Muffler Shops offer fast, courteous service in the merchandising of automotive exhaust systems, brakes, shock absorbers, struts, CV joints, and oil changes. Unique inventory control and group purchasing power enable Meineke to adhere to a "Discount Concept" and deliver quality service. No mechanical skills required.

Equity Capital Needed: Varies

Franchise Fee: $22,500

Royalty: 7-5 percent

Advertising Co-op Fee: 10 percent

Financial Assistance: Our representatives will work with you on financial details.

Management Assistance: National advertising, product support, national suppliers, field operations support, national dealer committees, and more.

Merlin's Muffler & Brake

One N. River Ln., Ste. 206
Geneva, IL 60134
Toll-Free Phone: (800) 652-9900
Phone: (630) 208-9900
Fax: (630) 208-8601
Contact: Director, Market Development

Number of Franchises: 58
Company-Owned Units: 3
Total Units: 61

In Business Since: 1975   **Franchising Since:** 1975

Description of Operation: Central to Merlin's retail concept is an upscale, six-bay automotive service facility, designed and developed as an important result of Merlin's complete real estate program. Merlin's typical franchise business plan and working cash requirement facilitates first-year cash flows appropriate to owner operation.

Equity Capital Needed: $45,000

Franchise Fee: $26,000-$30,000

Royalty: 4.9 percent

Advertising Co-op Fee:

Financial Assistance: Subject to individual qualifications, the franchise is readily financeable by third parties—for example, SBA, bank, equipment lease provider, inventory vendor, and so on. The franchisor provides extensive assistance to franchisees relative to securing financing.

Management Assistance: New franchisee assistance includes, but is not limited to, the following: five weeks of training, operations and personnel manuals, hot line phone services, grand opening, marketing, on-site corporate staff for at least two to four weeks, vendor assistance on product, video library in shop, and so on.

Training Assistance: Merlin's provides a comprehensive five-week technical and management training program at the headquarter's training facility and operating service center. Topics include personnel, marketing, product and purchasing, customer service, bookkeeping and accounting, equipment use and maintenance, and so on.

Midas International Corporation

225 N. Michigan Ave.
Chicago, IL 60601
Web Address: www.midasfran.com
E-mail Address: mchong.midas@mcimail.com
Toll-Free Phone: (800) 621-0144
Phone: (312) 565-7500
Fax: (312) 565-7818
Contact: V.P. of Franchise Development

Number of Franchises: 2349
Company-Owned Units: 369
Total Units: 2718

In Business Since: 1956   **Franchising Since:** 1956

Description of Operation: Midas Muffler & Brake is reknown for its chain of under-the-car specialty automotive repair shops. Services include exhaust replacement; brake repair; front end, steering, suspension, and drivetrain parts; alignment services; cooling systems—flush and fill; air-conditioning services (available at some locations); and products for vehicle maintenance.

Equity Capital Needed: $100,000

Franchise Fee: $20,000

Royalty: 10 percent

Advertising Co-op Fee:

Financial Assistance: Midas provides no direct financial assistance but will put applicants in contact with a list of lending institutions experienced in financing Midas Muffler & Brake Shops.

Management Assistance: Site selection, design, and construction; training; advertising and marketing; purchasing of both inventory and equipment; research and

development, Mystery Shopper Programs; national and local public relations; and field support.

Training Assistance: The entire training program takes approxiamtely six to eight weeks. Prework, which is on-the-job training, takes approximately three weeks to complete. After the prework assignment is completed, the franchisee must complete a three-week classroom training program at the Midas Institute of Technology in Palatine, IL.

Mister Front End

192 N. Queen St.
Etobicoke, ON M9C 1A8
Toll-Free Phone:
Phone: (416) 622-9999
Fax: (416) 622-9999
Contact: President

Number of Franchises: 1
Company-Owned Units: 1
Total Units: 2

In Business Since: 1973   **Franchising Since:** 1983

Description of Operation: Heavy duty spring, suspenion, air-conditioning, and alignment specialists.

Equity Capital Needed: Data not available

Franchise Fee: $15,000

Royalty: 5 percent

Advertising Co-op Fee:

Financial Assistance: Data not available

Management Assistance: Complete support for as long as necessary.

Training Assistance: We offer three months of training at the home base, followed by consultation at any time and for as long as necessary.

Mister Transmission

30 Wertheim Ct., Ste. 5
Richmond Hill, ON L4B 1B9
Web Address: www.mistertransmission.com
Toll-Free Phone: 800-373-8432
Phone: (905) 886-1511
Fax: (905) 886-1545
Contact: Vice President of Corporate Development

Number of Franchises: 89
Company-Owned Units: 0
Total Units: 89

In Business Since: 1963   **Franchising Since:** 1969

Description of Operation: Canada's largest transmission repair specialists. Our service is offered coast-to-coast. The Mister Transmission franchise system is a proven sales and marketing program, in business for over 30 years.

Equity Capital Needed: $100,000-$125,000

Franchise Fee: $25,000

Royalty: 7 percent

Advertising Co-op Fee:

Financial Assistance: The financing program through a chartered bank is available to qualified applicants.

Management Assistance: We provide a management training course at the head office, ongoing training sessions and in-store assistance, a complete training manual, advertising support, computer system, real estate support, and operations support.

Training Assistance: Training is available for owners, their managers, and employees.

Mr. Transmission

4444 W. 147th St.
Midlothian, IL 60445
Toll-Free Phone: (800) 377-9247
Phone: (708) 389-5922
Fax: (708) 389-5922
Contact: Vice President of Franchise Development

Number of Franchises: 88
Company-Owned Units: 1
Total Units: 89

In Business Since: 1956   **Franchising Since:** 1976

Description of Operation: Mr. Transmission provides transmission and drive-train service and repairs of trucks, cars, 4X4s, and RVs. Foreign and domestic. Retail, wholesale, and fleet.

Equity Capital Needed: $100,000-$130,000

Franchise Fee: $27,500

Royalty: 7 percent

Advertising Co-op Fee:

Financial Assistance: We provide referrals to third-party financing, based on only the prospect's credit.

Management Assistance: We provide operations, training, sales, owner's school, and ongoing assistance from operations, technical, legal, and accounting departments, as well as assistance with national accounts and vendors.

Training Assistance: We offer center manager's school for center training and owner's school. We also have an 800 number for operations and technical questions.

Multistate Transmission

4444 W. 147th St.
Midlothian, IL 60445
Toll-Free Phone: (800) 377-9247
Phone: (708) 389-5922
Fax: (708) 389-9882
Contact: Vice President of Franchise development

Number of Franchises: 33
Company-Owned Units: 1
Total Units: 34

In Business Since: 1973   **Franchising Since:** 1973

Description of Operation: Multistate Transmission provides transmission and drive-train service and repairs of trucks, cars, 4X4s, and RVs. Foreign and domestic. Retail, wholesale, and fleet.

Equity Capital Needed: $100,000-$130,000

Franchise Fee: $27,500

Royalty: 7 percent

Advertising Co-op Fee:

Financial Assistance: We provide referrals to third-party financing, based on only the prospect's credit.

Management Assistance: We provide operations, training, sales, owner's school and ongoing assistance from operations, technical, legal and accounting departments, as well as assistance with national accounts and vendors.

Training Assistance: Center manager's school for center training and owner's school. An 800# service for operations and technical questions.

Precision Tune

748 Miller Dr., S.E,
P.O. Box 5000
Leesburg, VA 20175
Toll-Free Phone: (800) 231-0588
Phone: (703) 777-9095
Fax: (703) 779-0137
Contact: Director of Franchise Recruitment

Number of Franchises: 538
Company-Owned Units: 3
Total Units: 541

In Business Since: 1975   **Franchising Since:** 1978

Description of Operation: Precision Tune, America's largest engine performance car care company, offers a variety of services: tune-up, quick oil and lube, brake service, engine performance repair, and maintenance. Franchisees are provided with comprehensive training programs, continual operating support, marketing and advertising support, and inventory and management support. Area franchise opportunities also available.

Equity Capital Needed: $137,100-$194,600

Franchise Fee: $25,000

Royalty: 7.5 percent

Advertising Co-op Fee:

Financial Assistance: While Precision Tune does not provide direct financal assistance, equipment leasing is available to qualified prospects through a third party. Assistance is also provided in SBA loan applications through an outside party. Precision Tune participates in the VelFran program and will finance 50 percent of the franchisee fee for 12 months at 0 percent interest for qualified veterans.

Management Assistance: A two-week management course is required for all franchisees. In addition, most franchisees are supported in their local market by an area subfranchisor who owns and operates centers. Area subfranchisors assist in business management, technical training, and ongoing support as needed. Those franchisees located in areas not covered by an area subfranchisor are assisted by corporate operations and marketing staff members.

Training Assistance: Training for each staff level: franchisee management training (two weeks), center management (one week), engine performance technical training (five weeks), and brake technical training (one week). We also offer classes in air-conditioning, cooling system service; fuel injection service; lighting service; lube, oil, and filter service; and transmission service.

SAF-T Auto Centers

121 N. Plains Industrial Rd., Ste. H
Wallingford, CT 06492
Web Address: www.saftauto.com
E-mail Address: saf-t@snet.net
Toll-Free Phone: (800) 382-7238
Phone: (203) 294-1094
Fax: (203) 269-2532
Contact: President

Number of Franchises: 12
Company-Owned Units: 1
Total Units: 13

In Business Since: 1978   **Franchising Since:** 1985

Description of Operation: SAF-T Auto Centers is an owner-operated, auto repair shop offering steering, suspension, brakes, mufflers, lubrication, and minor repairs. Our main effort is to put good mechanics in a business opportunity where they capitalize on their ability.

Equity Capital Needed: $25,000

Franchise Fee: $15,000

Royalty: $500 per month

Advertising Co-op Fee:

Financial Assistance: Assistance for third-party financing to qualified applicants.

Management Assistance: Provided as needed.

Training Assistance: One month on-site.

Shine Factory, The

3519 14th St. S.W. 2nd Floor
Calgary, AB T2T 3W2
Toll-Free Phone:
Phone: (403) 243-3030
Fax: (403) 243-3031
Contact: President

Number of Franchises: 26
Company-Owned Units: 0
Total Units: 26

In Business Since: 1979   **Franchising Since:** 1979

Description of Operation: Canada's largest automotive and polishing franchise.

Equity Capital Needed: $90,000-$150,000

Franchise Fee: $10,000-$50,000

Royalty: 8 percent

Advertising Co-op Fee:

Financial Assistance: We assist in bank negotiations.

Management Assistance: Each franchisee receives assistance in location, sales, bookkeeping, employee relations, operations, and advertising.

Training Assistance: Two weeks of hands-on and theory training, one week of marketing at the franchisee's location, and ongoing follow-up.

Speedy Auto Service

8430 W. Bryn Mawr Ave., Ste. 400
Chicago, IL 60631
Web Address: www.speedy.com
E-mail Address: dmaltzma@speedy.com
Toll-Free Phone: (800) 359-2359
Phone: (773) 693-1000
Fax: (773) 693-0309
Contact: Franchise Development Manager

Number of Franchises: 81
Company-Owned Units: 825
Total Units: 906

In Business Since: 1956   **Franchising Since:** 1986

Description of Operation: Speedy Auto Service is a regional chain with over 200 shops in the eastern United States. With our distribution in other countries, we have over 900 shops worldwide. We are retail automotive specialists providing service in brakes, exhaust, road handling, steering systems, and oil changes for all makes of cars and light trucks.

Equity Capital Needed: $65,000 minimum

Franchise Fee: $18,500

Royalty: 5 percent of gross sales

Advertising Co-op Fee: 5-10 percent

Financial Assistance: Third-party financing for SBA-guaranteed loans to qualified applicants.

Management Assistance: We will initially train franchisee in all aspects of the shop's operation. Ongoing managerial assistance will be provided by telephone, personal shop visits, or vendor participation.

Training Assistance: We provide five weeks of training at our headquarters and shop, plus two weeks of training at franchisee's shop. Ongoing training programs are available to franchisees and employees.

Speedy Muffler King

8430 W. Byrn Mawr Ave., Ste. 400
Chicago, IL 60631
Web Address: www.speedy.com
Toll-Free Phone: (800) 359-2359
Phone: (773) 693-1000
Fax: (773) 693-0309
Contact: Director of Franchise Operations

Number of Franchises: 107
Company-Owned Units: 258
Total Units: 365

In Business Since: 1956   **Franchising Since:** 1986

Description of Operation: Retail automotive repair shops that specialize in exhaust, suspension, front end, and brake repair.

Equity Capital Needed: $226,000 (excluding land and building)

Franchise Fee: $18,500

Royalty: 5 percent

Advertising Co-op Fee:

Financial Assistance: Local source and SBA.

Management Assistance: We provide 6-8 weeks of training, with field operations support. Management is by the dealer.

Training Assistance: Same as above.

Speedy Transmission Centers

902 Clint Moore Rd., Ste. 216
Boca Raton, FL 33487
Web Address: www.speedytransmission.com
Toll-Free Phone: (800) 336-0310
Phone: (561) 995-8282
Fax: (561) 995-8005
Contact: President

Number of Franchises: 28
Company-Owned Units: n/a
Total Units: 28

In Business Since: 1983   **Franchising Since:** 1983

Description of Operation: Centers repair, rebuild, and recondition automatic and standard transmissions and provide the general public a high-quality reasonably priced transmission repair service. Drive-train repair service is also available. Each unit is self-contained. Fleet programs and referral programs are developed for each location. A strong warranty system exists throughout the United States and Canada. Existing and new locations are available.

Equity Capital Needed: $50,000

Franchise Fee: $19,500

Royalty: 7 percent

Advertising Co-op Fee: $100 per month

Financial Assistance: Each franchisee new to the transmission repair business pays an initial franchisee fee of $19,500. We will defer the balance of $10,000 or any portion of it at the franchisee's option, provided no fees are payable to a broker or other third party for introducing them to our franchise. Throughout the term of the franchise, franchisee pays interest of ten percent (10 percent) on the unpaid balance. Payments on the principal may be paid at any time, but none are required. Balance is repaid on the sale of the center or expiration of the agreement.

Management Assistance: Operations support team in the field provides advice and guidance to operate the business through visits to the center or when the franchisee contacts the regional or national offices. Regular newsletters, technical and management bulletins, and sales information are part of the complete communication program. Hard hitting, effective, professional advertising programs are developed to alert motorists to a clear-cut choice in obtaining quality transmission service at competitive prices.

Training Assistance: General training courses conducted at the Speedy Transmission training center. Franchisees also receive complete on-the-job experience under the careful watch of supervisors who teach all aspects of operating a transmission center. Inspections include all procedures, accounting, insurance, customer service, business management, purchasing, and the basics of transmission service.

Tilden Associates, Inc.

1325 Franklin Ave., Ste. 165
Garden City, NY 11530
Toll-Free Phone: (800) 845-3367
Phone: (516) 746-7911
Fax: (516) 742-4499
Contact: Director of Franchise Development

Number of Franchises: 11
Company-Owned Units: 0
Total Units: 11

In Business Since: 1923   **Franchising Since:** 1996

Description of Operation: We're not just brakes. The total Car Care Concept allows you to offer a full menu of automotive services for maximum consumer procurement, rather than a limited niche market. You benefit from a management team whose concept, methods, and system were proven and perfected for 75 years before we began to offer franchises.

Equity Capital Needed: $60,000

Franchise Fee: $25,000

Royalty: 6 percent

Advertising Co-op Fee: 3 percent

Financial Assistance: Financing assistance provided through local sources and a national SBA lender. Equipment financing also available.

Management Assistance: Company will train the franchisee and the manager(s) in all aspects of managing a Tilden for Brakes Car Care Center.

Training Assistance: Two-week comprehensive training program at our national headquarters and corporate training center. Initial training and continual operations, technical, business, and management support. Grand opening program includes on-site assistance.

Tuffy Auto Service Centers

1414 Baronial Plaza Dr.
Toledo, OH 43615
Web Address: www.tuffy.com
E-mail Address: tuffy@primenet.com
Toll-Free Phone: (800) 228-8339
Phone: (419) 865-6900
Fax: (419) 865-7343
Contact: Director of Franchising

Number of Franchises: 206
Company-Owned Units: 16
Total Units: 222

In Business Since: 1970   **Franchising Since:** 1971

Description of Operation: Sales and installation of exhaust systems, brakes, shocks; front-end alignment and suspension; oil changes; air-conditioning service; and so forth.

Equity Capital Needed: $50,000 cash minimum

Franchise Fee: $20,000

Royalty: 5 percent

Advertising Co-op Fee:

Financial Assistance: Equipment lease financing is available to qualified applicants.

Management Assistance: Ongoing training and supervision are provided by the operations and training departments. Marketing and advertising assistance is provided by the marketing department.

Training Assistance: We offer three weeks of new franchisee training, two weeks of in-shop assistance at opening, and ongoing support.

Tunex Automotive Specialists

556 E. 2100 S.
Salt Lake City, UT 84106
Web Address: www.tunex.com
Toll-Free Phone: (800) 448-8639
Phone: (801) 486-8133
Fax: (801) 484-4740
Contact: Franchise Sales Department

Number of Franchises: 15
Company-Owned Units: 4
Total Units: 19

In Business Since: 1974   **Franchising Since:** 1975

Description of Operation: Diagnostic "tune-up" services and repairs of engine-related systems (for example, ignition, carburetion, fuel injection, emission, computer controls, cooling, and air-conditioning) for maximum customer satisfaction. We analyze all systems for problems so that the customer can make service and repair decisions.

Equity Capital Needed: $105,000-$120,000

Franchise Fee: $19,000

Royalty: 5 percent

Advertising Co-op Fee:

Financial Assistance: Some financing is provided, as well as equipment lease assistance.

Management Assistance: We provide quarterly training sessions, annual evaluations, and a toll-free "assist line."

Training Assistance: Initial training: classroom (one week), grand opening (one week), and follow-up (one week).

Vehicare

701 E. Franklin St.
Richmond, VA 23219
Web Address: www.vehicare.com
Toll-Free Phone:
Phone: (804) 225-0982
Fax: (804) 225-0946
Contact: Director of Marketing Services

Number of Franchises: 3
Company-Owned Units: 31
Total Units: 34

In Business Since: 1988   **Franchising Since:** 1989

Description of Operation: On-site mobile preventive maintenance for commercial fleets.

Equity Capital Needed: $200,000-$400,000

Franchise Fee: $80,000 per million population

Royalty: 5 percent

Advertising Co-op Fee:

Financial Assistance: Data not available.

Management Assistance: New operations are mostly joint ventures with Vehicare as managing general partner. Independent franchisees are invited to participate in all facility manager's training seminars.

Training Assistance: We offer one week of initial training at the company's headquarters, ongoing sales training, and facility manager seminars regularly.

Automobile—Oil Change

Express Oil Change, LLC

P.O. Box 19968
Birmingham, AL 35219
Toll-Free Phone:
Phone: (205) 945-1771
Fax: (205) 940-6026
Contact: V.P. of Franchise Development

Number of Franchises: 31
Company-Owned Units: 31
Total Units: 31

In Business Since: 1979   **Franchising Since:** 1983

Description of Operation: Fast automotive service.

Equity Capital Needed: $175,000-$375,000

Franchise Fee: $17,500

Royalty: 5 percent

Advertising Co-op Fee:

Financial Assistance: None

Management Assistance: We provide initial training, counsel, and advice in evaluating prospective sites; provide initial and continuing advisory service in the operation; provide franchisee with an initial set of recommended accounting, inventory, and inspection forms; and provide an experienced manager for up to five days to assist in the opening of the outlet. Other services on request.

Training Assistance: The training program consists of an orientation and training program for the franchisee and/or franchisee's manager at the Birmingham, AL, training center for up to two weeks. The initial orientation and training program covers all aspects of the licensed business. The franchisor will also review the operating manual with the franchisee and provide on-the-job training in the retail automotive business. An initial training program is mandatory.

Grease Monkey International

216 16th St., Ste. 1100
Denver, CO 80202
E-mail Address: gmmonkey@rmi.net
Toll-Free Phone: (800) 364-0352
Phone: (303) 534-1660
Fax: (303) 534-2906
Contact: V.P. Franchise Sales, Development & Real Estate

Number of Franchises: 184
Company-Owned Units: 31
Total Units: 215

In Business Since: 1978   **Franchising Since:** 1979

Description of Operation: Grease Monkey International (GMI) ranks fourth in size among all fast-lube organizations and is the largest fast-lube franchise organization not owned by a major oil company. GMI's sole business is providing convenient preventative maintenance services for motor vehicles. Since the majority of Grease Monkey centers are franchisee-owned, we take care to develop solid, mutually supportive relationships with each franchise owner and offer continued support, guidance, and leadership. In a world of same-sounding, fast-lube centers, Grease Monkey has the advantage of a distinctive name our customers easily remember.

Equity Capital Needed: $150,000

Franchise Fee: $28,000

Royalty: 5 percent

Advertising Co-op Fee: Up to 1 percent

Financial Assistance: Third-party financing available for qualified franchisees.

Management Assistance: Regional support through Regional Directors, Franchise Training Consultants, and Field Marketing Managers.

Training Assistance: Extensive training and certification prior to center opening. Ongoing regional marketing and operational workshops.

Indy Lube 10-Minute Oil Change

6515 E. 82nd St., Ste. 209
Indianapolis, IN 46250
Web Address: www.indylube.com
Toll-Free Phone: (800) 326-5823
Phone: (317) 845-9444
Fax: (317) 577-3169
Contact: President

Number of Franchises: 6
Company-Owned Units: 10
Total Units: 16

In Business Since: 1986   **Franchising Since:** 1989

Description of Operation: Indy Lube is a chain of 10-minute oil change centers that specialize in automotive fluid maintenance. Indy Lube sets itself apart from the competition by providing fast, quality service in a pleasant setting. All Indy Lube stores have landscaped exteriors; brightly painted buildings; and interior reception areas; complete with wallpaper, cloth chairs, and a courtesy telephone.

Equity Capital Needed: $50,000-$100,000

Franchise Fee: $18,000

Royalty: 5 percent

Advertising Co-op Fee:

Financial Assistance: No direct financial assistance; however, there is assistance available with business plan preparation for presentations to financial institutions.

Management Assistance: Indy Lube provides criteria and assistance in interviewing. Franchise store managers and owners are invited to train at a corporate store for two weeks prior to the opening of the franchise. There are ongoing training meetings each month for managers, assistant managers, employees, and franchise owners.

Training Assistance: Same as managerial assistance.

Jiffy Lube International

P.O. Box 2967
Houston, TX 77252-2967
Web Address: www.jiffylube.com
Toll-Free Phone: (800) 327-9532
Phone: (713) 546-4100
Fax: (713) 546-8792
Contact: Franchise Development

Number of Franchises: 667
Company-Owned Units: 412
Total Units: 1079

In Business Since: 1979   **Franchising Since:** 1979

Description of Operation: Largest quick-lube system in the industry.

Equity Capital Needed: Approximate total investment—$173,000-$194,000

Franchise Fee: $35,000

Royalty: 5 percent

Advertising Co-op Fee:

Financial Assistance: None

Management Assistance: Jiffy Lube International provides continual management services, for the life of the franchise, in such areas as accounting, advertising, policies, procedures, and operations. Complete manuals are provided. Regional managers are available to work closely with franchisees and visit service centers regularly to assist in solving problems.

Training Assistance: Jiffy Lube International provides a mandatory course to the franchisee or approved manager, which consists of working at a Jiffy Lube Service Center for four weeks. You must also attend a standard operations training course for an additional week at Jiffy Lube headquarters.

LubePro's Inc.

1630 Colonial Pkwy.
Inverness, IL 60067
Toll-Free Phone: (800) 654-5823
Phone: (847) 776-2500
Fax: (847) 776-2542
Contact: Chairman

Number of Franchises: 24
Company-Owned Units: 12
Total Units: 36

In Business Since: 1978   **Franchising Since:** 1986

Description of Operation: LubePro's service centers provide fast-service oil changes, lubrication, replacement of certain filters and fluids, and certain related courtesy services for motor vehicles.

Equity Capital Needed: $170,000-$200,000

Franchise Fee: $25,000

Royalty: 5 percent

Advertising Co-op Fee:

Financial Assistance: We direct the franchisee to build-to-suit developers.

Management Assistance: Field service and seminars are provided periodically.

Training Assistance: We provide ten days of training, including on-site training.

Oil Butler International

1599 Rt. 22
Union, NJ 07083
Toll-Free Phone:
Phone: (908) 687-3283
Fax: (908) 687-7617
Contact: Vice President, Franchise Development

Number of Franchises: 107
Company-Owned Units: 1
Total Units: 108

In Business Since: 1987   **Franchising Since:** 1991

Description of Operation: Mobile, on-site oil change and windshield repair service. We deliver quality service—quickly and affordably—to fleets, employees at their workplace, and residents. Our oil change trailer is light years ahead of anything else on the market, allowing you to perform your service at the highest level of safety and speed, part-time or full-time. Complete training, ongoing support, exclusive territory, repeat customers, and high profits can be yours.

Equity Capital Needed: $10,000

Franchise Fee: $7,000

Royalty: 7 percent

Advertising Co-op Fee:

Financial Assistance: Third party.

Management Assistance: Our ongoing support team is there to answer questions, assist with technical problems, help with sales techniques, and help to acquire accounts. We arrange for all of your suppliers, and we service national fleet accounts.

Training Assistance: Complete training is provided: technical, in-field, and classroom training; sales techniques; vehicle maintenance; and inventory control, billing, and bookkeeping.

Oil Can Henry's
(OCH International, Inc.)

1200 N.W. Front Ave., Ste. 690
Portland, OR 97209
Web Address: www.oilcanhenry.com
Toll-Free Phone: (800) 765-6244
Phone: (503) 243-6311
Fax: (503) 228-5227
Contact: President

Number of Franchises: 35
Company-Owned Units: 1
Total Units: 36

In Business Since: 1972   **Franchising Since:** 1989

Description of Operation: Only Oil Can Henry's offers the "Famous 20 Point Full Service Oil Change." Our unique logo, uniforms, building design, and operating procedures are a winning combination that distinguishes us from the competition. Franchisees receive real estate and site selection assistance, assistance securing SBA guaranteed loans, and extensive and comprehensive training for franchisees and their managers. We offer grand opening assistance, pre- and post-grand opening marketing plan, continuing and regular marketing assistance, and initial and ongoing regular management and business assessment and consulting.

Equity Capital Needed: $100,000

Franchise Fee: $25,000

Royalty: 5 percent of gross

Advertising Co-op Fee:

Financial Assistance: n/a

Management Assistance: n/a

Training Assistance: Comprehensive, state-of-the-art, initial and ongoing training for franchisees and managers.

SpeeDee Oil Change & Tune-Up

159 Highway 22 East, P.O. Box 1350
Madisonville, LA 70447
Toll-Free Phone: (800) 451-7461
Phone: (504) 845-1919
Fax: (504) 845-1936
Contact: Executive Vice President

Number of Franchises: 135
Company-Owned Units: 2
Total Units: 137

In Business Since: 1980   **Franchising Since:** 1982

Description of Operation: SpeeDee offers preventative auto maintenance services, specializing in a 17-point quick oil change, diagnostic tune-up, brake emissions/smog checks, and transmission/differential service. No appointment necessary. Service performed while you wait. Successful franchisees are enthusiastic and have a strong commitment to customer service and people management skills. Retail experience preferred.

Equity Capital Needed: $186,000-$767,500

Franchise Fee: $30,000

Royalty: 6 percent

Advertising Co-op Fee:

Financial Assistance: Not available

Management Assistance: Two to four weeks of management review at corporate headquarters with in-center practical training at a nearby service center. Also included are operations assistance, marketing and advertising assistance, manuals, videos, and so on.

Training Assistance: One to two weeks training in-center at opening. Ongoing quarterly franchisee meetings, field representative visits, conventions, and so on.

Valvoline Instant Oil Change

301 E. Main St., Ste. 1200
Lexington, KY 40507
Toll-Free Phone: (800) 622-6846
Phone: (606) 264-7070
Fax: (606) 264-7049
Contact: Franchise Department

Number of Franchises: 66
Company-Owned Units: 344
Total Units: 410

In Business Since: 1986   **Franchising Since:** 1988

Description of Operation: Fluid maintenace for passanger cars and light trucks.

Equity Capital Needed: $100,000-$200,000

Franchise Fee: $15,000-$25,000

Royalty: 4 percent, 5 percent, 6 percent, graduated

Advertising Co-op Fee:

Financial Assistance: The licensor and/or its affiliates will offer (to qualified prospects) leasing programs for land, building, equipment, signage, and POS systems.

Management Assistance: We provide support in all areas of franchise operations and marketing, site selection, construction, POS system, and administration.

Training Assistance: We offer a four-stage training program, as well as proprietary manuals, videos, on-site support, and training.

Automobile—Parts & Supplies

Aid Auto Stores

275 Grand Blvd., P.O. Box 281
Westbury, NY 11590
Web Address: www.aidauto.com
Toll-Free Phone: (800) 432-9339
Phone: (516) 338-7889

Fax: (516) 338-7803
Contact: Director of Advertising

Number of Franchises: 79
Company-Owned Units: 3
Total Units: 82

In Business Since: 1953   **Franchising Since:** 1953

Description of Operation: Franchisor, distributor, and retailer of automotive parts and accessories in the NY, NJ, and CT metro automotive aftermarkets. Aid Auto Stores sells automotive parts and accessories to franchisees to resell to retail customers. Aid Auto Stores operates company-owned stores in a retail capacity.

Equity Capital Needed: $175,000-$180,000

Franchise Fee: $22,500

Royalty: $1,175 per month

Advertising Co-op Fee:

Financial Assistance: 30-day terms on merchandise.

Management Assistance: Each franchise opened receives assistance regarding location, information on product set-ups, and actual product literature and information.

Training Assistance: Store set-up and training are provided and are ongoing. Initial merchandising, product knowledge, operations, and training support the set-up of each franchise. Auto parts technical knowledge is provided.

Batteries Plus—America's Battery Stores

625 Walnut Ridge Dr., Ste. 106
Hartland, WI 53029
Web Address: www.batteriesplus.com
E-mail Address: batplus@batteriesplus.com
Toll-Free Phone: (800) 274-9155
Phone: (414) 369-0690
Fax: (414) 369-0680
Contact: Director of Franchise Sales

Number of Franchises: 153
Company-Owned Units: 19
Total Units: 96

In Business Since: 1988   **Franchising Since:** 1992

Description of Operation: Retail specialty stores selling thousands of batteries for thousands of cars to both retail and commercial customers. Our stores feature the hard-to-find items and can troubleshoot or rebuild battery power packs in their in-store technical centers. Free delivery for commercial accounts and installation for the retail customers are value-added features.

Equity Capital Needed: $100,000

Franchise Fee: $25,000

Royalty: 3-4 percent, declining as volume grows

Advertising Co-op Fee: 1 percent

Financial Assistance: Referral to major financial companies that have experience in franchise lending, are familiar with Batteries Plus, and are preferred SBA lenders.

Management Assistance: New owners orientation, comprehensive owner/operator's manual, and ongoing on-site business development assistance.

Training Assistance: Owner's orientation (two days); store manager training (four weeks); in-store, start-up assistance (two weeks); ongoing training in-store (periodically); and an in-store training videocassette series.

Big O Tires

11755 E. Peakview Ave., Ste. A
Englewood, CO 80111
Web Address: www.bigotires.com
Toll-Free Phone: (800) 622-2446
Phone: (303) 790-2800
Fax: (303) 790-0225
Contact: Franchise Sales Cocrdinator

Number of Franchises: 402
Company-Owned Units: 13
Total Units: 415

In Business Since: 1962   **Franchising Since:** 1967

Description of Operation: Retail tire and undercar service centers.

Equity Capital Needed: $300,000 net worth; $100,000-$150,000 cash.

Franchise Fee: $25,000

Royalty: 2 percent

Advertising Co-op Fee:

Financial Assistance: Assistance will be provided in locating, financing, and preparing loan and lease applications.

Management Assistance: Training is provided at the national training center.

Training Assistance: Training consists of opening and closing procedures, merchandising and display, and overall store management. Hands-on training with a 10-bay service area.

End-A-Flat Tire Safety Sealant

1155 Greenbriar Dr.
Bethel Park, PA 15102
Toll-Free Phone:
Phone: (412) 831-1255
Fax: (412) 833-3409
Contact: Vice President

Number of Franchises:
Company-Owned Units:
Total Units: 10

In Business Since: 1980   **Franchising Since:**

Description of Operation: Sales of tire-safety sealant.

Equity Capital Needed: $10,000

Franchise Fee: None

Royalty: Data not available

Advertising Co-op Fee:

Financial Assistance: n/a

Management Assistance: Yes

Training Assistance: Yes

Endrust Auto Appearance Centers

1155 Greenbriar Dr.
Bethel Park, PA 15102
Toll-Free Phone:
Phone: (412) 833-1255
Fax: (412) 833-3409
Contact: Vice President

Number of Franchises:
Company-Owned Units:
Total Units: 55

In Business Since: 1969   **Franchising Since:**

Description of Operation: Complete auto appearance centers.

Equity Capital Needed: $30,000

Franchise Fee: None

Royalty: Data not available.

Advertising Co-op Fee:

Financial Assistance:

Management Assistance: Yes

Training Assistance: Yes

Matco Tools

4403 Allen Rd.
Stow, OH 44224
Web Address: www.matcotools.com
Toll-Free Phone: (800) 368-6651
Phone: (330) 929-4949
Fax: (330) 929-1526
Contact:

Number of Franchises: 1,186
Company-Owned Units: 30
Total Units: 1,216

In Business Since: 1979   **Franchising Since:** 1993

Description of Operation: Matco Tools is a provider of precision mechanics hand tools, service equipment, and diagnostic computers that are distributed through financial mobile tool distributors. As a Danaher Company, Matco uses the resources of eight manufacturing facilities, two computerized Distribution Centers, and a staff 400 strong to support more than 1,200 Franchised Distributors. From

well-stocked, attractive Matco Tools Trucks, Matco Distributors service, an inventory of quality products, warranties, customer financing and relationships, and repeat sales.

Equity Capital Needed: Not provided

Franchise Fee: 0

Royalty: 0

Advertising Co-op Fee: None

Financial Assistance: Financing is available through Matco for qualified candidates. Matco can finance up to $40,500 of the total investment required.

Management Assistance: Field support for Matco Distributors is provided by the District Business Manager (DBM). Locally based, DBMs work with Matco Distributors in the market they serve, providing individualized guidance and support. With an average of one DBM for each 15 distributors, Matco has one of the strongest field support organizations in Franchising.

Training Assistance: All new Matco Distributors are required to attend and successfully complete the Matco Tools New Distributor Training Program. This program is presented as classroom training for six days at Stow, OH, and through three-week, on-truck training with a designated trainer.

Mighty Distributing System of America, Inc.

50 Technology Park
Norcross, GA 30092
Web Address: www.mightyap.com
E-mail Address: tracy.sidelko@mightyap.com
Toll-Free Phone: (800) 829-3900
Phone: (770) 448-3900
Fax: (770) 446-8627
Contact: Franchise Sales

Number of Franchises: 146
Company-Owned Units: 4
Total Units: 150

In Business Since: 1963   **Franchising Since:** 1970

Description of Operation: Wholesale automotive parts to professional technicians. Franchisees operate in exclusive territories supplying automotive maintenance and repair facilities with original equipment quality, as well as "Mighty" branded auto parts, such as filters, belts, tune-up products, and brake products.

Equity Capital Needed: Data not provided

Franchise Fee: $.035 per registered vehicle

Royalty: 5 percent of gross monthly sales

Advertising Co-op Fee: Data not available.

Financial Assistance: n/a

Management Assistance: Technical support, national advertising, warranty programs, promotional campaigns, and information systems support.

Training Assistance: Initial and ongoing classroom and field training for franchisees and salespeople.

Pick-Ups Plus

3532 Irwin-Simpson Rd., Ste. 85
Mason, OH 45040
Web Address: www.pickups-plus.com
Toll-Free Phone: (888) 249-7587
Phone: (513) 398-4344
Fax: (513) 398-4271
Contact: Franchise Coordinator

Number of Franchises: 3
Company-Owned Units: 1
Total Units: 4

In Business Since: 1993   **Franchising Since:** 1995

Description of Operation: Pick-Ups Plus stores resemble a toy store for truck and SUV enthusiasts. Whether it's to make their trucks more attractive, more practical, more comfortable, more durable, or simply more unique, a growing number of truck owners are purchasing aftermarket parts and accessories. Pick-Ups Plus is now offering to the right candidate the opportunity to participate in this niche franchise. We sell accessories such as bed liners, running boards, caps, and many more. Our technicians are trained in factory-recommended installation procedures. If you like the idea of owning a business that combines fast-climbing market potential with comprehensive, tested business techniques, you should consider a Pick-Ups Plus franchise. Call toll-free 1-888-249-7587.

Equity Capital Needed: $150,000

Franchise Fee: $25,000

Royalty: 6 percent

Advertising Co-op Fee:

Financial Assistance: None available

Management Assistance: Training is provided for three weeks at the corporate store location. Then additional training is given at your location. Corporate assistance is provided also during your grand opening. Site selection assistance and facility requirements are offered as well. Continual contact with the corporate office is available.

Training Assistance: Data not available.

Snap On Tools

2801 80th St.
Kenosha, WI 53141
Web Address: www.snapon.com
Toll-Free Phone: (800) 775-7630
Phone: (414) 656-5770
Fax: (414) 656-5088
Contact: Director of Franchise Operations

Number of Franchises: 3700
Company-Owned Units: N/A
Total Units: 3700

In Business Since: 1920   **Franchising Since:** 1991

Description of Operation: The opportunity to visit a group of regular customers weekly and offer the world's finest quality tools and automotive equipment. Snap-on will provide the customer base, training, and assistance. You provide the face-to-face contact with the customers. There are no employee or real-estate-related hassles, unless you choose to apply for additional franchises in the future. If you haven't thought about the tool business, think about this: cars are getting more complicated, and there are more cars out there every day. Do something you enjoy; call Snap-on to learn more.

Equity Capital Needed: $35,000/varies

Franchise Fee: $5,000

Royalty: $50 per month

Advertising Co-op Fee: 0

Financial Assistance: Snap-on has the resources to assist you if you qualify. We have a flexible program. Call for the details.

Management Assistance: As a Snap-on Dealer, you would belong to a group of approximately ten Dealers. Snap-on employs and trains a Field Manager "coach" for the group locally. It's the best way for us to assist you.

Training Assistance: Training is not an event; it is an ongoing process. Snap-on begins with several weeks of intensive on-the-job training and continues support through personal supervision.

Tires Plus Auto Service Centers

701 Ladybird Ln.
Burnsville, MN 55337
Web Address: www.tiresplus.com
Toll-Free Phone: (800) 754-6519
Phone: (612) 895-4927
Fax: (612) 895-4981
Contact: Vice President

Number of Franchises: 20
Company-Owned Units: 35
Total Units: 55

In Business Since: 1976   **Franchising Since:** 1981

Description of Operation: Tires Plus is the largest independently owned tire retailer in the Midwest. We are single and multistore franchises in large and medium markets. Our concept is unique and competitively aggressive. We seek to dominate the market that we enter.

Equity Capital Needed: $100,000-$200,000

Franchise Fee: $30,000

Royalty: 3 percent

Advertising Co-op Fee:

Financial Assistance: Yes.

Management Assistance: Tires Plus has tremendous buying power that can be used for the benefit of the

franchisee. We provide site selection, construction drawings, and design assistance. We also provide support for field operations, computer training, marketing, and financial analysis.

Training Assistance: We provide two weeks of classroom training. We also provide in-store training and pay your salary for up to six months at one of our corporate stores. We supply a comprehensive operations management manual.

US1 Auto Parts

5 Dakota Dr., # 210
Lake Success, NY 11042
Toll-Free Phone:
Phone: (516) 358-5100
Fax: (516) 358-2717
Contact: President

Number of Franchises: 21
Company-Owned Units: 2
Total Units: 23

In Business Since: 1983   **Franchising Since:** 1990

Description of Operation: Automotive discount supermarket.

Equity Capital Needed: $125,000-$175,000

Franchise Fee: $25,000

Royalty: 6 percent

Advertising Co-op Fee:

Financial Assistance: All our franchisees received financial assistance of up to 8 percent on a turnkey operation.

Management Assistance: We offer training in stores that are already running for an limited time.

Training Assistance: Same as above.

Automobile—Miscellaneous

Auto One/Sun Country Auto Centers

15965 Jeanette St.
Southfield, MI 48075
Toll-Free Phone:
Phone: (810) 559-1415
Fax: (810) 557-7931
Contact:

Number of Franchises: 40
Company-Owned Units: 0
Total Units: 40

In Business Since: 1988   **Franchising Since:** 1988

Description of Operation: Auto appearance and protective services.

Equity Capital Needed: $45,000-$90,000

Franchise Fee: $20,000

Royalty: 5 percent

Advertising Co-op Fee:

Financial Assistance: Yes.

Management Assistance: Data not available.

Training Assistance: Yes.

Auto Purchase Consulting

9841 Airport Blvd., Ste. 1517
Los Angeles, CA 90045
Web Address: www.autopurchaseconsulting.com
Toll-Free Phone: (800) 756-4227
Phone: (310) 670-2886
Fax: (310) 670-5603
Contact: President

Number of Franchises: 2
Company-Owned Units: 1
Total Units: 3

In Business Since: 1984   **Franchising Since:** 1997

Description of Operation: For new car buyers who can't afford to overpay, don't have time to shop, and want to avoid conflict altogether, Auto Purchase Consulting offers its 14-year, proven, professional buying and leasing service. APC handles all 41 makes and more than 550 models with guaranteed savings of money, time, and aggravation. APC is a high-income, low-start-up, low-overhead, fast-return-on-investment franchise business investment. Call for a free information package including video- and audiocassettes.

Equity Capital Needed: $62,000

Franchise Fee: $25,000

Royalty: The greater of 8 percent or $600 minimum

Advertising Co-op Fee: 0

Financial Assistance: None

Management Assistance: APC finance manager provides daily assistance to franchisee, assisting with auto loan and lease approval and funding for customer transactions, using APC's leading bank sources with interest rates available way below market rates.

Training Assistance: Custom-tailored training up to 10 days based on experience; includes classroom and on-the-job training at corporate headquarters, plus on-site follow-up. Continual ongoing guidance and daily assistance provided.

Dealer Specialties, Inc.

60 American Way, Ste. A
Monroe, OH 45050
Web Address: www.getauto.com
E-mail Address: ds.ohio@getauto.com
Toll-Free Phone: (800) 647-8425

Phone: (513) 539-2200
Fax: (513) 539-2202
Contact: Operations Manager

Number of Franchises: 141
Company-Owned Units: 0
Total Units: 141

In Business Since: 1989   **Franchising Since:** 1995

Description of Operation: Dealer Specialties provides automobile dealerships with descriptive used-vehicle window stickers, and Internet advertising using the collected used-vehicle data.

Equity Capital Needed: $10,200-$34,400

Franchise Fee: $2,500

Royalty: $.60/label

Advertising Co-op Fee: $.02/label

Financial Assistance: None

Management Assistance: Dealer Specialties maintains an 800# hot line for technical support to all DS franchisees. The hot line is available Monday through Friday, 8 a.m. to 5 p.m. EST, with the exception of company holidays. From time to time, improvements and additions to the business are made available to all franchisees. Dealer Specialities also loans out copies of the confidential operations manual.

Training Assistance: Dealer Specialties trains every franchisee at the DSI headquarters. Training includes history of Dealer Specialties, computer orientation, and in-depth training in using the AutoStik program. Training also includes practice sessions so that the franchisee receives practice in creating labels.

J. D. Byrider Systems

5780 W. 71st St.
Indianapolis, IN 46278
Toll-Free Phone:
Phone: (317) 387-2345
Fax: (317) 668-1572
Contact: Vice President of Franchise Development

Number of Franchises: 68
Company-Owned Units: 1
Total Units: 69

In Business Since: 1979   **Franchising Since:** 1989

Description of Operation: J. D. Byrider is a full-service franchisor providing a complete package franchise for the sale and financing of five-year-and-older cars to customers who cannot qualify for conventional financing.

Equity Capital Needed: $225,000-$584,000

Franchise Fee: $29,000

Royalty: 3 percent or minimum of $1,000 per month

Advertising Co-op Fee:

Financial Assistance: None at this time.

Management Assistance: Thorough training in the methods, disciplines, and controls to accompany the proprietary software. The variances are all designed to indicate where a small problem is prior to escalation.

Training Assistance: Initial training is a five- to six-week process, conducted both in headquarters and in the field. The process includes basic presentation skills, credit scoring, management of sales counselors, how to buy the automobiles for profitable return, and proper and productive collection methods.

Spot-Not Car Washes

2011 W. 4th St.
Joplin, MO 64801
Toll-Free Phone: (800) 682-7629
Phone: (417) 781-2140
Fax: (417) 781-3906
Contact: Vice President

Number of Franchises: 26
Company-Owned Units: 0
Total Units: 26

In Business Since: 1968   **Franchising Since:** 1985

Description of Operation: High-pressure spray, frictionless automatic and self-service combination car washes.

Equity Capital Needed: $250,000-$350,000

Franchise Fee: $25,000

Royalty: 5 percent

Advertising Co-op Fee:

Financial Assistance: SBA funding and leasing arrangements with approved sources.

Management Assistance: Ongoing operations and marketing. Assistance through periodic visits and field meetings.

Training Assistance: We provide seven days at the corporate office, plus five days of field training in an operating unit.

Ziebart Tidycar

1290 E. Maple Rd.
Troy, MI 48007
Web Address: www.ziebart.com
E-mail Address: info@ziebart.com
Toll-Free Phone: (800) 877-1312
Phone: (248) 588-4100
Fax: (248) 588-0718
Contact: Director of Franchise Development

Number of Franchises: 525
Company-Owned Units: 19
Total Units: 544

In Business Since: 1954   **Franchising Since:** 1963

Description of Operation: Automotive application of detailing— accessories and protection services.

Equity Capital Needed: $99,000-$161,000

Franchise Fee: $24,000

Royalty: 8-5 percent

Advertising Co-op Fee:

Financial Assistance: Leasing is available.

Management Assistance: We provide regional advertising support and regional sales support in the field.

Training Assistance: All training is provided by franchisor, including sales, management, and all technical training.

Beauty Care—Cosmetics & Toiletries

Caryl Baker Visage Cosmetics (Canada)

801 Eglinton Ave. W.
Toronto, ON M5N 1E3
Toll-Free Phone:
Phone: (416) 789-7191
Fax: (416) 789-2594
Contact: Vice President

Number of Franchises: 30
Company-Owned Units: 1
Total Units: 31

In Business Since: 1969   **Franchising Since:** 1977

Description of Operation: Retail cosmetic and skin-care salons located in regional shopping malls.

Equity Capital Needed: Total investment of $90,000-$95,000

Franchise Fee: $15,000

Royalty: 0 percent

Advertising Co-op Fee:

Financial Assistance: Financial assistance is not available from the franchisor.

Management Assistance: We provide ongoing assistance, covering an analysis of store performance, updates of computer programs used in the store, and regular supervisor visits, as well as head office staff available at all times.

Training Assistance: We offer two weeks of training at our school and company store, covering product knowledge, marketing, and all facets of store operations. In addition, a supervisor provides one week of training at a new franchise store.

Elizabeth Grady Face First

200 Boston Ave.
Medford, MA 02155

Toll-Free Phone: (800) 322-4257
Phone: (781) 391-9380
Fax: (781) 391-4772
Contact: President

Number of Franchises: 15
Company-Owned Units: 8
Total Units: 23

In Business Since: 1974   **Franchising Since:** 1982

Description of Operation: Skin care salons, with emphasis on individual consultation and clinical analysis, treatments by professional estheticians, and a prescribed home care regime. Elizabeth Grady Face First's goal has always been to promote the healthiest skin for all people. Our commitment to serve the best interests of our customers is reflected in the quality of our complete line of products, many of which are specially developed for Elizabeth Gray salons.

Equity Capital Needed: $125,000

Franchise Fee: $25,000

Royalty: 6 percent

Advertising Co-op Fee:

Financial Assistance: Finanacial assistance is available to qualified applicants.

Management Assistance: Training includes periodic updates on all industry trends, new products, and services, as well as new advertising and promotional techniques. In addition, franchisees are provided with total ongoing supervision and support in the form of periodic visits by our experienced staff to consult with your staff on all aspects of operations. Other assistance is provided as needed.

Training Assistance: Everything you need to know to operate is included in our training program. The tuition is included in your franchise fee. Furthermore, one of our representatives will work with you for one week during your first month of operation. Franchisees will also receive an operations manual covering all areas of importance.

H2O +

676 N. Michigan Ave., Ste. 3900
Chicago, IL 60611
Web Address: www.h2oplus.com
Toll-Free Phone: (800) 537-1119
Phone: (312) 850-9283
Fax: (312) 642-9207
Contact: Director of Franchising

Number of Franchises: 1
Company-Owned Units: 54
Total Units: 55

In Business Since: 1989   **Franchising Since:** 1993

Description of Operation: Retailer of innovative and progressive cosmetic, skin-care, fragrance, and bath products.

Equity Capital Needed: $240,000-$380,000

Franchise Fee: $38,500

Royalty: 4 percent (1st year); 5 percent (2nd year); 5 percent (3rd year)

Advertising Co-op Fee:

Financial Assistance: None

Management Assistance: Our franchisees participate in a weekly conference call with their regional field manager. They receive visits from their regional manager a minimum of every two months. They have access to daily corporate contacts for support in marketing and promotions, human resources and training, finance and accounting, POS system, and legal. They receive newsletters, training tips, new products, and operational information from our corporate office weekly. An International Managers Meeting is held annually.

Training Assistance: Training is in four parts. Part one is on the seven-volume operating manual. In Part two, prior to store opening, franchisees participate in an intensive classroom/in-field training program that demonstrates "live" all material in seven volumes, including hands-on register and computer training. Part three consists of three to five days in company stores for orientation to customers, sales, and store operations. Part four is on-site training on store set-up and store opening.

I Natural Skin Care & Cosmetics

3202 Queens Blvd.
Long Island, NY 11101
Toll-Free Phone: (800) 962-5387
Phone: (718) 786-3204
Fax:
Contact: Franchise Co-ordinator

Number of Franchises: 0
Company-Owned Units: 3
Total Units: 3

In Business Since: 1970   **Franchising Since:** 1970

Description of Operation: Operation of a retail shop that specializes in skin care, cosmetics, and related services. The franchisor offers private label and other products and accessories for sale to the shops.

Equity Capital Needed: $106,500-$183,500

Franchise Fee: $15,000

Royalty: 0-6 months: 1 percent gross sales; 7-12 months: 2 percent; 13 months through balance: 3 percent

Advertising Co-op Fee:

Financial Assistance: No.

Management Assistance: Data not available.

Training Assistance: Franchisor will provide an initial training program for the franchisee. The training is held at franchisor's corporate office. The program is approximatey one week.

Rose Valenti

205 Rockaway Ave.
Valley Stream, NY 11580
Web Address: www.rosevalenti.com
Toll-Free Phone:
Phone: (516) 825-0273
Fax: (516) 825-9285
Contact: Vice President

Number of Franchises: 0
Company-Owned Units: 8
Total Units: 8

In Business Since: 1983   **Franchising Since:** 1992

Description of Operation: Fragrance and cosmetic retail sales.

Equity Capital Needed: $100,000-$110,000

Franchise Fee: $25,000

Royalty: 10 percent

Advertising Co-op Fee:

Financial Assistance: None

Management Assistance: Data not available.

Training Assistance: We will train the franchisee for four weeks in our stores. We will then help to open store and generally help the franchisee. We will then be available for any further assistance by phone or fax and, if need be, in person.

Top of the Line Cosmetics & Fragrances

1900 Military Rd. P.O. Box 11
Niagara Falls, NY 14304
Toll-Free Phone: (800) 929-3083
Phone: (732) 229-0014
Fax: (732) 222-1762
Contact: Director of Franchise Sales

Number of Franchises: 8
Company-Owned Units: 17
Total Units: 25

In Business Since: 1983   **Franchising Since:** 1987

Description of Operation: Retail sales of prestigious designer fragrances and brand-name cosmetics. Carry products for men, women, and children. Bath lines, gift sets, make-up, facial treatments, and fragrances are carried. Services provided are make-overs and color analysis.

Equity Capital Needed: $80,000-$125,000

Franchise Fee: $23,900

Royalty: 5 percent

Advertising Co-op Fee:

Financial Assistance: We will not provide loans, but will assist in getting loans through SBA.

Management Assistance: The franchisor provides set-up and training, ongoing assistance through training tapes, promotional material and events, and manuals. On-site training minimum of one week, plus training in a company store for one week.

Training Assistance: Training provided on-site and in the company store totals two weeks. Store set-up and paperwork training; management training; personnel training, including product knowledge, color, and make-over training; plus management and employee training mauals, videos, and tapes. Training is ongoing through the life of the franchise.

Aloette Cosmetics, Inc.

1301 Wrights Lane East
West Chester, PA 19380
Web Address: www.aloettecosmetics.com
E-mail Address: aletacct@erols.com
Toll-Free Phone: (800) 256-3883
Phone: (610) 692-0600
Fax: (610) 692-2334
Contact: Director of Franchise Operations

Number of Franchises: 82
Company-Owned Units: 2
Total Units: 84

In Business Since: 1978   **Franchising Since:** 1978

Description of Operation: Aloette Cosmetics, Inc., is a company that offers franchising opportunity of aloe-vera-based skin care line and color line in a direct sales (home show) approach.

Equity Capital Needed: $10,000-25,000

Franchise Fee: $20,000

Royalty: 5 percent of monthly sales

Advertising Co-op Fee: 0

Financial Assistance: Will hold note for franchise fee.

Management Assistance: Will train at franchise site on running business—but will run on own essentially with support from home office.

Training Assistance: Both marketing and sales and running the franchise as a business.

Beauty Care—Hair Care

Cost Cutters Family Hair Care

300 Industrial Blvd. N.E.
Minneapolis, MN 55413
Toll-Free Phone: (800) 858-2266
Phone: (612) 331-8500
Fax: (612) 331-2821
Contact: Development Administration

Number of Franchises: 499
Company-Owned Units: 1
Total Units: 500

In Business Since: 1963   **Franchising Since:** 1967

Description of Operation: A value-priced, full-service salon concept that provides low-cost, no-frills hair services for the family. The franchisor created Cost Cutters to meet the demand for providing the public with quality hair services and products at a moderate price.

Equity Capital Needed: Data not available

Franchise Fee: $19,500

Royalty: 6 percent

Advertising Co-op Fee:

Financial Assistance: Loan programs are available for qualified start-up franchisees. Also an equipment-lease program for existing (second store) franchisees is also available. There is also an SBA assistance program (paperwork assistance) for both start-up and existing operations.

Management Assistance: Managerial programs taught during training classes and during 10-day opening assistance.

Training Assistance: One week at national headquarters and 10 days on-site. Ongoing training is available on request. Continuing training available.

Fantastic Sam's

1400 Kellogg Dr. Ste. E
Anaheim, CA 92807
Web Address: www.fantasticsams.com
Toll-Free Phone: (800) 441-6588
Phone: (714) 779-3910
Fax:
Contact: VP of Operations/Development

Number of Franchises: 1304
Company-Owned Units: 6
Total Units: 1310

In Business Since: 1974   **Franchising Since:** 1976

Description of Operation: Full service family hair care centers.

Equity Capital Needed: $75,000-$100,000

Franchise Fee: $25,000

Royalty: $175.56 per week

Advertising Co-op Fee:

Financial Assistance: Some equipment leasing is available.

Management Assistance: Yes.

Training Assistance: Yes.

First Choice Haircutters

6465 Millcreek Dr. # 210
Mississauga, ON L5N 5R6
Web Address: www.firstchoice.com
Toll-Free Phone: (800) 387-8335
Phone: (905) 821-8555
Fax: (905) 567-7000
Contact: President

Number of Franchises: 136
Company-Owned Units: 73
Total Units: 209

In Business Since: 1980   **Franchising Since:** 1981

Description of Operation: Value-priced family hair care centers. High-volume, low-cost, à la carte hair care for men, women, and children.

Equity Capital Needed: approximately $40,000

Franchise Fee: $25,000

Royalty: 7 percent

Advertising Co-op Fee:

Financial Assistance: Data not available.

Management Assistance: Yes.

Training Assistance: Yes.

Great Clips

3800 W. 80th St., Ste. 400
Minneapolis, MN 55431
Web Address: www.greatclips.com
Toll-Free Phone: (800) 999-5959
Phone: (612) 893-9088
Fax: (612) 844-3443
Contact: Franchise Development Administrator

Number of Franchises: 991
Company-Owned Units: 12
Total Units: 1,003

In Business Since: 1982   **Franchising Since:** 1983

Description of Operation: This is a hair care franchise opportunity. The profile of a franchisee includes these characteristics: no previous hair care experience is needed, previous management experience preferred, strong people skills, and desire to succeed. Great Clips offers a low-investment franchise that provides repeat business.

Equity Capital Needed: $150,000

Franchise Fee: $17,500

Royalty: 6 percent franchise fee

Advertising Co-op Fee: 5 percent advertising fee

Financial Assistance: Great Clips offers a preset financing program through Textron Financial, which provides financing based on the assets of the business. Details in the UFOC.

Management Assistance: Local market support. Point of sale computer for complete business tracking. Full training center and operational support staff available in every market.

Training Assistance: Comprehensive three-day program in Minneapolis, MN. Training facilities are built in every market and staffed by local support personnel to assist franchisees once training is complete. Managers, stylists, and franchisees are all trained in the Great Clips system to ensure that each salon can provide excellent customer service.

Lemon Tree
"A Unisex Haircutting Establishment"

3301 Hempstead Tpk.
Levittown, NY 11756
Toll-Free Phone: (800) 345-9156
Phone: (516) 735-2828
Fax: (516) 735-1851
Contact: Vice President

Number of Franchises: 75
Company-Owned Units: n/a
Total Units: 75

In Business Since: 1974   **Franchising Since:** 1976

Description of Operation: Lemon Tree meets the hair care needs of the entire family at low affordable prices, with name-brand quality products, and hours from early morning to late evening.

Equity Capital Needed: $30,000-$42,000

Franchise Fee: $10,000

Royalty: 6 percent weekly royalty of gross sales

Advertising Co-op Fee: $400/month

Financial Assistance: Franchisor may assist the franchisee in obtaining financing for franchise fee and equipment. We may agree to finance one-half of the franchisee's purchase of equipment and franchise fee.

Management Assistance: Franchisee will be trained one week at franchisor's headquarters in the operation of the Lemon Tree. Franchisee will receive one week in-shop training on salon's grand opening, including supplemental training programs, seminars, and workshops, as franchisor deems necessary.

Sport Clips

P.O. Box 3000-266
Georgetown, TX 78627
Toll-Free Phone: (800) 872-4247
Phone: (512) 869-1201
Fax: (512) 869-0366
Contact: Director of Franchise Development

Number of Franchises: 11
Company-Owned Units: 5
Total Units: 16

In Business Since: 1993   **Franchising Since:** 1995

Description of Operation: Sport Clips provides haircuts for men and boys. We feature a sport theme environment. Sports on TV is offered at every station. No appointments. No perms or colors are offered.

Equity Capital Needed: $30,000-$50,000 cash; $95,000-$150,000

Franchise Fee: $15,000 multiple franchise package

Royalty: 6 percent

Advertising Co-op Fee:

Financial Assistance: Third-party vendors

Management Assistance: Area coaches are available.

Training Assistance: Two weeks of training are provided.

Beauty Care—Nail Salons

Encore Nails Franchising LLC

123 Cook St., Ste. 200
Denver, CO 80206
E-mail Address: encorenails@msn.com
Toll-Free Phone: (800) 498-8318
Phone: (303) 388-2665
Fax: (303) 388-0413
Contact: Managing Partner

Number of Franchises: 2
Company-Owned Units: 0
Total Units: 2

In Business Since: 1997   **Franchising Since:** 1997

Description of Operation: Upscale retail salon caters to upscale clientele, providing the finest in nail care and beautification. Exclusive providers of the "Polished Image Nail System"—the natural-looking odorless alternative to acrylics. Unique product, plus unique delivery and service.

Equity Capital Needed: $50,000-80,000

Franchise Fee: $15,000

Royalty: 5 percent of gross sales

Advertising Co-op Fee: 1 percent

Financial Assistance: Financial assistance not available directly from franchisor. Leasing options for equipment may be available.

Management Assistance: Marketing/Management/Personnel/Operations

Training Assistance: Train one owner/manager in retail/marketing/operational aspects of the business. Train lead nail technician (must be licensed) in the application of the product, care of nails, and so forth.

Beauty Care—Miscellaneous

Hair Replacement Systems/HRS

400 S. Dixie Highway
Hallandale, FL 33009
E-mail Address: hrshome@bellsouth.net
Toll-Free Phone: (800) 327-7971
Phone: (954) 457-0050
Fax: (954) 457-0054
Contact: Franchise Director

Number of Franchises: 32
Company-Owned Units: 0
Total Units: 32

In Business Since: 1980   **Franchising Since:** 1984

Description of Operation: Sales and service of nonsurgical men's and women's hair replacement systems.

Equity Capital Needed: $60,000-$150,000

Franchise Fee: $9,500 for 1st 100,000 population. $1,000 for additional 100,000 population.

Royalty: Flat rate based on territory population.

Advertising Co-op Fee:

Financial Assistance: No financing.

Management Assistance: Site selection, office design, computer systems, staffing, and contracts with new employees.

Training Assistance: Includes one week in the home office and a portion of a week in the new franchise location. Training covers telemarketing sales, styling, hair additions, computer use, marketing, and receptionist.

Tan World

1919 S. 40th Street, Ste. 202
Lincoln, NE 68506
Toll-Free Phone: (800) 865-2378
Phone: (402) 434-5620
Fax: (402) 434-5624
Contact: President

Number of Franchises: 2
Company-Owned Units: 2
Total Units: 4

In Business Since: 1995   **Franchising Since:** 1996

Description of Operation: Tan World offers megasalons, each featuring 20 or more tanning beds. We offer full-service tanning (with no appointments) and tanning products. In an air-conditioned, consumer-oriented environment.

Equity Capital Needed: $100,000

Franchise Fee: $20,000

Royalty: 6 percent

Advertising Co-op Fee: 2 percent

Financial Assistance: Current financial review, support on a business plan, and third-party lending options are provided.

Management Assistance: Complete training, software program, manuals, follow-up, and an 800# are provided.

Training Assistance: One week at the home office and one week on-site.

Business Services— Accounting

Accounting Business Systems

1760 Palmetto Ave. Ste. C
Winter Park, FL 32789
Web Address: www.absystems.com
E-mail Address: msilverburg@parkave.net
Toll-Free Phone:
Phone: (407) 644-5400
Fax: (407) 869-0077
Contact: President

Number of Franchises: 38
Company-Owned Units: 1
Total Units: 39

In Business Since: 1990   **Franchising Since:** 1992

Description of Operation: Complete accounting and tax franchise, including software, client marketing, training, and support. Designed to put qualified individuals into public practice to serve small business.

Equity Capital Needed: $11,500 includes franchise fee

Franchise Fee: $9,500

Royalty: $150 per month

Advertising Co-op Fee:

Financial Assistance: None

Management Assistance: Initial management training and counseling. Full ongoing telephone support.

Training Assistance: An extensive five days of training in Orlando, FL, covers client marketing, software operation, practice management, and tax practice development.

Advantage Payroll Services

126 Merrow Rd. P.O. Box 1330
Auburn, ME 04211
Toll-Free Phone: (800) 876-0178
Phone: (207) 784-0178
Fax: (207) 786-0490
Contact: President

Number of Franchises: 27
Company-Owned Units: 1
Total Units: 28

In Business Since: 1967   **Franchising Since:** 1983

Description of Operation: Payroll and payroll tax filing. Franchise computers are linked to franchisor's mainframe system. All tax deposits and quarterly reporting done by franchisor.

Equity Capital Needed: $20,000-$40,000

Franchise Fee: $14,500

Royalty: 0 percent

Advertising Co-op Fee:

Financial Assistance: $5,000 note; 10 percent for four years.

Management Assistance: Data not available.

Training Assistance: Two weeks at home office; 10 days in field. Ongoing 800# support.

Franklin Traffic Service

5251 Shawnee Rd. P.O. Box 100
Ransomville, NY 14131
Toll-Free Phone:
Phone: (716) 731-3131
Fax: (716) 731-2705
Contact: President

Number of Franchises: 2
Company-Owned Units: 1
Total Units: 3

In Business Since: 1969

Franchising Since: 1986

Description of Operation: Franklin Traffic Service is a prominent company providing its nationwide clientele with audit and payment of freight bills; management reporting; management services; and complete auditing and payment, customhouse brokerage audit, and international logistics.

Equity Capital Needed: $25,000-$28,000

Franchise Fee: $25,000

Royalty: 0 percent

Advertising Co-op Fee:

Financial Assistance: $11,000-$14,000 is required in advance. Financing on balance to qualified applicants.

Management Assistance: Franklin Traffic Service maintains a bona fide interest in all franchisees. Manuals of operations, forms, and directions are provided. In-the-field assistance is provided regularly. The franchisees benefit from all new marketing concepts that are developed. Franklin Traffic encourages regular franchise contact and continually upgrades and maintains the highest level of quality possible.

Training Assistance: We provide an intensive three-week, mandatory training program for all new franchisees. Training consists of in-house programs and time in the field with Franklin Traffic training personnel.

LedgerPlus

401 St. Francis St.
Tallahassee, FL 32301
Web Address: www.ledgerplus.com
Toll-Free Phone:
Phone: (904) 681-1941
Fax: (904) 561-1374
Contact:

Number of Franchises: 215
Company-Owned Units: 2
Total Units: 217

In Business Since: 1989   **Franchising Since:** 1990

Description of Operation: Local franchisees operate an accounting and tax practice, using special marketing techniques, in addition to operational and computer systems, to provide tax, record keeping, and other services to their clients.

Equity Capital Needed: $12,400-$25,000

Franchise Fee: $12,000

Royalty: 6 percent

Advertising Co-op Fee:

Financial Assistance: Available for franchise fee.

Management Assistance: Ongoing assistance from the home office and regional owner to the local franchisee.

Training Assistance: Five days of training: three days of home-office seminars, and two days of in-the-field training.

Padgett Business Services

160 Hawthorne Park
Athens, GA 30606
Web Address: www.smallbizpros.com
Toll-Free Phone: (800) 323-7292
Phone: (706) 548-1040
Fax: (706) 543-8537
Contact: V.P.

Number of Franchises: 410
Company-Owned Units: 0
Total Units: 410

In Business Since: 1966   **Franchising Since:** 1975

Description of Operation: Monthly tax, accounting, and consulting to the small business market represents 85 percent of all business.

Equity Capital Needed: $40,000-60,000

Franchise Fee: $22,000

Royalty: 9 percent

Advertising Co-op Fee: 0

Financial Assistance: Third-party financing assistance from $20,000 to $50,000

Management Assistance: Customer demographics, operations and sales manuals, technical support, press releases, grand opening support, strategic planning,

management seminars, practice management, newsletter, tax publication, and research and development.

Training Assistance: Initial training includes 13 days of classroom training and seven days of field training. Ongoing training includes marketing seminar and five-day tax seminar.

Parson-Bishop Services, Inc.

7870 Camargo Rd.
Cincinnati, OH 45243
Web Address: www.parsonbishop.com
Toll-Free Phone: (800) 543-0468
Phone: (513) 561-5560
Fax: (513) 527-8919
Contact: President

Number of Franchises: 62
Company-Owned Units: 0
Total Units: 62

In Business Since: 1973   **Franchising Since:** 1987

Description of Operation: P-B's executive franchisees market P-B's guaranteed effective, low-cost accounts receivable management, collection, and cash flow improvement plans. These exclusive plans provide solutions to an ongoing basic business need. More than 90 percent of businesses are prospects. Build equity from long-term, repeat customers. You must have a sales, marketing, or management background and be qualified to call on upper-level management in corporations of all sizes.

Equity Capital Needed: $23,000-$29,500

Franchise Fee: $18,000

Royalty: 0 percent

Advertising Co-op Fee:

Financial Assistance: None

Management Assistance: We provide constant advertising, marketing, and public relations support, plus videos and manuals. Computerized franchise management system.

Training Assistance: We offer one week of classroom training at the home office, two training visits to franchisee's area in the first six months, and quarterly national and regional seminars. Continual one-on-one support.

Business Services—Advertising

Adventures in Advertising

400 Crown Colony Dr.
Quincy, MA 02169
Toll-Free Phone: (800) 637-8668
Phone: (617) 472-9900
Fax: (617) 472-9976

Contact: Franchise Director

Number of Franchises: 0
Company-Owned Units: 0
Total Units: 0

In Business Since: 1981   **Franchising Since:** 1994

Description of Operation: Adventures in Advertising provides medium to large companies with imprinted promotional products to be used in trade shows, product introductions, safety programs, service awards, incentive programs, and recognition.

Equity Capital Needed: $57,000-$75,000

Franchise Fee: $17,500

Royalty: 4-7 percent

Advertising Co-op Fee:

Financial Assistance: None available.

Management Assistance: Each franchisee will be provided with a business operations manual and training in how to develop an office, sales force, and market presence. Constant updates on product and market developments are provided.

Training Assistance: Each franchisee receives one week of training and detailed manuals, which include industry, sales development, client development, and effective office management. Two conferences per year and regular, ongoing training programs are available.

Bingo Bugle Newspaper

P.O. Box 51189
Seattle, WA 98115
Web Address: www.bingobugle.com
Toll-Free Phone: (800) 447-1958
Phone: (206) 527-4958
Fax: (206) 527-9756
Contact: President

Number of Franchises: 68
Company-Owned Units: 0
Total Units: 68

In Business Since: 1982   **Franchising Since:** 1982

Description of Operation: Sell franchises for the Bingo Bugle Newspaper nationally. The Bingo Bugle is a monthly publication for bingo players. We also train and help the franchisees.

Equity Capital Needed: $5,500-$9,000

Franchise Fee: $1,500-$6,000

Royalty: 10 percent

Advertising Co-op Fee:

Financial Assistance: None

Management Assistance: Data not available.

Training Assistance: Two-day training session, tailored to prospect's experience in publishing and selling. Training subjects include checklist of everything franchisee needs to do at start-up.

Cathedral Directories

1401 W. Girard Ave.
Madison Heights, MI 48071
Toll-Free Phone: (800) 544-6903
Phone: (248) 545-1415
Fax: (248) 544-1611
Contact: Franchise Sales Director

Number of Franchises: 2
Company-Owned Units: 6
Total Units: 8

In Business Since: 1948   **Franchising Since:** 1993

Description of Operation: We publish church directories. Every directory is unique to the particular church. There is no charge to the church because the directory is advertising supported. Ads are sold on an annually renewed basis to funeral homes, florists, banks, and so on.

Equity Capital Needed: $35,000-$50,000 total

Franchise Fee: $5,000-$15,000

Royalty: 0 percent

Advertising Co-op Fee:

Financial Assistance: Third-party financial referrals. We design our assistance program to meet the needs of the franchisee. The franchisee is expected to provide computer hardware and basic office equipment. We provide free training and ongoing support.

Management Assistance: We provide three days of training at no charge. We also provide basic advice about business set-up. We have ongoing support and sales assistance in the field.

Training Assistance: We provide, at no charge, three days of on-site training at company's headquarters—one day for marketing training and two days for computer software training. We schedule additional training in the field after the franchise is in operation.

Effective Mailers

1151 Allen Dr.
Troy, MI 48083
Toll-Free Phone: (800) 360-6360
Phone: (248) 588-9880
Fax: (248) 588-4299
Contact: President

Number of Franchises: 15
Company-Owned Units: 1
Total Units: 16

In Business Since: 1982   **Franchising Since:** 1993

Description of Operation: EM offers direct-mail advertising franchises. Direct-mail advertising is an inexpensive but very effective way for local businesses (retail, service, and professionals) to advertise in their local markets. Each franchisee sells advertising to these local businesses in his or her franchised territory. Effective

Mailers provides excellent support, including production of graphics, printing, and mailing through the U.S. Post Office.

Equity Capital Needed: $25,000-$60,000

Franchise Fee: $500

Royalty: None

Advertising Co-op Fee:

Financial Assistance: None

Management Assistance: Effective Mailers' corporate office sells advertising to one million homes itself. Whatever it learns from the field, it relays practical information through letters, updated manuals, and aids.

Training Assistance: Three weeks of training include one week in the classroom and two weeks of in-field training in the local territory.

Finder/Binder Sourcebook Directories

8546 Chevy Chase Dr.
La Mesa, CA 91941
Toll-Free Phone: (800) 255-2575
Phone: (619) 463-5050
Fax: (619) 463-5097
Contact: President

Number of Franchises: 18
Company-Owned Units: 1
Total Units: 19

In Business Since: 1973 **Franchising Since:** 1978

Description of Operation: This is an add-on profit center for existing businesses in marketing, consulting, fund-raising, public relations, and so on.

Equity Capital Needed: $15,000

Franchise Fee: $1,000

Royalty: 5-10 percent

Advertising Co-op Fee: 0

Financial Assistance: n/a

Management Assistance: We provide training, operations manual, and telephone contact.

Training Assistance: A full day of training is all that is needed.

Greetings, Inc.

3415 Pimlico Parkway; P.O. Box 25623
Lexington, KY 40524
E-mail Address: greetings1@juno.com
Toll-Free Phone:
Phone: (606) 272-5624
Fax:
Contact: President

Number of Franchises: 5
Company-Owned Units: 3
Total Units: 8

In Business Since: 1984 **Franchising Since:** 1990

Description of Operation: We feel that every ad has to clear two hurdles. Hurdle #1 is that the ad must be seen, read, or heard. Hurdle #2 is that the ad must be placed with someone who has a need. We feel that Greetings clears both hurdles better than any other method of advertising. We are a target-market advertising company that addresses new home and apartment residents with the most timely, effective, and cost-efficient method of reaching new customers possible. We place a coupon magazine with College and University at the beginning of each semester.

Equity Capital Needed: $21,000

Franchise Fee: $15,000

Royalty: 5 percent

Advertising Co-op Fee: 0

Financial Assistance: None

Management Assistance: A computer operating program. Managerial assistance is given through the review and analysis of weekly and monthly reports, with follow-up as needed. Guidance is given on accounting, market areas, and systems.

Training Assistance: Training consists of one week of comprehensive training at the corporate office and one week at the franchise location. There are annual franchise meetings along with special franchise meetings addressing special areas of business.

Merchant Advertising Systems

4115 Tiverton Rd.
Randallstown, MD 21133
Toll-Free Phone:
Phone: (410) 655-3201
Fax: (410) 655-0262
Contact: President

Number of Franchises: 4
Company-Owned Units: 9
Total Units: 13

In Business Since: 1985 **Franchising Since:** 1987

Description of Operation: Provide major supermarkets and enclosed shopping malls with a free-standing, advertising kiosk that gives complimentary advertising. We then sell local target-market advertising to local merchants using custom-made signs and literature to attract shoppers in their respective areas.

Equity Capital Needed: $13,500-$25,500

Franchise Fee: $3,500

Royalty: 0 percent

Advertising Co-op Fee:

Financial Assistance: We finance 5 percent of the franchise fee at 10 percent over the first 12 months. We can provide miscellaneous sources of other financing if needed.

Management Assistance: We drop-ship all necessary materials and signs. We also provide sales catalogs, training tapes (audio), demo signs and photo albums, complete business operations manuals, testimonials (written), and the starting inventory of display centers.

Training Assistance: Training includes one week at our headquarters in Baltimore, MD. Full phone consultation, newsletters and annual follow-up training sessions are available.

Pennysaver

80 Eighth Ave.
New York, NY 10011
Toll-Free Phone:
Phone: (212) 243-6800
Fax: (212) 243-7457
Contact: President

Number of Franchises: 10
Company-Owned Units: 0
Total Units: 10

In Business Since: 1979 **Franchising Since:** 1990

Description of Operation: Free distribution shopping guide.

Equity Capital Needed: $34,900-$44,900

Franchise Fee: $29,900

Royalty: $200 plus per month

Advertising Co-op Fee:

Financial Assistance: The company provides no direct financing; however, financial assistance is available to franchisees based on adequate home equity through company contacts in the financial community.

Management Assistance: The company offers a franchisee ongoing revenue and support services. In-depth financial analysis is conducted on each issue of franchisee's publication, plus free, unlimited consulting.

Training Assistance: We provide a minimum of five days of classroom training and a minimum of five days of on-site training at the franchisee's location, at the company's expense.

Premium Shopping Guide

1235 Sunset Grove Rd.
Fallbrook, CA 92584
Toll-Free Phone: (800) 343-1056
Phone: (760) 723-8133
Fax: (760) 728-3145
Contact: National Sales Manager

Number of Franchises: 13
Company-Owned Units: 76
Total Units: 89

In Business Since: 1984 **Franchising Since:** 1992

Description of Operation: Print, label, and mail four-color direct-mail coupon and display magazines for independent publishers in over 36 states.

Equity Capital Needed: $3,000-$3,500

Franchise Fee: $2,950

Royalty: 0 percent

Advertising Co-op Fee:

Financial Assistance: Financing is available on franchise fee.

Management Assistance: Continuous 800# help line provided.

Training Assistance: In-house and field training provided.

Rental Guide

1600 Capital Circle S.W.
Tallahassee, FL 32310
Toll-Free Phone: (800) 277-4357
Phone: (904) 574-2111
Fax: (904) 574-2525
Contact:

Number of Franchises: 24
Company-Owned Units: 5
Total Units: 29

In Business Since: 1973 **Franchising Since:** 1988

Description of Operation: Full-color magazines for apartment property advertising. Free to consumers. Franchisees handle promotion, sales, layout, and distribution. Franchisor offers production, printing, training, and marketing support services.

Equity Capital Needed: $44,750-$105,000

Franchise Fee: $20,000

Royalty: 10.5 percent

Advertising Co-op Fee:

Financial Assistance: Partial financing of initial fee to qualified veterans. Lease program for distribution street racks.

Management Assistance: Assistance from regional managers and account executives. Training manuals, forms, sales aids, periodic newsletter, franchisee advisory council.

Training Assistance: We provide an initial two weeks of classroom training in Tallahassee, FL. Regional and national meetings with seminars. Toll-free 800# for technical assistance.

Resort Maps

Rte. 100 Old High School P.O. Box 726
Waitsfield, VT 05673
Web Address: www.resortmaps.com
Toll-Free Phone: (800) 788-5247
Phone: (802) 496-6277
Fax: (802) 496-6278
Contact: Director of Franchise

Number of Franchises: 29
Company-Owned Units: 0
Total Units: 29

In Business Since: 1993   **Franchising Since:** 1993

Description of Operation: RMFI Maps is engaged in the sales, nurturing, and support of franchised publishers of business and tourist information maps under the tradename of Resort Maps. It depends on and utilizes the business systems generated by Resort Maps, a company dedicated to providing a unique and creative method of alternative advertising media in the form of tourist and visitor information maps. Advertising space is supported by restaurants, resorts, retail stores, local attractions, and so forth.

Equity Capital Needed: $21,000 to $24,250 (includes $15,000 franchise fee.)

Franchise Fee: $15,000

Royalty: First year, 2 percent of GAS; second year and after, 5 percent of GAS

Advertising Co-op Fee:

Financial Assistance: No financing available.

Management Assistance: We provide ongoing 800# support, visits from a franchise coordinator, and any other assistance and consultation as needed.

Training Assistance: A comprehensive five-day training program is conducted in the home office in Waitsfield, VT, and is designed to instruct the franchisee in how to operate and maintain a Resort Maps territory and includes indoctrination on what a Resort Maps franchisee is required to do. Covered are basic principles of management skills, scheduling, cost control, ordering procedures, equipment, operation, and sales skills.

Supercoups

180 Bodwell St.
Avon, MA 02322
Web Address: www.supercoups.net
E-mail Address: desire@supercoups.net
Toll-Free Phone: (800) 626-2620
Phone: (508) 580-4340
Fax: (508) 588-3347
Contact: Sales

Number of Franchises: 290
Company-Owned Units: 0
Total Units: 290

In Business Since: 1983   **Franchising Since:** 1983

Description of Operation: SuperCoups is a cooperative direct-mail advertising franchise. The head offices, located in Avon, MA, provide all production functions. The franchisee operates the sales office out of his or her home—no inventory to carry. No coupon printing or graphics experience necessary—just a salesperson.

Equity Capital Needed: Franchise fee

Franchise Fee: $22,900

Royalty: $148 per mailing.

Advertising Co-op Fee:

Financial Assistance: None

Management Assistance: SuperCoups provides each franchisee with a complete set of managerial manuals, outlining everything from office supplies to sales techniques. Our large franchise system provides a network of managers to help any new franchisee get up and running.

Training Assistance: Franchisees receive one week of in-house training and one week of in-field training at their franchise location. We provide two 800#s for continual assistance, along with corporate-sponsored conferences twice a year, featuring classes on new procedures and industry-related topics. Also, we offer the first two mailings free to help start your business off right!

TriMark, Inc.

184 Quigley Blvd.
New Castle, DE 19720
Web Address: trimarkinc.com
E-mail Address: trimark2@universal.dca.net
Toll-Free Phone: (888) 321-6275
Phone: (302) 322-2143
Fax: (302) 322-9910
Contact: Vice President, Franchise Operations

Number of Franchises: 35
Company-Owned Units: 0
Total Units: 35

In Business Since: 1969   **Franchising Since:** 1978

Description of Operation: Multiunit direct-mail advertising Master Franchises available at $29,500 fee. No storefront, no inventory, no experience necessary (we train!). Each Master Franchise territory has a minimum of 300,000 households. Master sets the fee for each individual franchise unit with the Master Territory. Master also sets the retail prices. Immediate and residual income potential commensurate with your effort. TriMark provides complete production support. Offer by prospectus only (including franchisor's complete disclosure).

Equity Capital Needed: $37,500-$57,000

Franchise Fee: $29,500

Royalty: $.50 per advertisement per 1,000 printed pieces

Advertising Co-op Fee: 0

Financial Assistance: Financing available.

Management Assistance: Two full weeks (80 hours) of classroom and field training, ongoing advice and consultation, monthly newsletters, annual training in the field.

Training Assistance: 40 hours of classroom training at corporate headquarters, plus 40 hours of field training at the franchisee's location. Training (including reasonable lodging, food, and travel) is included in franchise fee.

TV News

80 Eighth Ave.
New York, NY 10011
Toll-Free Phone:
Phone: (212) 243-6800
Fax: (212) 243-7457
Contact: President

Number of Franchises: 5
Company-Owned Units: 1
Total Units: 6

In Business Since: 1979   **Franchising Since:** 1990

Description of Operation: Free distribution TV guide.

Equity Capital Needed: $15,500

Franchise Fee: $29,900

Royalty: $150 per month

Advertising Co-op Fee:

Financial Assistance: The company provides no direct financing; however, financial assistance is available to franchisees based on adequate home equity through company contacts in the financial community.

Management Assistance: The company offers a franchisee ongoing revenue and support services. In-depth financial analysis is conducted on each issue of franchisee's publication plus free, unlimited consulting.

Training Assistance: We offer a minimum of five days of classroom training and a minimum of five days on-site training at the franchisee's location, at the company's expense.

United Coupon Corporation

8380 Alban Rd. Ste. 100
Springfield, VA 22150
Toll-Free Phone: (800) 368-3501
Phone: (703) 644-0200
Fax: (703) 569-2031
Contact: Director of Franchise Development

Number of Franchises: 86
Company-Owned Units: 0
Total Units: 86

In Business Since: 1981   **Franchising Since:** 1982

Description of Operation: National corporation is expanding its operation. This is an excellent opportunity to join one of the leading companies involved in franchising in the direct-mail advertising field. Strong repeat business potential. Sales and/or marketing experience is preferred.

Equity Capital Needed: Three months of living expenses

Franchise Fee: $18,900-$21,900

Royalty: 0 percent

Advertising Co-op Fee:

Financial Assistance: Financing is available to qualified prospective franchisees.

Management Assistance: United provides production services such as artwork, layout, typesetting, platemaking, printing, inserting, addressing, mailing, labeling, and so on. Other assistance available through business management software, nationwide 800#, and regional and national seminars.

Training Assistance: We provide classroom and field training to new franchisees, training tapes on sales and business development, as well as sales force, time management, product knowledge, and customer relations.

Val-Pak Direct Marketing

8605 Largo Lakes Dr.
Largo, FL 34643
Toll-Free Phone: (800) 237-6266
Phone: (813) 393-1270
Fax: (813) 397-4968
Contact: Executive Vice President

Number of Franchises: 191
Company-Owned Units: 0
Total Units: 191

In Business Since: 1968   **Franchising Since:** 1988

Description of Operation: The nation's largest local cooperative direct-mail advertising company annually mails 310 million envelopes to consumers in all 50 states. More than 80,000 businesses are clients. The franchisor handles graphics, printing, and mailing.

Equity Capital Needed: $25,000-$250,000

Franchise Fee: $500

Royalty: 0 percent

Advertising Co-op Fee:

Financial Assistance: The franchisor offers purchase financing in limited cases.

Management Assistance: V.P. Link office management software.

Training Assistance: Training consists of a three-day, home-study program; five days of classroom training; and a three-day, on-site visit, plus three-day annual training meetings three times a year.

Wedding Pages, The

11106 Mockingbird Dr.
Omaha, NE 68137
Web Address: www.weddingpages.com
E-mail Address: wedpages @weddingpages.com
Toll-Free Phone: (800) 843-4983
Phone: (402) 331-7755
Fax: (402) 331-2887
Contact: Vice President of Marketing

Number of Franchises: 58
Company-Owned Units: 28
Total Units: 86

In Business Since: 1982   **Franchising Since:** 1985

Description of Operation: Complete database marketing system for wedding professionals to solicit business from brides and grooms. The system includes an ad and a mailing list.

Equity Capital Needed: $30,000-$35,000

Franchise Fee: $15,000

Royalty: 10 percent

Advertising Co-op Fee:

Financial Assistance: Not available.

Management Assistance: We provide two and one-half days of in-house training; two and one-half days of field training, and ongoing assistance with a toll-free number, conventions, and field visits.

Training Assistance: Same as above.

Yellow Jacket Direct Mail Advertising

23101 Moulton Pkwy. Ste. 110
Laguna Hills, CA 92653
Web Address: www.yellow-jacket.com
Toll-Free Phone: (800) 893-5569
Phone: (714) 951-9500
Fax: (714) 859-0899
Contact: Franchise Sales

Number of Franchises: 7
Company-Owned Units: 1
Total Units: 8

In Business Since: 1988   **Franchising Since:** 1990

Description of Operation: Yellow Jacket Direct Mail Advertising sells franchises on a national level, with master franchises available. Yellow Jacket is a fast-growing franchise opportunity. It offers business owners a proven method of advertising that significantly improves their sales and profits. Complete production support, artwork, printing, and mailing through the U.S. mail are provided.

Equity Capital Needed: $25,000

Franchise Fee: $10,000-$19,000

Royalty: 6 percent

Advertising Co-op Fee:

Financial Assistance: Financial assistance is available, depending on the applicant's qualifications.

Management Assistance: We produce training manuals, sales aids, and all applicable forms.

Training Assistance: A complete three-week training program includes classroom as well as field training. Ongoing field training support is also provided.

Business Services—Consulting

ABX-Associates Business Xchange

12221 Merit Dr., Ste. 950
Dallas, TX 75251
Toll-Free Phone:
Phone: (972) 233-3300
Fax: (972) 233-3306
Contact:

Number of Franchises:
Company-Owned Units:
Total Units:

In Business Since: 1962   **Franchising Since:**

Description of Operation: Nationwide franchise brokers network.

Equity Capital Needed:

Franchise Fee:

Royalty:

Advertising Co-op Fee:

Financial Assistance:

Management Assistance:

Training Assistance:

E. K. Williams & Company

1020 N. University Parks Dr.
Waco, TX 76707
Toll-Free Phone: (800) 992-0706
Phone: (254) 745-2424
Fax: (254) 745-2566
Contact: Franchise Sales Manager

Number of Franchises: 309
Company-Owned Units: 1
Total Units: 310

In Business Since: 1935   **Franchising Since:** 1947

Description of Operation: Franchised accounting, tax, and business counseling for small businesses. Monthly reports include profit and loss, balance sheet, cash flow, payroll check writing, and other management tools. Our internal software allows for regular modification and updates.

Equity Capital Needed: $38,000-$95,000

Franchise Fee: $25,000

Royalty: 8 percent, 6 percent, 4 percent sliding scale

Advertising Co-op Fee:

Financial Assistance: None at present.

Management Assistance: We offer ongoing training and assistance on-site. Semiannual meetings and national conventions every other year. Toll-free phone assistance with hardware, software, marketing, and other areas of need.

Training Assistance: We provide an intensive two weeks of classroom and in-field training. The first week is at the national support center; the second week is in a live office dealing with real situations. Training in all areas is covered.

Empire Business Brokers

336 Harris Hill Rd
Buffalo, NY 14221
Web Address: www.empirebusinessbrokers.com
E-mail Address: nickgug1@aol.com
Toll-Free Phone:
Phone: (716) 677-5229
Fax: (716) 677-0955
Contact: President

Number of Franchises: 47
Company-Owned Units: 1
Total Units: 48

In Business Since: 1981 **Franchising Since:** 1989

Description of Operation: The sale of existing businesses to qualified buyers.

Equity Capital Needed: $10,000-$15,000

Franchise Fee: $8,900

Royalty: 0 percent

Advertising Co-op Fee:

Financial Assistance: We will finance half the fee for qualified individuals.

Management Assistance: Five-day training at franchisor's office.

Training Assistance: Franchisees are led through the listing and sale process of a business.

Fortune Practice Management

9191 Towne Centre Dr. Ste. 175
San Diego, CA 92122
Web Address: www.fortunepractice.com
Toll-Free Phone: (800) 628-1052
Phone: (619) 535-1784
Fax: (619) 535-6387
Contact: Director of Franchise Support

Number of Franchises: 31
Company-Owned Units: 2
Total Units: 33

In Business Since: 1990 **Franchising Since:** 1991

Description of Operation: Fortune Practice Management provides business consulting and seminar services. The dental and health care industries, specializing in private practitioners in solo or group practice.

Equity Capital Needed: $35,000-$55,000

Franchise Fee: $42,000

Royalty: 10 percent, 5 percent

Advertising Co-op Fee:

Financial Assistance: We will finance $30,000. Terms for three years.

Management Assistance: A complete operations manual is given to each franchisee and weekly coaching calls are made between the franchisee and the home office. A franchise support hot line is available.

Training Assistance: Initial training consists of 10 intensive classroom days at home office, plus five to 10 training days on-site.

Gateway Franchise Credit Products— West Coast Commercial Credit

P.O. Box 19241
San Diego, CA 92159
Web Address: www.nzone.com/gateway
Toll-Free Phone: (800) 451-9041
Phone: (619) 463-0734
Fax: (800) 451-9044
Contact: President

Number of Franchises:
Company-Owned Units:
Total Units:

In Business Since: 1987 **Franchising Since:**

Description of Operation: Full-service commercial finance. No application or commitment fees. Nationwide funding for start-up, expansion, area development, and resale. SBA loans, conventional bank financing, equipment leasing, real estate-construction financing, inventory flooring, and accounts receivable financing. Minimum approximately $35,000 to $5,000,000 including private debt placement through investment banking. All franchise categories. Dual agent intermediary compensated by lender. No fees to franchisee for our prequalification, processing, packaging, and placement of your funding request. Referrals to CPAs, attorney, and so on.

Equity Capital Needed:

Franchise Fee:

Royalty:

Advertising Co-op Fee:

Financial Assistance:

Management Assistance:

Training Assistance:

General Business Services

1020 N. University Parks Dr.
Waco, TX 76707
Toll-Free Phone: (800) 583-6181
Phone: (817) 756-6181
Fax: (817) 756-0322

Contact: Senior Vice President

Number of Franchises: 339
Company-Owned Units: 0
Total Units: 339

In Business Since: 1961   **Franchising Since:** 1961

Description of Operation: GBS offers tax counseling, business counseling, financial counseling, management counseling, personnel services, computer services, financial record keeping, and wealth accumulation services to small and medium-sized companies.

Equity Capital Needed: Six months of personal expenses.

Franchise Fee: $30,000

Royalty: 10 percent to 2.5 percent based on volume and tenure with GBS.

Advertising Co-op Fee:

Financial Assistance: None

Management Assistance: A field-support manager works with franchisees in the field, and a marketing director works with them from the home office. Both are responsible for the building of the franchisee's business. The franchisees have a tax research department and business research department available to assist them in counseling their clients.

Training Assistance: The first year the franchisee is in business, he or she completes a 50-week training period. The first two weeks are in Waco, TX, completing basic training, which consists of both technical and marketing training. A custom-designed, 28-week, home-study course is next. After 90 days of business, there are eight different schools in their area. An annual convention is held in different locations yearly.

Interactive Media Broadcasting Company (I.M.B.C.)

25820 Southfield Rd., Ste. 201
Southfield, MI 48075
Web Address: www.wfcnet.com
E-mail Address: wfcnet@cris.com
Toll-Free Phone:
Phone: (248) 559-1415
Fax: (248) 557-7931
Contact:

Number of Franchises: 1
Company-Owned Units: 1
Total Units: 2

In Business Since: 1996   **Franchising Since:** 1997

Description of Operation: Franchise network of broadcasting associates. Provides interactive audio entertainment to the Internet.

Equity Capital Needed: $32,000

Franchise Fee: $62,000

Royalty: $5,000 per month

Advertising Co-op Fee: 0

Financial Assistance: n/a

Management Assistance: n/a

Training Assistance: n/a

International Mergers & Acquisitions

4300 N. Miller Rd., Ste.230
Scottsdale, AZ 85251
E-mail Address:
internationalmergersandacquisitionsworldhdq@
 worldnet.att.net
Toll-Free Phone:
Phone: (602) 990-3899
Fax: (602) 990-7480
Contact: President

Number of Franchises: 65
Company-Owned Units: 0
Total Units: 65

In Business Since: 1969   **Franchising Since:** 1977

Description of Operation: International Mergers and Acquisitions is an international affiliation of Members engaged in the profession of serving M&A-minded companies in the areas of consulting, financing, divestitures, mergers, and acquisitions; in essence, a one-stop service for corporate needs. We have offices in America, Mexico, Latin America, and South East Asia.

Equity Capital Needed: n/a

Franchise Fee: $10,000

Royalty: $375/quarter

Advertising Co-op Fee: 0

Financial Assistance: None

Management Assistance: IMA holds three to four Orientation Sessions and three to four Creative Work Sessions each year, plus personal workshops if needed.

Training Assistance: Explained in managerial assistance.

Priority Management Systems

2035 120th Ave. NE, Ste. 201
Bellevue, WA 98005
Web Address: www.prioritymanagement.com
Toll-Free Phone: (800) 221-9031
Phone: (206) 454-7686
Fax: (206) 454-5506
Contact: Vice President-Franchise Development

Number of Franchises: 250
Company-Owned Units: 1
Total Units: 251

In Business Since: 1981   **Franchising Since:** 1984

Description of Operation: An international management training and human resources development organization, committed to providing clients with a curriculum

of training programs designed to teach essential management skills. This curriculum is provided through a series of group workshops and face-to-face consultations.

Equity Capital Needed: $35,000-$45,000

Franchise Fee: $29,500

Royalty: 9 percent

Advertising Co-op Fee: 1 percent

Financial Assistance: Not available

Management Assistance: Corporate support and development teams, as well as a regional coach, for each of our 10 regions. Newsletters, national public relations programs, and participation in national trade shows.

Training Assistance: Initial owner's training is nine days and the international conference. Owner training is one-on-one with a regional coach in the field. Learning options are provided at the two regional meetings and the international conference.

Professional Dynametric Programs (PDP)

750 E. Highway 24, Building I
Woodland Park, CO 80863
Web Address: www.pdp-inc.com
E-mail Address: pdpnet@earthlink.net
Toll-Free Phone: (800) 632-1127
Phone: (719) 687-6074
Fax: (719) 687-8587
Contact: **Executive Vice President**

Number of Franchises: 27
Company-Owned Units: 0
Total Units: 27

In Business Since: 1980   **Franchising Since:** 1980

Description of Operation: A business-to-business franchise. Management tools with 20 years of research and development. Services, products, and trainings are designed around the proprietary behavioral assessment instruments. Applications are proven programs used for hiring, matching people to tasks, managing, evaluating, motivating, and much more. The behavioral assessment processes are more scientific, predictable, and effective than any known instruments, providing clients large and small, profit and nonprofit, national and international, with accurate and beneficial results.

Equity Capital Needed: $20,000

Franchise Fee: $29,500

Royalty: 0-30 percent on products, training, and services

Advertising Co-op Fee: 0

Financial Assistance: Franchise fee terms. Either cash discount or one-year, interest-free terms on $14,500.

Management Assistance: Technical support on operations of business: pricing, software programs, marketing support, field visits, and initial contact visits. First client-

training support: on-site expertise to conduct training and implementation. Ongoing support: newsletters, annual conferences, marketing strategies.

Training Assistance: First week of training will certify you in PDP products, services, operations, and Level 1 Sales and Marketing. Field Training: individualized training takes place at your business to help you apply the knowledge acquired in the classroom. Assistance in developing tactical plans to obtain client sales. Continuing education: executive development programs.

Sunbelt Business Brokers

2 Amherst St.
Charleston, SC 29413
Web Address: www.sunbeltnetwork.com
E-mail Address: sunbelt@sunbeltnetwork.com
Toll-Free Phone: (800) 771-7866
Phone: (803) 853-4781
Fax: (803) 853-4125
Contact: **Chief Executive Officer**

Number of Franchises: 137
Company-Owned Units: 1
Total Units: 138

In Business Since: 1979   **Franchising Since:** 1992

Description of Operation: Sunbelt franchisees engage in general business brokerage. The downsizing of major companies has flooded the market with thousands of unemployed people looking for businesses to buy. Sunbelt franchisees use their executive talents to help people buy and sell businesses to benefit themselves and their families.

Equity Capital Needed: $7,000-$50,000

Franchise Fee: $5,000-$10,000

Royalty: $3,000-$5,000 per year; semiannual payment

Advertising Co-op Fee:

Financial Assistance: None available.

Management Assistance: Complete operating systems are provided, as well as on-site assistance with set-up and hiring brokers. Follow-up, on-site visits ensure a smooth start-up.

Training Assistance: New broker training is held every month at regional training centers. Franchisees may send as many trainees as they wish as often as they wish, at no additional cost. Follow-up and special training sessions are provided as needed at the franchisee's location. Advanced training sessions are available at the regional training sites.

Triple Check Income Tax Service

2441 Honolulu Ave.
Montose, CA 91020
Toll-Free Phone: (800) 283-1040
Phone: (818) 236-2944
Fax: (818) 249-5344

Contact: President

Number of Franchises: 318
Company-Owned Units: 2
Total Units: 320

In Business Since: 1941 **Franchising Since:** 1979

Description of Operation: Franchisor offers a full range of support services to independent tax practitioners, including training, technical (hot line), marketing (including group referral programs), proprietary worksheet schedule system, and reduced computer costs. Through a sister company (Triple Check Financial Services), franchisees have an opportunity to engage in financial and investment planning services. The newest profit center—Triple Check Business Services—allows franchisees to offer sophisticated business counseling.

Equity Capital Needed: $500-$8,000

Franchise Fee: None

Royalty: Varies

Advertising Co-op Fee:

Financial Assistance: Short-term loans are available through a local area bank.

Management Assistance: Assistance is in the form of written manuals and telephone communication with specialists in each area of managing a tax preparation, business services, and financial services business.

Training Assistance: We provide 80 hours of training each year to be done at a licensed location. Advanced tax preparation training includes audiocassette tapes, extensive manuals, form modules in the Triple Check worksheet system, and a "sales and marketing" section to help the conservative-thinking accountant learn how you actually take advantage of our competitive advantages.

VR Business Brokers

1151 Dove St., Ste. 100
Newport Beach, CA 92660
Toll-Free Phone: (800) 377-8722
Phone:
Fax: (714) 975-1940
Contact: Director of Franchise Sales

Number of Franchises: 55
Company-Owned Units: 0
Total Units: 55

In Business Since: 1979 **Franchising Since:** 1979

Description of Operation: VR sells more businesses in the United States than anyone. Franchises are sold with a money-back guarantee. We help buyers to buy and sellers to sell small to mid-size businesses in many different industries.

Equity Capital Needed: Approximately $41,150 and up

Franchise Fee: 0

Royalty: 0

Advertising Co-op Fee:

Financial Assistance: No.

Management Assistance: Ongoing support by office visits and telephone. Goal setting, action plan assistance, and tracking system implementation are all a part of the ongoing assistance.

Training Assistance: Two weeks and five phases of detailed training covering the many aspects of business brokerage including pricing a business, strategic targeted marketing, recruiting, servicing the listing, working with buyers, prospecting, and so on.

World Trade Network, Inc.

580 Lincoln Park Blvd., Ste. 255
Dayton, OH 45429
E-mail Address: wtnet@infinet.com
Toll-Free Phone:
Phone: (937) 298-3383
Fax: (937) 298-2550
Contact: President/Chief Executive Officer

Number of Franchises: 17
Company-Owned Units: 1
Total Units: 18

In Business Since: 1983 **Franchising Since:** 1993

Description of Operation: The World Trade Network is the first and only franchise and licensing entity to provide a global strategy linking trading partners worldwide. WTN offers both already established and new traders to the industry the benefit of other offices to market and source products worldwide. WTN can efficiently represent a company in purchasing direct from foreign manufacturers and marketing directly to foreign distributors and retailers. WTN can provide a total turnkey import and export service.

Equity Capital Needed: $75,000

Franchise Fee: $15,000

Royalty: 7 percent of gross profits or commissions

Advertising Co-op Fee:

Financial Assistance: Yes.

Management Assistance: WTN has produced training manuals, forms, contracts, and many sales aids. After our one-week training course, assistance is only a phone call away. Convention seminars and a newsletter offer continual help to each office.

Training Assistance: An extensive one-week training program at our home office in Dayton, OH, is conducted to show each new office owner typical transactions from beginning to end. Training for the import/export business includes letters of credit, shipping, documentation agreements, marketing methods, and importing, along with many other aspects of the business.

Worldwide Canadian Management Consultants, Inc.

1480 Bayly Street, Ste. 7
Pickering, ON L1V 3T3
Toll-Free Phone:
Phone: (905) 831-2832
Fax: (905) 686-0469
Contact: Director

Number of Franchises: 37
Company-Owned Units: 2
Total Units: 37

In Business Since: 1976   **Franchising Since:** 1980

Description of Operation: International Business Opportunities. A different kind of business. Booming Industries. Low start-up and low overhead. Great profit potential. Worldwide Network. Home-based business. On-the-job training program. Unlimited business opportunities. Exclusive territories. Over 23 different countries and 21 years in consulting business.

Equity Capital Needed: $20,000-$60,000

Franchise Fee: $6,000-$20,000

Royalty: 5-8 percent

Advertising Co-op Fee: 3 percent

Financial Assistance: Financial assistance available.

Management Assistance: On-the-job training program.

Training Assistance: Full training

Business Services— Mail Centers

Mail Boxes Etc.

6060 Cornerstone Ct. West
San Diego, CA 92121-3795
Toll-Free Phone:
Phone: (619) 455-8800
Fax: (619) 546-7498
Contact: Tele-Sales Representative

Number of Franchises: 2953
Company-Owned Units: 1
Total Units: 2954

In Business Since: 1980   **Franchising Since:** 1981

Description of Operation: Mail Boxes Etc. (MBE) is the world's largest franchisor of postal, business, and communication service centers. Among the many services offered at MBE Centers are packing and shipping anything, anywhere ("Big or small, we ship it all."), mail box rental, mail receiving and forwarding, package receiving, copying, printing, public tax network, telex and Western Union, office and packing supplies, notary public, and national account programs for distribution and repair outlets for companies such as Xerox.

Equity Capital Needed: $30,000-$50,000

Franchise Fee: $24,950

Royalty: 5 percent

Advertising Co-op Fee: 2 percent

Financial Assistance: 70 percent financing through MBE's in-house finance program, which is easy to qualify for and does not require previous business experience or business credit history.

Management Assistance: Franchise owners get additional operating systems support through functional programs, such as programs regarding UPS and how to package properly. They receive management support operation reviews, which is an analysis of their centers. They also receive support through monthly newsletters and a national computer support network.

Training Assistance: Three weeks of management and operations training, often at the area franchisee's local pilot store. Franchise owners get continued training through ad association meetings, as well as at local and national conventions.

Pack 'N' Mail Packaging and Shipping Specialists

5211 85th St. Ste. 104
Lubbock, TX 79424
Toll-Free Phone: (800) 877-8884
Phone: (806) 794-0602
Fax: (806) 794-9997
Contact: President

Number of Franchises: 404
Company-Owned Units: 6
Total Units: 410

In Business Since: 1981   **Franchising Since:** 1988

Description of Operation: Complete business communications center, including shipping, packaging, fax service, complete copying service, mail box rentals, and much more.

Equity Capital Needed: $25,000-$35,000

Franchise Fee: $24,500

Royalty: 0 percent

Advertising Co-op Fee:

Financial Assistance: We offer $15,000 in a leased equipment program with another $15,000 in build-out allowance for a total of $30,000 of possible financing.

Management Assistance: We have 11 corporate officers and trainers with 30 years of combined experience.

Training Assistance: We offer two weeks of training at one of four corporate centers in the United States.

Packaging Plus Services

20 S. Terminal Dr.
Plainview, NY 11803
Toll-Free Phone: (800) 922-7225
Phone: (516) 349-1300
Fax: (516) 349-8036
Contact: President

Number of Franchises: 72
Company-Owned Units: 6
Total Units: 78

In Business Since: 1986   **Franchising Since:** 1986

Description of Operation: The company's primary goals are to provide consumers and small businesses with products and services efficiently and inexpensively. Packaging Plus Centers offer the convenient and cost-effective delivery of goods, which are properly packaged, wrapped, and shipped. In short, we ship just about anything, anywhere in the continental United States and internationally. Packaging Plus Services uses a variety of packaging techniques and environmentally friendly materials with reliable shippers. A one-step convenience!

Equity Capital Needed: $30,000

Franchise Fee: $19,500

Royalty: 3 percent

Advertising Co-op Fee:

Financial Assistance: The franchisee will be given a $25,000 long-term note at 5 percent interest after the $30,000 equity capital down payment is made. The total turnkey cost of the entire store is $55,000.

Management Assistance: National and regional advertising programs provided by PPS. PPS will provide also all of the technical knowledge, business, and marketing support necessary for the operation of the business.

Training Assistance: Hands-on training. PPS trainers spend several days in your new center with you. Marketing techniques, customer relations, positive attitude and general business skills are also covered. Plus an 800# hot line!

Pak Mail

3033 S. Parker Rd.; Ste. 1200
Aurora, CO 80014
Web Address: www.pakmail.com
E-mail Address: pakmailnsc@aol.com
Toll-Free Phone: (800) 833-2821
Phone: (303) 752-3500
Fax: (303) 755-9721
Contact: Franchise Development Manager

Number of Franchises: 327
Company-Owned Units: 0
Total Units: 327

In Business Since: 1984   **Franchising Since:** 1984

Description of Operation: Pak Mail, the premier franchise company in our industry, specializes in packing and shipping anything, anywhere in the world. We offer both residential and small and large business customers a complete array of packaging, shipping, and support services. Pak Mail centers provide convenient access to all carriers, custom packaging and moving supplies, private mail box rental, public fax, copies, and mail services. Our shipping department for businesses of all sizes. Our customer-service orientation and our focused niche set us apart from others in our industry.

Equity Capital Needed: $100,000

Franchise Fee: $22,950

Royalty: Sliding scale up to 5 percent

Advertising Co-op Fee: 2 percent

Financial Assistance: Pak Mail is a "preferred franchise company" with both SBA and private lenders. Pak Mail will provide assistance in securing financing up to 70 percent.

Management Assistance: Only Pak Mail provides custom software that focuses our franchise partners on their daily, weekly, monthly, and annual goals. The software includes pricing, projections, and planning and is tied to the point of sale system that manages each transaction. In addition, managerial advice is available online and by telephone.

Training Assistance: Pak Mail offers 10-day comprehensive training covering all aspects of our business—planning, franchising, purchasing, retail merchandising, computer training, marketing, packaging and shipping domestic and international, insurance, personnel, and customer service. There is never an additional charge for initial training or for additional attendees—that's just a part of our commitment to excellence!

Pony Mail Box and Business Center

13110 N.E. 177th Pl.
Woodinville, WA 98072
Web Address: www.pony.com
Toll-Free Phone: (800) 767-7668
Phone: (425) 483-0360
Fax: (425) 486-6495
Contact: President

Number of Franchises: 26
Company-Owned Units: 1
Total Units: 27

In Business Since: 1982   **Franchising Since:** 1986

Description of Operation: Commercial mail receiving, shipping, fax, word processing, mail boxes, Western Union, mailing supplies, answering service, wedding announcements, business cards, stationery, stamps, rubber stamps, envelopes, and packaging materials.

Equity Capital Needed: $50,000-$65,000

Franchise Fee: $19,950

Royalty: $3,000/year

Advertising Co-op Fee:

Financial Assistance: None

Management Assistance: Highly trained location assistance, specifications and drawings of build-out of offices, thorough training program, manual of operations, constant communications with each franchisee during term of contract. Expansion program in place.

Training Assistance: None

POSTALANNEX+

9050 Friars Rd., Ste. 400
San Diego, CA 92108
Web Address: www.postalannex.com
Toll-Free Phone: (800) 456-1525
Phone: (619) 563-4800
Fax: (619) 563-9850
Contact: Vice President of Development

Number of Franchises: 170
Company-Owned Units: 1
Total Units: 171

In Business Since: 1985   **Franchising Since:** 1986

Description of Operation: Postal, parcel, copy shop, business, and communications services. Complete postal, packaging, and parcel shipping services. Copy and high-speed duplicating, facsimile. Electronic funds transfer and office and packaging supplies.

Equity Capital Needed: $55,000-$80,000, including franchise fee

Franchise Fee: $19,500

Royalty: 5 percent

Advertising Co-op Fee:

Financial Assistance: Financing of up to $56,000 for those who qualify, for equipment, signage, cabinetry, and merchandise. POSTALANNEX+ offers financing through various outside companies under a variety of terms and rates.

Management Assistance: Assistance is available 24 hours a day, seven days a week with store operation, marketing, accounting, legal merchandising, promotions, and advertising. An 800# is available to all franchisees.

Training Assistance: Three weeks of comprehensive training is available at the home office-one and a half weeks in the classroom and one and a half weeks in the corporate training store. During training, every aspect of our business is covered in detail.

PostNet Postal and Business Centers

2501 N. Green Valley Park Way Ste. 101
Henderson, NV 89014
Web Address: www.postnet.net

E-mail Address: info@postnet.net
Toll-Free Phone: (800) 338-7401
Phone: (704) 792-7100
Fax: (702) 792-7115
Contact: Vice President

Number of Franchises: 107
Company-Owned Units: 4
Total Units: 111

In Business Since: 1985   **Franchising Since:** 1992

Description of Operation: PostNet International Franchise Corporation, with a staff that has developed over 500 postal and business centers throughout the United States, Alaska, Hawaii, Puerto Rico, and Guam, began franchising in the spring of 1993 and currently has a network of over 130 franchisees. PostNet offers a turnkey operation that includes a complete store development package and provides assistance in site selection and store design, merchandising, marketing, and daily store operations.

Equity Capital Needed: $57,000-$85,000

Franchise Fee: $22,500

Royalty: 3 percent

Advertising Co-op Fee:

Financial Assistance: If required, PostNet assists new franchisees in obtaining financing by preparing a comprehensive business plan with financial projections to take to loan providers, including SBA-affiliated banks.

Management Assistance: PostNet assists franchisees with managing their businesses by maintaining a constant line of communication with headquarters through an 800# and contact with PostNet Area Representatives. The development of the franchisee's business is monitored closely to ensure that PostNet franchisees grow according to plan. The Area Representative stays in contact with the franchisee and visits the store regularly. Regional meetings on business building and a five-volume operations manual.

Training Assistance: Each franchisee is trained up to one week in an area store and five to seven days on-site. The corporate trainer leads the new business owner through set-up and merchandising, including pricing, interior signage, and display. Training includes customer service techniques, staffing, record keeping, advertising, marketing, and daily operations. The trainer assists the franchise with the opening of the PostNet Center and ensures that the franchisee feels comfortable in all aspects of business operation.

Aim Mail Centers

20381 Lake Forest Dr. Ste. B-2
Lake Forest, CA 92630
Toll-Free Phone: (800) 969-0502
Phone: (714) 837-4151
Fax: (714) 837-4537
Contact: Franchise Director

Number of Franchises: 18
Company-Owned Units: 1
Total Units: 19

In Business Since: 1985 **Franchising Since:** 1989

Description of Operation: Aim Mail Centers take care of all your business service needs—from renting mailboxes, buying stamps, sending faxes, and making copies to gift wrapping, greeting cards, and passport photos. We offer it all, quickly and efficiently, without the runaround.

Equity Capital Needed: $55,000-$75,000

Franchise Fee: $17,500

Royalty: 1-5 percent

Advertising Co-op Fee:

Financial Assistance: SBA loans, FranVet, third-party financing.

Management Assistance: Two weeks of training, 800# help line, field support, workshops, newsletter (almost weekly), updates (both firmware and software at no charge), annual conventions, and franchisee advisory committee.

Training Assistance: Same as above.

Business Services—Tax Preparation

Econotax Tax Services

P.O. Box 13829
Jackson, MS 39236
Web Address: www.econotax.com
Toll-Free Phone: (800) 748-9106
Phone: (601) 956-0500
Fax: (601) 956-0583
Contact: President

Number of Franchises: 54
Company-Owned Units: 0
Total Units: 54

In Business Since: 1965 **Franchising Since:** 1968

Description of Operation: Econotax franchisees offer the public a complete range of tax services, including tax preparation, electronic return filing, refund loans, audit assistance, and tax planning.

Equity Capital Needed: $10,000-$15,000

Franchise Fee: $10,000

Royalty: 1.5 percent

Advertising Co-op Fee:

Financial Assistance: None

Management Assistance: Support is provided for all aspects of conducting a successful tax practice.

Training Assistance: A one-week, new-owner workshop is held annually at company headquarters. Regional seminars are held throughout the year. Self-study materials and 800# support are available.

Electronic Tax Filers

1600 Kilarney Dr., P.O. Box 2077
Cary, NC 27512
Toll-Free Phone:
Phone: (919) 469-0651
Fax: (919) 467-2094
Contact:

Number of Franchises: 32
Company-Owned Units: 1
Total Units: 33

In Business Since: 1990 **Franchising Since:** 1991

Description of Operation: We provide convenient, local, walk-in, retail locations where individual taxpayers can bring their completed tax returns for electronic filing of same to both state and federal taxing authorities. We also facilitate refund-anticipation loans for those taxpayers who want their refunds in one to three days rather than in the nine to 13 days needed for direct deposit of their refunds into their bank account. Most of the states, as well as the IRS, now consider Electronic Filing as the method of choice for transfer of tax information and are heavily promoting its use.

Equity Capital Needed: $25,000

Franchise Fee: $7,500

Royalty: 8 percent of gross revenue

Advertising Co-op Fee: 4 percent of gross revenue

Financial Assistance: We will finance part of the initial franchise fee for qualified applicants.

Management Assistance: Training in all facets of franchised location management is given during certification classes required of all new franchisees.

Training Assistance: Operational and managerial training is given during certification classes required of all new franchisees.

Peyron Tax Service

3212 Preston St.
Louisville, KY 40213
Toll-Free Phone:
Phone: (502) 637-7483
Fax:
Contact: President

Number of Franchises: 500
Company-Owned Units: 1
Total Units: 501

In Business Since: 1960 **Franchising Since:** 1965

Description of Operation: Peyron license others to operate tax preparation offices in stores, malls, and

storefront locations. Secured by company, which also provides warranty package, electronic filing, refund loans, technical assistance, signs, flyers, tax newsletters, and other materials and services. We also provide TV advertising for area operations.

Equity Capital Needed: $3,000 +

Franchise Fee: $3,000 +

Royalty: 5 percent

Advertising Co-op Fee:

Financial Assistance: Partial

Management Assistance: Hire and train all personnel for area operators (minimum 10 locations) and supervise closely first year. No managerial assistance provided for single-location operators.

Training Assistance: Basic tax preparation course, usually 10 weeks if operator elects to prepare all tax returns and has had no experience.

Business Services—Training

American Institute of Small Business

7515 Wayzata Blvd. Ste. 201
Minneapolis, MN 55426
Toll-Free Phone: (800) 328-2906
Phone: (612) 545-7001
Fax: (612) 545-7020
Contact: President

Number of Franchises: 4
Company-Owned Units: 1
Total Units: 5

In Business Since: 1986   **Franchising Since:** 1989

Description of Operation: Publisher of educational materials, including books, software, and videos on small business start-up, operation, and entrepreneurship. Puts on seminars and workshops on small business start-up, operations, and specific business subjects.

Equity Capital Needed: $5,000-$10,000

Franchise Fee: $2,000

Royalty: 0 percent

Advertising Co-op Fee:

Financial Assistance: Credit is extended on books, videos, and software purchases sold by franchisee.

Management Assistance: Complete training is provided on putting on a seminar or workshop, with the franchisor actually putting on the first workshop. Complete advertising materials, including literature, are provided.

Training Assistance: Franchisees come to Minneapolis, MN, for a two-day training program, or the company will send a representative to do training on location. The company will do the first workshop for the franchisee and will provide complete materials for the one-day workshop.

Control-O-Fax Systems

P.O. Box 5800 3022 Airport Blvd.
Waterloo, IA 50704
Toll-Free Phone: (800) 553-0070
Phone: (319) 234-4896
Fax: (319) 236-7350
Contact: Franchise Director

Number of Franchises: 60
Company-Owned Units: 0
Total Units: 60

In Business Since: 1969   **Franchising Since:** 1971

Description of Operation: Medical and dental office management systems and solutions.

Equity Capital Needed: $20,000-$50,000

Franchise Fee: $11,895-$26,395

Royalty: 0 percent

Advertising Co-op Fee:

Financial Assistance: $5,000-$10,000 of the initial franchise fee can be financed on a two- to four-year note.

Management Assistance: Regional manager assigned to each franchise. Dealer forum held twice a year, in which eight franchisees serve. Four are selected by management, and four are elected by franchisees. Dealer forum goals include dealer relations and problem solving.

Training Assistance: Formal classroom training is provided. One week of basic training. Three days of advanced training. Regional learning seminars routinely held.

Business—Miscellaneous

ACCTCORP International, Inc.

7414 N.E. Hazel Dell Ave., Ste. 209
Vancouver, WA 98665
Web Address: www.acctcorp.com
E-mail Address: admin@acctcorp.com
Toll-Free Phone: (800) 844-4024
Phone: (360) 694-4221
Fax: (360) 694-5924
Contact: Franchise Director

Number of Franchises: 16
Company-Owned Units: 3
Total Units: 19

In Business Since: 1987   **Franchising Since:** 1994

Description of Operation: We are a collection agency! We collect money that is past due from a variety of clients: hospitals, governments, utilities, property management, retail, restaurants, and so on. We train each franchise how to run and operate an ACCTCORP franchise based on our 40 plus years of experience.

Equity Capital Needed: $20,000-$50,000

Franchise Fee: $10,000-$20,000

Royalty: 8 percent of net

Advertising Co-op Fee: 3 percent

Financial Assistance: None at this time.

Management Assistance: Up to three weeks of training.

Training Assistance: In-house and on-site.

Cash Plus Financial Centers

3002 Dow Avenue, Ste. 510
Tustin, CA 92680
Web Address: www.cashplusinc.com
E-mail Address: chekthis1@aol.com
Toll-Free Phone: (888) 707-2274
Phone: (714) 731-2274
Fax: (714) 731-2099
Contact: V.P. Business Development

Number of Franchises: 22
Company-Owned Units: 1
Total Units: 23

In Business Since: 1985 **Franchising Since:** 1988

Description of Operation: Is there CASH in your future? Are you looking for a simple-to-run franchise? Want to be part of a growth industry? If you answered "yes" to these questions and can invest $51,000 to $78,000 in your future, we should talk. More than a traditional check-cashing company and less than a bank, we're about as close to a bank as you can get in franchising. Our designers created a retail environment that customers love, and our low-cost "Quick Start" marketing system focuses on your success. So if you're not already rich, check out CASH PLUS' approach to check cashing.

Equity Capital Needed: $50,000

Franchise Fee: $17,500

Royalty: 6 percent

Advertising Co-op Fee: 3 percent

Financial Assistance: CASH PLUS gladly provides guidance on credit applications and business plans used by franchisees seeking third-party financing.

Management Assistance: CASH PLUS offers a sophisticated approach to site selection, lease negotiations, and store design.

Training Assistance: In our comfortable classroom setting, we'll teach you easy-to-run computerized operating systems, many exciting community-oriented promotions, and our thorough check verification process.

Additional on-the-job instruction, in our store and yours, is included.

Check Express USA

1231 Greenway Dr. Ste. 800
Irving, TX 75038
Web Address: www.allcashexpress.com
Toll-Free Phone: (800) 713-3338
Phone: (972) 753-2211
Fax:
Contact: Vice President

Number of Franchises: 78
Company-Owned Units: 640
Total Units: 718

In Business Since: 1968 **Franchising Since:** 1996

Description of Operation: Retail financial services, check cashing, small loans, money orders, wire transfers, and phone products.

Equity Capital Needed: $150,000

Franchise Fee: $15,000/$30,000 small products/store

Royalty: 5 percent or $750 minimum

Advertising Co-op Fee:

Financial Assistance: Third-party leasing.

Management Assistance: The franchisor provides manual for cashing checks, collections, marketing, managing the store, and use of computer system. Support staff available seven days a week.

Training Assistance: Two weeks in corporate training center-classroom and in-store training.

Direct Opinions

23600 Mercantile Rd.
Beachwood, OH 44122
E-mail Address: directopinion@aol.com
Toll-Free Phone:
Phone: (216) 831-7979
Fax: (216) 464-0621
Contact: Director of Franchise Development

Number of Franchises: 2
Company-Owned Units: 1
Total Units: 3

In Business Since: 1983 **Franchising Since:** 1992

Description of Operation: Direct Opinions specializes in customer satisfaction surveys for retail sales and service clients, market business surveys, and business services. Direct Opinions utilizes a system of home-based telemarketers to conduct the actual phone interviews. The Direct Opinions business provides the franchisee with easy-to-operate software systems. Reporting and record keeping are accomplished through the use of proprietary computer software programs.

Equity Capital Needed: $15,000 + working capital

Franchise Fee: $10,000-$25,000

Royalty: 6 percent of first $100,000; 4 percent thereafter

Advertising Co-op Fee:

Financial Assistance: No royalties for first six months.

Management Assistance: Management training is provided during the initial training phase. Thereafter, management consultation is available by phone daily. Additionally, at the franchisee's expense, the franchisor will send representatives to the franchisee's location for additional training.

Training Assistance: Initial training is provided at the franchisor's corporate headquarters in Cleveland, OH. Training is for a maximum of one week (composed of five business days, eight to 10 hrs/day) or a minimum of three days, depending on progress. Training is provided in sales, marketing, customer service, management techniques, computer operations, general accounting, bookkeeping, and related business procedures.

Fast Bucks Check Cashing Service

1919 S. 40th St., Ste. 202
Lincoln, NE 68506
Toll-Free Phone: (800) 865-2378
Phone: (402) 434-5620
Fax: (402) 434-5624
Contact: President

Number of Franchises: 21
Company-Owned Units: 3
Total Units: 24

In Business Since: 1994 **Franchising Since:** 1995

Description of Operation: Fast Bucks Check Cashing Service has proved to be a highly attractive alternative to traditional banking, offering an array of services like check cashing, pay day loans, Western Union telegrams, and electronic tax filing.

Equity Capital Needed: $75,000

Franchise Fee: $20,000

Royalty: 5 percent

Advertising Co-op Fee: 2 percent

Financial Assistance: Current financial review, support on a business plan, and third-party lending options.

Management Assistance: Complete training, software program, manuals, follow-up, and an 800# are provided.

Training Assistance: One week at home office and one week on-site are provided.

Shred-It

2359 Royal Windsor Dr., #15
Mississauga, ON L5J 1K5
Web Address: www.shredit.com
Toll-Free Phone: 800-697-4733
Phone: (905) 855-2856

Fax: (905) 855-0466
Contact: Vice President of Franchise Development

Number of Franchises: 2
Company-Owned Units: 2
Total Units: 4

In Business Since: 1989 **Franchising Since:** 1992

Description of Operation: Mobile paper shredding and recycling business, serving medical, financial, government, and large and small business. Provide on-site shredding and recycling of shredded material. Business-to-business franchise.

Equity Capital Needed: $80,000-$160,000

Franchise Fee: $35,000

Royalty: 5 percent

Advertising Co-op Fee:

Financial Assistance: Business plan development and introduction to banks and leasing companies.

Management Assistance: We provide market research, start-up assistance, training, proprietary accounting, operating and shredding systems, field support, group purchasing, marketing, customer satisfaction, manuals, newsletters, and public relations.

Training Assistance: We provide two weeks in the head office and one week in the field at time of opening. Eight manuals on all aspects of the business.

Tradebank International, Inc.

4220 Pleasantdale Rd.
Atlanta, GA 30340
Web Address: tradebankonline.com
Toll-Free Phone: (800) 899-1111
Phone: (770) 239-3100
Fax: (770) 239-3113
Contact: Vice President

Number of Franchises: 18
Company-Owned Units: 8
Total Units: 26

In Business Since: 1987 **Franchising Since:** 1995

Description of Operation: Tradebank is an International Retail/Commercial Barter Exchange arranging barter transactions for manufacturers, wholesalers, distributors, retailers, professional services, or anyone with a product or service to sell. We provide all of the accounting and bookkeeping services for all barter transactions. For these services, we collect a 10 percent of brokerage fee.

Equity Capital Needed: $20,000

Franchise Fee: $30,000

Royalty: 0

Advertising Co-op Fee: 0

Financial Assistance: To qualified prospects, Tradebank will finance up to 50 percent of the Franchise Fee.

Tradebank also provides an operating stipend to its franchisees.

Management Assistance: Tradebank provides all of the accounting for barter transactions for all of franchisee's clients. We also collect and disperse all funds. We issue monthly statements to the clients.

Training Assistance: Tradebank gives one week of classroom training at the Atlanta, GA, headquarters, and one week of training in the franchised area. We also have quarterly conferences and provide ongoing support to all franchisees.

United Check Cashing

325 Chestnut St., Ste. 1005
Philadelphia, PA 19106
Web Address: www.unitedcheckcashing.com
E-mail Address: unitedcc12@unitedcheckcashing.com
Toll-Free Phone: (800) 626-0787
Phone: (215) 238-0300
Fax: (215) 238-9056
Contact: Development Director

Number of Franchises: 20
Company-Owned Units: 1
Total Units: 21

In Business Since: 1977   **Franchising Since:** 1991

Description of Operation: Convenience store of banking. Check cashing, money orders, write transfers, authorized bill payments, fax, copies, notary, consumer loans, ATMs, lottery, credit card advances, tax service, photo ID systems, and beeper sales.

Equity Capital Needed: $75,000-$125,000

Franchise Fee: $17,500

Royalty: 3 percent of 1 percent of check volume.

Advertising Co-op Fee:

Financial Assistance: We can assist with $7,500 of the franchise fee. Equipment leasing.

Management Assistance: We provide classroom training at the corporate headquarters and hands-on training at our training store. Grand opening assistance and toll-free hot line for ongoing daily assistance. We also offer computer programs for those with PCs.

Training Assistance: Classroom training consists of everything from daily work processing to information on state and local laws, licensing, banking procedures, and legal processes. The new franchisees also receive training in customer servicing, sales, and human resources. One of the most important aspects of the training is the information provided on loss prevention and risk management.

Campgrounds

Kampgrounds of America, Inc.
550 N. 31st TWIII P.O. Box 30558
Billings, MT 59114

Web Address: www.koakampgrounds.com
Toll-Free Phone: (800) 548-7239
Phone: (406) 248-7444
Fax: (406) 248-7414
Contact: Vice President of Licensing

Number of Franchises: 543
Company-Owned Units: 11
Total Units: 554

In Business Since: 1961   **Franchising Since:** 1962

Description of Operation: Franchisor of campgrounds.

Equity Capital Needed: $85,000 minimum

Franchise Fee: $20,000

Royalty: 10 percent of campsite rental income.

Advertising Co-op Fee: 0

Financial Assistance: None

Management Assistance: Management schools, regional meetings, convention (annual), and consultants.

Training Assistance: Orientation school, plus management schools, regional meeting, convention, and consultants.

Yogi Bear's Jellystone Park Camp-Resort-Leisure Systems, Inc.

6201 Kellogg Ave.
Cincinnati, OH 45245
Web Address: www.campjellystone.com
E-mail Address: leisuresys@aol.com
Toll-Free Phone: (800) 626-3720
Phone: (513) 232-6800
Fax: (513) 231-1191
Contact: President/COO

Number of Franchises: 72
Company-Owned Units: 0
Total Units: 72

In Business Since: 1969   **Franchising Since:** 1970

Description of Operation: The Jellystone Camp-Resorts are family-oriented camping resorts with special amenities including a retail store, swimming pools, game rooms, playgrounds, modern restroom facilities, laundry facilities, planned activities, pavilions, and special-event weekends.

Equity Capital Needed: $150,000 plus

Franchise Fee: $18,000

Royalty: 6 percent of gross revenues

Advertising Co-op Fee: 1 percent of gross evenues

Financial Assistance: None

Management Assistance: On-site consultants and inspections.

Training Assistance: Training programs administered at corporate headquarters with a duration of five (5) days. Additional training on-site as appropriate.

Children—Child Care

Goddard School, The

381 Brooks Rd.
King of Prussia, PA 19406
Toll-Free Phone: (800) 272-4901
Phone: (610) 265-8510
Fax: (610) 265-8867
Contact: Director of Center Development

Number of Franchises: 11
Company-Owned Units: 3
Total Units: 14

In Business Since: 1986   **Franchising Since:** 1988

Description of Operation: High-quality preschool, offering day-care hours. All Goddard teachers hold four-year degrees in early childhood or elementary education.

Equity Capital Needed: $115,000

Franchise Fee: $25,000

Royalty: 7 percent

Advertising Co-op Fee:

Financial Assistance: The finance department will prepare pro formas and present them to at least three banks, including one SBA source.

Management Assistance: Five full-time operations personnel (average experience in child care industry of 10 years) assist in ALL aspects of running the school and business.

Training Assistance: We offer two weeks of formal training on the business aspects. Every school has a director to handle education.

Wee Watch Private Home Day Care

105 Main St.
Unionville, ON L3R 2G1
Toll-Free Phone:
Phone: (905) 479-4227
Fax: (905) 479-9047
Contact: Vice President

Number of Franchises: 40
Company-Owned Units: 0
Total Units: 40

In Business Since: 1984   **Franchising Since:** 1987

Description of Operation: Private home day-care agency, where a franchisee recruits, trains, and supervises women to do day care in their own homes. Parents needing care contact the agency for placement. A full day-care program is in place.

Equity Capital Needed: $15,000

Franchise Fee: $6,000

Royalty: 8 percent

Advertising Co-op Fee:

Financial Assistance: Not available.

Management Assistance: Complete manuals, field visits, convention, ongoing training seminars, and advertising campaigns are provided.

Training Assistance: We offer one week at the home office and three days on-site.

Children—Education

FutureKids

5777 W. Century Blvd., Ste. 1555
Los Angeles, CA 90045
Web Address: www.futurekids.com
E-mail Address: kandrew@futurekids.com
Toll-Free Phone: (800) 765-8000
Phone: (310) 337-7006
Fax: (310) 337-9346
Contact: Vice President of Franchise Development

Number of Franchises: 850+
Company-Owned Units: 0
Total Units: 850+

In Business Since: 1983   **Franchising Since:** 1989

Description of Operation: FutureKids, a privately held company, is the world's largest chain of computer learning centers for children ages three to 13. Currently operating over 300 centers domestically and in 24 countries internationally. FutureKids' mission is to prepare young children for the future, where success will depend on the ability to work well with technology.

Equity Capital Needed: $70,000-$100,000 (includes franchise fee)

Franchise Fee: $35,000

Royalty: 10 percent + $360 per month

Advertising Co-op Fee:

Financial Assistance: None

Management Assistance: Assigned regional managers offer field support and continual support through telephone and computer network communications. Also available is 24-hour support through corporate newsletters, field seminars, annual conventions, and franchisee-led committees.

Training Assistance: Training at FutureKids involves an extensive two-week course at corporate headquarters in Los Angeles, CA, followed by one week of field training. Ongoing educational, technical, marketing, and operational materials, plus telephone and computer network support, are readily available and extended as routine corporate procedure.

Gymboree

700 Airport Blvd. Ste. 200
Burlingame, CA 94010
Web Address: www.gymboree.com
Toll-Free Phone:
Phone: (415) 579-0600
Fax: (415) 696-7452
Contact: Vice President of Franchise Sales

Number of Franchises: 409
Company-Owned Units: 5
Total Units: 414

In Business Since: 1976   **Franchising Since:** 1978

Description of Operation: Parent and child participation play program. Specialized equipment, songs, and games. Classes offered for children from newborn through five years of age.

Equity Capital Needed: $35,000-$50,000

Franchise Fee: $27,000 for one site.

Royalty: 6 percent

Advertising Co-op Fee:

Financial Assistance: Not available.

Management Assistance: Data not available.

Training Assistance: 10 days of training at the corporate offices cover all aspects of running a Gymboree program—management, hiring, office, computer, and teaching classes. Biannual visits from consultants and annual seminar, with updates of business as a whole.

Imagine That

P.O. Box 493
New Vernon, NJ 07976
Toll-Free Phone: (800) 820-1145
Phone: (973) 267-2907
Fax: (973) 455-1917
Contact: Director

Number of Franchises: 2
Company-Owned Units: 1
Total Units: 3

In Business Since: 1993   **Franchising Since:** 1994

Description of Operation: Imagine That is a children's hands-on museum with over 50 hands-on exhibits. We have approximately 15,000 square feet under one roof. We generate our income from birthday parties, field trips, a cafe, an educational gift shop, general admission, enrichment programs, and drop-off services.

Equity Capital Needed: $200,000

Franchise Fee: $25,000

Royalty: 6 percent

Advertising Co-op Fee:

Financial Assistance: None

Management Assistance: We provide a two-week training program at headquarters. We continually offer support six days a week by telephone.

Training Assistance: We provide ongoing marketing assistance, supply outside sales assistance, and visit our franchisees quarterly.

Kiddie Academy International

108 Wheel Rd. Ste. 200
Bel Air, MD 21015
Toll-Free Phone: (800) 554-3343
Phone: (410) 515-0788
Fax: (410) 569-9165
Contact: Director of Franchise Development

Number of Franchises: 37
Company-Owned Units: 12
Total Units: 49

In Business Since: 1979   **Franchising Since:** 1981

Description of Operation: Kiddie Academy has been a premier developer of Early Learning Centers since 1979. A strong focus in Northeast, Mid-Atlantic, and Midwest areas. Kiddie Academy offers an advanced, tested, state-of-the-art curriculum incorporating traditional development milestones, with emphasis on reading skills, language development, and social skills. Classes in computers and foreign languages. Infant through age 12.

Equity Capital Needed: $75,000-$150,000

Franchise Fee: $30,000

Royalty: 7 percent

Advertising Co-op Fee:

Financial Assistance: Kiddie Academy has identified third-party lenders interested in providing financing to qualified franchisees and will assist in contacting lenders, developing loan packages, and preparing business plans.

Management Assistance: Comprehensive training and support without additional cost. Kiddie Academy's step-by-step program assists with demographic and competitive surveys, site selection, lease negotiation, staff recruitment, training, licensing, grand opening, accounting, marketing, advertising, and curriculum. A true turnkey program that provides full support so that you can focus on running a successful business.

Training Assistance: Kiddie Academy provides two intensive weeks of classroom and on-site training for franchise owners in Baltimore, MD. A one-week training session is provided for the center director, as well as on-site, hands-on training for the complete staff. Kiddie Academy has prepared a complete set of training manuals and understands that ongoing support is one of the most important factors in a long and successful partnership.

Kinderdance International

268 N. Babcock St., Ste. A
Melbourne, FL 32935
E-mail Address: kinder@in.net.infonews.com/franchise/
kinderdance
Toll-Free Phone: (800) 666-1595
Phone: (407) 254-0590
Fax: (407) 254-3388
Contact: Vice President

Number of Franchises: 68
Company-Owned Units: 1
Total Units: 69

In Business Since: 1979   **Franchising Since:** 1985

Description of Operation: You don't need to be a dancer to be a Kinderdance franchisee. If you enjoy children and have high energy, you can qualify to join the nation's leader in quality preschool education through dance, gymnastics, and creative movement. No studio is required. Our program has been taught to thousands of children in hundreds of child care centers since 1979. Enjoy flexible hours, fulfilling work, and adorable customers. Rated one of the top 15 franchises for women by *Working Woman* magazine.

Equity Capital Needed: $4,000-$6,000

Franchise Fee: $6,500-$15,000

Royalty: 6 percent-1.5 percent

Advertising Co-op Fee:

Financial Assistance: Kinderdance will finance (in-house) up to 50 percent of the initial franchise fee.

Management Assistance: We provide perpetual assistance as needed, an 800# hot line available 24-hours a day, an operations manual, newsletters, and an active franchisee advisory counsel.

Training Assistance: We offer an initial seven-day training session at the home office in Melbourne, FL. Follow-up, on-site training within six months of start-up. Annual conferences (with updated training material) are held at various locations in Melbourne Beach, FL.

Primrose Schools Franchising Company

199 S. Erwin St.
Cartersville, GA 30120
Toll-Free Phone:
Phone: (770) 606-9600
Fax: (770) 606-0020
Contact: Executive Vice President

Number of Franchises: 21
Company-Owned Units: 1
Total Units: 22

In Business Since: 1982   **Franchising Since:** 1988

Description of Operation: Quality educational child care, with proven, traditional curriculum for infants through four to five; kindergarten; and after-school explorers club for ages five to 12 years. Spanish, computer intergenerational program, and strong parental communication. Programs develop positive self-esteem and a joy of learning.

Equity Capital Needed: $100,000-$150,000

Franchise Fee: $48,500

Royalty: 7 percent

Advertising Co-op Fee:

Financial Assistance: Referral to consultants.

Management Assistance: Data not available.

Training Assistance: We provide two weeks of corporate training; one week of on-site preopening support; four months of detailed, preopening operations; and marketing plans monitored by management staff. Strong operations, programming, and marketing support are ongoing after opening.

Wonders of Wisdom Children's Centers

3114 Golansky Blvd. Ste. 201
Prince William, VA 22192
Toll-Free Phone: (800) 424-0550
Phone: (703) 670-9344
Fax: (703) 670-2851
Contact: Director of Franchise Sales

Number of Franchises: 4
Company-Owned Units: 1
Total Units: 5

In Business Since: 1989   **Franchising Since:** 1989

Description of Operation: Quality child care, together with developmental educational approach to early education, emphasizing language and social development, motor skills, and reading. Infant through age 12. Programs developed over 25 years.

Equity Capital Needed: $112,005-$221,005

Franchise Fee: $25,000

Royalty: 6 percent

Advertising Co-op Fee:

Financial Assistance: The franchisor will help locate financing. The SBA may be available for qualified applicants.

Management Assistance: Wonders of Wisdom provides all needed forms, handbooks and manuals, location assistance, and state licensing package preparation. In addition, we design your facility and provide a list of approved suppliers and complete inventory. Monthly newsletters for franchisees and parents. Staff training manuals and curriculum units.

Training Assistance: We offer an extensive two-week training period at the home office in basic business skills, computer skills, education and child care systems, and marketing. Thereafter, we provide one week of training per year at your site for your employees, plus one week per year at our home office for the franchisee.

Children—Merchandise

Baby News Children Stores

23521 Foley St.
Hayward, CA 94545
Toll-Free Phone:
Phone: (510) 786-3460
Fax: (510) 785-1580
Contact: President

Number of Franchises: 42
Company-Owned Units: 1
Total Units: 43

In Business Since: 1962   **Franchising Since:** 1962

Description of Operation: Complete children's store, carrying juvenile furniture, clothing, preschool toys, accessories, and safety equipment.

Equity Capital Needed: $150,000

Franchise Fee: $15,000

Royalty: 1 percent or $700 per month

Advertising Co-op Fee:

Financial Assistance: We will assist with paperwork and budgets to submit to lending institutions.

Management Assistance: We have a distribution center in Haywood, CA, available to all stores.

Training Assistance: Have continual training available. Recommend a minimum of two weeks.

Children's Orchard

315 E. Eisenhower Pkwy., Ste. 316
Ann Arbor, MI 48108
Web Address: www.childorch.com
E-mail Address: childorch@aol.com
Toll-Free Phone: (800) 999-5437
Phone: (313) 994-9199
Fax: (313) 994-9323
Contact: President

Number of Franchises: 54
Company-Owned Units: 1
Total Units: 55

In Business Since: 1980   **Franchising Since:** 1985

Description of Operation: Upscale children's products resale, boutiques, and large stores. These stores also feature brand new products. Children's Orchard empha-

sizes comprehensive training and franchisee support services. Locations from Maine to Hawaii.

Equity Capital Needed: $52,000-$80,000

Franchise Fee: $14,500-$19,500

Royalty: Declining scale, starting at 6 percent.

Advertising Co-op Fee:

Financial Assistance: We assist with SBA or other business financing.

Management Assistance: We provide regular shop evaluations, hot line, newsletters, individualized business consulting, management seminar by mail, and published and custom statistical performance analysis.

Training Assistance: We offer two weeks of basic training on all aspects of business system, general management, and in-store practice. Five or more additional days of on-site training include grand opening assistance.

Children—Services

Babies First Diaper Service

5273 Hanson Ct.
Minneapolis, MN 55429
Toll-Free Phone:
Phone: (612) 533-1616
Fax: (612) 533-5915
Contact: Vice President of Franchise Development

Number of Franchises: 1
Company-Owned Units: 2
Total Units: 3

In Business Since: 1990   **Franchising Since:** 1991

Description of Operation: A home pickup and delivery service of laundered diapers for infants or incontinent adults. Markets of over 300,000 population may require laundry processing facilities as part of franchising package.

Equity Capital Needed: $90,000-$300,000

Franchise Fee: $10,000-$55,000

Royalty: 6 percent

Advertising Co-op Fee:

Financial Assistance: Not available at this time.

Management Assistance: Complete and ongoing.

Training Assistance: Complete in all phases and ongoing as required.

Explorations

902 Clint Moore Rd.; Ste. 136
Boca Raton, FL 33487
Toll-Free Phone: (800) 557-2669
Phone: (561) 998-3435

Fax: (561) 998-3425
Contact: COO

Number of Franchises: 8
Company-Owned Units: 1
Total Units: 9

In Business Since: 1992   **Franchising Since:** 1993

Description of Operation: Explorations is a children's fitness and entertainment center. The naturally themed indoor centers, designed for kids ages one to 12, are approximately 15,000 square feet and include proprietary play structures, licensed characters, a full-menu restaurant, birthday party rooms, adult and kiddie lounges, an electronic gameroom, and a kiddie ride area.

Equity Capital Needed: $275,000-$760,000

Franchise Fee: $30,000

Royalty: 5 percent

Advertising Co-op Fee:

Financial Assistance: We assist in the preparation of a business plan.

Management Assistance: We provide full ongoing support.

Training Assistance: Training includes two weeks at headquarters and one week in store.

Ident-A-Kid Services of America, Inc.

2810 Scherer Dr., Ste. 100
St. Petersburg, PA 33716
Toll-Free Phone:
Phone: (813) 577-4646
Fax: (813) 576-8258
Contact: President

Number of Franchises: 219
Company-Owned Units: 1
Total Units: 220

In Business Since: 1986   **Franchising Since:** 1987

Description of Operation: Ident-A-Kid program provides parents with a laminated child ID card containing a child's photograph, physical description, and fingerprint. In case of an emergency, parents can provide the card to law enforcement or others to help in the quick, safe recovery of their child. Total turnkey package is $12,500 including computer, camera, assembly equipment, supplies, and so on.

Equity Capital Needed: $12,500

Franchise Fee: 0

Royalty: 0

Advertising Co-op Fee: 0

Financial Assistance:

Management Assistance: Operations manual and phone support.

Training Assistance: On-site, three-day training.

SAFE & SOUND

301 North Main Street, Ste. 5
New City, NY 10956
Web Address: www.123safe.com
E-mail Address: bshandelmane.com@123safe.com
Toll-Free Phone: (800) 332-2229
Phone: (914) 638-4111
Fax: (914) 638-3978
Contact: Director of Franchise Development

Number of Franchises: 0
Company-Owned Units: 1
Total Units: 1

In Business Since: 1992   **Franchising Since:** 1998

Description of Operation: SAFE & SOUND's comprehensive child-safety service is one of the most exciting and fastest-growing segments for the safety industry. SAFE & SOUND's comprehensive program combines home-safety solutions and parental education to provide a positive environment where children can grow and explore free from unnecessary dangers. SAFE & SOUND gives parents in-home child safety education, expert advice on products and their application, a top-quality product line, and professional installation. Our home-based franchisees are backed by our 30 years of experience in the safety business.

Equity Capital Needed: $30,700-43,100

Franchise Fee: $19,500

Royalty: 5 percent of gross sales

Advertising Co-op Fee: 2 percent of gross sales

Financial Assistance: Assistance with third-party financing, business plans, and coordination with the SBA.

Management Assistance: Managerial assistance includes toll-free call center, lead generation program, Internet marketing, and operations support infrastructure.

Training Assistance: Franchise fee includes comprehensive training at corporate headquarters, in-field training, and ongoing and responsive technical and marketing support.

Cleaning & Sanitation Business—Industrial Cleaning

Aire-Master of America

P.O. Box 2310 Hwy. CC
Nixa, MO 65714
Web Address: www.airemaster.com
Toll-Free Phone: (800) 525-0957
Phone: (417) 725-2691

Fax: (417) 725-5737
Contact: Franchise Director

Number of Franchises: 53
Company-Owned Units: 5
Total Units: 58

In Business Since: 1958   **Franchising Since:** 1975

Description of Operation: Room deodorizing, restroom deodorizing and disinfecting service.

Equity Capital Needed: $25,000-$75,000

Franchise Fee: $15,000

Royalty: 5 percent

Advertising Co-op Fee:

Financial Assistance: 50 percent of franchise fee to qualified applicants.

Management Assistance: Included with five days of in-house training.

Training Assistance: An extensive 10-day training program: five days in-house and five days in territory.

Al-Vin Siding Cleaning

1233 Main St. Ste. 301
Buffalo, NY 14209
Toll-Free Phone:
Phone: (716) 883-2103
Fax: (716) 883-0802
Contact: President

Number of Franchises: 33
Company-Owned Units: 1
Total Units: 34

In Business Since: 1987   **Franchising Since:** 1987

Description of Operation: Cleaning the exterior of homes, offices, and so on. The franchisee is supplied with a turnkey operation.

Equity Capital Needed: $15,000-$25,000

Franchise Fee: $15,000

Royalty: $1,000-$2,000 per unit

Advertising Co-op Fee:

Financial Assistance: Data not available.

Management Assistance: You will receive three to four days of on-site training.

Training Assistance: You will receive three to four days of on-site training.

Americare Services

P.O. Box 2004
Elmhurst, IL 60126
Toll-Free Phone: (800) 745-6191
Phone: (708) 595-6200
Fax:
Contact: Vice President of Finance

Number of Franchises: 3
Company-Owned Units: 7
Total Units: 10

In Business Since: 1991   **Franchising Since:** 1993

Description of Operation: Restroom sanitation, hygienic services, order control, and janitorial supplies.

Equity Capital Needed: $4,750-$24,000

Franchise Fee: $9,500

Royalty: 30 percent

Advertising Co-op Fee:

Financial Assistance: At our option, half the franchise fee may be financed.

Management Assistance: We basically do all office functions, including accounts receivable, weekly routes, scheduling, and providing supplies.

Training Assistance: Two weeks of training, including how to run routes, sales, and office procedures.

Cleaning Consultant Services

1512 Western Ave. P.O. Box 1273
Seattle, WA 98111
Web Address: www.cleaningconsultants.com
Toll-Free Phone:
Phone: (206) 682-9748
Fax: (206) 622-6876
Contact: President

Number of Franchises: 4
Company-Owned Units: 2
Total Units: 6

In Business Since: 1976   **Franchising Since:** 1981

Description of Operation: In an effort to meet the growing demand for our services in the United States and internationally, we have begun a licensing program to provide qualified professionals with an opportunity to become associate consultants in their local areas. Our sole purpose is to provide support services to those who own, manage and/or supervise cleaning operations. Our services include software support, books, videos and software sales, cleaning business magazine, temporary agency, seminars, inspections, and consulting.

Equity Capital Needed: $3,000-$10,000

Franchise Fee: $2,500

Royalty: $50/month

Advertising Co-op Fee:

Financial Assistance: Partial payments are available. Inventory on a time payment plan. Shipping service, brochures, catalogues, and promotional materials provided at no cost.

Management Assistance: We provide phone support and procedural guides on-site.

Training Assistance: We offer training manuals, on-site visits, and two to three days at our training site in Seattle, WA.

Cove Ceiling Doctor

17810 Davenport Rd. Ste. 108
Dallas, TX 75252
Toll-Free Phone:
Phone: (972) 250-3311
Fax: (972) 250-3929
Contact: President

Number of Franchises: 118
Company-Owned Units: 2
Total Units: 120

In Business Since: 1984   **Franchising Since:** 1986

Description of Operation: Industrial and commercial cleaning and restoration of ceiling and other specialty surfaces, both interior and exterior.

Equity Capital Needed: $25,000

Franchise Fee: $12,500

Royalty: 8 percent

Advertising Co-op Fee: 2 percent

Financial Assistance: Third-party financial assistance is available for the entire franchise fee and start-up package requirement based on the credit history and assets of the new franchise prospect.

Management Assistance: Two of the seven days of training are spent in franchise business start-up time management, account identification, telemarketing, and sales. Monthly newsletters with "how to" tips and successes from organization.

Training Assistance: Training is seven days. We combine one-third of the time in business set-up and management, along with one-third in account development and one-third in technical aspects and hands-on training.

Coverall Cleaning Concepts

3111 Camino del Rio N., Ste. 950
San Diego, CA 92108
Web Address: www.coverall.com
E-mail Address: info@coverall.com
Toll-Free Phone: (800) 537-3371
Phone: (619) 584-1911
Fax: (619) 584-4923
Contact: Vice President of Marketing

Number of Franchises: 2887
Company-Owned Units: 0
Total Units: 2887

In Business Since: 1985   **Franchising Since:** 1985

Description of Operation: Turnkey commercial cleaning franchise. Initial fee includes training, equipment and supplies, customer accounts, ongoing support in

billing and accounts receivable, public relations, and monitoring quality service. Insurance, additional business, and additional training are also available. Nine different levels of business to choose from.

Equity Capital Needed: $2,050-$30,100

Franchise Fee: $3,250-$33,600

Royalty: 5 percent

Advertising Co-op Fee:

Financial Assistance: All packages are financed over a period of 24-36 months, depending on package purchased. Down payment, ranging from $1,700-$26,600, required.

Management Assistance: Billing and accounts receivable assistance, ongoing quality assurance checks and assistance, insurance, and equipment lease options available. Management advice.

Training Assistance: Training is provided in business development and cleaning techniques. Various training and technical manuals supplied. Ongoing training seminars offered in product knowledge, usage, and so forth.

Jan-Pro Cleaning Systems

500 E. Washingtons St.
North Atleborough, MA 02760
E-mail Address: janpro1@aol.com
Toll-Free Phone: (800) 668-1001
Phone: (617) 461-9091
Fax: (508) 695-3974
Contact: President

Number of Franchises: 516
Company-Owned Units: 3
Total Units: 519

In Business Since: 1991   **Franchising Since:** 1992

Description of Operation: Jan-Pro Cleaning Systems is a franchise in the commercial cleaning industry. We provide the resources that people need to establish themselves in their own cleaning business.

Equity Capital Needed: $2,800-$26,000

Franchise Fee: $1,450

Royalty: 8 percent

Advertising Co-op Fee:

Financial Assistance: Financing is available for all of our franchise plans.

Management Assistance: Jan-Pro provides the franchisees with full support from the moment they first start their business. This includes guidance from our operations staff, cash flow management, marketing assistance, and customer relations.

Training Assistance: Jan-Pro provides all franchisees with formal classroom and on-the-job expert training in every aspect of proper cleaning techniques.

Jani-King International

4950 Keller Springs Rd. Ste. 190
Dallas, TX 75248
Web Address: www.janiking.com
Toll-Free Phone: (800) 995-5264
Phone: (214) 991-0900
Fax: (214) 991-5723
Contact: President

Number of Franchises: 3860
Company-Owned Units: 25
Total Units: 3885

In Business Since: 1969   **Franchising Since:** 1974

Description of Operation: Commercial cleaning franchisor, offering entrepreneurs a proven system for operating a business involved in the cleaning of office buildings, retail, medical, and other facilities. Franchisees in this growth industry are owners/operators of these businesses who also have access to regional support centers.

Equity Capital Needed: Under $25,000

Franchise Fee: $6,500-$14,000

Royalty: 10 percent

Advertising Co-op Fee:

Financial Assistance: Yes.

Management Assistance: A complete range of support services, from billings to business growth, are offered through regional support centers. More than 50 centers are located throughout North America and abroad.

Training Assistance: The most comprehensive training course in the industry is available through regional support centers near the franchisee. Training covers cleaning, personnel, client relations, proposals, and sales.

Jantize America

15449 Little Belt Rd.
Livonia, MI 48154
Toll-Free Phone: (800) 968-9182
Phone: (313) 421-4733
Fax: (313) 421-4936
Contact:

Number of Franchises: 19
Company-Owned Units: 3
Total Units: 22

In Business Since: 1985   **Franchising Since:** 1988

Description of Operation: Commercial office cleaning.

Equity Capital Needed: $2,500-$12,500

Franchise Fee: $3,200-$16,000

Royalty: 6 percent-9 percent

Advertising Co-op Fee:

Financial Assistance: Up to 50 percent of franchise fee.

Management Assistance: Data not available.

Training Assistance: Yes.

Laser Chem "White Glove" Commercial Cleaning

7022 South 400 West
Midvale, UT 84047
Toll-Free Phone: (800) 272-2741
Phone: (801) 569-9500
Fax: (801) 569-8400
Contact: President

Number of Franchises: 18
Company-Owned Units: 1
Total Units: 19

In Business Since: 1978   **Franchising Since:** 1990

Description of Operation: Laser Chem offers a "White Glove" commercial cleaning franchise, which includes training on residential carpet and upholstry cleaning. We get accounts for you and support you from day to day.

Equity Capital Needed: $795

Franchise Fee: $6,795

Royalty: 7 percent

Advertising Co-op Fee: 0

Financial Assistance: We finance an initial franchise fee up to $6,000 and equipment purchases.

Management Assistance: We provide accounting, consultation, and other support services.

Training Assistance: Up to 34 hours of training ranging from owning a business to operating a janitorial company and carpet cleaning company.

National Maintenance Contractors

1801 130th Ave. N.E.
Bellevue, WA 98005
Toll-Free Phone: (800) 347-7844
Phone: (425) 881-0500
Fax: (425) 883-4785
Contact: President

Number of Franchises: 310
Company-Owned Units: 2
Total Units: 312

In Business Since: 1970   **Franchising Since:** 1973

Description of Operation: Janitorial service business. Master franchise needed in major metro market, which in turn will generate janitorial accounts and sell them to unit franchisees who do the work. Complete training at home office and through manuals and videos. Ongoing support in the local markets.

Equity Capital Needed: Unit franchise-$1,000; Master Franchise-$100,000

Franchise Fee: Unit franchise: $500; Master Franchise: $25,000

Royalty: Unit Franchise: 20 percent; Master Franchise: 4-5 percent

Advertising Co-op Fee:

Financial Assistance: Financing is available through the company and is interest-free for unit franchisees. Master franchise finance terms are flexible, based on market cost and working capital needed.

Management Assistance: Support provided as needed through on-site visits, 800#, newsletters, letters, account pricing support, and legal and accounting assistance.

Training Assistance: Master franchise: 30 days of training, three manuals and videos, start-up support in local market, as needed. Ongoing meetings. Unit franchise: five days of training, manual and videos, ongoing meetings, and consultation.

O.P.E.N. Cleaning Systems

2398 E. Camelback Rd. Ste. 740
Phoenix, AZ 85016
Web Address: www.opencleaning.com
Toll-Free Phone: (800) 777-6736
Phone: (602) 224-0440
Fax: (602) 468-3788
Contact: President

Number of Franchises: 589
Company-Owned Units: 3
Total Units: 592

In Business Since: 1983   **Franchising Since:** 1983

Description of Operation: Franchisor of office and commercial cleaning business. Franchisees are provided with guaranteed initial customers, training, and equipment. In addition, franchisor provides ongoing administrative and sales support to the franchisee. Ability to start part-time or full-time.

Equity Capital Needed: $2,500

Franchise Fee: $3,800

Royalty: 1.5 percent

Advertising Co-op Fee:

Financial Assistance: The franchisor generally finances up to 50 percent of the initial franchise fee.

Management Assistance: The franchisor's local office provides billing and collection services to all the franchisee's customers. It also assists the franchisees in customer service and acts as the contact person for all customer calls or inquiries. In addition, franchisees can use (free) bidding and proposal preparation service provided by the franchisor.

Training Assistance: The initial training covers all areas of the janitorial industry, including efficiency, material usage, and customer calls. Later courses teach franchisees how to bid and secure additional clients and perform specialty work. Franchisor's local office provides ongoing support.

ServiceMaster

860 Ridge Lake Boulevard
Memphis, TN 38120
Toll-Free Phone: (800) 752-6688
Phone: (901) 684-7500
Fax: (901) 684-7580
Contact: Vice President of Market Expansion

Number of Franchises: 4149
Company-Owned Units: 4
Total Units: 4153

In Business Since: 1947   **Franchising Since:** 1952

Description of Operation: ServiceMaster provides heavy cleaning services for homes, including carpet, upholstery, draperies, windows, and disaster restoration. Janitorial services are also provided for the commercial market. As you would expect from a $2.5 billion company, we provide all the research, equipment, supplies, and initial and continual training you will need.

Equity Capital Needed: $7,500-$12,500

Franchise Fee: $12,350-$23,350

Royalty: 4-10 percent or .5-1 percent

Advertising Co-op Fee:

Financial Assistance: We offer financing on the franchise fee, products, and equipment. The term of financing is 5 years. We offer level and graduated payments.

Management Assistance: ServiceMaster has 78 different distributors in different regions around the United States. These distributors serve as local support for the franchisees. Also, regional operations managers assist the franchisees in the growth and development of their business. All the departments within ServiceMaster have at least one person who handles franchise relations. Each distributor has owned and operated a ServiceMaster for at least five years, as have regional operations managers.

Training Assistance: ServiceMaster has a 10-phase training program, which includes manuals and videos; ServiceMaster orientation; self-study; on-the-job training; assistance with basic start-up tasks; two weeks spent with their distributor or own representative in actual on-the-job training; one week at the ServiceMaster Academy of Management, which is held every other month; specific personalized training in marketing and sales; financial counseling; goal determination; and personal review for future plans.

Serv U-1st

10151 SW Barbur Blvd. Bldg. D Ste. 10D
Portland, OR 97219
Toll-Free Phone:
Phone: (503) 244-7628
Fax: (503) 244-0287
Contact: President

Number of Franchises: 12
Company-Owned Units: 1
Total Units: 13

In Business Since: 1988   **Franchising Since:** 1988

Description of Operation: Complete janitorial service franchise, teaching complete janitorial management—financial control, getting started, production management, marketing, bidding, and selling. Ongoing assistance in finding new accounts in your franchise area.

Equity Capital Needed: $3,000-$12,000

Franchise Fee: $2,500

Royalty: 3 percent-1.5 percent

Advertising Co-op Fee:

Financial Assistance: 7.5 percent of total initial fees to us if you have excellent credit and sufficient assets.

Management Assistance: On-the-job training. Eight annual group meetings and trainings. Open-door policy. Manuals.

Training Assistance: Usually eight initial trainings of two hours each in getting started and on-the-job training in production and production control.

Swisher Hygiene

6849 Fairview Rd.
Charlotte, NC 28210
E-mail Address: pswis53866@aol.com
Toll-Free Phone: (800) 444-4138
Phone: (704) 364-7707
Fax: (704) 364-1202
Contact: Vice President Sales

Number of Franchises: 115
Company-Owned Units: 2
Total Units: 117

In Business Since: 1983   **Franchising Since:** 1990

Description of Operation: Swisher offers a package of unique products and cleaning services that do three basic things. First, we enhance our customer's image to their customers by offering a clean, safe, and fresh environment in the washroom. Secondly, we offer our customers an alternative to the high cost of inventory, pilferage, and waste by eliminating the need to store products on-site and giving customers a controllable, budgetable cost. Third, by eliminating washroom maintenance supply costs, such as soap, disinfectants, air fresheners, brushes, gloves, scouring cleansers, and so on. Swisher saves its customers money. Practically any business that has a public washroom is a potential customer. Swisher provides its franchisees with excellent support services.

Equity Capital Needed: $40,000+

Franchise Fee: $35,000-$75,000

Royalty: 6 percent

Advertising Co-op Fee: 2 percent

Financial Assistance: Limited financing available for the franchise fee.

Management Assistance: Swisher provides its franchisees with excellent support services, including customer invoicing, monthly statements, customer collection, centralized supply ordering, 800# telephone answering service, monthly P & L reports, and in-field assistance.

Training Assistance: Initial training of one week at corporate office on operations and one week in territory on sales. Ongoing guidance and assistance beyond training.

Uniclean Systems

236 Brooksbank Ave.
North Vancouver, BC V7J 2C1
Toll-Free Phone:
Phone: (604) 986-4750
Fax: (604) 987-6838
Contact: President

Number of Franchises: 289
Company-Owned Units: 1
Total Units: 290

In Business Since: 1976   **Franchising Since:** 1981

Description of Operation: Professional office cleaning.

Equity Capital Needed: $6,500+

Franchise Fee: $7,000-$12,000

Royalty: 10 percent

Advertising Co-op Fee:

Financial Assistance: None

Management Assistance: Telephone hot line.

Training Assistance: We offer one week of training at the franchisee's hometown location.

Value Line Maintenance Systems

P.O. Box 6450
Great Falls, MT 59406
Toll-Free Phone: (800) 824-4838
Phone: (406) 761-4471
Fax: (406) 761-4486
Contact: General Counsel

Number of Franchises: 29
Company-Owned Units: 0
Total Units: 29

In Business Since: 1959   **Franchising Since:** 1982

Description of Operation: Contract cleaning, providing janitorial services to large, single-floor retail outlets, such as supermarkets and general merchandise stores.

Equity Capital Needed: $50,800

Franchise Fee: $30,000

Royalty: 10 percent

Advertising Co-op Fee:

Financial Assistance: Financing of the franchise fee after an initial payment of $18,000. Financing is available on machine purchases through company-owned supplier.

Management Assistance: We provide invoicing service; marketing assistance; updated training in new techniques and products; supply purchasing program; machine repair; and other business, legal, and technical assistance.

Training Assistance: We provide a two-week training course, plus additional site training in operations, financial control, marketing, service techniques, labor training, advertising, and quality control.

Cleaning & Sanitation— Carpet & Upholstery Cleaning

AWC Commercial Window Covering

825 W. Williamson Way
Fullerton, CA 92832
Web Address: www.ibos.com/pub/ibos/awc
Toll-Free Phone: (800) 252-2280
Phone: (714) 879-3880
Fax: (714) 879-8419
Contact: President

Number of Franchises: 6
Company-Owned Units: 4
Total Units: 10

In Business Since: 1963 **Franchising Since:** 1992

Description of Operation: Mobile nontoxic drapery dry cleaning services provided on location for commercial customers, as well as sales, installation, and repairs of all types of window coverings at competitive prices through centralized buying. Nationwide accounts will be serviced by the franchisees as they are established. Using the customer base, references, and reputation of the franchisor developed over the past 34 years makes this an exceptional opportunity with endless possibilities and immediate credibility.

Equity Capital Needed: $112,520-$181,350

Franchise Fee: $25,000

Royalty: 5-12.5 percent

Advertising Co-op Fee: 2.5 percent

Financial Assistance: Yes, third party.

Management Assistance: We offer continual consultation with franchisees on all aspects of the business by phone. Constant updates on product, market research, and sales leads. Nationwide contracts are transferred to the franchisee's location. A well-coordinated marketing effort makes this an ideal growth opportunity.

Training Assistance: One week of hands-on and classroom training is provided at the home office in Fullerton, CA, including operational techniques, manuals, and product samples. One week of set-up and sales assistance at the franchisee's location. Continual, open communication is maintained and encouraged.

Canway Carpet Cleaning

2315 St. Laurent Blvd.
Ottawa, ON K1G 4J8
Toll-Free Phone: (800) 267-9249
Phone: (613) 247-7774
Fax: (613) 247-7822
Contact: Vice President of Organization

Number of Franchises: 97
Company-Owned Units: 0
Total Units: 97

In Business Since: 1984 **Franchising Since:** 1989

Description of Operation: Canway offers a unique opportunity for carpet cleaners—or would-be carpet cleaners—to operate as a nationally recognized brand name. Access to the client card list of national, U.S. retail department stores.

Equity Capital Needed: $10,000

Franchise Fee: $15,000

Royalty: 6 percent

Advertising Co-op Fee:

Financial Assistance: May finance up to 7.5 percent of the franchise fee.

Management Assistance: Complete range of managerial assistance, including advertising support, computer support, field and office support, newsletter, 800# telephone line, and technical support.

Training Assistance: Depending on the range of experience, up to one week of on-site and/or head office training.

Chem-Dry Carpet, Drapery and Upholstery Cleaning

1530 North 1000 West
Logan, UT 84321
Web Address: www.chemdry.com
E-mail Address: charlie@chemdry.com
Toll-Free Phone: (800) 841-6583
Phone: (435) 755-0099
Fax: (435) 755-0021
Contact: National Franchise Director

Number of Franchises: 4,200
Company-Owned Units: 0
Total Units: 4,200

In Business Since: 1977 **Franchising Since:** 1978

Description of Operation: BE YOUR OWN BOSS! When you join the Chem-Dry family, you get everything you need to go into business for yourself, including all equipment, solutions, paperwork, and training. Chem-Dry has been rated #1 by *Entrepreneur* magazine for the past nine years in the field of Carpet, Drapery, and Upholstery Cleaning. With over 4,000 franchisees in 50 different countries, you will have the advantage of a name trusted by customers; a proven, patented (we currently hold eight patents) process; and a research and development company that will keep you years ahead of the competition.

Equity Capital Needed: n/a

Franchise Fee: $18,950

Royalty: $70 per month

Advertising Co-op Fee: 0

Financial Assistance: $5,950 down; $13,000 financed over 56 months at zero percent interest.

Management Assistance: Easily accessible parent company with a technical department always just a phone call away. Training provided on everything from book-keeping to hiring employees. Kept up-to-date by monthly newsletters and various conventions.

Training Assistance: Franchisee is flown to our world headquarters in Logan, Utah, for an intensive two-day training seminar. Also provided with a video and manual training package. Updated training provided annually.

Chem-Dry Cleaning (Canada)

8361 B Noble Rd.
Chilliwack, BC V2P 7X7
Web Address: www.chemdry.com
Toll-Free Phone:
Phone: (604) 795-9918
Fax: (604) 795-7071
Contact: Franchise Licensing/Sales

Number of Franchises: 90
Company-Owned Units: 0
Total Units: 90

In Business Since: 1991   **Franchising Since:** 1991

Description of Operation: Jandor Enterprises (Canada) Ltd. is master franchiser and owns the exclusive right to offer Chem-Dry carpet and upholstery cleaning franchise in Canada. Jandor is the wholesale distributor of Chem-Dry cleaning products and equipment. As Chem-Dry headquarters for Canada, Jandor provides the independently owned and operated franchises with the latest developments in innovative new products and state-of-the-art equipment, ongoing technical support, and updated training.

Equity Capital Needed: $12,950 plus goods/services tax (GST) down payment

Franchise Fee: $9,500

Royalty: $260/month; cost of living increase in five-year term

Advertising Co-op Fee:

Financial Assistance: Interested parties may purchase a Chem-Dry franchise with a down payment of $12,950+ GST and pay the balance by making 48 payments of $280, interest included.

Management Assistance: The initial training includes written and verbal instruction regarding the successful management of the franchise business. Additional managerial assistance is provided through monthly newsletters, seminars, and one-on-one help by telephone or during personal visits to the franchise.

Training Assistance: New franchises are provided with one week of extensive on-the-job training at a designated location within Canada (travel and accommodations not included), as well as training manuals, videotapes, and accompanying workbook tests. Training includes how to mix and apply cleaning solutions, use equipment, compute estimates, solicit and maintain business, and the overall conduct of a Chem-Dry franchise. Updated training is provided at least once a year by seminars, videotapes, and newsletters.

Duraclean International

2151 Waukegan Rd.
Deerfield, IL 60015
Web Address: www.duraclean.com
Toll-Free Phone:
Phone: (847) 945-2000
Fax: (847) 945-2023
Contact: Director of Marketing

Number of Franchises: 522
Company-Owned Units: 1
Total Units: 523

In Business Since: 1930   **Franchising Since:** 1945

Description of Operation: District service markets and revenue center packages to fit your needs for independence and growth on your own terms. Carpet cleaning, upholstery and drapery cleaning, ceiling and wall cleaning, water/fire/smoke damage restoration, janitorial and hard surface floor care, ventilation, duct cleaning, pressure washing, and ultrasource blind cleaning.

Equity Capital Needed:

Franchise Fee: $6,400

Royalty: 2-8 percent

Advertising Co-op Fee: None

Financial Assistance: Financing arrangements are available from Duraclean International. Lease packaging on vans also available.

Management Assistance: See below.

Training Assistance: Duraclean puts an extraordinary amount of energy and attention into proper training techniques so that you will render a professional services market effectively and manage efficiently, using training manuals, videotapes, schools, local hands-on assistance, 800# phone line support, magazines, bulletins, conventions, and area meetings.

Heaven's Best Carpet & Upholstery Cleaning

247 N. 1st E. P.O. Box 607
Rexburg, ID 83440
Toll-Free Phone: (800) 359-2095
Phone: (208) 359-1106
Fax: (208) 359-1236
Contact: Chief Executive Officer

Number of Franchises: 113
Company-Owned Units: 4
Total Units: 117

In Business Since: 1983 **Franchising Since:** 1983

Description of Operation: Heaven's Best is a unique, low-moisture cleaning process that provides a great alternative to the traditional total-saturation methods of cleaning. Our customers love our dry-in-one-hour process. Our franchise is very affordable. Our business is one of quality and customer satisifaction.

Equity Capital Needed: $5,000-$20,000

Franchise Fee: $9,500

Royalty: $80 per month

Advertising Co-op Fee:

Financial Assistance: Some financial assistance may be available to qualified franchisees.

Management Assistance: The home office support is supplemented by a network of regional managers. An 800# hot line is available. Our procedures manual and regional seminars, coupled with our newsletter, keep each franchisee up-to-date on changes that occur within the industry. Our ongoing support is tremendous.

Training Assistance: We provide a complete and comprehensive four-day training program at our corporate headquarters in Rexburg, ID. All aspects of the business are covered during the training. All franchisees must attend the training.

Langenwalter Carpet Dyeing

1111 South Richfield Rd.
Placentia, CA 92870
E-mail Address: Langdye@aol.com
Toll-Free Phone: (800) 422-4370
Phone: (714) 528-7610
Fax: (714) 528-7620
Contact: President

Number of Franchises: 160
Company-Owned Units: 3
Total Units: 163

In Business Since: 1975 **Franchising Since:** 1980

Description of Operation: Complete carpet color restoration. Run a multivan operation, serving business as well as residential customers. Fading, bleach, punch, rust, and pet stains can all be color corrected at a fraction of the cost of replacement.

Equity Capital Needed: $60,000

Franchise Fee: $18,000

Royalty: $300/month

Advertising Co-op Fee: $95/month

Financial Assistance: None

Management Assistance: Complete management training to help hire employees and train technicians.

Training Assistance: Eight days of training covering every aspect of carpet dyeing.

Professional Carpet Systems

5182 Old Dixie Hwy.
Forest Park, GA 30050
Toll-Free Phone: (800) 925-5055
Phone: (404) 362-2300
Fax: (404) 362-2888
Contact: Franchise Counselor

Number of Franchises: 180
Company-Owned Units: 1
Total Units: 181

In Business Since: 1978 **Franchising Since:** 1981

Description of Operation: Professional Carpet Systems is the leader in on-site carpet redyeing, servicing thousands of apartment complexes, hotels, and motels worldwide. Other PCS services include carpet cleaning, rejuvenation, repair, water and flood damage restoration and "guaranteed odor control." PCS has a total carpet care concept.

Equity Capital Needed: $9,700+

Franchise Fee: $10,000

Royalty: 6 percent

Advertising Co-op Fee:

Financial Assistance: Some financing of initial franchise fee may be available to qualified applicants.

Management Assistance: Franchisees receive complete operations manuals, an accounting and bookkeeping system, and ongoing support from the franchisee's home office. PCS also offers ongoing training quarterly. PCS' newsletter keeps franchisees updated on marketing and product information.

Training Assistance: PCS franchisees attend a two-week training program at the PCS home office. During the training program, franchisees gain hands-on experience.

Rainbow International

1010 N. University Park Dr.
Waco, TX 76707
Toll-Free Phone: (800) 583-9100
Phone: (817) 756-2122
Fax: (817) 752-0661
Contact: President

Number of Franchises: 750
Company-Owned Units: 1
Total Units: 751

In Business Since: 1981   **Franchising Since:** 1981

Description of Operation: Rainbow franchisees offer services to commercial and residential clients. Services include disaster restoration—water, fire and smoke; carpet care and cleaning, including carpet repair; pet decontamination; and protective oversprays. Rainbow specializes in carpet dying and tinting. Other services offered are upholstery, drapery, and ceiling cleaning.

Equity Capital Needed: $23,000

Franchise Fee: $15,000

Royalty: 7 percent

Advertising Co-op Fee:

Financial Assistance: Financing is available for qualified individuals.

Management Assistance: Rainbow provides extensive initial and ongoing managerial assistance, including personnel management, financial management, and administrative and marketing systems.

Training Assistance: Rainbow provides extensive training for new franchisees that includes all phases of the Rainbow System. The initial training assists in launching a career for a new franchisee.

Stanley Steemer Carpet Cleaner

5500 Stanley Steemer Pkwy.
Dublin, OH 43017
Web Address: www.stanleysteemer.com
Toll-Free Phone: (800) 848-7496
Phone: (614) 764-2007
Fax: (614) 764-1506
Contact: Vice President/General Counsel

Number of Franchises: 225
Company-Owned Units: 22
Total Units: 247

In Business Since: 1947   **Franchising Since:** 1972

Description of Operation: Carpet and upholstery cleaning and related services.

Equity Capital Needed: $52,930-$77,840

Franchise Fee: Based on population; $20,000 per 100,000

Royalty: 7 percent monthly

Advertising Co-op Fee:

Financial Assistance: Depending on creditworthiness, financial assistance is available.

Management Assistance: Initial training is provided. Assistance, as needed.

Training Assistance: Initial training is provided. Assistance, as needed.

Steam Brothers

933 1/2 Basin Ave. P.O. Box 2656
Bismarck, ND 58502
Web Address: www.gcentral.com/steambrothers
E-mail Address: steambro@gcentral.com
Toll-Free Phone: (800) 767-5064
Phone: (701) 222-1263
Fax: (701) 222-1372
Contact: President

Number of Franchises: 21
Company-Owned Units: 0
Total Units: 21

In Business Since: 1977   **Franchising Since:** 1984

Description of Operation: Steam Brothers provides carpet, drapery, and upholstery cleaning; fire, smoke, and water damage restoration; furnace and air-duct cleaning; and acoustical ceiling cleaning.

Equity Capital Needed: $11,000-$55,000

Franchise Fee: 0

Royalty: 5-6.5 percent

Advertising Co-op Fee:

Financial Assistance: The initial franchise fee includes start-up equipment and inventory.

Management Assistance: We provide manuals, seminars, field representatives, newsletters, troubleshooting hot lines, monthly advertising material and suggested uses, promotional recommendations, an ongoing new product and services package, and more.

Training Assistance: We offer training at headquarters in Bismarck, ND, for five days. Training at franchisee's location is for two days.

Cleaning & Sanitation— Enviromental Products

Environmental Biotech, Inc.

4404 N. Tamiami Tr.
Sarasota, FL 34234
Web Address: www.envbiotech.com
E-mail Address: envbio@ix.netcom.com
Toll-Free Phone: (800) 314-6263
Phone: (941) 358-9112
Fax: (941) 359-9744

Contact: Vice President Franchise Development

Number of Franchises: 101
Company-Owned Units: 1
Total Units: 102

In Business Since: 1991   **Franchising Since:** 1991

Description of Operation: Environmental Biotech has developed four product lines to meet the goal set forth when the company was founded in 1991: to provide environmentally friendly solutions to customers' waste problems. Grease Eradication System (GES™), SES® Sugar and Starch Eradication System, and GEL-OUT™ contain all-natural, vegetative bacteria that actually eat these pollutants from the drainage systems and grease traps of a variety of facilities. These "bugs" convert waste products into simple water and carbon dioxide, thereby keeping drain lines and grease traps free of backups and clogs. The company recently introduced E Chem®, a line of biodegradable cleaning products for industrial and commercial applications. Additionally, E Chem works cooperatively with EBI's bacteria. Environmental Biotech's global network includes 95 territories in 14 countries. In 1997 EBI moved to its new World Headquarters situated on 13 acres of citrus trees in Sarasota, FL. EBI runs its own research laboratory, manufactures all its bacteria, teaches extensively to governmental agencies and its franchisees, and provides ongoing operational support for all its franchisees.

Equity Capital Needed: $50,000

Franchise Fee: $29,000

Royalty: 3 percent

Advertising Co-op Fee: 1 percent

Financial Assistance: None

Management Assistance: Ongoing managerial support is provided through field support personnel. Technical assistance is provided by our in-house technical team.

Training Assistance: Three weeks of training at corporate headquarters in Sarasota. Additional week at franchisee's location in the field.

Hydro Physics Pipe Inspection Corp.

1855 W. Union Ave., Ste. N
Englewood, CO 80110
Toll-Free Phone: (800) 781-3164
Phone: (303) 781-2474
Fax: (303) 781-0477
Contact: President/CEO

Number of Franchises: 2
Company-Owned Units: 1
Total Units: 3

In Business Since: 1991   **Franchising Since:** 1996

Description of Operation: Hydro Physics was founded in 1991 to serve the needs of people in residential, commercial, and industrial segments, and to provide objective analysis of the condition of virtually all types of three- to six-inch pipelines. Hydro Physics specializes in discovering, understanding, and diagnosing pipe problems. Like an appraiser, we don't buy, sell, or repair pipes. Instead, using the finest video pipe inspection equipment, Hydro Physics pinpoints the exact location of problems in pipelines, including depth. To inspect a pipe, a small camera is inserted into the line and for a view of the pipe's condition. Information is recorded on professional-grade videotape and is accompanied by a fully documented description of the images captured. By providing a pipe "appraisal," Hydro Physics offers customers an objective view of the situation *before* digging begins, often saving them thousands of dollars in unnecessary repair costs.

Equity Capital Needed: $30,000

Franchise Fee: $15,500

Royalty: 8 percent

Advertising Co-op Fee: 2 percent

Financial Assistance: We offer third-party leasing and financing assistance.

Management Assistance: We provide daily assistance to all franchisees in day-to-day operations.

Training Assistance: Hydro Physics provides complete training to franchisees. Franchisees receive one full week of training in Englewood, CO. In addition, H.P. provides one week of training on-site. Continual contact and emergency assistance provided.

Cleaning & Sanitation— Household Cleaning

Coit Services

897 Hinckley Rd.
Burlingame, CA 94010
Toll-Free Phone: (800) 243-8797
Phone: (415) 697-5471
Fax: (415) 697-5471
Contact: Franchise Director

Number of Franchises: 44
Company-Owned Units: 7
Total Units: 51

In Business Since: 1950   **Franchising Since:** 1962

Description of Operation: Coit is a multiservice cleaning company, offering drapery cleaning, carpet cleaning, upholstery cleaning, area-rug cleaning, air-duct cleaning, and more.

Equity Capital Needed: $20,000-$70,000

Franchise Fee: $9,950

Royalty: 6 percent

Advertising Co-op Fee:

Financial Assistance: We will assist with third-party financing.

Management Assistance: Management assistance is available in all areas of the operation, including advertising, marketing, financial, operational, reporting procedures, information systems, sales, and so on.

Training Assistance: The initial training program will cover up to two weeks of basic training in all areas of the operation at any of the company-owned operations.

Custom Care for Homes

1608 N. Miller Rd. Ste. 5
Scottsdale, AZ 85257
Toll-Free Phone:
Phone: (602) 941-2993
Fax:
Contact: President

Number of Franchises: 15
Company-Owned Units: 1
Total Units: 16

In Business Since: 1986 **Franchising Since:** 1990

Description of Operation: Home cleaning, carpet cleaning, and window cleaning for residential homes, plus commericial cleaning.

Equity Capital Needed: $1,500-$10,000

Franchise Fee: $2,900

Royalty: $100 per month

Advertising Co-op Fee:

Financial Assistance: Data not available.

Management Assistance: Assistance is always at your fingertips—a phone call. Detailed documentation and manuals answer almost all of your management concerns. If not, speedy telephone assistance is immediately available.

Training Assistance: Start your training with four hours of video instruction at your home. Then advance to a 190-page manual, which gives detailed instruction in every aspect of the business—marketing, advertising, sales, budgets and projections, accounting, record keeping, insurance, employee training, and employee contracts and forms.

Home Cleaning Centers of America

P.O. Box 14070
Palm Desert, CA 92255
E-mail Address: MCalhoon@aol.com
Toll-Free Phone: (800) 767-1118
Phone: (760) 360-0202
Fax: (760) 360-2611
Contact: President

Number of Franchises: 28
Company-Owned Units: 0
Total Units: 28

In Business Since: 1981 **Franchising Since:** 1984

Description of Operation: We have very large Franchise Zones; our System includes house, office, carpet, and window cleaning. We are looking for owners who want to make six-figure incomes, do not want to clean houses themselves, and have a very special talent for managing people. Our #1 goal is to increase existing franchise sales. That's why we award only a few new franchises each year. Our selection process is simple: Are we right for each other, and can we have fun?

Equity Capital Needed: $30,000-$40,000

Franchise Fee: $16,500

Royalty: 4.5-5 percent

Advertising Co-op Fee: 0

Financial Assistance: We will help you with every aspect of securing a loan. We have two-year pro formas, demographic studies, and market analysis on every franchise zone.

Management Assistance: We have district managers who also own a franchise. Each franchisee will receive whatever assistance is required.

Training Assistance: We begin with a one-week training session in Denver or St. Louis, followed by annual seminars.

Maid Brigade Systems, Inc.

850 Indian Trail Rd.
Lilbum, GA 30047
Web Address: www.maidbrigade.com
E-mail Address: cem@maidbrigade.com
Toll-Free Phone: (800) 722-6243
Phone: (770) 564-2400
Fax: (770) 564-2400
Contact: Director, Franchise Recruitment

Number of Franchises: 260
Company-Owned Units: 2
Total Units: 262

In Business Since: 1979 **Franchising Since:** 1980

Description of Operation: Cleaning homes profitably—that's what the entire Maid Brigade System is all about. Larger territory, lower overhead, generous sliding scale royalty, no cars necessary, on-site start-up, and much more.

Equity Capital Needed: $40,000-45,000

Franchise Fee: $16,900

Royalty: 3-7 percent

Advertising Co-op Fee: 2 percent max

Financial Assistance: Financial assistance available with purchase of additional territories.

Management Assistance: Manuals, formal training at our home office in Atlanta, on-site support, as well as our state-of-the-art MicroMaid software management system. All support staff have been successful franchisees, AND support lasts forever.

Training Assistance: Nobody but Maid Brigade puts a team of experienced professionals at your office for five days on opening—in addition to videos, manuals, formal training in Atlanta, and our outstanding MicroMaid software management system. All support staff have been successful franchisees, AND support lasts forever! All of this is designed to increase your profitability.

Maid to Perfection

7133 Rutherford Rd.
Baltimore, MD 21244
E-mail Address: maidsvc@aol.com
Toll-Free Phone: (800) 648-6243
Phone: (410) 944-6466
Fax: (410) 944-6469
Contact: Vice President

Number of Franchises: 120
Company-Owned Units: 1
Total Units: 121

In Business Since: 1980   **Franchising Since:** 1990

Description of Operation: Ranked #1 in Success Gold 100, Maid to Perfection is positioned so that our franchisees benefit from both the demographically driven demand for traditional home cleaning services and the less common but potentially more lucrative specialized cleaning services that are not offered by other maid service franchisees. You put the high net profit dollars generated by these additional services into your own pockets. And it keeps getting better! The profitable commercial market represents a world of opportunity that just doesn't exist for franchisees of other maid services. Contracts in this segment of the business can run into the millions of dollars.

Equity Capital Needed: $80,000 minimum

Franchise Fee: $8,995

Royalty: 4-7 percent

Advertising Co-op Fee: 0

Financial Assistance: 100 percent financing available for additional franchise.

Management Assistance: On-site visits, both home office and Regional Developers, annual seminars.

Training Assistance: Six-week preopening assistance. Five-day, easy-to-learn classroom training program includes personnel, office management, customer relations, advertising, estimating payroll, preparation, chemical/equipment use, demonstrations, business plan, and more. Extensive field and hands-on training. Strong follow-up. Ongoing support for life of your business.

Maids International, The

4820 Dodge St.
Omaha, NE 68132
Toll-Free Phone: (800) 843-6243
Phone: (402) 558-5555
Fax: (402) 558-4112
Contact: Sales

Number of Franchises: 216
Company-Owned Units: 0
Total Units: 216

In Business Since: 1979   **Franchising Since:** 1980

Description of Operation: Residential maid service franchise.

Equity Capital Needed: $13,500-$23,500

Franchise Fee: $17,500

Royalty: 5.5-7 percent

Advertising Co-op Fee:

Financial Assistance: We will finance up to 50 percent of franchise fee.

Management Assistance: Six weeks of pretraining counseling; 6 days of adminstrative corporate training, with complete hands-on computer training; and 90-day posttraining follow-up. Monthly newsletter, toll-free phone support, regional seminars, annual meetings, and advertising and public relations programs.

Training Assistance: Six weeks of pretraining counseling, 6 weeks of technical corporate training, and 90-day posttraining follow-up. Toll-free technical phone support.

Merry Maids

860 Ridge Lake Blvd.
Memphis, TN 38120
Web Address: www.merrymaids.com
Toll-Free Phone: (800) 798-8000
Phone: (901) 537-8100
Fax: (901) 537-8140
Contact: Franchise Sales Manager

Number of Franchises: 700
Company-Owned Units: 1
Total Units: 701

In Business Since: 1980   **Franchising Since:** 1981

Description of Operation: Merry Maids is the largest and most successful maid service in the United States. *Money* and *Success* magazines have ranked Merry Maids a "Top 10 US Franchise." The company's commitment to marketing, training, and ongoing support is unmatched. Merry Maids provides the most comprehensive software, equipment, and supply package. Merry Maids is a member of the ServiceMaster quality service network.

Equity Capital Needed: $15,000-$20,000

Franchise Fee: $12,500-$20,500

Royalty: 7-5 percent

Advertising Co-op Fee:

Financial Assistance: Up to $11,500 is available toward the franchise fee for qualified buyers.

Management Assistance: Complete managerial focus and application, from initial training and extending through the company's Advanced Performance Seminars for established franchise owners.

Training Assistance: Five days of headquarters training and all start-up equipment and supplies for two teams. Ongoing support includes 21 field regional coordinators, a "Buddy Program," weekly modem bulletin board, newsletters, regional meetings, national convention, and an 800# for assistance. Products and supplies are available at savings up to 80 percent.

Molly Maid

1340 Eisenhower Pl.
Ann Arbor, MI 48108
Web Address: www.mollymaid.com
E-mail Address: info@mollymaid.com
Toll-Free Phone: (800) 666-6559
Phone: (313) 975-1000
Fax: (313) 975-9000
Contact: Vice President-Sales and Marketing

Number of Franchises: 342
Company-Owned Units: 3
Total Units: 345

In Business Since: 1979 **Franchising Since:** 1979

Description of Operation: Customers choose Molly Maid for their professional image and proven results worldwide. *Inc.* Magazine rated Molly Maid as on of the 500 fastest-growing companies for three years. Molly Maid has a proven system, with over four million cleanings performed.

Equity Capital Needed: $10,000-$14,000

Franchise Fee: $9,900-$24,900

Royalty: 6-3 percent

Advertising Co-op Fee:

Financial Assistance: Up to 50 percent of the initial franchise fee or $10,000, whichever sum is lesser, with an APR of 9.75 percent over 36 equal monthly installments.

Management Assistance: A six-month "Right Start" program, which includes a business plan and marketing plan especially created for each franchisee, individually based on how quickly he or she wants to grow the business. A field representative will spend two days on-site with the franchisee at no charge after 45-60 days of operation.

Training Assistance: Five days of intense training in Ann Arbor, MI. Management, marketing, accounting, computer training, and hands-on activities.

Cleaning & Sanitation— Maintenance

American Leak Detection

888 Research Dr.; Ste. 100
Palm Springs, CA 92262
Web Address: www.leakbusters.com
Toll-Free Phone: (800) 755-6697
Phone: (760) 320-9991
Fax: (760) 320-1288
Contact: Marketing Director

Number of Franchises: 170
Company-Owned Units: 3
Total Units: 173

In Business Since: 1974 **Franchising Since:** 1985

Description of Operation: Pinpoint detection of water or sewer leaks under concrete slabs of homes, pools, spas, fountains, commercial buildings, and so on, with electronic equipment manufactured by the company.

Equity Capital Needed: $65,000

Franchise Fee: $29,500+

Royalty: 8-10 percent

Advertising Co-op Fee:

Financial Assistance: Financing is available on approved credit for up to 50 percent of the franchise fee.

Management Assistance: Advertising, data processing, directory assistance, field technical consultant visitations, publicity, business group insurance, trade show booths, marketing, and training.

Training Assistance: Six weeks of technical, hands-on training at corporate office in Palm Springs, CA, including marketing and sales training. Ongoing technical assistance available as needed to current and new franchisees. Annual convention to exchange and share technology and skills.

CleanNet USA

9861 Broken Land Pkwy. Ste. 208
Columbia, MD 21046
Toll-Free Phone: (800) 735-8838
Phone: (410) 720-6444
Fax: (410) 720-5307
Contact: Vice President

Number of Franchises: 2115
Company-Owned Units: 6
Total Units: 2121

In Business Since: 1987 **Franchising Since:** 1988

Description of Operation: CleanNet provides professional building maintenance services to commercial properties and institutions throughout the United States. CleanNet offers a complete turnkey system that provides the franchisee with business accounts, supplies, equipment, and insurance.

Equity Capital Needed: $2,950-$32,000

Franchise Fee: $2,950-$32,000

Royalty: 3 percent

Advertising Co-op Fee:

Financial Assistance: CleanNet will finance approximately 50 percent of the franchise fee.

Management Assistance: CleanNet provides a complete program of managerial support, including training, quality control, and customer support.

Training Assistance: CleanNet's program provides intensive training, including classroom, video, and on-the-job training.

Ductbusters

29160 U.S. Hwy. 19 N.
Clearwater, FL 34621-2400
Web Address: www.ductbusters.com
E-mail Address: info@ductbusters.com
Toll-Free Phone: (800) 786-3828
Phone: (813) 787-7087
Fax: (813) 789-0060
Contact: President

Number of Franchises: 27
Company-Owned Units: 1
Total Units: 28

In Business Since: 1985   **Franchising Since:** 1992

Description of Operation: Ductbusters offers a patented method of cleaning air-conditioning and heating systems.

Equity Capital Needed: $30,045-81,500

Franchise Fee: $7,500-24,000

Royalty: 7 percent

Advertising Co-op Fee: None

Financial Assistance: Data not provided

Management Assistance: We have a set of 14 manuals set up so that they cover every aspect of running a Ductbusters franchise. We also offer telephone and computer support whenever needed.

Training Assistance: When you join the Ductbusters franchise network, your production, sales, and management staff will receive a one-week training course in a classroom and practical setting. We will visit your location at least six days each year.

Mr. Rooter

1220 N. University Parks Dr.
Waco, TX 76707

Toll-Free Phone: (800) 583-8003
Phone: (254) 745-2500
Fax: (254) 745-2501
Contact: President

Number of Franchises: 182
Company-Owned Units: 0
Total Units: 182

In Business Since: 1968   **Franchising Since:** 1974

Description of Operation: Franchise of full-service plumber and drain repair business.

Equity Capital Needed: $17,500

Franchise Fee: $17,500

Royalty: 6 percent, declining on volume.

Advertising Co-op Fee:

Financial Assistance: Up to 70 percent financing is available to creditworthy applicants.

Management Assistance: Complete management and marketing assistance by home and field staff.

Training Assistance: Mandatory one week of training at home office. Field training provided, as needed.

National Leak Detection

P.O. Box 3191
Palos Verdes Estate, CA 90274
Toll-Free Phone: (800) 444-9421
Phone: (310) 377-2699
Fax: (310) 328-3342
Contact: Vice President of Marketing

Number of Franchises: 42
Company-Owned Units: 6
Total Units: 48

In Business Since: 1989   **Franchising Since:** 1989

Description of Operation: Leak detection and repair on swimming pools, spas, fountains, ponds, domestic water supply lines, slabs, irrigation systems, walls, and gas leaks.

Equity Capital Needed: $15,000

Franchise Fee: Varies

Royalty: 8 percent

Advertising Co-op Fee:

Financial Assistance: In-house financing is available.

Management Assistance: Ongoing support and assistance available to all franchisees, including workshops and seminars. New technology available to franchisee. Updated information given to franchisee through the "National Update." Corporate trainer will assist in helping new franchisees on technical knowledge.

Training Assistance: Continued workshops and meetings on new technology and laws on industry. One-on-one training with corporate trainer. In-house workshop on administrative responsibilities.

Paul Davis Systems

9000 Cypress Green Dr.
Jacksonville, FL 32256
Toll-Free Phone: (800) 722-1818
Phone: (904) 730-0320
Fax: (904) 730-8972
Contact: Director of Franchise Sales

Number of Franchises: 207
Company-Owned Units: 1
Total Units: 208

In Business Since: 1967 **Franchising Since:** 1970

Description of Operation: Paul W. Davis Systems is the world's largest international restoration company. It was founded in 1967 and has over 200 network franchises in the United States, Canada, and the United Kingdom. A Paul W. Davis Systems franchise is for the mature, entrepreneurial person who is service-oriented and who has the ability and patience to build and manage an organization. The demand for restoration is constant and not dependent on the economy, real estate, or weather. The franchise restores residential and commercial property with insurable losses.

Equity Capital Needed: $75,000-$150,000

Franchise Fee: $19,900-$46,000

Royalty: 3.5-5 percent

Advertising Co-op Fee:

Financial Assistance: None at this time.

Management Assistance: One week of field consulting for franchise start-ups, followed by 6 months of ongoing telephone support for new owners. Also one week of field consulting for job cost accounting.

Training Assistance: A five-week, mandatory, new-owner training class that includes franchise management, estimating, project management, job cost accounting, trades supervision, and marketing. Also an optional two-week signature, professional cleaning school. Two weeks of training for associates and contractors are provided for a nominal fee.

Precision Powerwash 2000

P.O. Box 463
W. Springfield, MA 01090
Web Address: www.cleanmachineinc.com
Toll-Free Phone:
Phone: (413) 734-4384
Fax: (413) 736-1785
Contact: President

Number of Franchises: 3
Company-Owned Units: 6
Total Units: 9

In Business Since: 1974 **Franchising Since:** 1993

Description of Operation: We specialize in cleaning the exterior of houses, cleaning truck fleets, and building restoration.

Equity Capital Needed: $35,000-$49,000

Franchise Fee: 0

Royalty: 0

Advertising Co-op Fee:

Financial Assistance: None

Management Assistance: We will assist in all aspects of conducting a new business from A to Z.

Training Assistance: We provide two weeks of training. Also, we will train as many new employees as needed.

Professional Polish

5450 E. Loop 820S
Fort Worth, TX 76119
Toll-Free Phone: (800) 255-0488
Phone: (817) 572-7353
Fax: (817) 561-6193
Contact: President

Number of Franchises: 32
Company-Owned Units: 2
Total Units: 34

In Business Since: 1982 **Franchising Since:** 1986

Description of Operation: Janitorial, lawn, landscape, and light building maintenance service at the local level. Master franchisor emphasis on marketing, training, and management of local franchisees.

Equity Capital Needed: Local: $11,500 total; Master: $50,000 liquid assets

Franchise Fee: 0

Royalty: Local: 1.5 percent; Master: 5 percent

Advertising Co-op Fee:

Financial Assistance: PPI will finance balance of purchase at 12 percent interest.

Management Assistance: Local: minimum 30 days of training—up to 90 days if needed—in sales, public relations, all accounts receivable, and bookkeeping, plus assistance with purchasing supplies, insurance, tax reports, and expense record keeping. Master: marketing and accounting.

Training Assistance: Local: minimum of 30 days, plus ongoing support. Master: minimum of 90 days, plus ongoing support.

Cleaning & Sanitation— Pest Control

Budget Pest Control

1 Parker Place 3616 Lake Rd.
Ponca City, OK 74604
Toll-Free Phone: (800) 364-5739

Phone: (316) 522-3800
Fax: (405) 765-4613
Contact: President

Number of Franchises: 3
Company-Owned Units: 6
Total Units: 9

In Business Since: 1968   **Franchising Since:** 1981

Description of Operation: Residential and commercial pest control business, using a patented P.E.S.T. machine along with proven marketing and management techniques.

Equity Capital Needed: $35,000-$70,000

Franchise Fee: $25,000

Royalty: 8 percent—first $100,000; 6 percent—second $100,000; 4 percent—third $100,000

Advertising Co-op Fee:

Financial Assistance: None

Management Assistance: Can share mainframe computer system. On-site assistance and phone assistance.

Training Assistance: 5-8 days of initial training in Ponca City, OK. Approximately 15 days of field training, then continual, ongoing training on-site and at corporate headquarter's training facility.

Terminix International

860 Ridge Lake Blvd.
Memphis, TN 38120
Toll-Free Phone: (800) 654-7848
Phone: (901) 766-1351
Fax: (901) 766-1107
Contact: Director of Franchise Recruitment

Number of Franchises: 224
Company-Owned Units: 401
Total Units: 625

In Business Since: 1927   **Franchising Since:** 1927

Description of Operation: World's largest structural pest control company, with over 600 service centers nationwide and in several foreign countries, offering termite and pest control services to residential, commercial, and industrial customers.

Equity Capital Needed: $29,500-$49,900

Franchise Fee: $25,000-$50,000

Royalty: 7 percent

Advertising Co-op Fee:

Financial Assistance: With approved credit, Terminix will finance up to 70 percent of the initial franchise fee.

Management Assistance: Ongoing technical, operational, sales, and marketing support.

Training Assistance: Training for new franchisees covers a wide variety of disciplines, including technical

aspects of termite and pest control, operations management and production, general business procedures, sales and sales management, and personnel administration.

Truly Nolen of America, Inc.

6375 E. Tanque Verde, Ste. 270
Tucson, AZ 85715
Web Address: www.truly.com
E-mail Address: Truly@truly.com
Toll-Free Phone: (800) 458-3664
Phone: (520) 546-2503
Fax: (520) 546-2511
Contact: Director of Franchising

Number of Franchises: 0
Company-Owned Units: 63
Total Units: 63

In Business Since: 1955   **Franchising Since:** 1997

Description of Operation: Truly Nolen is an operation Pest Control Company, leading in innovation services and control methods. Truly Nolen uses the most recognized marketing motif in the industry (The Mouse Car). Pest control includes residential pest control, commercial pest control, termite control, and lawn care. Truly Nolen proprietary services include Tru-guard, Truly-Proof, Truly Care EF, Truly Scape, and others.

Equity Capital Needed: $5,000

Franchise Fee: $7,500-$35,000

Royalty: 7 percent

Advertising Co-op Fee: None

Financial Assistance: Guidance in capital and asset franchising. Truly Nolen may finance the initial fee.

Management Assistance: Review of options and planning.

Training Assistance: Depending on background, basic business operations and basic pest management. Ongoing benchmarking.

Cleaning & Sanitation— Miscellaneous

Coustic-Glo International

7111 Ohms Ln.
Minneapolis, MN 55439
Web Address: www.cgi-online.com
E-mail Address: cgiinc@aol.com
Toll-Free Phone: (800) 333-8523
Phone: (612) 835-1333
Fax: (612) 835-1395
Contact: Vice President of Marketing

Number of Franchises: 160
Company-Owned Units: 1
Total Units: 161

In Business Since: 1970   **Franchising Since:** 1980

Description of Operation: The Coustic-Glo concept offers a unique opportunity for an individual to pursue financial independence in a virtually untapped industry. The need for ceiling and wall cleaning and restoration is all around you in every structure you enter daily. As a Coustic-Glo franchisee, you will be provided with all of the equipment, products, cleaning solutions, and the training necessary to prosper in the field.

Equity Capital Needed: $9,750-$25,000, depending on the area assigned

Franchise Fee: $37,500

Royalty: 6 percent

Advertising Co-op Fee:

Financial Assistance: Some company financing is available.

Management Assistance: The home office of Coustic-Glo International provides continual support in all areas of this business. Toll-free phones are maintained to give direct and constant access to the home office and assistance with field problems, technical questions, and so on. Complete test reports on all products are provided, with updating as necessary. A very aggressive national advertising campaign is pursued. Local ad mats and all product identification are provided.

Training Assistance: Each new franchisee is provided with a very intensive two to three-day training program that takes place in his or her respective exclusive area, under the direct supervision of an experienced franchisee who is brought in from that individual's area to assist in the establishment of the new franchisee's business. Also available to the new franchisee is the option of a training course provided at the home office under the direct supervision of home office personnel.

Fabri-Zone Cleaning Systems

3135 Universal Dr., Unit 6
Mississauga, ON L4X 2E2
Web Address: www.fabrizone.com
E-mail Address: fabrizone@fabrizone.com
Toll-Free Phone:
Phone: (905) 602-7691
Fax: (905) 602-7891
Contact: President

Number of Franchises: 25
Company-Owned Units: 1
Total Units: 26

In Business Since: 1981   **Franchising Since:** 1984

Description of Operation: Patented purification cleaning process for the cleaning of carpets, upholstery, ceilings, walls, blinds and drapes, plus smoke and damage restoration and cleaning.

Equity Capital Needed: $3,000-$10,000

Franchise Fee: $4,000

Royalty: 6 percent

Advertising Co-op Fee:

Financial Assistance: Business plan.

Management Assistance: Manager assistance.

Training Assistance: One week of initial telephone support and regional seminars.

Marble Renewal

6805 W. 12th St., Ste. H
Little Rock, AR 72204
Web Address: www.marblerenewal.com
E-mail Address: marble@aristotle.net
Toll-Free Phone: (888) 978-5409
Phone: (501) 663-2080
Fax: (501) 663-2401
Contact: Senior Vice President

Number of Franchises: 27
Company-Owned Units: 1
Total Units: 28

In Business Since: 1988   **Franchising Since:** 1988

Description of Operation: Marble Renewal is a franchise system with proprietary techniques and exclusive chemistries in floor treatment and floor upkeep for all dimensional stone, wood flooring, and walls. This includes marble, granite, terrazzo, slate, tile, limestone, travertine, quarry, hardwood, and so on. Marble Renewal supplies comprehensive training and field support in marketing and technical aspects. With its ongoing research and development, Marble Renewal is far ahead in modern technology. All areas are protected with very little overhead and high profit margins. Marble Renewal offers the finest technology in fashionable stone and hardwoods.

Equity Capital Needed: $10,000-$20,000

Franchise Fee: $5,000-$25,000

Royalty: 4-8 percent

Advertising Co-op Fee: 0

Financial Assistance: None

Management Assistance: Marketing and technical assistance can be offered.

Training Assistance: Two week initially and four weeks during the year.

Restorx

1135 Braddock Ave.
Braddock, PA 15104
Toll-Free Phone: (800) 323-3278
Phone: (412) 351-8686
Fax: (412) 351-1394
Contact: Vice President of Marketing

Number of Franchises: 40
Company-Owned Units: 1
Total Units: 41

In Business Since: 1982   **Franchising Since:** 1982

Description of Operation: Train franchisees to do restoration work for insurance company property losses. Areas of Restorx expertise are fire and smoke damage, water removal, electronic reclamation, fine arts and book reclamation, damage assessment, improvement of indoor quality, and deodorization.

Equity Capital Needed: $17,500-$60,000

Franchise Fee: $17,500

Royalty: $145 weekly

Advertising Co-op Fee:

Financial Assistance: Up to 60 percent financing is available at 1 percent above prime. Financing period for franchise fee is 24 months.

Management Assistance: Initially, six days of training at home office. Also, three days of marketing assistance in field. Seminars are conducted in the field to assist franchisees on request. Ongoing marketing and advertising help is continually given to franchisee.

Training Assistance: In addition to the above, a 24-hours-a-day, seven-days-a-week, 365-days-a-year hot line is available with technical assistance.

Roto-Rooter Plumbing, Sewer and Drain Service

300 Ashworth Rd.
Des Moines, IA 50265
Web Address: www.rotorooter.com
Toll-Free Phone:
Phone: (515) 223-1343
Fax: (515) 223-4220
Contact: Director of Franchise Administration

Number of Franchises: 570
Company-Owned Units: 84
Total Units: 654

In Business Since: 1935   **Franchising Since:** 1935

Description of Operation: Largest national provider of repair service plumbing and sewer-drain cleaning. Active in all 50 states, U.S. possessions, Canada, and Japan.

Equity Capital Needed: $24,500-$99,500

Franchise Fee: $1,000

Royalty: Based on population.

Advertising Co-op Fee:

Financial Assistance: None

Management Assistance: Regional management conferences; annual plumbing symposium; and traveling specialists in marketing, service, and sales.

Training Assistance: Provided as needed.

Service-Tech Corporation

21012 Aurora Rd.
Warrensville Heights, OH 44146
Toll-Free Phone:
Phone: (216) 663-2600
Fax: (216) 663-8804
Contact: President

Number of Franchises: 3
Company-Owned Units: 4
Total Units: 7

In Business Since: 1960   **Franchising Since:** 1989

Description of Operation: Indoor air quality remediation and industrial cleaning services. Opportunity to join 33 years of experience in solving the growing concerns associated with indoor air pollution. The list of cleaning services offered include air duct systems, industrial exhaust systems, industrial ovens, overhead structural steel, restaurant hood exhaust systems, laboratory hood exhaust systems, computer room subfloors, and laundry and restroom exhaust systems. A wide range of customers.

Equity Capital Needed: $49,000

Franchise Fee: $19,000

Royalty: 4-6 percent

Advertising Co-op Fee:

Financial Assistance: Assistance in obtaining financing from outside sources.

Management Assistance: Franchisees receive assistance with office set-up, field preparation, business and accounting forms, reference manuals, advertising and marketing supplies, open line communication with main office, and continual updates on industry-related matters and safety.

Training Assistance: 14-day training schedule conducted at the corporate training center, with hands-on field instruction at job sites. Training in marketing, sales, field operations, accounting, personnel, and management.

Sparkle International, Inc.

26851 Richmond Rd.
Bedford Heights, OH 44146
E-mail Address: pfunku@en.com
Toll-Free Phone: (800) 321-0770
Phone: (216) 464-4212
Fax: (216) 464-8869
Contact: President

Number of Franchises: 218
Company-Owned Units: 1
Total Units: 219

In Business Since: 1965   **Franchising Since:** 1967

Description of Operation: Sparkle Wash is the world's leading power wash company because no other system cleans as well or is so adaptable. Sparkle Wash services

the transportation, residential, industrial, and commercial industries. We provide you with complete training, patented equipment, environmentally friendly cleaning products, open territories, and ongoing support. Local competitors lack the knowledge and resources to master environmental regulations. However, you will have all that information available to you from the start. As a Sparkle Wash franchisee, you have the benefit of owning your own business with the support of the world's top power-washing franchise.

Equity Capital Needed: $15,000

Franchise Fee: $12,000 minimum

Royalty: 3-5 percent on sliding scale on adjusted gross sales

Advertising Co-op Fee: None

Financial Assistance: Sparkle Wash offers third-party financing based on your credit. Typical terms are 60 months. You may increase the down payment, purchase outright, or obtain your own financing. We also provide an initial line of credit for your orders.

Management Assistance: Sparkle Wash hosts an annual convention and seminars throughout the year to assist you in managing your business. Topics include marketing, sales, accounting, new cleaning processes, finding quality employees, and many more. We also provide monthly updates as well as advice and support daily.

Training Assistance: We help you learn how to operate a Sparkle Wash business with five days of factory training covering equipment operation; maintenance procedures; cleaning solutions; applications procedures; sales and marketing techniques; bookkeeping; and complete, easy-to-use reference manuals. We also provide on-site field training.

Steamatic

303 Arthur St.
Fort Worth, TX 76107
Web Address: www.Steamatic.com
Toll-Free Phone: (800) 527-1295
Phone: (817) 332-1575
Fax: (817) 332-5349
Contact: Senior Vice President of Franchise Development

Number of Franchises: 327
Company-Owned Units: 10
Total Units: 337

In Business Since: 1948   **Franchising Since:** 1968

Description of Operation: Steamatic provides water, fire, and storm insurance restoration (disaster recovery services); indoor environmental services; air duct and coil cleaning; carpet cleaning; furniture cleaning; drapery cleaning; deodorizing; wood restoration; document restoration; corrosion control; and ceiling and wall cleaning.

Equity Capital Needed: $40,000-$75,000

Franchise Fee: $5,000-$12,000-$16,000-$18,000 by territory size

Royalty: 8-5 percent

Advertising Co-op Fee:

Financial Assistance: Equipment, supplies, cleaning agents, and chemicals can be financed.

Management Assistance: We provide continual training and assistance in the franchisee's territory; regional and annual seminars; training and marketing tapes; and TV, radio, and print advertising, plus direct mail and 24-hour toll-free numbers.

Training Assistance: Initial training is two weeks. Advanced training is optional. The first week concentrates on the various cleaning and restoration services. The second week is a mini–business school session. Classes consist of advertising and marketing procedures, selling techniques, accounting methods, financial management, telemarketing skills, commercial pricing, insurance, residential jobs, writing programs, maintenance contracts, brainstorming, role playing, and much more.

Construction & Remodeling— Home Repair

Archadeck

2112 W. Laburnum Avenue, Ste. 100
Richmond, VA 23227
Web Address: www.archadeck.com
Toll-Free Phone: (800) 789-3325
Phone: (804) 353-6999
Fax: (804) 353-2364
Contact: Qualifications Specialist

Number of Franchises: 71
Company-Owned Units: 0
Total Units: 71

In Business Since: 1980   **Franchising Since:** 1986

Description of Operation: Archadeck is the nation's largest builder of custom-designed wooden decks, porches, and other outdoor-structure-related products. Archadeck believes in thorough and extensive training, and as an Archadeck franchisee you will receive the following: pretraining, 20-day training at corporate headquarters, start-up field training, regional seminars, drafting services, training services, and collateral materials (forms, software, brochures, and more).

Equity Capital Needed: $50,000-75,000

Franchise Fee: $24,500-39,500

Royalty: 3.5-5.5 percent

Advertising Co-op Fee: Data not provided

Financial Assistance: Some financing available, determined individually.

Management Assistance: Managerial assistance in sales, marketing, construction, and administration is ongoing to our franchisees.

Training Assistance: Archadeck provides to their franchisees pretraining, 20-day training at corporate headquaters, and start-up field training.

Handyman Connection

277 Northland Blvd.
Cincinnati, OH 45246
Web Address: www.handymanconnection.com
Toll-Free Phone: (800) 466-5530
Phone: (513) 771-1122
Fax: (513) 771-4975
Contact:

Number of Franchises: 65
Company-Owned Units: 1
Total Units: 64

In Business Since: 1990 **Franchising Since:** 1991

Description of Operation: Handyman Connection provides small to middle-sized home repairs and remodeling.

Equity Capital Needed: $25,000-$75,000

Franchise Fee: $25,000-$75,000

Royalty: 5 percent

Advertising Co-op Fee:

Financial Assistance: 50 percent down and 50 percent in equal installments paid monthly, with interest at two points over prime. For the first six months, no principal or interest payments are due.

Management Assistance: We completely train the franchisee for two weeks at our flagship operation in Cincinnati, OH, and then spend the first week assisting the franchisee in opening the operation in his or her city. From then on, we supply the advertising copy and new marketing and recruiting concepts. The Franchise Coordinator makes regular visits to all franchisees.

Training Assistance: As described in the preceding section, franchisees receive training at our home base and also receive an operations manual and videotapes that cover all the systems necessary to operate successfully one of our franchises.

Kitchen Tune-Up

131 N. Roosevelt
Aberdeen, SD 57401
E-mail Address: www.kituneup@nvc.net
Toll-Free Phone: (800) 333-6385
Phone: (605) 225-4049
Fax: (605) 225-1371

Contact: Senior Vice President

Number of Franchises: 300
Company-Owned Units: 0
Total Units: 300

In Business Since: 1986 **Franchising Since:** 1988

Description of Operation: Kitchen Tune-Up provides inexpensive wood care service to both the residential home owner and the commercial property owner. This #1-rated franchise also offers door replacement materials. This is a home-based, no-inventory, high-profit-margin business. Kitchen Tune-Up offers potential franchise owners the unique opportunity to attend training and evaluate the franchise before signing the franchise agreement.

Equity Capital Needed: $15,000-$25,000

Franchise Fee: $11,500

Royalty: 7 percent

Advertising Co-op Fee:

Financial Assistance: None

Management Assistance: Ongoing training programs, operations manuals and updates, national convention, monthly newsletter, advertising and promotional materials, and substantial discounts. Perpetual assistance, as needed.

Training Assistance: You must complete a one-week pretraining program before attending a one-week initial training seminar at the franchisor's home office. Initial training is then followed up with a 12-week training plan of action.

Miricle Method Bathroom Restoration

19402 Rim of the World Dr.
Monument, CO 80132
Web Address: miraclemethodusa.com
E-mail Address: cpistor@miraclemethodusa.com
Toll-Free Phone: (800) 444-8827
Phone: (719) 481-0849
Fax: (719) 481-1088
Contact: President

Number of Franchises: 101
Company-Owned Units: 0
Total Units: 101

In Business Since: 1977 **Franchising Since:** 1980

Description of Operation: Excellent income potential! Join a company committed to excellence. As a progressive industry leader, Miracle Method provides opportunities for hardworking entrepreneurs to get into business for themselves. Our procedures and systems for refinishing bathroom and kitchen fixtures provide a superior value to our customers. Bathtubs, ceramic tile, fiberglass showers, counter tops, and spas. Commercial and residential.

Equity Capital Needed: $23,000-$49,500

Franchise Fee: $16,500

Royalty: 5-7.5 percent

Advertising Co-op Fee: 3 percent

Financial Assistance: Financing of initial franchise fee is available subject to approval.

Management Assistance: Toll-free access to capable management. Written administration manuals. Up-front training in administration and management. Seminars and national conference. Periodic tips and newsletters. Access to internal network of experienced refinishers.

Training Assistance: Complete hands-on training in all necessary aspects of refinishing. Administrative and marketing training. Individualized advertising programs. Creative and responsive support in all areas of growing and managing your business.

Perma Ceramic Enterprises

65 Smithtown Blvd.
Smithtown, NY 11788
Toll-Free Phone: (800) 645-5039
Phone: (516) 724-1205
Fax: (516) 724-9626
Contact: President

Number of Franchises: 201
Company-Owned Units: 1
Total Units: 208

In Business Since: 1975   **Franchising Since:** 1976

Description of Operation: Resurfacing and repair of porcelain and fiberglass bathroom fixtures, such as tubs, sinks, and wall tile, with Perma Ceram's Porcelaincote. The process is used in private homes, apartments, hotels/motels, institutions, and so on, and is available in white and all colors. Established national accounts.

Equity Capital Needed: $24,500 total investment

Franchise Fee: 0

Royalty: 0 percent

Advertising Co-op Fee:

Financial Assistance: None

Management Assistance: Advertising, sales, and promotional materials, as well as ongoing managerial and technical assistance, are provided. Continual updating of information is provided through bulletins, newsletters, and personal contact. Return visits to the training facility are available if necessary.

Training Assistance: We offer five days of training at an established location with all expenses included in the cost of the dealership. Technical training, sales training, management, marketing, and so on. An operations manual is provided.

PTR Tub & Tile Restoration

3398 Sanford Dr.
Marietta, GA 30066
Toll-Free Phone: (800) 476-9271
Phone: (404) 429-0232
Fax: (404) 429-0232
Contact: President

Number of Franchises: 75
Company-Owned Units: 1
Total Units: 76

In Business Since: 1973   **Franchising Since:** 1990

Description of Operation: Restore beauty to old, dull, hard-to-clean bathtubs and tile. No painting or mess. Can be used the same day.

Equity Capital Needed: $5,995

Franchise Fee: Data not available

Royalty: 20 percent

Advertising Co-op Fee:

Financial Assistance: Varies.

Management Assistance: Data not available.

Training Assistance: Hands-on training and computer use for office. Manual.

Re-Bath Corporation

1055 S. Country Club Dr.
Mesa, AZ 85202
Web Address: www.re-bath.com
E-mail Address: mdebenedetto@re-bath.com
Toll-Free Phone: (800) 426-4573
Phone: (602) 844-1575
Fax: (602) 833-7199
Contact: General Manager

Number of Franchises: 77
Company-Owned Units: 1
Total Units: 78

In Business Since: 1979   **Franchising Since:** 1991

Description of Operation: Re-Bath offers custom-manufactured, high-impact acrylic bathtub liners, wall systems, and shower liners designed to go over existing bathtubs, ceramic tile walls, and shower bases. Re-Bath offers a permanent solution at a fraction of the cost of replacement.

Equity Capital Needed: $38,000-$78,000

Franchise Fee: $10,000+ and $5,000 start-up kit

Royalty: $25 per unit.

Advertising Co-op Fee:

Financial Assistance: Re-Bath offers no financial assistance for the franchise fee. However, Re-Bath, under certain circumstances, will finance a required start-up package for a period of up to 6 months.

Management Assistance: Re-Bath Corporation provides its franchisees with complete training manuals, forms, and marketing materials. Ongoing support is available in all areas of operation, installation, marketing, and sales. Monthly operational and marketing updates and informational newsletters keep the network informed. Annual conventions provide training updates.

Training Assistance: The new franchise owners attend a 5-6 day mandatory training program prior to opening. Training takes place at Re-Bath National Headquarters in Mesa, AZ, and covers all phases of installation, operations, sales, and marketing. Both classroom and hands-on training are provided.

Rich's Chimney Fix-It

15965 Jeanette St.
Southfield, MI 48075
E-mail Address: wfcnet@cris.com
Toll-Free Phone:
Phone: (810) 559-1415
Fax: (810) 557-7931
Contact:

Number of Franchises: 0
Company-Owned Units: 1
Total Units: 1

In Business Since: 1977   **Franchising Since:** 1997

Description of Operation: Brick and mortar repair and replacement.

Equity Capital Needed: $20,000

Franchise Fee: $15,000-$17,500

Royalty: $1,000 per month maximum

Advertising Co-op Fee: None

Financial Assistance: Help with third-party financing, including help with a business plan.

Management Assistance: Complete management training to help franchisees administer and manage their Chimney Fix-It franchise, including accounting procedures, billing, collection, human resource development, scheduling of work teams, hiring, firing, and so on.

Training Assistance: Four weeks of intensive training at both the franchsor's corporate location and the franchisee's location. Includes all aspects of chimney and mortar repair and restoration, marketing techniques, estimating procedures, and customer service.

Surface Doctor

6849 Fairview Rd.
Charlotte, NC 28210
E-mail Address: pswish53866@aolc.om
Toll-Free Phone: (800) 735-5055
Phone: (704) 442-0811
Fax: (704) 364-1202
Contact: Vice President Sales

Number of Franchises: 135
Company-Owned Units: 0
Total Units: 135

In Business Since: 1993   **Franchising Since:** 1994

Description of Operation: Surface Doctor is an alternative to conventional kitchen and bath remodeling at a 70-80 percent cost savings. We provide kitchen cabinet resurfacing and refacing services along with resurfacing of appliances and countertops. Our bathroom services include resurfacing of bathtubs, ceramic tile, and cultured marble. Our unique low-cost renovation techniques provide a greatly needed service for home owners, property management companies, hotels, commercial buildings, and more.

Equity Capital Needed: $10,000

Franchise Fee: $14,800

Royalty: 4-6 percent

Advertising Co-op Fee: 2 percent

Financial Assistance: Limited financing available to qualified individuals.

Management Assistance: Complete business services, which include monthly statement of accounts, P & L statements, accounts receivable statements, specialized computer software, telephone answering services, and telemarketing services.

Training Assistance: Four-week training program consisting of two weeks of home-study courses and comprehensive two weeks of hands-on technical training and business management at world headquarters in Charlotte, NC. Ongoing support, updating, newsletter, and toll-free support help line.

Surface Specialists Systems, Inc.

5168 Country Club Dr.
High Ridge, MO 63049
E-mail Address: surfspec@nothnbut.net
Toll-Free Phone: (888) 376-4468
Phone: (314) 376-4468
Fax: (314) 376-8889
Contact: Marketing/Sales Director

Number of Franchises: 26
Company-Owned Units: 0
Total Units: 26

In Business Since: 1981   **Franchising Since:** 192

Description of Operation: Whether customers have a chip, crack, gouge, burn,or scratch, or are in need of refinishing an entire surface, as a Surface Specialists franchisee, you will provide the solution to their problem. Using our proven repair and refinishing systems, which are the best in the nation, you can save customers up to 80 percent off the cost of replacing existing surfaces. You will become an expert in repairing and refinishing bathroom and kitchen surfaces, including fiberglass tubs and showers, porcelain tubs, acrylic tubs and showers,

acrylic spas, ceramic tile, cultured marble, swimming pools, and Formica countertops.

Equity Capital Needed: $4,500-$12,000

Franchise Fee: $14,500/250,000-500,000 population

Royalty: 5 percent

Advertising Co-op Fee: None

Financial Assistance: Franchisees may finance up to 15 percent of any franchise fee exceeding $10,000.

Management Assistance: Franchise fee includes operations manual; all equipment and materials to provide $10,000 in sales; a 24-hour, toll-free, franchise-dedicated phone; periodic retraining; and a quarterly newsletter.

Training Assistance: Three-week comprehensive training program conducted at home office. Includes classroom, field, and office management training.

Worldwide Refinishing Systems Inc.

1020 University Parks. Dr.
Waco, TX 76707
Toll-Free Phone: (800) 583-9099
Phone: (254) 745-2477
Fax: (254) 745-2588
Contact:

Number of Franchises: 408
Company-Owned Units: 0
Total Units: 408

In Business Since: 1970   **Franchising Since:** 1971

Description of Operation: Repairing and recoloring of ceramic, countertops, fiberglass showers, appliances, sinks, and so on.

Equity Capital Needed: $10,000-$30,000

Franchise Fee: $12,500 per 100,000 population

Royalty: 3-6 percent

Advertising Co-op Fee: 2 percent

Financial Assistance: Data not available.

Management Assistance: We provide separate 800#'s for technical and marketing assistance, regional meetings, and an annual convention. Marketing and management goals are set periodically with the marketing department.

Training Assistance: Data not available.

Construction & Remodeling— Roofing

American Roof-Brite

4492 Acworth Ind. Dr. Ste. 102
Acworth, GA 30101
Toll-Free Phone: (800) 476-9271

Phone: (770) 966-1080
Fax: (770) 975-4647
Contact: President

Number of Franchises: 11
Company-Owned Units: 1
Total Units: 12

In Business Since: 1973   **Franchising Since:** 1990

Description of Operation: Clean ugly, stained asphalt roofing shingles. Work performed for roofing manufacturers and home owners.

Equity Capital Needed: $5,995

Franchise Fee: $0

Royalty: 6 percent

Advertising Co-op Fee:

Financial Assistance: None

Management Assistance: Data not available.

Training Assistance: Phone consultation and manual with instructions.

Insulated Dry-Roof System

152 SE 5th Ave.
Hillsboro, OR 997123
Web Address: www.dryroof.com
E-mail Address: info@dryroof.com
Toll-Free Phone: (800) 779-1357
Phone: (503) 693-1619
Fax: (503) 693-1993
Contact: President

Number of Franchises: 28
Company-Owned Units: 0
Total Units: 28

In Business Since: 1989   **Franchising Since:** 1989

Description of Operation: Mobile and manufactured home roofing of a patented roofing system. Some commercial and non–mobile/manufactured residential sales.

Equity Capital Needed: $40,000-$60,000

Franchise Fee: Varies with size of the exclusive territory.

Royalty: 3 percent; minimum of $300 per month.

Advertising Co-op Fee:

Financial Assistance: None

Management Assistance: The franchisor provides initial training on business management and ongoing support through nonmandatory training meetings. Annual review of business activities and updating of business plan.

Training Assistance: We train all franchisees on marketing, selling, and installing the Insulated Dry-Roof System roof. Mandatory training prior to opening franchise territory and ongoing training after opening.

National International Roofing Corp.

11804 S. Rte. 47
Huntley, IL 60142
Toll-Free Phone: (800) 221-7663
Phone: (847) 669-3444
Fax: (847) 669-3173
Contact:

Number of Franchises: 2
Company-Owned Units: 12
Total Units: 14

In Business Since: 1991   **Franchising Since:** 1993

Description of Operation: Construction tradesman, make your roofing experience work for you! As part of the NIR Project Team, you'll own and operate your own roofing business while sharing in the benefits of cooperative marketing, shared purchasing power, a managed referral network, and more. The NIR franchise program has been designed as a network and a way for qualified entrepreneurs to build their own business futures. Individual or master franchises are now available to qualified candidates.

Equity Capital Needed: $28,600-$38,250

Franchise Fee: $17,500

Royalty: 10 percent

Advertising Co-op Fee:

Financial Assistance: No financing is provided through NIR; however, the franchisor will consult with and aid in presentation of loan package to lenders, investors, or the SBA.

Management Assistance: Data not available.

Training Assistance: NIR provides a comprehensive, confidential operations manual, a 10-day training course, which includes sales and marketing techniques, administration and financial controls, skills in roofing applications and repairs, and customer service procedures. In addition, NIR provides an 800# line, protected territories, and ongoing consulting support.

Roof Defender

5959 W. Loop South, Ste. 175, P.O. Box 27884
Bellaire, TX 77227
E-mail Address: JFHiggs@worldne.att.net
Toll-Free Phone: (800) 766-3669
Phone: (713) 661-9000
Fax: (713) 661-9096
Contact: V.P. Marketing

Number of Franchises: 1
Company-Owned Units: 0
Total Units: 1

In Business Since: 1997   **Franchising Since:** 1997

Description of Operation: Roof Defender Master franchisees will have three income streams. The first task is to franchise installers who, although they require no previous experience, will run a high-profit reroofing, deck maintenance, and roof mold removal business using newly developed hi-tech systems. The second task is to choose local building supply stores to retail the exclusive reroofing products. The third function is to service the branches of National accounts in the exclusive area. National accounts will be set up by Roof Defender National although profits from these accounts go to the Master Frachisee. This opportunity has a high-income probability. Knowledge of the industry is not necessary because extensive and comprehensive training and field support are provided by Roof Defender National.

Equity Capital Needed: $35,000-50,000

Franchise Fee: Varies: $25,000 and up

Royalty: Data not available

Advertising Co-op Fee: 0

Financial Assistance: None

Management Assistance: Daily ongoing assistance provided to franchisees, by the Internet and telephone.

Training Assistance: Initial one-week training plus ongoing training as needed.

Construction & Remodeling—Windows

Screenmobile Corp., The

457 W. Allen
San Dimas, CA 91773
Web Address: www.screenmobile.com
E-mail Address: mmwal@earthlink.net
Toll-Free Phone:
Phone: (909) 394-4581
Fax: (909) 394-0273
Contact: President

Number of Franchises: 50
Company-Owned Units: 1
Total Units: 51

In Business Since: 1980   **Franchising Since:** 1982

Description of Operation: We screen at your place. A mobile window and door screening business. We specialize in solar screens and heavy-duty, high-quality screen doors.

Equity Capital Needed: $28,000

Franchise Fee: $49,300

Royalty: 5 percent of gross sales

Advertising Co-op Fee: 0

Financial Assistance: We finance $24,300 of the franchise fee.

Management Assistance: Classroom training—total turnkey setup. Field training and marketing training are also provided.

Training Assistance:

Budget Blinds, Inc.

1570 Corporate Dr., Ste. B
Costa Mesa, CA 92626
Web Address: www.budgetblinds.com
E-mail Address: bbinfo@budgetblinds.com
Toll-Free Phone: (800) 420-5374
Phone: (714) 708-3338
Fax: (714) 708-3339
Contact: **Executive Vice President**

Number of Franchises: 155
Company-Owned Units: 3
Total Units: 158

In Business Since: 1992   **Franchising Since:** 1994

Description of Operation: Total window covering company with mobile units.

Equity Capital Needed: $40,000

Franchise Fee: $24,950

Royalty: 5-7 percent

Advertising Co-op Fee: 1-3 percent

Financial Assistance: Outside financing.

Management Assistance: Unlisted 800# hot line, newsletters, regional meetings, and annual meetings.

Training Assistance: One week, all expenses paid.

Construction & Remodeling— Miscellaneous

Aire Serv

1010 University Parks Dr.
Waco, TX 76707
Web Address: www.aireserv.com
Toll-Free Phone: (800) 583-2662
Phone: (254) 757-2662
Fax: (254) 745-2546
Contact: **President/General Manager**

Number of Franchises: 6
Company-Owned Units: 0
Total Units: 6

In Business Since: 1993   **Franchising Since:** 1994

Description of Operation: National heating, ventilating, and air-conditioning franchise organization, focused on the residential and light commercial service and replacement market. Franchisees are typically progressive, professional, state-licensed HVAC contractors.

Equity Capital Needed: $20,000-$100,000

Franchise Fee: $12,500+

Royalty: 6-3 percent

Advertising Co-op Fee:

Financial Assistance: Financing is available.

Management Assistance: Aire Serv franchisees are provided with extensive sales, marketing, operations, and management material, systems, and support. Ongoing support is provided through national conferences, regional consultants, and a toll-free hot line for immediate counseling and assistance.

Training Assistance: Intensive sales, marketing, and management training is provided for new franchisees (and their new hires). Additional training is provided throughout the year with four national conferences, each focused on a topic of concern to the HVAC contractor.

Ambic Building Inspection Consultants

1200 Rte. 130
Robbinsville, NJ 08691
Toll-Free Phone: (800) 882-6242
Phone: (609) 448-3900
Fax: (609) 426-1230
Contact: **President**

Number of Franchises: 20
Company-Owned Units: 0
Total Units: 20

In Business Since: 1987   **Franchising Since:** 1988

Description of Operation: Home and building inspections and related environmental tests of residential, commercial, and industrial properties.

Equity Capital Needed: $5,000-$10,000

Franchise Fee: $10,000-$16,500

Royalty: 6 percent ongoing

Advertising Co-op Fee: 3 percent

Financial Assistance: Ambic will assist in locating financing.

Management Assistance: Toll-free "Help line," marketing assistance, technical support, computer software updates, public relations and marketing material, business operations, and site visits.

Training Assistance: Approximately four weeks, including inspector training, hands-on and classroom experience, business operations, computer, public relations and marketing, customer response, and initial marketing campaign.

American Restoration Services

2061 Monongahela Ave.
Pittsburgh, PA 15218
Toll-Free Phone: (800) 245-1617
Phone: (412) 351-7100

Fax: (412) 351-2544
Contact: President

Number of Franchises: 267
Company-Owned Units: 1
Total Units: 268

In Business Since: 1970   **Franchising Since:** 1976

Description of Operation: General restoration of homes and commercial structures, using our unique line of cleaning and sealing products.

Equity Capital Needed: $30,000

Franchise Fee: $10,000

Royalty: $1,500 per year

Advertising Co-op Fee:

Financial Assistance: Total cost paid to American Restoration is $22,500, of which $10,000 is through a lease, and $5,000 is company financed.

Management Assistance: Phone support, on-site visits, and correspondence with master dealers.

Training Assistance: A.R.S. trains dealers in marketing, sales, accounting, and equipment operation.

B-Dry System

1341 Copley Rd.
Akron, OH 44320
Toll-Free Phone: (800) 321-0985
Phone: (330) 867-2576
Fax: (330) 867-7693
Contact: Vice President

Number of Franchises: 69
Company-Owned Units: 0
Total Units: 69

In Business Since: 1958   **Franchising Since:** 1978

Description of Operation: B-Dry System licensees receive territorial rights to their own area(s). Licensees are trained to install B-Dry's exclusive patented interior drainage system, designed to alleviate basement water leakage. The B-Dry system offers its customers a full life of the structure warranty on areas waterproofed. Transferable from owner to owner.

Equity Capital Needed: $25,000-$45,000

Franchise Fee: $15,000-$60,000 ($60,000 area with 1,000,000 pop.)

Royalty: 6 percent

Advertising Co-op Fee:

Financial Assistance: B-Dry System will finance up to 7.5 percent of the franchise fee with no interest. The balance is payable at a rate of $150 per installed job.

Management Assistance: B-Dry licensees receive managerial assistance through regional seminars, workshops, audio- and videotapes, on-site visits, and teleconferencing.

Training Assistance: At B-Dry System's training center in Akron, OH, you will be taught technical basement waterproofing procedures, with the aid of one-on-one lessons, written manuals, audiotape and videotape presentations, classroom discussion, and on-the-job instruction. Ongoing field training is also provided regularly, and the monthly newsletters keep you further informed about refinements to the system. You will also receive B-Dry's advertising package of promotional materials, honed by 30 years of experience.

California Closet Company

1000 4th St.
San Rafael, CA 94901
Toll-Free Phone:
Phone: (415) 433-9999
Fax: (415) 433-2911
Contact: Franchise Development Manager

Number of Franchises: 94
Company-Owned Units: 3
Total Units: 97

In Business Since: 1978   **Franchising Since:** 1982

Description of Operation: California Closets sells and installs custom storage and organization systems for the home and office: closets, garages, entertainment centers, home offices, and small business offices.

Equity Capital Needed: $75,000-$200,000

Franchise Fee: $9,000-$38,000

Royalty: 6 percent

Advertising Co-op Fee:

Financial Assistance: Outside financing for equipment purchases on start-up.

Management Assistance: Data not available.

Training Assistance: Three-week training program for new franchisees. Site selection; site build-out assistance; equipment purchase assistance; and on-site, start-up assistance.

Certa Propainters

1776 Old Spring House Lane
Atlanta, GA 30338
Toll-Free Phone:
Phone: (770) 455-4300
Fax: (770) 983-9884
Contact:

Number of Franchises: 39
Company-Owned Units: 0
Total Units: 39

In Business Since: 1992   **Franchising Since:** 1993

Description of Operation: Full-service residential and commercial painting franchise. Training, ongoing support, marketing, and business development. Ideal franchisee has little or no painting experience, but has

solid leadership and management abilities and skills. We are putting business men and women into the painting business.

Equity Capital Needed: $25,000-$30,000

Franchise Fee: $15,000

Royalty: $9,000 1st year; $12,000 2nd year and thereafter

Advertising Co-op Fee:

Financial Assistance: The franchisor will finance up to 50 percent of the franchise fee, and suppliers will finance other specific costs as well.

Management Assistance: Initial training: two weeks. Weekly follow-ups until year three. Three-day annual conference, quarterly reviews, and annual budgeting. Monthly newsletters, weekly meetings, and monthly marketing planning.

Training Assistance: Two weeks of training prior to start-up; quarterly training in field. After year one, advanced training is available to franchisees and their employees. Manuals, videos, and one-on-one training.

Closet Factory, The

12800 S. Broadway
Los Angeles, CA 90061
Toll-Free Phone: (800) 692-5673
Phone: (310) 516-7000
Fax: (310) 538-2676
Contact: Vice President/Franchise Director

Number of Franchises: 29
Company-Owned Units: 1
Total Units: 30

In Business Since: 1983 **Franchising Since:** 1985

Description of Operation: The Closet Factory markets, designs, manufactures, constructs, and installs custom closets and storage systems for consumers and sells other related products and services.

Equity Capital Needed: Total investment about $185,000; $100,000 liquid.

Franchise Fee: $39,500

Royalty: 5.75 percent

Advertising Co-op Fee:

Financial Assistance: The franchisor does not provide any financing, but equipment and vans may be financed by franchisees through their sources.

Management Assistance: Closet Factory provides complete operations and sales manuals, collateral, advertising materials, and sales aids. Franchise newsletter and meetings. Perpetual on-site and telephone assistance.

Training Assistance: Two weeks at our Los Angeles, CA, headquarters. On-site preopening training. Additional training is available if necessary.

Closettec

55 Carnegie Row
Norwood, MA 02062
Toll-Free Phone: (800) 365-2021
Phone: (781) 769-9997
Fax: (781) 769-9996
Contact: President

Number of Franchises: 17
Company-Owned Units: 0
Total Units: 17

In Business Since: 1985 **Franchising Since:** 1986

Description of Operation: Marketing, sales, design, manufacturing, and installation of residential and commercial closet systems, storage systems, home/office/garage systems, and so on.

Equity Capital Needed: $15,000-$185,000

Franchise Fee: $30,000

Royalty: 5.5 percent

Advertising Co-op Fee:

Financial Assistance: None

Management Assistance: Initial 7-10 days for opening of new operation. Continuing information via "Hottecs" and "Memotecs," annual conferences, and franchise interaction with 24-hour hot line.

Training Assistance: A minimum two weeks of training at corporate training facility for owner and all staff. If desired, 7-10 days on-site.

Comprehensive Painting

4705 Chromium
Colorado Springs, CO 80918
Toll-Free Phone:
Phone: (719) 599-8983
Fax: (719) 599-7933
Contact: President

Number of Franchises: 1
Company-Owned Units: 1
Total Units: 2

In Business Since: 1986 **Franchising Since:** 1992

Description of Operation: Comprehensive Painting provides residential home painting services and wood restoration, which includes treatment of decks, homes, wallpapering, and painting services.

Equity Capital Needed: $11,500-$30,000 (including fee).

Franchise Fee: $9,500

Royalty: 6 percent

Advertising Co-op Fee:

Financial Assistance: Royalty may be partially financed to qualified applicants. Equipment and signage financed by Sherwin Williams Paint Company to qualified applicants.

©JIST Works, Inc., Indianapolis, IN 46202

Management Assistance: Assistance includes customer newsletter, semiannual advertising promotions, database, and accounting services, as well as ongoing marketing with four-color documentation and the use of videos for training and marketing.

Training Assistance: Six to eight weeks of personal training in marketing, management, sales, estimating, applications, and color recommending, as well as customer relations and personnel management.

Eldorado Stone Corporation

P.O. Box 489
Carnation, WA 98014
E-mail Address: general@eldoradostone.com
Toll-Free Phone: (800) 925-1491
Phone: (425) 333-6722
Fax: (425) 333-4755
Contact: Director of Franchising

Number of Franchises: 26
Company-Owned Units: 0
Total Units: 26

In Business Since: 1969 **Franchising Since:** 1969

Description of Operation: Eldorado Store licenses the technology to manufacture and distribute lightweight concrete stone veneers and landscape stepstones and pavers. The products look just like their natural counterparts. The products are easy to install and very durable. For use in exterior or interior applications. Franchisees market and distribute through masonry and building suppliers and contractor direct.

Equity Capital Needed: $80,000-$149,000

Franchise Fee: $50,000

Royalty: 10 cents per square foot

Advertising Co-op Fee: 0

Financial Assistance: None

Management Assistance: Ongoing technical and R & D support.

Training Assistance: One week at training facility in Washington State. One week opening assistance at franchisee's facility.

Kitchen Saver of Canada

94 Besser Ct.
London, ON N6E 1K7
Toll-Free Phone: (800) 265-0933
Phone: (519) 686-8820
Fax: (519) 685-7283
Contact: President

Number of Franchises: 17
Company-Owned Units: 0
Total Units: 17

In Business Since: 1986 **Franchising Since:** 1986

Description of Operation: Manufacturer of cabinet doors and drawer fronts for refacing purposes.

Equity Capital Needed: Varies.

Franchise Fee: Varies.

Royalty: 0 percent

Advertising Co-op Fee:

Financial Assistance: Not available.

Management Assistance: Set-up procedures, accounting package, and on-site assistance.

Training Assistance: Measuring, training, and sales training.

Nationwide Floor and Window Covering

15965 Jeanette
Southfield, MI 48075
Web Address: www.wfcnet.com
E-mail Address: wfcnet@crisis.com
Toll-Free Phone:
Phone: (810) 559-1415
Fax: (810) 557-7931
Contact:

Number of Franchises: 15
Company-Owned Units: 0
Total Units: 15

In Business Since: 1992 **Franchising Since:** 1992

Description of Operation: We are a mobile floor covering and window treatment franchise. We provide a free shop-at-home service to today's time-starved consumer. Our franchisees bring carpet, vinyl, hardwood, ceramic tile, area rugs, and a huge selection of name brand window treatment samples right to their customer's home or office.

Equity Capital Needed: $22,477

Franchise Fee: $16,900

Royalty: 5 percent

Advertising Co-op Fee: None

Financial Assistance:

Management Assistance:

Training Assistance:

Perma Glaze

1638 S. Research Loop Road Ste. 160
Tucson, AZ 85710
Web Address: www.permaglaze.com
E-mail Address: permaglaze@the river.com
Toll-Free Phone: (800) 332-7397
Phone: (520) 722-9718
Fax: (520) 296-4393
Contact: President/V.P. International Development

Number of Franchises: 187
Company-Owned Units:
Total Units: 187

In Business Since: 1978 **Franchising Since:** 1981

Description of Operation: Perma-Glaze, the most progressive company in multisurface restoration, specializes in the renewal of worn/damaged fixtures and surfaces, including bathtubs, tile, porcelain, metal, acrylic, fiberglass, appliances, Formica, cultured marble, countertops, floors, and much more. Investment provides four distinct profit opportunities in one all-inclusive business package. Perma-Glaze licensed representatives provide valued services to hotels/motels, private residences, apartments, schools, hospitals, contractors, property managers, and many others. Experience is not necessary.

Equity Capital Needed:

Franchise Fee: $19,500-$39,500

Royalty:

Advertising Co-op Fee:

Financial Assistance:

Management Assistance:

Training Assistance: Extensive initial training; aggressive advertising and marketing campaigns; intensified field training; an extremely active research and development department; a continual support structure with regional meetings; newsletters; monthly technical tips; toll-free, 24-hour assistance; and so on.

Perma-Dry Systems

P.O. Box 2697
Darmouth, NS B2W 4R4
Toll-Free Phone: (800) 565-5325
Phone: (902) 468-1700
Fax: (902) 468-7474
Contact:

Number of Franchises: 17
Company-Owned Units: 1
Total Units: 18

In Business Since: 1983 **Franchising Since:** 1990

Description of Operation: Permacrete and Perma-Dry Systems Limited provide customers with a permanent solution to water control and shut-off problems through guaranteed concrete restoration services.

Equity Capital Needed: $35,000-$40,000

Franchise Fee: $18,500-$37,000

Royalty: 4 percent, plus 2 percent advertising fee.

Advertising Co-op Fee:

Financial Assistance: Not available.

Management Assistance: Managerial assistance to the franchisee includes reports of improvements in the Perma-Dry System, such as administrative, bookkeeping,

accounting, inventory control, and general operating procedures.

Training Assistance: The training for new franchisees includes a minimum of five days of hands-on training, procedures, bookkeeping, personnel management, basic marketing, and public relations techniques.

Profusion Systems

2851 S. Parker Rd., # 650
Aurora, CO 80014
Toll-Free Phone: (800) 777-3873
Phone: (303) 337-1949
Fax: (303) 337-0790
Contact: Director of Franchising

Number of Franchises: 218
Company-Owned Units: 2
Total Units: 220

In Business Since: 1980 **Franchising Since:** 1982

Description of Operation: Plastic, vinyl, leather, and laminate repair. Servicing commercial businesses such as restaurants, hotels, airports, hospitals, and so on. Franchisees can offer lifetime repairs on tears, rips, cuts, and burns. Mobile repair capability—almost all work performed on-site.

Equity Capital Needed: $15,000-$30,000

Franchise Fee: $20,500+

Royalty: 6 percent

Advertising Co-op Fee:

Financial Assistance: After qualification, the franchisor may finance up to 50 percent of the franchise fee.

Management Assistance: Franchisees receive operations, technical, and field supervision manuals, plus 800# telephone assistance.

Training Assistance: Nine days at headquarters include technical, management, sales, and accounting training. Four days of field supervision follow approximately six weeks after completion of initial training.

Screen Machine, The

19636 8th St. W.
Sonoma, CA 95476
Web Address: www.screenmachine.com
Toll-Free Phone:
Phone: (707) 996-5551
Fax: (707) 996-0139
Contact: President

Number of Franchises: 18
Company-Owned Units: 1
Total Units: 19

In Business Since: 1986 **Franchising Since:** 1988

Description of Operation: Mobile unit doing job-site window and door screening (new or rescreen) and other related services.

Equity Capital Needed: $47,000-$63,000

Franchise Fee: $25,000

Royalty: 5 percent

Advertising Co-op Fee:

Financial Assistance: None

Management Assistance: Training includes marketing, accounting, operations, and advertising.

Training Assistance: Each prospective franchisee is thoroughly trained in the various aspects of conducting The Screen Machine business. This training includes marketing strategies, advertising techniques, basic accounting methods, operational procedures, and hands-on technical instruction on how to custom-fabricate screens and perform screen repair and other related work. To ensure smooth operation, each franchisee is provided with advertising materials, audiovisual training, and new products information.

Service Center

7655 E. Gelding Dr., # A-3
Scottsdale, AZ 85260
Toll-Free Phone: (800) 729-7424
Phone: (602) 998-1616
Fax: (602) 948-7308
Contact: President

Number of Franchises: 18
Company-Owned Units: 3
Total Units: 21

In Business Since: 1991   **Franchising Since:** 1992

Description of Operation: Supply various services to both residential and commercial customers. Franchise creates a shell or umbrella, within which various skilled tradespeople can perform services. The franchisee is the management head of the company, and various trades are performed by independent service people. The franchisee essentially performs the business management expertise and provides the capital, while trained tehnicians actually perform the work.

Equity Capital Needed: $39,000-$51,000

Franchise Fee: $25,000

Royalty: 7 percent plus $75 per month for software maintenance

Advertising Co-op Fee:

Financial Assistance: Service Center will carry 50 percent of the $25,000 franchise fee. Terms are five years at 8 percent, with no interest on repayments on the note during the first year of operation. The note is secured only by the francise. No personal guarantee.

Management Assistance: Service Center will literally create a turnkey business so that on the first day of operation, there will be technicians to run the calls, as well as staff to answer the phones, dispatch technicians, and run the office. The advertising program will be in place, and customers will be calling for service—in short, a complete operating business.

Training Assistance: Each franchise and his or her staff will be taught every function of the business operation. Should any staff member need to be replaced, each of the other people trained in the operation will be able to assume the duties of the missing person. In addition, we are tied to each franchise office by modem and can operate a remote site franchise from our corporate office.

Stained Glass Overlay

1827 N. Case St.
Orange, CA 92665
Toll-Free Phone: (800) 944-4746
Phone: (714) 974-6124
Fax: (714) 974-6529
Contact: Vice President of Franchising

Number of Franchises: 351
Company-Owned Units: 0
Total Units: 351

In Business Since: 1974   **Franchising Since:** 1981

Description of Operation: Stained Glass Overlay is the world's largest franchisor of decorative glass products, with locations in 32 countries. The exclusive SGO-patented process can decorate any glass or acrylic surface, adding incomparable beauty to homes, churches, restaurants, hotels, and so on. We are looking for industrious, motivated individuals who have the desire to own their own successful business.

Equity Capital Needed: $45,000-$80,000

Franchise Fee: $34,000

Royalty: 5 percent

Advertising Co-op Fee:

Financial Assistance: SGO is currently offering financing, in the United States only, for up to $20,000 of the purchase price ($45,000), payable over a period of up to three years and at an interest rate of 10 percent per year. Because SGO has introduced this financing program on a trial basis only, there is no certainty about how long it will be offered.

Management Assistance: In addition to the comprehensive training program, we offer new franchisees a follow-up visit by one of our management team to their SGO studio between three to six months after opening. The purpose is to help them overcome any sort of difficulties in operating their business by hands-on, field training.

Training Assistance: Training includes all aspects of operating a successful SGO franchise, with emphasis on the SGO process, marketing, sales, and management of the business.

Dry Cleaning & Laundries

Comet One-Hour Cleaners

406 W. Division St. (Hwy. 80)
Arlington, TX 76011
Toll-Free Phone:
Phone: (817) 461-3555
Fax: (817) 861-4779
Contact: Sales Representative

Number of Franchises: 267
Company-Owned Units: 11
Total Units: 278

In Business Since: 1955   **Franchising Since:** 1967

Description of Operation: Dry cleaning and laundry packages. A complete turnkey operation. Our service includes site evaluation, market analyses, floor plan design and layout, two week training program, grand opening, advertising, and on-hand consultation in-store after store opening. Parts, service, and support for all equipment sold. All questions, parts, and service are just a phone call away. Members of IFA, IFI, and TLDA.

Equity Capital Needed: $135,000-$200,000

Franchise Fee: $15,000

Royalty: $1,000 per year

Advertising Co-op Fee:

Financial Assistance: Financing through Stephens Finance, Little Rock, AR. Five-year fixed rate.

Management Assistance: Part of training process. Consulting available as needed.

Training Assistance: Two weeks of comprehensive training in all facets of store operation—use of equipment, maintenance, marketing strategies, bookkeeping, and customer service. Training provided in local store and in franchisee's store after opening.

Dry Cleaning Station

1000 Shelard Pkwy., Ste. 320
Minneapolis, MN 55426
Toll-Free Phone: (800) 655-8134
Phone: (612) 541-0832
Fax: (612) 542-2246
Contact: CEO

Number of Franchises: 16
Company-Owned Units: 3
Total Units: 19

In Business Since: 1987   **Franchising Since:** 1993

Description of Operation: Value priced high quality dry cleaning plant stores and drop stores.

Equity Capital Needed: Not provided

Franchise Fee: $22,500

Royalty: 5 percent (4 percent-3 percent-2 percent)

Advertising Co-op Fee: 0

Financial Assistance: Resources for up to 90 percent financing lease or financing through third parties.

Management Assistance: Full home office and on-site training. Field operational profit reviews.

Training Assistance:

Duds 'N' Suds

1000 Shelard Parkway, Ste. 320
Minneapolis, MN 55426
Toll-Free Phone:
Phone: (612) 541-1514
Fax:
Contact: Vice President

Number of Franchises: 80
Company-Owned Units: 6
Total Units: 86

In Business Since: 1989   **Franchising Since:** 1989

Description of Operation: Coin-operated laundry with amenities. Large screen TV, TV lounge, pool table, video arcade games, snack bar, drop-off dry cleaning, and wash-dry-fold. Some locations have beer in snack bar.

Equity Capital Needed: $40,000

Franchise Fee: $20,000

Royalty: 5 percent

Advertising Co-op Fee:

Financial Assistance: We will help a franchisee locate financing. We construct a professional business plan and present the business plan to locate financial institutions. We also have leasing resources. SBA loans are very popular among previous franchisees of Duds 'N' Suds.

Management Assistance: Ongoing support both by telephone and visits to your location. A franchise advisory board is also part of our system. A yearly franchise-franchisee convention. Periodic training updates. At least one yearly visit from headquarters personnel.

Training Assistance: Each new franchisee attends a five-day training course at one of our educational facilities. Franchisees learn all parts of the operation. Both classroom and store time. A five-volume operations manual is at the heart of the system.

Pressed 4 Time

124 Boston Post Rd.
Sudbury, MA 01776
E-mail Address: franchiseinfo@pressed4time.com
Toll-Free Phone: (800) 423-8711
Phone: (978) 443-9200
Fax: (978) 443-0709
Contact: President

Number of Franchises: 98
Company-Owned Units: 0
Total Units: 98

©JIST Works, Inc., Indianapolis, IN 46202

In Business Since: 1987   **Franchising Since:** 1990

Description of Operation: Dry cleaning and shoe repair pick-up and delivery service, serving executives and staff at local businesses. A high repeat business, a low stress operation (five day workweek, local cleaning plants do the actual cleaning) and incomparable training and support.

Equity Capital Needed: $14,000-$21,000

Franchise Fee: $12,900

Royalty: The greater of 3.5 percent or $300/month

Advertising Co-op Fee:

Financial Assistance: Not available.

Management Assistance: Ongoing support is available by telephone and in the territory by special request. All necessary supplies, forms and materials for the operation are available. Complete training, procedures and operations manual.

Training Assistance: Training includes two days at the corporate offices, including one day of hands-on operations, the corporate vehicle and one day of intensive classroom training, covering start-up, record keeping, administration, dry cleaning, operations and sales. Also, two days of training in the franchisee's territory, consisting of marketing training in the field to establish initial accounts.

Apparelmaster

P.O. Box 62687
Cincinnati, OH 45262
Toll-Free Phone: (800) 543-1678
Phone: (513) 772-7721
Fax: (513) 772-5616
Contact: Vice President

Number of Franchises: 175
Company-Owned Units: 0
Total Units: 175

In Business Since: 1974   **Franchising Since:** 1974

Description of Operation: Apparelmaster enables dry cleaners and/or launderers to establish an industrial uniform and dust control rental business.

Equity Capital Needed: $15,000-$20,000

Franchise Fee: $15,000

Royalty: 6 percent, 2 percent, 1 percent

Advertising Co-op Fee:

Financial Assistance: Installment plan of $575 per month.

Management Assistance: We offer follow-up consultation visits through the life of the agreement, 800# hot line assistance, special reports, monthly information mailings, suppliers' corporate discount savings, and large buying power.

Training Assistance: We provide three weeks at the licensee's place of business, plus yearly visits.

Clean 'n' Press

500 Airport Blvd. Ste. 100
Burlingame, CA 94010
Toll-Free Phone: (800) 237-1711
Phone: (650) 579-6674
Fax: (650) 579-0650
Contact: President

Number of Franchises: 47
Company-Owned Units: 0
Total Units: 47

In Business Since: 1991   **Franchising Since:** 1991

Description of Operation: Clean 'N' Press is a franchisor of dry cleaning and laundry stores and plants. We also offer the "Home Express" pick-up and delivery service. We provide franchisees with a complete turnkey system for everything from a single "Home Express" van to a multiple store/plant combination. Our plant with satellite stores is highly efficient. We also provide marketing assistance.

Equity Capital Needed: $22,000-$200,000+

Franchise Fee: $10,000-$25,000+

Royalty: 9 percent

Advertising Co-op Fee:

Financial Assistance: Third-party financing assistance is available.

Management Assistance: Each franchisee will receive assistance regarding company-approved location, forms, management, accounting, and marketing. All operational aspects are covered by the instruction manual.

Training Assistance: We provide an extensive, one- to two-week training period at an existing operation, which varies depending on the background and experiences of the franchisee. Complete operations manuals are provided.

One Hour Martinizing Dry Cleaning

2005 Ross Ave.
Cincinnati, OH 45212
Toll-Free Phone: (800) 827-0345
Phone: (513) 351-6211
Fax: (513) 731-5513
Contact: Vice President

Number of Franchises: 844
Company-Owned Units: 0
Total Units: 844

In Business Since: 1949   **Franchising Since:** 1949

Description of Operation: New franchisees receive the full benefit of One Hour Martinizing's 40 plus years of experience in site-selection, training, and marketing. Martinizing focuses totally on assisting its franchisees before, during, and after opening. Martinizing offers instant brand awareness in any market for new franchisees.

Equity Capital Needed: $65,000 (minimum)

Franchise Fee: $25,000

Royalty: 4 percent

Advertising Co-op Fee:

Financial Assistance: Veterans of U.S. Armed Forces are offered financing of the initial fee (VetFran). Others are assisted in locating funding sources, but direct financing is not provided.

Management Assistance: We provide complete start-up assistance, a comprehensive training program, location/site assistance with ads, computerized demographics capabilities, grand opening marketing package, ongoing local store and marketwide promotional programs, and field and operations assistance.

Training Assistance: We offer a three-week, comprehensive training program, which includes one week of classroom training and two weeks of in-store training, training manuals, and operational and marketing ideas.

Educational Products & Services—Business

Academy of Learning

5 Bank St. Ste. 202
Attleboro, MA 02703
Toll-Free Phone:
Phone: (508) 222-0000
Fax: (508) 222-0005
Contact:

Number of Franchises: 78
Company-Owned Units: 2
Total Units: 80

In Business Since: 1987   **Franchising Since:** 1987

Description of Operation: Computer and business skills training centers, using unique "Integrated Learning System." This system provides short, effective self-paced computer and related courses for the office, using a combination of audiotapes, computers, original software, and workbooks. This method of training gives students full control over their attendance, pace, and time of learning. Facilitators are on-site at all times, to assist, advise, and motivate students.

Equity Capital Needed:

Franchise Fee: $41,000

Royalty: 0 percent

Advertising Co-op Fee:

Financial Assistance: Assistance in obtaining bank financing.

Management Assistance: Full assistance in locating premises, lease negotiations, equipment purchases, and miscellaneous applications as needed. Franchisee will receive a full "Administration Start-Up Kit," comprising all forms needed in the day-to-day running of the business. Comprehensive operations manual provided, along with ongoing newsletters and updates from home office.

Training Assistance: Up to three weeks of in-house and on-site training in marketing and operations provided. On-site support in initial set-up of operation and ongoing support. Both personal and home-office hot line.

Alamo Learning Systems

3160 Crow Canyon Rd. Ste. 280
San Ramon, CA 94583
Web Address: www.alamols.com
E-mail Address: alamols@alo.com
Toll-Free Phone: (800) 829-8081
Phone: (510) 277-1818
Fax: (510) 277-1919
Contact: President

Number of Franchises: 13
Company-Owned Units: 0
Total Units: 13

In Business Since: 1976   **Franchising Since:** 1993

Description of Operation: International only. Alamo is an international leader in corporate education. We do business with 200 of the Fortune 500 companies. We specialize in IOSO 1400, QS 9000, process improvement consulting, rational thinking skills, innovation, and fast-track ISO 9000 registration.

Equity Capital Needed: $50,000

Franchise Fee: $200,000

Royalty: 7 percent

Advertising Co-op Fee:

Financial Assistance: None

Management Assistance: Alamo provides franchisee with complete turnkey operation, including modem for proposal writing, trained consultants and instructors, sales support, and national marketing and telemarketing services.

Training Assistance: Complete program for sales, product knowledge, and train-the-trainer instruction. Also, ongoing training support and client management systems.

Citizens Against Crime

111 Jupiter Rd. Ste. 101C
Plano, TX 75074
E-mail Address: cacnat@comutech.net
Toll-Free Phone: (800) 466-1010
Phone: (972) 578-2287
Fax: (972) 509-0054
Contact: President

Number of Franchises: 24
Company-Owned Units: 1
Total Units: 25

In Business Since: 1980   **Franchising Since:** 1986

Description of Operation: CAC is a recognized leader in the field of safety education. Our professionally trained speakers present the program "Don't Be the Next Victim" to businesses and organizations within each franchisee's protected geographic territory. The acclaimed program discusses ways to avoid, escape, or survive crime. Profits are generated from the sale of high-quality safety items to seminar participants.

Equity Capital Needed: $10,000 (in addition to franchise fee).

Franchise Fee: $12,500

Royalty: 0 percent

Advertising Co-op Fee:

Financial Assistance: Up to 50 percent of the franchise fee may be financed.

Management Assistance: We provide phone support, a personal coach for each franchisee, two weeks of training when the franchise is purchased, and a minimum of two trainings per year for management issues. Specialized retreats for improving sales skills and management skills.

Training Assistance: We offer training in sales, marketing, operations, interviewing, hiring and training new employees, media, public relations, crime prevention, and running a small business. Training is provided by video, audio, and interaction with a corporate trainer. One week of training, held at corporate headquarters, and one week in franchisee's office.

Crestcom International, Ltd.

6900 E. Belleview Ave.
Englewood, CO 80111
Web Address: www.crestcom.com
E-mail Address: crestcom@ix.netcom.com
Toll-Free Phone: (800) 276-5439
Phone: (303) 267-8200
Fax: (303) 267-8207
Contact: Director of International Marketing

Number of Franchises: 101
Company-Owned Units: 0
Total Units: 101

In Business Since: 1987   **Franchising Since:** 1991

Description of Operation: Crestcom International, Ltd., is the business opportunity for executive-level individuals. Crestcom is a world leader in management sales and personnel training. Crestcom franchisees specialize in marketing/delivering video-based, live facilitated management and sales training. The videos feature internationally renowned training personalities. Crestcom franchisees are active in more than 40 countries. The training is available

in 20+ language versions. Many of the world's best-maintained companies are using Crestcom dynamic and unique training. Crestcom offers qualified applicants the opportunity to attend Crestcom franchisee training before making a decision to become a franchisee.

Equity Capital Needed: $9,355-19,860

Franchise Fee: $35,000 Standard /$52,500 Executive

Royalty: 1.5 percent

Advertising Co-op Fee: None

Financial Assistance: Data not provided

Management Assistance: Crestcom offers a lead referral program, ongoing training, training for franchisees' employees, newsletters, awards and incentive programs, and regional and international conferences.

Training Assistance: Crestcom offers qualified applicants the opportunity to attend a week to ten days of franchisee training (includes attending actual training seminars with Crestcom clients, as well as classroom and field training with a Crestcom representative) before making a decision to become a franchisee.

Executrain

1000 Abernathy Rd. Ste. 400
Atlanta, GA 30328
Toll-Free Phone: (800) 843-6984
Phone: (770) 667-7700
Fax: (770) 665-2000
Contact: Franchise Sales Representative

Number of Franchises: 59
Company-Owned Units: 3
Total Units: 61

In Business Since: 1984   **Franchising Since:** 1987

Description of Operation: Executrain is the worldwide computer training leader, specializing in the education of business professionals. We teach clients how to use popular business-related software through hands-on classroom training.

Equity Capital Needed: $150,000-$200,000

Franchise Fee: $30,000 for a U.S. franchise; $50,000, master

Royalty: 6-9 percent

Advertising Co-op Fee:

Financial Assistance: For the U.S. franchises, $20,000 of the $30,000 franchise fee is financed over a two-year period.

Management Assistance: General management training is provided for all franchise owners, focusing on business planning. Continual training and support are provided.

Training Assistance: Sales training, instructor training, management information systems training, and leadership training are all provided continually for franchisees and their employees to attend, depending on the franchise growth stage.

Gwynne Learning Academy

1432 W. Emerald Ste. 735
Mesa, AZ 85202
Toll-Free Phone:
Phone: (602) 644-1434
Fax: (602) 644-1434
Contact: Treasurer

Number of Franchises: 14
Company-Owned Units: 1
Total Units: 15

In Business Since: 1991   **Franchising Since:** 1991

Description of Operation: Video-based, interactive communications training, based on the latest scientific training technology for individuals and blue chip groups in business, government, and education.

Equity Capital Needed: $45,000

Franchise Fee: $25,000

Royalty: 7 percent

Advertising Co-op Fee:

Financial Assistance: Indirect financial assistance is available.

Management Assistance: The franchisee is assisted with site selection, lease negotiations, record keeping materials, and an initial training session.

Training Assistance: A seven-day initial training session is provided to all new franchisees.

New Horizons Computer Learning Center

1231 E. Dyer Rd., Ste. 110
Santa Ana, CA 92705
Web Address: www.newhorizons.com
Toll-Free Phone:
Phone: (714) 438-9491
Fax: (714) 432-9491
Contact: Director of North American Franchise Sales

Number of Franchises: 210
Company-Owned Units: 8
Total Units: 218

In Business Since: 1982   **Franchising Since:** 1992

Description of Operation: New Horizons Computer Learning Center is a complete PC, Macintosh, Novell, and UNIX training company. You provide one-day and two-day classes to businesses and individuals at your center or at the client's location.

Equity Capital Needed: $250,000-$400,000

Franchise Fee: $20,000-$100,000

Royalty: 6 percent

Advertising Co-op Fee:

Financial Assistance: We finance 50 percent of the franchise fee for one year with interest at 1.5 percent per annum.

Management Assistance: Franchisees are trained for three weeks at the headquarters and one week at their center on all aspects of running the business.

Training Assistance: Same as above.

Success Motivation Institute

1600 Lake Air Dr. P.O. Box 2508
Waco, TX 76710
Web Address: www.success-motivation.com
Toll-Free Phone: (800) 678-6103
Phone: (817) 776-1230
Fax: (817) 741-0001
Contact: Marketing Director

Number of Franchises: 700
Company-Owned Units: 0
Total Units: 700

In Business Since: 1960   **Franchising Since:** 1962

Description of Operation: We are the world leader in self-improvement programs, such as personal goal setting, sales management training, management training, sales training, time management, and personal effectiveness. As an SMI representative, an individual receives the benefit of 32 years of experience, comprehensive training, and ongoing support.

Equity Capital Needed: $50-$650

Franchise Fee: 0

Royalty: 0 percent

Advertising Co-op Fee:

Financial Assistance: None

Management Assistance: Data not available.

Training Assistance: Comprehensive long-term training and support, including home office training conferences, regional training, and field training. Our representative success system training program uses manuals and audiocassettes. On-call support.

Educational Products & Services—Career & Vocational Services

Barbizon Schools of Modeling

2240 Woolbright Rd., Ste. 300
Boynton Beach, FL 33426
Web Address: www.modelingschools.com

Phone: (561) 369-8600
Fax: (561) 361-1299
Contact: President

Number of Franchises: 65
Company-Owned Units: 0
Total Units: 65

In Business Since: 1939 Franchising Since: 1968

Description of Operation: Proprietary, vocational, schools of modeling and related creative arts.

Equity Capital Needed: $49,900-$89,000

Franchise Fee: $19,500-$35,000

Royalty: 7.5 percent

Advertising Co-op Fee:

Financial Assistance: Up to 50 percent of the franchise fee.

Management Assistance: Initial training at home office, plus on-site training of franchisee and staff. Ongoing advice and assistance.

Training Assistance: Training at home office and on-site.

Educational Products & Services—Youth

Fourth R, The

1715 Market St., Ste. 103
Kirkland, WA 98033
Toll-Free Phone: (800) 821-8653
Phone: (425) 828-0336
Fax: (425) 828-0192
Contact: President

Number of Franchises: 36
Company-Owned Units: 1
Total Units: 37

In Business Since: 1991 Franchising Since: 1992

Description of Operation: Franchisees teach computer skills to children 3-14 years old. Business can be conducted as home-based business or from commercial location. Broad curriculum includes ESL program and introductory classes for adults.

Equity Capital Needed: $17,000-$20,000

Franchise Fee: $16,000 1st franchise; $7,500 each additional

Royalty: 5-9 percent

Advertising Co-op Fee:

Financial Assistance: Franchisor-provided financing is available to qualified candidates.

Management Assistance: The franchisor provides continuing assistance and consultation to franchisee in all aspects of franchise operations, including continuing enhancements and additions to curriculum and product offerings.

Training Assistance: Training is 40-60 hours, depending on qualifications and experience of franchisee, and covers all aspects of sales and operations.

Genius Kid Academy

398 Steeles Ave. W. Ste. 214
Thornhill, ON L4J 6X3
Toll-Free Phone:
Phone: (905) 886-1920
Fax: (905) 886-4919
Contact: President

Number of Franchises: 1
Company-Owned Units: 1
Total Units: 2

In Business Since: 1992 Franchising Since: 1993

Description of Operation: Delivering high-quality computer education to children ages 3-12, as well as adults. Nothing is more satisfying than preparing children for the future.

Equity Capital Needed: $60,000

Franchise Fee: $50,000

Royalty: 1.5 percent

Advertising Co-op Fee:

Financial Assistance: Data not available.

Management Assistance: Custom-made software will take care of all the aspects of running a computer learning center.

Training Assistance: One month of training at the corporate location.

Grade Expectations Learning Systems, Inc.

105 Main St.
Unionville, ON M8X 2P5
E-mail Address: Grade@ICAN.NET
Toll-Free Phone: (800) 208-3826
Phone: (416) 410-6851
Fax: (416) 236-0078
Contact: President

Number of Franchises: 13
Company-Owned Units: 1
Total Units: 14

In Business Since: 1993 Franchising Since: 1995

Description of Operation: At Grade Expectations Learning Centres we provide supplementary education from grade 1 to 12. Enrichment and remedial programs use both traditional and computerized models.

Equity Capital Needed: $48,000

Franchise Fee: $22,000

Royalty: 10 percent of gross sales

Advertising Co-op Fee: 2 percent

Financial Assistance: $30,000 in load through CIBC banking institution.

Management Assistance: Complete business plan and follow through. Advertising plans, field visits, manuals, and seminars are provided.

Training Assistance: Initial three weeks of training. Followed by regular support through continuing seminars.

Honors Learning Center, The

5959 Shallowford Rd., Ste. 517
Chattanooga, TN 37421
Toll-Free Phone:
Phone: (423) 892-1800
Fax: (423) 892-1800
Contact: President

Number of Franchises: 2
Company-Owned Units: 0
Total Units: 2

In Business Since: 1987　**Franchising Since:** 1992

Description of Operation: The Honors Learning Center is an educational facility, offering academic testing and individualized programs in reading, math, SAT/ACT prep, study skills, and so on, for grades K-12. These remedial and enrichment programs are offered during after-school hours and Saturdays. The educational programs are comprehension skill-based, and the student success rate is fully documented.

Equity Capital Needed: $64,663-$131,845 includes franchise fee

Franchise Fee: $15,000

Royalty: 8 percent

Advertising Co-op Fee:

Financial Assistance: None

Management Assistance: Each franchisee has a personal consultant at the corporate office available for answering questions and making suggestions about center operations on an ongoing basis by telephone.

Training Assistance: We provide up to two weeks at the corporate office and four business days leading up to the grand opening.

Sylvan Learning Systems

1000 Lancaster St.
Baltimore, MD 21202
Web Address: www.educate.com
Toll-Free Phone: (800) 284-8214
Phone: (410) 843-8000
Fax: (410) 843-8717

Contact: Director of Franchise Systems Development

Number of Franchises: 572
Company-Owned Units: 38
Total Units: 600

In Business Since: 1979　**Franchising Since:** 1980

Description of Operation: Sylvan is the leading private provider of supplemental education services in North America. Programs, directed at preschool through adult, include reading, math, algebra, writing, study skills, SAT/ACT prep, and more.

Equity Capital Needed: $79,000-$114,000

Franchise Fee: $34,000-$42,000

Royalty: 8-9 percent

Advertising Co-op Fee:

Financial Assistance: Some financing is available in selected locations.

Management Assistance: Complete start-up and ongoing assistance is provided through highly trained field consultants.

Training Assistance: Comprehensive basic and ongoing training are provided in all programs and operations.

Educational Products & Services—Miscellaneous

ELS International

5761 Buckingham Parkway
Culver City, CA 90230
E-mail Address: tcooper@els.com
Toll-Free Phone: (800) 468-8978
Phone: (310) 342-4100
Fax: (310) 342-4150
Contact: President

Number of Franchises: 52
Company-Owned Units: 26
Total Units: 78

In Business Since: 1961　**Franchising Since:** 1978

Description of Operation: "English as a foreign language" schools abroad.

Equity Capital Needed: $150,000-$300,000

Franchise Fee: $30,000 per center

Royalty: 5 percent

Advertising Co-op Fee:

Financial Assistance: Not available.

Management Assistance: Complete operations manual and start-up guidance is provided prior to opening. Ongoing consultation and services as needed. Management academy.

Training Assistance: Management training is provided prior to opening. Annual on-site visits and attendance at grand opening. Ongoing consultation.

LearnRight

1315 W. College Ave. Ste. 303
State College, PA 16801
Web Address: www.learnright.com
Toll-Free Phone: (800) 876-3450
Phone: (814) 234-9658
Fax: (814) 237-9095
Contact: President

Number of Franchises: 0
Company-Owned Units: 1
Total Units: 1

In Business Since: 1978   **Franchising Since:** 1993

Description of Operation: Founded in 1978 and incorporated in 1992, LearnRight is the parent company of LearnRight franchises, licensor of private schools dedicated to teaching people of all ages how to become more effective learners. LearnRight's specialized one-on-one instruction establishes a positive learning pattern, provides a foundation for improved academic performance, strengthens conceptual understanding, and develops the student's confidence in learning. Also, thinking skills instruction.

Equity Capital Needed: $40,000-$80,000

Franchise Fee: $29,900

Royalty: 6 percent

Advertising Co-op Fee:

Financial Assistance: Financing is available for the franchise fee only.

Management Assistance: Franchisees are provided with full educational and business support.

Training Assistance: Franchisees attend LearnRight's three-week franchise training program, consisting of classroom instruction and facility training.

Employment Services—
Executive Placement

Dunhill Staffing Systems, Inc.

150 Motor Parkway
Hauppauge, NY 11788
Web Address: www.dunhillstaff
E-mail Address: Pe@dunhillstaff.com
Toll-Free Phone: (800) 386-7823
Phone: (516) 952-3000
Fax: (516) 952-3500

Contact: Director of New Business Development

Number of Franchises: 161
Company-Owned Units: 19
Total Units: 161

In Business Since: 1952   **Franchising Since:** 1961

Description of Operation: Dunhill offers professional search and temporary staffing franchises. Our franchisees provide permanent executives, mid-level management, professionals, technical staffing, and temporaries. Professional search franchisees benefit from the industry's best interview to placement ratio and leading edge computerized placement matching system. For temporary staffing, Dunhill's computerized system handles back-office accounting allowing franchisees to focus on sales and service. There is a 1-800 help line available.

Equity Capital Needed: Prof.: $30,000-$50,000; Temp.: $110,000-$140,000

Franchise Fee: Prof. Search: $38,000 (4.7 percent financed); Temp.: $15,000

Royalty: 7 + 1 percent Prof. Search; Temp. depends on productivity.

Advertising Co-op Fee: For Perm., 1 percent of royalty is for this.

Financial Assistance: Dunhill offers up to 4.7 percent in-house financing on our professional search franchise fee. Beyond that, we are a preferred customer of AT&T Capital Corp and can provide prospects with SBA loan applications and information.

Management Assistance: Recruitment and training of staff for our franchisees offices including conducting in-person seminars and videoconferencing to screen sales consultants for our professional search offices. A collection department dedicated to collecting fees due to our franchisees. Payroll and risk management services to assist our temp franchisees with their daily operations.

Training Assistance: Intense training for both franchises at corporate offices and in franchise marketplace. A strong emphasis on quality service and client relationships. All executive and support staff has "front line" industry experience and provides ongoing, consistent support. Regional and national meetings plus specialty and strategy meetings.

Franchise Recruiters, LTD

3500 Innsbruck/Lincolnshire Country Club
Village of Crete, IL 60417
E-mail Address: franchise@worldnet.att.net
Toll-Free Phone: (800) 334-6257
Phone: (708) 757-5595
Fax: (708) 758-8222
Contact: Founder

Number of Franchises: 1
Company-Owned Units: 1
Total Units: 2

In Business Since: 1984   **Franchising Since:** 1984

Description of Operation: Jerry Wilkerson has been in franchising for 20 years. He is the former president and executive of the International Franchise Association. FRL is the largest franchise search firm in the United States and Canada. An international executive search corporation dedicated exclusively to franchising. Unconditional one-year guarantee. Excellent client references. Placement of professionals in sales, operations, executive, marketing, training, finance, legal, and international development of franchising.

Equity Capital Needed: This and following information not available

Franchise Fee:

Royalty:

Advertising Co-op Fee:

Financial Assistance:

Management Assistance:

Training Assistance:

Management Recruiters

200 Public Square, 31st Floor
Cleveland, OH 44114
Toll-Free Phone: (800) 875-4000
Phone: (216) 696-1122
Fax: (216) 696-3221
Contact: Vice President of Franchise Marketing

Number of Franchises: 402
Company-Owned Units: 25
Total Units: 427

In Business Since: 1957   **Franchising Since:** 1965

Description of Operation: Management level and general personnel placement, search, and recruiting service on an employer-paid, contingency-fee basis.

Equity Capital Needed: $30,000-$50,000

Franchise Fee: $40,000

Royalty: 7 percent

Advertising Co-op Fee:

Financial Assistance: None

Management Assistance: The licensee is provided with a detailed operations manual, containing information, procedures, and know-how for operating the business, computer hardware and software, an account executive, plus accounting and administrative assistant's manuals. Also receives a VCR/color TV, plus 38 video training films and a 90-day supply of all necessary operating forms, brochures, and so on. Continuing advice, guidance, and assistance through national meetings, seminars, and training films.

Training Assistance: An intensive initial training program of approximately three weeks at headquarters, plus an additional on-the-job training program of approxi-

mately three additional weeks in licensee's first office. Training thereafter as needed. Staff will also assist and advise the licensee in securing suitable office space, lease negotiations, design and layout, office furniture, equipment, telephone systems, and so on.

Sanford Rose Associates

265 South Main Street, P.O. Box 80596
Akron, OH 44308
Web Address: www.sanfordrose.com
E-mail Address: SRAIntl@aol.com
Toll-Free Phone: (800) 731-7724
Phone: (330) 762-7162
Fax: (330) 762-1007
Contact: Vice President

Number of Franchises: 54
Company-Owned Units: 0
Total Units: 54

In Business Since: 1969   **Franchising Since:** 1970

Description of Operation: Executive search services are provided following our own proprietary process, Dimensional Search®. This methodology gives your clients tangible ways to experience and be accustomed to receiving many value-added services to the hiring effort. This process sells easily, helps you command premium fees, and keeps your clients coming back. We will train and support you and your employees, and furnish a complete set of tools, such as software, databases, an Internet connection, sales literature, and operations manuals. Since the fees you earn are usually from $15,000 to $75,000 per completed assignment, you can afford to provide a lot of services to your client companies about important career decisions. Interpersonal effectiveness, good communications skills, and a solid business background are prerequisites for SRA office ownership. Membership in our smaller, congenial style firm is exclusive. We are not a franchise factory.

Equity Capital Needed: $60,000

Franchise Fee: $32,000

Royalty: 3-7 percent

Advertising Co-op Fee: None

Financial Assistance: A portion of the franchise fee may be financed.

Management Assistance: We use industry experts on the SRA staff and outside experts to provide our franchisees the methods and tools to be at least one step ahead of the competition. Picking the best elements from the most innovative entrepreneurs to the tried and true systems developed by large corporations.

Training Assistance: The transition between training and operations support is seamless at SRA. Classroom theories and operating systems are immediately put to use in real-world, income-generating situations. No franchisee is ever too experienced to ask for our help. In fact, the top performing offices do it most often. The training never ends.

Employment Services—Temporary Staffing

1st Agency Professionals

5428 Northland Dr. N.E.
Grand Rapids, MI 49525
Web Address: www.firstagency.com
Toll-Free Phone:
Phone: (616) 791-4260
Fax: (616) 791-7039
Contact: President

Number of Franchises: 0
Company-Owned Units: 1
Total Units: 1

In Business Since: 1990   **Franchising Since:** 1992

Description of Operation: Provides nurses and nurse aides temporarily to hospitals, nursing homes, and other health care facilities.

Equity Capital Needed: $23,500-$110,500

Franchise Fee: $25,000

Royalty: 6.5 percent

Advertising Co-op Fee:

Financial Assistance: Not available.

Management Assistance: Training at home office and at the franchise office. On-call, 24-hour assistance.

Training Assistance: Home office and franchise office.

Accountants on Call

Park 80 West, Plaza II, 9th Fl.
Saddle Brook, NJ 07662
Web Address: www.accountantsoncall.com
Toll-Free Phone:
Phone: (201) 843-0006
Fax: (201) 843-4936
Contact: Vice President of Operations

Number of Franchises: 13
Company-Owned Units: 50
Total Units: 63

In Business Since: 1979   **Franchising Since:** 1981

Description of Operation: Temporary and permanent placement of accounting, bookkeeping, and financial personnel.

Equity Capital Needed: $90,000-$110,000

Franchise Fee: $25,000

Royalty: 7 percent

Advertising Co-op Fee:

Financial Assistance: Accounts receivable financing.

Management Assistance: Advise on-site selection and staff hiring. Manuals and consulting assistance always available.

Training Assistance: Approximately two to three weeks in corporate office and in a branch location. Ongoing training and seminars.

Express Personnel Services

6300 Northwest Expy.
Oklahoma City, OK 73132
Web Address: www.expresspersonnel.com
Toll-Free Phone: (800) 652-6400
Phone: (405) 840-5000
Fax: (405) 773-6442
Contact: Vice President of Franchising

Number of Franchises: 363
Company-Owned Units: 0
Total Units: 363

In Business Since: 1983   **Franchising Since:** 1985

Description of Operation: Full-service temporary help service. Permanent and executive search divisions for recruiting also.

Equity Capital Needed: $55,000-$95,000

Franchise Fee: $14,500-$17,500 includes training fee

Royalty: 40 percent of gross margin temp./6 percent executive search

Advertising Co-op Fee:

Financial Assistance: 100 percent financing of the temporary payroll and indirect financing for selected items, such as yellow page advertising, signage, computer software, and industrial testing packages.

Management Assistance: Comprehensive assistance with site selection, help in negotiating leases, manuals and video training aids, testing, and selection materials for temporary staffing. Continual updates. An assigned field representative.

Training Assistance: Two full weeks of training at the corporate headquarters, followed by one full week in the new office as it opens with the assigned field representative. Continual follow-up training in the field and in annual and regular seminars and workshops.

Flex-Staff/Pro-Tem

214 N. Main St Ste. 202
Natick, MA 01760
Toll-Free Phone:
Phone: (508) 650-0026
Fax: (508) 650-0035
Contact: President

Number of Franchises: 8
Company-Owned Units: 1
Total Units: 9

In Business Since: 1970   **Franchising Since:** 1975

Description of Operation: Eligibility for our franchise opportunity is restricted to those individuals having substantial prior experience in the temporary services industry. We require a minimum of two years of successful, hands-on experience at the level of branch manager or above. By eliminating the need to train and closely supervise franchisees lacking temporary services experience, we are able to offer services at a significantly lower cost.

Equity Capital Needed: $15,000-$40,000

Franchise Fee: $1,000

Royalty: Varies by market.

Advertising Co-op Fee:

Financial Assistance: Financing of temporary employee payroll and related payroll taxes is an integral part of our service to franchisees. We may also make available financing of Worker's Compensation deposit premiums.

Management Assistance: We provide substantial assistance in the back-office work of the franchisee, including payroll, invoicing, accounts receivable control, credit and collection, and remittances.

Training Assistance: Because we restrict our opportunity to individuals with substantial industry experience, our training program is limited to brief training in our operating methods and systems.

Hostess Helper

20 Whittlesey Rd.
Newton Centre, MA 02159
Toll-Free Phone:
Phone: (617) 332-3516
Fax: (617) 630-1744
Contact: President

Number of Franchises: 0
Company-Owned Units: 1
Total Units: 1

In Business Since: 1973   **Franchising Since:** 1990

Description of Operation: A temporary waitstaff and party-planning service. Hostess Helper provides waiters, waitresses, and bartenders for functions of all sizes. Can arrange for food, decorations, entertainment, and so on.

Equity Capital Needed: $17,000-$25,000 including franchise fee.

Franchise Fee: $10,000

Royalty: 7 percent

Advertising Co-op Fee:

Financial Assistance: Data not available.

Management Assistance: Ongoing assistance is always available by telephone. If location allows, on-site assistance is available.

Training Assistance: Initial training takes five days at the head office in Massachusetts. Ongoing assistance is available after that.

Labor Force

5225 Katy Frwy., Ste. 600
Houston, TX 77007
Toll-Free Phone: (800) 299-4312
Phone: (713) 802-1284
Fax: (713) 802-1288
Contact: President

Number of Franchises: 20
Company-Owned Units: 0
Total Units: 20

In Business Since: 1970   **Franchising Since:** 1991

Description of Operation: We supply temporary personnel to almost every type of business or industry. We fill: clerical, electrical assembly, drivers, carpenters, plumbers, electricians, furniture manufacturing, carpet manufacturing, food processing, inventory crews, retail store helpers, recycling helpers, warehouse workers, and many more positions.

Equity Capital Needed: $125,000-$130,000

Franchise Fee: $25,000

Royalty: 4.5-2 percent depending on volume.

Advertising Co-op Fee:

Financial Assistance: 60-day accounts receivable funding with affliate company.

Management Assistance: Help with site selection, office set-up, manuals, forms, promotional material, bulk mailing, and consulting, as needed. Periodic visits and an annual meeting with all franchisees.

Training Assistance: Two weeks of classroom and actual office training in a working environment. Personnel support available for travel expense charge.

Nursefinders

1200 Copeland, Ste. 200
Arlington, TX 76011
Web Address: www.nursefinders.com
Toll-Free Phone: (800) 445-0459
Phone: (817) 460-1181
Fax: (817) 460-1969
Contact: Vice President of Franchising

Number of Franchises: 50
Company-Owned Units: 50
Total Units: 100

In Business Since: 1974   **Franchising Since:** 1978

Description of Operation: Nursefinders is a national provider of nurses and other health care professionals for home health care services and supplemental staffing to hospitals and other health care facilities.

Equity Capital Needed: $110,000-$150,000

Franchise Fee: $19,600

Royalty: 7 percent

Advertising Co-op Fee:

Financial Assistance: Partial financing is available to qualified prospects.

Management Assistance: The franchisor assists the franchisee with site analysis and selection, plus office layout and design. Regional representatives visit the franchise sites at least annually to consult with franchisees about business operations and to offer suggestions for implementing Nursefinders' policies and procedures.

Training Assistance: The franchisor provides one week of training at one of its established offices, two weeks at its corporate headquarters in Arlington, TX (or other locations designated by franchisor), and one week at the franchisee's site. Additional training includes on-site training visits and periodic management workshops.

Remedy Temporary Services

32122 Camino Capistrano
San Juan Capistrano, CA 92675
Toll-Free Phone: (800) 722-8367
Phone: (714) 661-1211
Fax: (714) 248-0813
Contact: Vice President of Franchise Development

Number of Franchises: 38
Company-Owned Units: 56
Total Units: 94

In Business Since: 1968   **Franchising Since:** 1987

Description of Operation: A full-service staffing franchise, specializing in office automation; clerical, legal, and accounting positions; and light industrial business. Fully automated office.

Equity Capital Needed: $75,000-$130,000

Franchise Fee: $15,000

Royalty: Varies with gross margin.

Advertising Co-op Fee:

Financial Assistance: Remedy provides funding of the temporary payroll.

Management Assistance: Help and advice with site location, lease, and space planning. Regular visit by operations department to help in sales, recruiting, problem solving, national accounts, workman's compensation issues, regular seminars, and national meeting.

Training Assistance: Two weeks of preopening training, covering all aspects of operating and promoting a successful office. One week of classroom and one week of hands-on training in a Remedy office.

Snelling Personnel Services

12801 N. Central Expy., Ste. 700
Dallas, TX 75243
Web Address: www.snelling.com
Toll-Free Phone: (800) 766-5556
Phone: (214) 239-7575
Fax: (214) 239-6881
Contact: Sr. V.P. of Marketing/Development

Number of Franchises: 278
Company-Owned Units: 28
Total Units: 306

In Business Since: 1951   **Franchising Since:** 1956

Description of Operation: Full-service temporary and permanent personnel service franchise. Computerized national matching network. Specialities include, but are not limited to, sales and marketing, accounting and finance, data processing, engineering, health care, and office support.

Equity Capital Needed: $84,000-$172,000

Franchise Fee: $9,000

Royalty: 8 percent: permanent; 4.5 percent of billing: temporary

Advertising Co-op Fee:

Financial Assistance: Payroll funding provided on temporary help. Third-party financing.

Management Assistance: We provide two weeks of training at corporate offices and up to 10 days of on-site training. Support and field training provided.

Training Assistance: Same as above.

Todays Temporary

18111 Preston Rd., Ste. 700
Dallas, TX 75252
Toll-Free Phone: (800) 822-7868
Phone: (214) 380-9380
Fax: (214) 713-4198
Contact: Franchise Development Co-ordinator

Number of Franchises: 24
Company-Owned Units: 59
Total Units: 83

In Business Since: 1982   **Franchising Since:** 1983

Description of Operation: A full-service, high-quality, office, clerical temporary employment service, using a distinctive sales, service, promotional, quality control, and accounting procedure known as "Todays Way Method" of operations.

Equity Capital Needed: $90,000-$145,000

Franchise Fee: Varies ($8,000-$18,000).

Royalty: Percentage varies with volume.

Advertising Co-op Fee:

Financial Assistance: Payroll, receivables, insurance, credit, and collections.

Management Assistance: Start-up, grand-opening assistance; site selection; initial and ongoing systems; procedures, sales, and operations support and training; manuals; customer satisfaction programs; technical and computer support; human resources; payroll; and receivables.

Training Assistance: Classroom and ongoing field support in business operations, sales, operations, and management; field sales development support; and operations field development. All support is ongoing.

TRC Staffing Services

100 Ashford Center North, Ste. 500
Atlanta, GA 30338
Web Address: www.trcstaffing.com
E-mail Address: mikebaer@aol.com
Toll-Free Phone: (800) 488-8008
Phone: (770) 392-1411
Fax: (770) 393-2742
Contact: V.P.—Franchise Division

Number of Franchises: 44
Company-Owned Units: 27
Total Units: 71

In Business Since: 1980　　**Franchising Since:** 1984

Description of Operation: A national staffing service company, providing office support, clerical, word processing, data processing, marketing, and light industrial personnel.

Equity Capital Needed: $25,000 liquid & good credit

Franchise Fee: No fee.

Royalty: 9.5 percent or a 40/60 gross margin split

Advertising Co-op Fee:

Financial Assistance: Available to qualified individuals.

Management Assistance: Each franchisee will be visited by his or her franchise support manager multiple times throughout the year. Also, our corporate offices provide marketing, payroll, credit, and human resources support continually. Offer credit collection insurance.

Training Assistance: The Atlanta, GA, corporate offices provide formal training for operations, sales, and branch management, as well as owner's training, which is provided for first-time franchise owners. Also, our franchise support managers will provide on-site training prior to opening and throughout the life of the franchise.

Western Staff Services

301 Lennon Ln.
Walnut Creek, CA 94598
Toll-Free Phone: (800) 872-8367
Phone: (510) 930-5345
Fax: (510) 256-1515

Contact: **President, Franchising Division**

Number of Franchises: 98
Company-Owned Units: 207
Total Units: 305

In Business Since: 1948　　**Franchising Since:** 1957

Description of Operation: Western Staff Services is a privately held, international, temporary help firm. Founded in San Francisco in 1948, Western today has over 350 offices in eight countries and is widely recognized as a leader in the temporary help industry. Western provides office, light industrial, medical, technical, accounting, outsourcing, marketing, and Santa/photo personnel. Exclusive-territory franchises are still available in prime markets.

Equity Capital Needed: $50,000-$100,000

Franchise Fee: $10,000-$50,000

Royalty: 0 percent; gross profit divided, based on sales volume

Advertising Co-op Fee:

Financial Assistance: Western provides unlimited financing of the temporary payroll and accounts receivable. Financing of a portion of the franchise fee is available to applicants with at least two years of management experience.

Management Assistance: Western handles all payrolling and invoices through our computerized corporate payroll facility and offers professional advertising and public relations materials and support, risk management, legal and credit assistance, video orientation and training resources, QWIZ testing and tutorial software and support, national accounts, sales leads, office automation systems, and more.

Training Assistance: Western provides five days of intensive classroom instruction at the corporate offices; two days of field office training in the San Francisco Bay Area; and a three-day, on-site, training-completion visit. Ongoing shared-cost workshops, peer groups, and seminars.

Employment Services—
Miscellaneous

AAA Employment

4914-A Creekside Dr.
Clearwater, FL 34620
Toll-Free Phone: (800) 237-2853
Phone: (813) 573-0202
Fax: (813) 572-8709
Contact: President

Number of Franchises: 22
Company-Owned Units: 24
Total Units: 46

In Business Since: 1957   **Franchising Since:** 1977

Description of Operation: Emphasizes a full-service, general employment agency, specializing in placement at all levels of employment. Applicant-paid and employer-paid positions are handled. Low placement fee with convenient terms sets AAA Employment apart from other agencies.

Equity Capital Needed: $7,500-$20,000

Franchise Fee: $10,000

Royalty: 9 percent

Advertising Co-op Fee:

Financial Assistance: No financial assistance is available.

Management Assistance: Support in all phases of the operation is an ongoing commitment. Seminars and annual conventions are held, and a weekly newsletter is provided, as well as an operations and training manual.

Training Assistance: Two to four weeks.

Checkmate Systems

P.O. Box 32034
Charleston, SC 29417
Toll-Free Phone: (800) 964-6298
Phone: (803) 763-9393
Fax: (803) 571-1851
Contact: Vice President of Marketing

Number of Franchises: 4
Company-Owned Units: 0
Total Units: 4

In Business Since: 1992   **Franchising Since:** 1993

Description of Operation: Checkmate provides total personnel administration services to small business owners through the new technique of employee leasing. Business owners are completely relieved of all payroll, employee benefit, and other personnel administrative duties when Checkmate assumes their employer duties and leases the employees back to them. Small business owners gain the purchasing power and tax advantages usually only available to large companies in providing employee benefits.

Equity Capital Needed: $25,000-$50,000

Franchise Fee: $15,000

Royalty: 3/10 of 1 percent of gross payroll processed.

Advertising Co-op Fee:

Financial Assistance: Checkmate does not provide financing, but will assist the franchisee in finding adequate funding.

Management Assistance: The franchisee is provided comprehensive software as a part of the franchise fee. The company provides back-up support for all of the functions the franchisee is required to perform for clients. The company also provides professional marketing materials and ongoing support.

Training Assistance: The franchisee receives a minimum of one week of training in an operating franchise location, covering the principles of employee leasing, software operation, and marketing.

Western Medical Services

220 N. Widget Ln.
Walnut Creek, CA 94598
E-mail Address: bgeorge@westf.com
Toll-Free Phone: (800) 872-8367
Phone: (510) 256-1561
Fax: (510) 952-2591
Contact: President, Franchise Division

Number of Franchises: 26
Company-Owned Units: 33
Total Units: 59

In Business Since: 1967   **Franchising Since:** 1967

Description of Operation: With over 55 offices, Western offers a full range of health care personnel services, including home health care. A program for Medicare certification is available. Franchise includes intensive training, computerized caregiver payroll and financing, professional risk management, credit and legal expertise, optional office automation systems, and much more.

Equity Capital Needed: $100,000

Franchise Fee: $30,000-$40,000

Royalty: 8 percent of gross sales

Advertising Co-op Fee:

Financial Assistance: Western provides complete financing of the caregiver payroll and accounts receivable. Financing of a portion of the franchise fee is available to applicants with at least two years of management experience in the health care or staffing industries.

Management Assistance: Western handles all payrolling and invoices through our computerized corporate payroll facility and offers professional advertising and public relations materials and support, risk management, legal and credit assistance, video orientation and training resources, sales leads, office automation systems, and more.

Training Assistance: Western provides five days of intensive classroom instruction at the corporate offices; five days of field office training in the San Francisco Bay Area; and a five-day, on-site, training-completion visit by a Western training representative. In addition, Western offers ongoing shared-cost affiliate workshops, peer groups, and seminars.

Florists

Buning the Florist

3860 W. Commercial Blvd.
Ft. Lauderdale, FL 33309
Toll-Free Phone: (800) 940-1778
Phone: (305) 488-3000
Fax: (305) 486-0622
Contact: President

Number of Franchises: 4
Company-Owned Units: 16
Total Units: 20

In Business Since: 1925   **Franchising Since:** 1960

Description of Operation: Buning the Florist offers unique retail florist shops. The franchise package includes assistance in site selection, store layout, and a complete training program at headquarters in Fort Lauderdale, FL.

Equity Capital Needed: $50,000

Franchise Fee: $15,000

Royalty: 4 percent

Advertising Co-op Fee:

Financial Assistance: No financial assistance is provided by the franchisor.

Management Assistance: The franchisor assists the franchisee in all aspects of shop operation, record keeping, advertising, promotion, and selling techniques. Manuals of operations and counseling are provided. Home office personnel are available for periodic visits.

Training Assistance: Two weeks of training are provided at company headquarters in Ft. Lauderdale, FL, plus continuing training in-store under company supervision.

Conroy's/1-800-FLOWERS

1600 Stewart Ave., 7th Floor
Westbury, NY 11590
Web Address: www.1800flowers.com
Toll-Free Phone:
Phone: (516) 237-6000
Fax: (516) 237-6087
Contact:

Number of Franchises: 92
Company-Owned Units: 22
Total Units: 114

In Business Since: 1962   **Franchising Since:** 1974

Description of Operation: The flower industry is blooming. There's no better way to become part of it than through a 1-800-FLOWERS franchise. As part of 1-800-

FLOWERS, you'll be associated with our growing reputation for quality, service, selection, and value.

Equity Capital Needed: $75,000-125,000

Franchise Fee: $28,500

Royalty: Not available

Advertising Co-op Fee:

Financial Assistance: Will provide assistance in obtaining financing from third-party sources.

Management Assistance: Retail shop development, nationwide name recognition, and sales support. Complete training program, site development, and merchandising assistance.

Training Assistance: No floral experience is necessary. An intensive four-week Retail Partner Training Program takes you through the fundamentals of flower care, retail selling, and business strategies, both in a classroom setting and on the job at an operating store.

Foliage Design Systems

4496 35th St.
Orlando, FL 32811
Toll-Free Phone: (800) 933-7351
Phone: (407) 245-7776
Fax: (407) 245-7533
Contact: President

Number of Franchises: 42
Company-Owned Units: 3
Total Units: 45

In Business Since: 1971   **Franchising Since:** 1980

Description of Operation: Sale, lease, and short-term rental of live, artifical, and preserved interior foliage and decorative containers. Related products include seasonal decorative items. Design, install, and maintain interior foliage in office buildings, hotels, residences, restaurants, and so on. Weekly professional plant care and maintenance by uniformed technicians.

Equity Capital Needed: $35,000-$150,000

Franchise Fee: $20,000-$100,000

Royalty: 6 percent

Advertising Co-op Fee:

Financial Assistance: None

Management Assistance: On-site training; ongoing phone support (800#); assistance with design and bidding, monthly information, and educational internal newsletter; network of leads and sources; annual meetings; marketing materials; and complete operating manuals.

Training Assistance: Initial 8-10 weekdays at corporate office, followed up by on-site training. Training covers all facets of business from plant care and plant identification, to sales and marketing, to office procedures. Complete operations manuals provided.

Parker Interior Plantscape

1325 Terrill Rd.
Scotch Plains, NJ 07076
Toll-Free Phone: (800) 526-3672
Phone: (908) 322-5552
Fax: (908) 322-4818
Contact: President

Number of Franchises: 2
Company-Owned Units: 1
Total Units: 3

In Business Since: 1948   **Franchising Since:** 1980

Description of Operation: Sell or rent live plants, flowers, trees, containers, and so on, to Fortune 500 corporations. We also guarantee and maintain them.

Equity Capital Needed: $1,000

Franchise Fee: $15,000

Royalty: 0 percent

Advertising Co-op Fee:

Financial Assistance: None

Management Assistance: We train in all aspects of the business and help the franchise get started.

Training Assistance: Same as above.

Food—Bagels, Donuts, & Buns

Benny's Bagels Franchising, Inc.

2636 Walnut Hill Lane, Ste. 110
Dallas, TX 75229
Web Address: www.bennysbagels.com
E-mail Address: info@bennysbagels.com
Toll-Free Phone:
Phone: (214) 351-2600
Fax: (214) 351-2604
Contact: President

Number of Franchises: 30
Company-Owned Units: 1
Total Units: 31

In Business Since: 1994   **Franchising Since:** 1995

Description of Operation: Benny's Bagels is a retailer and franchisor of retail bagel stores. Our concept consists of an authentic bagel bakery with our bagels baked on hearth oven stones in full view of the customer. We offer the lowest investment in the industry with the highest-quality product and concept.

Equity Capital Needed: $70,000

Franchise Fee: $25,000

Royalty: 5 percent

Advertising Co-op Fee: 2 percent

Financial Assistance: We have a $2 million SBA franchisor line of credit available.

Management Assistance: We provide site selection and architectural design; oversee store construction; and offer one-week, on-site, opening assistance, hiring, support, and so on.

Training Assistance: Two full weeks of intensive training. 7.5 percent is in-store operations; and 2.5 percent is managerial, corporate office-related.

Best Bagels in Town

480-19 Patchogue—Holbrook Rd.
Holbrook, NY 11741
Toll-Free Phone:
Phone: (516) 472-4104
Fax:
Contact: President

Number of Franchises: 5
Company-Owned Units: 1
Total Units: 6

In Business Since: 1988   **Franchising Since:** 1990

Description of Operation: Quick-service bagel and bakery restaurant. Eat in or take out fresh bagels, rolls, breads, and pastries. Hot and cold drinks.

Equity Capital Needed: $50,000-$90,000

Franchise Fee: $12,500

Royalty: 4 percent

Advertising Co-op Fee:

Financial Assistance: Yes.

Management Assistance: Assistance is provided as needed through the duration of contract term of 10 years.

Training Assistance: Yes. Periods vary at both new owner's location and at home office.

Blue Chip Cookies

100 First St., Ste. 2030
San Francisco, CA 94105
Toll-Free Phone: (800) 888-9866
Phone: (415) 546-3840
Fax: (415) 546-9717
Contact: President

Number of Franchises: 32
Company-Owned Units: 13
Total Units: 45

In Business Since: 1983   **Franchising Since:** 1984

Description of Operation: Gourmet bakery products, produced from scratch and baked fresh daily. Our menu includes cookies, brownies, muffins, cinnamon rolls, fruit bars, and espresso drinks, as well as coffee, tea, sodas, bottled water, yogurt, and ice cream.

Equity Capital Needed: $170,000-$195,000 (includes fee)

Franchise Fee: $29,500

Royalty: 4 percent

Advertising Co-op Fee:

Financial Assistance: We refer the franchisee to an outside lender.

Management Assistance: Site selection assistance is provided on request. Review of construction plans and equipment. Operational, marketing, and financial analysis is provided.

Training Assistance: An extensive two-week training period before store opening at a home-based company store will give you hands-on training. Operations representatives will be present at your store location for three to five days at the opening to assist in opening your store. Continued support is available by biannual operational visits and telephone consultations.

Cindy's Cinnamon Rolls

1432 S. Mission Rd. Ste. A
Fallbrook, CA 92028
Toll-Free Phone:
Phone: (760) 723-1121
Fax: (760) 723-4143
Contact: President

Number of Franchises: 33
Company-Owned Units: 0
Total Units: 33

In Business Since: 1985　　**Franchising Since:** 1986

Description of Operation: Hot cinnamon rolls in major regional malls.

Equity Capital Needed: $120,000-$150,000

Franchise Fee: $25,000

Royalty: 5 percent

Advertising Co-op Fee:

Financial Assistance: We provide help in leasing equipment.

Management Assistance: One week of training at a training center and one week of training in-store when opening. After store is open, we provide newsletters and personal visits.

Training Assistance: Same as above.

Coffee Time Donuts

477 Ellesmere Rd
Scarborough, ON M1R 4E5
Toll-Free Phone:
Phone: (416) 288-8515
Fax: (416) 288-8895
Contact: Executive Vice President

Number of Franchises: 120
Company-Owned Units: 2
Total Units: 122

In Business Since: 1982　　**Franchising Since:** 1989

Description of Operation: Coffee Time Donuts is one of the largest franchisors of stores that sell coffee and donuts in Ontario. Coffee Time Donut stores offer a wide variety of menu items and are open 24 hours a day to attract customers for an any-time-of-the-day "minimeal." In addition to a wide variety of donuts, muffins, croissants, pastries, and a gourmet blend coffee as snack foods, the menu expands to include soups, chili, salads, sandwiches, and choices of various hot and cold beverages.

Equity Capital Needed: Data not available.

Franchise Fee: $15,000

Royalty: 4.75 percent

Advertising Co-op Fee:

Financial Assistance: Coffee Time Donuts does not, in the normal course of business, provide financing directly to a potential franchisee. What Coffee Time Donuts has done is to arrange financial assistance packages with various chartered banks experienced in franchising matters.

Management Assistance: In addition to the initial training program covered below, Coffee Time supports the franchise network by providing ongoing store visitations by qualified field representatives. Franchisees are encouraged to view their opinions during the council meeting held every two months, or at the regional meeting held semiannually.

Training Assistance: Coffee Time's training program covers all facets of the coffee and donut selling business. There is particular emphasis on those aspects of the business and store that make for a successful franchisee. Coffee Time goes beyond the simple operating aspects of the business to include maintaining a clean, attractive store; serving customers in a warm and efficient manner; and fostering good employee relationships.

Donut Inn

22120 Clarendon; Ste. 110
Woodland Hills, CA 91367
Web Address: www.donutinn.com
Toll-Free Phone: (800) 422-5379
Phone: (818) 888-2220
Fax: (818) 888-2893
Contact: Franchise Development Director

Number of Franchises: 116
Company-Owned Units: 3
Total Units: 119

In Business Since: 1975　　**Franchising Since:** 1982

Description of Operation: Upscale, California-style, donut, pastry, muffin, scone, cookie, croissant, and bagel shops.

Equity Capital Needed: Equipment package approximately $45,000-$65,000

Franchise Fee: $23,750-$95,000 (varies with area)

Royalty: 5.5 percent

Advertising Co-op Fee:

Financial Assistance: SBA-approved.

Management Assistance: We provide a comprehensive recipe and procedures manual that guides the franchisee in the everyday operation relating to product and quality control, service, sales, bookkeeping, inventory, ordering, marketing, and so on. Whenever the franchisee has a question or needs advice on anything relating to the Donut Inn shop, there is a 24-hours-a-day, seven-days-a-week hot line.

Training Assistance: We provide three to four weeks of concentrated training in all phases of the business in our training facility. Continual updating and retraining, as needed, on the newest and most innovative concepts and equipment. One week of training in your store on opening.

Goldberg's All American Food Groups

104 New Era Dr.
South Plainfield, NJ 07080
Toll-Free Phone: (800) 776-5940
Phone:
Fax: (908) 757-8857
Contact: Franchise Development

Number of Franchises: 36
Company-Owned Units: 6
Total Units: 42

In Business Since: 1983   **Franchising Since:** 1990

Description of Operation: A fast-food restaurant, serving 36 varieties of New York-style bagels, appetizers, sandwiches, salads, desserts, beverages, gourmet coffee, and more.

Equity Capital Needed: $220,000-$250,000

Franchise Fee: $25,000

Royalty: 5 percent

Advertising Co-op Fee:

Financial Assistance: None

Management Assistance: Franchisees are provided with record keeping and administrative control forms; operations and employee manuals; multimedia advertising programs; approved product, equipment, and vendor lists; insurance specifications, quality assurance and guideline checklists; build-out specifications; and recommended contractors.

Training Assistance: Franchisees are provided with preopening training, grand opening assistance, and ongoing training for franchisees and their staff.

Manhattan Bagel Company

246 Industrial Way W.
Eatontown, NJ 07724

Toll-Free Phone:
Phone: (732) 544-0155
Fax: (732) 544-1315
Contact: Director of Franchise Development

Number of Franchises: 28
Company-Owned Units: 0
Total Units: 28

In Business Since: 1987   **Franchising Since:** 1988

Description of Operation: Upscale bagel eateries, offering deli items, soups, and full breakfast fare. Operations are configured 100 percent turnkey, with site selection and lease negotiation.

Equity Capital Needed: $75,000-$100,000

Franchise Fee: $30,000

Royalty: 5 percent

Advertising Co-op Fee:

Financial Assistance: Assistance with SBA loan processing.

Management Assistance: Comprehensive, hands-on training, with detailed operations manual and regular field assistance in marketing, merchandising, food preparation, and other business facets.

Training Assistance: One week of managerial and administrative classroom training, plus two weeks of required hands-on, in-store training. Refresher courses are also given, as needed.

Robin's Donuts

725 Hewitson St.
Thunder Bay, ON P7B 6B5
Toll-Free Phone:
Phone: (807) 623-4453
Fax: (807) 623-4682
Contact: Franchise Sales

Number of Franchises: 185
Company-Owned Units: 5
Total Units: 190

In Business Since: 1975   **Franchising Since:** 1977

Description of Operation: Coffee, donuts, submarine sandwiches, soups, salads, and so on. Fast-food restaurants.

Equity Capital Needed: $100,000

Franchise Fee: $35,000

Royalty: 4 percent

Advertising Co-op Fee:

Financial Assistance: Financing is provided through major banks. Guidance provided.

Management Assistance: We assist in accounting, costing, staffing, sales/marketing, advertising, purchasing, operations, research and development, and construction.

Training Assistance: Five weeks of hands-on training at our national training center. Two additional weeks with training team on-site.

Saint Cinnamon Bakery

7181 Woodbine Ave., Ste. 222
Markham, ON L3R 1A3
Web Address: www.saintcinnamon.com
E-mail Address: info@saintcinnamon.com
Toll-Free Phone:
Phone: (905) 470-1517
Fax: (905) 470-8112
Contact: Vice President

Number of Franchises: 130
Company-Owned Units: 2
Total Units: 132

In Business Since: 1986   **Franchising Since:** 1986

Description of Operation: Freshy baked gourmet cinnamon rolls made in front of customers daily. Hot from the oven and served with our Columbian coffee. Only the finest ingredients are used, including high-quality cinnamon. Franchisee must be hands-on at her or his location.

Equity Capital Needed: $50,000-60,000

Franchise Fee: $25,000

Royalty: 6 percent

Advertising Co-op Fee: 3 percent

Financial Assistance: Not applicable.

Management Assistance: Head office management provides ongoing assistance in all aspects of the business.

Training Assistance: Two weeks of intensive training is done at our head office. This includes rolling the dough and all the required paperwork.

Winchell's Donut

1800 E. 16th St.
Santa Ana, CA 92701
Toll-Free Phone: (800) 347-9347
Phone: (714) 565-1800
Fax: (714) 565-1801
Contact: Franchise Representative

Number of Franchises: 75
Company-Owned Units: 300
Total Units: 375

In Business Since: 1948   **Franchising Since:** 1950

Description of Operation: Winchell's offers coffee, soft drinks, muffins, donuts, and other bakery products.

Equity Capital Needed: $85,000

Franchise Fee: $20,000

Royalty: 5 percent

Advertising Co-op Fee:

Financial Assistance: None

Management Assistance: Store visits by a Winchell's representative, plus market support.

Training Assistance: Complete donut training is conducted at a designated training store, normally taking 3-4 weeks.

Big Apple Bagels

8501 W. Higgins Rd., Ste. 320
Chicago, IL 60631
Toll-Free Phone: (800) 251-6101
Phone: (773) 380-6100
Fax: (773) 380-6183
Contact: Director of Franchise Development

Number of Franchises: 111
Company-Owned Units: 26
Total Units: 137

In Business Since: 1992   **Franchising Since:** 1993

Description of Operation: Exciting bagel concept with over 20 varieties of bagels and gourmet cream cheeses. Also offering muffins and coffee with a tri-branding from My Favorite Muffin and Brewsters Coffee.

Equity Capital Needed:

Franchise Fee: $25,000

Royalty: 5 percent

Advertising Co-op Fee: 2 percent

Financial Assistance: None with the second unit.

Management Assistance: Ten days of intensive training with additional days of on-site assistance; includes an operations and marketing manual.

Training Assistance:

Food—Bakery

Carole's Cheesecake Company

1272 Castlefield Ave.
Toronto, ON M6B 1G3
Toll-Free Phone:
Phone: (416) 256-0000
Fax:
Contact: Executive Vice President

Number of Franchises: 8
Company-Owned Units: 1
Total Units: 9

In Business Since: 1979   **Franchising Since:** 1980

Description of Operation: Manufacturer and retailer of a line of 100 flavors of premium-brand cheesecakes and 20 baked gourmet cake dessert items.

Equity Capital Needed: $8,500-$125,000 (6.5 percent may be borrowed).

Franchise Fee: $15,000-$25,000

Royalty: 0 percent

Advertising Co-op Fee:

Financial Assistance: Major Canadian banks may provide up to 65 percent or more of required total capital expenditure, depending on the credit rating of the applicant.

Management Assistance: Full training is offered at a company-owned outlet. Ongoing assistance. No prior knowledge or experience is required.

Training Assistance: Full training is offered at a company-owned unit. On-site supervision and assistance are given at the franchisee's location during opening stage.

Great Harvest Franchising, Inc.

28 S. Montana St.
Dillon, MT 59725
Web Address: www.greatharvest.com
E-mail Address: info@greatharvest.com
Toll-Free Phone: (800) 442-0424
Phone: (406) 683-6842
Fax: (406) 683-5537
Contact: Development

Number of Franchises: 140
Company-Owned Units: 1
Total Units: 141

In Business Since: 1976   **Franchising Since:** 1978

Description of Operation: Retail premium bread bakeries, specializing in whole wheat products.

Equity Capital Needed: $83,300-$293,300 (at least $100,000 liquid assets)

Franchise Fee: $24,000

Royalty: 7 percent: first five yrs; 6 percent: second five yrs; 5 percent: thereafter

Advertising Co-op Fee:

Financial Assistance: No direct financial assistance is available. Franchisee/lender technical and negotiation assistance offered.

Management Assistance: In addition to access to the world's best baking wheat, the Great Harvest provides strong managerial assistance in all areas of business start-up, opening, and postopening business operations. Ongoing support.

Training Assistance: In addition to close, thorough ongoing training and assistance throughout the start-up phase, Great Harvest provides a minimum of 200 hours of hands-on training.

MMMARVELLOUS MMMUFFINS

3300 Bloor St. W., Ste. 2910
Etobicoke, ON M8X 2X3
Toll-Free Phone:

Phone: (416) 236-0055
Fax: (416) 236-0054
Contact: Franchising Administrator

Number of Franchises: 109
Company-Owned Units: 5
Total Units: 114

In Business Since: 1979   **Franchising Since:** 1980

Description of Operation: Muffins, baked on premises.

Equity Capital Needed: $40,000-$60,000

Franchise Fee: $25,000

Royalty: 7 percent

Advertising Co-op Fee:

Financial Assistance: We provide guidance in preparing the business plan for bank submission as well as bank introductions if required.

Management Assistance: A store service representative provides continuing assistance in all areas of store operation. Field consultants provide leadership and support, assist in implementing standards of operation, consult, and identify profitability opportunities to achieve maximum potential. Regular store visits. Marketing programs are set up to assist the franchisee in marketing and promotion necessary in his or her business.

Training Assistance: We have an intensive 10-day training program for new franchisees. This program has been designed to provide all students with the knowledge, tools, and equipment necessary to maximize the potential of their stores.

Paradise Bakery & Cafe

1610 Arden Way, Suite 145
Sacramento, CA 95815
Toll-Free Phone: (800) 951-9582
Phone: (916) 568-2310
Fax: (916) 568-1240
Contact: V.P. Franchise Sales

Number of Franchises: 37
Company-Owned Units: 16
Total Units: 53

In Business Since: 1976   **Franchising Since:** 1987

Description of Operation: Over 20 years of bakery and cafe experience offering our signature fresh baked goods, made from scratch and baked right on premises all day long. The "food with a flair" menu includes an appetizing selection of made-to-order sandwiches, heavy soups, delicous pastas, and crispy salads. Gourmet coffee lovers will be delighted with the specialty beverages and freshly brewed coffees prepared with 100 percent Arabica coffee beans.

Equity Capital Needed: $150,000

Franchise Fee: $35,000

Royalty: 6 percent

Advertising Co-op Fee: 2 percent of gross sales

Financial Assistance: Third-party financing assistance.

Management Assistance: Operational training and manuals for operations and marketing provided during training sessions. Field representatives in constant contact with franchisees.

Training Assistance: Intensive three-week seminar at our Paradise Bakery & Cafe training facility, plus an additional two weeks preopening training sessions for staff at your cafe. Ongoing support and consultation from area supervisors.

Food—Candy

Americandy

1401 Lexington Rd.
Louisville, KY 40206
E-mail Address: americandy@aol.com
Toll-Free Phone: (800) 822-6392
Phone: (502) 583-1776
Fax: (502) 583-6627
Contact: President

Number of Franchises: 0
Company-Owned Units: 1
Total Units: 1

In Business Since: 1992   **Franchising Since:** 1992

Description of Operation: The marketing of confections and chocolates representing 50 states in beautiful red and gold AmeriCandy presentation boxes. The company owns retail stores and also distributes its products through specialty shops and catalogs. Currently developing an overseas market in Asia.

Equity Capital Needed: $185,000

Franchise Fee: $25,000

Royalty: 6 percent of gross sales

Advertising Co-op Fee: 0

Financial Assistance: We have sources for financing across the country.

Management Assistance: Will set up store and spend two weeks with training of personnel.

Training Assistance:

Bourbon Street Candy Company

266 Elmwood Ave., Ste. 287
Buffalo, NY 14222
E-mail Address: bscc@inter-pc.on.ca
Toll-Free Phone:
Phone: (905) 894-4819
Fax: (905) 894-3072
Contact: President

Number of Franchises: 24
Company-Owned Units: 2
Total Units: 26

In Business Since: 1990   **Franchising Since:** 1991

Description of Operation: Candy and related gift items. Self-serve concept. Makes fresh fudge daily.

Equity Capital Needed: $60,000-$150,000 (kiosk or in-line)

Franchise Fee: $20,000

Royalty: 3 percent

Advertising Co-op Fee: 1 percent

Financial Assistance: Yes.

Management Assistance: The franchise includes ongoing support, as requested or required.

Training Assistance: Each new franchisee receives operations manuals, in addition to having one week of training at an operating location and the assistance of a representative of the franchisor's staff in the opening of the franchisee's store for up to one week.

Kilwin's Chocolates and Ice Cream

355 N. Division Rd.
Petoskey, MI 49770
Web Address: www.kilwins.com
Toll-Free Phone:
Phone: (616) 347-3800
Fax: (616) 347-6951
Contact: President

Number of Franchises: 31
Company-Owned Units: 2
Total Units: 33

In Business Since: 1947   **Franchising Since:** 1982

Description of Operation: Full-line confectionery shops, featuring Kilwin's hand-made chocolates, fudge, and Kilwin's own original-recipe ice cream.

Equity Capital Needed: $90,000-$175,000

Franchise Fee: $20,000

Royalty: 5 percent

Advertising Co-op Fee:

Financial Assistance: None

Management Assistance: Interviewing, hiring, training, and employee supervision guides, plus ongoing training. Includes a 140-page operations manual.

Training Assistance: Initial training for 10 days at headquarters and store. Ongoing training as needed.

Rocky Mountain Chocolate Factory

265 Turner Dr.
Durango, CO 81301
Toll-Free Phone: (800) 438-7623
Phone: (970) 259-0554

Fax: (970) 259-5895
Contact: Franchise Development

Number of Franchises: 186
Company-Owned Units: 36
Total Units: 222

In Business Since: 1981 **Franchising Since:** 1982

Description of Operation: Retail sale of packaged and bulk gourmet chocolates, brittles, truffles, sauces, cocoas, coffees, assorted hard candies, and related chocolate and nonchocolate items. In-store preparation of fudges, caramel apples, and dipped fruit through interactive cooking demonstrations. Complete line of gift and holiday items. Supplemental retail sale of soft drinks, ice cream, cookies, and brewed coffee.

Equity Capital Needed: net worth—$200,000

Franchise Fee: $19,500

Royalty: 5 percent, plus 1 percent marketing and promotional fee = 6 percent total

Advertising Co-op Fee:

Financial Assistance: None at this time.

Management Assistance: Ongoing support and training provided by field staff. Annual national meetings and biannual regional meetings.

Training Assistance: Complete training provided in customer service, record keeping, merchandising, inventory control, and marketing during 10-day program at corporate headquarters, in addition to several days on-site for store opening.

Food—Coffee & Tea

Tim Hortons

4288 W. Dublin-Granville Road
Dublin, OH 43017
Toll-Free Phone:
Phone: (614) 764-3100
Fax: (614) 766-3868
Contact: Manager of Franchising

Number of Franchises: 1,425
Company-Owned Units: 100
Total Units: 1,525

In Business Since: 1964 **Franchising Since:** 1965

Description of Operation: Tim Hortons is Canada's largest franchised retail coffee, donut, and specialty baked goods chain, with over 1,500 locations across Canada and the United States. The franchisee purchases a turnkey operation, the right to use Tim Hortons' trademarks and tradenames, a comprehensive seven-to eight-week training program, and ongoing operational and marketing support.

Equity Capital Needed: 30 percent of purchase price

Franchise Fee: $35,000

Royalty: 4.5 percent of gross sales

Advertising Co-op Fee: 4 percent of gross sales

Financial Assistance: Through financing institutions.

Management Assistance: Assistance of the operations staff with the initial store opening and ongoing support and guidance of the Head Office personnel, experienced in all aspects of this business.

Training Assistance: An eight-week intensive and extensive program at the training center in Oakville, Ontario.

My Favorite Muffin, Too, Inc.

8501 W. Higgens Road
Chicago, IL 60631
Toll-Free Phone: (800) 251-6101
Phone: (773) 380-6100
Fax: (773) 380-6183
Contact: Director of Franchise Development

Number of Franchises: 62
Company-Owned Units: 9
Total Units: 71

In Business Since: 1987 **Franchising Since:** 1988

Description of Operation: Exciting concept featuring a selection from over 300 regular and fat-free muffins. Also, offering bagels and coffee with branding from Big Apple Bagels and Brewsters Coffee.

Equity Capital Needed:

Franchise Fee: $25,000

Royalty: 5 percent

Advertising Co-op Fee: 1 percent

Financial Assistance: None until the second unit.

Management Assistance: Ten days of intensive training, plus three days of additional on-site assistance. Includes operations and marketing manual.

Training Assistance:

Nutter's Bulk & Natural Foods

1601 Dunmore Rd. S.E. Ste. 107
Medicine Hat, AB T1A 1Z8
Toll-Free Phone: (800) 665-5122
Phone: (403) 529-1664
Fax: (403) 529-6507
Contact: Franchise Licensing Director

Number of Franchises: 31
Company-Owned Units: 3
Total Units: 34

In Business Since: 1982 **Franchising Since:** 1983

Description of Operation: Nutter's offers a huge selection of products, ranging from exotic tea and coffee, natural and organic products, aromatic spices, pastas, grains, beans and deli products, to everyday, fine-quality baking needs. All of these are offered in a clean, healthy, friendly store atmosphere. No messy containers or bins, but rather a brightly decorated store with attractive dispensing containers.

Equity Capital Needed: $150,000-$200,000

Franchise Fee: $30,000

Royalty: 4 percent

Advertising Co-op Fee:

Financial Assistance: No financing is available at this time.

Management Assistance: New franchisees are provided with location analysis, including site selection and lease negotiations. We provide complete store layouts and store equipment packages. Also provided are complete operating packages, from accounting systems to extensive merchandising to promotional programs and staff training. We offer capital and operating budgets, coordinated franchise-wide promotional programs, sample advertising layouts, and ongoing advertising assistance.

Training Assistance: We provide a 30-day training program at our head office. The program includes all aspects of day-to-day business. On-site training is provided also at the time of opening.

Food—Cookies

Cookie Bouquet/Cookies By Design

1865 Summit Ave. Ste. 605
Plano, TX 75074
Web Address: www.cookiebouquet.com
Toll-Free Phone: (800) 945-2665
Phone: (972) 881-4311
Fax: (972) 881-8116
Contact: Vice President of Franchise Development

Number of Franchises: 166
Company-Owned Units: 1
Total Units: 167

In Business Since: 1983 **Franchising Since:** 1987

Description of Operation: Unique retail opportunity! Gift bakery, specializing in hand-decorated cookie arrangements and gourmet cookies, created for special events, holidays, centerpieces, and so on. Clientele includes both individual and corporate customers. A wonderful, delicious alternative to flowers or balloons.

Equity Capital Needed: $50,250-$110,000

Franchise Fee: $20,000

Royalty: 6 percent

Advertising Co-op Fee:

Financial Assistance: None

Management Assistance: Cookie Bouquet produces complete training, operations, design, decorating, and employee manuals. Stores receive periodic visits from corporation representatives. The corporation publishes a monthly newsletter and holiday bulletins and also holds an annual convention.

Training Assistance: An extensive two-week "Cookie College" at the corporate headquarters in Plano, TX, will show new franchise owners a working store, where they can have hands-on training in every aspect of the business.

Cookies in Bloom

5437 N. MacArthur Blvd.
Irving, TX 75038
Toll-Free Phone: (800) 222-3104
Phone: (972) 518-1749
Fax: (972) 580-1831
Contact: Owner

Number of Franchises: 14
Company-Owned Units: 0
Total Units: 14

In Business Since: 1988 **Franchising Since:** 1992

Description of Operation: Hand-decorated cookies, gourmet cookies, and whimsical cookie arrangements for retail sale. Available in baskets, tote sacks, and wooden or ceramic containers.

Equity Capital Needed: $53,000-$108,000

Franchise Fee: $12,500

Royalty: 5 percent

Advertising Co-op Fee:

Financial Assistance: None

Management Assistance: Cookies in Bloom personnel are trained completely in all areas of the managerial skills needed to operate a Cookies in Bloom shop—everything from employee hiring to tax report preparation.

Training Assistance: Each Cookies in Bloom franchisee is fully trained in all areas of the preparation of the cookie arrangements, as well as in sales training.

Great American Cookie Company, Inc.

4685 Frederick Dr., S.W.
Atlanta, GA 30336
Web Address: www.greatamericancookies.com
Toll-Free Phone: (800) 336-2447
Phone: (404) 696-1700
Fax: (404) 699-0887
Contact: Senior Vice President of Franchising

Number of Franchises: 250
Company-Owned Units: 80
Total Units: 330

In Business Since: 1977　　**Franchising Since:** 1978

Description of Operation: Retail cookie stores, primarily in major regional malls nationwide.

Equity Capital Needed: $170,000

Franchise Fee: $25,000

Royalty: 7 percent

Advertising Co-op Fee:

Financial Assistance: None

Management Assistance: Complete training is provided in all operations of a cookie store.

Training Assistance: A six-day training program at the corporate office and in-store. Ongoing operation and marketing assistance.

Food—Frozen Dessert

All American Frozen Yogurt & Ice Cream Shops

812 S.W. Washington St., Ste. 1110
Portland, OR 97205
Toll-Free Phone:
Phone: (503) 224-6199
Fax: (503) 224-5042
Contact: President

Number of Franchises: 17
Company-Owned Units: 2
Total Units: 19

In Business Since: 1986　　**Franchising Since:** 1988

Description of Operation: Retail shop, selling frozen yogurt and ice cream. Majority of shops are in enclosed shopping centers. Upscale design.

Equity Capital Needed: $45,000

Franchise Fee: $7,500-$20,000

Royalty: 5 percent

Advertising Co-op Fee:

Financial Assistance: The company offers no direct financing arrangements. The company has financial contacts with lenders.

Management Assistance: Comprehensive training program: one week at corporate office and one week in store. Complete operations training, including manuals, accounting, menu items, personnel, and day-to-day operations.

Training Assistance: See above.

Emack & Bolio's

P.O. Box 703
Brookline Village, MA 02147

E-mail Address: enbic@aol.com
Toll-Free Phone:
Phone: (617) 739-7995
Fax: (617) 232-1102
Contact: President

Number of Franchises: 40
Company-Owned Units: 1
Total Units: 41

In Business Since: 1975　　**Franchising Since:** 1977

Description of Operation: We sell at retail super-premium ice cream and yogurt along with a juice bar, vitamins, coffee, teas, and pastries.

Equity Capital Needed: Data not avaiable.

Franchise Fee: none

Royalty: none

Advertising Co-op Fee:

Financial Assistance: None

Management Assistance: Training and assistance on-site when opening. Telephone support, newsletter, video, and so on.

Training Assistance: 10 days at our company store in Macy's New York City.

Everything Yogurt Express

1000 South Street
Staten Island, NY 10314
Toll-Free Phone: (800) 205-6050
Phone: (718) 494-8888
Fax: (718) 494-8776
Contact: Director of Sales

Number of Franchises: 12
Company-Owned Units: 0
Total Units: 12

In Business Since: 1976　　**Franchising Since:** 1981

Description of Operation: Everything Yogurt Express is Restaurant Systems International's first franchise concept. While its first location was opened over twenty years ago, Everything Yogurt Express continues to capitalize on the nonfat, great-tasting, wholesome appeal of frozen yogurt. Everything Yogurt Express has everything going for you. Sales per square foot are considerably greater than any of our competitors. Substantial profit return on each dollar invested. And far more years building a loyal following.

Equity Capital Needed: $50,000

Franchise Fee: $15,000

Royalty: 5 percent monthly

Advertising Co-op Fee: 1 percent

Financial Assistance: Our company uses third-party lenders to help franchisees secure financing.

Management Assistance: All franchisees must complete a two-week training program consisting of in-store training and classroom instruction.

Training Assistance: Training consists of two-week, in-store, hands-on work and classroom instruction covering all aspects of operating a successful business.

Petrucci's Dairy Barn

507 W. Corporate Dr.
Langhorne, PA 19047
Toll-Free Phone: (888) 550-8020
Phone: (215) 860-4848
Fax: (215) 860-6123
Contact: Vice President

Number of Franchises: 112
Company-Owned Units: 0
Total Units: 112

In Business Since: 1983   **Franchising Since:** 1996

Description of Operation: 50 flavors of soft-serve ice cream and frozen yogurt, cones, shakes, sundaes, Mega Blend™, cakes, pies, Italian ices, hand-dipped ice cream, frozen novelties, soft pretzels, and much more.

Equity Capital Needed: $150,000

Franchise Fee: $20,000

Royalty: 5 percent of gross sales

Advertising Co-op Fee: To be announced

Financial Assistance: Third-party financing to qualified individuals.

Management Assistance: Complete operations manual and ongoing assistance; refresher courses offered periodically.

Training Assistance: Training at corporate headquarters, on-site training, manuals, and an individual store representative.

Rita's Italian Ices

1525 Ford Road P.O. Box 1329
Bensalem, PA 19020
Web Address: www.ritasice.com
Toll-Free Phone: (800) 677-7482
Phone: (215) 633-9899
Fax: (215) 633-9922
Contact: Director of Franchise Licensing

Number of Franchises: 154
Company-Owned Units: 3
Total Units: 157

In Business Since: 1984   **Franchising Since:** 1990

Description of Operation: Rita's Italian Ices is this country's largest retail specialty ice chain. Our stores offer customer gourmet Italian ices made fresh on premises daily along with premium frozen custard; soft pretzels; and our newest product, "Misto," which is a "smoothie" type of drink. Stores operate 11 hours per day, seven days per week, with the majority of the stores open March through October. Rita's is currently offering individual franchises and area development agreements to qualified franchises.

Equity Capital Needed: $70,000

Franchise Fee: $22,500

Royalty: 6.5 percent

Advertising Co-op Fee: Yes. 2 1/2 percent

Financial Assistance: While Rita's does not provide any direct financial assistance to franchisees, we have several banks and leasing companies that have expressed interest in financing qualified franchisees.

Management Assistance: The company provides a comprehensive five-day training program for all franchisees. In addition, corporate assistance is provided by executives trained in real estate acquisition, construction, marketing, and operations.

Training Assistance: Initial training in site selection process is followed by a comprehensive five-day operating training at our Bensalem, PA, corporate office. Areas covered in the training include administration, personnel marketing, product preparation, and customer service.

Yogen Fruz

8300 Woodbine Ave., Ste. 500
Markham, ON M2M 328
Web Address: www.yogenfruz.com
Toll-Free Phone:
Phone: (905) 479-8762
Fax: (905) 479-5235
Contact: Director of Franchising & Retail Expansion

Number of Franchises: 3800+
Company-Owned Units: 6
Total Units: 3800+

In Business Since: 1986   **Franchising Since:** 1987

Description of Operation: Frozen yogurt and frozen dairy-related treats.

Equity Capital Needed: 50 percent

Franchise Fee: $25,000

Royalty: 6 percent

Advertising Co-op Fee: 2 percent

Financial Assistance: Third-party financing.

Management Assistance: The franchisor negotiates the lease, handles the preparation of plans, contracts the construction, equips the entire store, sets up suppliers, and arranges distribution.

Training Assistance: Training includes one week at a corporate store and one week of training at the franchisee's store. Operations manual, marketing manual, and manager's manual.

Baskin 31 Robbins Ice Cream

31 Baskin Robbins Pl.
Glendale, CA 91201
Toll-Free Phone: (800) 331-0031
Phone: (818) 956-0031

Fax:

Contact: National Franchise Director

Number of Franchises: 197
Company-Owned Units: 0
Total Units: 197

In Business Since: 1940   **Franchising Since:** 1971

Description of Operation: Retail sale of hard and soft ice cream and frozen desserts.

Equity Capital Needed: $45,000-$50,000

Franchise Fee: $25,000

Royalty: .5 percent of 1 percent

Advertising Co-op Fee:

Financial Assistance: We have packages set up with banks that detail our operation, but assistance depends on the franchisee's application and relationship with the bank.

Management Assistance: A district manager is assigned to every location, operating as the franchisee's business advisor and operational consultant.

Training Assistance: Participation in an extensive three-week training program in California is mandatory.

Haagen-Dazs Shoppe Company, The

GlenPointe Centre East
Teaneck, NJ 07666
Toll-Free Phone: (800) 793-6872
Phone:
Fax:
Contact: Franchise Development Manager

Number of Franchises: 257
Company-Owned Units: 2
Total Units: 259

In Business Since: 1961   **Franchising Since:** 1978

Description of Operation: Haagen-Dazs operates retail shops, which represent excellent sampling and marketing opportunities for entrepreneurs who recognize quality in products and services, and who will represent the undisputed leader in the super-premium ice cream segment with distinction. Applicants must be U.S. citizens or permanent resident aliens and have $75,000 in liquid assets.

Equity Capital Needed: $250,000 net worth excluding residence

Franchise Fee: $35,000

Royalty: $1.16 per gallon of ice cream purchased.

Advertising Co-op Fee:

Financial Assistance: None

Management Assistance: Franchisees receive assistance with site selection and negotiation, attend an 11-day training school, and receive ongoing operations consulting

and advice from company representatives. Company franchise area managers are trained professionals.

Training Assistance: Potential franchisees must attend and successfully complete an 11-day training school, located in Fairfield, NJ. This school offers training development in the day-to-day operation of the business.

Ice Cream Churn

3361 Boyington Ste. 200
Carrollton, TX 75006
Web Address: www.icecreamchurn.com
Toll-Free Phone:
Phone: (972) 788-5294
Fax: (972) 233-4129
Contact: Vice President of Sales

Number of Franchises: 542
Company-Owned Units: 0
Total Units: 542

In Business Since: 1973   **Franchising Since:** 1981

Description of Operation: Ice Cream Churn establishes ice cream parlors, offering 32 flavors of ice cream and yogurt, within another business, such as delis, bakeries, video stores, convenience stores, donut shops, truckstops, etc. Churn's regional agents assist in setting up the locations and signs, train employees, and then support the location with ongoing promotional support. Kiosks for malls are available. Packages available in malls and WalMart Super Centers.

Equity Capital Needed: $15,000-$50,000

Franchise Fee: $10,000

Royalty: $1.00 per tub

Advertising Co-op Fee:

Financial Assistance: Financing is available for equipment and sign packages in most areas.

Management Assistance: Regional agents train managers and all employees on the opening of locations and on regular monthly visits. Additional training is available as needed. ICC also provides promotions to increase sales, and works with managers to implement these programs.

Training Assistance: For each location, ICC provides training and training manuals, which cover all phases of the operation. This training is performed at the actual location before and after the opening of a Churn.

Marble Slab Creamery

3100 S. Gessner, Ste. 305
Houston, TX 77063
Web Address: www.marbleslab.com
E-mail Address: marbleslab@marbleslab.com
Toll-Free Phone:
Phone: (713) 780-3601
Fax: (713) 780-0264
Contact: Development Coordinator

Number of Franchises: 26
Company-Owned Units: 2
Total Units: 28

In Business Since: 1983   **Franchising Since:** 1984

Description of Operation: Retail ice cream stores, featuring super-premium, quality ice cream, cones baked fresh daily, fresh-frozen yogurt, cookies, brownies, frozen pies, and cakes. Ice cream is custom-designed for customers on frozen marble slabs and made daily in each store. Open seven days a week.

Equity Capital Needed: $35,000-$45,000

Franchise Fee: $19,000-$25,000

Royalty: 5 percent in year one; 6 percent thereafter

Advertising Co-op Fee:

Financial Assistance: None. However, the franchisor will provide assistance in locating financing through independent financial institutions.

Management Assistance: Marble Slab Creamery maintains an ongoing business relationship with its franchisees, with assistance available in all phases of store operations. A complete operations manual is provided to all franchisees. Company field personnel visit stores regularly to ensure the consistency of operations throughout the franchise system. Marble Slab Creamery constantly updates advertising programs and evaluates new products for its franchised locations.

Training Assistance: 10 days of training in the company's training facilities in Houston, TX. Six additional days of training at franchisee's store (three days before opening and three days after opening).

TCBY Systems

1200 TCBY Tower, 425 W. Capitol Ave.
Little Rock, AR 72201
Web Address: www.tcby.com
Toll-Free Phone:
Phone: (501) 688-8229
Fax: (501) 688-8549
Contact: Director of Franchise Sales

Number of Franchises: 2765
Company-Owned Units: 1
Total Units: 2766

In Business Since: 1981   **Franchising Since:** 1982

Description of Operation: Frozen yogurt and ice cream served in a variety of specialty desserts.

Equity Capital Needed: $116,000-$341,900

Franchise Fee: $2,500-$20,000

Royalty: 4 percent

Advertising Co-op Fee:

Financial Assistance: No financial assistance is available.

Management Assistance: You will receive operations manuals, a library of training tapes (which are updated

regularly) and a trained division manager will be present to guide you through your three to five days of operation to ensure a smooth, efficient, and successful opening period. The division manager will evaluate your operation and advise you regularly.

Training Assistance: A seven-day training program at corporate headquarters in Little Rock, AR, is provided for you and your manager. This program has been designed to cover vital areas of importance in your success as a franchise owner. It covers the operations manual, library of training tapes, equipment layout, methods of inventory control, bookkeeping and accounting, equipment maintenance, advertising, promotion methods, standards of quality, personnel policies, training of employees, and operational techniques.

White Mountain Creamery

3600 Chamberlain Ln. Ste. 720
Louisville, KY 40241
Toll-Free Phone:
Phone: (502) 423-8962
Fax: (502) 423-8421
Contact: President

Number of Franchises: 28
Company-Owned Units: 3
Total Units: 31

In Business Since: 1985   **Franchising Since:** 1987

Description of Operation: White Mountain Creamery is a unique concept, featuring on-site production of super-premium ice cream, frozen yogurt, and bakery goods. We appeal to a wide market niche by offering products for the entire family—everything from fat-free, sugar-free diet desserts and bakery products to rich, award-winning ice cream. We also offer frozen cakes and pies, as well as specialty coffees in a friendly, family atmosphere. Our locations include strip centers, some with a drive-thru window, enclosed malls, and free-standing stores.

Equity Capital Needed: $60,000-$75,000

Franchise Fee: $20,000

Royalty: 4 percent

Advertising Co-op Fee: 1 percent

Financial Assistance: We assist in the evaluation of your business plan for submission to commercial leaders or SBA personnel. We do not offer internal financing at this time.

Management Assistance: We offer floor plans and store layout, site selection and lease negotiation, construction assistance, preopening equipment planning, preopening crew training and product production assistance, and grand opening planning assistance. Postopening service continues throughout the term of the franchise to help you manage your store's growth and profitability. There is a 1 percent cooperative marketing and advertising fund.

Training Assistance: Training consists of a 14-day combination classroom and in-store training at headquarters for profit-making knowledge, which includes philosophy and sales strategy, customer sales and service, cash control management, merchandising, hiring, and training. Confidential and comprehensive training manuals. Extensive continuing education programs. Special training sessions available.

Food—Popcorn, Nuts & Pretzels

Boardwalk Peanuts

P.O. Box 1134
Pleasantville, NJ 08232
E-mail Address: leopeanuts@msn.com
Toll-Free Phone:
Phone: (609) 272-1511
Fax: (609) 407-0937
Contact: President

Number of Franchises: 1
Company-Owned Units: 6
Total Units: 7

In Business Since: 1971 **Franchising Since:** 1987

Description of Operation: Retail nuts, chocolates, popcorn, and seasonal confectionaries. Ideal for boardwalk or resort areas.

Equity Capital Needed: $60,000-$100,000

Franchise Fee: $12,000

Royalty: 5 percent

Advertising Co-op Fee:

Financial Assistance: Assistance with bank loans. Loan package.

Management Assistance: We provide an operations manual and two days of on-site opening assistance.

Training Assistance: We offer a five-day training program, plus an 800# for instant response to problems.

Gretel's Pretzels

1000 South Ave.
Staten Island, NY 10314
Toll-Free Phone: (800) 205-6050
Phone: (718) 494-8888
Fax: (718) 494-8776
Contact: Director of Sales

Number of Franchises: 16
Company-Owned Units: 1
Total Units: 17

In Business Since: 1993 **Franchising Since:** 1994

Description of Operation: Gretel's Pretzels is a single-concept franchise with more than a single product—two

in fact: homemade, hand-rolled soft pretzels and frosty fruit shakes. This is a big competitive advantage over single-product concepts: the consumer is stopped with a double-action taste appeal. The franchisee gets a double shot at better-than-average sales per square foot. Gretel's Pretzels is an ever-appealing concept from a long established leader in the healthy fast-food industry—the Restaurant Systems management team.

Equity Capital Needed: $50,000

Franchise Fee: $20,000

Royalty: 5 percent monthly

Advertising Co-op Fee: 1 percent

Financial Assistance: Our company uses third-party lendors to assist franchisees secure financing.

Management Assistance: All franchisees must complete a two-week training program consisting of in-store training and classroom instruction.

Training Assistance: Training consists of a two-week program of in-store, hands-on work and classroom instruction covering all aspects of operating a successful business.

Topsy's International

221 W. 74th Terrace
Kansas City, MO 64114
Toll-Free Phone:
Phone: (818) 523-5555
Fax: (819) 523-4747
Contact: President

Number of Franchises: 16
Company-Owned Units: 1
Total Units: 17

In Business Since: 1950 **Franchising Since:** 1967

Description of Operation: Retail popcorn and ice cream shop. Regional malls provide the best location. Topsy's is the leader in the popcorn gift canister business. Topsy's enhances its store volumes by its corporate and mail order canister program.

Equity Capital Needed: $100,000-$150,000

Franchise Fee: $20,000

Royalty: 5 percent

Advertising Co-op Fee:

Financial Assistance: Because of the number of years the company has been in business and the success of most of its franchisees, this franchise concept has been approved for many levels of SBA financing.

Management Assistance: Managerial and marketing programs are ongoing throughout the term of the franchise.

Training Assistance: The franchisee is required to train in Kansas City, MO, in an existing shop and commissary for at least one week. The franchisor provides a representative for a period of approximately three to five days during the opening of each franchised location. These periods can be extended, depending on the franchisee's background and expertise.

Food—Miscellaneous

B.Y.O.B. Water Store

1288 W. Main #103
Lewisville, TX 75067
Toll-Free Phone:
Phone: (972) 219-1551
Fax:
Contact: President

Number of Franchises: 10
Company-Owned Units: 0
Total Units: 10

In Business Since: 1984   **Franchising Since:** 1985

Description of Operation: A B.Y.O.B. Water Store is a specialty store which sells its main product "processed water" to the consumer in his or her own bottle. Because we manufacture our main product on-site and ask the consumer to "Bring Your Own Bottle" to fill up with our "tea totaling water," there is very little cost to the consumer. We sell also ice, bottles, crocks, coolers, and so on.

Equity Capital Needed: Not applicable

Franchise Fee: The company licenses the process to you.

Royalty: Not applicable

Advertising Co-op Fee:

Financial Assistance: Data not provided

Management Assistance: Newsletter optional.

Training Assistance:

Bananas Ultimate Juice Bar

1000 South Avenue
Staten Island, NY 10314
Toll-Free Phone: (800) 205-6050
Phone: (718) 494-8888
Fax: (718) 494-6050
Contact: Director of Sales

Number of Franchises: 89
Company-Owned Units: 3
Total Units: 92

In Business Since: 1976   **Franchising Since:** 1981

Description of Operation: Bananas Ultimate Juice Bar is a single-product concept that's a natural. First, it offers consumers a choice of 25 blended or mixed fresh fruits, fruit and frozen yogurt smoothies, traditional favorites, and exotic fruit mixtures—all with natural additives like

ginseng, wheat grass, protein powder, and bee pollen. Second, Bananas Ultimate Juice Bar's enticing envrinoment, colors, and specially designed counters provide extra consumer appeal. Finally, Bananas Ultimate Juice Bar is a perfect healthy complement to an Everything Yogurt and Salad Cafe or Gretel's Pretzels . . . sharing the same facilities, utilities, and management. The result is a marked increase in operating efficiency and considerable cost savings.

Equity Capital Needed: $50,000

Franchise Fee: $20,000

Royalty: 5 percent monthly

Advertising Co-op Fee: 1 percent

Financial Assistance: Our company uses third-party lenders to assist franchisees secure financing.

Management Assistance: All franchisees must complete a two-week training program with some classroom instruction.

Training Assistance: Training consists of a two-week program consisting of in-store, hands-on work and classroom instruction covering all aspects of operating a successful business.

Creative Croissants

6335 Ferris Square Ste. G
San Diego, CA 92121
Toll-Free Phone: (800) 735-3182
Phone: (619) 587-7300
Fax: (619) 587-7309
Contact:

Number of Franchises: 30
Company-Owned Units: 3
Total Units: 33

In Business Since: 1981   **Franchising Since:** 1986

Description of Operation: Upscale restaurant, featuring gourmet coffees, espresso and cappuccino drinks, freshly tossed salads, gourmet sandwiches, baked potatoes, and unique hot meal croissants. Also, featuring baked goods, freshly baked on the premises—dessert croissants, Danish, puff pastry, and muffins.

Equity Capital Needed: $99,000-$145,000

Franchise Fee: $17,500

Royalty: 4.5 percent

Advertising Co-op Fee:

Financial Assistance: Not available.

Management Assistance: Ongoing business planning, site selection assistance, lease negotiations, promotional support, marketing support, and national contracts with food and beverage vendors.

Training Assistance: Two weeks of training in operational store, as well as classroom training. Opening week help and staff support, as well as assistance with promotional items for grand opening.

Edelweiss Deli Express

Unit 7—3331 Viking Way
Richmond, BC V6V 1X7
Toll-Free Phone:
Phone: (604) 270-2360
Fax: (604) 270-6560
Contact: President

Number of Franchises: 12
Company-Owned Units: 0
Total Units: 12

In Business Since: 1973   **Franchising Since:** 1988

Description of Operation: We find the location and build a turnkey operation. We help hire people and train the new employees. We help order all food and work with the food distribution. We stay with the franchisee for 1-2 weeks at opening. We will do biweekly checks and can be called any time for assistance.

Equity Capital Needed: $85,000-$115,000

Franchise Fee: $20,000

Royalty: 6 percent

Advertising Co-op Fee: 2 percent

Financial Assistance: We will work with banks or any other finance institution.

Management Assistance: Director of Marketing, Director of Franchising, Director of Food Service, and Training Supervisor.

Training Assistance: We train new franchisees for four or more weeks. We give ongoing assistance for 10 years. We have training manuals, forms, sales aids, and franchise meetings every second month, plus product seminars.

M&M Meat Shops

640 Trillium Drive, P.O. Box 2488
Kitchener, ON N3L 2V1
E-mail Address: chrisf@mmms.ca
Toll-Free Phone:
Phone: (519) 895-1075
Fax: (519) 895-0762
Contact: Administrative Assistant, Franchising

Number of Franchises: 227
Company-Owned Units: 1
Total Units: 228

In Business Since: 1980   **Franchising Since:** 1981

Description of Operation: Canada's largest specialty frozen food chain, providing high-quality meats and specialty frozen foods items to the public at reasonable prices. Our product caters to a variety of life styles—homemakers, seniors, professionals, and tradespeople. M&M Meat Shops sells a select variety of frozen meats, seafood, desserts, party foods, cheese, and vegtables. M&M Meat Shops also features convenient heat-and-serve products geared to today's fast-paced consumer.

Equity Capital Needed: $150,000

Franchise Fee: $30,000

Royalty: 3 percent

Advertising Co-op Fee: 1.5 percent

Financial Assistance: M&M Meat Shops has an excellent working relationship with all major banks. We have banking packages for candidates who can meet preset qualifications. M&M Meat Shops does not finance.

Management Assistance: A field consultant works directly with the franchisee in the store for a period leading up to and immediately following the grand opening. This same field consultant is available at all times for assistance to the franchisee as required.

Training Assistance: Mandatory 14-day training period is held in Kitchener, Ontario, at both our head office location and our corporate store. All aspects of the operation are covered.

Mr. Mugs

P.O. Box 20019
Brantford, ON N3P 2A4
Toll-Free Phone:
Phone: (519) 752-9890
Fax: (519) 752-0978
Contact: President

Number of Franchises: 19
Company-Owned Units: 2
Total Units: 21

In Business Since: 1984   **Franchising Since:** 1986

Description of Operation: A very active coffee and donut chain with a deli bar, combined with homemade soups and chili. A complete line of fresh-baked muffins is offered, along with freshly baked bread.

Equity Capital Needed: $60,000-$70,000

Franchise Fee: $20,000

Royalty: 4 percent

Advertising Co-op Fee:

Financial Assistance: Support with loan applications and sources of funding. Partial financing available only in Canada.

Management Assistance: On-site head office staff available for assistance whenever necessary in all aspects of business.

Training Assistance: Extensive training in baking, marketing, advertising, and all aspects of successfully running a franchise.

Murphy's Pizza/Papa Aldo's

8000 N.E. Parkway Ste. 350
Vancouver, WA 98662
Toll-Free Phone:
Phone: (360) 260-7272

Fax: (360) 260-0500
Contact: President

Number of Franchises: 110
Company-Owned Units: 5
Total Units: 115

In Business Since: 1984   Franchising Since: 1986

Description of Operation: High-quality products (pizza, calzone, and lasagna), made from scratch for the customer to bake at home. We offer the highest-quality products and sell them to the consumer at a great value.

Equity Capital Needed: $80,000-$100,000

Franchise Fee: $17,500

Royalty: 5 percent plus 1 percent marketing

Advertising Co-op Fee:

Financial Assistance: None

Management Assistance: The franchisee must be the owner/operator. No investors. Managerial skills are taught during training program. On-site representative assists franchisee in developing management skills.

Training Assistance: One week of training at corporate headquarters. Three weeks at other franchise stores. Field representative works with you for the first week at your store and during your grand opening promotions.

Orange Julius of America

P.O. Box 39286
Minneapolis, MN 55439
Web Address:
E-mail Address:
Toll-Free Phone: (800) 285-8515
Phone: (612) 830-0327
Fax: (612) 830-0450
Contact:

Number of Franchises: 493
Company-Owned Units: 0
Total Units: 493

In Business Since: 1926   Franchising Since: 1930

Description of Operation: Franchising of specialty drink and hot dog shops.

Equity Capital Needed: $150,000 net worth; $70,000 liquid assets.

Franchise Fee: $15,000

Royalty: 6 percent

Advertising Co-op Fee:

Financial Assistance: OJA will finance 50 percent of initial franchise fee.

Management Assistance: We provide complete, ongoing operations assistance.

Training Assistance: We offer a comprehensive training program.

White Hen Pantry

660 Industrial Dr.
Elmhurst, IL 60126
Toll-Free Phone: (800) 726-8791
Phone: (630) 833-3100
Fax: (630) 833-0292
Contact: Franchise Manager

Number of Franchises: 224
Company-Owned Units: 1
Total Units: 225

In Business Since: 1965   Franchising Since: 1965

Description of Operation: Neighborhood convenience store; coffee, deli, sandwiches, salads, produce, and bakery.

Equity Capital Needed: $25,000-$30,000

Franchise Fee: $60,000-$65,000 total investment

Royalty:

Advertising Co-op Fee: None

Financial Assistance: Financing is provided by White Hen Pantry.

Management Assistance: Field personnel provide regular business counseling.

Training Assistance: Selected candidates will be trained in customer service, food service, sales development, and accounting procedures.

Franchise—Consulting

Docucorp

2217 West Elizabeth Street
Fort Collins, CO 80521
Toll-Free Phone:
Phone: (970) 484-5145
Fax: (970) 484-5145
Contact: President

Number of Franchises: 0
Company-Owned Units: 1
Total Units: 1

In Business Since: 1983   Franchising Since:

Description of Operation: Docucorp is a franchise consulting firm offering the following services: Drafting of operations manuals, franchise development, and business consulting.

Equity Capital Needed: n/a

Franchise Fee: n/a

Royalty: n/a

Advertising Co-op Fee: n/a

Financial Assistance: Possible funding for franchise development.

Management Assistance: Full consulting services.

Training Assistance: Full training programs are available.

Entrepreneur's Source, The

900 Main St. South, Bldg. 2
Southbury, CT 06488
Web Address: www.franchisesearch.com
E-mail Address: info@entrepreneursource.com
Toll-Free Phone: (800) 289-0086
Phone: (203) 264-2006
Fax: (203) 264-3516
Contact: President

Number of Franchises: 0
Company-Owned Units: 6
Total Units: 6

In Business Since: 1984   **Franchising Since:** 1997

Description of Operation: Franchise consulting, coaching, placement/selection, and development firm providing services to prospective and existing franchisees and franchisors. The Entrepreneur's Source has helped hundreds of people choose the right franchise. We also assist companies seeking to expand through franchising. Our experienced staff can provide you with everything you need to package, launch, and maintain a successful and profitable franchise system.

Equity Capital Needed: $25,000-$85,000

Franchise Fee: $19,500-$$50,000

Royalty: 0

Advertising Co-op Fee: $350/month

Financial Assistance:

Management Assistance: This is an excellent opportunity for individuals with a record of accomplishment in management or sales careers. Specific experience in franchising is not required. The ideal candidate is an innovative self-starter, solves problems effectively, and possesses strong interpersonal skills.

Training Assistance: Two-week training period and ongoing support provided.

Franchise Consultants, Inc.

7119 E. Shea Blvd., Ste. 109-187
Scottsdale, AZ 85254
Web Address:
E-mail Address: bobservcen@aol.com
Toll-Free Phone: (888) 513-1672
Phone: (602) 348-1021
Fax: (602) 443-4653
Contact: President

Number of Franchises:
Company-Owned Units:
Total Units:

In Business Since: 1995   **Franchising Since:** 1995

Description of Operation: Advice and hands-on assistance in helping a potential franchise purchase, or a business desiring to build, a regional or national franchise operation.

Equity Capital Needed:

Franchise Fee:

Royalty:

Advertising Co-op Fee:

Financial Assistance: Advice

Management Assistance: Advice and document preparation.

Training Assistance: Whatever is needed.

Grocery

Oky Doky Foods

1250 Iowa St.
Dubuque, IA 52001
Toll-Free Phone:
Phone: (319) 556-8050
Fax: (319) 582-6334
Contact: General Manager

Number of Franchises: 8
Company-Owned Units: 8
Total Units: 16

In Business Since: 1916   **Franchising Since:** 1964

Description of Operation: Convenience stores.

Equity Capital Needed: $25,000

Franchise Fee: $0

Royalty: 2 percent

Advertising Co-op Fee:

Financial Assistance: Depends on the applicant.

Management Assistance: As much as required.

Training Assistance: On-the-job training.

Quickway Convenience Store

44 Grand St.
Sidney, NY 13838
Toll-Free Phone:
Phone: (607) 561-2700
Fax: (607) 563-1460
Contact: V.P. of Marketing

Number of Franchises: 3
Company-Owned Units: 35
Total Units: 38

In Business Since: 1952   **Franchising Since:** 1992

Description of Operation: Gasoline station and convenience store, featuring the sale of groceries, tobacco products, candy, made-to-order sandwiches, snacks, soda, beer, and gasoline.

Equity Capital Needed: $75,000-$400,000

Franchise Fee: $7,500

Royalty: 3 percent

Advertising Co-op Fee:

Financial Assistance: None

Management Assistance: We will train store management and personnel, and our store supervisors will make a minimum of two visits per month.

Training Assistance: The owners will be given the opportunity to work in a company-owned outlet for two to three weeks, along with any personnel hired by the franchisee. Franchisees will also be given the opportunity to attend all company-owned store meetings and training sessions.

Quix Systems

4 N. Third St.
Temple, TX 76501
Web Address: www.seiquix.com
Toll-Free Phone:
Phone: (254) 778-3547
Fax: (254) 778-0910
Contact: Director of Franchising

Number of Franchises: 3
Company-Owned Units: 37
Total Units: 40

In Business Since: 1958   **Franchising Since:** 1994

Description of Operation: Quix Convenience Food Stores with fuel installations. Standard franchise offering is on existing locations in Texas. Quix Systems also has a dealer franchise program geared toward the development of new sites.

Equity Capital Needed: $75,000 (approximately)

Franchise Fee: $25,000

Royalty: 5 percent

Advertising Co-op Fee:

Financial Assistance: Quix Systems does not offer any financing, but will provide assistance in obtaining financing.

Management Assistance: Ongoing operations support provided by franchise advisor. Other marketing assistance includes manuals, newsletters, vendor negotiations, promotional programs, bulletins and signage, layouts, schematics, advertising media, and grand opening support.

Training Assistance: An intensive two weeks of classroom and in-field training are provided. An additional 80 hours of on-site training are provided within the first three weeks of operation.

Health & Fitness — Exercise & Fitness Centers

Form-You-3 Weight Control & Aerobics

4790 Douglas Cir., N.W.
Canton, OH 44718
Toll-Free Phone: (800) 525-6315
Phone: (330) 499-3334
Fax: (330) 499-8231
Contact: Vice President

Number of Franchises: 157
Company-Owned Units: 15
Total Units: 172

In Business Since: 1982   **Franchising Since:** 1984

Description of Operation: Form-You-3 offers weight control and aerobics as well as other secondary services such as food products, clothing, and convenience items related to services. Structured diet and aerobics program is monitored by trained counselors and aerobics instructors. They meet almost all of the guidelines set and approved by regulatory agencies. 800-3,000 square feet, is required for building space, depending on the market.

Equity Capital Needed: $39,000-$89,000

Franchise Fee: $9,800-$13,300

Royalty: 6 percent or $500

Advertising Co-op Fee:

Financial Assistance: Some assistance offered.

Management Assistance: Support in the areas of advertising and training. Seminars on hiring, recruiting, sales, service, basic business operations, and financial guidance. Ongoing support through visits, video, and newsletter.

Training Assistance: Marketing, sales and service training, as well as owner and management training. Training is comprehensive and ongoing.

World Gym Fitness Centers

2210 Main St.
Santa Monica, CA 90405
Web Address: www.worldgym.com
Toll-Free Phone:
Phone: (310) 450-0080
Fax: (310) 450-3455
Contact: CEO

Number of Franchises: 250
Company-Owned Units: 0
Total Units: 250

In Business Since: 1980   **Franchising Since:** 1986

Description of Operation: We believe World Gym Fitness Centers are the most exciting business opportunity in health and fitness today. Through the affiliation of Joe Gold and a global network of approximately 250 World Gym licensees, we are forging a new direction that is reshaping the fitness industry.

Equity Capital Needed: $350,000-750,000

Franchise Fee: $12,000

Royalty: $6,000/year

Advertising Co-op Fee:

Financial Assistance: Not available

Management Assistance: Operation manuals giving you a road map to run your business. Presale manual, corporate accounts manual, interior design manual, lead boxes, ad slicks, and standard forms for the operation of your gym. 800# hotline for ongoing services and support. Real estate and site location services available.

Training Assistance: Ongoing sales training and marketing programs through World Gym Seminars.

Health & Fitness—Medical and Pharmaceutical Supplies

Drug Emporium

155 Hidden Ravines Dr.
Powell, OH 43065
Web Address: www.drugemporium.com
Toll-Free Phone:
Phone: (614) 548-7080
Fax: (614) 548-6541
Contact: Director of Franchise Operations

Number of Franchises: 81
Company-Owned Units: 135
Total Units: 216

In Business Since: 1977   **Franchising Since:** 1979

Description of Operation: Retail deep discount drug store.

Equity Capital Needed: Data not available.

Franchise Fee: $25,000

Royalty: 1 percent-$3-6 million; 2 percent-$6-8 million; 3 percent-$8-10 million

Advertising Co-op Fee:

Financial Assistance: Not available.

Management Assistance: The complete corporate staff assists in servicing the franchise community. This process is coordinated through the franchise department.

Training Assistance: We provide initial training of six weeks in various facets of the business, i.e. purchasing, receiving, accounting, cash management, operations, start-up, and so on. Continual training as needed.

Medicap Pharmacies, Inc.

4700 Westown Pkwy., Ste. 300
West Des Moines, IA 50266-6730
Web Address: www.medicap.com
Toll-Free Phone: (800) 445-2244
Phone: (515) 224-8400
Fax: (515) 224-8415
Contact: Vice President Franchise Development

Number of Franchises: 167
Company-Owned Units: 0
Total Units: 144

In Business Since: 1971   **Franchising Since:** 1974

Description of Operation: Pharmacy franchise company. Apothecary-type pharmacies that average 1,500 square feet. Stores have counseling rooms, drive-thru windows, and drop boxes. We help registered pharmacists open new stores and convert existing drug stores and independent pharmacies to the Medicap concept. We require that the pharmacist-manager own at least 20 percent of the operation.

Equity Capital Needed:

Franchise Fee: $15,000 new/$8,500 store conversion

Royalty: 4 percent new/2 percent store conversion

Advertising Co-op Fee: 1 percent

Financial Assistance: Medicap will provide up to $16,000 of required equity for those who cannot do it on their own.

Management Assistance: We provide assistance in advertising, marketing, accounting, inventory control, negotiation of managed care and third party contracts, negotiation of purchasing contracts, and much more.

Training Assistance: We provide a five-day training program to all franchisees.

Medicine Shoppe, The

1100 N. Lindbergh Blvd.
St. Louis, MO 63132
Web Address: www.medshoppe.com
Toll-Free Phone: (800) 325-1397
Phone: (314) 993-6000
Fax: (314) 872-5500
Contact: National Sales Director

Number of Franchises: 1,270
Company-Owned Units: 7
Total Units: 1,277

In Business Since: 1970   **Franchising Since:** 1972

Description of Operation: The Medicine Shoppe is a franchisor of professional pharmacies selling health-related products.

Equity Capital Needed: $63,000-$111,800 (exclusive of origination fee).

Franchise Fee: $18,000 for orgination fee for new store.

Royalty: 5.5 percent

Advertising Co-op Fee:

Financial Assistance: $63,000-$111,800 initial investment (excluding origination fee) includes remodeling of premises, purchase of equipment, fixtures, opening inventory, supplies, and working capital. MSI will finance up to 90 percent upon loan approval. Loan is repaid on a schedule of up to ten years.

Management Assistance: Operations personnel (district and regional managers) provide ongoing support to franchisees. A team to find real estate. MSI also provides field marketing support for grand opening assistance, lease negotiation, lease-hold improvement specifications and coordination, accounting system, and third-party contract procurement.

Training Assistance: Operations manuals are provided. New franchisees attend an intensive six-day training school at MSI corporate offices. District and regional meetings and field seminars are conducted throughout the year at various locations within the various districts.

Health & Fitness—Optical

Nu-Vision

2284 S. Ballenger Hwy. Box 2600
Flint, MI 48501
Toll-Free Phone: (800) 733-5468
Phone: (313) 767-0900
Fax: (313) 767-6390
Contact: Manager of Franchise Operations

Number of Franchises: 38
Company-Owned Units: 73
Total Units: 111

In Business Since: 1949   **Franchising Since:** 1983

Description of Operation: Retailer of eyeglasses, contact lenses, accessories, and supplies, with complete optometric facilities. Nu-Vision is currently reviewing their franchise.

Equity Capital Needed: $75,000-$500,000

Franchise Fee: $15,000

Royalty: 8.5 percent

Advertising Co-op Fee: 7 percent

Financial Assistance: Yes, to qualifying applicants.

Management Assistance: Complete corporate staff support.

Training Assistance: Ongoing.

Procare Vision Centers Inc.

926 N. 21st St.
Newark, OH 43055

Toll-Free Phone: (800) 837-5569
Phone: (740) 366-7341
Fax: (740) 366-5453
Contact: Vice President

Number of Franchises: 18
Company-Owned Units: 1
Total Units: 19

In Business Since: 1981   **Franchising Since:** 1985

Description of Operation: ProCare provides vision care products and services through franchises owned and operated by licensed vision care professionals. The success of each franchisee has always been a high priority, achieved by constant support and assistance of an experienced corporate staff. ProCare Vision Centers help caring vision professionals compete through franchising.

Equity Capital Needed: $30,000-$200,000

Franchise Fee: $8,000

Royalty: 5 percent

Advertising Co-op Fee:

Financial Assistance: Established relationships with lending and leasing institutions allow the franchisee the opportunity to acquire funds.

Management Assistance: Each prospective and current franchisee receives extensive ongoing information on merchandise, supplies, products, equipment, location, construction, marketing, and computer support. Complete training manuals, weekly communications, and monthly newsletters are used to enhance the ongoing support of the franchisor.

Training Assistance: Training for the franchisee, managers, and staff is available at the corporate headquarters and at the franchisee's office. The prescribed training at the corporate headquarters takes place 1-2 weeks before the opening of the office and for a period of 3-8 business days. On-site training is available at the franchisee's office for 1 week before opening. Additional training for new staff members is available on an ongoing basis.

Health & Fitness—Weight Loss

Beverly Hills Weight Loss and Wellness

200 Highpoint Ave., Ste. B-5
Portsmouth, RI 02871
Web Address: www.beverlyhillsintl.com
E-mail Address: bhwlw@wsii.com
Toll-Free Phone: (800) 825-4500
Phone: (401) 683-6620
Fax: (401) 683-6885
Contact: President

Number of Franchises: 97
Company-Owned Units: 0
Total Units: 97

In Business Since: 1986   **Franchising Since:** 1989

Description of Operation: Beverly Hills Weight Loss and Wellness is medically supervised. Patients must have lab work performed and doctor approval before starting the program. Our patients are taught to modify their eating habits and eat regular store-bought food from the start. The company takes pride in its success with weight loss and especially with maintaining the loss.

Equity Capital Needed: $45,000

Franchise Fee: $15,000

Royalty: 8 percent

Advertising Co-op Fee:

Financial Assistance: Not available.

Management Assistance: Area supervisors are available to assist with on-site training, advertising, site location, and general problem solving.

Training Assistance: 2 weeks of classroom training is provided.

Diet Center

395 Springside Dr.
Akron, OH 44333
Web Address: www.dietcenterworldwide.com
E-mail Address: info@dietcenterworldwide.com
Toll-Free Phone: (800) 656-3294
Phone:
Fax: (330) 666-2197
Contact: Director of Franchise Development

Number of Franchises: 942
Company-Owned Units: 0
Total Units: 942

In Business Since: 1970   **Franchising Since:** 1972

Description of Operation: Diet Center counselors work one-on-one with clients, helping them develop a personalized, low-fat eating style and more active lifestyle. With the aid of a new behavior management program, clients design their own practical solutions for losing and maintaining desired weight. Diet Center clients learn to improve their health and appearance by focusing on reducing body fat, instead of obsessing over an "ideal" number on the scale.

Equity Capital Needed: $31,000-$43,600

Franchise Fee: $6,500

Royalty: 8 percent

Advertising Co-op Fee:

Financial Assistance: None.

Management Assistance: Diet Center provides marketing, advertising, real estate, lease negotiations, and a complete nutritional staff. 800 number assistance

is also available to all owners. On-site grand opening support.

Training Assistance: Diet Center assists in all training aspects, from grand opening assistance to program and nutritional training. Training is provided both at our home office and in regional areas.

Diet Light

300 Market St., Ste. 101
Lebanon, OR 97355
Web Address: www.busdir.com\dietlight
E-mail Address:
Toll-Free Phone: (800) 248-7712
Phone: (541) 259-3573
Fax: (541) 259-3506
Contact: President

Number of Franchises: 12
Company-Owned Units: 11
Total Units: 23

In Business Since: 1983   **Franchising Since:** 1988

Description of Operation: Individual weight loss counseling with our portion-controlled meals and optional fitness facilities with toning tables and cardiovascular equipment.

Equity Capital Needed: $12,000-$15,000

Franchise Fee: None.

Royalty: 0 percent

Advertising Co-op Fee: None

Financial Assistance: None.

Management Assistance: Training at headquarters. Support from main office. Training manuals and videos also given.

Training Assistance: 3 days of training. Training 2 times a year at headquarters.

Health & Fitness— Miscellaneous

Amigo Mobility Center

6693 Dixie Hwy.
Bridgeport, MI 48722
Web Address: www.concentric.net\~mcihq
E-mail Address: mcihq@concentric.net
Toll-Free Phone: (800) 821-2710
Phone: (517) 777-6370
Fax: (517) 777-6537
Contact: Franchise Operations

Number of Franchises: 23
Company-Owned Units: 5
Total Units: 28

In Business Since: 1968   **Franchising Since:** 1984

Description of Operation: Amigo Mobility Centers sell and service mobility products to individuals with walking disabilities. The centers operate in protected territories throughout the US. They sell and service mobility products, such as electric scooters, lift chairs, wheelchairs and other adaptive equipment. Sold to individuals whose mobility is affected by an illness such as stroke, MS, joint replacement, or older people to maintain their independence.

Equity Capital Needed: $76,100-$115,100

Franchise Fee: Varies with size of territory

Royalty: 5 percent declining

Advertising Co-op Fee:

Financial Assistance: We assist franchisees with proposals to lending institutions and the development of their business plans.

Management Assistance: The franchisee receives operations manuals, advertising manuals and service manuals. Assistance also includes site selection, lease negotiation, store set-up, and grand opening staffing. On-site visits and a step-by-step operational system to follow.

Training Assistance: An intensive three-week classroom/in-field initial training program that includes 1 week of classroom on operations, advertising, sales, and service. 1 week of in-store training at a company-owned unit and 1 week in the franchisee's area. Training includes phone, written, and on-site instruction on all aspects of the business.

Great Earth Companies

140 Lauman Ln.
Hicksville, NY 11801
Web Address: www.greatearth.com
E-mail Address: hillary@spec.net
Toll-Free Phone: (800) 374-7328
Phone: (516) 822-1230
Fax: (516) 822-1252
Contact: Director of Franchise Development

Number of Franchises: 140
Company-Owned Units: 5
Total Units: 150

In Business Since: 1971   **Franchising Since:** 1988

Description of Operation: Retail vitamin stores.

Equity Capital Needed: $80,000-$140,000

Franchise Fee: $30,000

Royalty: 6 percent

Advertising Co-op Fee:

Financial Assistance: 33 percent franchise.

Management Assistance: Includes site selection, lease negotiations, and operating procedures.

Training Assistance: We offer a four-week course at Vita-U, the company's California training facility, that covers product knowledge, sales training, store operations, and the new store opening.

Lorraine's TropicTan

5152 Commerce Rd.
Flint, MI 48507
Toll-Free Phone: (800) 642-4826
Phone: (810) 230-0090
Fax: (810) 230-1115
Contact: President
Number of Franchises: 4
Company-Owned Units: 6
Total Units: 10
In Business Since: 1979   **Franchising Since:** 1985

Description of Operation: Indoor suntanning salon and related sales and services.

Equity Capital Needed: $30,000-$70,000

Franchise Fee: $7,000

Royalty: 3.5 percent or $4,200

Advertising Co-op Fee:

Financial Assistance: While TropiTan does not provide actual monetary financial assistance, we do provide help with securing bank loans, the preparation of any required documents, forms, and so on.

Management Assistance: Managers of company-owned salons can be reached at a toll-free number 7 days a week. Upper management can be queried by appointment.

Training Assistance: Franchise management is required to complete a two-week training program at a corporate salon before opening the franchised store. Also included in the franchise fee is 1 week of on-site training, during which time TropiTan management will assist in preparation for store opening at the franchise location.

Home Furnishings— Carpeting & Flooring

Carpet Network

109 Gaither Dr. #302
Mt. Laurel, NJ 08054
Web Address: www.carpetnetwork.com
E-mail Address: cptnetwork@aol.com
Toll-Free Phone: (800) 428-1067
Phone: (609) 273-9393
Fax: (609) 273-0160
Contact: President

Number of Franchises: 48
Company-Owned Units: 1
Total Units: 49

In Business Since: 1991   **Franchising Since:** 1992

Description of Operation: Carpet Network is a mobile retailer offering carpet, window treatments, vinyl, and laminate floors. Our "Traveling Floor & Window Store" is fully equipped with samples from leading manufacturers that are presented in the customer's home or business. Large exclusive territory. Creative marketing strategy. Comprehensive training and support.

Equity Capital Needed:

Franchise Fee: $15,500

Royalty: 5 percent gross sales

Advertising Co-op Fee: None

Financial Assistance: Data not provided

Management Assistance: Assist in business plan development.

Training Assistance: Extensive home training. Six days at Carpet Network corporate offices. Five-week training after corporate training; 24-hour support program.

Home Furnishings—Drapery

Decor-At-Your-Door International

P.O. Box 2290
Pollock Pines, CA 95726
Toll-Free Phone: (800) 936-3326
Phone: (916) 644-6056
Fax: (916) 644-3326
Contact: President

Number of Franchises: 25
Company-Owned Units: 2
Total Units: 27

In Business Since: 1983   **Franchising Since:** 1995

Description of Operation: Selling national brand carpet and window coverings direct to the home owner from a mobile unit. National buying power gives wholesale prices. No quotas, no renewal charges, no transfer fees. This is a great franchise and lots of fun to operate. Set your own hours and start to enjoy life.

Equity Capital Needed: $5,000

Franchise Fee: $9,000

Royalty: 3 percent

Advertising Co-op Fee: 1 percent

Financial Assistance: We will finance up to half the cast with a $5,000 down payment. Balance at $50 per month at 5 percent interest for 5 years.

Management Assistance: Marketing assistance with promotions, and great support from the home office.

Training Assistance: Complete training. No experience necessary.

Drapery Works Systems

4640 Western Ave.
Lisle, IL 60532
Toll-Free Phone: (800) 353-7273
Phone: (708) 963-2820
Fax: (708) 963-1370
Contact: President

Number of Franchises: 5
Company-Owned Units: 1
Total Units: 6

In Business Since: 1978   **Franchising Since:** 1993

Description of Operation: Custom drapery and soft bedding accessories mobile service. Offers franchise owners the opportunity to own business, work flexible hours, and have the potential to earn substantial money. Designed for people who like to work with people.

Equity Capital Needed: $5,000

Franchise Fee: $15,000

Royalty: 5 percent

Advertising Co-op Fee:

Financial Assistance: None available at this time.

Management Assistance: Owner/management support is available by telephone. Training, assistance, proven systems, and corporate marketing support.

Training Assistance: We teach independent business owners the selling techniques necessary to succeed in the custom window treatment industry. Strongest emphasis on selling, measuring, and calculating each treatment.

Home Furnishings—Furniture

Expressions Custom Furniture

3636 S. I-10 Service Rd. S. Ste. 103
Metairie, LA 70001
Toll-Free Phone:
Phone: (714) 577-8407
Fax:
Contact: Vice President of Franchise Development

Number of Franchises: 58
Company-Owned Units: 3
Total Units: 61

In Business Since: 1978   **Franchising Since:** 1983

Description of Operation: Expressions is a manufacturer and retailer of fine, designer, custom upholstery.

Stores are arranged and displayed with unique accessories, appealing to affluent and fashion-oriented individuals.

Equity Capital Needed: $70,000-$80,000

Franchise Fee: $30,000

Royalty: 3.5 percent

Advertising Co-op Fee:

Financial Assistance: The company provides no direct financing, but has relationships established with financial firms.

Management Assistance: Grand opening, as well as assistance in all facets of its business.

Training Assistance: Training for 3 weeks before opening, as well as on-site training provided by regional managers.

Furniture Medic

860 Ridge Lake Blvd.
Memphis, TN 38120
Web Address: www.furnituremedic.com
E-mail Address: chris_beck@svm.com
Toll-Free Phone: (800) 877-9933
Phone: (901) 820-8600
Fax: (901) 820-8660
Contact:

Number of Franchises: 500
Company-Owned Units: 0
Total Units: 500

In Business Since: 1992

Franchising Since: 1993

Description of Operation: Furniture Medic is an on-site furniture/wood restoration and repair franchise. Everyone has furniture—hotels, restaurants, homes, and so on. Wood furniture is easily damaged during manufacturing, warehousing, transporting and by daily wear and tear. Furniture Medic restoration techniques can save this furniture for a fraction of replacement or refinishing costs. Furniture Medic provides franchisees with specialized equipment and territory.

Equity Capital Needed: $5,600-$10,000

Franchise Fee: $11,400 or $16,400

Royalty: 7 percent

Advertising Co-op Fee:

Financial Assistance: Financing available.

Management Assistance: Franchisees receive complete operations, training, and marketing manuals. Furniture Medic provides support and has a toll-free telephone hotline that franchisees use to reach the home office. Franchisees receive newsletters and product updates. Training updates, marketing information and other important information is provided through Furniture Medic's annual convention.

Training Assistance: The three-week comprehensive training program that Furniture Medic provides includes a one-week home study course and 2 weeks of training and hands-on experience at Furniture Medic's home office in Memphis, TN. Furniture Medic's training program is designed to turn out well-rounded business people. Along with teaching our systems and products, high priority is given to teaching customer service, time management, monitoring sales, profit, motivation, discipline, and people skills.

Guardsmen Woodpro

4999 36th St. S.E.
Grand Rapids, MI 49546
Toll-Free Phone: (800) 496-6377
Phone:
Fax: (616) 285-7882
Contact: Franchise Development Manager

Number of Franchises: 0
Company-Owned Units: 1
Total Units: 1

In Business Since: 1915 **Franchising Since:** 1993

Description of Operation: On-site, mobile, wood touch-up, and repair service.

Equity Capital Needed: $35,000-$50,000

Franchise Fee: $25,000-$35,000

Royalty: Varies

Advertising Co-op Fee:

Financial Assistance: Third-party assistance.

Management Assistance: Guardsmen Woodpro provides its franchise partners with support, such as initial promotional assistance programs, continuing education courses, research and development on new products, and financial management assistance.

Training Assistance: Guardsmen Woodpro offers 2 weeks of training, concentrating on the enhancement of managerial marketing and accounting skills, and a thorough program on touch-up and repair procedures and techniques.

Norwalk-The Furniture Idea

100 Furniture Pkwy.
Norwalk, OH 44857
Web Address: www.norwalkfurniture.com
Toll-Free Phone: (888) 667-9255
Phone: (419) 668-4461
Fax: (419) 663-0021
Contact: Vice President

Number of Franchises: 85
Company-Owned Units: 9
Total Units: 92

In Business Since: 1902 **Franchising Since:** 1987

Description of Operation: Custom living room furniture specialty stores, offering 2,000 fabrics and leathers available on over 500 styles with delivery in just 35 days.

Equity Capital Needed: $100,000-175,000

Franchise Fee: $35,000

Royalty: None

Advertising Co-op Fee: None

Financial Assistance: Third-party financing is available.

Management Assistance: Multiple training sessions and seminars are required before franchise opens. Extensive assistance is provided.

Training Assistance: Management training, videotape program, on-site sales staff training, service manager training, and seminars.

Summit Naked Furniture

P.O. Box F 1157 Lackawanna Trail
Clarks Summit, PA 18411
Web Address: www.nakedfurniture.com
E-mail Address: nkdfurn@epix.net
Toll-Free Phone: (800) 352-2522
Phone: (717) 587-7800
Fax: (717) 586-8587
Contact: President

Number of Franchises: 39
Company-Owned Units: 2
Total Units: 41

In Business Since: 1972   **Franchising Since:** 1976

Description of Operation: Naked Furniture is the nation's largest retailer of custom-finished and ready-to-finish solid wood home furnishings, offering a wide range of innovative and affordable choices. We serve our market with attractive, professionally run stores and a diverse selection of quality products that allow our store owners to maintain their leadership position in the rapidly growing specialty furniture market.

Equity Capital Needed: $71,500-$122,500 start-up; cash, ability to borrow.

Franchise Fee: $19,500

Royalty: 4 percent

Advertising Co-op Fee:

Financial Assistance: Will assist in financing up to $40,000 of initial investment.

Management Assistance: The franchisor assists with merchandising, site selection, lease negotiation, interior display, accounting, advertising, customer service, office procedures, product knowledge, and selection. Computer-linked distribution center.

Training Assistance: We provide two weeks of training at the corporate office and the franchisee's store or a prototype store, as well as field support as needed by individual franchisee.

Home Furnishings— Interior Design

Decor & You, Inc.

900 Main St., South Building #2
Southbery, CT 06488
E-mail Address: franchising@TheEsource.com
Toll-Free Phone: (800) 477-3326
Phone: (203) 264-3500
Fax: (203) 264-3516
Contact:

Number of Franchises: 0
Company-Owned Units: 5
Total Units: 5

In Business Since: 1994   **Franchising Since:** 1998

Description of Operation: Decor & You is the industry's decorating franchise, featuring state-of-the-art computerized room renderings, thousands of samples, and the personalized services of professionally trained interior decorators who come to you. No prior experience is needed. Decor & You also offers the opportunity to own a Regional Development Franchise. By assisting in the recruiting and support of Decor Designers, you will receive 50 percent of franchise fees and royalties.

Equity Capital Needed: $10,000-$25,000

Franchise Fee: $12,000 individual/$50,000 regional

Royalty: 10 percent

Advertising Co-op Fee: 3 percent

Financial Assistance: None

Management Assistance: Decor & You provides its franchisees with a regional director to support them through the developmental stages of their growing businesses. Support also includes continual training in product knowledge, marketing, order placement, and follow-up. The regional director also provides coaching and problem-solving assistance while tracking and nurturing the success of each franchise.

Training Assistance: Decor & You provides a ten-day training program for all franchisees, with a twelve-day program for regional directors. All aspects of the decorating business are covered, including color and design, trends, product knowledge, client development, follow-up skills, advertising, and virtual decorating through computer graphics. No prior experience in decorating is needed. The regional director training program focuses on marketing, the process of screening and selecting franchisees, coaching, problem-solving skills, and monitoring and directing the success of each franchisee. A regional director is not required to operate a decorating franchise to own the region.

Home Furnishings—
Miscellaneous

Almost Heaven, Ltd.

Rt. 5-FS
Renick, WV 24966
Toll-Free Phone:
Phone: (304) 497-3163
Fax: (304) 497-2698
Contact: Vice President of Franchise Sales

Number of Franchises: 1953
Company-Owned Units: 0
Total Units: 1953

In Business Since: 1971   Franchising Since: 1976

Description of Operation: The most complete line of hot water, health, and leisure products made today. Almost Heaven manufactures wooden hot tubs, spas, whirlpool bathtubs, and steamrooms. Hot tub and spa systems include Jacuzzi-brand whirlpool equipment.

Equity Capital Needed: $5,000-$10,000

Franchise Fee: $0

Royalty: 0 percent

Advertising Co-op Fee:

Financial Assistance: We provide help in securing bank financing.

Management Assistance: Assistance by telephone and fax after initial training at factory.

Training Assistance: Complete factory training, video, and free consulting.

Bath Genie

20 River St.
Marlboro, MA 01752
Toll-Free Phone: (800) 255-8827
Phone: (508) 481-8827
Fax: (508) 624-6444
Contact: General Manager

Number of Franchises: 26
Company-Owned Units: 1
Total Units: 27

In Business Since: 1974   Franchising Since: 1984

Description of Operation: Bathtub repair and resurfacing.

Equity Capital Needed: $10,000-$50,000

Franchise Fee: $24,500

Royalty: 0 percent

Advertising Co-op Fee:

Financial Assistance: None.

Management Assistance: Total training to start up the business. A complete package is provided.

Training Assistance: Both in the field and at corporate headquarters.

Bathcrest

2425 S. Progress Dr.
Salt Lake City, UT 84119
Web Address: www.bathcrest.com
Toll-Free Phone: (800) 826-6790
Phone: (801) 972-1110
Fax: (801) 977-0328
Contact: Vice President of Sales

Number of Franchises: 163
Company-Owned Units: 1
Total Units: 164

In Business Since: 1979   Franchising Since: 1985

Description of Operation: Bathroom refinishing. The bathroom is the number-one refinished room in the home. Bathcrest is in a unique position to make money by saving the homeowner up to 80 percent of replacement cost. Our proven process and product is used in commercial and residential homes.

Equity Capital Needed: $24,500-$41,000

Franchise Fee: $3,500

Royalty: $1,200 annual renewal fee

Advertising Co-op Fee:

Financial Assistance: Will finance franchise fee.

Management Assistance: Comprehensive operations manual; on-the-job training of marketing, advertising, daily operation procedures, estimating, and sales; newsletter; ad slicks; and manuals to help in all phases of the business. Two toll-free lines for support and ordering.

Training Assistance: To help ensure your success, we offer one week of on-the-job training with paid airfare, room, and board. Complete equipment, printing, and enough material to recoup your investment. National and regional conferences. Two toll-free lines for technical support.

Living Lighting

4699 Keele St. Ste. 1
Downsview, ON M3J 2N8
Web Address: www.livinglighting.com
Toll-Free Phone:
Phone: (416) 661-9916
Fax: (416) 661-9706
Contact: Vice President of Franchising

Number of Franchises: 32
Company-Owned Units: 0
Total Units: 32

In Business Since: 1971   Franchising Since: 1971

Description of Operation: Living Lighting provides retail and residential lighting.

Equity Capital Needed: $250,000-$350,000

Franchise Fee: $30,000

Royalty: 6 percent

Advertising Co-op Fee:

Financial Assistance: None.

Management Assistance: Ongoing visits by operations, supervisors, advice, lease advice, advertising materials, buying assistance, and so on. Supported by home office specialists.

Training Assistance: Training is on-site at other locations. Theory training seminars.

Hotels & Motels

Americinn Motel

18202 Mnnetonka Blvd.
Deephaven, MN 55391
Web Address: www.americinn.com
Toll-Free Phone: (800) 634-3444
Phone: (612) 476-9020
Fax: (612) 476-7601
Contact: Vice President of Franchise Marketing

Number of Franchises: 36
Company-Owned Units: 0
Total Units: 36

In Business Since: 1987   **Franchising Since:** 1987

Description of Operation: Upper and economy lodging.

Equity Capital Needed: $350,000-$500,000

Franchise Fee: $20,000

Royalty: 4.5 percent

Advertising Co-op Fee:

Financial Assistance: None.

Management Assistance: Americinn provides complete training manuals, continual consultation with the local franchisees, annual convention, and regional workshops.

Training Assistance: Americinn provides complete training for managers, front-desk personnel, and housekeepers.

Best Inn of America

1205 Skyline Dr., P. O. Box 1719
Marion, IL 62959
Web Address: www.bestinn.com
Toll-Free Phone:
Phone: (618) 997-5454

Fax: (618) 993-5974
Contact: Director of Franchise and Real Estate Development

Number of Franchises: 4
Company-Owned Units: 18
Total Units: 22

In Business Since: 1968   **Franchising Since:** 1983

Description of Operation: Limited service, upscale motel. All suites and regular motels with 100 percent satisfaction program.

Equity Capital Needed: $400,000-$500,000

Franchise Fee: $10,000 for 75 units and under.

Royalty: 2 percent of total sales.

Advertising Co-op Fee:

Financial Assistance: Assistance is available through several services.

Management Assistance: Complete training for all new franchisees on management level.

Training Assistance: Total training program and update training.

Cendant Corporation

339 Jefferson Rd., P. O. Box 278
Parsipanny, NJ 07054
Toll-Free Phone: (800) 932-4677
Phone: (973) 428-9700
Fax: (973) 428-6057
Contact:

Number of Franchises: 3790
Company-Owned Units: 0
Total Units: 3790

In Business Since: 1990   **Franchising Since:** 1990

Description of Operation: HFS is the world's largest hotel franchisor, with over 3,700 Days Inn, Howard Johnson, Park Inns, Ramada, and Super 8 motels with over 370,000 rooms. A pure franchisor, HFS does not own or operate any of the hotel properties. Through royalty payments and reservation and marketing fees, HFS franchisees are entitled to not only use the brand names but the support services the company offers, including marketing/advertising campaigns, training programs, central reservation systems and financial expertise.

Equity Capital Needed: Data not available.

Franchise Fee: $350 per room.

Royalty: 4 percent-6.5 percent

Advertising Co-op Fee:

Financial Assistance: HFS franchisees can now access financial resources for refinancing, acquisitions, new construction, renovation and leasing by simply calling a toll-free number. We have lenders that will provide competitive rates for qualifying franchisees and who are sensitive to the needs of our industry.

Management Assistance: An extensive three- to four-day orientation for new general managers, conducted at our home office. This is a mandatory program for all general managers new to the system within six months of taking over the position. This program trains managers on how to use the resources from Hospitality Franchise Systems. If further assistance is needed, the general managers from each property have a franchise service manager who is assigned to help them with any questions or anything else needed.

Training Assistance: Several training seminars and sessions are available in housekeeping, front office, sales, food and beverage, management and supervisory skills, guest service, safety, and security.

Choice Hotels International

10750 Columbia Pike
Silver Spring, MD 20901
Web Address: www.hotelchoice.com
Toll-Free Phone: (800) 547-0007
Phone: (301) 593-5600
Fax: (301) 979-6205
Contact: Resource Specialist

Number of Franchises: 3485
Company-Owned Units: 0
Total Units: 3485

In Business Since: 1934   **Franchising Since:** 1939

Description of Operation: Hotel/motel franchise. Products range from economy to mid-price to upscale.

Equity Capital Needed: Varies.

Franchise Fee: Varies by brand ($25,000-$45,000 minimum)

Royalty: 3.5-5.25 percent of gross room revenue

Advertising Co-op Fee:

Financial Assistance: Choice has third-party financing programs for franchisees.

Management Assistance: Includes national and world-wide marketing ($40 million annual budget), worldwide reservations, advertising, public relations, monthly newsletter, product purchasing, renovation, guest relations, employee training, and more.

Training Assistance: Education and training program for all franchisees.

Condotels International

2703 Hwy. 17 S.
N. Myrtle Beach, SC 29582
Toll-Free Phone: (800) 845-0631
Phone: (803) 272-8400
Fax: (803) 272-6556
Contact: Franchise Analyst

Number of Franchises: 4
Company-Owned Units: 1
Total Units: 5

In Business Since: 1982   **Franchising Since:** 1989

Description of Operation: Operates as a hotel franchisor, except that the accommodations provided are condominium homes rather than hotel rooms. Franchisees manage rentals of resort condos for the condo homeowners and provide check-in and daily maid service.

Equity Capital Needed: $42,500-$192,500

Franchise Fee: $35,000

Royalty: 4 percent

Advertising Co-op Fee:

Financial Assistance: None.

Management Assistance: Ongoing support.

Training Assistance: 10 days at corporate headquarters. 2 days on-site.

Country Inns & Suites by Carlson

P.O. Box 59159, Carlson Pkwy.
Minneapolis, MN 55459-8203
Web Address: www.countryinns.com
Toll-Free Phone: (800) 477-4200
Phone: (612) 449-1326
Fax: (612) 449-1338
Contact: Vice President of Development

Number of Franchises: 118
Company-Owned Units: 4
Total Units: 122

In Business Since: 1987   **Franchising Since:** 1987

Description of Operation: Upscale, limited service lodging facilities (inns, suites, resorts). Old-world charm, exterior architecture, and interior decor.

Equity Capital Needed: $300,000

Franchise Fee: $35,000

Royalty: 3-4 percent

Advertising Co-op Fee: 2-3 percent marketing fee

Financial Assistance: Introduction to potential leaders.

Management Assistance: Complete operations manual, assistance with opening, training, operation set-up, teach PICI hiring (Passion, Intelligence, Compassion, Intensity), philosophical and technical training programs for easy application by manager, sales and marketing tools, graphic design, and advertising support.

Training Assistance: Guest service training, technical departmental training, management skills training, housekeeping skills seminar, sales training, and 10-day on-site opening support.

Courtyard by Marriott

1 Marriott Dr.
Washington, DC 20058
Web Address: www.courtyard.com
Toll-Free Phone: (800) 638-8108

Phone: (301) 380-8521
Fax: (301) 380-6699
Contact:

Number of Franchises:
Company-Owned Units:
Total Units: 300+

In Business Since: 1983   **Franchising Since:** 1991

Description of Operation: Moderate-priced hotel chain with more than 220 hotels throughout the United States.

Equity Capital Needed: Not available

Franchise Fee: $66,650-116,569/$400 per room

Royalty: 5.5 percent of Gross Room Revenue

Advertising Co-op Fee: 1.2 percent of Gross Room Revenue

Financial Assistance: Not available

Management Assistance: Each hotel has a direct representative to assist with marketing, sales, operations, and training. In addition, each hotel receives division support for systems, procurement, and operations.

Training Assistance: We provide classroom and on-site operation training, ranging from two to six weeks, manual and videos included. Other classroom training is offered in marketing and sales, guest services, and finances.

Days Inns of America

339 Jefferson Rd.
Parsippany, NJ 07054-0278
Web Address: www.daysinn.com
Toll-Free Phone: (800) 932-6726
Phone: (201) 428-9700
Fax: (201) 428-0526
Contact: Executive Vice President-Franchise Development

Number of Franchises: 1450
Company-Owned Units: 0
Total Units: 1450

In Business Since: 1970   **Franchising Since:** 1970

Description of Operation: Days Inn of America is the licensor of Days Inn guest lodging facilities.

Equity Capital Needed: $1.6-$20.2 million

Franchise Fee: $26,000 or $300 per room.

Royalty: 5 percent

Advertising Co-op Fee:

Financial Assistance: Mortgage financing, assistance in processing SBA loans, and preferred vendor leasing are available.

Management Assistance: Full services are available, including site selection, design and construction, opening and operational support, and sales and marketing support.

Training Assistance: Complete hotel/motel management and operations training are available, including classroom instruction, videos, and on-site training.

Doubletree Club Hotel Systems

410 N. 44th St., # 700
Phoenix, AZ 85008
Toll-Free Phone: (800) 222-6722
Phone: (602) 220-6666
Fax: (602) 220-6753
Contact:

Number of Franchises: 11
Company-Owned Units: 3
Total Units: 14

In Business Since: 1984   **Franchising Since:** 1985

Description of Operation: Limited-service lodging concept, combining 4-star quality accommodations, an airline style "club" room, and an affordable room rate. Targeted primarily toward the commercial business traveler, families on weekends, and small groups. Doubletree Club Hotels offer the guest an exceptional price-value relationship.

Equity Capital Needed: $3-$5 million

Franchise Fee: $30,000

Royalty: 3 percent

Advertising Co-op Fee:

Financial Assistance: None.

Management Assistance: Franchisor offers marketing and operations support, which are provided on an ongoing basis from the corporate office in Phoenix, AZ. In addition, Doubletree has a regional manager of operations responsible for overseeing all Doubletree Club Hotels in the system.

Training Assistance: A minimum five-day training program, including system management, management techniques, personnel policies, and so on. Periodically, training courses, conferences, and seminars are also offered. Additional training programs are implemented as needed.

Downtowner Inns

1726 Montreal Circle
Tucker, GA 30084
Toll-Free Phone: (800) 247-4677
Phone: (770) 270-1180
Fax: (770) 270-1077
Contact: President of Sales

Number of Franchises: 5
Company-Owned Units: 0
Total Units: 5

In Business Since: 1973   **Franchising Since:** 1991

Description of Operation: Moderately priced accommodations with all amenities.

Equity Capital Needed: Varies.

Franchise Fee: $100 per room. $10,000 minimum

Royalty: 4 percent or $395

Advertising Co-op Fee:

Financial Assistance: We assist in locating potential lenders in preparation of the loan package.

Management Assistance: A mandatory management seminar is conducted semiannually.

Training Assistance: On-site training for front desk and housekeeping staff is provided.

Fairfield Inn & Suites by Marriott

1 Marriott Dr., Dept. 51/514.01
Washington, DC 20058
Web Address: www.fairfieldinn.com/fairfieldinn/facts.asp
Toll-Free Phone:
Phone: (301) 380-5237
Fax: (301) 380-6699
Contact:

Number of Franchises:
Company-Owned Units:
Total Units: 300

In Business Since: 1987　**Franchising Since:** 1990

Description of Operation: Fairfield Inn by Marriott has set a new quality standard in economy lodging and has grown to nearly 300 hotels. Fairfield Suites, all suites hotels, is an extension of Fairfield Inn offering more space and amenities in the economy segment.

Equity Capital Needed: Varies by project.

Franchise Fee: $55,000-69,764

Royalty: 4.5 percent of Gross Room Revenue

Advertising Co-op Fee: 2.5 percent of Gross Room Revenue

Financial Assistance: Standard programs are not currently available.

Management Assistance: Each franchised hotel is managed in conjunction with the franchise partner's management team by the Fairfield Inn area management team.

Training Assistance: Not available.

Fairfield Inn by Marriott

1 Marriott Dr.
Washington, D.C. 20058
Web Address: www.fairfieldinn.com/fairfieldinn/facts.asp
Toll-Free Phone:

Phone: (301) 380-5237
Fax: (301) 380-6699
Contact: Manager of Franchise Development

Number of Franchises: 52
Company-Owned Units: 80
Total Units: 132

In Business Since: 1987　**Franchising Since:** 1990

Description of Operation: Economy lodging with a rooms-only concept.

Equity Capital Needed: Varies by project.

Franchise Fee: $200-$375 per room.

Royalty: 4 percent of room sales.

Advertising Co-op Fee:

Financial Assistance: Standard programs are not currently available. Financial assistance is considered case-by-case, limited to labor, multiunit, multiproduct franchise partners, or strategically important conversions.

Management Assistance: Each franchised hotel is managed in conjunction with the franchise partner's management team by the Fairfield Inn area management team.

Training Assistance: Data not available

First Interstate Inns

1919 S. 40th Street, Ste. 202
Lincoln, NE 68506
Toll-Free Phone: (800) 865-2378
Phone: (402) 434-5620
Fax: (402) 434-5624
Contact: President

Number of Franchises: 20
Company-Owned Units: 0
Total Units: 20

In Business Since: 1963　**Franchising Since:** 1997

Description of Operation: First Interstate Inns provides two levels of lodging. Value priced and mid-priced conversions are accepted.

Equity Capital Needed: $500,000

Franchise Fee: $15,000-25,000

Royalty: 6 percent

Advertising Co-op Fee: 2 percent

Financial Assistance: Current financial review, support on a business plan, and third-party lending options are provided.

Management Assistance: Complete training, software program, manuals, follow-up, and an 800 number are provided.

Training Assistance: One to two weeks at home office and one to two weeks on-site.

Hampton Inn & Suites

6800 Poplar Ave., #200
Memphis, TN 38138
Toll-Free Phone:
Phone: (903) 374-5000
Fax: (901) 756-9479
Contact:

Number of Franchises: 0
Company-Owned Units: 0
Total Units: 0

In Business Since: 1983   **Franchising Since:** 1994

Description of Operation: Franchising and operation of Hampton Inn & Suites.

Equity Capital Needed: $1-$2.5 million

Franchise Fee: $400 per room with a minimum of $40,000

Royalty: 4 percent

Advertising Co-op Fee:

Financial Assistance: Second mortgage financing is available.

Management Assistance: Yes

Training Assistance: Numerous programs are available.

Hampton Inn Hotel Division

6800 Poplar Ave. Ste. 200
Memphis, TN 38138
Toll-Free Phone:
Phone: (901) 374-5000
Fax: (901) 756-9479
Contact: Senior Vice President of Development

Number of Franchises: 339
Company-Owned Units: 39
Total Units: 378

In Business Since: 1983   **Franchising Since:** 1983

Description of Operation: Franchising and operation of Hampton Inn Hotels.

Equity Capital Needed: $500,000-$2,500,000

Franchise Fee: $400 per room, minimum of $40,000.

Royalty: 4 percent

Advertising Co-op Fee:

Financial Assistance: Lender referrals.

Management Assistance: Yes

Training Assistance: Numerous programs are available.

Holiday Inn Worldwide

3 Ravina Dr., #2000
Atlanta, GA 30346-2149
Toll-Free Phone:
Phone:
Fax: (404) 604-2107

Contact: Director of Franchise Marketing

Number of Franchises: 1608
Company-Owned Units: 175
Total Units: 1783

In Business Since: 1951   **Franchising Since:** 1952

Description of Operation: Franchisor of hotel/motel properties, which include Holiday Inn Hotel, Holiday Inn Crown Plaza, Holiday Inn Crown Plaza Resorts, Holiday Inn Express, Holiday Inn Garden Court, and Holiday Inn SunSpree Resorts.

Equity Capital Needed: 5-30 percent

Franchise Fee: $300 per room.

Royalty: 5 percent

Advertising Co-op Fee:

Financial Assistance: Through an in-house agency, GIAC, loans for refurbishment and development are available to qualified applicants.

Management Assistance: The franchise development team coordinates the application until just before opening. Our Road Scholars will open the hotel and provide instant training to the hotel personnel. Our field representatives will offer continual on-site training programs to hotel personnel, including workshops. In-house representatives dedicated to specific hotels are available via a toll-free line to any answering questions the hotel or franchisee may have.

Training Assistance: Same as above.

Homewood Suites

755 Crossover Ln.
Memphis, TN 38117
Web Address: www.homewood_suites.com
Toll-Free Phone:
Phone: (901) 374-5000
Fax: (901) 374-5008
Contact: Senior Vice President of Development

Number of Franchises: 36
Company-Owned Units: 15
Total Units: 51

In Business Since: 1988   **Franchising Since:** 1988

Description of Operation: Franchising and operation of Homewood Suites.

Equity Capital Needed: $1.5-$3.5 million

Franchise Fee: $400 per room, with a minimum of $40,000

Royalty: 4 percent

Advertising Co-op Fee:

Financial Assistance: Second mortgage financing is available.

Management Assistance: Yes.

Training Assistance: Numerous programs are available.

Hospitality International

1726 Montreal Circle
Tucker, GA 30084
Toll-Free Phone: (800) 247-4677
Phone: (770) 270-1180
Fax: (770) 270-1077
Contact:

Number of Franchises: 348
Company-Owned Units: 0
Total Units: 348

In Business Since: 1982   **Franchising Since:** 1982

Description of Operation: Hotel franchisor of Master Hosts Inns and Resorts, Red Carpet Inns, Scottish Inns, Passport Inns, and Downtowner Inns. Has over 375 franchised properties in 32 states, the Bahamas, Canada, and South America. Hospitality International is one of the fastest-growing hotel systems in the industry. Provides tremendous support services, 24-hour reservation "ReservaHost" system, group sales, marketing, housekeeping, management training, creative services, reasonable fees, and interest in the franchisee's success.

Equity Capital Needed: Varies.

Franchise Fee: $100-$150 per room; $10,000-$15,000 minimum

Royalty: 2.5-4.5 percent, or $350-$435, whichever is greater

Advertising Co-op Fee:

Financial Assistance: We assist the franchisee in contacting potential lenders.

Management Assistance: Mandatory management seminar conducted semiannually.

Training Assistance: On-site training for front desk and housekeeping staff.

Howard Johnson Franchise Systems

339 Jefferson Rd.
Parsippany, NJ 07054
Toll-Free Phone: (800) 932-6726
Phone: (201) 428-9700
Fax: (201) 428-9700
Contact: Executive Vice President-Franchise Development

Number of Franchises: 600
Company-Owned Units: 0
Total Units: 600

In Business Since: 1954   **Franchising Since:** 1954

Description of Operation: Howard Johnson Franchise Systems is the licensor of Howard Johnson guest lodging facilities.

Equity Capital Needed: $1.6-$20.2 million

Franchise Fee: Data not available

Royalty: 5 percent

Advertising Co-op Fee:

Financial Assistance: Mortgage financing, assistance in processing SBA loans and preferred vendor leasing are available.

Management Assistance: Full services available, including site selection, design, construction, opening and other operational support, and sales and marketing support.

Training Assistance: Complete hotel/motel management and operations training is available, including classroom instruction, videos, and on-site training.

InnSuites Hotels

1615 E. Northern Ave., Ste. 105
Phoenix, AZ 85020
Web Address: www.innsuites.com
E-mail Address: isphoenix@attmail.com
Toll-Free Phone: (888) 466-7848
Phone:
Fax: (602) 777-9893
Contact: Customer Service & Trademark Manager

Number of Franchises: 0
Company-Owned Units: 9
Total Units: 9

In Business Since: 1980   **Franchising Since:** 1980

Description of Operation: InnSuites Hotels offer a cost-effective trademark license for a new, or to reposition an existing, motel or hotel in a mid-market studio and two room suite hotel. Featuring microwave, fridge, coffee maker, hand dryer in the suite, free breakfast, social hour, and more in value to the guest. InnSuites is successful in Arizona and California with more growth potential in the West.

Equity Capital Needed: Varies with size of operation.

Franchise Fee: $15,000 deferred

Royalty: 1.5 percent of business sent

Advertising Co-op Fee:

Financial Assistance: None

Management Assistance: We provide continual managerial and technical assistance as needed.

Training Assistance: Management is required to attend a two-week program at a designated corporate facility for classroom and hands-on management training. The designated person representing the owner must complete a two-day seminar at the corporate office. Training is available for all positions of employment if desired.

Knights Inn

339 Jefferson Rd.
Parsippany, NJ 07054
Web Address: www.knightsinn.com
Toll-Free Phone: (800) 758-8999

Phone: (973) 428-9700
Fax: (973) 428-6057
Contact: Executive Vice President-Franchise Development

Number of Franchises: 150
Company-Owned Units: 29
Total Units: 179

In Business Since: 1991   **Franchising Since:** 1992

Description of Operation: Hotel/motel franchise and management company.

Equity Capital Needed: $100,000 +

Franchise Fee: $15,000

Royalty: 8 percent

Advertising Co-op Fee:

Financial Assistance: We provide access to cooperating financial institutions.

Management Assistance: Initial training at national business and education conference, then property managers can obtain daily support through 800 number and manuals supplied by franchisor.

Training Assistance: American Hotel/Motel Association Educational Institution provides training and video support, as well as a corporate team twice yearly. Regional training classes.

Master Hosts Inns and Resorts

1726 Montreal Ct.
Tucker, GA 30084
Toll-Free Phone: (800) 247-4677
Phone: (770) 270-1180
Fax: (770) 270-1077
Contact: Vice President of Sales

Number of Franchises: 40
Company-Owned Units: 0
Total Units: 40

In Business Since: 1973   **Franchising Since:** 1982

Description of Operation: Moderately-priced accommodations with all amenities.

Equity Capital Needed: Varies with size and complexity of project

Franchise Fee: $150 per room. $15,000 minimum

Royalty: 4.5 percent or $435.

Advertising Co-op Fee:

Financial Assistance: We assist in locating potential lenders and in the preparation of the loan package.

Management Assistance: A mandatory management seminar is conducted semi-annually.

Training Assistance: We offer on-site training for front desk and housekeeping staff.

Microtel

One Airport Way, Ste. 200
Rochester, NY 14624
Toll-Free Phone:
Phone: (404) 321-4045
Fax: (716) 436-4045
Contact: Senior Vice President of Franchise Development

Number of Franchises: 14
Company-Owned Units: 0
Total Units: 14

In Business Since: 1986   **Franchising Since:** 1987

Description of Operation: Budget sector hotel chain.

Equity Capital Needed: $600,000

Franchise Fee: $25,000

Royalty: 2.5 percent

Advertising Co-op Fee:

Financial Assistance: Assistance is limited to providing introductions to potential lenders.

Management Assistance: In-house "consultants" available to work with franchisees as problem solvers and program developers.

Training Assistance: Training programs are tailored to meet the franchisee's specific needs.

Park Inns International

339 Jefferson Rd.
Parsippany, NJ 07054
Toll-Free Phone: (800) 932-6726
Phone: (201) 428-9700
Fax: (201) 428-0526
Contact: Executive Vice President-Franchise Development

Number of Franchises: 108
Company-Owned Units: 0
Total Units: 108

In Business Since: 1986   **Franchising Since:** 1986

Description of Operation: Park Inns International is the licensor of Park Inn International and Park Plaza guest lodging facilities. From five-star Park Plaza to Park Inn International—full and/or limited service hotels.

Equity Capital Needed: $1.6-$20.2 million

Franchise Fee: $100 per room

Royalty: 1.9 percent

Advertising Co-op Fee:

Financial Assistance: Mortgage financing, assistance in processing SBA loans, and preferred vendor leasing are available.

Management Assistance: Full services available, including site selection, design and construction, opening

and other operational support, and sales and marketing support.

Training Assistance: Complete hotel/motel management and operations training is available, including classroom instruction, videos, and on-site training.

Passport Inn

1726 Montreal Ct.
Tuckere, GA 30084
Toll-Free Phone: (800) 247-4677
Phone: (770) 270-1180
Fax: (770) 270-1077
Contact: Vice President of Sales

Number of Franchises: 20
Company-Owned Units: 0
Total Units: 20

In Business Since: 1973   **Franchising Since:** 1982

Description of Operation: Budget motels. Limited amenity lodging.

Equity Capital Needed: Varies with size and complexity of project.

Franchise Fee: $100 per room. $10,000 minimum.

Royalty: 3.5 percent or $350.

Advertising Co-op Fee:

Financial Assistance: We assist in locating potential lenders and in the preparation of the loan package.

Management Assistance: A mandatory management seminar is conducted semiannually.

Training Assistance: We provide on-site training for front desk and housekeeping staff.

Ramada Inns

339 Jefferson Rd.
Parsippany, NJ 07054
Web Address: www.ramada.com
Toll-Free Phone: (800) 758-8999
Phone: (973) 428-9700
Fax: (973) 428-6057
Contact: Executive Vice President-Franchise Development

Number of Franchises: 650
Company-Owned Units: 0
Total Units: 650

In Business Since: 1959   **Franchising Since:** 1959

Description of Operation: Ramada Franchise Systems is the licensor of Ramada guest lodging facilities.

Equity Capital Needed: $1.6-$20.2 million

Franchise Fee: $30,000 or $300 per month.

Royalty: 4 percent

Advertising Co-op Fee:

Financial Assistance: Mortgage financing, assistance in processing SBA loans, and preferred vendor leasing are available.

Management Assistance: Full services are available, including site selection, design and construction, opening and other operational support, and sales and marketing support.

Training Assistance: Complete hotel/motel management and operational training is available, including classroom instruction, videos, and on-site training.

Red Carpet Inn

1726 Montreal Ct.
Tucker, GA 30084
Web Address: www.redcarpet.com
Toll-Free Phone: (800) 247-4677
Phone: (770) 270-1180
Fax: (770) 270-1077
Contact: Vice President of Sales

Number of Franchises: 140
Company-Owned Units: 0
Total Units: 140

In Business Since: 1969   **Franchising Since:** 1982

Description of Operation: Moderately priced motel accommodations with all amenities.

Equity Capital Needed: Varies with size and complexity of project.

Franchise Fee: $150 per room. $15,000 minimum.

Royalty: 4 percent or $395

Advertising Co-op Fee:

Financial Assistance: We assist in locating potential lenders and in the preparation of the loan package.

Management Assistance: A mandatory management seminar is conducted semiannually.

Training Assistance: We provide on-site training for front desk and housekeeping staff.

Residence Inn by Marriott

1 Marriott Dr., Dept. 51/514.01
Washington, DC 20058
Web Address: www.residenceinn.com/residenceinn/facts.asp
Toll-Free Phone: (800) 638-8108
Phone: (301) 380-8521
Fax: (301) 380-6699
Contact:

Number of Franchises:
Company-Owned Units:
Total Units: 225+

In Business Since: **Franchising Since:**

Description of Operation: Residence Inn by Marriott leads the extended-stay hotel segment as the only national extended-stay brand with over 225 plus hotels.

176

Equity Capital Needed: Not available

Franchise Fee: $75,000-108,000

Royalty: 4 percent of gross room revenues/1st two yrs./5 percent after

Advertising Co-op Fee: 2.5 percent of gross room revenues

Financial Assistance: Not available

Management Assistance: Not available

Training Assistance: Not available

Scottish Inns

1726 Montreal Ct.
Tucker, GA 30084
Toll-Free Phone: (800) 247-4677
Phone: (770) 270-1180
Fax: (770) 270-1077
Contact: Vice President of Sales

Number of Franchises: 140
Company-Owned Units: 0
Total Units: 140

In Business Since: 1973   **Franchising Since:** 1982

Description of Operation: Budget motels. Limited amenity lodging.

Equity Capital Needed: Varies with size and complexity of project.

Franchise Fee: $100 per room. $10,000 minimum.

Royalty: 3.5 percent or $350.

Advertising Co-op Fee:

Financial Assistance: We assist in locating potential lenders and in the preparation of the loan package.

Management Assistance: A mandatory management seminar is conducted semiannually.

Training Assistance: We offer on-site training for front desk and housekeeping staff.

Super 8 Motels

339 Jefferson Rd.
Parsippany, NJ 07054
Web Address: www.super8.com
Toll-Free Phone: (800) 758-8999
Phone: (973) 428-9700
Fax: (973) 428-6057
Contact: Executive Vice President-Franchise Development

Number of Franchises: 1083
Company-Owned Units: 0
Total Units: 1083

In Business Since: 1972   **Franchising Since:** 1972

Description of Operation: Super 8 Motels is the franchisor of "Economy Motels," which offer a full-size room with color TV, direct-dial phones, attractive decor, and VIP Frequent Traveler Club.

Equity Capital Needed: $450,000-$3 million

Franchise Fee: $20,000

Royalty: 4 percent

Advertising Co-op Fee:

Financial Assistance: Mortgage financing, assistance in processing SBA loans, and preferred vendor leasing are available.

Management Assistance: Full services are available, including site selection, design and construction, opening and other operational support, and sales and marketing support.

Training Assistance: Complete hotel and motel management and operations training are available, including classroom instruction and video and on-site training.

TownePlace by Marriott

1 Marriott Dr., Dept. 51/514.01
Washington, DC 20058
Web Address: www.towneplace.com/towneplace/facts/asp
Toll-Free Phone:
Phone: (301) 380-5237
Fax: (301) 380-6699
Contact:

Number of Franchises:
Company-Owned Units:
Total Units:

In Business Since: **Franchising Since:**

Description of Operation: TownePlace Suites by Marriott, a new mid-market lodging product, target to extended travelers whose stay exceeds five consecutive nights.

Equity Capital Needed: Not available

Franchise Fee: $68,000

Royalty: 5 percent of Gross Room Revenue

Advertising Co-op Fee: 1.5 percent of Gross Room Revenue

Financial Assistance: Not available

Management Assistance: Not available

Training Assistance: Not available

Lawn & Garden

Clintar Groundskeeping Services

4210 Midland Ave.
Scarborough, ON M1V 4S6
E-mail Address: clintar01@aol.com
Toll-Free Phone: (800) 361-3542
Phone: (416) 291-1611
Fax: (416) 291-6792

Contact: President

Number of Franchises: 9
Company-Owned Units: 0
Total Units: 9

In Business Since: 1973   **Franchising Since:** 1985

Description of Operation: Clintar is Canada's largest and most successful grounds care company. We offer management and sales professionals an opportunity to build their own "large" business in a stable industry. We provide exclusive territories, complete and constant support training, and a chance to put your sales and people skills to work building long-term customer relationships in a commercial/industrial setting.

Equity Capital Needed: $150,000

Franchise Fee: $30,000

Royalty: 8 percent of gross revenue

Advertising Co-op Fee: None

Financial Assistance: Before business startup, Clintar works with the new franchisee to complete an exhaustive business plan and budget that is ready for presentation to financial institutions. This process is repeated with each franchise annually, and throughout the year we conduct rolling quarter reviews with each franchise.

Management Assistance: Ongoing classroom training sessions are held a minimum of four times per year. The majority of these sessions are to upgrade skills in sales, customer services, and financial management. On-site follow-up visits are conducted monthly.

Training Assistance: Classroom type and "on-the-job" training sessions are conducted throughout the year. All aspects of operating a successful business are covered.

Cut Only, Inc.

15965 Jeanette St.
Southfield, MI 48075
Web Address: www.wfcnet.com
E-mail Address: wfcnet@cris.com
Toll-Free Phone:
Phone: (810) 557-2784
Fax: (810) 557-7931
Contact:

Number of Franchises:
Company-Owned Units:
Total Units:

In Business Since: 1973   **Franchising Since:**

Description of Operation: Customer-controlled lawn care. Offers home owners dependable, quality workmanship, customer-selected service options, and low prices. Combines 20 years of lawn care knowledge with a unique and original marketing tool.

Equity Capital Needed: $35,000

Franchise Fee: $10,000

Royalty: 5 percent

Advertising Co-op Fee: None

Financial Assistance:

Management Assistance:

Training Assistance:

Emerald Green Lawn Care

9333 N. Meridian St.
Indianapolis, IN 46260
Toll-Free Phone: (800) 783-0981
Phone: (317) 846-9940
Fax: (317) 846-1696
Contact:

Number of Franchises: 12
Company-Owned Units: 1
Total Units: 13

In Business Since: 1984   **Franchising Since:** 1985

Description of Operation: Full-service residential lawn, tree, and shrub care program.

Equity Capital Needed: $60,000-$90,000

Franchise Fee: $15,000

Royalty: 6.5-8.5 percent

Advertising Co-op Fee:

Financial Assistance: Not available.

Management Assistance: We provide an initial twelve days of training, ongoing field service, technical support, marketing, administration, staff training, financial planning, and safety. Operations and technical manuals provided. Annual seminars and regional meetings.

Training Assistance: The initial training, 12 days at the company headquarters, and in-field experience cover all phases of the business.

Enviro Masters Lawn Care

Box 178
Caledon East, ON L0N 1E0 CAN
Toll-Free Phone:
Phone: (905) 584-9592
Fax:
Contact: President

Number of Franchises: 17
Company-Owned Units: 2
Total Units: 19

In Business Since: 1987   **Franchising Since:** 1991

Description of Operation: Lawn care company specializing in organic products and environmentally considerate applications. We provide seasonal programs throughout the growing season.

Equity Capital Needed: $15,000-$20,000

Franchise Fee: $15,000-$20,000

Royalty: 5 percent

Advertising Co-op Fee:

Financial Assistance: None.

Management Assistance: Enviro Masters provides a complete manual with continual consultation and ongoing support. Franchisees receive regular newsletters and attend regular meetings and seminars.

Training Assistance: Our training program is ongoing through the first year of business. This includes in-field training, as well as marketing, sales, administration, and turf management.

Lawn Doctor Inc.

142 Hwy. 34 Box 401
Holmdel, NJ 07733-0401
Toll-Free Phone: (800) 631-5660
Phone: (732) 946-0029
Fax: (908) 946-9089
Contact: National Franchise Director

Number of Franchises: 335
Company-Owned Units: 0
Total Units: 335

In Business Since: 1967   **Franchising Since:** 1967

Description of Operation: Offering an automized lawn-care service, Lawn Doctor provides all-natural and regular fertilization, plus control applications using the exclusive Turf Tamer equipment manufactured and used only by Lawn Doctor. Additionally, a broad range of cultural care practices, using Integrated Pest Management to develop the health and beauty of turf and landscape areas with environmentally balanced care.

Equity Capital Needed: $20,000

Franchise Fee: None.

Royalty: 10 percent

Advertising Co-op Fee:

Financial Assistance: Up to 50 percent financing.

Management Assistance: Ongoing operations support, seminars and group meetings. Two-year new dealer support assistance.

Training Assistance: Two-week intensive training program; two-year concentrated new dealer support assistance.

Liqui-Green Lawn Care Corporation

9601 N. Allen Rd.
Peoria, IL 61615
Toll-Free Phone: (800) 747-5211
Phone: (309) 243-5211
Fax: (309) 243-5247
Contact: Director

Number of Franchises: 25
Company-Owned Units: 1
Total Units: 26

In Business Since: 1953   **Franchising Since:** 1971

Description of Operation: Lawn-care maintenance and sales.

Equity Capital Needed: $5,000-$6,000

Franchise Fee: $5,000

Royalty: $2,500 to start and graduated up to cap of $6000.

Advertising Co-op Fee:

Financial Assistance: To qualified buyers, we can put you in business for as low as $2,500, but you must have at least another $2,500 to purchase phone, insurance, advertising, and working capital.

Management Assistance: Purchasing power, agronomics, technical assistance, an 800 number, availability to answer any questions, monthly newsletter, and annual seminars.

Training Assistance: All training will be in the assigned territory with a sales representative.

Nitro-Green Professional Lawn and Tree Care

2791-F N. Texas St., Ste. 300
Fairfield, CA 94533
Toll-Free Phone: (800) 982-5296
Phone: (707) 428-5297
Fax: (707) 428-5297
Contact: President/Chief Executive Officer

Number of Franchises: 38
Company-Owned Units: 2
Total Units: 40

In Business Since: 1977   **Franchising Since:** 1979

Description of Operation: Automated professional lawn and tree care services.

Equity Capital Needed: $40,000-$45,000

Franchise Fee: $17,400

Royalty: 7 percent

Advertising Co-op Fee:

Financial Assistance: Financing of equipment and a portion of franchise fee is available.

Management Assistance: We provide a toll-free hotline, complete business planning, market planning and guidance, and periodic on-site visits.

Training Assistance: We offer one week of training at the corporate headquarters and one week of on-site opening.

Nutri-Lawn Ecology Friendly Lawn Care

5397 Ellinton Ave. West, Ste. 110
Toronto, ON M90 5K6
Web Address: www.nutri-lawn.ca

Toll-Free Phone: (800) 396-6096
Phone: (416) 620-7100
Fax: (416) 620-7771
Contact: President

Number of Franchises: 38
Company-Owned Units: 0
Total Units: 38

In Business Since: 1985 **Franchising Since:** 1987

Description of Operation: The opportunity to grow a large lawn care business based on our ecology friendly approach. Our target market is residential homeowners who are sensitive to pesticide usage. We offer exclusive territories and a complete system of marketing, computer administration, and promotion.

Equity Capital Needed: $25,000-60,000

Franchise Fee: $15,000

Royalty: 6 percent

Advertising Co-op Fee: 2 percent

Financial Assistance: Financing of franchise fee $5,000 down and $10,000 over 2 years.

Management Assistance: Ongoing business planning, marketing plans, and execution.

Training Assistance: One-week classroom in head office. Minimum two visits to your place with field instruction.

Nutritte-Division of Hidro-Agri

P. O. Box 1000
Brossard, PQ J4Z 3N2 CAN
Toll-Free Phone:
Phone: (514) 462-2555
Fax: (514) 462-3634
Contact: Director

Number of Franchises: 46
Company-Owned Units: 0
Total Units: 46

In Business Since: 1964 **Franchising Since:** 1984

Description of Operation: Lawn care.

Equity Capital Needed: $50,000

Franchise Fee: $70,000

Royalty: $3,550

Advertising Co-op Fee:

Financial Assistance: None.

Management Assistance: Courses are given during the season to all franchisees.

Training Assistance: Training is provided all year for franchisees and employees of franchisees. There are three major meetings per year for training with our specialists.

Spring-Green Lawn Care Corp.

11927 Spaulding School Dr.
Plainfield, IL 60544
Toll-Free Phone: (800) 435-4051
Phone: (815) 436-8777
Fax: (815) 436-9056
Contact: Director of Franchise Development

Number of Franchises: 119
Company-Owned Units: 11
Total Units: 130

In Business Since: 1977 **Franchising Since:** 1977

Description of Operation: A national network of lawn and tree care businesses committed to beautifying our earth.

Equity Capital Needed: $50,000-$60,000

Franchise Fee: $30,000

Royalty: 6-9 percent

Advertising Co-op Fee:

Financial Assistance: Data not available.

Management Assistance: We offer a thorough one-week initial training program. This program is classroom and practical training, consisting of goal setting and planning, lawn-care theory and technology, field operations, equipment operation and maintenance, computerized and bookkeeping management, sales, and promotion. This is all backed with customized reference and audio/video tools that become part of your personal reference library.

Training Assistance: Data not available.

Weed Man

2399 Royal Windsor Dr.
Mississauga, ON L5J 1K9
Toll-Free Phone:
Phone: (905) 823-8550
Fax: (905) 823-4594
Contact: Director of Franchise Development

Number of Franchises: 110
Company-Owned Units: 3
Total Units: 113

In Business Since: 1970 **Franchising Since:** 1977

Description of Operation: Residential lawn care services.

Equity Capital Needed: $25,000-$750,000

Franchise Fee: $25,000

Royalty: $7,600 per production truck per year.

Advertising Co-op Fee:

Financial Assistance: None.

Management Assistance: Complete support in technical, administration, marketing, and sales is provided.

Training Assistance: We offer one week of orientation, followed by ongoing seminars.

Pet Care

Canine Counselors

1660 Southern Blvd.
West Palm, FL 33404
Web Address: www.caninecounselors.com
Toll-Free Phone: (800) 456-3647
Phone: (407) 640-3970
Fax: (407) 640-3973
Contact: President

Number of Franchises: 1
Company-Owned Units: 3
Total Units: 4

In Business Since: 1982   **Franchising Since:** 1987

Description of Operation: Professional dog training and behavior problem solving. Schools provide services on location, in client's home or business, with lifetime training warranty.

Equity Capital Needed: $39,000

Franchise Fee: $29,000

Royalty: 7 percent, or $100 per week minimum.

Advertising Co-op Fee:

Financial Assistance: Ongoing training and support of franchisees and their employees. Sale and training services provided by franchisor. Operations manual, all data entry provided by franchisor, monthly report, and newsletter.

Management Assistance: Franchise meetings provide various workshops on business and employee management skills. Individual assistance quarterly on location by franchisor provides franchisee with local support.

Training Assistance: Two weeks at home office in West Palm Beach, FL, followed by two weeks on location in franchisee's new territory.

Pet-Tenders

3305 Adams Ave., Ste, 60, P.O. Box 23622
San Diego, CA 92193
Web Address: www.pet-tenders.com
E-mail Address: pettenders@aol.com
Toll-Free Phone: (800) 738-8363
Phone: (619) 298-3033
Fax:
Contact: President

Number of Franchises: 4
Company-Owned Units: 1
Total Units: 5

In Business Since: 1983   **Franchising Since:** 1990

Description of Operation: Pet-Tenders is an in-home pet/housesitting service that cares for pets in the comfort of their own home! Pet-Tenders provides feeding, exercis-ing, plant care, housesitting, and above all—spoiling! The perfect opportunity for the devoted animal lover.

Equity Capital Needed:

Franchise Fee: $8,500

Royalty: 5 percent

Advertising Co-op Fee: 2 percent

Financial Assistance: For qualified applicants, franchise fee assistance for one year.

Management Assistance: A toll-free line that is available nationwide for assistance.

Training Assistance: Five days at company headquarters in San Diego, CA, covering marketing, telephone work, customer service, and pet care.

Pets Are Inn

7723 Tanglewood Ct., Ste. 150
Minneapolis, MN 55439
Web Address: www.petsareinn.com
E-mail Address: jplatt@petsareinn.com
Toll-Free Phone: (800) 248-7387
Phone: (612) 944-8298
Fax: (612) 941-4919
Contact: Chief Financial Officer

Number of Franchises: 17
Company-Owned Units: 0
Total Units: 17

In Business Since: 1982   **Franchising Since:** 1986

Description of Operation: Finally! Pet boarding without cages! When most people go on vacation, they impose on friends or family or look to a kennel facility for the care of their pet. How special is your pet? Pets Are Inn focuses on the family/individual who considers a pet one of the family—a person disguised as a dog or cat. Pets Are Inn provides a unique home environment for each pet by using "host families" to care for pets. Round-trip transportation is provided by Pets Are Inn. Both pet and owner prefer the "piece of mind" and "worry free" services provided. This business is designed to be run from the home.

Equity Capital Needed: $25,000

Franchise Fee: $15,000

Royalty: 0.5-10 percent

Advertising Co-op Fee: 1 percent

Financial Assistance: Co-sign for business loan with 75 percent down and acceptable credit.

Management Assistance: Opening assistance and follow-up coaching weekly. 30-60-90 during first year at start program. 90-180-270-365-day review and evaluation during first year.

Training Assistance: Thirty-day pretraining countdown schedule; 5 days at corporate before opening. Ongoing training first year.

Pet Sales & Supplies

Petland

195 N. Hickory St.
Chillicothe, OH 45601
Toll-Free Phone: (800) 221-5935
Phone: (614) 775-2464
Fax: (614) 775-2575
Contact: **Executive Vice President of Franchising**

Number of Franchises: 134
Company-Owned Units: 1
Total Units: 135

In Business Since: 1967 **Franchising Since:** 1972

Description of Operation: Full-service pet retail store, offering expert pet counseling to consumers and offering over 3,000 merchandise items. Fifty percent of merchandise is proprietary, exclusive to Petland franchisees. Primary retail focus is on the "hobby pets," such as tropical fish, pet birds, reptiles, amphibians, and small mammals such as rabbits, guinea pigs, and hamsters. Comprehensive animal husbandry systems, employee training programs, and proprietary animal fixtures focus consumer attention to tropical fish and pet sales.

Equity Capital Needed: $50,000-$125,000

Franchise Fee: $25,000

Royalty: 4.5 percent

Advertising Co-op Fee:

Financial Assistance: Petland will provide assistance with the loan request package and assist the franchisee with bank presentation and the ongoing banking relationship.

Management Assistance: Petland will assist the new franchisee with site location, lease negotiations, construction, and grand opening marketing. Petland will assist the new franchisee with the development of a comprehensive business plan. Petland requires the production of monthly financial statements and executive-level management monitors actual results as compared to plan with the new franchisee.

Training Assistance: Petland requires all franchisees to attend 4 weeks of training. The 4 weeks are comprised of 1 week of classroom training, 1 week of hands-on training in a corporate training store, 1 week in the new store before opening, and 1 week of post-opening training. Video and audio training tapes and comprehensive operating manuals are provided, in addition to field service representative visits to the retail store. Bi-annual franchise meetings are held for idea exchanges. Monthly marketing guides.

Pet Supplies

Bone Appetit Bakery, The
1919 S. 40th Street
Lincoln, NE 68506
Toll-Free Phone: (800) 865-2378
Phone: (402) 434-5620
Fax: (402) 434-5624
Contact: **President**

Number of Franchises: 2
Company-Owned Units: 1
Total Units: 3

In Business Since: 1996 **Franchising Since:** 1997

Description of Operation: The Bone Apetit Bakery offers wholesome all-natural treats for dogs and cats. The treats are hand-cut and freshly baked. With the addition of the Pet Gift Boutique, you can be a part of the multi-billion dollar pet industry.

Equity Capital Needed: $50,000

Franchise Fee: $17,500

Royalty: 6 percent

Advertising Co-op Fee: 1 percent

Financial Assistance: Will help review current financial status, supply information on business plans, and refer to a third party vendors.

Management Assistance: Complete training, software program, manuals, follow-up, and 800 number provided.

Training Assistance: One week at home office and 2-3 days on-site. Additional training provided as required.

Cherrybrook

P. O. Box 15, Rte. 57
Broadway, NJ 08808
Web Address: www.cherrybrook.com
Toll-Free Phone: (800) 524-0820
Phone: (908) 689-7979
Fax: (908) 689-7988
Contact: **President**

Number of Franchises: 8
Company-Owned Units: 1
Total Units: 9

In Business Since: 1968 **Franchising Since:** 1990

Description of Operation: Full-service dog and cat supplies with retail convenience, at wholesale prices.

Equity Capital Needed: $70,000-$100,000

Franchise Fee: $16,000

Royalty: None.

Advertising Co-op Fee:

Financial Assistance: The franchisee provides his/her own financing.

Management Assistance: Representatives from franchisor visit franchise locations monthly to help with promotions, merchandising, and so on.

Training Assistance: 1 week of training provided at company headquarters before franchise opening.

Paws & Claws Pet Nutrition Centers

6465 Millcreek Dr., #205
Mississauga, ON L5N 5R3 CAN
Toll-Free Phone: (800) 387-8335
Phone: (905) 567-4180
Fax: (905) 567-5355
Contact: Director of Franchise Development

Number of Franchises: 4
Company-Owned Units: 2
Total Units: 6

In Business Since: 1986 **Franchising Since:** 1990

Description of Operation: Specialty retailer, dedicated to providing for the total nutritional needs of pets by offering a complete line of quality pet foods and supplies. Knowledgeable staff which is extensively trained on animal care and maintenance.

Equity Capital Needed: $35,000

Franchise Fee: $25,000

Royalty: 6 percent

Advertising Co-op Fee:

Financial Assistance: Financial assistance through lending institution.

Management Assistance: Ongoing management support, store visits, newsletters and central purchasing.

Training Assistance: 2 weeks of on-site training, educating the franchisees on the day-to-day procedures necessary for the successful operation of the business.

Pet Pals

8301 E. Prentice Ave., #300
Englewood, CO 80111
Toll-Free Phone: (800) 275-9000
Phone: (303) 771-8251
Fax: (303) 773-1332
Contact: Franchise Development

Number of Franchises: 0
Company-Owned Units: 11
Total Units: 11

In Business Since: 1983 **Franchising Since:** 1993

Description of Operation: Boutique strip center retail site, offering accessories to the public for pet products, including a propriety line of foods and other products.

Equity Capital Needed: $95,000-$100,000

Franchise Fee: $22,500

Royalty: 6 percent

Advertising Co-op Fee:

Financial Assistance: In special cases, the franchisor may provide up to 50 percent financing. The franchisor gives assistance in obtaining financing.

Management Assistance: We provide operational on-site learning, manuals, merchandising, annual meeting, promotional program, newsletters, continual support, and an 800 number support line.

Training Assistance: Training includes 6 days of training in the home office and 1 week of on-site training. Opening support.

Pet Valu

121 McPherson
Markham, ON L3R 9Z6
Web Address: www.petvalu.com
Toll-Free Phone:
Phone: (905) 946-1200
Fax: (905) 946-0659
Contact:

Number of Franchises: 143
Company-Owned Units: 23
Total Units: 166

In Business Since: 1976 **Franchising Since:** 1987

Description of Operation: Sale of pet foods and pet supplies.

Equity Capital Needed: $35,000-$135,000

Franchise Fee: $12,000

Royalty: 6 percent

Advertising Co-op Fee:

Financial Assistance: None.

Management Assistance: Dedicated franchise field consultant.

Training Assistance: 3 weeks of total training provided; 1 week of classroom training and 2 weeks of store training.

PetPeople

722 Genevieve St., Ste. E
Solana Beach, CA 92075
E-mail Address: PetPeople@aol.com
Toll-Free Phone: (800) 655-6595
Phone: (619) 481-3335
Fax: (619) 481-3337
Contact: President

Number of Franchises: 0
Company-Owned Units: 10
Total Units: 10

In Business Since: 1990 **Franchising Since:** 1996

Description of Operation: PetPeople is a convenience store for premium pet foods and supplies. The average store is 3,800 square feet. Most stores are located next to the neighborhood's highest volume supermarket. PetPeople does not sell pets or any live animals. Focusing on pet foods and supplies makes it possible for us to offer our shoppers extremely clean stores with sales associates that have time to take care of our customers needs. Our stores are large enough to compete effectively, offering our customers a complete assortment of exciting products for the pets, yet small enough to be relatively simple to operate.

Equity Capital Needed: $50,000

Franchise Fee: $25,000

Royalty: 4 percent of sales

Advertising Co-op Fee: 2 percent of sales

Financial Assistance: PetPeople does not offer financial assistance.

Management Assistance: Each PetPeople franchise store is linked to our merchandise database. Our merchandising staff regularly reviews the sales data advising our franchisees of the products that are performing well chain-wide, target pricing, costs, upcoming promotions, and so on. Each franchise store is visited on a regular basis by our field operations supervisors. This in-store assistance is ongoing.

Training Assistance: PetPeople requires each franchisee to attend an initial training program that includes one week of classroom training, and two weeks of in-store operations training. Immediately before your store's grand opening, a PetPeople field training supervisor will assist you in training your new sales staff.

Petxtra/Petmart

7805 Arjons Dr.
San Diego, CA 92126
Toll-Free Phone: (800) 748-5577
Phone: (619) 693-3639
Fax: (619) 693-1120
Contact: Director of Franchise Development

Number of Franchises: 21
Company-Owned Units: 6
Total Units: 27

In Business Since: 1973   **Franchising Since:** 1982

Description of Operation: Pet Xtra/PetMart is a petless pet store concept. The focus is on selling pet food and supplies within the community. We are a service-driven organization that provides our customers with top-quality pet products by friendly, knowledgeable owners.

Equity Capital Needed: $75,000

Franchise Fee: $125,000-total turn-key package.

Royalty: 6 percent

Advertising Co-op Fee:

Financial Assistance: We can put prospective franchisees in touch with several financial institutions that specialize in franchise financing.

Management Assistance: Our operations department is extremely thorough in assisting new franchisees throughout their term as a franchisee within the system. Support includes business goals, local marketing efforts, employee financial guidance and overall operational support. A training manager is specifically hired for continual on-site and off-site support. The operations department will make periodic store reviews to help improve any areas in need of assistance and make sure the system is working effectively.

Training Assistance: We have an extensive two-week training program which incorporates both in-store operations and training at the corporate office. Training is covered in the following areas; management, product knowledge, merchandising, inventory control, record keeping, advertising, public relations, and basic animal care.

Pet Care

Shampoo Chez

1380 Soquel Ave.
Santa Cruz, CA 95062
Web Address:
E-mail Address:
Toll-Free Phone:
Phone: (408) 427-2284
Fax: (408) 457-2845
Contact: President

Number of Franchises: 1
Company-Owned Units: 1
Total Units: 2

In Business Since: 1983   **Franchising Since:** 1986

Description of Operation: Self-service dog wash. Natural, non-toxic pet supplies and professional dog and cat grooming.

Equity Capital Needed: $25,000

Franchise Fee: $15,000

Royalty: 3.5 percent for 1st 6 months; 5 percent thereafter

Advertising Co-op Fee:

Financial Assistance: None.

Management Assistance: Custom computer software program, product seminars, assistance in site selection, lease negotiations, central data processing and purchasing, field training and evaluation of field operations, inventory control, operations manual, monthly operational and marketing ideas, bi-monthly customer newsletter, and pricing guide.

Training Assistance: On-the-job training at company headquarters in Santa Cruz, CA for 5 days during the month before opening to familiarize the franchisee with the proven business practices and procedures of opera-

tion. Assistance in setting up store and opening for business. A minimum of 1 on-site visit per month during first 6 months of operation. Personal visits to store periodically throughout the term of franchise.

Printing & Copying

Alphagraphics Printshops of the Future

3760 N. Commerce Dr.
Tucson, AZ 85705
Web Address: www.alphagraphics.com
Toll-Free Phone: (800) 955-6246
Phone: (520) 293-9200
Fax: (520) 887-2850
Contact: Franchise Development

Number of Franchises: 350
Company-Owned Units: 1
Total Units: 351

In Business Since: 1970   **Franchising Since:** 1980

Description of Operation: AlphaGraphics' high-tech rapid response printing stores offer a complete line of reprographic services which include high-speed duplication, single and multi-color printing, desktop design and publishing, custom presentation materials, and an international satellite computer network that transmits camera-ready text and graphics in minutes to any AlphaGraphics store worldwide. AlphaGraphics also does Web page and CD-ROM publishing.

Equity Capital Needed: $75,000-$100,000 plus living expenses for 1 year

Franchise Fee: $25,900

Royalty: 8-5-3-1.5 percent

Advertising Co-op Fee:

Financial Assistance: The franchisor supplies sources of financing to franchisee and at the franchisee's request, the franchisor will assist in completing necessary applications.

Management Assistance: The franchisor provides a full compliment of field based and home office support.

Training Assistance: 1 month of training is provided at the corporate training center. 2 weeks of training are provided in the franchisee's store, as well as 1 week of advanced franchisee training 9-12 months after the store's opening. After the first month of training, there is a week of training at a training store.

American Speedy Printing, Inc.

1800 W. Maple Rd.
Troy, MI 48084
Web Address: www.americanspeedy.com
E-mail Address: ASPCH@aol.com

Toll-Free Phone: (800) 726-9050
Phone:
Fax: (248) 614-3789
Contact:

Number of Franchises: 450
Company-Owned Units: 0
Total Units: 450

In Business Since: 1976   **Franchising Since:** 1977

Description of Operation: Printing centers offering high quality printing, desktop publishing, color copying, 4-color printing, digital printing, free pick-up, and delivery.

Equity Capital Needed: $188,000-200,000

Franchise Fee: $19,500

Royalty: 3-6 percent

Advertising Co-op Fee: Yes

Financial Assistance:

Management Assistance: Two-week training class provided.

Training Assistance: On-site training is available, along with continuing support for franchisees in a number of areas.

American Wholesale Thermographics(R), Inc.

12715 Telge Rd.
Cypress, TX 77429
Web Address: www.awt.com
E-mail Address: awtsales@awt.com
Toll-Free Phone: (888) 280-2053
Phone:
Fax: (281) 373-4450
Contact: Franchise Sales

Number of Franchises: 21
Company-Owned Units: 0
Total Units: 21

In Business Since: 1980   **Franchising Since:** 1981

Description of Operation: Wholesale printing providing next day raised-letter printed materials to retail printers, copy centers, and business service centers. Products include quality business cards, stationary, announcements, and invitations.

Equity Capital Needed: $90,000

Franchise Fee: $30,000

Royalty: 5 percent

Advertising Co-op Fee: None

Financial Assistance: Assistance, Yes.

Management Assistance: Ongoing workshops and weekend seminars at our 125 acre International Headquarters campus. Monthly publications and technical bulletins and an intranet linking all centers and our World Headquarters resources. Ongoing research of the

next generation of equipment, annual convention and trade show, ongoing in store, and telephone support.

Training Assistance: 2 people, 216 hours in classroom, 48 hours on the job.

BCT, INC.

3000 NE 30th Place, 5th Fl.
Ft. Lauderdale, FL 33306
Toll-Free Phone: (800) 627-9998
Phone: (954) 563-1224
Fax: (954) 565-0742
Contact:

Number of Franchises: 95
Company-Owned Units: 0
Total Units: 95

In Business Since: 1975   **Franchising Since:** 1977

Description of Operation: World's largest wholesale printing chain, specializing in next-day delivery of thermographed business products (business cards, stationery, teledex cards and promotional items), two-day delivery of thermographed social products (wedding invitations and social stationery), and next-day delivery of custom-made marking devices (standard and self-inking rubber stamps). Also, distributors of Pelican Paper products.

Equity Capital Needed: $175,000 min. cash including franchise fee

Franchise Fee: $35,000

Royalty: 6 percent of monthly gross sales.

Advertising Co-op Fee:

Financial Assistance: Outside sourcing for five-year/60-month equipment lease program.

Management Assistance: 2 weeks of classroom and hands-on training at the Ft. Lauderdale, FL headquarters, followed by 2 weeks of on-site training and opening assistance by operations field representatives.

Training Assistance: Operations manuals, proprietary computer software package, management information systems department, and R & D. Franchisee seminars, conventions, regular plant visits by operations field representatives, special training classes, advertising, marketing campaigns and mailing programs. Annual Dealer Appreciation Program. Dealer catalog training videos. Corporate Print Shop provides product catalogs, price lists, display items, and technical advice and assistance.

Copies Now.
A Franchise of Sir Speedy

26722 Plaza P.O. Box 9077
Mission Viejo, CA 92690
Web Address: www.sirspeedy.com
E-mail Address: fdelucia@sirspeedy.com

Toll-Free Phone: (800) 854-3321
Phone: (714) 348-5000
Fax: (714) 348-5068
Contact:

Number of Franchises: 30
Company-Owned Units: 0
Total Units: 30

In Business Since: 1983   **Franchising Since:** 1984

Description of Operation: Full-service business communications center providing high-speed copying, electronic publishing, color reproduction, engineering, copying, bindery, and fax services for small to mid-sized businesses.

Equity Capital Needed: $135,500 including franchise fee

Franchise Fee: $45,500

Royalty: 4-6 percent

Advertising Co-op Fee:

Financial Assistance: 100 percent financing is available for the franchise fee and equipment. Minimum cash $40,000.

Management Assistance: Financing, site selection, market survey, floor planning, design of store, complete starting inventory, monthly mailers, newsletter and advertising repros, resident business management consultant for store, systemwide advertising, print media, direct mail, regional roundtable training sessions, all pro seminars, national convention and vendor show, ongoing research and development, complete operations, and marketing and administrative manuals.

Training Assistance: We offer 2 weeks in our University in Mission Viejo, CA for 2 people. Airfare and hotel are included. 2 weeks on-site during opening with a field representative.

Copy Club

12715 Telge Road
Cypress, TX 77429
Web Address: www.copyclub.com
E-mail Address: ccsales@copyclub.com
Toll-Free Phone: (888) 280-2053
Phone:
Fax: (281) 373-4450
Contact: Franchise Sales

Number of Franchises: 15
Company-Owned Units: 0
Total Units: 15

In Business Since: 1992   **Franchising Since:** 1994

Description of Operation: Full service copying and digital imaging communications center in a dynamic retail environment. Also offering self-service copying and computer rental. Open 24 hours a day, 7 days a week.

Equity Capital Needed: $100,000

Franchise Fee: $30,000

Royalty: 7 percent

Advertising Co-op Fee: None

Financial Assistance: Assistance, Yes.

Management Assistance: Ongoing workshops and weekend seminars at our 125 acre international headquarters campus. Monthly publications and technical bulletins, an intranet linking all centers and our world headquarters resources. Ongoing research of the next generation of equipment, annual convention and trade show, ongoing in-store and telephone support.

Training Assistance: 5 weeks of classroom training, 2 weeks in store training.

Franklin's® Systems

12715 Telge Road
Cypress, TX 77429
Web Address: www.franklins-printing.com
E-mail Address: fpsales@franlins-printing.com
Toll-Free Phone: (888) 280-2053
Phone:
Fax: (281) 373-4450
Contact: Franchise Sales

Number of Franchises: 67
Company-Owned Units: 0
Total Units: 67

In Business Since: 1971   **Franchising Since:** 1977

Description of Operation: Printing, copying, and digital imaging, producing upscale commercial printing and color copying with connectivity. Franklin's starts owners from day one with outside sales consultants targeting volume repeat corporate accounts.

Equity Capital Needed: $80,000

Franchise Fee:

Royalty: 5 percent

Advertising Co-op Fee: 1-1 1/2 percent

Financial Assistance: Assistance, Yes.

Management Assistance: Ongoing workshops and weekend seminars at our 125 acre international headquarters campus. Monthly publications and technical bulletins, an intranet linking all centers and our world headquarters resources. Ongoing research of the next generation of equipment, annual convention and trade show, ongoing in store and telephone support.

Training Assistance: 4 weeks of classroom training and 2 weeks training in your store.

Ink Well® of America, Inc., The

12715 Telge Road
Cypress, TX 77429
Web Address: www.iwa.com
E-mail Address: iwasales@iwa.com
Toll-Free Phone: (888) 280-2053
Phone:
Fax: (281) 373-4450
Contact: Franchise Sales

Number of Franchises: 44
Company-Owned Units: 0
Total Units: 44

In Business Since: 1972   **Franchising Since:** 1981

Description of Operation: Printing, copying, and digital imaging, producing upscale commercial printing and color copying with connectivity. The Ink Well starts owners from day one with outside sales consultants targeting volume repeat corporate sales.

Equity Capital Needed: $80,000

Franchise Fee:

Royalty: 4-6 percent

Advertising Co-op Fee: None

Financial Assistance: Assistance, Yes.

Management Assistance: Ongoing workshops and weekend seminars at our 125 acre international headquarters campus. Monthly publications and technical bulletins, an intranet linking all centers and our world headquarters resources. Ongoing research of the next generation of equipment, annual convention and trade show, ongoing in store and telephone support.

Training Assistance: 4 weeks of classroom training and 1 1/2 weeks in your shop.

Insty-Prints, Inc.

15155 Technology Dr.
Eden Prairie, MN 55344
Web Address: www.instyprints.com
Toll-Free Phone: (800) 779-1000
Phone: (612) 975-6299
Fax: (800) 369-1234
Contact: Vice President of Development

Number of Franchises: 277
Company-Owned Units: 2
Total Units: 279

In Business Since: 1965   **Franchising Since:** 1967

Description of Operation: Insty-Print Centers are the businessperson's choice of computerized graphic design, volume copying and commercial printing services. Franchise partners receive guidance, training and support in market analysis, sales and advertising, operations, and bottom-line business management. Previous experience in printing is not necessary. However, a strong desire to succeed, the ability to market aggressively, and a passion for superior customer service are required.

Equity Capital Needed: $60,000-$90,000

Franchise Fee: $29,500

Royalty: 4.5 percent

Advertising Co-op Fee:

Financial Assistance: Financially-qualified individuals may finance the cost of the fixtures, equipment and signage necessary to open an Insty-Prints business through a lease plan arranged by franchisor. FBS Business Finance Corporation offers a seven-year lease at very competitive rates.

Management Assistance: Insty-Prints' professional field support teams are on-call business consultants that advise franchisees in all phases of business planning, financial analysis, operations, human resource development, and marketing. Proven sales building marketing programs and the industry's best automated direct mail program are available to all Insty-Prints franchise partners.

Training Assistance: From the signing of the franchise agreement, training never ends. Marketing and site evaluation, pre-training assistance, 4 weeks of classroom and hands-on training, on-site opening support, specialized video and audio programs and regional and national conferences are all part of Insty-Prints' commitment to success.

Kwik Copy® Corporation

12715 Telge Road
Cypress, TX 77429
Web Address: www.kwikkopy.com
E-mail Address: kksales@kwikkopy.com
Toll-Free Phone: (888) 280-2053
Phone:
Fax: (281) 373-4450
Contact: Franchise Sales

Number of Franchises: 848
Company-Owned Units: 0
Total Units: 848

In Business Since: 1967　　**Franchising Since:** 1967

Description of Operation: Printing, copying, and digital imaging, producing upscale commercial printing and color copying with connectivity. Kwik Kopy Printing starts owners from day one with outside sales consultants targeting volume repeat corporate accounts.

Equity Capital Needed: $80,000

Franchise Fee:

Royalty: 4-8 percent

Advertising Co-op Fee: None

Financial Assistance: Assistance, Yes.

Management Assistance: Ongoing workshops and weekend seminars at our 125 acre international headquarters campus. Monthly publications and technical bulletins, an intranet linking all centers and our world headquarters resources. Ongoing research of the next generation of equipment, annual convention and trade show, ongoing in store and telephone support.

Training Assistance: 4 weeks of classroom training and 1 to 1 1/2 weeks in your store.

Lazerquick Copies

27375 S.W. Parkway Ave.
Wilsonville, OR 97070
Web Address: www.lazerquick.com
Toll-Free Phone:
Phone: (503) 682-9025
Fax: (503) 682-7816
Contact: Vice President of Franchising

Number of Franchises: 17
Company-Owned Units: 34
Total Units: 51

In Business Since: 1968　　**Franchising Since:** 1990

Description of Operation: Lazerquick Copies centers are complete, one-stop, printing and copying centers. All centers feature state of the art electronic publishing and electronic graphics and imaging services that support our wide range of quality, fast service offset printing, high-speed copying, laser copying and related bindery and finishing services. The Lazerquick franchise is based on value and performance. Affiliates benefit from our unique and innovative programs.

Equity Capital Needed: $135,000-$190,000 (inclusive of franchise fee)

Franchise Fee: $20,000

Royalty: 5 percent first 5 yrs.; 2.5 percent of increased sales yr. 6

Advertising Co-op Fee:

Financial Assistance: Financing is offered through indirect sources only. Lazerquick does not carry financing for franchise operations.

Management Assistance: Assistance is ongoing and on an as-needed basis. The assistance is preferably offered via telephone, fax, modem, and mail.

Training Assistance: Franchise affiliates receive 5 weeks of intensive, hands-on training in our training facility, with additional optional weeks of training in a working location, plus on-site assistance during the first week of operation. Regular field visits, manuals, bulletins and an 800 number hotline provide ongoing support.

Pip Printing

27001 Agoura Rd. Ste. 200
Agoura Hills, CA 91301
Toll-Free Phone: (800) 292-4747
Phone: (818) 880-3800
Fax: (818) 880-3857
Contact:

Number of Franchises: 768
Company-Owned Units: 0
Total Units: 768

In Business Since: 1943　　**Franchising Since:** 1968

Description of Operation: PIP Printing locations offer a full range of business communications, from initial

concept to finished printed product, PIP's services include short-run, full-run, multicolor printing; high-volume copying; desktop publishing; layout; design; and finishing on an array of products, including newsletters, brochures, bound presentations, business stationery, and forms. PIP works to meet the needs of small and medium-sized businesses. PIP is currently changing their franchising package.

Equity Capital Needed: $189,000-$297,500

Franchise Fee: $40,000

Royalty: 1-7 percent (sliding scale)

Advertising Co-op Fee:

Financial Assistance: We do not offer financing, but we will assist potential franchisees through the review process with their financial institution.

Management Assistance: PIP's franchisees get ongoing assistance from our staff. After the initial 2 weeks of training, the owners may request a visit from business consultants trained in sales, marketing, operations, and finance. This service is free of charge. We also conduct workshops, regional meetings, and biennial conclaves that are held nation-wide and cover a wide range of topics, from customer service to the future of the printing industry. We also supply owners with training, operations, and safety manuals.

Training Assistance: A two-week business printing management course is offered in our corporate offices for new franchise owners. Ongoing training workshops offered nationwide. Specialized field visits from business consultants on marketing, sales, operations, and finance.

Quik Print

9415 E. Harry Suite 203
Wichita, KS 67207
Toll-Free Phone: (800) 825-2679
Phone: (316) 685-4800
Fax: (316) 685-9351
Contact: Senior Vice President

Number of Franchises: 142
Company-Owned Units: 63
Total Units: 205

In Business Since: 1963   **Franchising Since:** 1967

Description of Operation: Quik Print is a full-service printing and copying center, offering a full range of services, from desktop publishing to bindery. Complete training and support, including site selection, improvements, bookkeeping, advertising and sales assistance, and so on.

Equity Capital Needed: $150,000

Franchise Fee: $35,000

Royalty: 5 percent

Advertising Co-op Fee:

Financial Assistance: Up to $100,000 SBA loan to qualified buyers.

Management Assistance: We provide site selection, lease negotiation, overseeing of leasehold improvements, and marketing and sales programs.

Training Assistance: Training includes 4 weeks at corporate headquarters plus 2 weeks at location.

Screen Printing USA

534 W. Shawnee Ave.
Plymouth, PA 18651
E-mail Address: spusa@tl.infi.com
Toll-Free Phone:
Phone: (717) 779-5175
Fax:
Contact: President

Number of Franchises: 27
Company-Owned Units: 0
Total Units: 27

In Business Since: 1988   **Franchising Since:** 1988

Description of Operation: Full-service silk screen printing franchise-hats, T-shirts, jackets, signs, posters, and labels, using full-service computer graphics.

Equity Capital Needed: $25,000-$60,000

Franchise Fee: $10,000-$25,000

Royalty: 5 percent

Advertising Co-op Fee:

Financial Assistance: 50 percent of franchise fee.

Management Assistance: 2 weeks of training, ongoing phone support, on-site visits and, on-line computer help.

Training Assistance: 2 weeks of training.

Signal Graphics Printing

6789 S. Yosemite St.
Englewood, CO 80112
Web Address: www.signalgraphics.com
E-mail Address: SAMPACORP@aol.com
Toll-Free Phone: (800) 852-6336
Phone: (303) 779-6789
Fax: (303) 779-8445
Contact: Director of Franchise Development

Number of Franchises: 51
Company-Owned Units: 2
Total Units: 53

In Business Since: 1974   **Franchising Since:** 1982

Description of Operation: Full-service printing centers, offering high-speed color copying, fax, digital imaging, and desktop publishing. Quick-printing and a special emphasis on quality commercial printing. Comprehensive training, a proven system of operations and a state of the art equipment package can help newcomers to the field

quickly dominated their marketplace. Ongoing franchise support is a specialty, with management and technical help always on call from headquarters.

Equity Capital Needed: $60,000-$70,000

Franchise Fee: $18,000

Royalty: 5 percent; declining to 0 percent

Advertising Co-op Fee:

Financial Assistance: The franchisee is required to have a minimum of $18,000 for the franchise fee and $45,000 in working capital in liquid funds. Franchisor will assist franchisee in locating third-party financing for the equipment package of $110,000.

Management Assistance: In addition to the initial training and start-up assistance, 2 on-site follow up visits are provided during the first year of operation. a toll-free 800 number hotline, signal-grams and newsletters are provided for ongoing management assistance.

Training Assistance: A member of the top management team assists owners with site procurement, lease negotiation and store layout. Operations and management training consists of 3 weeks at headquarters, followed by 1 week on-site during opening.

Sir Speedy Printing Centers

26722 Plaza P.O. Box 9077
Mission Viejo, CA 92690
Web Address: www.sirspeedy.com
E-mail Address: fdelucia@sirspeedy.com
Toll-Free Phone: (800) 854-3321
Phone: (714) 348-5000
Fax: (714) 348-5068
Contact:

Number of Franchises: 861
Company-Owned Units: 19
Total Units: 880

In Business Since: 1968   **Franchising Since:** 1968

Description of Operation: Sir Speedy, Inc., headquartered in Mission Viejo, CA., is the world's largest and most successful franchisor of printing, copying and digital networking centers. Celebrating its 30th anniversary in 1998, Sir Speedy expects to exceed $400 million in network sales in 1997 for a record fifth straight year. Sir Speedy centers offer a wide range of services including graphic design; digital and conventional printing; high-speed, color and oversized copying; binding and finishing; mailing and shipping; and electronic data transfer to hundreds of national and international locations. The Sir Speedy Global Digital Network spans more than 900 centers around the world. For more information about Sir Speedy and its services, visit the Sir Speedy Web site at www.sirspeedy.com.

Equity Capital Needed: $75,000

Franchise Fee: $20,000

Royalty: 6 percent; 4 percent 1st yr./subject to rebate

Advertising Co-op Fee:

Financial Assistance: Sir Speedy provides assistance to franchise applicants in obtaining financing from either a leasing company, which finances equipment only; a non-bank lender, which finances equipment and soft costs; or with an SBA national underwriter, which will do either. A franchisee may use his/her own local sources.

Management Assistance: Sir Speedy provides operations manuals, toll-free hotlines, regional business management consultants, local franchisee associations, an audio and video resource library, seminars at regional roundtables, and annual conventions. A development service representative will help set up and conduct initial on-site training.

Training Assistance: Training provided includes an intense two-week classroom session at corporate headquarters, and a 1 1/2 week on-site session with a franchisee consultant on-site. Includes a three-day follow-up visit, five weeks of training are provided.

Real Estate—Apartments

Apartment Selector

P.O. Box 600355
Dallas, TX 75360
Web Address: www.aptselector.com
E-mail Address: askl@aptselector.com
Toll-Free Phone: (800) 324-3733
Phone: (214) 361-4420
Fax: (214) 361-8677
Contact: Chairman

Number of Franchises: 20
Company-Owned Units: 0
Total Units: 20

In Business Since: 1959   **Franchising Since:** 1987

Description of Operation: A rental referral agency (apartment locator). We assist renters for free. All fees are paid by property owner. Founded in 1959. Extensive training. Computer programs included.

Equity Capital Needed: $5,000-$20,000

Franchise Fee: $2,500

Royalty: 5 percent

Advertising Co-op Fee:

Financial Assistance: None

Management Assistance: Management will visit location, at franchisee's expense, during the year. Complete phone and computer support.

Training Assistance: Video, tapes, computer, and extensive manuals cover prospecting and listings.

Real Estate—For Sale By Owner

Picket Fence Franchise Co.

1 Kennedy Dr.
South Burlington, VT 05403
Web Address: www.picketfence-vt-fsbo.com
E-mail Address: billfsbo@sover.net
Toll-Free Phone: (800) 761-6060
Phone: (802) 660-3167
Fax:
Contact: President

Number of Franchises: 7
Company-Owned Units: 2
Total Units: 9

In Business Since: 1993   **Franchising Since:** 1994

Description of Operation: Publish a full color "for sale by owner" real estate advertising magazine. Provide and sell real estate yard signs, books, and videos (all trademark and copyright protected). Also available is a full-service, in-house mortgage company, US Direct Mortgage. Full training in desktop publishing, Internet publishing, for sale by owner marketing concepts, and more.

Equity Capital Needed: $120,000-150,000

Franchise Fee: $40,000

Royalty: 5 percent after 3 years.

Advertising Co-op Fee: None

Financial Assistance: Financing available for additional markets and franchise fee.

Management Assistance: Complete ongoing consultation as needed for first year.

Training Assistance: Desktop publishing, Internet publishing, and office structure. Optional: mortgage brokerage operation.

Real Estate—Inspection

Advantage Radon Control Centers

804 Second St. Pike
Southampton, PA 18966
Toll-Free Phone: (800) 535-8378
Phone: (215) 935-9200
Fax: (215) 953-8837
Contact: Chief Executive Officer

Number of Franchises: 1
Company-Owned Units: 5
Total Units: 6

In Business Since: 1984   **Franchising Since:** 1991

Description of Operation: Environmental testing with emphasis placed upon those services attached to the transfer of real estate. We are actively pursuing trained home inspectors who wish to expand their services to include environmental inspections. Specializing in radon testing and mitigation, we can improve performance and increase sales.

Equity Capital Needed: $15,000-$25,000

Franchise Fee: $17,500

Royalty: 8 percent

Advertising Co-op Fee:

Financial Assistance: 65-80 percent financing for qualified individuals.

Management Assistance: Excellent training and ongoing assistance for all franchisees.

Training Assistance: In-house and on-the-job training program. Assistance in obtaining federal and state licensing. Development of QA/QC plans. Periodic updating during course of year as prescribed by EPA.

AmeriSpec, Inc.

860 Ridge Lake Blvd.
Memphis, TN 38120
Web Address: www.SVM.com
E-mail Address: AMSHQ@aol.com
Toll-Free Phone: (800) 426-2270
Phone: (901) 820-8500
Fax: (901) 820-8520
Contact: Vice President of Sales

Number of Franchises: 280
Company-Owned Units: 0
Total Units: 280

In Business Since: 1987   **Franchising Since:** 1988

Description of Operation: AmeriSpec provides residential home inspection services. Typically conducted as a part of the real estate transaction. Includes systems, components, and some structural analysis. Ancillary inspections can be included such as radon, water, and lead testing, to name a few.

Equity Capital Needed: $50,000-$74,900

Franchise Fee: $11,900-$22,900

Royalty: 7 percent

Advertising Co-op Fee: 3 percent

Financial Assistance: A wholly owned subsidiary of ServiceMaster Co., SMAC provides financing up to seventy percent of franchise fee for up to a 5 year term. Rate is determined by prime through First Chicago Bank plus 3 percent. AmeriSpec discounts to retired military personnel.

Management Assistance: Complete written operations, sales and marketing, inventory control, accounting, and contact management manuals and software.

Training Assistance: Two week technical and marketing related training at corporate location and on-site training as requested at start-up.

HomeTeam Inspection Service

6355 E. Kemper Rd., Ste. 250
Cincinnati, OH 45241
Web Address:
Toll-Free Phone: (800) 598-5297
Phone: (513) 469-2100
Fax: (513) 469-2226
Contact: President

Number of Franchises: 52
Company-Owned Units: 0
Total Units: 52

In Business Since: 1991 **Franchising Since:** 1993

Description of Operation: National franchisor of home inspections. The HomeTeam is unique and approaches this rapidly growing business in a different way.

Equity Capital Needed: $4,050-$12,270

Franchise Fee: $8,950-$20,900

Royalty: 6 percent

Advertising Co-op Fee:

Financial Assistance: We will finance up to 50 percent of the initial franchise fee.

Management Assistance: The franchisee will be trained in all aspects of operating the business. Marketing, accounting, and management will all be included. Ongoing assistance will be available throughout the franchise term.

Training Assistance: Each franchisee will receive a 14-day, comprehensive training program at the corporate office.

HouseMaster

421 West Union Avenue
Bound Brook, NJ 08805
Web Address: www.housemaster.com
E-mail Address: rrestaino@housemaster.com
Toll-Free Phone: (800) 526-3939
Phone: (908) 469-6565
Fax: (908) 469-7405
Contact: Director of Franchise Sales

Number of Franchises: 277
Company-Owned Units: 0
Total Units: 277

In Business Since: 1979 **Franchising Since:** 1979

Description of Operation: Home inspections for home buyers and sellers. With the high price of housing and the growing need for full disclosure, a home inspection is becoming a must in the course of real estate transactions.

Equity Capital Needed: $15,750-$51,500

Franchise Fee: $8,500-$24,000

Royalty: 7.5 percent

Advertising Co-op Fee: 2.5 percent

Financial Assistance: Not available

Management Assistance: Not applicable

Training Assistance: 1 week sales and operations classroom training, 1 week technical classroom training, 1 week technical field training.

National Property Inspections, Inc.

11620 Arbor St., Ste. 100
Omaha, NE 68144
E-mail Address: hpi@radiks.net
Toll-Free Phone: (800) 333-9807
Phone: (402) 333-9807
Fax: (800) 933-2508
Contact: Director of Marketing

Number of Franchises: 84
Company-Owned Units: 0
Total Units: 84

In Business Since: 1987 **Franchising Since:** 1987

Description of Operation: Nationally respected leader in residential/commercial property inspection franchises. Industry is booming. Savvy consumers nationwide want to protect home purchase. U.S. Postal Services says 46,000 households move each day. NPI's stellar reputation and success are widely recognized corporation of highly motivated, competent professionals dedicated to your success. Most generous package available. Exclusive territories. Innovative training. Sophisticated, on-site computer system. Cutting edge marketing. Ongoing technical support. Business expansion expertise. All you need for first year of business! Franchisees benefit from award-winning referral program in the billion dollar relocation industry.

Equity Capital Needed:

Franchise Fee: $17,800-$25,800

Royalty: 8 percent monthly

Advertising Co-op Fee: None

Financial Assistance: Partial financing of franchise fee.

Management Assistance: Founder and president Roland Bates is available for technical and managerial support in addition to a staff of eighteen full time employees with expertise in construction, real estate, sales and marketing, computers, and much more.

Training Assistance: Franchise fee includes comprehensive two-week training at corporate headquarters, in field training, ongoing and responsive technical and marketing support, annual meeting with technical and marketing speakers/workshops.

Real Estate—Residential Sales

Assist-2-Sell, Inc.

535 E. Plumb Lane, Ste. 102
Reno, NV 89502
Web Address: assist2sell.com
E-mail Address: lyle@assist2sell.com
Toll-Free Phone: (800) 528-7816
Phone: (702) 688-6060
Fax: (702) 688-6069
Contact: CEO

Number of Franchises: 40
Company-Owned Units: 1
Total Units: 40

In Business Since: 1987   **Franchising Since:** 1994

Description of Operation: America's "full service for less" real estate franchise. The future of real estate is moving towards lower commissions and "menu of services" type brokerages. If you are a licensed real estate broker with 2 or more years experience, check us out. Find out how to increase you volume and your profits while charging less.

Equity Capital Needed: $25,000

Franchise Fee: $6,995

Royalty: $100 per closing (sale)

Advertising Co-op Fee: None

Financial Assistance: None

Management Assistance:

Training Assistance: Comprehensive one week training class plus ongoing support.

Better Homes & Garden Real Estate Service

2000 Grand Ave.
Des Moines, IA 50312
Web Address: www.bhgrealestate.com
Toll-Free Phone: (800) 274-7653
Phone: (515) 284-2355
Fax: (515) 284-3342
Contact:

Number of Franchises: 658
Company-Owned Units: 0
Total Units: 658

In Business Since: 1902   **Franchising Since:** 1978

Description of Operation: The Better Homes and Gardens Real Estate service is a national residential real estate marketing service which licenses selected real estate firms to an exclusive territory. Members and affiliates total 652 in the United States and 6 in Canada. The real estate service typically receives a joining fee from new member firms and thereafter a franchise fee based on a percentage of the member's gross commission income on residential housing sales. Member firms may purchase marketing programs/materials.

Equity Capital Needed: $40,000-$200,000

Franchise Fee: Sliding scale.

Royalty: 5 percent maximum

Advertising Co-op Fee:

Financial Assistance: Deferred payment program on identity materials: 50 percent down, 18 installment payments with no interest. Initial franchise, if required, may also be paid on the deferred plan.

Management Assistance: Better Homes & Gardens Management Training Institute, Better Homes & Gardens Management Orientation Session, Better Homes & Gardens Recruiting System, Better Homes & Gardens In-Touch Service Program.

Training Assistance: Better Homes & Gardens Sales Associate Orientation Program, Better Homes and Gardens Advantage Training Program, Better Homes and Gardens Medallion Club Summit Program, Better Homes and Gardens International Business Conference and Convention, Better Homes and Gardens In-Touch Service Program.

Buyer's Agent, Inc., The

1255 Lynnfield, Ste.273
Memphis, TN 38119
Web Address: www.forbuyers.com
E-mail Address: REBUYRAGT@aol.com
Toll-Free Phone: (800) 766-8728
Phone: (901) 767-1077
Fax: (901) 767-3577
Contact: Director of Marketing

Number of Franchises: 72
Company-Owned Units: 0
Total Units: 72

In Business Since: 1988   **Franchising Since:** 1988

Description of Operation: The Buyer's Agent is the nation's leading real estate franchisor specializing in exclusive buyer representation. The company offers the most complete and technically advanced office management system with assistance in office setup, recruiting, training, marketing, and daily operations. They Buyer's Agent remains the only real estate franchisor with 100 percent of its franchisees linked by its own national computer network.

Equity Capital Needed: $30,000-50,000

Franchise Fee: $14,900

Royalty: 5 percent

Advertising Co-op Fee: 1 percent

Financial Assistance: The Buyer's Agent offers short-term financing on the initial franchise fee only.

Management Assistance: Assistance with site selection, agent recruitment and development, electronic referral network, computer hardware and software, national 800 number, Internet Website, in-house legal counsel, whole-sale mortgage loan program, newsletters, and a client follow-up program.

Training Assistance: Five-day certified broker/owner training program at corporate headquarters in Memphis, TN. Four-day certified agent training program. Annual and mid-year conferences. Agent recognition and awards program.

Buyer's Resource

393 Hanover Center
Etna, NH 03750
Web Address: www.buyersresource.com
E-mail Address: info@buyersresource.com
Toll-Free Phone: (800) 359-4092
Phone: (603) 643-9300
Fax: (603) 643-0404
Contact:

Number of Franchises: 30
Company-Owned Units: 0
Total Units: 30

In Business Since: 1989   **Franchising Since:** 1989

Description of Operation: Franchisor of exclusive buyer-broker real estate firms, representing buyers exclusively in real estate transactions.

Equity Capital Needed: $35,000-$65,000

Franchise Fee: $9,000-rural/resort $12,500-metropolitan

Royalty: 5 percent, plus 2 percent advertising fee.

Advertising Co-op Fee:

Financial Assistance: No standards. Done on case-by-case basis.

Management Assistance: Corporate officers bring their strong and deep personal commitment to buyer agency and to each Buyer's Resource franchise office. Direct support and consulting services are provided by all.

Training Assistance: 5 days of initial training, ongoing seminars, annual conventions, telephone training, and in-house training.

By Owner Realty Network

2115 E. Sherman Ave. Ste. 101
Coeur d'Alene, ID 83814
Toll-Free Phone:
Phone: (208) 667-6184
Fax: (208) 664-4539
Contact: Vice President

Number of Franchises: 7
Company-Owned Units: 1
Total Units: 8

In Business Since: 1985   **Franchising Since:** 1986

Description of Operation: Real estate centers in retail locations, offering sellers money-saving marketing and services, in addition to full broker and realtor services.

Equity Capital Needed: $14,850

Franchise Fee: $16,500

Royalty: 10 percent, including advertising fees.

Advertising Co-op Fee:

Financial Assistance: Owner does not currently offer financing for franchisees.

Management Assistance: Franchise locations within the existing master franchise areas receive ongoing and hands-on support from the master (sub) franchisor. Franchise locations in other areas will be managed directly from the corporate headquarters of franchisor. Ongoing support is considered a top priority for network success.

Training Assistance: Initial: a minimum of 3 days training at corporate headquarters. Before opening—hands-on training and preparation for opening. On-site at new location. Grand opening—franchisor representative on hand for grand opening. Ongoing: Ongoing training and education is encouraged by all parties—franchisees and franchisor representatives.

Century 21 Real Estate

393 Jefferson Rd. P.O. Box 278
Parsippany, NJ 07054
Web Address: www.century21.com
Toll-Free Phone: (800) 932-4677
Phone: (973) 428-9700
Fax: (973) 428-6057
Contact:

Number of Franchises: 6000
Company-Owned Units: 0
Total Units: 6000

In Business Since: 1972   **Franchising Since:** 1972

Description of Operation: World's largest real estate franchising organization, established to provide a marketing support system for independently-owned and operated real estate brokerage offices. We offer international advertising, VIP referral system, residential and commercial sales training, management training, national accounts center, client follow-up, and other real estate-related services. Subsidiary of Metropolitan Life Insurance Company.

Equity Capital Needed: $15,000-$30,000

Franchise Fee: $15,000-$30,000

Royalty: Determined by region, usually 6 percent

Advertising Co-op Fee:

Financial Assistance: Some financing may be available.

Management Assistance: New members attend the International Management Academy, a five-day orientation/management training seminar. Other courses in sales management, business management, leadership, reloca-

tion, and commercial brokerage are offered at the regional level. A performance-based program, Operation Orbit, is delivered at a variety of locations throughout the organization and helps attendees use the various elements of Century 21 office management.

Training Assistance: Performance-based training is available to Century 21 sales associates, covering a wide range of topics. The 21 Plus program sets the standard for customer-oriented real estate sales and epitomizes a quality service approach. Programs in relocation, investment, career management, finance, and quality service are also offered.

Group Trans-Action Brokerage Services

550 Sherbrooke, W. Ste.775
Montreal, PQ H3A 1B9
Toll-Free Phone:
Phone: (514) 288-6777
Fax: (514) 288-7543
Contact: General Manager

Number of Franchises: 48
Company-Owned Units: 0
Total Units: 48

In Business Since: 1978   **Franchising Since:** 1982

Description of Operation: Complete real estate services—purchase, sale, relocation, homefinding, and so on.

Equity Capital Needed: $50,000

Franchise Fee: $16,500

Royalty: $130 per agent per month

Advertising Co-op Fee:

Financial Assistance: 25 percent minimum down payment—balance can be repaid in 12 consecutive months without interest.

Management Assistance: Back-up support in all areas of franchise operations.

Training Assistance: The franchise includes basic and advanced seminars. Other training is available as required.

Help-U-Sell Real Estate

225 W. Hospitality Ln. Ste. 200
San Bernadano, CA 92408
Web Address: www.helpusell.net
E-mail Address: franchising@helpusell.com
Toll-Free Phone: (800) 366-1177
Phone: (909) 890-0682
Fax: (909) 890-2624
Contact:

Number of Franchises: 148
Company-Owned Units: 0
Total Units: 148

In Business Since: 1976   **Franchising Since:** 1978

Description of Operation: Help-U-Sell continues to develop a menu of services that is offered to buyers and sellers. The Help-U-Sell method provides specific services to the seller for a set fee. In addition, sellers can choose to place their property into the Multiple Listing Service. Buyers can view properties on their own, but are encouraged to be shown by an agent and be represented by a buyer's agent. The marketing system can generate hundreds of buyer and seller leads without the need to cold-call.

Equity Capital Needed: Varies, depending on existing or start-up office.

Franchise Fee: $4,500 +

Royalty: 5.5 percent

Advertising Co-op Fee:

Financial Assistance: None.

Management Assistance: Either a regional or corporate person is assigned to each office.

Training Assistance: We offer 4 1/2 days of intensive, initial training at corporate headquarters in San Bernadano, CA. Ongoing support and training through either a regional or corporate person as well as regional and national conventions.

Her Real Estate

4656 Executive Dr.
Columbus, OH 43220
Toll-Free Phone: (800) 848-7400
Phone: (614) 459-7400
Fax: (614) 457-6807
Contact: President

Number of Franchises: 12
Company-Owned Units: 25
Total Units: 37

In Business Since: 1976   **Franchising Since:** 1981

Description of Operation: Personalized approach to real estate franchising. Brokers keep their own identity and marks of franchisor do not detract or dominate. On-location educational opportunities. Franchisees offered exclusive territories. Also provided are test-marketed, award-winning, marketing tools and techniques.

Equity Capital Needed: $6,800-$23,000

Franchise Fee: $2,500-$80,000

Royalty: 5 percent, plus 1 percent advertising.

Advertising Co-op Fee:

Financial Assistance: A portion of the initial franchisee fee is used for conversion of office.

Management Assistance: Support programs through field representation, continuing education, and other unique educational opportunities.

Training Assistance: Initial 2 weeks of training for anyone new to the company. Ongoing follow-up programs, along with monthly continuing education.

Homeowners Concept, Inc.

611 N. Mayfair Rd.
Milwaukee, WI 53226
Web Address: http://homeownersconcept.com
E-mail Address: hoc@excpc.com
Toll-Free Phone: (800) 800-9890
Phone: (414) 258-7778
Fax: (414) 258-8276
Contact: President

Number of Franchises: 34
Company-Owned Units: 0
Total Units: 34

In Business Since: 1982   **Franchising Since:** 1984

Description of Operation: Homeowners Concept offers a flat fee real estate program of consulting /sales. Extremely profitable, highly satisfying business on the cutting edge of the "do it yourself" megatrend. No cold calling, no open houses, no showing! Large exclusive territory.

Equity Capital Needed: $15,000

Franchise Fee: $4,500

Royalty: 3 percent

Advertising Co-op Fee: None

Financial Assistance: None

Management Assistance: Operations manual proprietary software, national conferences, newsletters, ongoing support.

Training Assistance: One on one training for up to 3 days.

Prudential Real Estate Affiliates

3333 Michaelson Dr. Ste. 1000
Irvine, CA 92612
Toll-Free Phone: (800) 666-6634
Phone:
Fax: (714) 794-7031
Contact:

Number of Franchises: 434
Company-Owned Units: 0
Total Units: 434

In Business Since: 1988   **Franchising Since:** 1988

Description of Operation: Offer and sale of franchises for the operation of real estate brokerage to selected real estate brokers throughout the US and certain foreign countries.

Equity Capital Needed: $25,565-$45,900 (excluding franchise fee)

Franchise Fee: $25,000-$73,000 and up.

Royalty: 1.25-6 percent

Advertising Co-op Fee:

Financial Assistance: The franchisor may allow the franchisee to defer payment of all or a portion of the initial franchise fee and may permit financing of other obligations owed to the franchisor. The annual rate of interest ranges from 9 to 15 percent for up to 36 months or equal to the highest rate permitted by law, whichever is lower.

Management Assistance: Each location manager is required to attend the franchisor's Management Academy. An initial orientation program is provided by the franchisor for managers.

Training Assistance: Optional staff training seminars are available.

RE/MAX International, Inc.

8390 East Crescent Parkway, Ste. 600
Englewood, CO 80155-3907
Web Address: www.remax.com
Toll-Free Phone: (800) 525-7452
Phone: (303) 770-5531
Fax: (303) 796-3884
Contact: Public Relations Manager

Number of Franchises: 2,890
Company-Owned Units: 0
Total Units: 2,890

In Business Since: 1973   **Franchising Since:** 1976

Description of Operation: Real estate brokerage franchise operating under unique RE/MAX Concept.

Equity Capital Needed: $10,000-25,000

Franchise Fee: $10,000-25,000

Royalty: $100 per sales associate

Advertising Co-op Fee:

Financial Assistance: Yes

Management Assistance: An intensive 2 days of individual instruction is given by national staff, teaching new owners how to operate the Realty Executives one-hundred percent concept, using methods with over twenty years of proven success. A comprehensive operations manual, coupled with the instant accessibility of a national staff, who also administer company-owned offices, provide ongoing assistance. New accounting software is available at additional expense.

Training Assistance: Unlimited consultation in proven, successful accounting procedures, recruiting techniques, clerical hiring, and advertising methods is provided. National and regional meetings cover topics of vital interest to owners. Operation of national referral network and volume purchasing to our brokers and associates.

Realty One

7310 Potomac Dr.
Boise, ID 83704
Toll-Free Phone: (800) 732-5891
Phone: (208) 322-2700
Fax: (208) 322-2756
Contact: President

Number of Franchises: 2
Company-Owned Units: 1
Total Units: 3

In Business Since: 1985   **Franchising Since:** 1987

Description of Operation: Full-service real estate franchise company, offering a new concept in real estate brokerage. Featuring "Real 100 percent" commissions—the Realty One concept. A method of real estate business operation uniquely different from conventional-type real estate offices.

Equity Capital Needed: $75,000-$100,000

Franchise Fee: $15,000

Royalty: Fixed monthly fee.

Advertising Co-op Fee:

Financial Assistance: None.

Management Assistance: We provide on-site managerial assistance for the start-up of a new franchise, as well as corporate office staff assistance.

Training Assistance: We offer on-site training in the franchisee's local board of realtors and realtor community, including site location, start-up assistance, operations, and recruitment of realtors.

Realty World

4100 Newport Pl. Ste. 720
Newport Beach, CA 92660
Toll-Free Phone: (800) 777-5565
Phone: (714) 245-1200
Fax: (714) 245-1066
Contact: Executive Vice President

Number of Franchises: 500
Company-Owned Units: 0
Total Units: 500

In Business Since: 1974   **Franchising Since:** 1974

Description of Operation: Realty World American Corporation has developed a plan designed to enable independent real estate brokerage offices to benefit from broad name identification and to enable such offices to compete more effectively in the real estate industry. The Realty World System is one of the largest real estate franchise organizations in North America, with independently-owned and operated offices throughout the US, Canada, Mexico and Israel.

Equity Capital Needed: $27,000-$38,000 (start up).

Franchise Fee: $15,900

Royalty: 1-5 percent

Advertising Co-op Fee:

Financial Assistance: Realty World Corporation makes financing available to new franchisees.

Management Assistance: The Realty World System includes the common use and promotion of the service mark Realty World and other marks, the production of

commercials for use in radio and TV and other media advertising, sales training programs, educational programs, training manuals, a program for referral of real estate listings and various forms, procedures and systems to assist in the operation and management of a real estate office.

Training Assistance: RWC holds the RealStart Management Training Academy for new franchisee broker/owners. It is a five-day orientation and business planning session highlighting Realty World programs and services.

Real Estate—Miscellaneous

Criterium Engineers

650 Brighton Ave.
Portland, ME 04102
Toll-Free Phone: (800) 242-1969
Phone: (207) 828-1969
Fax: (207) 775-4405
Contact: Director of Marketing/Development

Number of Franchises: 63
Company-Owned Units: 0
Total Units: 63

In Business Since: 1957   **Franchising Since:** 1959

Description of Operation: Criterium Engineers is a nationwide franchise network of registered professional engineers, specializing in buildings and related consulting services. Services include residential and commercial inspections, insurance investigations, environmental assessments, capital reserve studies, design, and related services. Clients include buyers, building owners and managers, lenders, attorneys, insurance companies, and government agencies.

Equity Capital Needed: $2,500

Franchise Fee: $22,500

Royalty: 6 percent

Advertising Co-op Fee:

Financial Assistance: A down payment of $10,000 is required. Franchisor will finance the balance of the franchise fee.

Management Assistance: 1 week of initial training is provided at the franchisor's main office. Annual business workshops are held in the fall with several business sessions. Customized software and unlimited toll-free phone support is provided to all franchisees.

Training Assistance: Data not available.

National Tenant Network

P.O. Box 1664
Lake Grove, OR 97034
Toll-Free Phone: (800) 228-0989

Phone: (503) 635-1118
Fax: (503) 635-9392
Contact: President

Number of Franchises: 12
Company-Owned Units: 4
Total Units: 16

In Business Since: 1980 **Franchising Since:** 1987

Description of Operation: Residential and commercial tenant performance reporting. Analysis of retail credit and tenant performance data maintained on a nationally networked mainframe computer. Low-overhead, high cash flow, turn-key opportunity. All equipment provided by franchisor. National accounts may be provided to business at start-up.

Equity Capital Needed: $30,000-$50,000

Franchise Fee: $30,000

Royalty: 10 percent

Advertising Co-op Fee:

Financial Assistance: Up to 50 percent financing is available on the purchase of developed territories.

Management Assistance: All that is required of a new NTN operation.

Training Assistance: Initially, 1 full week at franchisee's site. Operational training and marketing manuals. Ongoing, close working relationship among all NTN offices, 6 days a week.

Room-Mate Referral Service Centers

P.O. Box 890575
Oklahoma City, OK 73189
Toll-Free Phone:
Phone: (405) 692-0947
Fax: (405) 634-3096
Contact: Chief Executive Officer

Number of Franchises: 22
Company-Owned Units: 2
Total Units: 24

In Business Since: 1979 **Franchising Since:** 1984

Description of Operation: A service company that handles the placement of persons as roommates, for economic and a variety of other needs.

Equity Capital Needed: $6,500-$15,000

Franchise Fee: $4,500-$11,000

Royalty: 3 percent

Advertising Co-op Fee:

Financial Assistance: 25 percent of the franchise fee is carried personally at no interest.

Management Assistance: After initial training, we are always available by phone. Once a year, we go back into the area at our expense for additional training or whatever help is needed.

Training Assistance: A manual and enough forms to last at least 3 months are provided. We go into the area of the new franchisee to train. We are there 2 1/2 to 3 days. Besides training, we help locate the site needed for business. We do the training at our own expense.

Recreation & Travel— Amusement Center

Fun Works

3216 Power Blvd.
Metairie, LA 70003
Toll-Free Phone:
Phone: (504) 887-5678
Fax: (504) 887-5437
Contact: President

Number of Franchises: 1
Company-Owned Units: 1
Total Units: 2

In Business Since: 1986 **Franchising Since:** 1992

Description of Operation: An indoor "soft play" amusement center, specializing in participating play for children, ages 2-twelve. Play area consists of child play toys such as Space Pillow, Sea of Balls, Cargo Net, Cheese Maze, and so on. Business consists of general admission birthday parties and groups. Play area is complimented with game area and concession stand.

Equity Capital Needed: $100,000

Franchise Fee: $25,000

Royalty: 6 percent

Advertising Co-op Fee:

Financial Assistance: None.

Management Assistance: Site selection assistance, installation of operational procedures for this type of business and necessary forms. 1 week of hands-on training at home office before opening. Operations manual and advertising material provided.

Training Assistance: 1 week of hands-on training at home office and 1 week of hands-on training at new site during opening. Additional follow-up training available on request for additional fee.

Gigglebees

519 S. Minnesota Ave.
Sioux Falls, SD 57104
Toll-Free Phone:
Phone: (605) 331-4242
Fax:
Contact: Franchise Development

Number of Franchises: 1
Company-Owned Units: 1
Total Units: 2

In Business Since: 1985   **Franchising Since:** 1994

Description of Operation: Gigglebees is a family entertainment center with pizza, games, and rides. Occupying 10,000 to 15,000 square feet, each franchise offers a wide variety of games and attractions for children ages 2-12 and their families. The fun center features video games, pinball redemption games, and coin operated rides. The restaurant employs remote control robots that look like stuffed animals riding tricycles. These robots deliver the food directly to the tables while they sing and play with the children. Gigglebees offers freedom and flexibility so that each franchise owner can model their store according to local tastes and trends.

Equity Capital Needed: $100,000-300,000

Franchise Fee: $25,000

Royalty: 4.5 percent of gross sales monthly

Advertising Co-op Fee: None

Financial Assistance: None

Management Assistance: Each franchise is initially served by a management team that provides the following services: hiring, training, vendor contracting, media purchasing, and floor management.

Training Assistance: Franchisees will attend a 21-day training event at the company headquarters in Sioux Falls, SD. This initial training will reach all areas of the Gigglebees operation, culminating in the franchisee actually managing an existing store. Ongoing training is semi-annual at the franchisee's operation.

Grove Recreations, Inc.

Rose Bud Lane-Socastee Area, P.O. Box 2435
Myrtle Beach, SC 29578
E-mail Address: chgrove@sccoast.net
Toll-Free Phone:
Phone: (803) 236-4733
Fax: (803) 236-0336
Contact: President

Number of Franchises: 10
Company-Owned Units: 3
Total Units: 13

In Business Since: 1977   **Franchising Since:** 1977

Description of Operation: Designer/builder themed contoured miniature golf, and family entertainment centers. Also, manufacture heavyweight fiberglass props, for theming.

Equity Capital Needed: $50,000-100,000

Franchise Fee: N/A

Royalty: N/A

Advertising Co-op Fee: None

Financial Assistance: We work with client to obtain funding.

Management Assistance: All assistance needed for operations.

Training Assistance: All assistance needed for operations.

Putt-Putt® Golf Courses of America, Inc.

P.O. Box 35237
Fayetteville, NC 28303-0237
Web Address: www.putt-putt.com
E-mail Address: scotland@putt-putt.com
Toll-Free Phone:
Phone: (910) 485-7131
Fax: (910) 485-1122
Contact: National Franchise Director

Number of Franchises: 264
Company-Owned Units: 8
Total Units: 264

In Business Since: 1954   **Franchising Since:** 1955

Description of Operation: We are the number one franchise of miniature golf and family recreation centers in the world. Our current franchised attractions are: Putt-Putt® Golf, arcade gamerooms, go karts, baseball batting cages, bumper boats, total play, and laser tag.

Equity Capital Needed: 20 percent of total project cost

Franchise Fee: $5,000-$30,000

Royalty: 2-3 percent

Advertising Co-op Fee: 1-2

Financial Assistance:

Management Assistance: Design services, site selection, business plan preparation, staff training, advertising, on-site training, national convention, and more.

Training Assistance: On-site training, monthly and quarterly memos, training manuals, convention, and seminar sessions.

Ultrazone

2880 E. Flamingo Rd. Ste. E
Las Vegas, NV 89121
Web Address: www.ultrazone.com
Toll-Free Phone: (800) 628-2829
Phone: (702) 734-3617
Fax: (702) 734-3618
Contact: Vice President

Number of Franchises: 35
Company-Owned Units: 3
Total Units: 38

In Business Since: 1993   **Franchising Since:** 1993

Description of Operation: Ultrazone, the ultimate laser adventure. The most exciting investment in franchising's newest industry—live-action laser games. An American company, offering the most advanced laser game technology on the planet, backed by seven years of research, development and operations. Ultrazone offers franchise owners service and support unequaled in the industry. Investment ranges from $320,000-$480,000.

Equity Capital Needed: $290,000-$400,000

Franchise Fee: $15,000

Royalty: 5 percent of gross, or $2,000 per month.

Advertising Co-op Fee:

Financial Assistance: No financing is currently available.

Management Assistance: Ongoing business support, from date of signing, through pre-opening training.

Training Assistance: We offer five days of on-site training, plus 10 days of preopening training.

Recreation & Travel—Cinema

Cinema Grill

P.O. Box 28467
Atlanta, GA 30358
Web Address: www.cinemagrill.com
E-mail Address: cinemagrill@aol.com
Toll-Free Phone:
Phone: (404) 250-9536
Fax: (404) 845-0718
Contact: Vice President

Number of Franchises: 27
Company-Owned Units: 2
Total Units: 29

In Business Since: 1975   **Franchising Since:** 1980

Description of Operation: Cinema Grill is a theater/restaurant format that is universally appealing and distinctive. We start with a proven recession-proof product—food, drink and film—combined in a stylish, art deco theater. Then we enhance its value by offering space for business seminars, sports telecasts and private parties for daytime use.

Equity Capital Needed: $100,000-$450,000

Franchise Fee: $40,000

Royalty: 3 percent

Advertising Co-op Fee:

Financial Assistance: Assistance provided in putting together business plans, landlord/developer negotiation and direction in SBA and various other programs.

Management Assistance: Initially, you and your theater manager will be required to attend a three-week training program, providing step-by-step operational techniques additional to pre-opening, and on-site training.

Training Assistance: Regular visits from regional managers ensure that the operations of the theater are kept up to standards. Also, assistance is provided with new products, accounting controls, promotions and personnel guidance.

Recreation & Travel—Pool

American Poolplayers Association, Inc.

1000 Lake St. Louis Blvd., Ste. 325
Lake St. Louis, MO 63367
Web Address: www.poolplayers.com
Toll-Free Phone: (800) 372-2536
Phone: (314) 625-8611
Fax: (314) 625-2975
Contact: Franchise Development Manager

Number of Franchises: 217
Company-Owned Units: 2
Total Units: 219

In Business Since: 1981   **Franchising Since:** 1982

Description of Operation: Franchisees operate amateur billiard leagues using a unique, copyrighted handicap system nationally sponsored by R.J. Reynolds "CAMEL" brand and now known as the "Camel Pool League." Franchisees receive customized software, complete training, marketing support, and networking opportunities. Work out of your home full or part-time with a business that is recognized throughout the billiard industry as the "Governing Body of Amateur Pool."

Equity Capital Needed: $4,320-$6,220

Franchise Fee: $5,000 plus $100 per 20,000 population

Royalty: 20 percent

Advertising Co-op Fee: None

Financial Assistance: In-house financing is available for qualified individuals.

Management Assistance: A full support department is staffed at the national office to give our franchisees any ongoing support needed.

Training Assistance: A six-day seminar is provided and required of all franchisees. Complete training of customized software program and league operation is covered during training and a full support staff is provided for continued ongoing support.

Recreation & Travel—
Travel & Cruises

Algonquin Travel

657 Bronson Ave.
Ottawa, ON K1S 4E7
Web Address: www.algtravel.com
E-mail Address: frnchise@algtravel.com
Toll-Free Phone: (800) 668-1743
Phone: (613) 233-7713
Fax: (613) 233-7805
Contact: Franchise Development

Number of Franchises: 107
Company-Owned Units: 1
Total Units: 108

In Business Since: 1964 **Franchising Since:** 1978

Description of Operation: Full-service travel agency, where the mission is to develop a team of successful travel agencies working together to exceed the expectations of the traveling consumer. Our goal is to be the dominant, best-quality, best-service, and best-value travel chain in each market in which we are active.

Equity Capital Needed: $75,000-$150,000

Franchise Fee: $35,000

Royalty: 6-10 percent

Advertising Co-op Fee:

Financial Assistance: Government small business loans, full assistance in loan applications, including business plan writing and financial forecasts.

Management Assistance: Three weeks of training in Ottawa, ON: one week on-site, staff recruiting and agency set-up, franchisee buddy system, automation training, six months of complimentary automation for new locations, toll-free and E-mail, and experienced field support staff.

Training Assistance: Full training curriculum.

Cruise Holidays International Inc.

9665 Chesapeake Dr., Ste. 401
San Diego, CA 92123
Web Address: www.cruiseholidayint.com
E-mail Address: frandev@cruiseholidayint.com
Toll-Free Phone: (800) 866-7245
Phone: (619) 279-4780
Fax: (619) 279-4788
Contact:

Number of Franchises: 203
Company-Owned Units: 0
Total Units: 203

In Business Since: 1984 **Franchising Since:** 1984

Description of Operation: Cruise Holidays International Inc. is the oldest and largest franchisor of retail travel centers in the world, specializing in the sale of cruise vacations to the general public. Cruising has become the fastest growing and most profitable segment of the travel industry. Cruise Holidays offers comprehensive training, national advertising and no inventory. Cruise Holidays represents all the major cruise lines.

Equity Capital Needed: $100,000-$130,000

Franchise Fee: $29,500

Royalty: 1 percent or $525

Advertising Co-op Fee:

Financial Assistance: SBA approved franchisor.

Management Assistance: We provide two weeks of comprehensive training in marketing, advertising, sales, customer service, product knowledge, business operations, and accounting. A free cruise is included as part of the training. On-site visits and assistance. Group and convention sales and advanced training available.

Training Assistance: Same as above.

Cruise Lines Reservation Center

9229 Kaufman Pl.
Brooklyn, NY 11236
Toll-Free Phone:
Phone: (718) 763-4259
Fax:
Contact: President

Number of Franchises: 24
Company-Owned Units: 1
Total Units: 25

In Business Since: 1989 **Franchising Since:** 1990

Description of Operation: Cruise-only travel agency.

Equity Capital Needed: $1,000-$2,000

Franchise Fee: $500

Royalty: 1 percent

Advertising Co-op Fee:

Financial Assistance: None.

Management Assistance: Unlimited consultation.

Training Assistance: Training is provided through comprehensive manuals and nationwide training seminars.

Empress Travel

465 Smith St.
Farmingdale, NY 11735
Toll-Free Phone:
Phone: (516) 420-9200

Fax: (516) 420-4752
Contact:

Number of Franchises: 63
Company-Owned Units: 0
Total Units: 63

In Business Since: 1958   **Franchising Since:** 1970

Description of Operation: East Coast, retail, travel agency network. Affiliated with one of the country's largest travel wholesalers. Franchisee enjoys the benefits of massive advertising, including weekly full-page advertisements in the *New York Times* and other papers such as *Newark Star Ledger, The Washington Post, The Philadelphia Inquirer, The Albany Times Union, The New York Post, Newsday,* and others.

Equity Capital Needed: $2,500-$100,000

Franchise Fee: $20,000

Royalty: From $7,500 per year.

Advertising Co-op Fee:

Financial Assistance: None from franchisor.

Management Assistance: Weekly communication via company newsletter. Monthly seminars on sales techniques, marketing ideas and operational know-how. Telephone support is five days a week, 52 weeks a year.

Training Assistance: We offer an extensive, two-week training course, plus ongoing assistance, as described above. In addition, training for each employee on an airline reservation system is completed by either American Airlines Sabre System or Continental on System One at no additional cost to the franchisee.

TPI Travel Services

3030 N. Rocky Point Rd. W. Ste, 100
Tampa, FL 33607
Web Address: www.tpitravel.com
Toll-Free Phone: (800) 393-7767
Phone: (813) 281-5670
Fax: (813) 281-2304
Contact: President

Number of Franchises: 345
Company-Owned Units: 1
Total Units: 346

In Business Since: 1987   **Franchising Since:** 1987

Description of Operation: Full-service travel agency. Set-up includes training, automation, computers, software, on-site assistance, ticket processing, higher commissions, support, and assistance.

Equity Capital Needed: $15,000-$20,000

Franchise Fee: $10,995

Royalty: $95

Advertising Co-op Fee:

Financial Assistance: We can finance a portion of the franchise fee.

Management Assistance: We provide full support through toll-free numbers and by communication through software.

Training Assistance: Training consists of five days at corporate office and includes airfare and hotel.

Travel Network

560 Sylvan Ave.
Englewood Cliffs, NJ 07632
Web Address: www.travelnetwork.com
E-mail Address: info@travelnetwork.com.
Toll-Free Phone: (800) 872-6638
Phone: (201) 567-8500
Fax: (201) 567-4405
Contact: Vice President of Marketing

Number of Franchises: 423
Company-Owned Units: 1
Total Units: 424

In Business Since: 1982   **Franchising Since:** 1983

Description of Operation: We provide complete start-up assistance (site selection, lease negotiations, staffing, industry accreditation, bonding, and furnishings package in a five-week intensive front-end training); accounting package; complete computerization; ongoing, continual, support and training, both locally and on-site; in-field plus regional and national meetings; saturated marketing program; and a high commissions earning program.

Equity Capital Needed: $80,000-$100,000

Franchise Fee: $29,900

Royalty: $350/month-yr. 1; $550/month-yr. 2; $750/month-yr. 3

Advertising Co-op Fee:

Financial Assistance: 90 percent financing of turn key store furnishings package.

Management Assistance: We provide automated accounting training, computer training, on-site field management training, and toll-free hotline. Inside support structure for assistance, and ongoing, targeted trainings on each aspect of travel agency management.

Training Assistance: One week each training for business development and marketing; agency operations (budgeting, preopening) and agency management; airline computer training; on-site at store level for preopening; automated accounting; and postopening budgeting.

TravelPlex International

655 Metro Place S., Ste. 250
Dublin, OH 43017
Toll-Free Phone: (800) 221-9581
Phone: (614) 766-6315
Fax: (614) 766-0540
Contact: President

Number of Franchises: 17
Company-Owned Units: 0
Total Units: 17

In Business Since: 1984   **Franchising Since:** 1989

Description of Operation: Retail travel agency franchise organization, specializing in business and vacation travel arrangements. This unique franchise has been created by working agency owner/managers. A comprehensive training program is provided for all staff levels. TravelPlex International provides recruitment services and productive office procedures. Franchisees receive sales and marketing programs, operational support, and effective networking with member agencies.

Equity Capital Needed: $50,000

Franchise Fee: $30,900

Royalty: $400 per month

Advertising Co-op Fee:

Financial Assistance: We will finance 24 percent of the franchise fee for 24 months.

Management Assistance: All manager applicants are screened, interviewed, rated, and tested by the TravelPlex International management team.

Training Assistance: 1 to 2 weeks at headquarters in Columbus, OH and 3 to 4 weeks on-site. Additional time as needed.

Uniglobe Travel (International) Inc.

1199 W. Pender St.; Ste. 900
Vancouver, BC V6E 2R1
Web Address: www.uniglobe.com
E-mail Address: opportunity@uniglobe.com
Toll-Free Phone: (800) 590-4111
Phone: (510) 463-2100
Fax: (604) 718-2642
Contact: Director of Franchise Licensing

Number of Franchises: 1000
Company-Owned Units: 0
Total Units: 1000

In Business Since: 1980   **Franchising Since:** 1981

Description of Operation: UNIGLOBE Travel is a world leader in retail travel agency franchising for both start-ups and existing agencies. UNIGLOBE provides the tools, systems, and support to franchisees to help them provide superior service to corporate and leisure clients. Benefits include training and professional development for owners and staff, money saving automation agreements, toll-free emergency rescue line service for clients, and top-notch incentive commission programs with airline, car rental, tour, and cruise companies. Currently franchising in U.S., Canada, Japan, U.K., Germany, Austria, and Benelux countries.

Equity Capital Needed: $10,000-$120,000

Franchise Fee: $5,000-$35,000

Royalty: 10 percent

Advertising Co-op Fee: Varies

Financial Assistance: Financial assistance to prospective fanchisees is determined by the regions and varies according to local conditions.

Management Assistance: The UNIGLOBE regions provide ongoing managerial assistance to franchisees. This includes training programs and the use of software programs designed so that franchisees can manage their agencies efficiently and profitably. As well, UNIGLOBE headquarters provides assistance on issues related to running a travel agency, such as sales and marketing, agency operations, and financial planning. Automation agreements with top suppliers of computer reservation system.

Training Assistance:

Wagonlit Travel Associates

12755 Hwy. 55, P.O. Box 59159
Minneapolis, MN 55459-8207
Web Address: www.enquest.com
Toll-Free Phone: (800) 678-8241
Phone:
Fax: (813) 579-0529
Contact:

Number of Franchises: 1,300
Company-Owned Units: 416
Total Units: 1,716

In Business Since: 1888   **Franchising Since:** 1984

Description of Operation: Offer start-up and conversion travel agency franchise program. Preferred supplier program, national and local marketing and advertising, newsletters, brochures, assistance with commercial business development, regional meetings, participation in the Carlson Selling System, Associate Consulting Service, hotel program, 24-hour service center, centralized support services department, international rate desk, and professional development programs. Leading technology available to maximize efficiency of operations.

Equity Capital Needed: $79,985-156,160/Conversion: $6,560-17,735

Franchise Fee: $34,500/Conversion: $3,950

Royalty: $400-750/month: Conversion .5-4.55 percent

Advertising Co-op Fee:

Financial Assistance: Not available

Management Assistance: See training.

Training Assistance: Start-up: two weeks in Minneapolis/on-site (conversion is two days.) Training at annual meeting. Agent education includes workshops, speakers, industry panels, and trade show of suppliers. Other management training: profitability, mergers, and acquisitions, performance improvement, leisure sales process, effective performance reviews, hiring process, and new

employee orientation to Carlson programs. Technology training: building basic technology skills, using Internet, develop agency Web page, provide "Tech Tips" in weekly mailing.

Travel Professionals International, Inc.

312 Whittington Parkway Suite 203
Louisville, KY 40222
Web Address: www.travelprof.com
Toll-Free Phone: (800) 626-2469
Phone: (502) 423-9966
Fax: (502) 327-9024
Contact: Vice President Franchise Development

Number of Franchises: 80
Company-Owned Units: 1
Total Units: 81

In Business Since: 1982   **Franchising Since:** 1983

Description of Operation: The Travel Professionals International franchise opportunity is a full service professional travel agency—we call them TRAVEL RESOURCE OFFICES. Our focus is: 1) marketing and sales, 2) traditional and nontraditional, high-margin travel products, and 3) fully integrated management and marketing technology. We specialize in business, leisure, and group travel products with higher commissions. Our marketing is powerful and award winning. Our Management and Marketing Information System takes the full measure of the information age.

Equity Capital Needed: $170,000

Franchise Fee: $27,500

Royalty: 5 percent with minimums

Advertising Co-op Fee: No

Financial Assistance: N/A

Management Assistance: Complete and ongoing managerial assistance by a support team qualified in all phases of marketing, management and operations.

Training Assistance: Initial training in the first year is extensive and tailored to fit the needs of the franchisee. Ongoing training thereafter in all phases of the system operations.

Recreation & Travel— Miscellaneous

Club Nautico

850 N.E. 3rd St., Ste. 204
Dania, FL 33004
Toll-Free Phone: (800) 628-8426
Phone: (954) 927-9800
Fax: (954) 927-1300
Contact: Vice President of Marketing

Number of Franchises: 55
Company-Owned Units: 7
Total Units: 62

In Business Since: 1984   **Franchising Since:** 1986

Description of Operation: Each Club Nautico retail center rents superior-quality powerboats to the qualified public and sells memberships. The Club Nautico network focuses on providing the consumer with an easy, convenient and affordable alternative to boat ownership, allowing members to enjoy highly preferential rates at any Club in the world. The company's service mark "Love Work," actually originated when a franchisee suggested the epithet to accurately describe the business. Club Nautico sells entertainment!

Equity Capital Needed: $100,000

Franchise Fee: $25,000

Royalty: 10 percent

Advertising Co-op Fee:

Financial Assistance: Equipment leasing available through franchisor.

Management Assistance: On-site training on request and toll-free number (800) BOATRENT.

Training Assistance: Franchisees must successfully complete a comprehensive, two weeks of training at the Club Nautico boot camp in Ft. Lauderdale, FL for classroom and "on the water" training. Technical training related to fleet and engine management is available free and is held at OMC regional training facilities on an ongoing basis. Five days of training at your Club Nautico is available by request. Toll-free assistance and 24-hour paging service are also available.

Complete Music

7877 L St.
Omaha, NE 68127
Web Address: www.cmusic.com
E-mail Address: djinfo@cmusic.com
Toll-Free Phone: (800) 843-3866
Phone: (402) 339-0001
Fax: (402) 339-1285
Contact: Director of Franchising

Number of Franchises: 142
Company-Owned Units: 1
Total Units: 143

In Business Since: 1972   **Franchising Since:** 1984

Description of Operation: Complete Music, the nation's largest franchised mobile entertainment service, provides entertainment for special events. Franchise owners hire and train a staff of D.J.'s to perform at these events.

Equity Capital Needed: $15,000-$20,000

Franchise Fee: $9,500 for major market

Royalty: 8 percent

Advertising Co-op Fee:

Financial Assistance: Partial assistance is available to qualified individuals.

Management Assistance: Complete Music provides ongoing support, in addition to initial training. The support team would include in-office managerial staff, as well as experienced owners' support in other cities.

Training Assistance: Training includes 10 days at Complete Music's corporate office, covering all aspects of day-to-day operations, including marketing, training of staff, hiring procedures, and so on. Initial training also includes a four-day visit to the franchisee's city.

Fun Services

4400 Tejasco
San Antonio, TX 78218
Web Address: www.funservices.com
Toll-Free Phone: (800) 562-5266
Phone: (210) 829-4666
Fax: (210) 824-6565
Contact:

Number of Franchises: 48
Company-Owned Units: 1
Total Units: 49

In Business Since: 1965   **Franchising Since:** 1965

Description of Operation: Fun Services provides a wide range of community entertainment and fund raising programs. Some of these are the original "Santa's Secret Shop" program; the "Fun Fair" school carnival program; and employee and company events, such as picnics and conventions. The fund raising areas are designed for school children in small groups or whole school projects. Some of the programs are "Great American Gift Wrap" and "Gifts for All Seasons," as well as the incentive prize program "Just for Fun."

Equity Capital Needed: $25,000

Franchise Fee: $75,000-$100,000

Royalty: $150 per month   **Advertising Co-op Fee:**

Financial Assistance: Some franchise financing may be available upon credit application.

Management Assistance: Three-day, on-site, start-up training school at an existing franchise location. Annual conventions and sales meetings are held throughout the year. The cost of the first rate training school is included in the franchise fee, which includes hotel and transportation.

Training Assistance: Same as above, plus on-site visits by franchisor staff continues throughout the franchise term.

Game Player

1919 S. 40th St., Ste. 202
Lincoln, NE 68506
Toll-Free Phone: (800) 865-2378
Phone: (402) 434-5620
Fax: (402) 434-5624

Contact: President

Number of Franchises: 1
Company-Owned Units: 0
Total Units: 1

In Business Since: 1993   **Franchising Since:** 1996

Description of Operation: Game Player has taken a new approach to video game stores by buying, selling, and trading new or used titles.

Equity Capital Needed: $100,000

Franchise Fee: $20,000

Royalty: 6 percent

Advertising Co-op Fee: 1 percent

Financial Assistance: Current financial review, support on a business plan, and third lending options provided.

Management Assistance: Complete training, software program, manuals, follow-up, and an 800 number is provided.

Training Assistance: One week at the home office and one week on-site.

Haunted Hayrides

16 Orangewood
Liverpool, NY 13090
Toll-Free Phone: (800) 344-2868
Phone: (315) 652-8295
Fax: (315) 652-8298
Contact: Chief Executive Officer

Number of Franchises: 21
Company-Owned Units: 3
Total Units: 24

In Business Since: 1985   **Franchising Since:** 1989

Description of Operation: Haunted Hayrides is an entertainment concept with a Halloween theme operated during the month of October. Actors and actresses are scheduled on a trail or road that in and of itself could be considered scary. These "haunts" increase that aspect. We consider a Haunted Hayride to be good old-fashioned, All-American fun.

Equity Capital Needed: $30,000-$45,000

Franchise Fee: $15,000

Royalty: 10 percent ($5,000 minimum)

Advertising Co-op Fee:

Financial Assistance: The franchisor does not provide any financial assistance.

Management Assistance: Franchisor actively participates and must approve the future site of a Haunted Hayrides. The franchisor will advise the prospective franchisee as to zoning, leasing and sources of supply for equipment. The franchisor must approve every phase of the operation before the season starts and visit each site during the season. The franchisee is responsible to the franchisor for all charges except the first visit.

Training Assistance: The franchisor provides 2 days of intensive training, generally at the home office in Liverpool, NY. A confidential manual is provided to each franchisee for study and reference. The manual is the focus of the two-day training but all phases of operating a hayride are studied by means of video tape and one-on-one discussions with other franchisees that are already in business.

Hoop Mountain

P.O. Box 242
Hathorne, MA 01937
Toll-Free Phone: (800) 519-8445
Phone: (508) 774-7730
Fax:
Contact: President

Number of Franchises: 6
Company-Owned Units: 1
Total Units: 7

In Business Since: 1985   **Franchising Since:** 1996

Description of Operation: Women's and men's basketball camp. College counseling service for basketball players. Run basketball tournaments.

Equity Capital Needed: $25,000

Franchise Fee: $20,000

Royalty: 5 percent

Advertising Co-op Fee: None

Financial Assistance: Financing

Management Assistance: Provide 2 weeks of training. Supply manager for the first year.

Outdoor Connection

1001 E. Cliff Rd.
Burnsville, MN 55124
Web Address: www.outdoor-connection.com
Toll-Free Phone:
Phone: (612) 890-0407
Fax: (612) 890-8133
Contact: President

Number of Franchises: 95
Company-Owned Units: 2
Total Units: 97

In Business Since: 1988   Franchising Since: 1988

Description of Operation: Outdoor Connection arranges and promotes fishing and hunting trips. The network of lodges and outfitters is located throughout North America. The franchisees represent those lodges to customers in their local area.

Equity Capital Needed: $1,100-$5,600

Franchise Fee: $5,800

Royalty: 3-5 percent

Advertising Co-op Fee:

Financial Assistance: The franchisor will provide a promissory note for up to 50 percent for 1 year for 1/2 the franchise fee.

Management Assistance: The franchisor helps with and suggest plans for planning for 6 month and 1 year objectives. Also, a plan to reach those objectives is suggested.

Training Assistance: A well-organized, 1 1/2 day training program includes product knowledge, paperwork for bookings, bookkeeping, advertising, trade show knowledge, sales hints and more.

Rental—Auto

Affordable Used Car Rental System

96 Freneau Ave. Ste. 2
Matawan, NJ 07747
Toll-Free Phone: (800) 631-2290
Phone: (732) 290-8300
Fax: (732) 290-8305
Contact: General Manager

Number of Franchises: 100
Company-Owned Units: 0
Total Units: 100

In Business Since: 1981   **Franchising Since:** 1981

Description of Operation: We provide training, insurance, and management support for a car rental profit center.

Equity Capital Needed: $15,000-$30,000

Franchise Fee: $3,500-$6,000

Royalty: $10-$15 per car/month, depends on number of cars

Advertising Co-op Fee:

Financial Assistance: The franchise fee can be financed at 0 percent interest.

Management Assistance: Two-day training school, manual and forms, personal on-site visits, and reinforcement tapes.

Training Assistance: 2 days at our corporate office for training in customer screening, vehicle selection, advertising, and telephone techniques.

Budget Rent A Car (Canada)

1027 Youge St. 3rd Floor
Toronto, ON M4W 2K9
Toll-Free Phone:
Phone: (416) 969-1190
Fax: (416) 969-9582
Contact:

Number of Franchises: 11
Company-Owned Units: 3
Total Units: 14

In Business Since: 1993   **Franchising Since:** 1993

Description of Operation: As part of the worldwide Dollar Rent A Car system, we offer franchisees a full support package, including fleet and insurance programs, a reservation system, marketing, advertising, training, and ongoing assistance.

Equity Capital Needed: $150,000 (minimum)

Franchise Fee: $25,000 (minimum)

Royalty: 7 percent, plus 2 percent national advertising.

Advertising Co-op Fee:

Financial Assistance: Extended payment terms for the franchise fee may be negotiated in some cases. Assistance and advice are provided for fleet and business financing.

Management Assistance: We provide assistance with rental location, lease negotiation, leasehold improvements, staff recruitment, local marketing and advertising, administration, and accounting set-up.

Training Assistance: We offer a combination of classroom and on-site training, a minimum of 1 week in each case, plus ongoing courses at all staff levels.

Budget Rent A Car Corporation

P.O. Box 111580
Carrollton, TX 75011
Web Address: www.budgetrentacar.com
Toll-Free Phone: (800) 621-2844
Phone:
Fax: (972) 404-7867
Contact: Director of Franchise Development

Number of Franchises: 2772
Company-Owned Units: 387
Total Units: 3159

In Business Since: 1958   **Franchising Since:** 1960

Description of Operation: Car and truck rental, both in airport and local markets.

Equity Capital Needed: Varies

Franchise Fee: $15,000 minimum

Royalty: 7.5 percent

Advertising Co-op Fee:

Financial Assistance: 80 percent of the initial franchise fee may be financed over 12 months at reasonable interest rates.

Management Assistance: Assistance is available through operational visits to discuss franchisee's performance. Also, regional meetings, workshops, and profit groups are held on a periodic basis.

Training Assistance: Training classes are conducted on an as-needed basis in both corporate headquarters and in the franchisee's city(s).

Dollar Rent A Car

5330 E. 31st
Tulsa, OK 74153-1167
Web Address: www.dollarcar.com
E-mail Address: pfritz@dollarcar.com
Toll-Free Phone: (800) 555-9893
Phone: (918) 669-3103
Fax: (918) 669-3006
Contact: Director of Franchise Development

Number of Franchises: 71
Company-Owned Units: 160
Total Units: 231

In Business Since: 1966   **Franchising Since:** 1967

Description of Operation: Dollar Rent A Car operates and licenses others to operate car rental operations. Licensees are granted exclusive territories and access to services which include, sales, marketing, worldwide reservations, risk management, fleet leasing, training, standards, and image and ongoing consultation.

Equity Capital Needed: $100,000 minimum

Franchise Fee: $12,500 minimum

Royalty: 6 percent local/7-8 percent Airport

Advertising Co-op Fee: None

Financial Assistance: Qualified licensees may participate in a fleet leasing program.

Management Assistance: Regional managers provide consultation on all facets of the car rental business.

Training Assistance: New licensees receive three-day orientation at headquarters, followed by one week on-site by the regional managers. Dollar has a training program conducted on-site lasting a week.

Dollar Rent A Car (Canada)

1027 Youge St. 3rd Floor
Toronto, ON M4W 2K9
Toll-Free Phone:
Phone: (416) 969-1190
Fax: (416) 969-9582
Contact:

Number of Franchises: 11
Company-Owned Units: 3
Total Units: 14

In Business Since: 1993   **Franchising Since:** 1993

Description of Operation: As part of the worldwide Dollar Rent A Car system, we offer our franchisees a full support package, including fleet and insurance programs, a reservation system, marketing, advertising, training and ongoing assistance.

Equity Capital Needed: $150,000 (minimum)

Franchise Fee: $25,000 (minimum)

Royalty: 7 percent, plus 2 percent national advertising

Advertising Co-op Fee:

Financial Assistance: Extended payment terms for the franchise fee may be negotiated in some cases. Assistance and advice are provided for fleet and business financing.

Management Assistance: We provide assistance with rental location, lease negotiation, leasehold improvements, staff recruitment, local marketing and advertising, administration, and accounting set-up.

Training Assistance: We offer a combination of classroom and on-site training, a minimum of 1 week in each case, plus ongoing courses at all staff levels.

Payless Car Rental

2350-N 34th St. N.
St. Petersburg, FL 33713
Web Address: www.paylesscar.com
Toll-Free Phone: (800) 729-5255
Phone: (813) 321-6352
Fax: (813) 321-1715
Contact: **Executive Director of Franchise Development**

Number of Franchises: 150
Company-Owned Units: 0
Total Units: 150

In Business Since: 1971　**Franchising Since:** 1971

Description of Operation: Automobile rental and licensing of car sales.

Equity Capital Needed: Varies by number of vehicles in fleet & site

Franchise Fee: Range $6,000-$250,000 Varies airport/nonairport

Royalty: Airport-8 percent; non-airport-4 percent

Advertising Co-op Fee:

Financial Assistance: None.

Management Assistance: Assistance is available for new and existing locations in operations, reservations, fleet, marketing, management information systems, and supplies. Assistance is offered and implemented in ongoing system bulletins, manual updates, and newsletters. Departments are available via 800 number for assistance.

Training Assistance: New locations receive a three-day orientation session at Payless headquarters, 1 week of on-site training at opening by an operations manager, and 1 week of computer training by an approved computer vendor. Ongoing support is available as needed by all departments. Operations visits are made as deemed necessary, with a minimum of 2 per year.

Practical Systems

1500 E. Tropicana Ave., Ste. 123
Las Vegas, NV 89119
Toll-Free Phone: (800) 424-7722
Phone: (702) 798-0025
Fax: (702) 798-4739
Contact:

Number of Franchises: 115
Company-Owned Units: 0
Total Units: 115

In Business Since: 1989　**Franchising Since:** 1989

Description of Operation: Practical Rent A Car is a daily rental, short-term leasing, automobile and truck franchise system. The operators of Practical have reservation systems, fleet programs, handicapped vehicle programs, insurance programs, national advertising, promotional items, and printing contracts.

Equity Capital Needed: $100,000-$500,000

Franchise Fee: Varies by location

Royalty: $20 per vehicle.　**Advertising Co-op Fee:**

Financial Assistance: None at this time.

Management Assistance: Ongoing training at corporate headquarters. Regional meetings and annual conventions. Quarterly newsletters. New employees may attend training at the Practical Academy.

Training Assistance: Each new office will receive assistance regarding office location, rate setting, fleet mix, necessary forms and office management, including hands-on experience, at a five-day training program at the home office.

Rent 'N Drive

1919 S. 40th, Ste. 202
Lincoln, NE 68506
Toll-Free Phone: (800) 865-2378
Phone: (402) 434-5620
Fax: (402) 434-2378
Contact: **President**

Number of Franchises: 0
Company-Owned Units: 1
Total Units: 1

In Business Since: 1990　**Franchising Since:** 1996

Description of Operation: Rent 'N Drive provides an affordable alternative to high-priced new car rentals, offering more flexible rental terms also means a larger customer base!

Equity Capital Needed: $100,000

Franchise Fee: $20,000

Royalty: 6 percent

Advertising Co-op Fee: 1 percent

Financial Assistance: Current financial review, support on a business plan, and third party lending options provided.

Management Assistance: Complete training, software program, manuals, follow-up, and an 800 number is provided.

Training Assistance: One week at home office and one week on-site.

Rent A Vette International

1025 W. Laurel, Ste. 102
San Diego, CA 92101
Web Address: www.bnm.com
E-mail Address: vette@cgl.com
Toll-Free Phone: (800) 627-0808
Phone: (619) 238-3883
Fax: (619) 238-4279
Contact: President

Number of Franchises: 3
Company-Owned Units: 1
Total Units: 4

In Business Since: 1981   **Franchising Since:** 1992

Description of Operation: Sports car rentals, requiring a minimum of 50 percent Corvettes; the balance can be any type of sports car from Mustang to Mercedes Benz. Criteria for franchisee: population of at least 1,000,000, airport arrivals of 7,500,000 and year-round good weather.

Equity Capital Needed: $300,000-$1,000,000

Franchise Fee: $12,500

Royalty: 3 percent-first year; 4 percent-second; 5 percent-ongoing.

Advertising Co-op Fee:

Financial Assistance: The company will guide the franchisee in the right direction, but provides no direct financing.

Management Assistance: We provide a 12-week countdown from site selection to opening, home office training and on-site training. Ongoing support for the length of the agreement.

Training Assistance: We offer software and computer training, advertising, accounting and day-by-day answers to any problem that might occur.

Rent-A-Wreck of America

11460 Cronridge Dr., Ste. 120
Owings Mills, MD 21117
Web Address: www.rent-a-wreck.com
E-mail Address: raw@rent-a-wreck.com
Toll-Free Phone: (800) 421-7253
Phone: (410) 581-5755
Fax: (410) 581-1566
Contact:

Number of Franchises: 463
Company-Owned Units: 0
Total Units: 463

In Business Since: 1973   **Franchising Since:** 1978

Description of Operation: Rent and lease new and used cars, trucks and vans to the public and businesses.

Equity Capital Needed: $60,000-$100,000 stand alone. $25,000-$40,000 add-on

Franchise Fee: $5,000-$23,000; average $12,500

Royalty: 6 percent, plus 2 percent advertising

Advertising Co-op Fee:

Financial Assistance: Rent-A-Wreck may finance up to 75 percent of the initial franchise fee (not including cars) to qualified individuals. We may finance cars after an initial 6 month period for qualified individuals.

Management Assistance: Managerial assistance is readily available to new franchisees, as is the assistance of the franchisee advisor council. Also available are seminars at the annual convention and the annual regional conferences. We also have counter training classes nationwide.

Training Assistance: All new franchisees are required to attend a five-day company school for which there is no cost, other than hotel and meals. The school provides all instructional material and manuals required.

Sensible Car Rental

96 Freneau Ave.
Matawan, NJ 07747
Toll-Free Phone: (800) 367-5159
Phone: (732) 583-8500
Fax: (732) 290-8305
Contact: General Manager

Number of Franchises: 110
Company-Owned Units: 0
Total Units: 110

In Business Since: 1986   **Franchising Since:** 1986

Description of Operation: We provide training, insurance, and management support for a car rental profit center.

Equity Capital Needed: $15,000-$30,000

Franchise Fee: $3,500-$6,000

Royalty: $10-$15 per car

Advertising Co-op Fee:

Financial Assistance: The franchise fee can be financed at zero interest.

Management Assistance: We provide a two-day training school, manual, forms, personal on-site visits, and reinforcement audio cassettes.

Training Assistance: 2 days at our corporate offices cover customer screening, vehicle selection, advertising, telephone techniques, and so on.

Sensible Car Rental, Inc.

96 Freneau Ave.
Matawan, NJ 07747
Web Address:
E-mail Address:
Toll-Free Phone: (800) 367-5153
Phone: (732) 583-8500
Fax: (732) 290-8305
Contact: General Manager

Number of Franchises: 115
Company-Owned Units: 0
Total Units: 115

In Business Since: 1986 **Franchising Since:** 1986

Description of Operation: Our program is designed to be a profit center to an existing auto related business. We offer the "How To" in being successful in car rental. Additionally, we offer the prospect an opportunity to join our A+ rated insurance program which is a vital part of the business. In addition to a comprehensive formal training program, we routinely visit our franchisees many times during the year to review procedures and retrain additional employees. We function as "professional staff" to your business.

Equity Capital Needed: Varies

Franchise Fee: $4,900 average

Royalty: $10-$15 per month per car

Advertising Co-op Fee: None

Financial Assistance: None

Management Assistance: In addition to formal training, all franchisees are routinely visited numerous times during the year to have procedures reviewed and to provide training necessary for new employees.

Training Assistance: Two days formal training at our corporate headquarters.

Thrifty Car Rental System

6050 Indian Line
Mississauga, ON L4V 1G5
Web Address: www.thrifty.com
E-mail Address: trental@thrifty.com
Toll-Free Phone:
Phone: (905) 612-1881
Fax: (905) 612-1893
Contact: Vice President

Number of Franchises: 139
Company-Owned Units: 9
Total Units: 148

In Business Since: 1968 **Franchising Since:** 1972

Description of Operation: Provide car and truck rental and leasing services.

Equity Capital Needed: Varies.

Franchise Fee: Varies.

Royalty: 8 percent

Advertising Co-op Fee:

Financial Assistance: We provide vehicle financing, computer financing, and franchise fee financing.

Management Assistance: Data not available.

Training Assistance: We provide pre-opening, in-store training, and opening on-site training. Areas covered are operations, accounting, computers, and fleet control.

U-Save Auto Rental of America

7525 Connelley Dr. Ste. A
Hanover, MD 21076
Toll-Free Phone: (800) 438-2300
Phone: (410) 760-8727
Fax: (410) 760-0452
Contact:

Number of Franchises: 510
Company-Owned Units: 2
Total Units: 512

In Business Since: 1978 **Franchising Since:** 1979

Description of Operation: U-Save Auto Rental rents cars, vans, and light-duty trucks to neighborhood and leisure customers, local businesses, and people in need of temporary replacement vehicles. We also service commercial and government travelers in selected off-airport locations.

Equity Capital Needed: Net worth at least $250,000, $60,000 liquid

Franchise Fee: $7,500-$15,000

Royalty: Based on fleet size.

Advertising Co-op Fee:

Financial Assistance: Partial fleet leasing assistance is available.

Management Assistance: U-Save Rental provides support services to help franchisees operate and build their rental business. Some of these services include operating manuals, field support, marketing materials and supplies, fleet leasing programs, vehicle insurance programs, nationwide reservation systems, and a president's advisory council.

Training Assistance: We offer initial classroom guidance from experienced instructors about how a U-Save Auto Rental business operates and how to function as a franchisee. Training through national conventions, regional meetings, and annual operational reviews. Also, a toll-free telephone connection to the U-Save Rental National Support Center for assistance.

Wheelchair Getaways, Inc.

3006 Tim Tam Trail
Versailles, KY 40383
Web Address: wheelchair-getaways.com
E-mail Address: wheelchair-getaways@aol.com
Toll-Free Phone: (800) 536-5518
Phone: (606) 873-4973
Fax: (606) 873-8039
Contact:

Number of Franchises: 31
Company-Owned Units: 0
Total Units: 31

In Business Since: 1989 **Franchising Since:** 1989

Description of Operation: Wheelchair Getaways franchisees rent modified wheelchair accessible full size and mini vans to wheelchair or scooter users on a daily, weekly, monthly, or extended basis. Wheelchair Getaways is the only franchise company renting wheelchair accessible vans in the United States. Franchise territory is based on population and only one franchise is sold in any area. A Wheelchair Getaways franchise can be operated out of one's home provided there are no zoning restrictions and ample parking is available.

Equity Capital Needed: $50,000

Franchise Fee: $17,500

Royalty: $550 per van per year

Advertising Co-op Fee: $550 per van per year

Financial Assistance: Financing is not available through the company.

Management Assistance: A toll-free number is provided to the franchisees as well as use of the Internet for any questions.

Training Assistance: One day of intense training is provided at one of the franchise locations nationwide. Follow-up is provided by Internet and telephone.

Rental—Formal Wear

Gingiss International, Inc.

2101 Executive Dr.
Addison, IL 60101
Web Address: www.gingiss.com
E-mail Address: gingiss@gingiss.com
Toll-Free Phone: (800) 621-7125
Phone: (630) 620-9050
Fax: (630) 620-8840
Contact: **Vice President of Franchise Development**

Number of Franchises: 205
Company-Owned Units: 38
Total Units: 243

In Business Since: 1936   **Franchising Since:** 1968

Description of Operation: World's largest men's formal wear rental and sales chain.

Equity Capital Needed: $119,680-$242,680

Franchise Fee: $0-$15,000

Royalty: For 1998 2.5 percent with stepped increases thereafter

Advertising Co-op Fee: 2 percent of gross rental revenues

Financial Assistance: Data not provided.

Management Assistance: Regional Advisors help in key areas, including merchandising, advertising, staffing, training, store operations, and financial management.

Training Assistance: Two weeks of extensive classroom and store training plus on location training at franchisees own Gingiss Center. Also, confidential operations manual.

Rental—Miscellaneous

Aaron's Rental Purchase

309 E. Paces Ferry Rd.
Atlanta, GA 30305
Toll-Free Phone: (800) 551-6015
Phone: (404) 237-4016
Fax: (404) 240-6594
Contact: **Director of Franchise Development**

Number of Franchises: 125
Company-Owned Units: 320
Total Units: 445

In Business Since: 1955   **Franchising Since:** 1992

Description of Operation: Provides electronics, appliances, furniture, and jewelry on a "cash and carry" basis or on a monthly rental program.

Equity Capital Needed: $175,000-$225,000

Franchise Fee: $35,000

Royalty: 5 percent

Advertising Co-op Fee:

Financial Assistance: Aaron's Rental Purchase does not offer direct financial assistance, but can provide sources for inventory financing.

Management Assistance: Provides support and assistance in all areas of franchise opportunities on an ongoing basis. A set of instruction manuals is also provided which covers all aspects of operation.

Training Assistance: All franchisees are invited to attend a comprehensive training course held at the training facility to supplement classroom training. Franchisees spend an average of about 4 weeks in an Aaron's Rental Purchase showroom for on-the-job training.

Baby's Away International

122 Jackson St.
Denver, CO 80226
Web Address: www.csd.net/~babyaway
Toll-Free Phone: (800) 984-9030
Phone:
Fax: (303) 394-3777
Contact: **Vice President of Business Development**

Number of Franchises: 16
Company-Owned Units: 9
Total Units: 23

In Business Since: 1990 **Franchising Since:** 1993

Description of Operation: Rental of baby supplies ranging from cribs to toys to VCRs and more.

Equity Capital Needed: $5,000-$8,000

Franchise Fee: $8,000

Royalty: 7 percent plus 5 percent advertising

Advertising Co-op Fee:

Financial Assistance: 50 percent down and 50 percent payable over 12 months.

Management Assistance: We offer complete assistance in getting the franchisee operational. We also provide a program for identifying and establishing contact with prospective clients, including advertising programs.

Training Assistance: We provide 3 days of training at the franchisee's location, as well as manuals, newsletters, a national 800 number referral service, and ongoing consulting.

ColorTyme

1231 Greenway Dr., Ste. 900
Irving, TX 75038
Web Address: www.colortyme.com
Toll-Free Phone: (800) 411-8963
Phone: (972) 751-1711
Fax: (972) 714-5423
Contact:

Number of Franchises: 262
Company-Owned Units: 0
Total Units: 262

In Business Since: 1979 **Franchising Since:** 1981

Description of Operation: ColorTyme provides a specialized inventory of rental products such as televisions, audio-video equipment, appliances, furniture, jewelry, pagers, and computers offered to consumers under a "Rent-To-Own" program.

Equity Capital Needed: $75,000-$125,000

Franchise Fee: $7,500-$25,000

Royalty: 4 percent

Advertising Co-op Fee:

Financial Assistance: ColorTyme has contracted with Suntrust Credit Corporation to provide funding to ColorTyme for financing offered by ColorTyme to franchisees. ColorTyme offers financing for all approved products purchased by the franchisee from the franchisor or any other supplier.

Management Assistance: The duration of the initial training program will be approximately 2-3 weeks, before the opening of the ColorTyme Rental Store.

Training Assistance: Data not available.

Restaurants—Chicken

Bojangles' Restaurants, Inc.

P.O. Box 240239
Charlotte, NC 28224
Web Address: www.bojangles.com
Toll-Free Phone: (800) 366-9921
Phone: (704) 527-2675
Fax: (704) 523-6803
Contact: Vice President of Franchise Development

Number of Franchises:
Company-Owned Units:
Total Units: 251

In Business Since: 1977 **Franchising Since:** 1978

Description of Operation: Bojangles' is a quick service restaurant with a core menu of spicy, Cajun-style chicken served with fresh buttermilk biscuits, and one-of-a-kind "fixen's", like dirty rice or Cajun pintos.

Equity Capital Needed: Minimum net worth of $400,000 for first store.

Franchise Fee: $20,000

Royalty: 4 percent

Advertising Co-op Fee:

Financial Assistance: None

Management Assistance: A franchise field service representative is available on a continual basis for franchisee support.

Training Assistance: Bojangles' University in Charlotte offers a variety of "hands-on" training classes for all corporate and franchise managers. These classes teach the mechanics of making our products as well as Bojangles' standards and values. Our franchise and company field supervisors provide additional training and ongoing support where it matters most—in the restaurants.

Brown's Chicken and Pasta, Inc.

1200 Jorie Blvd.
Oak Brook, IL 60523
Toll-Free Phone:
Phone:
Fax: (630) 571-5300
Contact: President

Number of Franchises: 62
Company-Owned Units: 12
Total Units: 74

In Business Since: 1964 **Franchising Since:** 1964

Description of Operation:

Equity Capital Needed: Financial statement required.

Franchise Fee: $25,000

Royalty: 5 percent

Advertising Co-op Fee: 4 percent

Financial Assistance: None. Recommendation to local bank.

Management Assistance: A complete training program in cooking, catering, paperwork, and personnel procedures are covered in a 6 week course. Field supervisors are available for every store and inspections and follow-up are provided. Quarterly meetings provide updates on industry. All franchisees are kept up-to-date on research and development.

Training Assistance:

BW-3 Franchise Systems

1919 Interchange Tower 600 S. Highway 169
Minneapolis, MN 55426
Web Address: www.bw3.com
Toll-Free Phone:
Phone: (513) 943-9293
Fax: (513) 943-9397
Contact: Franchise Sales Director

Number of Franchises: 68
Company-Owned Units: 10
Total Units: 78

In Business Since: 1982   **Franchising Since:** 1991

Description of Operation: BW-3 (Buffalo Wild Wings) feature buffalo-style chicken wings, ranging from mild to wild. They have an extensive menu, with burgers, chicken breasts and beef, all featured on the Weck roll. All BW-3 restaurants have full bars with 12-20 beers on tap and forty-two offered. Most restaurants feature one hundred inch screen televisions and NTN, the National Trivia Sports game.

Equity Capital Needed: $450,000-$750,000

Franchise Fee: $25,000

Royalty: 5 percent

Advertising Co-op Fee:

Financial Assistance: Not available.

Management Assistance: There is a thorough 3 week training program in Cincinnati, OH. An opening team will be at the location for at least 1 week. A team leader will visit once a month to evaluate the franchise and management.

Training Assistance: Same as above.

Chef's Fried Chicken

20 Audobon Oaks Blvd.
Lafayette, LA 70506
Toll-Free Phone:
Phone: (318) 233-1621
Fax: (318) 233-1621
Contact: President

Number of Franchises: 3
Company-Owned Units: 0
Total Units: 3

In Business Since: 1970   **Franchising Since:** 1971

Description of Operation: Fast-food fried chicken, with a touch of Cajun.

Equity Capital Needed: $75,000

Franchise Fee: $20,000

Royalty: 4 percent

Advertising Co-op Fee:

Financial Assistance: None.

Management Assistance: Assistance is provided during the opening until the franchisee is able to manage the operation. Then, when there is a problem, the individual can call in for assistance.

Training Assistance: Franchisees are trained in operations until they are satisfied that they know the complete operation.

Chicken Delight

395 Berry St.
Winnipeg, MB R3J 1N6
Toll-Free Phone:
Phone: (204) 885-7570
Fax: (204) 831-6176
Contact: Director of Franchise Development

Number of Franchises: 45
Company-Owned Units: 18
Total Units: 63

In Business Since: 1952   **Franchising Since:** 1952

Description of Operation: Chicken Delight has been in business for over 40 years, featuring our famous pressure-fried chicken and fresh-dough pizza, plus other tasty selections. We cater to the fast-food market with dine-in, take-out, delivery, and drive-thru.

Equity Capital Needed: $75,000

Franchise Fee: $20,000

Royalty: 5 percent

Advertising Co-op Fee: 2 percent

Financial Assistance: Yes.

Management Assistance: We provide on-site operational training, manuals and marketing ideas. We also monitor the progress of all franchisees on a monthly basis.

Training Assistance: We offer an intensive four-week, in-field training program at our corporate stores. During the course of the training, the operational manager periodically checks the new franchisee's progress.

Golden Fried Chicken

11488 Luna Rd.
Dallas, TX 75234
Web Address: www.goldenchicken.com
Toll-Free Phone:
Phone: (972) 831-0911
Fax: (972) 831-0411
Contact:

Number of Franchises: 85
Company-Owned Units: 8
Total Units: 93

In Business Since: 1967   **Franchising Since:** 1972

Description of Operation: Franchisor of Golden Fried Chicken fast-food restaurants, specializing in quality fried chicken and appropriate side orders. A typical restaurant requires 2,000 square feet and a drive-thru window.

Equity Capital Needed: $25,000-$125,000

Franchise Fee: $15,000-1st; $10,000 each other location

Royalty: 4 percent

Advertising Co-op Fee:

Financial Assistance: None.

Management Assistance: GFC provides continual support for the life of the franchise, including pre-opening assistance, marketing programs, negotiation of national purchase contracts, operations manuals, regular visits by field personnel and product, equipment, and market research.

Training Assistance: 2 weeks of pre-opening training at a company location, plus on-site opening assistance.

KFC/Kentucky Fried Chicken

1441 Gardiner Ln.
Louisville, KY 40213
Web Address: www.kfc.com
Toll-Free Phone: (800) 544-5774
Phone: (874) 454-2021
Fax: (874) 456-8255
Contact:

Number of Franchises: 3079
Company-Owned Units: 2121
Total Units: 5200

In Business Since: 1954   **Franchising Since:** 1957

Description of Operation: Quick-service restaurant with a chicken-dominated menu.

Equity Capital Needed: $125,000-$150,000

Franchise Fee: $25,000

Royalty: 4 percent

Advertising Co-op Fee:

Financial Assistance: Data not available.

Management Assistance: Site selection assistance, engineering and construction advise, equipment, materials and supplies advice, operating quality control, meetings, and seminars for methods in processing and marketing approved products. Periodic inspections to ensure franchisee compliance with standards and specifications.

Training Assistance: Seven-week training course before opening outlet. Classes average eight hours per day. Three days are spent in a classroom, and 30 days are spent in an outlet. In addition to initial training, KFC offers continual assistance in the areas of customer service, general outlet management, quality control and employee training. All courses are optional and free of charge, with the exception of out-of-pocket expenses.

Lee's Famous Recipe Chicken

1727 Elm Hill Pike Ste. B-9
Nashville, TN 37210
Toll-Free Phone:
Phone: (615) 315-5300
Fax: (652) 231-3453
Contact: Vice President of Franchise Operations

Number of Franchises: 225
Company-Owned Units: 59
Total Units: 284

In Business Since: 1966   **Franchising Since:** 1966

Description of Operation: Sit-down and take-out chicken restaurant.

Equity Capital Needed: $578,000-$778,000 average investment required.

Franchise Fee: $15,000

Royalty: 3 percent

Advertising Co-op Fee:

Financial Assistance: Finance sources are provided.

Management Assistance: Each franchisee attends an extensive 4-8 week training program in Nashville, TN in a company-operated Lee's Famous Recipe training restaurant.

Training Assistance: Training includes crew training and scheduling, equipment use and maintenance, service and product standards, accounting, inventory and cost control procedures. An experienced restaurant training team will train all employees on site before the opening.

Wings To Go

170 Jennifer Rd., Ste. 250
Annapolis, MD 21401
Toll-Free Phone: (800) 552-9464
Phone:
Fax:
Contact: Executive Vice President

Number of Franchises: 48
Company-Owned Units: 2
Total Units: 50

In Business Since: 1987   **Franchising Since:** 1990

Description of Operation: Retail restaurants, specializing in authentic buffalo-style chicken wings.

Equity Capital Needed: $40,000-$65,000

Franchise Fee: $15,000

Royalty: 3 percent

Advertising Co-op Fee:

Financial Assistance: We will help prepare business plans to submit to lending institutions to secure financing. Direct financing is not available from the corporation at this time.

Management Assistance: Training consists of 1 week at the home office or other corporate facility. 2 weeks of on-site, hands-on training, with monthly follow-up visits or contact with a regional manager. Complete training manuals, forms and advertising aids.

Training Assistance: We offer 1 week of training in corporate store and 2 weeks of on-site training.

Yaya's Flame Broiled Chicken

521 S. Dort Hwy.
Flint, MI 48503
Toll-Free Phone: (800) 754-1242
Phone: (810) 235-6550
Fax: (810) 235-5210
Contact: President

Number of Franchises: 20
Company-Owned Units: 1
Total Units: 21

In Business Since: 1985 **Franchising Since:** 1988

Description of Operation: Flame-broiled chicken, marinated with Yaya's special blend of herbs and spices. Side dishes include baked beans, mashed potatoes, rice pilaf, cole slaw, and potato salad. No fried or frozen products. We specialize in flavor and nutrition.

Equity Capital Needed: $200,000-$250,000

Franchise Fee: $20,000

Royalty: 4 percent

Advertising Co-op Fee:

Financial Assistance: None.

Management Assistance: We provide periodic inspections with operational evaluation and financial review and recommendations.

Training Assistance: Complete operational and management training is provided.

Village Inn Restaurants

400 W. 48th Ave., P.O. Box 16601
Denver, CO 80216
Web Address: www.villageinn.com
Toll-Free Phone: (800) 891-9978
Phone: (303) 672-2229

Fax: (303) 672-2212
Contact: Franchise Operations Coordinator

Number of Franchises: 108
Company-Owned Units: 97
Total Units: 205

In Business Since: 1958 **Franchising Since:** 1961

Description of Operation: Full service, family-style restaurant, offering a variety of menu items and special features emphasizing our breakfast heritage in all day parts.

Equity Capital Needed: $200,00-300,000

Franchise Fee: $25,000

Royalty:

Advertising Co-op Fee: None

Financial Assistance: None

Management Assistance: None

Training Assistance: A minimum of two managers must complete a 12-20 week management training program in addition to one other person from the franchisee's organization. An opening team is on-site for approximately four weeks. Specific training requests provided at franchisee's expense.

Restaurants—Fast Food

A & W Restaurants, Inc.

1 A & W Dr.
Farmington Hill, MI 48331
Toll-Free Phone: (800) 222-2337
Phone: (888) 269-6847
Fax: (248) 699-2000
Contact: Director of Franchise Development

Number of Franchises: 1000
Company-Owned Units: 3
Total Units: 1003

In Business Since: 1919 **Franchising Since:** 1925

Description of Operation: Restaurants, serving hamburgers, hot dogs and the world's #1-selling root beer.

Equity Capital Needed: $20,000-$80,000

Franchise Fee: Varies $5,000-$20,000

Royalty: Varies 4 percent + 4 percent marketing fee; 6 percent

Advertising Co-op Fee:

Financial Assistance: Available.

Management Assistance: A & W provides operational, marketing, and facilities management support to the franchisees. Assistance with architecture and design as well as equipment, purchasing, development and real estate advising.

Training Assistance: Eighteen days of training over a three-week period at A & W corporate facilities.

Arby's

1000 Corporate Dr.
Ft. Lauderdale, FL 33334
Toll-Free Phone: (800) 487-2729
Phone: (305) 351-5100
Fax: (305) 351-5190
Contact: Vice President of Franchising

Number of Franchises: 2406
Company-Owned Units: 263
Total Units: 2669

In Business Since: 1964   **Franchising Since:** 1964

Description of Operation: Fast-food restaurant, specializing in roast beef sandwiches.

Equity Capital Needed: $250,000 liquid; $500,000 net worth

Franchise Fee: $37,500

Royalty: 4 percent

Advertising Co-op Fee:

Financial Assistance: No direct assistance. However, Arby's will guide franchisees in obtaining financing.

Management Assistance: Manuals, advice and counseling are available, covering all aspects of Arby's operation.

Training Assistance: Training includes classroom and in-store training—1 week of training for the owner and 5 weeks for the operator.

Arthur Treacher's Fish & Chips

7400 Baymeadows Way Ste. 300
Jacksonville, FL 32256
Toll-Free Phone: (800) 321-3113
Phone: (904) 739-1200
Fax: (904) 739-2500
Contact: Director of Franchise Development

Number of Franchises: 130
Company-Owned Units: 20
Total Units: 150

In Business Since: 1969   **Franchising Since:** 1969

Description of Operation: The franchisor develops, owns, operates, and licenses others to own and operate a unique fast-food restaurant with a limited menu and system. This system includes a method of operation, customer service, quality control, trade secrets, technical knowledge, specially-designed decor, equipment, lay-out plans, signs, food distribution programs, and accounting systems.

Equity Capital Needed: $72,500-$157,500

Franchise Fee: $19,500

Royalty: 6 percent

Advertising Co-op Fee:

Financial Assistance: The franchisor does not offer financing to franchisees either directly or through affiliates. The franchisor receives no revenues or other commissions from anyone who offers or arranges financing for franchisees.

Management Assistance: Management assistance covers all facets of the operation.

Training Assistance: The initial training program is 3 weeks in duration and takes place at the national headquarters in Jacksonville, FL and at a designated restaurant location. Training covers all facets of the restaurant operation.

Back Yard Burgers, Inc.

2768 Colony Park Dr.
Memphis, TN 38118
Toll-Free Phone: (800) 292-6939
Phone: (901) 367-0888
Fax: (901) 367-0999
Contact: Director of Franchise Sales

Number of Franchises: 45
Company-Owned Units: 32
Total Units: 77

In Business Since: 1987   **Franchising Since:** 1988

Description of Operation: Back Yard Burgers, Inc. operates and franchises quick casual restaurants under the name Back Yard Burgers. The restaurants are designed to project a theme that emphasizes charbroiling fresh, great tasting food including hamburgers, gourmet hamburgers, chicken filet sandwiches, and other sandwich items as customers would cook in their own backyards.

Equity Capital Needed: $200,000 liquid, $300,000 net worth

Franchise Fee: $25,000

Royalty: 4 percent

Advertising Co-op Fee: 3 percent

Financial Assistance: None

Management Assistance: Site selection assistance, lease review, interior and exterior design, manuals, and advice in all areas of Back Yard Burgers operations. Periodic visits to franchising restaurants by district managers to assist with operations, marketing, training, and any other areas needed. New store opening assistance provided.

Training Assistance: Eight weeks of training provided in Memphis at the corporate office and in corporate stores covering all aspects of Back Yard Burgers operations. Training assistance provided for new store opening.

Bassett's Original Turkey

228 Lakeside Dr.
Harsham, PA 19044
Web Address: www.bassetts.com
E-mail Address: BOTurkey@aol.com
Toll-Free Phone: (800) 282-8875

Phone: (215) 675-9670
Fax: (215) 675-9690
Contact: V.P. Franchise Development

Number of Franchises: 16
Company-Owned Units: 3
Total Units: 19

In Business Since: 1983   **Franchising Since:** 1991

Description of Operation: Quick-serve restaurant specializing in fresh-roasted turkey sandwiches, salads, and hot platters.

Equity Capital Needed: $60,000-90,000

Franchise Fee: $25,000

Royalty: 5 percent of net sales

Advertising Co-op Fee: 1 percent of net sales

Financial Assistance: Third-party referrals for financing.

Management Assistance: Opening team stays at store for 10 days after opening day, then company representatives make regular site visits.

Training Assistance: Three-week program; 2 weeks in company store, 1 week in corporate office.

Burger King Corporation

17777 Old Cutler Rd.
Miami, FL 33157
Web Address: www.burgerking.com
Toll-Free Phone:
Phone: (305) 378-7157
Fax: (305) 378-7262
Contact: Director of Franchise Administration

Number of Franchises: 8,827
Company-Owned Units: 817
Total Units: 9,644

In Business Since: 1954   **Franchising Since:** 1954

Description of Operation: Burger King is a highly recognized, world-wide brand, with over 6,800 points of distribution. New lower cost facility design and flexible ownership guidelines continue to make Burger King an attractive franchise investment. BURGER KING IS NOT CURRENTLY ACCEPTING UNSOLICITED FRANCHISE INQUIRIES.

Equity Capital Needed: Thirty-five percent non-real estate investment ($73,000-$511,000)

Franchise Fee: $40,000

Royalty: 3.5 percent

Advertising Co-op Fee:

Financial Assistance: Data not available.

Management Assistance: Burger King franchisees have a group of support personnel available to them who specialize in all phases of business activities, including operations, training, marketing, profit and loss control, real estate, and construction.

Training Assistance: Burger King offers a full range of training to its franchisees, including basic and advanced operations courses, equipment seminars, human relations training, franchisee business courses, and so on.

Captain D's

1717 Elm Hill Pike Ste. A-10
Nashville, TN 37210
Web Address: www.captainds.com
Toll-Free Phone:
Phone: (615) 231-2987
Fax: (615) 231-2790
Contact:

Number of Franchises: 210
Company-Owned Units: 376
Total Units: 586

In Business Since: 1969   **Franchising Since:** 1969

Description of Operation: Quick-service, dine-in or take-out seafood restaurant. Serves baked, broiled, and fried fish; shrimp and chicken entrees; and a variety of vegetables and desserts.

Equity Capital Needed: $300,000 net worth; $150,000 liquid assets

Franchise Fee: $20,000

Royalty: 3 percent

Advertising Co-op Fee:

Financial Assistance: None.

Management Assistance: On-site opening assistance.

Training Assistance: We offer 6-8 weeks of in-store training.

Charley's Steakery

6610 Busch Blvd., Ste. 100
Columbus, OH 43229
Web Address: www.charleyssteakery.com
Toll-Free Phone: (800) 437-8325
Phone: (614) 847-8100
Fax: (614) 847-8110
Contact: Manager of Franchising

Number of Franchises: 52
Company-Owned Units: 9
Total Units: 61

In Business Since: 1986   **Franchising Since:** 1991

Description of Operation: Charley's Steakery features Philly style fresh grilled steak and chicken subs, salads, fresh-cut fries with signature toppings and old-fashioned real lemonade. Everything is made-to-order right in front of the guests. Charley's has received several local, regional, and national awards for its concept and food.

Equity Capital Needed: $78,300-$187,000

Franchise Fee: $19,500

Royalty: 5 percent

Advertising Co-op Fee: 3 percent; for LSM, up to 5 percent

Financial Assistance:

Management Assistance: Charley's provides system-wide support services including assistance in site selection and lease negotiations, local store marketing, store opening assistance, and business consulting services.

Training Assistance: Charley's requires a three-week training program in Columbus, Ohio. Some of the topics include developing a business plan, staffing and training, customer service, store operations, and local store marketing.

Del's Lemonade and Refreshments

1260 Oaklawn Ave.
Cranston, RI 02920
Web Address: www.dels.com
Toll-Free Phone:
Phone: (401) 463-6190
Fax: (401) 463-7931
Contact: Executive Vice President

Number of Franchises: 30
Company-Owned Units: 5
Total Units: 35

In Business Since: 1948   **Franchising Since:** 1965

Description of Operation: Soft frozen lemonade, pretzels, nachos, popcorn, pizza, candy and hot dogs. 16 ounce bottle of beverage line.

Equity Capital Needed: $50,000-$80,000 minimum

Franchise Fee: $15,000 and up

Royalty: None.

Advertising Co-op Fee:

Financial Assistance: Del's provides no financial assistance, but we will work with franchisee to put the business plan together.

Management Assistance: Del's has top-quality people working in the organization to assist and train all new franchises.

Training Assistance: Assistance includes Del's manuals and on-the-job training.

Everything Yogurt & Salad Cafe

1000 South Avenue
Staten Island, NY 10314
Toll-Free Phone: (800) 205-6050
Phone: (718) 494-8888
Fax: (718) 494-8776
Contact: Director of Sales

Number of Franchises: 88
Company-Owned Units: 3
Total Units: 91

In Business Since: 1976   **Franchising Since:** 1981

Description of Operation: A single-concept franchise that combines the timeless appeal of frozen yogurt with the healthful qualities of fresh and wholesome salads, sandwiches, soups, and baked stuffed potatoes. Our newest menu addition is a line of Combo Meals giving consumers an even greater selection of healthy foods. It's a big plus for consumers looking for a healthy alternative to standard fast food.

Equity Capital Needed: $50,000

Franchise Fee: $25,000

Royalty: 5 percent monthly

Advertising Co-op Fee: 1 percent

Financial Assistance: Our company uses third party lenders to assist franchisees secure financing.

Management Assistance: All franchisees must complete a 2 week training program consisting of in-store training and classroom instruction.

Training Assistance: Training consists of a two-week program consisting of in-store, hands-on work and classroom instruction covering all aspects of operating a successful business.

Flamer's Charbroiled Hamburgers

500 3rd St. S
Jacksonville Beach, FL 32250
Web Address: www.flamersgrill.com
Toll-Free Phone:
Phone: (904) 241-3737
Fax: (904) 241-1301
Contact:

Number of Franchises: 73
Company-Owned Units: 9
Total Units: 82

In Business Since: 1987   **Franchising Since:** 1988

Description of Operation: Fast food gourmet hamburger and chicken chain, located primarily in regional malls across the country. All food is cooked to order in plain view of the consumer. The food is cooked on a gas grill using lava rocks.

Equity Capital Needed: $170,000-$200,000

Franchise Fee: $25,000

Royalty: 5 percent

Advertising Co-op Fee:

Financial Assistance: Third party and SBA.

Management Assistance: Regional management from parent company oversees the store after the grand opening crew has left.

Training Assistance: 2 weeks of training in Jacksonville, FL or Boston, MA.

International Dairy Queen

P.O. Box 39286
Minneapolis, MN 55439
Toll-Free Phone: (800) 285-8515
Phone: (612) 830-0200
Fax: (612) 830-0450
Contact: Vice President of Franchise Development

Number of Franchises: 5449
Company-Owned Units: 1
Total Units: 5450

In Business Since: 1940   **Franchising Since:** 1940

Description of Operation: Quick-service food restaurant

Equity Capital Needed: $150,000 net worth, plus $85,000 liquid assets

Franchise Fee: $30,000

Royalty: 4 percent

Advertising Co-op Fee:

Financial Assistance: 50 percent of franchise fee. We will assist in locating additional financing.

Management Assistance: Complete ongoing operations assistance.

Training Assistance: Comprehensive training.

Interstate Dairy Queen

4601 Willard Ave.
Chevy Chase, MD 20815
Toll-Free Phone: (800) 546-5923
Phone: (301) 913-5923
Fax: (301) 913-5424
Contact: President

Number of Franchises: 99
Company-Owned Units: 3
Total Units: 102

In Business Since: 1977   **Franchising Since:** 1977

Description of Operation: Fast food and treat franchisor on interstate highways. Specialists in marketing to the highway traveler.

Equity Capital Needed: $50,000-$150,000

Franchise Fee: $25,000

Royalty: 4 percent

Advertising Co-op Fee:

Financial Assistance: None.

Management Assistance: Full-time professional field force consultants. 2 week training school. Financial management analysis and recommendations.

Training Assistance: 2 weeks of school and preopening assistance from opening team covering 4 people weeks.

Krystal Company, The

One Union Square, 10th Floor
Chattanooga, TN 37402
Web Address: www.krystalco.com
E-mail Address: kryfran@mindspring.com
Toll-Free Phone: (800) 458-5912
Phone: (423) 757-1535
Fax: (423) 757-5623
Contact: Franchise Development Manager

Number of Franchises: 97
Company-Owned Units: 249
Total Units: 346

In Business Since: 1932   **Franchising Since:** 1989

Description of Operation: Krystal is a quick-service restaurant with a drive-thru window and inside seating. Menu includes breakfast and features the unique Krystal Burger prepared on a grill with steamed onions for flavor. Open 24 hours offering full line of Krystal products.

Equity Capital Needed: $200,000

Franchise Fee: $32,500

Royalty: 4.5 percent of weekly gross

Advertising Co-op Fee: None

Financial Assistance: Not available

Management Assistance: All the tools you need to successfully open and run your own Krystal restaurant are at your fingertips. With Krystal's tried-and-true operational systems, the process to handle every task—from ordering supplies to preparing food—are already established. You get comprehensive management training and ongoing field support. Complete operations manuals for easy reference any time of day. An accessible and knowledgeable corporate management team to keep you updated on the latest food service innovations. You also benefit from broadcast and print advertising created to draw more customers to your restaurant and marketing materials and strategies created for you to use on a local level. Field support is provided through assistance by phone and through franchise field consultants.

Training Assistance: We provide complete and comprehensive training for you and your key managers. You will be prepared for an efficient, productive Grand Opening and smooth operations thereafter. Your comprehensive training program includes three distinct phases. There is training at our Tennessee headquarters, when appropriate. Further training is provided at an operating certified Krystal training restaurant. Finally, there is training support at your location for a minimum of five days during your first month.

Long John's Silver's Restaurants

P.O. Box 11988
Lexington, KY 40579
Web Address: www.ljsilvers.com
E-mail Address: scegnar@ljsilvers.com

Toll-Free Phone: (800) 545-8360
Phone:
Fax: (606) 388-6190
Contact:

Number of Franchises: 502
Company-Owned Units: 932
Total Units: 1434

In Business Since: 1969   **Franchising Since:** 1969

Description of Operation: Long John Silver's Restaurants is the largest quick-service seafood chain in the fish and seafood segment. We are approximately 1,500 units strong and are aggressively developing. We offer a menu of fish, seafood, and chicken. Eat-in, take-out, and drive-thru.

Equity Capital Needed: $500,000

Franchise Fee: $20,000

Royalty: 4 percent

Advertising Co-op Fee:

Financial Assistance: None.

Management Assistance: Directors of Franchise Operations work directly with new franchisees during the establishment and opening of new stores. Along with field marketing directors, the DFO's continue to maintain support. The franchise director acts as a liaison between the company and the franchisee.

Training Assistance: We provide an initial 5 1/2 weeks of training. Continual training is offered through workshops, seminars, conferences, and so on.

McDonald's Corporation

7111 Jorie Blvd.
Oak Brook, IL 60521
Web Address: www.mcdonalds.com
Toll-Free Phone: (888) 800-7257
Phone: (630) 623-6196
Fax: (630) 623-5645
Contact:

Number of Franchises:
Company-Owned Units:
Total Units: 23,000

In Business Since: 1955   **Franchising Since:** 1955

Description of Operation: McDonald's is the world's leading food-service retailer in the global consumer market place, with nearly 23,000 restaurants in 109 countries. 85 percent of McDonald's restaurant businesses in the US are locally-owned and operated by independent entrepreneurs.

Equity Capital Needed: $75,000 in non-borrowed personal resources

Franchise Fee: $45,000

Royalty: 4 percent plus monthly base rent

Advertising Co-op Fee:

Financial Assistance: McDonald's does not provide financing or loan guarantees.

Management Assistance: Operations, training, maintenance, accounting, and equipment manuals are provided. McDonald's makes available promotional advertising material, plus field operations support.

Training Assistance: Prospective franchisees are required to participate in a training and evaluation program which may, on a part-time basis, take 2 years or longer to complete.

Mr. Sub

720 Spadina Ave., Ste. 300
Toronto, ON M5S 2T9
Web Address: www.mrsub.ca
Toll-Free Phone: (800) 668-7827
Phone: (416) 962-6232
Fax: (416) 962-9995
Contact: Vice President of Business Development

Number of Franchises: 550
Company-Owned Units: 1
Total Units: 551

In Business Since: 1968   **Franchising Since:** 1970

Description of Operation: Fast food—submarines, salad, soups, beverages, and baked goods.

Equity Capital Needed: $45,000

Franchise Fee: $12,000

Royalty: 5 percent + 3 percent advertising

Advertising Co-op Fee:

Financial Assistance: Data not available.

Management Assistance: Ongoing field assistance, national advertising, local marketing, and design development.

Training Assistance: Comprehensive training program. Classroom and in-store practical training. 3 weeks at corporate center and 1 week at training store.

Sammi's Deli

114 Wilton Hill Rd.
Columbia, SC 29212
Toll-Free Phone:
Phone: (808) 781-7977
Fax:
Contact: President

Number of Franchises: 1
Company-Owned Units: 0
Total Units: 1

In Business Since: 1984   **Franchising Since:** 1991

Description of Operation: Fast food with free delivery.

Equity Capital Needed: $60,000-$80,000

Franchise Fee: $9,500

Royalty: 5 percent or $350, whichever is higher.

Advertising Co-op Fee:

Financial Assistance: None available at this time.

Management Assistance: 5 days of training in the new location.

Training Assistance: A two-week training course, comprised of hands-on instruction at our training store and classroom orientation at our headquarters. At opening, our staff remains for at least 5 days, assisting in all aspects of the opening.

Sonic Drive In Restaurants

101 Park Avenue, Ste. 1400
Oklahoma City, OK 73102
Web Address: www.sonicdrivein.com
Toll-Free Phone: (800) 569-6656
Phone: (405) 280-7654
Fax: (405) 272-8298
Contact: Vice President of Franchising

Number of Franchises:
Company-Owned Units: 267
Total Units: 1,700

In Business Since: 1953 **Franchising Since:** 1959

Description of Operation: 50's concept, drive-in fast-food restaurant, serving hamburgers, hot dogs, french fries and onion rings.

Equity Capital Needed: $250,000

Franchise Fee: $30,000

Royalty: 4 percent-increases with sales

Advertising Co-op Fee:

Financial Assistance: Sonic has an affiliation with several major financing sources that are well established in the business community. Financing is available for real estate and equipment through these financial sources.

Management Assistance: Management school (1 week), videos, field representatives, and so on.

Training Assistance: Same as above.

South Philly Steaks & Fries

1000 South Ave.
Staten Island, NY 10314
Toll-Free Phone: (800) 205-6050
Phone: (718) 494-8888
Fax: (718) 494-8776
Contact: Director of Sales

Number of Franchises: 16
Company-Owned Units: 0
Total Units: 16

In Business Since: 1983 **Franchising Since:** 1983

Description of Operation: South Philly Steaks & Fries, a concept that begins with the classic Philadelphia style cheese steak and ends with success. The South Philly steak sandwich is available with a variety of toppings such as; onions, peppers, lettuce, tomatoes, mushrooms, and bacon. The South Philly Steaks & Fries menu appeals to a wide customer base and offers sub-sandwich favorites and, of course, delicious french fries.

Equity Capital Needed: $50,000

Franchise Fee: $25,000

Royalty: 5 percent monthly

Advertising Co-op Fee: 1 percent

Financial Assistance: Our company uses third party lenders to assist franchisees secure financing.

Management Assistance: All franchisees must complete a two week training program consisting of in-store training and classroom instruction.

Training Assistance: Training consists of a two-week program consisting of in-store, hands-on work and classroom instruction covering all aspects of operating a successful business.

Ward's Restaurants

7 Professional Pkwy. Ste. 102
Hattiesburg, MS 39402
Toll-Free Phone: (800) 748-9273
Phone: (601) 268-9273
Fax: (601) 268-9283
Contact: President

Number of Franchises: 38
Company-Owned Units: 10
Total Units: 48

In Business Since: 1978 **Franchising Since:** 1981

Description of Operation: Fast-food restaurant chain featuring chili-dogs, chili-burgers, and homemade root beer served in frosty mugs. The menu also includes a complete breakfast line featuring homemade buttermilk biscuits and a variety of sandwiches. Restaurants have inside seating, as well as drive-thru service.

Equity Capital Needed: $90,000-$120,000

Franchise Fee: $20,000

Royalty: 3-5 percent

Advertising Co-op Fee:

Financial Assistance: None available.

Management Assistance: The franchisor provides site selection, building, equipment, recruiting and training assistance before opening. Special opening support crew is provided during opening week. After opening, a franchise consultant makes periodic contacts and visits to the store.

Training Assistance: A four-week training program is provided for the owner and manager at the company headquarters. The owner must pay for transportation and living expenses while attending the training program.

Wendy's Old Fashioned Hamburgers

P.O. Box 256
Dublin, OH 43017
Web Address: www.wendys.com
Toll-Free Phone:
Phone: (614) 764-3094
Fax: (614) 764-6894
Contact: Director of Franchise Administration

Number of Franchises: 3,995
Company-Owned Units: 1,202
Total Units: 5,197

In Business Since: 1969   **Franchising Since:** 1971

Description of Operation: Wendy's is a quick-service hamburger restaurant.

Equity Capital Needed: $250,000

Franchise Fee: $30,000

Royalty: 4 percent

Advertising Co-op Fee:

Financial Assistance: None.

Management Assistance: We offer a two-day corporate business orientation in conjunction with ongoing regional support.

Training Assistance: We provide 16-20 weeks of in-store and classroom training, conducted in a certified training store.

Great Wraps!

57 Executive Park S., Ste. 440
Atlanta, GA 30329
Toll-Free Phone: (888) 489-7277
Phone: (404) 248-9900
Fax: (404) 248-0180
Contact:

Number of Franchises: 45
Company-Owned Units: 2
Total Units: 47

In Business Since: 1974   **Franchising Since:** 1981

Description of Operation: Fast-food franchisor with 50+ units open in 12 states. Operates in major regional mall food courts. Serves hot, grilled, pita-wrapped sandwiches with beef and lamb, steak and cheese, fresh vegetables and strips of chicken breast, plus fresh salads, such as Greek and caesar, kurly fries, and soft drinks.

Equity Capital Needed: $180,000-$250,000

Franchise Fee: $25,000

Royalty: 5 percent

Advertising Co-op Fee:

Financial Assistance: We will assist in finding financing, but make no claims to guarantee any loans.

Management Assistance: Ongoing field support, audits and 3 weeks of up-front training at the corporate training

store. Store opening team (3-5 people) for up to 1 week after opening. Thorough pre-opening training manual and post-opening operations manual.

Training Assistance: Same as above.

Restaurants—Grills & Bars

Chelsea Street Pub & Grill

P.O. Box 9989
Austin, TX 78766
E-mail Address: ranken@worldnet.att.net
Toll-Free Phone:
Phone: (512) 454-7739
Fax: (512) 454-1801
Contact: President

Number of Franchises: 5
Company-Owned Units: 13
Total Units: 18

In Business Since: 1973   **Franchising Since:** 1983

Description of Operation: Restaurant and pub, located in regional malls in Texas, Louisiana, Colorado or New Mexico. Live entertainment after 9:00 PM. Serves hamburgers to steaks—over 75 menu items—liquor, beer and wine served. Table service. Giant TV screen.

Equity Capital Needed: $600,000-$700,000

Franchise Fee: $30,000

Royalty: 5 percent

Advertising Co-op Fee:

Financial Assistance: None.

Management Assistance: We provide training, advertising, purchasing, bookkeeping, band booking, on-line E-mail, computer assistance, market research, construction supervision, and day and night on-call.

Training Assistance: We offer an extensive (6 weeks) of in-store training and 2 weeks in general office. Management assists in franchisee's unit for first 2 weeks when opened.

Mickey Finn's Sports Cafe—Castle Rose, Inc.

207 Galvin Road North
Bellevue, NE 68005
Toll-Free Phone: (888) 478-8463
Phone: (402) 341-2424
Fax: (402) 291-2345
Contact: President

Number of Franchises: 7
Company-Owned Units: 1
Total Units: 8

In Business Since: 1988   **Franchising Since:** 1988

Description of Operation: Mickey Finn's Sports Cafe is a neighborhood restaurant and full-service bar featuring sports, games, and fun. The menu provides a wide range of appetizers, sandwiches, and light entrees. There is an emphasis on national and regional sports broadcasts with big screen TVs and many smaller sets visible from all seating areas. The concept was founded in 1988.

Equity Capital Needed: $50,000-$75,000

Franchise Fee: $17,500

Royalty: 5 percent

Advertising Co-op Fee: None

Financial Assistance: Assistance in preparation of business plan.

Management Assistance: Operations manual, forms, telephonic and on-site consultation.

Training Assistance: 2 weeks management/key personnel training in Omaha, Nebraska. 3 to 6 weeks on-site training at opening. Periodic on-site visitations, seminars, and training sessions.

Philadelphia Bar & Grill—Castle Rose, Inc.

207 Galvin Road North
Bellevue, NE 68005
Toll-Free Phone: (888) 478-8463
Phone: (402) 341-2424
Fax: (402) 291-2345
Contact: President

Number of Franchises: 8
Company-Owned Units: 0
Total Units: 8

In Business Since: 1985   **Franchising Since:** 1985

Description of Operation: Philadelphia Bar & Grill is a neighborhood bar & grill restaurant featuring a value-oriented menu of appetizers, light entrees and sandwiches with a full-service bar. The restaurants are casual, comfortable, and experience a high percentage of repeat business, particularly from neighboring business and residential areas. The concept was founded in 1985.

Equity Capital Needed: $50,000-$70,000

Franchise Fee: $17,500

Royalty: 5 percent

Advertising Co-op Fee: None

Financial Assistance: Assistance in preparation of business plan.

Management Assistance: Operations manual, forms, telephonic, and on-site consultation.

Training Assistance: 2 weeks management/key personnel training in Omaha, Nebraska. 3 to 6 weeks on-site training at opening. Periodic on-site visitations, seminars, and training sessions.

R. J. Gator's Florida Food 'N Fun

609 Hepburn Ave. Suite 103
Jupiter, FL 33458
E-mail Address: jrgator@msn.com
Toll-Free Phone: (800) 438-4286
Phone: (561) 575-0326
Fax: (561) 575-9220
Contact: CEO/President

Number of Franchises: 9
Company-Owned Units: 3
Total Units: 12

In Business Since: 1986   **Franchising Since:** 1992

Description of Operation: R. J. Gator's is a family, casual dining restaurant which features a wide range of menu items from chicken wings and burgers to crab cakes and seafood dinners. R. J. Gator's also offers a full liquor bar. Our fast, friendly service and casual Florida atmosphere appeals to kids of all ages. Currently we have twelve units in Florida and North Carolina and are looking to open four more units in 1998.

Equity Capital Needed: $500,000

Franchise Fee: $30,000

Royalty: 5 percent of sales

Advertising Co-op Fee: 1 percent of sales

Financial Assistance: R. J. Gator's provides assistance in obtaining financing from an outside source. We do not directly finance franchisees.

Management Assistance: R.J. Gator's can provide assistance in selecting personnel for managerial positions. We do not provide personnel for staffing our units.

Training Assistance: R. J. Gator's requires franchisees to attend and complete our management training program along with opening management team. Training on-site during opening weeks with corporate trainers are also provided.

Restaurants—Hot Dogs

Wienerschnitzel

4440 Von Karman Ave., Ste. 222
Newport Beach, CA 92660
Web Address: www.bison1.com
Toll-Free Phone: (800) 764-9353
Phone: (714) 851-2609
Fax: (714) 851-2615
Contact: Franchise Sales Director

Number of Franchises: 315
Company-Owned Units: 315
Total Units: 315

In Business Since: 1961 **Franchising Since:** 1965

Description of Operation: In 1961 John N. Galardi, Founder of Galardi Group, Inc. opened his first Wienerschnitzel restaurant in Wilmington, CA. The first menu consisted of hot dogs and sodas. Today, hot dogs remain the central items on the Wienerschnitzel menu. Galardi Group, Inc. (GGI) is a privately held restaurant franchisor headquartered in Newport Beach, California. Wienerschnitzel is the largest, privately owned hot dog restaurant chain in the World. Wienerschnitzel's Market presence is expanding with the recent co-branding of its Original Hamburger Stand concept and new store growth. Today there are over 300 Wienerschnitzel Restaurants operating in California and throughout the Southwest. Galardi Group continues to expand through franchising, as well as through additional limited franchised owned locations. A Galardi Group franchise offers an ambitious individual an opportunity to own their own business and to be a part of the hot dog segment leader of the fast food industry or a price competitive hamburger chain.

Equity Capital Needed: $100,000-$150,000

Franchise Fee: $20,000

Royalty: 5 percent franchise service fee/1 percent national advertising

Advertising Co-op Fee: 3-5 percent local advertising

Financial Assistance: SBA assistance through approved lenders and equipment only financing through approved lenders.

Management Assistance: We have a Franchise Area Director for every 30-35 restaurants. Franchisees have access to any and all corporate personnel.

Training Assistance: We provide six weeks of training for the new franchisee and any desired management personnel; one week of opening support and ongoing management development programs.

Restaurants—Italian

Fazoli's Systems

2470 Palumbo
Lexington, KY 40509
Toll-Free Phone:
Phone: (606) 268-1668
Fax: (606) 268-2263
Contact: Vice President of Franchising

Number of Franchises: 5
Company-Owned Units: 38
Total Units: 43

In Business Since: 1988 **Franchising Since:** 1991

Description of Operation: Italian food—fast. A walk-up, take-out, and drive-thru operation with approximately 100 seats.

Equity Capital Needed: $400,000-$800,000

Franchise Fee: $20,000

Royalty: 4 percent

Advertising Co-op Fee:

Financial Assistance: None.

Management Assistance: A five-week training program is required for a minimum of 3 persons per unit. Opening assistance is provided by company personnel. Monthly supervision. Semi-annual meetings.

Training Assistance: Same as above.

Mike's Restaurants

8250 Decarle Blvd.
Montreal, PQ H4P 2P5
Web Address: www.mikes.ca
Toll-Free Phone:
Phone: (514) 341-5544
Fax: (514) 341-6236
Contact:

Number of Franchises: 107
Company-Owned Units: 24
Total Units: 131

In Business Since: 1968 **Franchising Since:** 1968

Description of Operation: M-Corp Inc. is a full-support franchise management company, currently operating a network of one-hundred thirty-one Mike's Restaurants, which is the dominant purveyor of Italian food in Quebec. Featuring pizzas, pastas, and Italian sandwiches; full table service in a family setting; and 30-minute delivery division that oversees the home delivery of Mike's food.

Equity Capital Needed: $125,000-$175,000 (Canadian)

Franchise Fee: $45,000

Royalty: 8 percent

Advertising Co-op Fee:

Financial Assistance: Franchise financing programs are negotiated with major financial institutions on behalf of franchisees, offering excellent terms and conditions.

Management Assistance: We provide complete set-up of operating manuals, with ongoing assistance offered by trained field consultants to assist franchisees in the maintenance of efficient employee working schedules, food costs, and so on.

Training Assistance: We offer pre-opening and takeover assistance. 8-ten weeks of full-time, in depth training by consultant in all aspects of franchise operations, plus 2 weeks of hands-on training team following opening.

Mrs. Vanelli's Pizza & Italian Food

2133 Royal Windsor Dr. Ste. 23
Mississauga, ON L5J 1K5
E-mail Address: info@denatogroup.com
Toll-Free Phone:
Phone: (905) 823-8883
Fax: (905) 823-5255
Contact: Director of Franchising

Number of Franchises: 80
Company-Owned Units: 1
Total Units: 81

In Business Since: 1981   **Franchising Since:** 1983

Description of Operation: Italian fast-food restaurant, operating in food courts of major shopping centers.

Equity Capital Needed: $40,000-$60,000

Franchise Fee: $25,000

Royalty: 6 percent

Advertising Co-op Fee:

Financial Assistance: We will assist in the financial presentation.

Management Assistance: We provide ongoing support. Operational and marketing support with periodic visits.

Training Assistance: We offer 2 weeks of theoretical and on-site training before opening, as well as 2 weeks of training during opening, if required.

Pasta to Go

25280 Southfield Rd. Ste. 201
Southfield, MI 48075
Web Address: www.wfcnet.com
Toll-Free Phone:
Phone: (248) 557-2784
Fax: (248) 557-7931
Contact:

Number of Franchises: 34
Company-Owned Units: 1
Total Units: 35

In Business Since: 1987   **Franchising Since:** 1991

Description of Operation: Fast-food Italian pasta. We serve pasta, along with a variety of sauces, salads, sandwiches, and pizza if necessary.

Equity Capital Needed: $65,000-$95,000

Franchise Fee: $20,000

Royalty: 5 percent + 2 percent advertising

Advertising Co-op Fee:

Financial Assistance: We have third-party financing for equipment for qualified applicants.

Management Assistance: Operations training, operations manual, monthly inspections, which in turn are formed into an action plan for marketing and operations, ideas, newsletter, hotline, and meetings.

Training Assistance: An extensive two-week training program is provided at one of our stores. This will be followed by 2 weeks at the new franchisee's store. Additional training is available beyond that.

Samuel Mancino's Italian Eatery

25820 Southfield Rd., Ste. 201
Southfield, MI 48075
Web Address: www.wfcnet.com
E-mail Address: wfc@cris.com
Toll-Free Phone:
Phone: (248) 559-1415
Fax:
Contact:

Number of Franchises: 25
Company-Owned Units: 1
Total Units: 26

In Business Since: 1948   **Franchising Since:** 1990

Description of Operation:

Equity Capital Needed: $70,000

Franchise Fee: $40,000

Royalty: 4 percent

Advertising Co-op Fee:

Financial Assistance:

Management Assistance:

Training Assistance:

Sbarro

763 Larkfield Rd.
Commack, NY 11725
Toll-Free Phone: (800) 766-4949
Phone: (516) 864-0200
Fax: (516) 462-9165
Contact: Vice President of Franchising

Number of Franchises: 140
Company-Owned Units: 540
Total Units: 680

In Business Since: 1955   **Franchising Since:** 1992

Description of Operation: Italian eateries.

Equity Capital Needed: $300,000+

Franchise Fee: $35,000

Royalty: 5 percent

Advertising Co-op Fee:

Financial Assistance: None.

Management Assistance: Full training and ongoing field support.

Training Assistance: 5 weeks (at 40 hours per week) of in-store training.

Uncle Tony's Pizza & Pasta Restaurants

1800 Post Rd. 27 Airport Plaza
Warwick, RI 02866
Toll-Free Phone:
Phone: (401) 738-1321
Fax: (401) 732-1936
Contact: President

Number of Franchises: 10
Company-Owned Units: 3
Total Units: 13

In Business Since: 1970   **Franchising Since:** 1976

Description of Operation: Providing 150-180 seat, family-style Italian-theme restaurants; specializing in old world pizza; and serving beer, wine, and various cocktails.

Equity Capital Needed: $300,000

Franchise Fee: $35,000

Royalty: 4 percent

Advertising Co-op Fee:

Financial Assistance: We assist in loan packaging, SBA presentation, and restaurant supply house financing.

Management Assistance: We provide every phase of management assistance, including on-site company staff for an indefinite period of time.

Training Assistance: We offer 12 weeks of on-the-job and classroom training.

Restaurants—Mexican

Casa Ole Mexican Restaurants, Inc.

1135 Edgebrook Dr.
Houston, TX 77034
Toll-Free Phone:
Phone: (713) 943-7574
Fax: (713) 943-9554
Contact:

Number of Franchises: 17
Company-Owned Units: 37
Total Units: 54

In Business Since: 1973   **Franchising Since:** 1979

Description of Operation: Full-service, freshly-prepared Mexican food served in our friendly, casual dining room. Menu price range: appetizers $3.35-$5.95, entrees $3.45-$7.95, children's menu $2.25-$2.95, margaritas, beer and wine.

Equity Capital Needed: $325,000-$1,000,000

Franchise Fee: $25,000

Royalty: 5 percent

Advertising Co-op Fee:

Financial Assistance: None available.

Management Assistance: 4-6 weeks' training in advance of opening for each manager and assistant manager. Fifteen days of training for the chef. Advice, assistance and training manuals for staff positions. Franchisor representatives on hand during first 2 weeks of new store opening. We also provide advice and guidance to the franchisee, beginning with site selection, through construction and grand opening. We utilize a comprehensive store development guidelines manual to aid the new franchisee throughout the development phase.

Training Assistance: Data not available.

Diamond Dave's Taco Company

201 S. Clinton St.; Ste. 281
Iowa City, IA 52240
Toll-Free Phone:
Phone: (319) 337-7690
Fax: (319) 337-4707
Contact: President

Number of Franchises: 36
Company-Owned Units: 4
Total Units: 40

In Business Since: 1979   **Franchising Since:** 1981

Description of Operation: Diamond Dave's is a casual theme, sit-down Mexican/American restaurant with a lounge. Family dining, predominantly located in regional shopping malls. Fun and festive atmosphere with family prices.

Equity Capital Needed: $125,000-$275,000

Franchise Fee: $15,000

Royalty: 4 percent

Advertising Co-op Fee:

Financial Assistance: In general, Diamond Dave's usually negotiates some cash contribution to construction from landlord. Equipment financing is available to qualified persons.

Management Assistance: Pre-training of owner/manager is required for 3-6 weeks before opening. Initial crew training for opening is provided. After opening, unit visits are performed; spring and fall franchise seminars are given.

Training Assistance: Pre-opening training of key employees is provided in our company-owned units. At opening, our trainers will be on-site to train the complete opening staff. Our people continue to train for up to a week afterwards.

El Chico Restaurants

12200 Stemmons Fwy. Ste. 100
Dallas, TX 75234
Toll-Free Phone:
Phone: (972) 241-5500

Fax: (972) 888-8198
Contact:

Number of Franchises: 29
Company-Owned Units: 56
Total Units: 85

In Business Since: 1940   **Franchising Since:** 1969

Description of Operation: Full-service Mexican food restaurant.

Equity Capital Needed: Data not available.

Franchise Fee: $35,000

Royalty: 4 percent

Advertising Co-op Fee:

Financial Assistance: We do not provide financial assistance.

Management Assistance: 2 regional managers for ongoing field support.

Training Assistance: A 12-week training program is required before opening. Ongoing training provided as needed. Training provided as needed. Training seminars provided throughout the year.

La Salsa

10474 Santa Monica Blvd. Ste. 300
Los Angeles, CA 90025
Web Address: www.lasalsa.com
Toll-Free Phone: (800) 527-2572
Phone: (310) 446-8744
Fax: (310) 446-8733
Contact:

Number of Franchises:
Company-Owned Units:
Total Units: 100

In Business Since: 1979   **Franchising Since:** 1988

Description of Operation: Fresh and healthy Mexican quick-service restaurant.

Equity Capital Needed: $103,300

Franchise Fee: $29,500

Royalty: 5 percent

Advertising Co-op Fee:

Financial Assistance: None.

Management Assistance: Complete managerial training. Field service representative.

Training Assistance: 5-8 weeks of in-store and class-room training. 1 week of new store training.

Nacho Nana's Worldwide Inc.

1220 S. Alma School Rd., Ste. 101
Mesa, AZ 85210
Toll-Free Phone: (800) 316-2627
Phone: (602) 644-1340

Fax: (602) 644-1506
Contact:

Number of Franchises: 7
Company-Owned Units: 0
Total Units: 7

In Business Since: 1993   **Franchising Since:** 1993

Description of Operation: Mexican fast food, catering to upscale market, with menu designed for the "lite" food conscious.

Equity Capital Needed: $37,700-$45,900

Franchise Fee: $9,500

Royalty: 2 percent

Advertising Co-op Fee:

Financial Assistance: Nacho Nana's does not directly provide financing. However, we can provide approved equipment financing sources who can deal directly with the franchisees.

Management Assistance: Six-day training school in Scottsdale, AZ, plus five days of training at the store to assist in new store opening.

Training Assistance: Six-day training school in Scottsdale, AZ, plus five days of training at the store to assist in new store opening.

Pedro's Tacos of America

2313 S. El Camino Real
San Clemente, CA 92672
Toll-Free Phone:
Phone: (714) 498-5904
Fax: (714) 498-0562
Contact: Owner

Number of Franchises: 1
Company-Owned Units: 1
Total Units: 2

In Business Since: 1985   **Franchising Since:** 1991

Description of Operation: Mexican fast-food with low, value-oriented prices and a very limited, fast-service menu. Drive-thru optional, but recommended. A unique and very profitable concept.

Equity Capital Needed: $30,000

Franchise Fee: $15,000 returnable after 10 years.

Royalty: 5 percent

Advertising Co-op Fee:

Financial Assistance: On approved credit, Pedro's and an affiliate will finance up to 50 percent of the equipment, start-up and construction costs, excluding land, above and beyond any SBA, local bank or landlord financed costs which the franchisee may have already secured. This offer is quite unique in the industry.

Management Assistance: Data not available.

Training Assistance: We offer a comprehensive, hands-on and intensive two-week training period for approved franchisees at our prototype unit in San Clemente, CA.

Pepe's Mexican Restaurants

1325 W. 15th St.
Chicago, IL 60608
Toll-Free Phone:
Phone: (312) 733-2500
Fax: (312) 733-2564
Contact: Corporate Counsel

Number of Franchises: 55
Company-Owned Units: 1
Total Units: 56

In Business Since: 1967 **Franchising Since:** 1967

Description of Operation: Full-service Mexican restaurant franchise, featuring a full range of Mexican items, including beer, wine and liquor.

Equity Capital Needed: $50,000-$250,000

Franchise Fee: $15,000

Royalty: 4 percent

Advertising Co-op Fee:

Financial Assistance: The franchisor helps the franchisee find financing and will consider some financing on a case-by-case basis.

Management Assistance: We train new franchisees for up to 1 month before opening. After opening, we spend 1-2 weeks at the restaurant helping to operate

Training Assistance: Training includes instruction in operating restaurant, preparation of food, training of employees, record keeping, and ordering of inventory.

Taco Casa

P.O. Box 4542
Topeka, KS 66604
Toll-Free Phone:
Phone: (913) 267-2548
Fax: (913) 267-2652
Contact: President

Number of Franchises: 20
Company-Owned Units: 1
Total Units: 21

In Business Since: 1963 **Franchising Since:** 1976

Description of Operation: Fast-food Mexican restaurant. Extensive menu, offering a wide variety of items.

Equity Capital Needed: $50,000-$150,000

Franchise Fee: $15,000

Royalty: 4 percent

Advertising Co-op Fee:

Financial Assistance: No direct financial assistance is provided. Assistance in providing lending sources.

Management Assistance: We provide site inspections, hotline assistance available at all times, seminars, training programs, operations manuals, headquarters staff at site with 10 days' notice, newsletter and legal updates.

Training Assistance: Two weeks of training at headquarters are provided.

Taco Grande

P.O. Box 780066
Wichita, KS 67278
Toll-Free Phone:
Phone: (316) 744-0200
Fax: (316) 744-0299
Contact: President

Number of Franchises: 14
Company-Owned Units: 10
Total Units: 24

In Business Since: 1960 **Franchising Since:** 1966

Description of Operation: Taco Grande offers a limited-menu Mexican restaurant, featuring drive-thru service. Our recipes are authentic Mexican recipes. We have been in successful operation for over thirty-four years. We offer excellent products, training and a cost-efficient and labor-saving building design.

Equity Capital Needed: $45,000 cash. Total investment—$250,000-$450,000

Franchise Fee: $20,000

Royalty: 3 percent

Advertising Co-op Fee:

Financial Assistance: None is available at this time.

Management Assistance: We provide headquarters and on-site training, manuals, a monthly newsletter, company-wide marketing fund provides POP materials, radio and TV ads, kids premiums, suggested reader board specials, and so on.

Training Assistance: We offer 3-4 weeks of training at a company store in Wichita, KS, operations and training manuals, and up to 2 weeks of on-site training at the store opening.

Taco Maker Inc., The

P.O. Box 9519
Ogden, UT 84401
Web Address: www.ttm@tacomaker.com
Toll-Free Phone:
Phone: (801) 476-9780
Fax: (801) 476-9788
Contact:

Number of Franchises: 134
Company-Owned Units: 3
Total Units: 137

In Business Since: 1978 **Franchising Since:** 1978

Description of Operation: Mexican fast-food franchise, available in both single outlet, multi-outlet, and master license with a variety of site options, including free-standing, mall, kiosk, double drive-thru, and cart.

Equity Capital Needed: $75,000-$100,000

Franchise Fee: $22,500

Royalty: 6 percent

Advertising Co-op Fee:

Financial Assistance: The franchisee obtains his/her own financing package.

Management Assistance: We help with the negotiation of the lease after assistance with the site selection. Operations manuals and ongoing marketing through national co-operative are available.

Training Assistance: Thirty days of extensive training in operations, personnel management and accounting procedures at corporate office. On-site training is provided to new owners by corporate trainers during the period.

Taco Mayo Franchise Systems, Inc.

10405 Greenbriar Pl.
Oklahoma City, OK 73159
Toll-Free Phone: (800) 291-8226
Phone: (405) 691-8226
Fax: (405) 691-8226
Contact: Franchise Qualification Specialist

Number of Franchises: 86
Company-Owned Units: 34
Total Units: 106

In Business Since: 1978   **Franchising Since:** 1980

Description of Operation: Taco Mayo (My-oh) is a quick service restaurant chain featuring a Tex-Mex menu. The menu features Tex-Mex favorites like Crispy Tacos, Burritos, Nachos, and Salads. Taco Mayo also features proprietary items like the Chimayo, Serape Tex-Mex wraps and the Nacho Mayo. Taco Mayo proudly pours Coca-Cola and Dr. Pepper brand soft drinks. As a franchise owner/operator you are given every opportunity to succeed in business through Taco Mayo's support systems that include but are not limited to field operations consultants, central purchasing, advertising co-operatives, and restaurant merchandising.

Equity Capital Needed: Not provided

Franchise Fee: $15,000

Royalty: 4 percent of gross sales

Advertising Co-op Fee: 3 percent

Financial Assistance: Taco Mayo Franchise Systems, Inc. (TMFSI) will assist with the preparation of a business plan for the purposes of arranging financial assistance from prospective lenders. However, TMFSI does not provide direct financial assistance.

Management Assistance: TMFSI provides each franchisee with a Franchised Field Consultants. These highly

experienced consultants are acutely aware of all aspects of operating a Taco Mayo restaurant and are available for assistance.

Training Assistance: Each franchisee is required to have four management personnel trained before the opening of their Taco Mayo. The cost of this training is included in the franchise fee. Ongoing training is available on an as needed basis.

Tasty Tacos

1420 E. Grand Ave.
Des Moines, IA 50316
Toll-Free Phone:
Phone: (515) 262-3940
Fax: (515) 263-8828
Contact: President

Number of Franchises: 2
Company-Owned Units: 5
Total Units: 7

In Business Since: 1961   **Franchising Since:** 1992

Description of Operation: Quick-service restaurant.

Equity Capital Needed: $30,000-$45,000

Franchise Fee: $7,500

Royalty: 4 percent

Advertising Co-op Fee:

Financial Assistance: We are working with an equipment leasing company.

Management Assistance: We provide on-site assistance and ongoing phone consultation.

Training Assistance: We offer 1 month of training at a company-owned restaurant and 2 weeks of on-site assistance.

Zuzu Handmade Mexican Food

2651 N. Harwood, Ste. 200
Dallas, TX 75201
Toll-Free Phone: (800) 824-8830
Phone: (214) 922-8226
Fax: (214) 720-1332
Contact:

Number of Franchises: 17
Company-Owned Units: 2
Total Units: 19

In Business Since: 1989   **Franchising Since:** 1992

Description of Operation: Fast, casual restaurant, serving consistent, fresh, regional, and Mexican food in a modern, clean, convenient facility.

Equity Capital Needed: $130,000-$267,000

Franchise Fee: $25,000

Royalty: 4 percent

Advertising Co-op Fee:

Financial Assistance: Zuzu does not provide direct financing, but will assist in acquiring financing.

Management Assistance: Fully-supervised certification training for general managers, kitchen manager or chef is provided at the corporate training center. State-of-the-art point-of-sales control equipment, plus the leading food service cost control inventory accounting package. As part of our commitment to the success of our franchisees, we offer friendly, knowledgeable field support for any operational issues or questions that management may have.

Training Assistance: We offer a comprehensive eight-week training program in the Dallas, TX area. The training program covers restaurant operations, product preparation and presentation, customer service, equipment maintenance and sanitation, marketing, management theory application and communication skills.

Restaurants—Oriental

Edo Japan

4838-32nd St. S.E.
Calgary, AB T2B 2S6
Toll-Free Phone:
Phone: (403) 215-8800
Fax: (403) 215-8801
Contact: President

Number of Franchises: 62
Company-Owned Units: 10
Total Units: 72

In Business Since: 1977 **Franchising Since:** 1986

Description of Operation: We are the original teppan/teriyaki-style, fast-food outlet that places emphasis on nutrition, high-quality food, and the availability of vegetarian-style dishes. All menu items are prepared fresh, in full view of the customers. The teppan-style menu brings customers back again and again. Edo Japan has a highly successful, very profitable, fast-food concept. In the food courts, where we are located, we are generally in the top 3, often number one in sales. There are 70+ Edo Japan restaurants in US and Canada.

Equity Capital Needed: $170,000-$250,000

Franchise Fee: $20,000

Royalty: 6 percent

Advertising Co-op Fee:

Financial Assistance: The franchisee is responsible for his or her own financing.

Management Assistance: Scheduling of staff for busy and slow periods, cash register training, ordering of supplies and product, training of staff, introduction to new equipment, training in new menu items, and basic control of the store.

Training Assistance: Two weeks at head office includes food and sauce preparation, cooking, store procedures, and training in accounting.

Happi House Restaurants

2901 Moorpark Ave. Ste. 255
San Jose, CA 95128
Toll-Free Phone: (800) 764-2774
Phone: (408) 244-0655
Fax: (408) 244-9262
Contact: President/Chief Executive Officer

Number of Franchises: 2
Company-Owned Units: 7
Total Units: 9

In Business Since: 1976 **Franchising Since:** 1991

Description of Operation: Asian fast/food restaurant (primarily Japanese food).

Equity Capital Needed: $200,000-$240,000

Franchise Fee: $25,000

Royalty: 5 percent

Advertising Co-op Fee:

Financial Assistance: None.

Management Assistance: Ongoing managerial assistance program. Larger training program available on request.

Training Assistance: An intensive two-week training program. Larger training program available at no extra cost when necessary. Excellent manuals and training materials.

Ho-Lee-Chow (Canada)

658 Danforth Ave. Ste. 201
Toronto, ON M4J 5B9
Toll-Free Phone:
Phone: (416) 778-6660
Fax: (416) 778-6818
Contact: General Manager

Number of Franchises: 23
Company-Owned Units: 1
Total Units: 24

In Business Since: 1989 **Franchising Since:** 1989

Description of Operation: Great Chinese food, delivered fast and fresh. Pick-up also available. No sit-down. Each dish cooked to order. No MSG added. Clean, bright, open kitchen concept.

Equity Capital Needed: $75,000

Franchise Fee: Not available.

Royalty: 6 percent

Advertising Co-op Fee:

Financial Assistance: Not available.

Management Assistance: We provide operational assistance for the general manager, group supervisor,

corporate chef, corporate managers, corporate cooks, central order processing department, and the accounting department.

Training Assistance: We offer a minimum 5 weeks of training, 2 weeks of theory (maximum), and 3 weeks (minimum) of practical, in-store training.

Made In Japan—A Teriyaki Experience

2133 Royal Windsor Dr.; Ste. 23
Mississauga, ON L5J 1K5
E-mail Address: info@denatogroup.com
Toll-Free Phone:
Phone: (905) 823-8883
Fax: (905) 823-5255
Contact: Director of Franchising/Development

Number of Franchises: 41
Company-Owned Units: 0
Total Units: 41

In Business Since: 1985   **Franchising Since:** 1987

Description of Operation: Japanese teriyaki-style fast food, operating in food courts of shopping centers.

Equity Capital Needed: $80,000-$150,000

Franchise Fee: $25,000

Royalty: 6 percent

Advertising Co-op Fee:

Financial Assistance: We will assist in the financial presentation.

Management Assistance: We provide ongoing operational and marketing support with periodic visits.

Training Assistance: We offer 2 weeks of training before opening; theoretical and on-site training. 2 weeks of training during opening is required.

Manchu Wok

816 S. Military Trail Ste. 6
Deerfield Beach, FL 33442
Toll-Free Phone: (800) 423-4009
Phone: (305) 481-9555
Fax: (305) 481-9670
Contact:

Number of Franchises: 133
Company-Owned Units: 62
Total Units: 195

In Business Since: 1980   **Franchising Since:** 1980

Description of Operation: Chinese fast food.

Equity Capital Needed: $200,000-$230,000

Franchise Fee: $20,000

Royalty: 7 percent, plus 1 percent advertising

Advertising Co-op Fee:

Financial Assistance: Yes.

Management Assistance: Ongoing.

Training Assistance: Training is provided in all operations of franchise.

Mark Pi's China Gate

3120 Valleyview Dr.
Columbus, OH 43204
Toll-Free Phone:
Phone: (614) 276-0901
Fax: (614) 276-0917
Contact: President

Number of Franchises: 12
Company-Owned Units: 0
Total Units: 12

In Business Since: 1978   **Franchising Since:** 1992

Description of Operation: Gourmet Chinese restaurants.

Equity Capital Needed: $201,800-$1,061,000

Franchise Fee: $30,000

Royalty: 2-3 percent

Advertising Co-op Fee:

Financial Assistance: Not available.

Management Assistance: We provide real estate, construction, marketing, purchasing, training, and operations assistance.

Training Assistance: Two-week training program for restaurant manager and owner. 5 days of new unit opening assistance.

Mark Pi's Express

3120 Valleyview Drive
Columbus, OH 43204
Toll-Free Phone:
Phone: (614) 276-0901
Fax: (614) 276-0917
Contact: President

Number of Franchises: 32
Company-Owned Units: 0
Total Units: 32

In Business Since: 1992   **Franchising Since:** 1992

Description of Operation: Chinese fast-food restaurant.

Equity Capital Needed: $109,600-479,600

Franchise Fee: $20,000

Royalty: 4 percent

Advertising Co-op Fee: Not data provided.

Financial Assistance: Not available

Management Assistance: We provide real estate, construction, marketing, purchasing, training, and operations assistance.

Training Assistance: Two-week training program for restaurant manager and owner. Five days of new unit operating assistance.

Restaurants—Pizza

Breadeaux Pisa, Inc. D.B.A. Breadeaux Pizza

Frederick Ave. at 23rd St., P.O. Box 6158
St. Joseph, MO 64506
Web Address: www.breadeauxpizza.com
Toll-Free Phone: (800) 835-6534
Phone: (816) 364-1088
Fax: (816) 364-3739
Contact: Vice President Franchise Development

Number of Franchises: 92
Company-Owned Units: 2
Total Units: 94

In Business Since: 1985 **Franchising Since:** 1985

Description of Operation: Pizza restaurants—Sale of pizza to general public. "Original French Crust". Dine-in, carryout and delivery.

Equity Capital Needed: $30,000

Franchise Fee: $15,000

Royalty: 5 percent

Advertising Co-op Fee: 3 percent

Financial Assistance: Third party

Management Assistance: Site-selection approval, architectural support, marketing, payroll, accounting, and owner/manager training both at corporate offices and on-site.

Training Assistance: All aspects of owning and operating a pizza restaurant.

Captain Tony's Pizza & Pasta Emporium

1159 E. Colonial
Orlando, FL 32817
Toll-Free Phone: (800) 332-8669
Phone: (407) 273-6674
Fax: (407) 467-0784
Contact: President

Number of Franchises: 19
Company-Owned Units: 1
Total Units: 20

In Business Since: 1972 **Franchising Since:** 1986

Description of Operation: Pizza franchise.

Equity Capital Needed: $95,000-$125,000

Franchise Fee: $9,500

Royalty: 4-5 percent

Advertising Co-op Fee:

Financial Assistance: Not available.

Management Assistance: Data not available.

Training Assistance: 1 week at company-designated training facility and 2 weeks on-site.

Cassano's Pizza & Subs

1700 E. Stroop Rd.
Dayton, OH 45429
Toll-Free Phone:
Phone: (937) 294-8400
Fax: (937) 294-8107
Contact:

Number of Franchises: 14
Company-Owned Units: 47
Total Units: 61

In Business Since: 1953 **Franchising Since:** 1957

Description of Operation: Cassano's grants franchises to operate Cassano's Pizza & Subs restaurants. The menu features pizza prepared to customer's orders from a selection of ingredients and including our crust, the formulation and preparation of which is a trade secret. Cassano's also offers specially-prepared sandwiches, salads, garlic bread, potato chips and beverages, including beer and wine where available. Cassano's restaurants provides on-premises dining, take-out service, and delivery.

Equity Capital Needed: $141,000-$390,000

Franchise Fee: $10,000

Royalty: 4 percent

Advertising Co-op Fee:

Financial Assistance: Currently, Cassano's does not provide financial assistance. There are, however, lending institutions who are willing to provide financing, based on the strength of the franchisee.

Management Assistance: Cassano's will furnish operating assistance to the franchisee as often as Cassano's deems necessary. This includes guidance in methods of food preparation; packaging and sales; sale of additional authorized products and services; hiring and training of employees; advertising and promotion programs; and establishment and maintenance of administrative, inventory control, and general operating procedures.

Training Assistance: Before opening, the franchisee or manager of the restaurant is required to satisfactorily complete a minimum four-week training program given by Cassano's in Dayton, OH. Cassano's will also provide training for up to 2 additional employees. Training is free of charge, but franchisee is responsible for travel, room, and living expenses while at training. The training program consists of lectures, demonstrations, discussions

and participation in the operation of Cassano's restaurants in the Dayton area.

Chicago's Pizza Franchise

1111 N. Broadway
Greenfield, IN 46140
Toll-Free Phone:
Phone: (317) 462-9878
Fax: (317) 467-1877
Contact: CEO

Number of Franchises: 11
Company-Owned Units: 1
Total Units: 12

In Business Since: 1979   **Franchising Since:** 1982

Description of Operation: Franchisor of pizza, sandwiches, and salads. Inside dining and carryout.

Equity Capital Needed: $75,000-150,000

Franchise Fee: $10,000

Royalty: 4 percent of net sales

Advertising Co-op Fee: 2 percent of net sales

Financial Assistance: None

Management Assistance: Ongoing training and product development.

Training Assistance: Open to close supervision. First two weeks of opening.

Cici's Pizza

1620 Rafe St., Ste. 114
Carrollton, TX 75006
Web Address: www.cicispizza.com
Toll-Free Phone: (800) 398-6259
Phone: (972) 389-2424
Fax: (972) 389-2425
Contact:

Number of Franchises: 90
Company-Owned Units: 10
Total Units: 100

In Business Since: 1985   **Franchising Since:** 1989

Description of Operation: Cici's Pizza provides its guests with delicious pizza, pasta, salad bar and dessert on an all-you-can-eat lunch and dinner buffet. Cici's Pizza also offers a value-priced take-out menu. Our low price, combined with great service and sparkling clean restaurants is making Cici's among the fastest-growing franchises in America!

Equity Capital Needed: $1150,000-$165,000

Franchise Fee: $25,000

Royalty: 0 percent

Advertising Co-op Fee:

Financial Assistance: Cici's provides no corporate funding.

Management Assistance: Full training program. Site selection and development. Overseeing the construction of the restaurant. Purchasing the highest quality products at phenomenally low prices through our distribution company that serves each of our 200+ restaurants. Maximize effectiveness of your restaurant's advertising dollar through market-specific, strategically sound marketing plans.

Training Assistance: Full training program. 12 weeks of hands-on training in a corporate training restaurant.

Domino's Pizza of Canada, Ltd.

Comac Food Group, 1121 Centre St. N., Ste. 440
Calgary, AL T2E 7K6
Toll-Free Phone: (800) 361-1151
Phone: (403) 230-1151
Fax: (403) 230-2182
Contact: Franchise Development Manager

Number of Franchises: 198
Company-Owned Units:
Total Units: 198

In Business Since: 1982   **Franchising Since:** 1982

Description of Operation: Domino's Pizza is an efficient, operations-focused delivery system. It starts with a proprietary pizza sauce, dough, and cheese blend that give each Domino's pizza consistent taste and quality. Each pizza is delivered hot and fresh to the customer within approximately 30 minutes.

Equity Capital Needed: Data not provided

Franchise Fee: Data not provided

Royalty: Data not provided

Advertising Co-op Fee: Data not provided

Financial Assistance: Data not provided

Management Assistance: Data not provided

Training Assistance: Data not provided

Donato's Pizza

935 Taylor Station Rd.
Columbus, OH 43230
Toll-Free Phone: (800) 366-2867
Phone: (614) 864-2444
Fax: (614) 575-4466
Contact:

Number of Franchises: 13
Company-Owned Units: 43
Total Units: 56

In Business Since: 1963   **Franchising Since:** 1991

Description of Operation: High-quality pizza, subs, and salads for dine-in, pick-up, and delivery.

Equity Capital Needed: $300,000-$350,000

Franchise Fee: $15,000

Royalty: 4 percent

Advertising Co-op Fee:

Financial Assistance: Not available.

Management Assistance: Each new franchisee is provided assistance in developing a business plan, securing financing, store development, site selection, ongoing training, and ongoing business consultation.

Training Assistance: The training period lasts between 4-8 weeks, depending upon the franchisee's prior experience. In addition, a field trainer is provided for the first 28 days. Additional assistance is available.

Edwardo's Natural Pizza Restaurants

205 W. Wacker, Ste. 1800
Chicago, IL 60606
Toll-Free Phone: (800) 944-3393
Phone: (312) 346-5455
Fax: (312) 346-8522
Contact: Vice President

Number of Franchises: 17
Company-Owned Units: 12
Total Units: 29

In Business Since: 1978   **Franchising Since:** 1988

Description of Operation: Chicago-style stuffed pizza and more.

Equity Capital Needed: $270,000-$500,000

Franchise Fee: $25,000

Royalty: 5 percent

Advertising Co-op Fee:

Financial Assistance: None.

Management Assistance: We provide on-site training and operational manuals.

Training Assistance: Training includes 8 week sessions in the Chicago training center and 4 training supervisors at the site for 2 weeks on opening of new store.

Fox's Pizza Den

3243 Old Frankstown Rd.
Pittsburgh, PA 15239
Toll-Free Phone: (800) 899-3697
Phone: (412) 733-7888
Fax:
Contact: President

Number of Franchises: 170
Company-Owned Units: 0
Total Units: 170

In Business Since: 1971   **Franchising Since:** 1974

Description of Operation: A complete pizza and sandwich operation, offering both fresh dough and shell pizza. Six different size pizzas, plus a large variety of

sandwiches and Fox's famous Wedgies (a sandwich made on a pizza shell). Franchisee may expand his or her menu as desired. Franchisee may choose a sit-down store or a take-out and delivery only. We have our own commissary to service all your franchise needs.

Equity Capital Needed: $50,000-$60,000

Franchise Fee: $8,000

Royalty: $200 per month

Advertising Co-op Fee:

Financial Assistance: We assist with the business plan and work with prospective franchise and local banks.

Management Assistance: Complete assistance with business plan, site location, assistance with lease, financing, equipment set-up, supervise renovation and on-site training of franchisee and employees. Assistance with bookkeeping and inventory control. We hold their hand from beginning to end.

Training Assistance: 10 days of on-site training at franchisee's own unit. No need to attend out-of-state training schools.

Godfather's Pizza

9140 W. Dodge Rd. Ste. 300
Omaha, NE 68114
Web Address: www.godfathers.com
Toll-Free Phone: (800) 456-8347
Phone: (402) 391-1452
Fax: (402) 255-2685
Contact: Vice President of Sales

Number of Franchises: 376
Company-Owned Units: 148
Total Units: 524

In Business Since: 1973   **Franchising Since:** 1974

Description of Operation: Pizza restaurant, serving 2 types of pizza crust, salads, beverages, and sandwiches.

Equity Capital Needed: $136,500-$291,000

Franchise Fee: $15,000

Royalty: 5 percent

Advertising Co-op Fee:

Financial Assistance: Not available.

Management Assistance: Regional Franchise Managers (RFM's) are assigned to all new franchisees to assist in getting their restaurant opened and operational. Additionally, the RFM's provide support in financial performance, business development, communications, and ongoing training.

Training Assistance: A four-week training program in Omaha, NE at GPI's corporate headquarters, which includes the research and development center, and their key operators. The franchisee is responsible for the cost.

Greco Pizza Donair

105 Walker St. P.O. Box 1040
Truro, NS B2N 5G9
Toll-Free Phone:
Phone: (902) 893-4141
Fax: (902) 895-7635
Contact: Director of Development

Number of Franchises: 48
Company-Owned Units: 6
Total Units: 54

In Business Since: 1977 **Franchising Since:** 1981

Description of Operation: The largest home-delivery chain of pizza, donair and oven-sub sandwiches in Atlantic Canada. Specializing in fast, free delivery.

Equity Capital Needed: $150,000-$180,000 (Canadian)

Franchise Fee: $15,000 (Canadian)

Royalty: 5 percent

Advertising Co-op Fee:

Financial Assistance: Not available.

Management Assistance: Four-week correspondence test before five-week training program, both on and off the site. Ongoing managerial assistance available on an "as required" basis.

Training Assistance: Same as above.

Jake's Pizza

16 Official Rd.
Addison, IL 60101
Toll-Free Phone: (800) 425-2537
Phone: (847) 368-1990
Fax: (847) 368-1995
Contact: President/Chief Executive Officer

Number of Franchises: 38
Company-Owned Units: 1
Total Units: 39

In Business Since: 1961 **Franchising Since:** 1965

Description of Operation: Jake's Pizza specializes in the sale of premium, thin crust, pan, and stuffed pizzas. Eat-in, pick-up and delivery service is provided. Each store has an open "display" kitchen, open to the customer's view.

Equity Capital Needed: $30,000-$50,000

Franchise Fee: $15,000

Royalty: 4-5 percent

Advertising Co-op Fee:

Financial Assistance: There is no direct financing assistance available from the company; however, we can suggest various outside lenders and leasing companies.

Management Assistance: We will aid the opening and ongoing management of the franchise through a "start-up" team and an ongoing support team.

Training Assistance: The training course is for a total of 4 weeks—2 weeks at headquarters and 2 weeks in the field at a corporate store. After the franchise opens, the corporate staff aids in training the franchisee's staff.

Jerry's Subs & Pizza

15942 Shady Grove Rd.
Gaithersburg, MD 20877
Toll-Free Phone:
Phone: (301) 921-8777
Fax: (301) 948-3508
Contact: Director of Franchise Development

Number of Franchises: 100
Company-Owned Units: 3
Total Units: 103

In Business Since: 1954 **Franchising Since:** 1980

Description of Operation: Fresh-dough pizza and over-stuffed submarine sandwiches, served in upscale retail outlets, featuring take-out service and self-service dining.

Equity Capital Needed: $60,000-$90,000

Franchise Fee: $25,000

Royalty: 6 percent

Advertising Co-op Fee:

Financial Assistance: Jerry's meets SBA loan requirements.

Management Assistance: All franchisees receive ongoing management assistance, which includes on-site visits and evaluations designed to maintain the integrity of the franchise. New franchisees receive as much as 10 days of full-time support to assist in their grand opening.

Training Assistance: All franchisees must satisfactorily complete a nine-week training program. Training, which is full-time during this period, is competency-based and includes both practical and classroom instruction. Franchisees will be certified as managers upon completion.

La Pizza Loca

7920 Orangethorpe Ave. Ste. 202
Buena Park, CA 90620
Toll-Free Phone:
Phone: (714) 670-0934
Fax: (714) 670-7849
Contact: Franchise

Number of Franchises: 7
Company-Owned Units: 29
Total Units: 36

In Business Since: 1986 **Franchising Since:** 1991

Description of Operation: Pizza delivery and carry-out company whose restaurants cater to the tastes and customs of the Hispanic community. Unique, Latin-flavored pizzas, competitively promoted price/value strategy, plus guaranteed free delivery in 30 minutes, provides La Pizza Loca customers outstanding quality, value, and service.

Equity Capital Needed: $125,000 total investment (cash-$40,000)

Franchise Fee: $15,000

Royalty: 5 percent

Advertising Co-op Fee:

Financial Assistance: La Pizza Loca will assist franchisees to secure their own independent financing.

Management Assistance: In addition to 4 weeks of formal training and 2 weeks on on-site opening assistance, La Pizza Loca will also provide grand opening and local store marketing planning assistance, as well as ongoing, periodic visits from a La Pizza Loca Franchise Operations Consultant, who will provide guidance and consultation regarding the operation of a La Pizza Loca restaurant.

Training Assistance: An initial training and familiarization course of about 4 weeks in duration is provided to the franchisee and his management team at La Pizza Loca's training school in Buena Park, CA. In addition to the initial training, a La Pizza Loca representative will also provide up to 2 weeks of on-site assistance at the commencement of restaurant operations.

Little Caesars Pizza

Fox Office Center 2211 Woodward Ave.
Detroit, MI 48201
Toll-Free Phone: (800) 553-5776
Phone: (313) 983-6000
Fax: (313) 983-6390
Contact:

Number of Franchises: 3400
Company-Owned Units: 1200
Total Units: 4600

In Business Since: 1959   **Franchising Since:** 1961

Description of Operation: The world's largest carry-out only pizza chain.

Equity Capital Needed: Data not available.

Franchise Fee: $20,000

Royalty: 5 percent

Advertising Co-op Fee:

Financial Assistance: Third-party financing is available in Canada and the USA.

Management Assistance: Each franchisee is assigned personnel qualified in marketing, operations, finance, real estate, architecture, and design.

Training Assistance: The initial training school is 7 weeks in duration and covers every aspect of the business. There are continuing, ongoing classes as well.

Mamma Ilardo's Pizzerias

3600 Clipper Mill Rd. Ste. 266
Baltimore, MD 21211
Toll-Free Phone:

Phone: (410) 662-1930
Fax: (410) 662-1936
Contact:

Number of Franchises: 50
Company-Owned Units: 2
Total Units: 52

In Business Since: 1976   **Franchising Since:** 1985

Description of Operation: Quick-service pizza by the slice, whole pizza, and calzone. In food courts, in-line and express units, hospitals, airports, and train stations.

Equity Capital Needed: $30,000-$100,000

Franchise Fee: $25,000 standard; $15,000 express.

Royalty: 6 percent or 4 percent express

Advertising Co-op Fee:

Financial Assistance: No.

Management Assistance: Eight weeks of training in operations-marketing, design support, and in-depth review of all phases of unit operation. Also, work three weeks on-site with approved extensions. Managerial support is limited except through training! Franchisee is responsible for all hiring and management.

Training Assistance: See above.

Marco's Pizza

5252 Monroe St.
Toledo, OH 43623
Web Address: www.marcospizza.com
Toll-Free Phone: (800) 262-7267
Phone: (419) 885-7000
Fax: (419) 885-5215
Contact: Director of Franchise Sales

Number of Franchises: 34
Company-Owned Units: 118
Total Units: 152

In Business Since: 1978   **Franchising Since:** 1979

Description of Operation: Marco's Pizza stores offer pizza, hot sub sandwiches, and cheese bread for carry-out and delivery. The company was established in Toledo, OH in 1978 and has grown steadily to over 100 stores in Ohio, Michigan, Indiana, and Pennsylvania. Marco's Pizza has built its business on a strong foundation of excellent quality products., superb customer service, and great value.

Equity Capital Needed: $45,000-65,000

Franchise Fee: $12,000

Royalty: 5 percent

Advertising Co-op Fee: Data not available.

Financial Assistance: No direct financing from Marco's is available. Marco's assists its new franchisees in obtaining bank financing or equipment leasing, depending on the franchisee's financial strength.

Management Assistance: Marco's Pizza franchisees are well-supported by the Marco's Franchise Department. Each franchisee is assigned an expert franchise representative to help ensure his/her success. Each store is visited a minimum of twice a month by the franchise representative to help the franchisee and consult with him/her on any necessary matters. Marco's Pizza provides its franchisees a complete set of training, operations, and administrative manuals.

Training Assistance: Each new Marco's Pizza franchisee is trained in each and every aspect of the Marco's Pizza system, including marketing, advertising, and administration. The training program is approximately 8 weeks in duration, 2-4 of which are held at the corporate training center. Prior food service or related experience is required.

Mary's Pizza Shack

P.O. Box 1049
Boyes Hot Spring, CA 95416
Toll-Free Phone:
Phone: (707) 938-3602
Fax: (707) 938-5976
Contact: President

Number of Franchises: 2
Company-Owned Units: 9
Total Units: 11

In Business Since: 1959   **Franchising Since:** 1990

Description of Operation: Full-service restaurant, serving pizza and Italian dishes developed by our founder Mary Fazio. We have successfully created a niche between typical pizza parlors and high-end Italian restaurants. We also have developed delivery systems in many of our locations.

Equity Capital Needed: $250,000

Franchise Fee: $30,000

Royalty: 5 percent

Advertising Co-op Fee:

Financial Assistance: Data not available.

Management Assistance: Each franchisee has the ongoing support of a district supervisor for overall restaurant operations and a kitchen supervisor for quality control and assistance of food preparation procedures. Also available is advertising and local marketing assistance from the corporate office.

Training Assistance: 6-8 weeks of in-field and classroom training is provided to the owner and manager. Also included is restaurant staff training one week before the opening and two weeks after the opening.

Mazzio's Pizza

4441 South 72nd East Ave.
Tulsa, OK 74145-4692
Toll-Free Phone: (800) 827-1910

Phone:
Fax: (918) 641-1236
Contact: Manager of Brand Development/Licensing

Number of Franchises: 145
Company-Owned Units: 105
Total Units: 250

In Business Since: 1961   **Franchising Since:** 1979

Description of Operation: Mazzio's Pizza was founded in 1979 by Mazzio's Corporation, which has been in the pizza business since 1961. Mazzio's Corporation is a privately held company and is still principally owned by its founder, Ken Selby. Mazzio's Pizza offers a clearly superior product in an exterior and interior design package that is second to none. Mazzio's offers pizza, pasta, appetizers, sandwiches, and salads, giving our guests the options of dine-in, carryout, and delivery. Mazzio's Pizza is able to provide today's demanding consumer with quality and high value in a "fun" and upscale atmosphere.

Equity Capital Needed: $200,000

Franchise Fee: $20,000

Royalty: 3 percent of net sales

Advertising Co-op Fee: 1 percent of net sales

Financial Assistance: Mazzio's Corporation does not offer and "direct" financing. AT&T Capital Corporation has designated Mazzio's Pizza as a Preferred Franchise Account for SBA guaranteed loans. Franchisees may qualify for this "indirect" financing.

Management Assistance: Franchisees are provided ongoing supervision and support from an experienced franchise operations representative through periodic visits. Franchisees are updated on all new products, suppliers, equipment, inventory control, advertising, and much more through weekly manager's reports, monthly newsletters, and regular direct contact from our staff.

Training Assistance: An 8 week training program at the corporate headquarters in Tulsa, Oklahoma is provided for the franchisee and management team consisting of three people. This program has been designed to cover vital areas of importance to your success as a franchise owner. Upon opening, 3 1/2 weeks will be provided.

Mellow Mushroom Pizza

695 North Ave. NE
Atlanta, GA 30308
Web Address: www.mellowmushroom.com
E-mail Address: franchise@mellowmushroom.com
Toll-Free Phone:
Phone: (404) 524-6133
Fax: (404) 223-5419
Contact: Vice President

Number of Franchises: 34
Company-Owned Units: 0
Total Units: 34

In Business Since: 1974   **Franchising Since:** 1985

Description of Operation: Pizza and sandwich restaurants.

Equity Capital Needed: $100,000

Franchise Fee: $40,000

Royalty: 5 percent

Advertising Co-op Fee:

Financial Assistance: Lease negotiations, equipment consulting and build-out consulting.

Management Assistance: We provide hands-on training in the operating location.

Training Assistance: Hands-on training in operating location.

Mr. Jim's Pizza

4276 Kellway Circle
Addison, TX 75244
Toll-Free Phone: (800) 583-5960
Phone:
Fax: (214) 247-5463
Contact: Executive Director

Number of Franchises: 48
Company-Owned Units: 2
Total Units: 50

In Business Since: 1977   **Franchising Since:** 1981

Description of Operation: Pizza carry out and delivery.

Equity Capital Needed: $50,000

Franchise Fee: $10,000

Royalty: 4 percent

Advertising Co-op Fee:

Financial Assistance: None.

Management Assistance: Business courses available.

Training Assistance: 300 hours in store for pre-opening. First 10 days at your location for pre-opening. Yearly seminars and meetings.

Papa Murphy's International

8000 N.E. Parkway Dr., #350
Vancouver, WA 98662
Toll-Free Phone: (800) 257-7272
Phone: (360) 260-7272
Fax: (360) 260-0500
Contact: V.P. of Franchising

Number of Franchises: 291
Company-Owned Units: 0
Total Units: 291

In Business Since: 1981   **Franchising Since:** 1982

Description of Operation: We are a take and bake pizza franchise. Offering customers a high quality meal replacement at a great value.

Equity Capital Needed:

Franchise Fee: $25,000

Royalty: 5 percent-weekly

Advertising Co-op Fee: 1 percent national ad

Financial Assistance: We will assist in providing information on third-party financing.

Management Assistance: Not provided

Training Assistance: We have 5 weeks of both corporate and in store training.

Paul Revere's Pizza

1570-42nd St. N.E.
Cedar Rapids, IA 52402
Web Address: www.paulreverespizza.com
E-mail Address: mrpr1000@aol.com
Toll-Free Phone: (800) 995-9437
Phone: (319) 395-9113
Fax: (319) 395-9115
Contact:

Number of Franchises: 50
Company-Owned Units: 6
Total Units: 56

In Business Since: 1975   **Franchising Since:** 1981

Description of Operation: Pizza delivery, take-out, and sit-down.

Equity Capital Needed: $53,000-$105,000

Franchise Fee: $10,000

Royalty: 4 percent

Advertising Co-op Fee:

Financial Assistance: None.

Management Assistance: We provide site selection, equipment, accounting, and store layout. POS installation.

Training Assistance: We offer 4 weeks of in-store training.

Peter Piper Pizza

236 E. Camelback Rd.
Phoenix, AZ 85016
Toll-Free Phone: (800) 899-3425
Phone: (602) 995-1975
Fax: (602) 995-8857
Contact: Director of Franchise Sales

Number of Franchises: 65
Company-Owned Units: 27
Total Units: 92

In Business Since: 1972   **Franchising Since:** 1976

Description of Operation: Quality, value-priced, family-fun pizza restaurants. Large facilities make us the favorite place for teams, large groups, and parties. Our casual, fun atmosphere of videos and redemption games, bawl crawl, and tubes and pinballs appeals to the entire family.

Equity Capital Needed: $250,000-$300,000

Franchise Fee: $25,000

Royalty: 5 percent

Advertising Co-op Fee:

Financial Assistance: We will provide sources for SBA and other lending organizations.

Management Assistance: 6 weeks of manager training and 3 weeks of opening team assistance. Ongoing operational visits at the facility.

Training Assistance: 6 weeks of training, as needed. Manuals for operations and marketing provided. Training videos available.

Pizza Factory, Inc.

49430 Road 426
Oakhurst, CA 93644
Web Address: www.pizzafactoryinc.com
E-mail Address: pfinc@sierratel.com
Toll-Free Phone: (800) 654-4840
Phone: (209) 683-3377
Fax: (209) 683-6879
Contact: National Marketing Director

Number of Franchises: 88
Company-Owned Units: 3
Total Units: 91

In Business Since: 1979 **Franchising Since:** 1985

Description of Operation: Family restaurant featuring homemade hand-tossed pizza, pasta, sandwiches. Dine-in, take-out, or delivery. Our company specializes in placing Pizza Factories in small communities of 15,000 or less. It's a wonderful opportunity to be your own boss while having the security of a proven franchise. People are looking for a simpler, safer way of life. We have a proven product in our award-winning pizza and are actively seeking people from all walks of life who want to make a career change. Community minded. Our motto and logo: "We toss'em, They're Awesome".

Equity Capital Needed: $150,000

Franchise Fee: $20,000

Royalty: 4 percent

Advertising Co-op Fee: 1 percent

Financial Assistance: Partial financing on equipment.

Management Assistance:

Training Assistance: Franchisees are required to train a minimum of 325 hours at one of our training facilities.

Pizza Pit

4253 Argosy Court
Madison, WI
Toll-Free Phone:
Phone: (608) 221-6777

Fax: (608) 221-6771
Contact: Vice President

Number of Franchises: 26
Company-Owned Units: 10
Total Units: 36

In Business Since: 1969 **Franchising Since:** 1984

Description of Operation: Free home delivery and carry-out of hand-crafted pizzas, specialty sandwiches, pasta and salads. The units are also adaptable to inside seating. Single and multiple-unit programs are available. Merged business concepts with family fun centers, bowling centers, and convenience stores.

Equity Capital Needed: $125,280-$264,740

Franchise Fee: $16,000-$17,500

Royalty: 5.5-6.5 percent + 1 percent advertising fee

Advertising Co-op Fee:

Financial Assistance: None.

Management Assistance: Pizza Pit offers ongoing assistance to all franchise locations. We have operations advisors that make routine visits to assist management in the operation of Pizza Pit.

Training Assistance: We provide a comprehensive training program that covers all aspects of the operation of a Pizza Pit Restaurant, from order taking to profit planning.

Pizza Pizza

580 Jarvis St.
Toronto, ON M4Y 2H9
Toll-Free Phone: (800) 263-5556
Phone: (416) 967-1010
Fax: (416) 967-0891
Contact: Vice President of Franchising

Number of Franchises: 265
Company-Owned Units: 76
Total Units: 341

In Business Since: 1968 **Franchising Since:** 1972

Description of Operation: Pizza Pizza Limited is Canada's leading pizza chain, consisting mainly of take-out and delivery stores with a menu that includes pizza, salads, wings, subs and Italian dinners. Even after twenty-five years in business, Pizza Pizza continues to be a fast-paced, entrepreneurial corporation.

Equity Capital Needed: $100,000-$200,000 (to purchase turn-key business).

Franchise Fee: $20,000 (included in above price).

Royalty: 6 percent

Advertising Co-op Fee:

Financial Assistance: Help to find financing.

Management Assistance: Each store is assigned an area market representative who provides assistance on an ongoing basis. In addition, the franchisor provides various

service departments, such as accounting, real estate, and marketing, which franchisees can access as needed.

Training Assistance: An intensive ten week program combines classroom and test kitchen training with in-store practical experience. A new franchisee who successfully completes this course should understand all aspects of a Pizza Pizza outlet.

Rocky Rococo Pan Style Pizza

105 E. Wisconsin Ave. Ste. 204
Oconomowoc, WI 53066
Toll-Free Phone: (800) 888-7625
Phone: (414) 569-5580
Fax: (414) 569-5591
Contact: President

Number of Franchises: 30
Company-Owned Units: 20
Total Units: 50

In Business Since: 1974   **Franchising Since:** 1974

Description of Operation: Pizza restaurant providing full dining, carry-out, drive-thru, delivery service and featuring pizza by the slice.

Equity Capital Needed: $50,000-$150,000

Franchise Fee: $15,000

Royalty: 4 percent

Advertising Co-op Fee:

Financial Assistance: None.

Management Assistance: We provide continual business assistance in areas such as real estate, construction, operations (from restaurant opening to regular visits), marketing, finance, and quality assurance.

Training Assistance: We offer a six-week manager training program, combination of classroom and in-restaurant, as well as various 1-2 day seminars.

Snappy Tomato Pizza Company

P.O. Box 336
Florence, KY 41022
Toll-Free Phone:
Phone: (606) 283-2770
Fax: (606) 525-4686
Contact:

Number of Franchises: 40
Company-Owned Units: 4
Total Units: 44

In Business Since: 1993   **Franchising Since:** 1993

Description of Operation: Snappy Tomato Pizza Company is a delivery, dine-in and carry-out pizzeria that offers the highest-quality pizza available. Our menu also includes hoagies, salads, and our award-winning "Ranch Pizza." As a franchisee, you will take part in the preparation of dough and other products on a daily basis for maximum freshness, without paying over-inflated commis-

sary prices. Franchise owners also enjoy multiple store buying power discounts.

Equity Capital Needed: $70,000

Franchise Fee: $15,000

Royalty: 5 percent royalty + 2.5 percent advertising

Advertising Co-op Fee:

Financial Assistance: Financing is not available.

Management Assistance: Corporate representatives will assist in opening of the store.

Training Assistance: A four-week training program covers every aspect of the business, including actual time in stores getting hands-on experience.

Straw Hat Cooperative Corporation

6400 Village Pkwy.
Dublin, CA 94568
Web Address: www.strawhatpizza.com
E-mail Address: info@strawhatpizza.com
Toll-Free Phone:
Phone: (510) 829-1500
Fax Number: (510) 829-9533
Contact: President

Number of Franchises: 60
Company-Owned Units: 0
Total Units: 60

In Business Since: 1961   **Franchising Since:** 1969

Description of Operation: Operating community-based pizza restaurants throughout the western states. Providing dine-in, take-out, and delivery service. Straw Hat Pizza is operated as a cooperative whereby individual store owners also own the parent "franchise" company. Initial and ongoing fees are extremely low giving store owners a decided advantage. Straw Hat offers all of the advantages of a nationally recognized brand without the high fees or control of conventional franchises. Straw Hat is best matched to the entrepreneur who has a clear idea of how their success will come in a competitive market.

Equity: $250,000

Franchise Fee: $10,000

Royalty: 2.75 percent total

Advertising Co-op Fee: None

Financial Assistance: Straw Hat does not provide financing. Straw Hat can provide referrals and assistance in obtaining financing.

Managerial Assistance: A comprehensive four-week hands-on training program is required and provided to new members. Following the opening of your store, field support is provided in an ongoing basis by a Region V.P. A full comprehensive set of operations manuals are provided as part of your membership.

Training Assistance: The initial training is provided in a four-week course at an actual operating restaurant. Additional training is provided thereafter in area owner

meetings, regional meetings, in-store consultations, and regular printer communications.

Stuft Pizza

1040 Calle Cordillera Ste. 103
San Clemente, CA 92673
Web Address: www.stuftpizzafran.com
Toll-Free Phone:
Phone: (714) 361-2522
Fax: (714) 361-2501
Contact: President

Number of Franchises: 26
Company-Owned Units: 1
Total Units: 27

In Business Since: 1976 **Franchising Since:** 1985

Description of Operation: Award-winning pizza—from take-out to restaurant and microbrewery.

Equity Capital Needed: $100,000-$300,000

Franchise Fee: $25,000

Royalty: 3 percent

Advertising Co-op Fee:

Financial Assistance: No company financing is available.

Management Assistance: Training and follow-up meetings.

Training Assistance: Data not available.

Tom's House of Pizza

7730 Macleod Tr. S.
Calgary, AB T2H 0L9
Toll-Free Phone:
Phone: (403) 252-0111
Fax:
Contact: Vice President

Number of Franchises: 2
Company-Owned Units: 2
Total Units: 4

In Business Since: 1963 **Franchising Since:** 1963

Description of Operation: Restaurant and lounge operation, specializing in thin-crusted pizza. Family atmosphere.

Equity Capital Needed: $130,000

Franchise Fee: $5,000

Royalty: $500 per month

Advertising Co-op Fee:

Financial Assistance: Assistance is available with either the head company, participating in ownership for first 3 years, or as a straight loan, 25 percent down payment.

Management Assistance: Data not available.

Training Assistance: Training is provided at the head office location for about 4-6 weeks.

Restaurants—Sandwich

Brown Baggers

1919 S. 40th St., Ste. 202
Lincoln, NE 68506
Toll-Free Phone: (800) 865-2378
Phone: (402) 434-5620
Fax: (402) 434-5624
Contact: President

Number of Franchises: 1
Company-Owned Units: 2
Total Units: 3

In Business Since: 1988 **Franchising Since:** 1993

Description of Operation: Brown Baggers offers a healthy alternative to "fast food" establishments. Inside a clean, comfortable sandwich shop you will find healthy and hearty sandwiches and side items. The sandwiches are served on homemade, freshly baked bread. We offer fresh meat, cheese, vegetables, an array of side salads, and desserts. In addition, we offer catering services and delivery to business customers.

Equity Capital Needed: $100,000

Franchise Fee: $20,000

Royalty: 5 percent

Advertising Co-op Fee: 1 percent

Financial Assistance: Current financial review, support on business plan, and third party lenders available.

Management Assistance: Complete training, software program, manuals, follow-up, and an 800 number provided.

Training Assistance: One week at home office and one week on-site. Additional training provided as required.

Cold Cut Kruise

25820 Southfield Rd., Ste. 201
Southfield, MI 48075
Web Address: www.wfcnet.com
E-mail Address: wfc@cris.com
Toll-Free Phone:
Phone: (248) 559-1415
Fax:
Contact: Sales Director

Number of Franchises: 0
Company-Owned Units: 1
Total Units: 1

In Business Since: 1996 **Franchising Since:** 1999

Description of Operation: Drive-through deli. Using the staffing and marketing based on one-price sandwich—regardless of the meats used—per broad type. For example, onion roll, bagel, rye bread, or white bread. Motif: "Cruising in the Car."

Equity Capital Needed: $100,000

Franchise Fee: $10,000

Royalty: 4 percent

Advertising Co-op Fee: None

Financial Assistance: Assistance with S.B.A.

Management Assistance: Complete store design, managerial systems, marketing plans, inventory control, and so on. Ongoing support.

Training Assistance: Four weeks, two in own location.

Cousins Subs

N83 W13400 Leon Rd.
Menomonee Falls, WI 53051
Web Address: www.cousinssubs.com
Toll-Free Phone: (800) 238-9736
Phone: (414) 253-7700
Fax: (414) 253-7710
Contact: **Executive Vice President of Franchise Development**

Number of Franchises: 92
Company-Owned Units: 35
Total Units: 127

In Business Since: 1972   **Franchising Since:** 1985

Description of Operation: Uniquely developed submarine sandwich operation, with over 25 years of expertise. Volume-oriented, fast-service concept in an upscale, in-line, strip, or free-standing location, some with drive-up windows. Outstanding, fresh-baked bread and the finest quality ingredients go into our hot and cold subs, delicious soups, and garden-fresh salads. Franchising opportunities are available for a select group of single, multiunit, and area developer franchisees.

Equity Capital Needed: $50,000-$100,000 liquid

Franchise Fee: $12,500

Royalty: 6-4 percent

Advertising Co-op Fee:

Financial Assistance: SBA source, equipment package leasing sources.

Management Assistance: Initially, Cousins provides design criteria and resource manual, franchise manual, operations manual, real estate site selection manual, sandwich making manual, modular video training program, and recommended supplier list. Additionally, Cousins provides ongoing seminars and training classes. A franchise area representative meets with each franchise location management 3 times per month to maintain communications and assist in problem solving.

Training Assistance: Training includes a store-building seminar for site selection, lease negotiation and construction, 24 days of hands-on training, plus 10 days of opening assistance and training. National and local store marketing support.

Erbert & Gerbert's Subs & Clubs

320 Graham Ave.
Eau Claire, WI 54701
Toll-Free Phone: (800) 283-5241
Phone: (715) 833-1375
Fax: (715) 833-8523
Contact: **President/Chief Executive Officer**

Number of Franchises: 15
Company-Owned Units: 1
Total Units: 16

In Business Since: 1988   **Franchising Since:** 1992

Description of Operation: Erbert and Gerbert's stores offer top-quality, gourmet submarine and club sandwiches on bread baked fresh on-site. A delivery service compliments eat-in and carry-out services.

Equity Capital Needed: $75,000-$150,000

Franchise Fee: $9,500

Royalty: 6.5 percent

Advertising Co-op Fee:

Financial Assistance: None available.

Management Assistance: Quarterly franchisee meetings cover advertising, labor and scheduling, cost control, quality control, and other key management issues. Annual conventions focus more intensely on those same issues over three-day periods. Newsletters supplement the face-to-face communication and training.

Training Assistance: A two-week training program involves 1 week of in-store, hands-on training in a company store. Scheduling, food preparation, cash control, and quality standards are covered in this weekly section. The second week involves administrative and management training required for cost control, payroll, financial management, and so on. This is followed by 1 week of training at the time of start-up in the franchisee's store.

Giff's Sub Shop

4 Cambridge Ave.
Fort Walton Beach, FL 32547
Toll-Free Phone:
Phone: (850) 864-5468
Fax:
Contact:

Number of Franchises: 6
Company-Owned Units: 1
Total Units: 7

In Business Since: 1977   **Franchising Since:** 1985

Description of Operation: Subs and salads—featuring steaksubs. Home of the famous "Fighter Pilot Sub." Some stores offer breakfast, subs, and biscuits. Average store employees 3-5 people.

Equity Capital Needed: $25,000-$30,000

Franchise Fee: $7,500

Royalty: 4 percent

Advertising Co-op Fee:

Financial Assistance: Giff's offers no financial assistance.

Management Assistance: None.

Training Assistance: The new franchisee is trained for 1 week at home office and in the field as long as needed to operate successfully. They are also taught public relations, hiring practices, bookkeeping, and food management. Our training manual covers everything needed to successfully operate a Giff's Sub Shop.

Gorin's Homemade Cafe & Grill

57 Executive Park S., Ste. 440
Atlanta, GA 30329-2213
Toll-Free Phone: (888) 489-7277
Phone: (404) 248-9900
Fax: (404) 248-0180
Contact: Franchise Development

Number of Franchises: 37
Company-Owned Units: 3
Total Units: 40

In Business Since: 1981   **Franchising Since:** 1983

Description of Operation: Quick serve restaurant featuring unique "grilled" sandwiches, cheesesteaks, and signature ice cream.

Equity Capital Needed: $85-95,000 liquid/$250-300,000 net worth

Franchise Fee: $18,500

Royalty: 5 percent

Advertising Co-op Fee: 2 percent

Financial Assistance: We will assist in finding financing but make no claims to guarantee any loans.

Management Assistance: We provide "hands on" training with accompanying manuals and guidelines for every aspect of restaurant management as well as continued supervision and constant support.

Training Assistance: We offer 3-4 weeks of comprehensive training in all aspects of the operation for up to 2 managers. Also at store opening, our District Managers provide training on-site for the restaurant employees as well as assist with the actual opening.

Jimmy John's

600 Tollgate Rd. Ste. B
Elgin, IL 60123
Toll-Free Phone:
Phone: (847) 888-7206
Fax: (847) 888-7070
Contact:

Number of Franchises: 0
Company-Owned Units: 11
Total Units: 11

In Business Since: 1983   **Franchising Since:** 1993

Description of Operation: Franchisor of Jimmy John's gourmet sandwich shops, which make, sell, and deliver an upscale signature line of french bread subs and wheat club sandwiches. Stores require small investment and can be located in strip centers, downtown store frontages, and food courts in malls.

Equity Capital Needed: $55,000-$127,000

Franchise Fee: $25,000

Royalty: 5.5 percent

Advertising Co-op Fee:

Financial Assistance: No direct financing assistance is available; however, we will provide necessary financial information to potential lending entities.

Management Assistance: 6 weeks of training is provided at corporate store location. This includes both operational and marketing assistance. Pre-opening assistance includes construction plans, site location, and lease management.

Training Assistance: Same as above.

Larry's Giant Subs

8616 Baymeadows Rd.
Jacksonville, FL 32256
Toll-Free Phone: (800) 358-6870
Phone: (904) 739-2498
Fax: (904) 739-2502
Contact:

Number of Franchises: 28
Company-Owned Units: 2
Total Units: 30

In Business Since: 1982   **Franchising Since:** 1986

Description of Operation: Own your own sandwich shop. Larry's Giant Subs is an upscale, New York-style, sandwich shop, featuring 50 varieties of subs and numerous salads. Franchise features easy operation, no experience necessary, non-cooking environment and low royalty.

Equity Capital Needed: $45,000-$55,000

Franchise Fee: $11,000

Royalty: 5 percent

Advertising Co-op Fee:

Financial Assistance: None.

Management Assistance: 24-hour hotline and problem assistance. Accounting systems.

Training Assistance: Site selection, complete demographics, equipment purchases, 30 days of training at franchise headquarters, and training of key employees. First-week opening assistance so things run smoothly. Advertising programs.

Mr. Goodcents Franchise Systems

16210 W. 110th St.
Lenexa, KS 66219
Web Address: www.mrgoodcent.com
E-mail Address: frandev@mrgoodcents.com
Toll-Free Phone: (800) 648-2368
Phone: (913) 888-9800
Fax: (913) 888-8427
Contact:

Number of Franchises: 113
Company-Owned Units: 5
Total Units: 118

In Business Since: 1988 **Franchising Since:** 1990

Description of Operation: Quick-service-dine-in, carry out, or delivery. Serving submarine sandwiches and pasta.

Equity Capital Needed: $73,750-$150,250

Franchise Fee: $12,500

Royalty: 5 percent of gross receipts

Advertising Co-op Fee:

Financial Assistance: Not available.

Management Assistance: Operations management field service for consultation, marketing, administration, real estate, and lease negotiating assistance.

Training Assistance: A minimum of thirty days of training for new owners on operations and administration. Operations and training manuals, site selecting, and sales building.

My Friend's Place

106 Hammond Dr.
Atlanta, GA 30328
Toll-Free Phone:
Phone: (404) 843-3803
Fax: (404) 843-0371
Contact: Vice President

Number of Franchises: 10
Company-Owned Units: 2
Total Units: 12

In Business Since: 1980 **Franchising Since:** 1990

Description of Operation: Sandwich shops, catering to quality-oriented customers interested in a quick, light, and

healthy lunch. Specializing in sandwiches, salads, soups, and homemade desserts. We are a "Fresh Food Express."

Equity Capital Needed: $95,000-$175,000

Franchise Fee: $17,500

Royalty: Fixed service fee. Contact franchisor.

Advertising Co-op Fee:

Financial Assistance: Not available.

Management Assistance: Assistance in site selection.

Training Assistance: Extensive training for a 4 week period. Additional training when and if required. Ongoing training seminars for new products, equipment, and techniques.

Nathan's Famous

1400 Old Country Rd., Ste. 400
Westbury, NY 11590
Web Address: www.nathansfamous.com
Toll-Free Phone: (800) 628-4267
Phone: (516) 338-8500
Fax: (516) 338-7220
Contact: Senior Vice President

Number of Franchises: 163
Company-Owned Units: 16
Total Units: 179

In Business Since: 1916 **Franchising Since:** 1979

Description of Operation: Nathan's Famous offers a large variety of menu items, featuring our world-famous, all-beef frankfurter and fresh-cut french fries in a contemporary atmosphere. Nathan's Famous offers 8 different prototypes, ranging from countertop modulars to free-standing restaurants-adaptable to all market considerations.

Equity Capital Needed: $150,000-$200,000

Franchise Fee: $30,000

Royalty: 4.5 percent

Advertising Co-op Fee:

Financial Assistance: Yes.

Management Assistance: The company offers site selection, lease negotiations, and ongoing support.

Training Assistance: We provide comprehensive training to principals, managers, and crew.

Pastel's Cafe

1121 Centre St. N. Ste. 440
Calgary, AB T2E 7K6
Toll-Free Phone: (800) 361-1151
Phone: (403) 230-1151
Fax: (403) 230-2182
Contact:

Number of Franchises: 18
Company-Owned Units: 0
Total Units: 18

In Business Since: 1980 Franchising Since: 1981

Description of Operation: Pastel's, founded in 1980, features a full menu of the finest-quality gourmet sandwiches, a mouth-watering array of specialty salads and hearty home-made soups, all prepared with fresh, healthy ingredients and presented with style.

Equity Capital Needed: $125,000-$200,000

Franchise Fee: $25,000

Royalty: 5 percent

Advertising Co-op Fee:

Financial Assistance: Royal Bank of Canada

Management Assistance: Day-to-day operations, marketing and promotions, administrative functions, supplier requirements, staff training, and quality control analysis done every quarter.

Training Assistance: Up to 21 days of hands-on training in every facet of the business.

Penn Station Steak & Sub

8276 Beechmont Ave.
Cincinnati, OH 45255
Toll-Free Phone:
Phone: (513) 474-3153
Fax: (513) 474-7116
Contact:

Number of Franchises: 16
Company-Owned Units: 0
Total Units: 16

In Business Since: 1985 Franchising Since: 1988

Description of Operation: Retail sale of various cheesecake and submarine sandwiches, fresh-cut fries, and fresh-squeezed lemonade.

Equity Capital Needed: $140,000-$180,000

Franchise Fee: $17,500

Royalty: 6 percent

Advertising Co-op Fee:

Financial Assistance: We will assist in the loan application process only.

Management Assistance: We have area representatives responsible for supervision of franchisees in a given area.

Training Assistance: We offer 7-10 days of training before opening and 7-10 days of training after opening.

Philly Connection

120 Interstate N. Pkway., E. Ste. 112
Atlanta, GA 30339
Toll-Free Phone: (800) 886-8826
Phone: (770) 952-6152
Fax: (770) 952-3168
Contact: Office Manager

Number of Franchises: 23
Company-Owned Units: 0
Total Units: 23

In Business Since: 1985 Franchising Since: 1987

Description of Operation: Fast-food franchise, specializing in Philly cheesesteaks, hoagies, and salads.

Equity Capital Needed: $100,000

Franchise Fee: $20,000

Royalty: 5 percent

Advertising Co-op Fee: 2 percent

Financial Assistance: None.

Management Assistance: Each new franchisee will receive assistance for the construction of his/her store, manuals will be provided for the operation, marketing ideas, and accounting services will be offered.

Training Assistance: New franchisees will train in Atlanta, GA, with other franchisees before the opening of their store. For the first week of opening, the corporate office will provide full-time on-site assistance. The corporate office periodically offers assistance to all franchisees.

Subway

325 Bic Dr.
Milford, CT 06460
Web Address: www.subway.com
Toll-Free Phone: (800) 888-4848
Phone: (203) 877-4281
Fax: (203) 876-6674
Contact: Director of Franchise Sales

Number of Franchises: 13016
Company-Owned Units: 0
Total Units: 13016

In Business Since: 1965 Franchising Since: 1974

Description of Operation: World's largest submarine sandwich and salad chain. Open in all 50 states and 64 countries. Rated the number one franchise 8 times by Entrepreneur Magazine. National TV advertising.

Equity Capital Needed: $65,000-$140,000

Franchise Fee: $10,000

Royalty: 8 percent

Advertising Co-op Fee:

Financial Assistance: Equipment leasing is available for qualified franchisees.

Management Assistance: Subway provides field assistance in site selection, lease negotiations, and opening week, plus a monthly unit inspection and evaluation.

Training Assistance: An intensive two-week training program covers the fundamentals of establishing and operating a Subway store. The training takes place in the classroom and in an actual Subway unit.

Thundercloud Subs

1102 W. 6th St.
Austin, TX 78703
Web Address: www.thundercloud.com
E-mail Address: thunder@onr.com
Toll-Free Phone:
Phone: (512) 479-8805
Fax: (512) 479-8806
Contact:

Number of Franchises: 28
Company-Owned Units: 8
Total Units: 36

In Business Since: 1975   **Franchising Since:** 1981

Description of Operation: Thundercloud prepares fresh submarine sandwiches, salads and soups as well as offering smoothies at some locations. The concept is based on a combination of unique character and fast, healthy food. The units occupy 800 to 1,200 square feet in retail strip centers, and free-standing sites. Full seating, limited seating, drive-thru, or drive-thru only.

Equity Capital Needed: $46,000-$126,500

Franchise Fee: $10,000

Royalty: 4 percent

Advertising Co-op Fee:

Financial Assistance: Not available.

Management Assistance: We provide hands-on, in-store assistance during the initial operating period, as well as periodic evaluations and in-store assistance as required, and training at headquarters.

Training Assistance: Training is tailored to the needs of the franchisee and is conducted in advance of opening in a company-owned store and on-site following opening.

Togo's Eatery

900 E. Campbell Ave., Ste. 1
Campbell, CA 95008
Toll-Free Phone: (800) 777-9983
Phone:
Fax: (404) 377-4130
Contact:

Number of Franchises: 150
Company-Owned Units: 9
Total Units: 159

In Business Since: 1977   **Franchising Since:** 1977

Description of Operation: Fast-food sandwiches

Equity Capital Needed: $140,000-$180,000

Franchise Fee: $12,500-$35,000

Royalty: 5 percent

Advertising Co-op Fee:

Financial Assistance: None.

Management Assistance: We provide purchasing, cost control, sanitation, product development, promotion, and general assistance for the life of the franchise.

Training Assistance: We offer 2 weeks of on-site training with periodic follow-up.

Tubby's Sub Shop

6029 E. 14 Mile Rd.
Sterling Heights, MI 48312
Web Address: www.tubby.com
E-mail Address: tonys@tubby.com
Toll-Free Phone: (800) 752-0644
Phone: (810) 978-8829
Fax: (810) 977-8083
Contact:

Number of Franchises: 87
Company-Owned Units: 3
Total Units: 90

In Business Since: 1968   **Franchising Since:** 1978

Description of Operation: Specialty submarine sandwich shop, featuring grilled sandwiches, soups, and salads.

Equity Capital Needed: $45,000-$100,000

Franchise Fee: $15,000 traditional; $8,000 non

Royalty: 3.5 percent plus 6 percent advertising

Advertising Co-op Fee:

Financial Assistance: We have relationships with third-party financiers.

Management Assistance: Every aspect of managing your business is addressed, from marketing to customer service classes to "how to structure your company and how to manage it financially." We also assist in site selection, lease negotiations, and provide construction drawings from our engineers. Complete equipment packages are available from subsidiary company, Subline, Inc. Ongoing advertising and local store marketing support is given, along with frequent visits to your site from experts. Complete grand opening package.

Training Assistance: We provide a comprehensive 2 week training program-both in-store and classroom sessions. Every facet of your business is covered. Additional on-site assistance is given just before opening and during your first few weeks of operation.

Zero's Mr. Submarine

2106 Pacific Ave.
Virginia Beach, VA 23451
E-mail Address: zeros@norfolk.infi.net
Toll-Free Phone: (800) 588-0782
Phone: (757) 425-8306
Fax: (757) 422-9157
Contact:

Number of Franchises: 39
Company-Owned Units: 6
Total Units: 45

In Business Since: 1967 **Franchising Since:** 1987

Description of Operation: Zero's Mr. Submarine is a fast-food, sit-down, and to-go restaurant; serving hot, oven-baked submarine sandwiches, salads, and pizza.

Equity Capital Needed: $30,000-$60,000

Franchise Fee: $10,000

Royalty: 5 percent plus 2 percent advertising

Advertising Co-op Fee:

Financial Assistance: We offer indirect financing.

Management Assistance: We assist in all areas of setting up a franchise.

Training Assistance: Extensive training is provided for franchisees and managers at the corporate headquarters (6 weeks) and also at the franchised location (2 weeks).

Restaurants—Steakhouse

Benihana of Tokyo

8685 N.W. 53rd Terr.
Miami, FL 33166
Toll-Free Phone:
Phone: (305) 593-0770
Fax: (305) 592-6371
Contact:

Number of Franchises: 11
Company-Owned Units: 50
Total Units: 61

In Business Since: 1964 **Franchising Since:** 1970

Description of Operation: The Benihana Steakhouse chain is known throughout the world for its top quality food and service. Each guest's meal is prepared right before his/her eyes by an entertaining chef who introduces all the ingredients before she masterfully cooks. Twice recognized as America's most popular full-service restaurant.

Equity Capital Needed: $300,000-$500,000

Franchise Fee: $50,000

Royalty: 5 percent

Advertising Co-op Fee:

Financial Assistance: None.

Management Assistance: Benihana will provide both pre-opening and post-opening support for the duration of the franchise. Also provided are forms, training manuals, posters, newsletters, and point-of-sale material.

Training Assistance: Before the opening of the restaurant, Benihana will provide training for both chefs and

managers alike. Such training programs require each trainee to work in a Benihana restaurant for a period of 12-16 weeks until properly trained in general restaurant management and preparation.

Golden Corral Restaurants

5151 Glenwood Ave. Ste. 300
Raleigh, NC 27612
Toll-Free Phone: (800) 284-5673
Phone: (919) 781-9310
Fax: (919) 881-5252
Contact: Vice President of Franchise Development

Number of Franchises: 137
Company-Owned Units: 288
Total Units: 425

In Business Since: 1973 **Franchising Since:** 1987

Description of Operation: Steaks, buffet, and bakery restaurant.

Equity Capital Needed: $1,200,000-$2,400,000

Franchise Fee: $30,000 or $40,000

Royalty: 4 percent

Advertising Co-op Fee:

Financial Assistance: Not available.

Management Assistance: Full assistance from site selection, training, opening assistance, and ongoing operations support.

Training Assistance: Twelve-week program in 3 phrases: 10 weeks in certified training restaurant and 2 weeks of classroom training.

K-Bob's USA

1600 Randolph S.E. Ste. 200
Albuquerque, NM 87106
Web Address:
E-mail Address: kbobs@/.net
Toll-Free Phone: (800) 225-8403
Phone: (505) 242-8403
Fax: (505) 764-0492
Contact: President

Number of Franchises: 33
Company-Owned Units: 7
Total Units: 40

In Business Since: 1966 **Franchising Since:** 1991

Description of Operation: Franchisor of steakhouses.

Equity Capital Needed: $250,000+

Franchise Fee: $25,000

Royalty: 3 percent

Advertising Co-op Fee:

Financial Assistance: None.

Management Assistance: K-Bob's USA's new store opening team is sent to a new unit 2 weeks before

opening and spends a total of 1,272 man-hours assisting new franchisees with the opening and operation of their unit opening. Opening team cost of $16,000 is included in the franchise fee.

Training Assistance: All new franchisees are required to attend our company-owned and operated unit training facility in Los Lunas, NM for a period of 4 weeks, learning all aspects of operations, marketing, procurement, and administration of a restaurant to K-Bob's USA standards.

Mr. Mike's Grill

611 Columbia St.
Westminister, BC V3M 1A7
Toll-Free Phone:
Phone: (604) 515-1190
Fax: (604) 515-1197
Contact:

Number of Franchises: 20
Company-Owned Units: 1
Total Units: 21

In Business Since: 1962　　**Franchising Since:** 1963

Description of Operation: Full service steakhouse and bar featuring premium steaks, burgers, and salad bar.

Equity Capital Needed: $100,000-$200,000

Franchise Fee: $37,500

Royalty: 5 percent plus 2 percent advertising

Advertising Co-op Fee:

Financial Assistance: Presentation package prepared for bank.

Management Assistance: On-site training minimum of 2 weeks. Off-site training for management. Ongoing head office support for marketing and advertising. Field representatives available for store use.

Training Assistance: Franchisees are exposed to existing store policies and procedures. In-store training for all staff.

Ponderosa

12404 Park Central Dr.
Dallas, TX 75251
Toll-Free Phone: (800) 543-9670
Phone:
Fax: (972) 404-5806
Contact: Director of Franchise Sales

Number of Franchises: 407
Company-Owned Units: 354
Total Units: 761

In Business Since: 1965　　**Franchising Since:** 1966

Description of Operation: America's family steakhouse. A modified full-service, affordable family steakhouse restaurant, open 7 days a week for lunch and dinner.

Menu features approximately 10 beef entrees, 4 seafood entrees, 3 chicken entrees, and the Grand Buffet.

Equity Capital Needed: $500,000 net worth, $125,000 liquid.

Franchise Fee: $30,000

Royalty: 4.8 percent

Advertising Co-op Fee:

Financial Assistance: The franchisor assists in identifying sources.

Management Assistance: Real estate, architecture and construction, training, marketing, purchasing and product distribution, product development, franchise field consultant and unit operating team.

Training Assistance: Training includes 5 weeks in field, then 1 week at headquarters, then 3 additional weeks in field. Follow-up training in steakhouse, as required.

Sirloin Stockade

2908 N. Plum
Hutchinson, KS 67502
Toll-Free Phone:
Phone: (316) 669-9372
Fax: (316) 669-0531
Contact:

Number of Franchises: 74
Company-Owned Units: 12
Total Units: 86

In Business Since: 1984　　**Franchising Since:** 1984

Description of Operation: Sirloin Stockade restaurants feature top-quality steaks, chicken, and fish entrees. A scatter-bar includes a deli/salad bar, a hot buffet, and a dessert bar, at family prices. Restaurant facilities are free-standing buildings of 8,700-10,000 square feet, seating 300-400 people. A minimum of 60,000 square feet of land is required.

Equity Capital Needed: $200,000-$250,000

Franchise Fee: $15,000

Royalty: 3 percent

Advertising Co-op Fee:

Financial Assistance: The franchisee must obtain financing through his/her personal resources.

Management Assistance: In addition to pre-opening assistance, SSI provides ongoing training, education, and assistance during the lifetime of the franchise agreement. Regular visits by SSI operation field consultants offer assistance in solving field problems, conducting quality control surveys and evaluating store operations. Franchisees are informed of new developments in the company and the industry, as well as techniques to improve productivity and profitability. A system-wide marketing program is administered.

©JIST Works, Inc., Indianapolis, IN 46202

Training Assistance: A comprehensive, twelve-week training program in all phases of the operation is provided for store management at a company training facility. The franchisee receives a complete set of confidential operations manuals, including recipes and food procedures, employee training, marketing, and equipment manuals.

Western Sizzlin

902 Kermit Dr.
Knoxville, TN 37912
Toll-Free Phone: (800) 247-8325
Phone: (423) 219-9000
Fax: (423) 219-9013
Contact:

Number of Franchises: 250
Company-Owned Units: 16
Total Units: 266

In Business Since: 1962   **Franchising Since:** 1968

Description of Operation: Semi-cafeteria style family steak house.

Equity Capital Needed: $250,000 liquid assets; $750,000 total net worth.

Franchise Fee: $25,000

Royalty: 2 percent

Advertising Co-op Fee:

Financial Assistance: No direct financial assistance is provided.

Management Assistance: Regional management consultants visit the franchise restaurants on a frequent basis.

Training Assistance: Training for new franchisees is an intensive eight-week training program, followed by 1 week classroom course.

Restaurants—Miscellaneous

Applebee's International

4551 W. 107th St., Ste. 100
Overland Park, KS 66207
Toll-Free Phone:
Phone: (913) 967-4000
Fax: (913) 341-1694
Contact: Director of Franchise Development

Number of Franchises: 310
Company-Owned Units: 65
Total Units: 375

In Business Since: 1983   **Franchising Since:** 1983

Description of Operation: Applebee's is positioned as a neighborhood grill and bar, where consumers can obtain a high-value experience through attractively-priced food and alcoholic beverages. The principles of fast food (convenience, quality, and service, coupled with limited time and money) can be applied to an adult consumer.

Equity Capital Needed: $4,000,000 net worth; $500,000 liquid assets

Franchise Fee: $35,000

Royalty: 4 percent

Advertising Co-op Fee:

Financial Assistance: Outside lenders.

Management Assistance: Training is provided for the general manager, the kitchen manager, and the franchisee's restaurant managers in our operations training facility for such period as the franchisor shall deem reasonably necessary. Franchisee personnel shall complete the course to the franchisor's reasonable satisfaction.

Training Assistance: Applebee's basically provides management training, pre-opening assistance, ongoing assistance, and follow-up assistance. Additionally, they help find site locations and offer assistance with purveyors for purchasing. Marketing program and formal assistance is provided.

Bennett's Pit Bar-B-Que

6551 S. Revere Pkwy., Ste. 285
Englewood, CO 80111
Toll-Free Phone:
Phone: (303) 792-3088
Fax: (303) 792-5801
Contact:

Number of Franchises: 12
Company-Owned Units: 3
Total Units: 15

In Business Since: 1984   **Franchising Since:** 1989

Description of Operation: Full-service and limited-service bar-b-que restaurants, featuring hickory-smoked barbeque in a fast-paced, friendly, family atmosphere.

Equity Capital Needed: $250,000 net worth; $100,000 liquid

Franchise Fee: $25,000

Royalty: 3.5 percent

Advertising Co-op Fee:

Financial Assistance: None.

Management Assistance: Site approval, lease negotiations, and construction management are available on a fee basis.

Training Assistance: Training consists of 4-8 weeks at the training center, plus 1-2 weeks of initial on-site training.

Big Boy, International

4199 Marcy
Warren, MI 48091
Toll-Free Phone: (800) 837-3003
Phone:
Fax: (810) 757-4737
Contact: Senior Executive Vice President

Number of Franchises: 406
Company-Owned Units: 74
Total Units: 480

In Business Since: 1938   **Franchising Since:** 1952

Description of Operation: Full-service family restaurant, featuring in-store bakery, breakfast, dinner, soup, and fruit bar.

Equity Capital Needed: $150,000

Franchise Fee: $25,000

Royalty: 3 percent

Advertising Co-op Fee:

Financial Assistance: The franchisor will provide a list of lenders.

Management Assistance: The franchisor will train all levels of the management team, including hourly personnel.

Training Assistance: 8 weeks of training is provided to new franchisees.

BJ's Kountry Kitchen

4325 N. Golden State Blvd. Ste. 102
Fresno, CA 93722
Toll-Free Phone:
Phone: (209) 275-1981
Fax: (209) 275-8786
Contact: Chairman

Number of Franchises: 8
Company-Owned Units: 0
Total Units: 8

In Business Since: 1981   **Franchising Since:** 1989

Description of Operation: Kountry Coffee Shop, operating 6 a.m. to 2 p.m., that bustles! Shorter hours and a single shift give you more time to do it right, as well as monitor the performance of others. Breakfast and lunch (especially breakfast) mean lower food cost with biscuits and gravy, omelets, hamburgers, and sandwiches. Good ol' basic food served quickly, simply, and economically with real hustle and bustle!

Equity Capital Needed: $65,000-$130,000

Franchise Fee: $25,000

Royalty: 5 percent

Advertising Co-op Fee:

Financial Assistance: Partial financing of the lease is available and subject to credit approval. Cost includes franchise fee and site acquisition.

Management Assistance: The franchise office is staffed with full-time management assistance.

Training Assistance: We train the beginner to become a pro by keeping our operation simple. The franchisee, plus 2 employees, get a two-week classroom and on-site program which offers the techniques and training to BUSTLE, including full operations, advertising, record keeping, personnel, and management. Full manuals and follow-up support.

Bobby Rubino's Place for Ribs

1990 E. Sunrise Blvd.
Ft. Lauderdale, FL 33304
E-mail Address: rubinousa@worldnet.att.net
Toll-Free Phone:
Phone: (954) 763-9871
Fax: (954) 467-1192
Contact:

Number of Franchises: 13
Company-Owned Units: 0
Total Units: 13

In Business Since: 1978   **Franchising Since:** 1980

Description of Operation: Full-service BBQ restaurant, specializing in ribs, chicken, and shrimp. All units have full-service lounges and take-out facilities. Serving steaks, prime-rib, and other popular items.

Equity Capital Needed: $400,000-$650,000

Franchise Fee: $50,000

Royalty: 4 percent

Advertising Co-op Fee:

Financial Assistance: None.

Management Assistance: Bobby Rubino's USA provides management material, training manuals and ongoing assistance for the term of the franchise. Visits to the franchisee occur on a regular basis. Assistance is offered in all areas of the business.

Training Assistance: Training provided for franchisee's management personnel in Florida for 6-8 weeks. Up to 5 people may attend. Provides a training team for store openings for up to 2 weeks. Ongoing training is provided for the franchisee.

Bridgeman's Restaurants

5700 Smetana Dr. Ste. 110
Minnetonka, MN 55343
Toll-Free Phone: (800) 297-5050
Phone: (612) 931-3099
Fax: (612) 931-3199
Contact:

Number of Franchises: 30
Company-Owned Units: 3
Total Units: 33

In Business Since: 1936   **Franchising Since:** 1967

Description of Operation: A full-service, family-style restaurant, featuring our famous ice cream specialty treats. Bridgeman's also awards franchise opportunities for the Dip Shoppe concept, offering ice cream treats and limited sandwich menu; or the soda fountain concept with the full line of ice cream treats; and finally, the Dip Station, which allows the franchisee to dispense all of our 22 natural rich and creamy flavors of ice cream.

Equity Capital Needed: We list no requirements.

Franchise Fee: $750-$25,000

Royalty: 2 percent

Advertising Co-op Fee:

Financial Assistance: Bridgeman's furnishes no financial assistance.

Management Assistance: District managers offer ongoing programs to provide better customer service and improve profitability. The company gives continual supervision and evaluation of service, cleanliness, and food quality. The district managers are on-site for several days each quarter and are also available on-call.

Training Assistance: Operational, training, and menu manuals are given to each new franchisee. The hands-on training program consists of 4-6 weeks at a corporate site. The length of the training will depend upon the experience of the trainee.

Cheddar's

616 Six Flags Dr. Ste. 116
Arlington, TX 76011
Toll-Free Phone:
Phone: (817) 640-4344
Fax: (817) 633-4452
Contact:

Number of Franchises: 15
Company-Owned Units: 12
Total Units: 27

In Business Since: 1978   **Franchising Since:** 1984

Description of Operation: Full-service, casual dining restaurant, with alcoholic beverage service. Cheddar's is based on mainstream, traditional concepts. Serves high-quality food frequently prepared fresh from scratch and portioned bountifullly at low prices with a very high perceived price/value ratio. The environment is casual, with natural colors and materials.

Equity Capital Needed: $250,000-$500,000

Franchise Fee: $30,000

Royalty: 3 percent

Advertising Co-op Fee:

Financial Assistance: None.

Management Assistance: Training for 12 weeks for every manager and director of operations. Opening and training team for 2-3 weeks. Assistance on all development. New product research and development. Full

accounting systems and services. Design and construction assistance.

Training Assistance: Same as above.

Company's Coming

Comac Food Group, 1121 Centre St. N., Ste. 440
Calgary, AL T2E 7K6
Toll-Free Phone: (800) 361-1151
Phone: (403) 230-1151
Fax: (403) 230-2182
Contact: Franchise Development Manager

Number of Franchises: 20
Company-Owned Units: 1
Total Units: 21

In Business Since: 1987   **Franchising Since:** 1987

Description of Operation: With consumer demand for wholesome fresh foods growing at an unprecedented rate, the time was right to begin a new tradition: the sale of freshly baked goods and gourmet beverages from family-oriented cafes under the Company's Coming name. Featuring over 65 varieties of freshly baked goods, including miniloaves, brownies, carrot cakes, and over 20 varieties of gourmet coffee.

Equity Capital Needed: $100,000-200,000

Franchise Fee: $25,000

Royalty: 8 percent

Advertising Co-op Fee: Not provided

Financial Assistance: Royal Bank of Canada

Management Assistance: Day-to-day operations, marketing, promotions, administration functions, supplier requirements, and staff training. Quality control analysis is done every quarter.

Training Assistance: Hands-on training of approximately 14 days in every aspect of the business.

Country Kitchen Restaurants

P.O. Box 44434, 6410 Enterprise Ln.
Madison, WI 53719
Toll-Free Phone: (888) 359-3235
Phone: (608) 274-5030
Fax: (608) 274-9999
Contact:

Number of Franchises: 235
Company-Owned Units: 0
Total Units: 235

In Business Since: 1939   **Franchising Since:** 1977

Description of Operation: Sit-down, full-service family dining restaurant. Breakfast, lunch, and dinner menu served 6 am-11 pm. Nontraditional sites in hotels, airports, and truckstops will be considered.

Equity Capital Needed: $125,000-$750,000

Franchise Fee: $25,000

Royalty: 4 percent

Advertising Co-op Fee:

Financial Assistance: Introduction to potential lenders.

Management Assistance: Full management training (8 weeks) included in initial franchise fee. Corporate trainers in new store for 4 weeks to help manager hire and train a staff.

Training Assistance: Ongoing management support, operational support, and re-training throughout the term of the agreement.

Cultures

20 Bay St. Waterpark Pl. Ste. 1605
Toronto, ON M5J 2N8
Toll-Free Phone:
Phone: (416) 368-1440
Fax: (416) 368-0804
Contact:

Number of Franchises: 33
Company-Owned Units: 11
Total Units: 44

In Business Since: 1978   **Franchising Since:** 1980

Description of Operation: Cultures is a "fresh food" concept, in which all products are prepared on the premises every day. Salad, soup, sandwiches, a wide variety of baked goods, and frozen yogurt specialties make up a healthy menu. We are dedicated to providing a "Better for You" customer experience, by offering great tasting, fresh food F.A.S.T. Friendly, Attentive, Speedy, Thoughtful.

Equity Capital Needed: $175,000-$225,000 (Canadian)

Franchise Fee: $35,000 (Canadian)

Royalty: 5 percent

Advertising Co-op Fee:

Financial Assistance: We are currently investigating financial assistance programs by institutional banks.

Management Assistance: We provide the franchisees with central purchasing, field operations evaluation, field training, inventory control, newsletters, and regional/national meetings.

Training Assistance: We offer a comprehensive, six-week, in-store training program and ongoing support from field representatives.

Dairy Belle Freeze

832 N. Hillview Dr.
Milpitas, CA 95035
E-mail Address: stone577@aol.com
Toll-Free Phone:
Phone: (408) 263-2612
Fax: (408) 263-1797
Contact: Executive Vice President

Number of Franchises: 15
Company-Owned Units: 0
Total Units: 15

In Business Since: 1957   **Franchising Since:** 1957

Description of Operation: A Dairy Belle restaurant is a place where the menu is large and diverse with soft-serve ice cream desserts, hamburgers, hot dogs, hot sandwiches, Mexican food, several types of french fries, and much more. We do not think of ourselves as a fast-food restaurant—more quick-service, because our food is "cooked to order," the way our customer would like it.

Equity Capital Needed: $51,000-$180,000

Franchise Fee: $12,500

Royalty: 4.5 percent

Advertising Co-op Fee:

Financial Assistance: We can assist in finding financing.

Management Assistance: In addition to our intensive training program, the company will have staff available to help new franchisees in their restaurant. We will continually assist our franchisees in all aspects of operations-from promotions through menu pricing, purchasing and customer relations.

Training Assistance: We offer a complete restaurant management training program of 3-5 weeks. We also train our franchisees in bookkeeping and personal growth and development through understanding relationships and customer service.

Dairy Queen Canada Inc.

5245 Harvester Rd. P.O. Box 430
Burlington, ON L7R 3Y3
Toll-Free Phone:
Phone: (905) 639-1492
Fax: (905) 681-3623
Contact: Franchise Development Manager

Number of Franchises: 500
Company-Owned Units: 0
Total Units: 500

In Business Since: 1940   **Franchising Since:** 1950

Description of Operation: Franchising of quick-service restaurants, serving fast food and frozen dairy treats.

Equity Capital Needed: $200,000 average

Franchise Fee: $30,000

Royalty: 4 percent

Advertising Co-op Fee:

Financial Assistance: DQC will finance 50 percent of the initial franchise fee of $30,000.

Management Assistance: Assistance from all departments, as required—accounting, lease negotiation, operations, building plans, and so on.

Training Assistance: 3 week training period at head office in Minneapolis, MN for owners and managers. Training team at store opening.

Denny's

203 E. Main St.
Spartanburg, SC 29319
Toll-Free Phone: (800) 304-0222
Phone: (864) 597-8000
Fax: (864) 597-7708
Contact:

Number of Franchises: 765
Company-Owned Units: 891
Total Units: 1656

In Business Since: 1953   **Franchising Since:** 1984

Description of Operation: Full-service family restaurant—24 hour operation.

Equity Capital Needed: Net worth—$750,000; liquid—$250,000

Franchise Fee: $35,000

Royalty: 4 percent

Advertising Co-op Fee:

Financial Assistance: Not available at this date. May change.

Management Assistance: Data not available.

Training Assistance: Currently a thirty-day training program in a Denny's restaurant, plus a training crew in the restaurant 1 week before opening and 2 weeks after opening.

Elmer's Pancake & Steak House

11802 SE Stark St. P.O. Box 16938
Portland, OR 97216
Toll-Free Phone: (800) 325-5188
Phone: (503) 252-1485
Fax: (503) 257-7448
Contact: Director of Franchising

Number of Franchises: 18
Company-Owned Units: 11
Total Units: 29

In Business Since: 1960   **Franchising Since:** 1966

Description of Operation: Full services—breakfast, lunch, and dinner. Special feature is breakfast, as well as all other menu items (unless special note), served all day. Banquet facilities, extensive menu. Some locations have lounges.

Equity Capital Needed: Minimum-$200,000+; ability to finance the rest.

Franchise Fee: $35,000

Royalty: 4 percent

Advertising Co-op Fee:

Financial Assistance: None.

Management Assistance: We provide approximately 3 months of initial training. The opening crew provides training to new employees. We stay in close touch, especially first 2 years. Annual seminar.

Training Assistance: Training takes place in Portland, OR and is one-on-one rather than classroom. All aspects of operating a restaurant are taught.

Friendly Banners Restaurant

1965 W. 4th Ave. Ste. 203
Vancouver, BC V6J 1M8
Toll-Free Phone:
Phone: (604) 737-7748
Fax: (604) 737-7993
Contact: President

Number of Franchises: 6
Company-Owned Units: 0
Total Units: 6

In Business Since: 1969   **Franchising Since:** 1969

Description of Operation: Family-style restaurant, featuring Baskin-Robbins ice cream desserts. Restaurants strategically located in neighborhood areas—usually part of a strip mall.

Equity Capital Needed: $200,000

Franchise Fee: $30,000

Royalty: 4 percent, plus 2 percent advertising

Advertising Co-op Fee:

Financial Assistance: Assistance will be given to acquire bank financing on behalf of the franchisee. This includes providing pro forma statements, cash flow projections, capital costs, and attending meetings.

Management Assistance: Published manuals are available as well as a requirement that the franchisee work and train in an existing franchise. Assistance will be given to hiring practices, accounting systems, and controls required to minimize labor and food costs. Site location and set-up requirements will be provided.

Training Assistance: On-site training is required at an existing franchise store. Opening advertising program is provided. Training team to assist with opening.

Fuddruckers

One Corporate Place, 55 Ferncroft Rd.
Danvers, MA 01923-4001
Toll-Free Phone:
Phone: (978) 774-6606
Fax: (978) 774-2974
Contact: Sr. V.P. Development

Number of Franchises: 87
Company-Owned Units: 112
Total Units: 199

In Business Since: 1980   **Franchising Since:** 1983

Description of Operation: Fuddruckers is an upscale restaurant, serving fresh ground beef patties from our on-premises butcher shop on our freshly-baked buns from our on-premises bakery. Breast of chicken, fish filet, hot dogs, a variety of salads, fries, onion rings, fresh cookies, brownies, pies, milk shakes, and beverages with unlimited refills are also available. Garnish your selection with your choices from our bountiful produce bar. Fuddruckers is where you get the world's greatest hamburger and you do your own thing.

Equity Capital Needed: $350,000-1,200,000

Franchise Fee: $50,000

Royalty: 5 percent

Advertising Co-op Fee: Data not provided.

Financial Assistance: None. We have some lenders who have asked to be referred to any potential franchisees if the franchisee requests it.

Management Assistance: We have full-time operations consultants who make weekly contact and who visit a minimum of 2 times per year. Secret shopper surveys are also conducted regularly. Help is a phone call away.

Training Assistance: 3-4 management people will be trained for 6 weeks in a Fuddruckers company restaurant. All positions in the restaurant will be learned. Testing is weekly. Profile tests are available to compare with successful management profiles of Fuddruckers personnel.

Gelato Amare

11504 Hyde Pl.
Raleigh, NC 27614
Toll-Free Phone:
Phone: (919) 847-4435
Fax:
Contact: President

Number of Franchises: 4
Company-Owned Units: 1
Total Units: 5

In Business Since: 1983   **Franchising Since:** 1986

Description of Operation: Gelato Amare stores feature products that appeal to the total frozen dessert market! We serve delicious Italian-style super-premium, low-fat, low-calorie, lactose-free ice cream made in the store; all natural sugar-free frozen yogurt, espresso, and more.

Equity Capital Needed: $225,000

Franchise Fee: $18,900 ($7,500 for additional store)

Royalty: 5 percent

Advertising Co-op Fee:

Financial Assistance: We provide cash flow and break-even analysis and all relevant data to lending institutions.

Management Assistance: We provide ongoing personnel pricing, marketing, advertising, public relations, promotion, merchandising, and operations assistance.

Training Assistance: We provide complete small business management training and all training specific to our business to help ensure franchisees success.

Grabbajabba

Comac Food Group, 1121 Centre St. N., Ste. 440
Calgary, AL T2E 7K6
Toll-Free Phone: (800) 361-1151
Phone: (403) 230-1151
Fax: (403) 230-2182
Contact: Franchise Development Manager

Number of Franchises: 58
Company-Owned Units: 4
Total Units: 62

In Business Since: 1987   **Franchising Since:** 1987

Description of Operation: The European style coffee house features the highest quality menu of whole and freshly brewed Arabic coffee specialty coffees, espresso, and cappuccino. European style sandwiches, soups, salads, and locally baked goods all served with a refreshing flair.

Equity Capital Needed: $125,000-200,000

Franchise Fee: $25,000

Royalty: 8 percent

Advertising Co-op Fee: Not provided

Financial Assistance: Royal Bank of Canada

Management Assistance: Day-to-day operations, marketing and promotions, administration functions, supplier requirements, and staff training. Quality control analysis is done every quarter.

Training Assistance: Hands-on training of approximately 14 days in every aspect of the business.

Ground Round, The

P.O. Box 9078 Braintree Hill Office Park
Braintree, MA 02184
Toll-Free Phone:
Phone: (617) 380-3116
Fax: (617) 380-3168
Contact: Director of Franchise Development

Number of Franchises: 38
Company-Owned Units: 125
Total Units: 163

In Business Since: 1969   **Franchising Since:** 1970

Description of Operation: Full-service, casual theme, family restaurant with liquor.

Equity Capital Needed: Net worth-$1,000,000; cash available-$400,000

Franchise Fee: $40,000

Royalty: 4 percent

Advertising Co-op Fee:

Financial Assistance: None available.

Management Assistance: Ground Round's district franchise manager will consult with and discuss all aspects of operating a Ground Round restaurant.

Training Assistance: We provide complete, comprehensive training and certification of the restaurant's management team, as well as employee training before and during the first weeks of operation.

Hobee's

4224 El Camino Real
Palo Alto, CA 94306
Web Address: www.hobees.com
Toll-Free Phone: (800) 462-3376
Phone: (650) 493-7117
Fax: (650) 493-0756
Contact: Vice President

Number of Franchises: 6
Company-Owned Units: 4
Total Units: 10

In Business Since: 1974   **Franchising Since:** 1986

Description of Operation: Hobee's franchises sit-down restaurants, serving healthy, California cuisine in a casual atmosphere. The chain is well known throughout Northern California and has won over 15 awards in 1993, which recognized Hobee's achievements in the areas of food quality customer service and community involvement. Franchisees receive extensive support from the corporate office in the form of legal guidelines, a company newsletter for customers, and assistance with advertising promotions.

Equity Capital Needed: $200,000-$400,000

Franchise Fee: $35,000

Royalty: 5 percent

Advertising Co-op Fee:

Financial Assistance: The franchisor does not provide financial assistance.

Management Assistance: Franchisees are free to enter Hobee's management program, provided space is available. Prior work experience at the restaurants is encouraged.

Training Assistance: The franchisee receives extensive pre-opening training at a designated training store. Length of training depends upon restaurant experience. A special team assists franchisee at his or her site for several weeks during post-opening.

Houlihan's

2 Brush Creek Blvd. P.O. Box 16000
Kansas City, MO 64112
Web Address: www.houlihans.com
Toll-Free Phone:
Phone: (816) 756-2200

Fax: (816) 561-2842
Contact: Senior Vice President of Franchising

Number of Franchises: 45
Company-Owned Units: 62
Total Units: 107

In Business Since: 1972   **Franchising Since:** 1987

Description of Operation: Houlihan's has been one of the most successful casual dining concepts in the country for the past 20 years. The restaurant has broad appeal with its unique, relaxed atmosphere and ambiance. The menu consists of a wide selection of items cutting across many ethnic cuisines. Our commitment is to make every guest a repeat guest.

Equity Capital Needed: $300,000-$450,000

Franchise Fee: $35,000

Royalty: 4 percent

Advertising Co-op Fee:

Financial Assistance: Financial assistance is available through third-party financial vendors that have approved the Houlihan's concept.

Management Assistance: On-site operational training manuals, videos, ongoing training sessions, quarterly owners meetings, and annual conference.

Training Assistance: An intensive sixty-day "hands-on" training program in the restaurant for all General Managers. Training is conducted in the corporate restaurants. All training materials are provided, including manuals and videos. An abbreviated training program s available for the franchisee.

Humpty's Restaurants International

2505 MacLeod Trail S.
Calgary, AB T2G 5J4
Web Address: www.humptys.com
Toll-Free Phone: (800) 661-7589
Phone: (403) 269-4675
Fax: (403) 266-1973
Contact: President

Number of Franchises: 29
Company-Owned Units: 2
Total Units: 31

In Business Since: 1977   **Franchising Since:** 1986

Description of Operation: 24-hour, full-service family family-type restaurant. Generous portions at very competitive prices. Very unique breakfast section of the menu. We promote children's meals and activities. Special promotions throughout the year, such as "2 for 1 Omelette Month."

Equity Capital Needed: $200,000-$350,000 (Canadian)

Franchise Fee: $25,000

Royalty: 5 percent

Advertising Co-op Fee:

Financial Assistance: Financial assistance is not available; however, business plans are provided by the company to assist the franchisee in approaching financial institutions.

Management Assistance: 4 weeks of training during the opening of the business. Ongoing monthly visits after opening. 800 number for franchisees to call.

Training Assistance: We offer 3 weeks of training before the opening for 2 people and 4 weeks during the opening period. Total of 7 weeks maximum.

International House of Pancakes

525 N. Brand Blvd., 3rd Floor
Glendale, CA 91203
Web Address: www.ihop.com
Toll-Free Phone: (888) 774-4467
Phone: (818) 240-6055
Fax: (818) 240-0270
Contact: Vice President of Franchising

Number of Franchises:
Company-Owned Units:
Total Units: 750

In Business Since: 1958   **Franchising Since:** 1960

Description of Operation: Full-service family restaurant, serving breakfast, lunch, dinner, snacks, and desserts, including a variety of pancake specialties and featuring the cook's Daily Special. Wine and beer are served in some locations.

Equity Capital Needed: Varies, depending on location.

Franchise Fee: Varies.

Royalty: Varies.

Advertising Co-op Fee:

Financial Assistance: None.

Management Assistance: The franchisor provides opening supervision, regular visits and assistance from field coordinators. A complete manual of operations specifies how each menu item is prepared and served and how the business is to be operated profitably.

Training Assistance: We provide 6 weeks of classroom and on-the-job instruction. Continued training is available.

Java Centrale

1610 Arden Way.; Ste. 145
Sacramento, CA 95815
Toll-Free Phone: (800) 551-5282
Phone: (916) 568-2310
Fax: (916) 568-1240
Contact: V.P. Franchise Development

Number of Franchises: 33
Company-Owned Units: 0
Total Units: 33

In Business Since: 1992   **Franchising Since:** 1992

Description of Operation: European-style gourmet coffee cafe, offering over 40 fine roasted coffees, available by the pound, fresh-brewed, and specialty beverages like espresso, cappuccino, latte, mocha—hot or iced. Fresh morning baked goods, deli sandwiches, salads, and desserts. Nothing is baked or cooked on the premises. Site selection assistance, extensive training, ongoing field support, and aggressive marketing are provided.

Equity Capital Needed: $175,000-382,000

Franchise Fee: $35,000

Royalty: 6 percent

Advertising Co-op Fee: Not provided

Financial Assistance: No financial assistance is available through the franchisor.

Management Assistance: We provide operational training at a company-owned facility and on-site training before the cafe opens. Manuals for operation and marketing. Field representatives to cafes, monthly newsletters, and continuing promotion ideas.

Training Assistance: We offer 2 weeks of franchisee and manager training, covering all aspects of cafe operations/training cafe. Then, the training crew spends 2 weeks at the new cafe before the opening to assist in employee training and final cafe preparation.

Joey's Only Seafood

514 - 42 Ave., S.E.
Calgary, AB 72G 1YG
Toll-Free Phone: (800) 661-2123
Phone: (403) 243-4584
Fax: (403) 243-8989
Contact:

Number of Franchises: 65
Company-Owned Units: 1
Total Units: 66

In Business Since: 1985   **Franchising Since:** 1992

Description of Operation: Family-style, seafood, sit-down restaurant, specializing in fish and chips. Licensed for beer and wine.

Equity Capital Needed: $75,000-100,000

Franchise Fee: $25,000

Royalty: 4.5 percent

Advertising Co-op Fee: 2 percent

Financial Assistance: No data provided.

Management Assistance: The District Manager assists in the pre-opening and opening of the location (2 weeks). Continual monthly visits to assist in better operating procedures.

Training Assistance: We offer a five-week training program, from dishwashing to cooking procedures, food handling, and customer service.

Joia Pastel

258250 Southfield Rd., Ste. 201
Southfield, MI 48075
Web Address: www.wfcnet.com
E-mail Address: wfc@cris.com
Toll-Free Phone:
Phone: (248) 559-1415
Fax: (248) 557-7931
Contact: Sales Director

Number of Franchises: 1
Company-Owned Units: 1
Total Units: 2

In Business Since: 1996   **Franchising Since:** 1999

Description of Operation: Brazilian food.

Equity Capital Needed: $90,000

Franchise Fee: $5,000

Royalty: 5 percent

Advertising Co-op Fee: None

Financial Assistance: Assist in S.B.A. and other financing programs.

Management Assistance: Turn key operation. Total follow-up support.

Training Assistance: 5 weeks. 2 in franchisee's own location.

Kelsey's Restaurants

450 S. Service Rd. W.
Oakville, ON L6K 2H4
Toll-Free Phone:
Phone: (905) 842-5510
Fax: (905) 842-5603
Contact:
Number of Franchises: 17
Company-Owned Units: 20
Total Units: 37

In Business Since: 1977   **Franchising Since:** 1981

Description of Operation: Licensed, full-service casual dining, offering lunch, dinner, and late-night menu with a wide variety of food items. Offering great value with large portions. The atmosphere is warm and the service is fast, friendly and efficient. We also cater to family dining. Stand-up bar available.

Equity Capital Needed: $200,000+

Franchise Fee: $20,000

Royalty: 5 percent

Advertising Co-op Fee:

Financial Assistance: Varies.

Management Assistance: We will assist the franchisee in hiring and training a management team. We will also assist with a "hands-on" support team for the first 30 days of operation.

Training Assistance: A twelve-week, in-store training program is mandatory to learn Kelsey's operations and systems.

Kettle Restaurants

2855 Magul Ste. 485
Houston, TX 77092
Web Address: www.kettle.com
Toll-Free Phone: (800) 929-2391
Phone: (713) 263-1237
Fax: (713) 263-1240
Contact: Franchise Development

Number of Franchises: 95
Company-Owned Units: 60
Total Units: 155

In Business Since: 1968   **Franchising Since:** 1968

Description of Operation: Full-service 24 hour family restaurant,

Equity Capital Needed: $150,000-$500,000

Franchise Fee: $20,000

Royalty: 5 percent

Advertising Co-op Fee:

Financial Assistance: None.

Management Assistance: Managerial instruction is given during the normal on-the-job training. Technical assistance is given by the franchisor to key personnel before opening for business and after opening until the operation stabilizes. Periodic visits thereafter, approximately every quarter, or more often, if deemed necessary or requested.

Training Assistance: We provided training for 4—10 weeks at our training center in Houston, TX.

Le Croissant Shop

227 W. 40th St.
New York, NY 10021
Toll-Free Phone:
Phone: (212) 719-5940
Fax: (212) 944-0269
Contact:

Number of Franchises: 23
Company-Owned Units: 3
Total Units: 26

In Business Since: 1981   **Franchising Since:** 1984

Description of Operation: French bakery cafe, serving croissants, sandwiches, salads, soups, muffins, and bread.

Equity Capital Needed: $200,000-$300,000

Franchise Fee: $22,500

Royalty: 5 percent

Advertising Co-op Fee:

Financial Assistance: No financial assistance.

Management Assistance: Ongoing visits and support by franchisor.

Training Assistance: 4 weeks of training at company headquarters. 1 week of support by franchise company crew at store opening.

Lisa's Tea Treasures

1151 Minnesota Ave.
San Jose, CA 95125
Web Address: www.lisateas.com
E-mail Address: ltt@aol.com
Toll-Free Phone: (800) 500-4832
Phone: (408) 371-1453
Fax: (408) 371-1875
Contact: Vice President of Sales

Number of Franchises: 5
Company-Owned Units: 1
Total Units: 6

In Business Since: 1988   **Franchising Since:** 1992

Description of Operation: Lisa's Tea Treasures Tea Room and Gift Parlour is a specialty purveyor of the finest quality teas and tea-related accessories. Tea is served in an elegant Victorian setting. We offer fine bulk teas, gourmet foods, tea ware, and Victorian-era gifts.

Equity Capital Needed: $130,000-$190,000

Franchise Fee: $25,000

Royalty: 6 percent

Advertising Co-op Fee:

Financial Assistance: We provide assistance in locating third-party financing.

Management Assistance: We provide a detailed operations manual, ordering guide, on-site assistance at grand opening, newsletters, and monthly promotional events and national and regional meetings.

Training Assistance: Each franchisee attends 10 days of training at a corporate location. This includes approximately 30 percent of classroom training on the history of tea, how to conduct a tea tasting, tea etiquette, and so on. In-depth training is provided in business areas as well.

Maurice's Gourmet Barbeque

1600 Charleston Hwy. P.O. Box 6847
West Columbia, SC 29171
Toll-Free Phone: (800) 628-7423
Phone: (803) 791-5887
Fax: (803) 791-8707
Contact: National Director of Marketing

Number of Franchises: 1
Company-Owned Units: 7
Total Units: 8

In Business Since: 1939   **Franchising Since:** 1990

Description of Operation: Maurice is offering the most unique barbeque concept in the world today, featuring

real old-fashioned, pit-cooked barbeque as cooked in the colonial days. We have created a high-tech system. The company will sell franchises to an individual or to an investor-owned franchises. 55 years of experience.

Equity Capital Needed: $150,000-$250,000

Franchise Fee: $48,500

Royalty: 5 percent

Advertising Co-op Fee:

Financial Assistance: A Piggie Park reserves the right to permit deferred payment of a portion of a fee when individual circumstances warrant. These circumstances are based on considerations such as the number of restaurants to be constructed, the total time for constructing the restaurants and the franchise owner's ability to pay the entire development fee in one lump sum.

Management Assistance: The franchisor will provide back-up support in all areas of franchise operations. If the franchisee does not wish to participate in the day-to-day management of the franchise owner's ability to pay the entire development fee in one lump sum.

Training Assistance: The franchisee will be trained in our system and methodology, including standards, methods, procedures, and techniques. This includes assistance in purchasing, advertising, marketing, promotions, operations, and human resources.

Melting Pot Restaurants, The

8406-G Benjamin Rd.
Tampa, FL 33634
Toll-Free Phone:
Phone: (813) 881-0055
Fax: (813) 889-9361
Contact:

Number of Franchises: 42
Company-Owned Units: 3
Total Units: 45

In Business Since: 1975   **Franchising Since:** 1984

Description of Operation: Rated number one specialty fondue restaurant franchise system by Entrepreneur Magazine in 1993. The Melting Pot offers a unique opportunity to stand apart from the competition. Select the franchise system that offers a unique concept, coupled with training, education, and outstanding support. To become a part of our expansion plans, call now for a "quick fax" package.

Equity Capital Needed: $160,000-$350,000

Franchise Fee: $15,600

Royalty: 4.5 percent

Advertising Co-op Fee:

Financial Assistance: This is the responsibility of the new franchisee.

Management Assistance: Melting Pot field representatives will be on hand before and during your restaurant

opening to assist in employee orientation meetings and to conduct on-site training.

Training Assistance: All franchisees and their managers must attend and successfully complete a comprehensive training program conducted at the Melting Pot Restaurants' headquarters in Tampa, FL. The cost of this program is included in the initial franchise fee. Franchisees and their managers pay their own costs of lodging, meals, and transportation during training.

Perkins Family Restaurants

6075 Poplar Ave.; Ste. 800
Memphis, TN 38119
Web Address: www.perkinsrestaurants.com
Toll-Free Phone: (800) 877-7375
Phone: (901) 766-6400
Fax: (901) 766-6445
Contact: Senior Franchise Director

Number of Franchises: 296
Company-Owned Units: 126
Total Units: 422

In Business Since: 958   **Franchising Since:** 1958

Description of Operation: Perkins Family Restaurants are full-service, family-style restaurants, offering a broad menu base, including breakfast, lunch, and dinner entrees. More than half of the restaurants feature our signature bakery.

Equity Capital Needed: 20 percent of total investment

Franchise Fee: $40,000

Royalty: 4 percent

Advertising Co-op Fee: 3 percent

Financial Assistance: We structure a Franchise Financing Program in conjunction with Bell Atlantic Tricon's Franchise Lending Division. The program is supported by Perkins with a limited guaranty of funds borrowed by the franchise.

Management Assistance: Ongoing supervision is provided for both pre-opening and post-opening activities. Support programs include training, marketing, purchasing, operations, site selection, construction, finance, and equipment purchasing.

Training Assistance: Licensee orientation and operations training. Management training and development. New store opening training assistance. Restaurant personnel training program and assistance.

Rocco Raccoons Indoor Playgrounds, Inc.

27 Minard St.
Lockport, NY 14094
Toll-Free Phone:
Phone: (716) 434-7553
Fax: (716) 647-1580
Contact: Director of Operations

Number of Franchises: 1
Company-Owned Units: 1
Total Units: 2

In Business Since: 1994   **Franchising Since:** 1994

Description of Operation: We specialize in family fun play centers with indoor supervised play areas, full menu, pizza, animated characters, gift shop, and skill testing games.

Equity Capital Needed: $250,000-500,000

Franchise Fee: $50,000

Royalty: 4 percent of gross

Advertising Co-op Fee: 1 percent of gross

Financial Assistance: Financing: Reality, computer, account administration.

Management Assistance: Complete training program and ongoing support.

Training Assistance: Complete training to operate all aspects of business.

Schlotzsky's Deli

203 Colorado St.
Austin, TX 78701
Toll-Free Phone: (800) 846-2867
Phone: (512) 236-3600
Fax: (512) 236-3601
Contact: Franchise Sales Director

Number of Franchises: 666
Company-Owned Units: 7
Total Units: 673

In Business Since: 1971   **Franchising Since:** 1977

Description of Operation: Sandwich, soup, salad, and pizza. Quick service. A proprietary product that is different from other sandwiches. All products are served hot on sourdough buns, baked fresh daily in store.

Equity Capital Needed: 30 percent of total project cost,

Franchise Fee: $20,000

Royalty: 6 percent

Advertising Co-op Fee:

Financial Assistance: Third party lenders approved for financial assistance.

Management Assistance: Local developers, who act as service representatives, provide hands-on assistance.

Training Assistance: Training consists of 3 weeks at the Austin training center. In addition, a 3-person opening team will be on location for the first week of operation.

Seafood America

645 Mearns Rd.
Warminister, PA 18974
Toll-Free Phone:
Phone: (215) 672-2211

Fax: (215) 675-8324
Contact: President

Number of Franchises: 17
Company-Owned Units: 0
Total Units: 17

In Business Since: 1976   **Franchising Since:** 1980

Description of Operation: Retail sale of seafood and related items.

Equity Capital Needed: $200,000-$250,000

Franchise Fee: $15,000

Royalty: 2 percent

Advertising Co-op Fee:

Financial Assistance: No financing is available.

Management Assistance: We will provide total training and initial assistance upon opening the store.

Training Assistance: Training is provided in an existing store for a period of 4 weeks.

Smitty's

501 18th Ave. Ste. 600
Calgary, AB T2S 0C7
Toll-Free Phone:
Phone: (403) 229-3838
Fax: (403) 229-3899
Contact: President

Number of Franchises: 110
Company-Owned Units: 10
Total Units: 120

In Business Since: 1959   **Franchising Since:** 1960

Description of Operation: Family restaurant operator and franchisor for over 30 years in Canada and Hawaii. Concept originated as a pancake house and has developed into a full-menu, complementing breakfast, lunch, and evening dining. Franchisee committees assist in design and implementation of menu and marketing programs.

Equity Capital Needed: $150,000-$200,000

Franchise Fee: $35,000

Royalty: 5 percent

Advertising Co-op Fee:

Financial Assistance: None.

Management Assistance: We provide extensive three-week training program in all aspects of running a restaurant. Restaurant opening assistance and ongoing assistance is available.

Training Assistance: In-depth food handling and preparation, front of the house operations, accounting, management, human resource, marketing, inventory, and food cost control.

Sonny's Real Pit Bar-B-Q

2605 Maitland Ctr. Pkwy.
Maitland, FL 32751
Toll-Free Phone:
Phone: (407) 660-8888
Fax: (407) 660-9050
Contact: Director of Franchise Services

Number of Franchises: 71
Company-Owned Units: 8
Total Units: 79

In Business Since: 1968   **Franchising Since:** 1976

Description of Operation: Sonny's Real Pit Bar-B-Q was founded in Gainesville, FL, featuring choice of cuts of beef, pork, chicken, and ribs, smoked over a hardwood fire and served at a great value in a full-service, sit-down restaurant. While every store features waitress service, the speed of service approximates or equals that of many fast-food restaurants. A significant portion of the business is through a take-out/walk-up window, while a drive-thru window is an option. Sonny's restaurants also offer catering.

Equity Capital Needed: $234,500-$1,335,000

Franchise Fee: $25,000

Royalty: 2.5 percent

Advertising Co-op Fee:

Financial Assistance: Introductions and assistance will be provided between SBA programs and certain independent sale and leaseback programs for franchise development.

Management Assistance: Each franchisee receives a package of operations, training, and accounting materials to guide in management. Manual revisions and updated. Sonny's representatives visit restaurants offering advice on many aspects of the business. Periodic franchisee meetings are held on various aspects of restaurant ownership. An advertising/sales promotion package is available. 1 percent of monthly revenue is paid into advertising fund that promotes Sonny's system. Corporate purchasing maintains quality control.

Training Assistance: The franchisee or operating manager will be required to take 400 hours of on-the-job training in one of Sonny's corporate restaurants. In addition, the assistant manager or head cook will be required to take 150 hours of training in kitchen operations. In the beginning, Sonny's will provide a complete training guide and operations manual in order to maintain consistency within the system.

Steak N Shake

36 S. Pennsylvania, 500 Century
Indianapolis, IN 46204
Web Address: www.steaknshake.com
Toll-Free Phone:
Phone: (317) 633-4100
Fax: (317) 656-4500

Contact: Franchise Development

Number of Franchises: 50
Company-Owned Units: 211
Total Units: 261

In Business Since: 1934   **Franchising Since:** 1939

Description of Operation: Steak N Shake is a unique restaurant concept serving quick-seared steak burgers, thin french fries, genuine chili, and hand dipped milk shakes. Steak N Shake offers full waitress service with food served on china, as well as drive-thru and take-out service, in a casual environment reminiscent of the 50's.

Equity Capital Needed: $500,000+

Franchise Fee: $30,000

Royalty: 4 percent

Advertising Co-op Fee: Data not available

Financial Assistance: None

Management Assistance: Steak N Shake will provide an opening crew to assist with the opening of the new restaurant. Complete building plans and consultation during the construction of the restaurant are provided.

Training Assistance: All new franchisee employees, including restaurant management personnel, are given a comprehensive, on-the-job training program, using personal instructions, training videos, and workbooks.

Steak-Out

8210 Stephanie Dr.
Huntsville, AL 35802
Toll-Free Phone:
Phone: (205) 883-2300
Fax: (205) 883-4300
Contact: Franchise Licensing Manager

Number of Franchises: 48
Company-Owned Units: 4
Total Units: 52

In Business Since: 1986   **Franchising Since:** 1987

Description of Operation: Steak-Out specializes in the delivery and carry-out of steaks, burgers, and chicken. Salads, sandwiches, baked potatoes and desserts round out the menu of this quality and customer-oriented concept.

Equity Capital Needed: $174,250-$247,000

Franchise Fee: $21,500 (included in start-up estimate).

Royalty: 4 percent; 2 percent advertising

Advertising Co-op Fee:

Financial Assistance: None available.

Management Assistance: Field training and support is provided on an ongoing basis by a field consultant and the home office.

Training Assistance: A six-week training program is provided to franchisees and their operational managers.

This program prepares them for every facet of the business, with a good comprehension of the industry and how Steak-Out relates to it.

Stuff 'n' Turkey

9199 Reistertown Rd. Ste. 215C
Owings Mills, MD 21117
Toll-Free Phone:
Phone: (410) 581-9393
Fax: (410) 363-3308
Contact: President

Number of Franchises: 14
Company-Owned Units: 7
Total Units: 21

In Business Since: 1986   **Franchising Since:** 1989

Description of Operation: Stuff 'N' Turkey is a specialty deli operation, featuring home-cooked turkey and glazed ham. A unique, healthy, and home-cooked approach.

Equity Capital Needed: $60,000-$175,000

Franchise Fee: $25,000

Royalty: 5 percent

Advertising Co-op Fee:

Financial Assistance: We will assist in obtaining financing.

Management Assistance: Ongoing.

Training Assistance: We offer 2 weeks of training at a company store and 1 week on-site.

Tony Roma's—A Place for Ribs

9304 Forest Ln., Ste. 400
Dallas, TX 75243
Web Address: www.tonyromas.com
Toll-Free Phone:
Phone: (214) 343-7800
Fax: (214) 343-2680
Contact:

Number of Franchises: 146
Company-Owned Units: 37
Total Units: 183

In Business Since: 1972   **Franchising Since:** 1978

Description of Operation: Full-service restaurant with alcoholic beverages, specializing in chicken and ribs.

Equity Capital Needed: $300,000 liquid; $800,000 est. total investment

Franchise Fee: $50,000

Royalty: 4 percent

Advertising Co-op Fee:

Financial Assistance: Referrals only to those firms that have expressed an interest in providing capital to franchisees.

Management Assistance: We provide a training program for all managers. Manuals for operations, purchasing, marketing, recipes, building plans, visits to units, and opening team are also provided.

Training Assistance: Training is for 3 or more unit managers and lasts 4-6 weeks, depending on experience. Training manuals. Opening teams sent to units before openings.

Village Inn Restaurants

400 W. 48th Ave., P.O. Box 16601
Denver, CO 80216
Web Address: www.villageinn.com
Toll-Free Phone: (800) 891-9978
Phone: (303) 672-2229
Fax: (303) 672-2212
Contact: Franchise Operations Coordinator

Number of Franchises: 108
Company-Owned Units: 97
Total Units: 205

In Business Since: 1958   **Franchising Since:** 1961

Description of Operation: Full service, family-style restaurant, offering a variety of menu items and special features emphasizing our breakfast heritage in all dayparts.

Equity Capital Needed: $200,00-300,000

Franchise Fee: $25,000

Royalty:

Advertising Co-op Fee: None

Financial Assistance: None

Management Assistance: None

Training Assistance: A minimum of two managers must complete a 12-20 week management training program in addition to one other person from the franchisee's organization. An opening team is on-site for approximately four weeks. Specific training requests provided at franchisee's expense.

Retail—Bird Supplies

Wild Bird Centers of America

7687 MacArthur Blvd.
Glen Echo, MD 20812
Web Address: www.wildbirdcenter.com
Toll-Free Phone: (800) 945-3247
Phone: (301) 229-9585
Fax: (301) 320-6154
Contact: President

Number of Franchises: 99
Company-Owned Units: 3
Total Units: 102

In Business Since: 1985   **Franchising Since:** 1989

Description of Operation: Franchising and supporting the ultimate wild bird specialty shops for people who want successful businesses that they can be proud to call their own.

Equity Capital Needed: $83,000-$131,000

Franchise Fee: $19,500

Royalty: 3-4.5 percent

Advertising Co-op Fee:

Financial Assistance: Wild Bird Centers of America provides a business plan kit, including a hard copy business plan, business plan on disk, site selection, and lease analysis workbook.

Management Assistance: All aspects of operating Wild Bird Centers and Wild Bird Crossings franchises are supported by an experienced staff, a bi-monthly customer newsletter and advertising support.

Training Assistance: The initial training for Wild Bird Centers and Wild Bird Crossings is 10 days long at the company headquarters and emphasizes practical hands-on activities. Ongoing activities are conducted through store visits and an annual national meeting.

Wild Bird Marketplace

1891 Santa Barbara Dr., Ste. 106
Lancaster, PA 17601
Web Address: www.wildbird.com
Toll-Free Phone: (888) 926-2473
Phone: (717) 581-5310
Fax: (717) 581-5312
Contact: President

Number of Franchises: 31
Company-Owned Units: 0
Total Units: 31

In Business Since: 1989   **Franchising Since:** 1989

Description of Operation: Wild Bird Marketplace offers a range of products for the birders, gardeners and naturalists interested in their immediate environment. Our primary focus is on birding activities. Our stores are bright, modern and inviting to today's shopper. Located in retail centers, they draw on the booming interest in backyard birding and in bird-related gifts and supplies.

Equity Capital Needed: $90,000-$125,000

Franchise Fee: $15,000

Royalty: 4 percent

Advertising Co-op Fee:

Financial Assistance: None.

Management Assistance: Data not available.

Training Assistance: Wild Bird Marketplace provides comprehensive training in all areas of operations and management, plus full advertising and marketing support. In addition, we train you in the basics of bird feeding and watching. Training is comprehensive and ongoing.

Wild Birds Unlimited

11711 N. College Ave., Ste. 146
Carmel, IN 46032
Toll-Free Phone: (800) 326-4928
Phone: (317) 571-7100
Fax: (317) 571-7110
Contact: **Director of Franchise Development**

Number of Franchises: 152
Company-Owned Units: 0
Total Units: 152

In Business Since: 1981   **Franchising Since:** 1983

Description of Operation: Wild Birds Unlimited is North America's original and largest group of retail stores catering to the backyard birdfeeding and nature enthusiast. We have over 150 stores in the US and Canada. Stores provide extensive educational programs to the public on backyard birdfeeding. Franchisees are provided with a full support system.

Equity Capital Needed: $60,000-$90,000

Franchise Fee: $15,000

Royalty: 3 percent

Advertising Co-op Fee:

Financial Assistance: No.

Management Assistance: Wild Birds Unlimited provides site selection and lease negotiation assistance. Franchisees attend an initial training session and are then given field training at their store. Support is given in all operational areas, including vendor discounts, business planning, marketing, and advertising.

Training Assistance: The franchisor provides a five-day initial training session, covering assorted topics, including customer service, employee training, store build-out, inventory, and suppliers, marketing and advertising and detailed business operations. Ongoing training is given in the form of monthly newsletters, quarterly marketing guides, visits by field representatives, and annual and regional meetings.

Retail—Bookstores

Lemstone Books

1123 Wheaton Oaks Ct.
Wheaton, IL 60187
Web Address: www.lemstone.com
Toll-Free Phone:
Phone: (630) 682-1400
Fax: (630) 682-1828
Contact: **Sales Manager**

Number of Franchises: 74
Company-Owned Units: 1
Total Units: 75

In Business Since: 1981   **Franchising Since:** 1982

Description of Operation: "America's Christian Bookstore Franchise." Lemstone specializes in high-volume mall retailing. Our franchisees come from a wide range of professions. Our stores retail Christ-centered and family-oriented retail products. Product categories include Christian books, Bibles, recorded music, videos, stationery products, T-shirts, and gift products.

Equity Capital Needed: Total: $140,000-$200,000
Equity: $60,000-$90,000

Franchise Fee: $30,000

Royalty: 4 percent plus 1 percent advertising

Advertising Co-op Fee:

Financial Assistance: We assist the franchisee in preparing and obtaining local bank financing.

Management Assistance: We offer a complete turn-key operation, including site-selection, lease negotiations, construction, inventory selection, store set-up, operating systems, and ongoing promotional support and training. National seminars and an annual convention are also offered. On-site operational support, as required.

Training Assistance: Franchisees attend an initial eight-day seminar at franchise headquarters in Wheaton, Illinois, covering all aspects of store management. This seminar takes place approximately one month before opening. At this time, franchisees are introduced to the comprehensive operations manual and procedures are worked through in detail. Valuable "hands on" experience is gained during in-store training at our nearby Lemstone Books corporate training store. At the time of store set-up Lemstone's operations team will assist you in getting your store up and running and will help you develop a successful Grand Opening strategy. Includes convention, seminars, employee training materials, newsletters, and promotional training.

Little Professor Book Centers

405 Little Lake Dr. Ste. C
Ann Arbor, MI 48103
Toll-Free Phone: (800) 899-6232
Phone: (734) 994-1212
Fax: (734) 994-9009
Contact: **Franchise Sales Manager**

Number of Franchises: 90
Company-Owned Units: 0
Total Units: 90

In Business Since: 1964   **Franchising Since:** 1969

Description of Operation: General full-service, community-oriented book stores.

Equity Capital Needed: $100,000

Franchise Fee: $35,000

Royalty: 3.5 percent

Advertising Co-op Fee:

Financial Assistance: Assistance in loan application process.

Management Assistance: We provide support in all areas of franchised book store operations on an ongoing basis.

Training Assistance: We offer an extensive 7 day training period at the home office in Ann Arbor, MI in all areas related to running and managing book store daily operations, including bookselling, personnel, daily operations, financial, computer operations, and so on. Also, on-site training of 5-7 days. More for a superstore.

Retail—Clothing

T-Shirts Plus

4732 W. Waco Dr.
Waco, TX 76710
Toll-Free Phone: (800) 880-0721
Phone: (254) 776-8872
Fax: (254) 776-6838
Contact: Director of Development

Number of Franchises: 113
Company-Owned Units: 0
Total Units: 113

In Business Since: 1974   **Franchising Since:** 1976

Description of Operation: The sale and enhancement of athletic family apparel and customizing while the customer waits.

Equity Capital Needed: $100,000-$50,000 cash/$50,000 collateral.

Franchise Fee: $35,000

Royalty: 6 percent or flat $1,250 per month

Advertising Co-op Fee:

Financial Assistance: We will assist in SBA financing, helping to prepare the package and submit to a lender.

Management Assistance: We provide ongoing support, monthly news and promotional packages, continual software, support, and assistance.

Training Assistance: We provide a seven-day "college" training that is mandatory for all new franchise owners-providing training in all aspects of the business in Waco, TX.

Retail—Collectibles

Sports Fantastic

1919 S. 40th Street, Suite 202
Lincoln, NE 68506
Toll-Free Phone: (800) 865-2378

Phone: (402) 434-5620
Fax: (402) 434-5624
Contact: President

Number of Franchises: 1
Company-Owned Units: 1
Total Units: 2

In Business Since: 1992   **Franchising Since:** 1996

Description of Operation: Sports Fantastic is the place where you can find unique gifts for sports fans of all ages, from trading cards to authentic sports collectibles.

Equity Capital Needed: $100,000

Franchise Fee: $20,000

Royalty: 5 percent

Advertising Co-op Fee: 1 percent

Financial Assistance: Current financial review, support on a business plan, and third party lending options provided.

Management Assistance: Complete training, software program, manuals, follow-up, and an 800 number is provided.

Training Assistance: One week at home office, and one week on-site.

Retail—Convenience Store

UncleSam's Convenient Store

300 E. Highway 107; P.O. Box 870
Elsa, TX 78543-0870
Toll-Free Phone: (888) 786-7373
Phone: (956) 262-7273
Fax: (956) 262-7290
Contact: Executive Vice President

Number of Franchises: 9
Company-Owned Units: 52
Total Units: 52

In Business Since: 1970   **Franchising Since:** 1996

Description of Operation: Become a part of this exciting convenience store franchise opportunity. Join a team of convenience store professionals with over 26 years of experience, and a whole new outlook on convenience store management. An UncleSam's Convenient Store franchise offers you a way of being your own boss and being in business for yourself. UncleSam's Convenient Store franchise program provides 1) a proven retail business, 2) an established system, 3) no experience required, 4) financing options, 5) store design and layout, 6) merchandising, 7) fuel supply, 8) construction assistance, 9) volume purchasing power, 10) a proprietary software package, 11) training, 12) a detailed operations manual, 13) a celebrity spokesman, and 14) a patriotic name.

Equity Capital Needed: Data not provided

Franchise Fee: $25,000

Royalty: 5 percent of gross sales excluding fuel sales.

Advertising Co-op Fee: 1 percent of gross sales excluding fuel sales.

Financial Assistance: Financing available through various lending sources.

Management Assistance: Ongoing management assistance.

Training Assistance: Initial training—4 consecutive weeks plus ongoing training.

Retail—Cutlery & Kitchen

Butterfields, And so on.

1040 Wm. Hilton Pkwy., The Circle Bldg.
Hilton Head, SC 29928
Toll-Free Phone:
Phone: (803) 842-6000
Fax: (803) 842-6999
Contact: President

Number of Franchises: 22
Company-Owned Units: 0
Total Units: 22

In Business Since: 1979 **Franchising Since:** 1986

Description of Operation: Retail gourmet kitchen store, located in upscale malls. Our merchandise mix includes high-quality cookware, a large assortment of kitchen gadgets, cookbooks, decorative ceramics, linens, cutlery, and fresh-roasted gourmet coffee beans.

Equity Capital Needed: $130,000-$185,000

Franchise Fee: $20,000

Royalty: 5-4 percent, based on units.

Advertising Co-op Fee:

Financial Assistance: We do not offer a financing plan, but we can offer suggestions and referrals to various sources of financing. We can assist you in preparing a business plan, along with pro forms for your banker, once you become a franchisee.

Management Assistance: The Butterfields operation manual contains procedures, policies and practices essential for each step of your business development. This confidential guide is a valuable reference and excellent tool for training new employees. You will receive periodic visits by our field representatives, who will consult with you and offer useful advice on all facets of your operation.

Training Assistance: Butterfields provides you with extensive training before, during, and after your grand opening. We teach you the operational and management techniques necessary to provide consistent, high-quality merchandising and customer service. We provide training in personnel development, buying, merchandising, advertising, and inventory control.

Pot Pourri

4699 Keele St., Unit 2
Downsview, ON M3J 2N8
Toll-Free Phone:
Phone: (416) 661-9916
Fax: (416) 661-9706
Contact: Vice President of Franchising

Number of Franchises: 27
Company-Owned Units: 1
Total Units: 28

In Business Since: 1991 **Franchising Since:** 1991

Description of Operation: Pot Pourri operates franchised kitchen and giftware retail stores.

Equity Capital Needed: $100,000-$300,000

Franchise Fee: $25,000

Royalty: 6 percent

Advertising Co-op Fee:

Financial Assistance: We do not provide financial assistance.

Management Assistance: We provide ongoing visits by operations specialists, financial advice by home office specialists, advertising preparation and materials, advice by headquarters specialists, buying assistance, and training seminars.

Training Assistance: Same as above.

Rolling Pin Kitchen Emporium

4264 Winters Chapel Road, Building 2
Atlanta, GA 30360
Web Address: www.rollingpin.com
E-mail Address: cpke@aol.com
Toll-Free Phone:
Phone: (710) 457-2600
Fax: (710) 457-3110
Contact: President

Number of Franchises: 22
Company-Owned Units: 14
Total Units: 36

In Business Since: 1978 **Franchising Since:** 1982

Description of Operation: Gourmet Housewares stores offering over 4,000 gadgets. Hard-to-find items, kitchen accessories, cookware, and cutlery.

Equity Capital Needed: $200,000

Franchise Fee: $20,000

Royalty: 5 percent royalty

Advertising Co-op Fee: .5 percent advertising fund

Financial Assistance: No data available.

Management Assistance: District messages do biannual visits, however individual telephone assistance every day.

Training Assistance: Training at headquarters 7 days then initial setup and ongoing thereafter.

Retail—Electronics

RadioShack

100 Throckmorton Street, Ste. 1000
Fort Worth, TX 76102
Web Address: www.radioshack.com
E-mail Address: pcrump1@tandy.com
Toll-Free Phone:
Phone: (817) 415-3499
Fax: (817) 339-8651
Contact: Associate Store Marketing Director

Number of Franchises: 1934
Company-Owned Units: 4969
Total Units: 6903

In Business Since: 1921 **Franchising Since:** 1968

Description of Operation: RadioShack Select is an opportunity for established retailers in communities that have a population between 1,500 and 15,000 and that want to add a "store-within-a-store" concept. The RadioShack Select package—from fixtures to products—requires less than 400 square feet. Merchandise includes approximately 1,800 of America's most popular electronic products and accessories, including direct-to-home satellite. In addition, RadioShack Select provides one-stop access to more than 110,000 additional electronic products and accessories through the RadioShack Unlimited special order program. RadioShack Select is available with an initial investment of less than $60,000.

Equity Capital Needed: $60,000

Franchise Fee: $7,500

Royalty: None

Advertising Co-op Fee: None

Financial Assistance: Financing available

Management Assistance: Toll-free support line for immediate answers

- Seminars
- Workshops
- Training Manual
- Store operations manual

Training Assistance: *One-on-one, on-site training provided by RadioShack representatives.

- Manuals
- Workshops
- Seminars

©JIST Works, Inc., Indianapolis, IN 46202

Retail—Furniture

Slumberland

3060 Centerville Rd.
Little Canada, MN 55117
Web Address: www.slumberland-furniture.com
Toll-Free Phone:
Phone: (612) 482-7500
Fax: (612) 482-0027
Contact: Franchise Coordinator

Number of Franchises: 33
Company-Owned Units: 0
Total Units: 33

In Business Since: 1967   **Franchising Since:** 1968

Description of Operation: Retail furniture.

Equity Capital Needed: $112,500-$295,000

Franchise Fee: $10,000

Royalty: 6 percent

Advertising Co-op Fee:

Financial Assistance: None.

Management Assistance: A complete management package is available to all franchisees. The assistance includes marketing, advertising, sales training, and office set-up.

Training Assistance: You and two of your employees will participate in a training course of 9 days in Orlando. This course provides instruction in the Balloons & Bears merchandising and customer service techniques, administrative procedures, and financial controls. A representative from Balloons & Bears will then spend one week at your store to provide assistance with the store set-up, grand opening events, and advertising. You may also be invited to attend refresher courses held in your area.

Retail—Gifts

Balloons & Bears

901 Douglas Ave., Ste. 204
Altamonte Springs, FL 32714
Web Address: www.balloonsandbears.com
Toll-Free Phone: (800) 771-2327
Phone: (407) 869-7422
Fax:
Contact: President/CEO

Number of Franchises: 0
Company-Owned Units: 4
Total Units: 4

In Business Since: 1989   **Franchising Since:** 1993

Description of Operation: Balloons, gift store, and florist—like none other. We are number one in our industry. A combination of balloons, gift baskets, flowers, and singing telegrams make us unique. High profit margins and low overhead make us profitable.

Equity Capital Needed: $45,000-$60,000

Franchise Fee: $19,500

Royalty: 6 percent

Advertising Co-op Fee:

Financial Assistance: Assistance in obtaining SBA or conventional loans. Our director of operations is president of a national bank and provides the insight into the financing process.

Management Assistance: 2-3 weeks of training at headquarters. One-week, on-site, and ongoing visits and support. Management effective seminars and T.Q.M.

Training Assistance: 2-3 weeks of intense training includes all operations, bookkeeping, accounting, management, and operations.

Country Clutter

3333 Vaca Valley Pkwy. Ste. 900
Vacaville, CA 95688
Web Address: www.countryclutter.com
Toll-Free Phone: (800) 425-8883
Phone: (707) 451-6890
Fax: (707) 451-0410
Contact: President

Number of Franchises: 2
Company-Owned Units: 2
Total Units: 4

In Business Since: 1991   **Franchising Since:** 1992

Description of Operation: A charming store for gifts, collectibles and home decor. A unique business that offers old-fashioned quality, selections and customer service. A complete franchise program that is professionally designed, computerized, and planned to sell a perfected blend of country merchandise, made up of primarily American manufacturers and crafters. Rich arrangements and displays of textures, colors and aromas make shopping at Country Clutter a true sensory delight.

Equity Capital Needed: $151,000-$251,000

Franchise Fee: $25,000

Royalty: 4 percent

Advertising Co-op Fee:

Financial Assistance: Country Visions (franchisor) does not directly assist in financing. However, we have established relationships with SBA and other financial sources.

Management Assistance: Graduate from our own Franchise Business Degree program! A complete home study course covers all business systems and operations. Also, enjoy a three-day training seminar at our corporate offices in California. Ongoing support will be provided which includes 5 days of on-site training before you open.

Training Assistance: Same as above.

John Simmons

36 W. Calhoun Ave.
Memphis, TN 38103
Toll-Free Phone: (800) 737-5567
Phone: (901) 526-5567
Fax: (901) 526-5605
Contact: President

Number of Franchises: 4
Company-Owned Units: 1
Total Units: 5

In Business Since: 1985   **Franchising Since:** 1985

Description of Operation: General gifts.

Equity Capital Needed: $100,000-$150,000

Franchise Fee: $15,000

Royalty: 4.5 percent

Advertising Co-op Fee:

Financial Assistance: Not available.

Management Assistance: Data not available.

Training Assistance: We offer 2-4 day training period.

John T's Unique Gifts

1018 Garden St., Ste. 206
Santa Barbara, CA 93101
E-mail Address: JOHNSB@JUNO.Com
Toll-Free Phone: (800) 782-8988
Phone: (805) 564-6943
Fax: (805) 564-6953
Contact: President

Number of Franchises: 2
Company-Owned Units: 6
Total Units: 8

In Business Since: 1967   **Franchising Since:** 1991

Description of Operation: John T's is a retail men's gift shop, selling games, gifts, pipes, and tobacco in mall locations.

Equity Capital Needed: $140,000-$250,000

Franchise Fee: $20,000

Royalty: 5 percent

Advertising Co-op Fee:

Financial Assistance: None.

Management Assistance: We provide 2 weeks of training in a corporate store before the franchise unit opens, then 1 week in the new franchise unit upon grand opening. We'll visit the unit once per month thereafter.

Training Assistance: We offer 2 weeks of in-store training (in one of the corporate stores), 1 week in the new store for grand opening, and visit once every month. In-store training at corporate store can be longer, depending on the need.

MacBirdie Golf Gifts

5250 W. 73rd St. Ste. I
Minneapolis, MN 55439
Web Address: www.macbirdie.com
Toll-Free Phone: (800) 343-1033
Phone: (612) 830-1033
Fax: (612) 830-1055
Contact: Director of Franchise Operations

Number of Franchises: 0
Company-Owned Units: 8
Total Units: 8

In Business Since: 1989   **Franchising Since:** 1994

Description of Operation: Mac Birdie offers a wide variety of flexible, year-round, and seasonal opportunities. Our exclusive Mac Birdie apparel line is supported by a variety of accessories, novelties, and executive gifts. Options for selling Mac Birdie merchandise such as kiosks, carts, catalog sales, gift racks and/or leased departments, depends on location and personal interests.

Equity Capital Needed: $30,000-$100,000

Franchise Fee: $5,000-$50,000

Royalty: 5 percent

Advertising Co-op Fee:

Financial Assistance: None.

Management Assistance: Business planning, site selection, lease negotiations, and grand opening assistance. An extensive operations manual is distributed and up-dated regularly. A franchise newsletter will be distributed regularly and a franchise advisory committee will be approved as the network grows.

Training Assistance: 1 week of professional training at the corporate headquarters is provided in merchandising, set-ups, product information, advertising, inventory, purchasing, personnel, customer service, and sales. Ongoing training is provided. You will leave with your individual plan in hand.

... it Store

1111 Flint Rd. Unit 36
Downsview, ON M3J 3C7
Toll-Free Phone:
Phone: (416) 487-8673
Fax: (416) 665-8839
Contact:

Number of Franchises: 34
Company-Owned Units: 20
Total Units: 54

In Business Since: 1981   **Franchising Since:** 1982

Description of Operation: Sales of gifts, cards and novelty items.

Equity Capital Needed: $150,000

Franchise Fee: $25,000

Royalty: 6 percent

Advertising Co-op Fee:

Financial Assistance: Franchisees to arrange their own financing.

Management Assistance: Services of supervisor for up to 1 week at opening. Semi-annual meetings. Regular visits to all locations to offer merchandising and sales assistance. Ongoing head office support.

Training Assistance: Initial 2 days of training in Toronto, ON. Training manuals.

Papyrus Franchise Corporation

954 60th St.
Oakland, CA 94608
Web Address: www.papyrus-stores.com
Toll-Free Phone: (800) 872-7978
Phone: (510) 428-0166
Fax: (510) 428-0615
Contact:

Number of Franchises: 85
Company-Owned Units: 39
Total Units: 124

In Business Since: 1973   **Franchising Since:** 1988

Description of Operation: A Papyrus store offers the finest in greeting cards, paper accessories, gifts, and custom-printed invitations, announcements, and stationery. Sophisticated and upscale, the stores are an exciting alternative to the traditional card store.

Equity Capital Needed: $75,000-$100,000

Franchise Fee: $29,500

Royalty: 6 percent

Advertising Co-op Fee:

Financial Assistance: We provide third-party referrals.

Management Assistance: Ongoing support service.

Training Assistance: We offer 9 days of training. Ongoing regional training seminars and meetings, plus frequent on-site visits.

Retail—Hobby

Hobbytown USA

6301 S. 58th St.
Lincoln, NE 68516
Web Address: www.hobbytown.com
E-mail Address: sales@hobbytown.com
Toll-Free Phone: (800) 858-7370
Phone: (402) 434-5052
Fax: (402) 434-5055
Contact: Director of Franchising

Number of Franchises: 126
Company-Owned Units: 1
Total Units: 127

In Business Since: 1969   **Franchising Since:** 1986

Description of Operation: Hobbytown USA allows the rare opportunity to work and play at the same time. Hobbytown USA carries radio-controlled vehicles of all types—model trains, adventure games, models, sports cards, and more! Hobbytown USA is the country's largest chain of hobby stores.

Equity Capital Needed: $50,000-$80,000

Franchise Fee: $19,500

Royalty: 2.5 percent

Advertising Co-op Fee:

Financial Assistance: None.

Management Assistance: The company will furnish timely computer up-dates, an evaluation of sales, an annual inventory and sales analysis, operations and pre-opening manuals, and a monthly company newsletter.

Training Assistance: The company requires a 1 week training program at the home office in Lincoln, NE. In addition, a field manager will assist the franchisee at the new store location, including grand opening.

Retail—Home

Spring Crest Drapery Centers

505 W. Lambert Rd.
Brea, CA 92621
Web Address: www.springcrest.com
Toll-Free Phone: (800) 552-5523
Phone: (714) 529-9993
Fax: (714) 529-2093
Contact: President

Number of Franchises: 153
Company-Owned Units: 1
Total Units: 154

In Business Since: 1955   **Franchising Since:** 1968

Description of Operation: Retail stores selling custom window coverings and related decorating accessories. The franchisor is the manufacturer of an exclusive drapery system sold only through franchised stores.

Equity Capital Needed: $25,000-$70,000

Franchise Fee: $15,000

Royalty: 3-5 percent

Advertising Co-op Fee:

Financial Assistance: Financing assistance is available.

Management Assistance: Spring Crest provides assistance with site location, design and set-up, operations

manual, forms, supplier arrangement, newsletter, meetings, and home office and regional support.

Training Assistance: We provide a combination of classroom and in-field training over a 3-4 week period. Ongoing training through regional meetings and conferences.

Stencil Home Gallery

2300 Pilgrim Rd.
Brookfield, WI 53005
Toll-Free Phone:
Phone: (414) 797-9974
Fax:
Contact: President

Number of Franchises: 0
Company-Owned Units: 2
Total Units: 2

In Business Since: 1988   **Franchising Since:** 1993

Description of Operation: Retail franchise, specializing in decorative border stencils for the home and also featuring gifts and home furnishing.

Equity Capital Needed: $47,800-$98,000

Franchise Fee: $15,000

Royalty: 5 percent

Advertising Co-op Fee:

Financial Assistance: None.

Management Assistance: The franchisor will provide initial training to one manager for each store developed.

Training Assistance: The initial training program will include, but is not limited to, advice and guidelines with respect to merchandising, advertising, store decoration, and store operation.

Wallpapers To Go

16825 Northchase Dr., Ste. 900
Houston, TX 77060
Web Address: www.wallpaperstogo.com
E-mail Address: tonya@wallpaperstogo.com
Toll-Free Phone: (800) 843-7094
Phone: (713) 874-0800
Fax: (713) 874-3655
Contact: Franchise Development Assistant

Number of Franchises: 61
Company-Owned Units: 16
Total Units: 77

In Business Since: 1986   **Franchising Since:** 1986

Description of Operation: The nation's largest franchisor of in-stock specialty wallpaper stores; offering extensive selection of coordinating products, including window coverings, fabrics, decorative accessories, paint, along with thousands of rolls of wallcovering.

Equity Capital Needed: $129,000-$155,000 (includes franchise fee)

Franchise Fee: $15,000-$25,000

Royalty: 6 percent

Advertising Co-op Fee:

Financial Assistance: We provide finance package-assistance with preparing a proposal for the bank and/or SBA. We participate in the VetFran program (finance up to 50 percent of the franchise fee.)

Management Assistance: We provide ongoing merchandising support and programs, promotions, ongoing store visits by operations field directors, lease negotiations, legal comments, site selection, national convention, store layout, and design.

Training Assistance: Training consists of 1 week of comprehensive training at corporate office. 1-2 weeks or more of in-store training before and during opening of store.

Retail—Music

Disc Go Round

4200 Dahlberg Dr.
Minneapolis, MN 55422
Web Address: www.discgoround.com
E-mail Address: info@dgr1.com
Toll-Free Phone: (800) 842-4356
Phone: (612) 520-8500
Fax: (612) 520-8623
Contact: Franchise Developers

Number of Franchises: 126
Company-Owned Units: 3
Total Units: 129

In Business Since: 1990   **Franchising Since:** 1992

Description of Operation: The Disc Go Round retail franchise chain focuses on buying and selling pre-owned as well as new CDs and related accessories, providing the value that today's consumers are seeking. Disc Go Round stores feature the kind of buying environment that makes it fun and easy for customers to buy and sell. Our customer look-up stations, CD reservation system, convenient listening stations, and more make Disc Go Round the store of choice for customers who want to find value in an inviting environment.

Equity Capital Needed: $86,300-$114,500

Franchise Fee: $20,000

Royalty: 5 percent of gross sales

Advertising Co-op Fee: $500/year

Financial Assistance: The company offers a 2 1/2 day training session at the headquarters in Minneapolis to train

new owners on putting together a business plan and presenting it to a banker.

Management Assistance:

Training Assistance: In addition to the financial and real estate training, Disc Go Round provides comprehensive training covering buying used products, customer service, the hiring and training of staff, merchandising, advertising planning, store operations, and more.

Records on Wheels

255 Shields Ct.
Markham, ON L3R 8V2
Toll-Free Phone:
Phone: (905) 475-3550
Fax: (905) 475-4163
Contact: Franchise Director

Number of Franchises: 24
Company-Owned Units: 18
Total Units: 42

In Business Since: 1974 **Franchising Since:** 1975

Description of Operation: Retail stores offering compact discs, cassettes, video, and music accessories. Retail operations across Canada. Stores which are successful tend to have managers with a general interest in music trends.

Equity Capital Needed: $75,000 +

Franchise Fee: $7,500

Royalty: 0 percent

Advertising Co-op Fee:

Financial Assistance: No financing.

Management Assistance: In most locations, stores are owner-operated. General guideline from head office are enforced with every location.

Training Assistance: Where possible, hands-on training is held in another location.

Top Forty

10333 - 174 St.
Edmonton, AB T5S 1H1
Toll-Free Phone: (800) 661-9931
Phone: (403) 489-2324
Fax: (403) 486-7528
Contact: Vice President

Number of Franchises: 18
Company-Owned Units: 20
Total Units: 38

In Business Since: 1977 **Franchising Since:** 1980

Description of Operation: Retailer of pre-recorded music products, such as compact discs, cassettes, videos, and other such paraphernalia.

Equity Capital Needed: $120,000-$200,000

Franchise Fee: $15,000

Royalty: 5 percent

Advertising Co-op Fee:

Financial Assistance: A franchise financing package has been developed with the cooperation of a major chartered bank. Assistance in preparing all of the necessary information and applications is provided.

Management Assistance: In addition to the new franchise start-up training, ongoing managerial training is provided through regular field visits, counseling from the head office, financial statement review, and annual franchise seminars.

Training Assistance: Initial training consists of 2 weeks; 1 week at the head office and 1 week at a store location. Upon opening a new store, further assistance and training in starting up a store is provided on-site. An extensive and constantly updated systems manual is provided. Regular operational memoranda are also provided.

Retail—Newsstand

Street Corner News, McColla Enterprises

2945 Wanamaker Drive
Topeka, KS 66614
Toll-Free Phone: (800) 789-6397
Phone: (913) 272-8529
Fax: (913) 272-2384
Contact: CEO

Number of Franchises: 11
Company-Owned Units: 7
Total Units: 18

In Business Since: 1988 **Franchising Since:** 1995

Description of Operation: Street Corner News is a newsstand/convenience store/tobacconist situation in high trafficked locations in regional mall settings offering broad selection of convenience products such as cigarettes, candies, snacks lottery, cigars, beverages, and over the counter medicines and sundry items.

Equity Capital Needed: $25,000

Franchise Fee: $17,500

Royalty: Data not provided

Advertising Co-op Fee: Data not provided

Financial Assistance: Help will be provided in assisting obtaining an SBA loan.

Management Assistance: National pricing, promotions, POS material, disseminating financial, marketing, and product updates.

Training Assistance: Initial intensive in-house training, comprehensive operational manual, ongoing telephone, e-mail, newsletter, and site support.

Gateway Newsstands

30 East Beaver Creek Road, Ste. 206
Richmond Hill, ON L4B 1J2
Web Address: www.gatewaynewstands.com
E-mail Address: info@gatewaynewstands.com
Toll-Free Phone: (800) 942-5351
Phone: (905) 886-8900
Fax: (905) 886-8904
Contact: CEO

Number of Franchises: 304
Company-Owned Units: 0
Total Units: 304

In Business Since: 1982   **Franchising Since:** 1982

Description of Operation: Franchised newsstands/candy/coffee outlets in shopping malls, office towers, and transit locations.

Equity Capital Needed: $75,000

Franchise Fee: $25,000-75,000

Royalty: 3 or 5 percent of gross sales

Advertising Co-op Fee: None

Financial Assistance: Based on individual franchised locations and costs to construct and set up.

Management Assistance: Training program in store for as long as is needed.

Training Assistance:

Retail—Miscellaneous

Bath Fitter

27 Berard Dr. Ste. 2701
S. Burlington, VT 05403
Web Address: www.bathfitter.com
Toll-Free Phone: (800) 892-2847
Phone: (802) 860-2919
Fax: (802) 862-7976
Contact:

Number of Franchises: 9
Company-Owned Units: 1
Total Units: 10

In Business Since: 1984   **Franchising Since:** 1992

Description of Operation: Sales and installation of custom-molded bathtub liners, made-to-measure acrylic bath walls, shower bases, shower walls, and related accessories.

Equity Capital Needed: $24,800-$48,400

Franchise Fee: $12,500

Royalty: 0 percent

Advertising Co-op Fee:

Financial Assistance: Data not available.

Management Assistance: Direct assistance with preparation of a business plan, regular on-site visits by area representatives, ad layouts, preprinted full-color marketing materials, and an 800-number hotline (24 hours).

Training Assistance: Office and administration procedures (1 day), sales methods (1 day), and installation techniques (3 days-owners and employees).

Candleman

P.O. Box 731 1021 Industrial Park Rd.
Brainerd, MN 56401
Web Address: www.candleman.com
Toll-Free Phone: (800) 328-3453
Phone: (218) 829-0592
Fax: (218) 825-2449
Contact: Vice President

Number of Franchises: 21
Company-Owned Units: 1
Total Units: 22

In Business Since: 1991   **Franchising Since:** 1992

Description of Operation: Sale of retail specialty stores, located in regional shopping malls, offering the widest selection of candles and accessories anywhere.

Equity Capital Needed: $50,000-$75,000

Franchise Fee: $25,000

Royalty: 6 percent

Advertising Co-op Fee:

Financial Assistance: Assistance in preparing loan presentations to third-party lenders such as SBA.

Management Assistance: Complete start-up assistance: begins with financing site location, lease and remodeling negotiation to training in an operating store, various manuals, videos, promotions, proprietary computerized operating system, on-site support, 800 number, newsletters, monthly reports, new products, and more.

Training Assistance: Data not available.

Cleaning Ideas

P.O. Box 7269
San Antonio, TX 78207
Toll-Free Phone:
Phone: (210) 227-9161
Fax: (210) 227-0002
Contact: Vice President

Number of Franchises: 0
Company-Owned Units: 12
Total Units: 12

In Business Since: 1979   **Franchising Since:** 1986

Description of Operation: Cleaning Ideas is a unique retail/wholesale store operation. Cleaning Ideas stores sell over 1,600 items and chemicals to be used for cleaning.

All chemical items are manufactured by Cleaning Ideas, thus gross profits run as high as 60 percent. All products are sold with a money-back guarantee. Each store is 1,000 square feet.

Equity Capital Needed: $6,000-$20,000

Franchise Fee: $1,000

Royalty: 0 percent

Advertising Co-op Fee:

Financial Assistance: Data not available.

Management Assistance: Cleaning Ideas provides ongoing managerial and technical assistance for the duration of the franchise agreement.

Training Assistance: An intensive six-day, mandatory training course is scheduled for all new franchisees. All training is performed in company-owned stores.

Dollar Discount Stores of America

1362 Naamans Creek Rd.
Boothwyn, PA 19061
Web Address: www.dollardiscount.com
Toll-Free Phone: (800) 227-5314
Phone: (610) 497-1991
Fax: (610) 485-6439
Contact: Franchise Director

Number of Franchises: 29
Company-Owned Units: 0
Total Units: 29

In Business Since: 1983   **Franchising Since:** 1985

Description of Operation: Retail franchise—dollar stores and variety discount stores.

Equity Capital Needed: $96,750-$126,925

Franchise Fee: $18,000

Royalty: 3 percent

Advertising Co-op Fee:

Financial Assistance: The franchisor will assist prospective franchise owner in preparing loan application, as well as referring prospective franchise owner to potential institutions which provide loans to qualified applicants.

Management Assistance: We assist the new owner in ordering fixtures and merchandise. Provide minimum of 7 day field rep assistance in preparing store for opening. New franchise owner will get extensive support and assistance during opening period.

Training Assistance: One-week training class, where all facets of the business are discussed and new owners are trained on how to run the business and how to strive for the maximum profit potential.

Fan-A-Mania

3855 S. 500 West #R
Salt Lake City, UT 84115
E-mail Address: Fanaman1@aol.com

Toll-Free Phone: (800) 770-9120
Phone: (801) 288-9120
Fax: (801) 288-9210
Contact: Director Franchise Sales

Number of Franchises: 10
Company-Owned Units: 5
Total Units: 15

In Business Since: 1994   **Franchising Since:** 1994

Description of Operation: The franchise features entertainment and sports products such as casual wear, souvenirs, collectibles, and novelty items. Marketed primarily through stores and kiosks located in malls. The product lines include Warner Brothers, Disney, Professional, and College sports licensed merchandise.

Equity Capital Needed: $100,000

Franchise Fee: $19,500

Royalty: 3.5 percent of gross sales

Advertising Co-op Fee: 1 percent local

Financial Assistance: No data provided

Management Assistance: Franchisee is provided with our operations manual, site selection, and lease negotiation. In-store sales and merchandise training. Buying assistance as well as volume discounts. Advisory services include analysis of sales, marketing, and financial data.

Training Assistance: Company training-3 days at corporate headquarters and 1 week onsite training. Includes all aspects of the operation of a store including financial, marketing, merchandising, staff hiring, buying, inventory controls, and company quality standards.

Four Season Sunrooms

5005 Veterans Memorial Hwy.
Holbrook, NY 11741
Toll-Free Phone: (800) 521-0179
Phone: (516) 563-4000
Fax: (516) 563-4010
Contact: Vice President of Sales

Number of Franchises: 267
Company-Owned Units: 5
Total Units: 272

In Business Since: 1975   **Franchising Since:** 1985

Description of Operation: Four Seasons offers an opportunity for qualified sales and marketing-oriented individuals to offer and sell the widest range of sunroom products available. No previous technical background or skills required.

Equity Capital Needed: $25,000-$40,000

Franchise Fee: $7,500-$10,000-$15,000 depends on dealer level

Royalty: None or 2.5 percent on non-Four Season products

Advertising Co-op Fee:

Financial Assistance: None.

Management Assistance: 3-5 days of initial training, training and operations manuals, videos and regional meetings, and national conventions.

Training Assistance: General business (pro forma), advertising and marketing, sales and lead management, and installation.

International Golf

9101 N. Thornydale Rd.
Tucson, AZ 85741
Toll-Free Phone: (800) 204-2600
Phone: (520) 744-1840
Fax: (520) 744-2076
Contact: Franchising Assistant

Number of Franchises: 47
Company-Owned Units: 4
Total Units: 51

In Business Since: 1977   **Franchising Since:** 1981

Description of Operation: Off-course retail golf store. May add tennis and/or ski lines.

Equity Capital Needed: $275,000-$300,000

Franchise Fee: $42,000

Royalty: 2 percent

Advertising Co-op Fee:

Financial Assistance: International Golf does not provide financing. However, help is provided in acquiring funds from financial institutions, including preparing the business plan.

Management Assistance: International Golf's support team is constantly available for advice and assistance, updating franchisees on new merchandise, advertising and marketing programs, and making improvements for daily operations.

Training Assistance: We provide 2 weeks of training in all facets of the business for the franchise owner and key employee(s) at International Golf headquarters in Oklahoma City, OK with the Vice President of Operations.

Just-A-Buck

301 N. Main St.
New City, NY 10956
Toll-Free Phone: (800) 332-2229
Phone: (914) 638-4111
Fax: (914) 638-3878
Contact: Director of Franchise Development

Number of Franchises: 22
Company-Owned Units: 6
Total Units: 28

In Business Since: 1980   **Franchising Since:** 1992

Description of Operation: Diverse selection of quality merchandise for Just-A-Buck. This is a retail operation that caters to the ever-evolving low price-point marketplace. We pay close attention to quality in customer service, merchandising, operations, and store design.

Equity Capital Needed: $70,000

Franchise Fee: $25,000

Royalty: 4 percent

Advertising Co-op Fee:

Financial Assistance: Financial assistance available to new franchisees consists of assistance in preparing a business plan, narrative with pro forma operating statements and cash flows. In addition, the franchisor will assist in making introductions to potential lenders.

Management Assistance: Just-A-Buck provides ongoing support in reordering merchandise, inventory control, store appearance, and seasonal merchandising (planning, projections and ordering). Our franchise office provides accounting assistance in analyzing sales figures, customer counts, average customer sales, cash sheets, office systems, and payroll percent. Just-A-Buck will also advise and help to set guidelines for personnel, as well as loss prevention measures, and assist in equipment purchasing and repairs.

Training Assistance: We provide fifteen-day training program—5 days of pre-opening assistance in company units and ten days on-site in a franchised unit. We will consult and advise with regard to initial inventory, merchandising and retailing display, design, store layout, sales techniques, personnel development, and other business operational and advertising matters that directly relate to the franchise operation.

Relax The Back Corporation

2101 Rosecrans Ave., Ste. 1250
El Segundo, CA 90245
Web Address: www.relaxtheback.com
E-mail Address: info@relaxtheback.com
Toll-Free Phone: (800) 290-2225
Phone: (310) 416-1077
Fax: (310) 416-1076
Contact: Franchise Development

Number of Franchises: 81
Company-Owned Units: 13
Total Units: 94

In Business Since: 1984   **Franchising Since:** 1988

Description of Operation: Relax The Back is the nation's largest franchisor of retail stores devoted exclusively to back-related products. The more than 500 items offered by each store range from simple back braces, support cushions, and books to elaborate Shiatsu-style massage loungers, ergonomic work stations, and air-adjustable lumbar support sleep systems. Featuring a trained, friendly staff eager to share its extensive knowledge on preventing and relieving back pain. Relax The Back caters to the 80 percent of the U.S. population that suffers from chronic or acute back problems. Franchised

stores, which average about 25,000 square feet of floor space, operate in strip centers, store-fronts, free standing buildings, and power centers.

Equity Capital Needed: $200,000

Franchise Fee: $25,000

Royalty: 4 percent

Advertising Co-op Fee: 1 percent

Financial Assistance: None

Management Assistance: Two weeks of complete training and ongoing operations support.

Training Assistance: Two weeks of complete training and ongoing operations support.

Roaden Jewelers

4259 Canada Way, Ste. 246
Burnaby, BC V5G 1H1
Toll-Free Phone:
Phone: (604) 438-1625
Fax: (604) 438-1635
Contact: General Manager

Number of Franchises: 12
Company-Owned Units: 0
Total Units: 12

In Business Since: 1976 **Franchising Since:** 1982

Description of Operation: Retail jewelry stores, specializing in fine gold and silver jewelry, diamonds, name brand watches, and giftware. Located on key corners in major regional shopping centers. The stores maintain a professional staff of goldsmiths, stone setters, managers, and sales people to provide our customers with the best and complete services possible. With on-site goldsmiths, we offer unique "While Customer Shops" jewelry and watch repair services. We offer customers the convenience to visit any of the Rodan Jewellers locations for after sale services, such as ring sizing, battery replacement, refund/exchange, redemption of gift certificates, and so on.

Equity Capital Needed: $250,000-500,000 Canadian

Franchise Fee: $50,000-75,000 Canadian

Royalty: 5 percent

Advertising Co-op Fee: 2-2.5 percent

Financial Assistance: Financial assistance is available. Details of financial assistance varies among franchise, depending upon the individual situation and needs.

Management Assistance: We provide grand opening assistance, marketing strategies, architectural planning and construction, and so on. Management meetings are held regularly to bring franchisees up-to-date on the current situation of the industry to help them respond quickly to the ever-changing market place. Ongoing assistance is also provided in all aspects of the business.

Training Assistance: An initial 80 hours of classroom and in-store training is provided to the franchisees and staff. A comprehensive curriculum includes instruction in all facets of the business and marketing operations. Other seminars are also offered from time to time on special topics.

Sangster's Health Centres

433 34th St. E.
Saskatoon, SK S7K 0S9
Web Address: www.sansters.sk
E-mail Address: franchise@sansters.sk.ca
Toll-Free Phone:
Phone: (306) 653-4481
Fax: (306) 654-4688
Contact: Franchise Department

Number of Franchises: 40
Company-Owned Units: 1
Total Units: 41

In Business Since: 1971 **Franchising Since:** 1978

Description of Operation: Retail sales of vitamins, herbs, natural cosmetics, natural foods, and body building supplies. We specialize in our own name-brand products and also national company brands. We are looking for a master franchise in the U.S.

Equity Capital Needed: $95,000-$115,000 CBN

Franchise Fee: $25,000 CBN

Royalty: 5 percent; 1 percent advertising fee

Advertising Co-op Fee:

Financial Assistance: We help arrange bank financing with business plans and projections.

Management Assistance: Franchisees are trained in supervision, accounting, and the various things that managers need.

Training Assistance: Franchisees will train in an existing operation, as well as be trained in their own location. Nutrition course provided.

Servistar Home & Garden Showplace

8600 Brynmawr
Chicago, IL 60631
Toll-Free Phone:
Phone: (773) 695-5000
Fax: (773) 695-7049
Contact: General Manager

Number of Franchises: 172
Company-Owned Units: 0
Total Units: 172

In Business Since: 1988 **Franchising Since:** 1988

Description of Operation: A full-line retail garden center, featuring nursery stock, soil, fertilizer, gift department, crafts, outdoor equipment, and much more.

Equity Capital Needed: $75,000 +

Franchise Fee: $1,500

Royalty: $4,800 a year.

Advertising Co-op Fee:

Financial Assistance: SBA and National Co-operative Bank.

Management Assistance: We provide store design, layout, set-up, ordering, advertising, supplies, and agricultural guidance.

Training Assistance: We offer owner clinics, along with field sales support.

Silkcorp

2101 Roberts Dr.
Broadview, IL 60153
Toll-Free Phone: (800) 843-7455
Phone: (708) 450-9800
Fax: (708) 450-1507
Contact: President

Number of Franchises: 1
Company-Owned Units: 41
Total Units: 42

In Business Since: 1991   **Franchising Since:** 1992

Description of Operation: Retail outlet of silk trees and plants.

Equity Capital Needed: $50,000-$100,000

Franchise Fee: $25,000

Royalty: 6.5 percent

Advertising Co-op Fee:

Financial Assistance: Not available.

Management Assistance: Site selection and financial assistance.

Training Assistance: 4-6 week training period.

Retail—Party Stores

Discount Party Warehouse

538 Larkfield Rd.
E. Northport, NY 11731
Toll-Free Phone:
Phone: (516) 368-5200
Fax: (516) 368-5213
Contact: President

Number of Franchises: 11
Company-Owned Units: 22
Total Units: 33

In Business Since: 1976   **Franchising Since:** 1984

Description of Operation: Retail store of paper and plastic party supplies, decorations, greeting cards and balloons. We are a warehouse concept that features a wide selection of merchandise that is deeply discounted. We are pioneers of the party goods business.

Equity Capital Needed: $250,000-$300,000

Franchise Fee: $25,000

Royalty: 5 percent

Advertising Co-op Fee:

Financial Assistance: None.

Management Assistance: Company provides experienced personnel to assist in the set-up of the store and for the initial opening week of business. Constant and continual communication is performed via telephone, fax, and mail.

Training Assistance: Franchisees receive a professional two-week training program at franchisor's corporate offices in NY.

Paper Warehouse

7630 Excelsior Blvd.
Minneapolis, MN 55426
Web Address: www.@paperwarehouse.com
E-mail Address: jan.pithey@paperwarehouse.com
Toll-Free Phone: (800) 229-1792
Phone: (612) 936-1000
Fax: (612) 936-9800
Contact: Director of Franchise Development

Number of Franchises: 51
Company-Owned Units: 73
Total Units: 124

In Business Since: 1983   **Franchising Since:** 1987

Description of Operation: Retail party stores.

Equity Capital Needed: $101,000-$195,000

Franchise Fee: $19,000-$25,000

Royalty: 4 percent

Advertising Co-op Fee:

Financial Assistance: None.

Management Assistance: Daily assistance (as needed) in finance operations, human resources, advertising, and merchandising.

Training Assistance: We provide 1 week of training.

Party Land

5215 Militia Hill Rd.
Plymouth Meeting, PA 19462
Web Address: www.partyland.com
E-mail Address: jbarry@partyland.com
Toll-Free Phone: (800) 778-9563
Phone: (610) 941-6200
Fax: (610) 941-6301

Contact: Vice President of Sales

Number of Franchises: 202
Company-Owned Units: 1
Total Units: 203

In Business Since: 1986   **Franchising Since:** 1988

Description of Operation: Retail party supplies, balloons, and party favors. World's largest international retail party supply franchise.

Equity Capital Needed: $164,000-$264,000

Franchise Fee: $35,000

Royalty: 5 percent

Advertising Co-op Fee:

Financial Assistance: Available to qualified applicants.

Management Assistance: 12 years of professional party supply retail experience. Location assistance, merchandising, marketing, promotion, buying power, and training at Party Land University.

Training Assistance: 1 week at Party Land University—the most comprehensive and in-depth training in the industry today.

Retail—Photography

Contempo Portraits

3415 W. Glendale Ste. 25
Phoenix, AZ 85051
Toll-Free Phone:
Phone: (602) 589-5050
Fax: (602) 926-2382
Contact: President

Number of Franchises: 0
Company-Owned Units: 0
Total Units: 0

In Business Since: 1987   **Franchising Since:** 1993

Description of Operation: Contempo Portraits franchise is a contemporary portrait studio, offering a new concept in portraiture. A unique blend of creative photography and effective marketing techniques distinguishes Contempo Portrait as a "first of its kind" in the industry.

Equity Capital Needed: $75,000

Franchise Fee: $25,000

Royalty: 7 percent plus 1 percent advertising.

Advertising Co-op Fee:

Financial Assistance: The franchisor will assist the franchisee in obtaining financing through a third party.

Management Assistance: Contempo Portrait provides complete training manuals and forms, as well as continual

support and consultation. Seminars, newsletters, and workshops will be scheduled on a regular basis.

Training Assistance: Training will be conducted in an actual franchise with classroom-type sessions. The training will be supervised by the founder of Contempo Portraits.

Glamour Shots

1300 Metropolitan Ave.
Oklahoma City, OK 73108
Web Address: www.glamourshots.com
E-mail Address: reesa@glamourshots.com
Toll-Free Phone: (800) 336-4550
Phone: (405) 947-8747
Fax: (405) 951-7343
Contact: Franchise Development Coordinator

Number of Franchises: 200
Company-Owned Units: 2
Total Units: 207

In Business Since: 1988   **Franchising Since:** 1992

Description of Operation: Glamour Shots is the world's leader in high fashion photography. We provide the customer with a makeover (including hair and makeup) with 4 wardrobe choices, complete accessories, and a 16 pose photo session. The customer is able to view their photos and place their orders the same day.

Equity Capital Needed: $100,000

Franchise Fee: $15,000

Royalty: None

Advertising Co-op Fee: None

Financial Assistance: Assist in obtaining third party financing.

Management Assistance: Many informational reports are available showing: sales, sales average, customer satisfaction, overall experience rating by employee, and more.

Training Assistance: A week long Glamour Camp covers all areas of store operations. A corporate provided field consultant will also assist in store openings and on a regular basis.

Retail—Shoe Stores

Athlete's Foot, The

1950 Vaughn Rd.
Kennesaw, GA 30144
Web Address: www.theathletesfoot.com
Toll-Free Phone: (800) 524-6444
Phone: (404) 514-4718
Fax: (404) 514-4903
Contact: Director of Franchise Development

Number of Franchises: 386
Company-Owned Units: 279
Total Units: 645

In Business Since: 1971 **Franchising Since:** 1972

Description of Operation: The Athlete's Foot is the largest franchisor of specialty athletic footwear retail stores. We operate in 21 countries including the US, Canada, Mexico, Australia, Europe, and Asia. We sell name-brand athletic footwear and apparel in a typical 2,000 SF store. Our stores are located in malls, strip centers, and downtown locations.

Equity Capital Needed: $175,000-$250,000

Franchise Fee: $25,000

Royalty: 3.5 percent, plus .5 percent advertising fee

Advertising Co-op Fee:

Financial Assistance: None.

Management Assistance: New franchisees are assigned a New Owner Coordinator and a Franchise Coordinator who guides the franchisee through all the steps, from the training session to store opening. The Franchise Coordinator continues to work with the franchisee on an ongoing basis. The Advertising Coordinator works with the franchisee to develop a marketing plan for the grand opening and beyond.

Training Assistance: New franchisees attend a five-day training session in Atlanta. Training encompasses financial planning, inventory planning and control, open-to-buy inventory assortment, visual merchandising, store construction, operations, human resources and advertising. New franchisees certified in 2 other training programs, the Certified Sales Associate and Fit Technician. New franchisees also attend our Fit University in Naperville, IL for 3 days, becoming certified as a Master Fit Technician to certify their staff.

Fleet Feet Sports

2311 J St.
Sacramento, CA 95816
E-mail Address: ffine@aol.com
Toll-Free Phone:
Phone: (916) 557-1000
Fax: (916) 557-1010
Contact: President

Number of Franchises: 31
Company-Owned Units: 0
Total Units: 31

In Business Since: 1976 **Franchising Since:** 1978

Description of Operation: Retailer of specialty athletic footwear and apparel for lifetime sports (running, walking, cycling, swimming, aerobics, and cross-training).

Equity Capital Needed: $125,000-$175,000

Franchise Fee: $20,000

Royalty: 2-4 percent

Advertising Co-op Fee:

Financial Assistance: Financial planning, business planning, review, and financing strategy.

Management Assistance: Operational expertise, financial training, retail sales expertise, computer networking, and product exchange.

Training Assistance: Depending on the status of the franchisee, training can range from 3 weeks-6 months. Combination of classroom, store, and research.

Sox Appeal

6321 Bury Dr. Ste. 1
Eden Prairie, MN 55346
Toll-Free Phone:
Phone: (612) 937-6162
Fax: (612) 934-5665
Contact: Vice President of Franchise Development

Number of Franchises: 28
Company-Owned Units: 0
Total Units: 28

In Business Since: 1984 **Franchising Since:** 1988

Description of Operation: Retail sale of men's, women's and children's shoes.

Equity Capital Needed: $90,000-$130,000

Franchise Fee: $20,000

Royalty: 5 percent

Advertising Co-op Fee:

Financial Assistance: None.

Management Assistance: Aside from the initial training, franchisees may call our toll-free 800 number for help and information on any subject at any time. We also provide detailed manuals to assist the franchisees.

Training Assistance: 4 days of intensive, extensive training, including order writing, hiring and training the staff, back room operations, and so on. Part of 1 day is spent in one of the local stores for hands-on training.

Retail—Sports Equipment & Supplies

A J. Barnes Bicycle Emporium

14230 Stirrup Lane
Wellington, FL 33414
Web Address: www.ajbarnes.com
E-mail Address: ajbarnes1@ajbarnes.com
Toll-Free Phone: (888) 252-2453
Phone: (901) 368-3333
Fax: (901) 368-1144
Contact: Director of Marketing

Number of Franchises: 24
Company-Owned Units: 0
Total Units: 24

In Business Since: 1989 **Franchising Since:** 1992

Description of Operation: A. J. Barnes Bicycle Emporium is the world's largest chain of franchised bicycle retail stores. A. J. Barnes features an "old-fashioned" theme with dark green oak wood, and brass accouterments giving a warm, nostalgic feeling. A unique open-kitchen service area permits customers to actually watch their bicycle being serviced.

Equity Capital Needed: $40,000

Franchise Fee: $25,000

Royalty: 6 percent of gross sales

Advertising Co-op Fee:

Financial Assistance: A. J. Barnes is SBA approved and parent company can assist in preparing the business plan and other start-up related issues.

Management Assistance: The A. J. Barnes Game Plan budgets quantitative and qualitative sales and operations data on a monthly basis. We plan quarterly and visit results monthly.

Training Assistance: 2 weeks at home office in Palm Beach, Florida; 5 days on-site.

Bike Line

1035 Andrew Dr.
West Chester, PA 19380
Web Address: www.bikeline.com
Toll-Free Phone: (800) 537-2654
Phone: (610) 429-4370
Fax: (610) 429-4295
Contact: Director of Franchise Development

Number of Franchises: 55
Company-Owned Units: 17
Total Units: 72

In Business Since: 1983 **Franchising Since:** 1991

Description of Operation: Retail sales and service of bicycle and fitness equipment.

Equity Capital Needed: $106,000-$152,000

Franchise Fee: $24,500

Royalty: 4 percent

Advertising Co-op Fee:

Financial Assistance: We will assist with third-party financing.

Management Assistance: We assist with site location and lease negotiating. We also provide a turn-key store, and will work closely with our contractors through the build-out. We provide a full-training program as well as ongoing support, monthly newsletters, and biannual meetings.

Training Assistance: 2 weeks of training at corporate headquarters covering all aspects of running a bike shop. 5 days of support during grand opening.

Golf USA

3705 W. Memorial Rd., Ste. 801
Oklahoma City, OK 73120
Toll-Free Phone: (800) 488-1107
Phone: (405) 751-0015
Fax: (405) 755-0065
Contact: Director of Franchising and Marketing

Number of Franchises: 75
Company-Owned Units: 1
Total Units: 76

In Business Since: 1986 **Franchising Since:** 1989

Description of Operation: Franchise of retail golf stores.

Equity Capital Needed: $75,000-$100,000

Franchise Fee: $30,000-$40,000

Royalty: 2 percent

Advertising Co-op Fee:

Financial Assistance: Assistance in business plan operation.

Management Assistance: On-site training by qualified Golf USA staff member in all phases of retail store operations. An operations manual is provided to use for daily operations.

Training Assistance: 1 week of training in all aspects of the operation of a retail store, i.e., hands-on computer training, basic accounting, merchandising, and so on, at the international headquarters in Edmond, OK. Professional speakers and manufacturer's representatives are invited to the training classes.

Las Vegas Discount Golf & Tennis

5325 S. Valley View Blvd., Ste. 10
Las Vegas, NV 89118
Web Address: www.vgolf.com
Toll-Free Phone: (800) 873-5110
Phone: (702) 798-5500
Fax: (702) 798-6847
Contact:

Number of Franchises: 35
Company-Owned Units: 10
Total Units: 45

In Business Since: 1974 **Franchising Since:** 1984

Description of Operation: Las Vegas Discount Golf & Tennis franchises are retail stores specializing in golf and tennis equipment and apparel at discounted prices. The franchise program provides market analysis, site selection assistance, a proprietary computer system, exceptional training, and all other services necessary to open and

operate a store. Each franchisee is given an exclusive protected territory.

Equity Capital Needed: $450,000-$750,000 including franchise fee

Franchise Fee: $40,000

Royalty: 3 percent

Advertising Co-op Fee:

Financial Assistance: Prospects must meet financial requirements: net worth $750,000 of this $250,000 must be liquid. Will assist in third-party financing.

Management Assistance: During the two-week training course, managerial and staff procedures are addressed in detail.

Training Assistance: LVG&T provides the industry's leading training and operational support. Each franchisee must complete an intensive two-week class that includes classroom and in-store training. Continual training and operational support is available throughout the term of the franchise agreement.

Nevada Bob's Pro Shop

4043 S. Eastern Ave.
Las Vegas, NV 89119
Toll-Free Phone: (800) 348-2627
Phone: (702) 451-3333
Fax: (702) 451-9378
Contact: Franchise Director

Number of Franchises: 275
Company-Owned Units: 6
Total Units: 281

In Business Since: 1974   **Franchising Since:** 1978

Description of Operation: Selling discount golf equipment in an attractive atmosphere, specializing in top-of-the-line products by major manufacturers.

Equity Capital Needed: $275,000

Franchise Fee: $47,500-$57,500

Royalty: 3 percent

Advertising Co-op Fee:

Financial Assistance: We assist in directing where and to whom to apply for financial assistance.

Management Assistance: Assistance in advertising, opening store, and ordering products for inventory. Assistance in accounting and obtaining product information and availability.

Training Assistance: We assist with a week of intensive training in Las Vegas, NV. Assist in site selection, lease negotiation, and design of the store layout.

Pro Golf of America, Inc.

32751 Middlebelt Rd.
Farmington Hills, MI 48334
Web Address: www.progolfamerica.com
Toll-Free Phone: (800) 776-4653
Phone: (248) 737-0553
Fax: (248) 737-9077
Contact: National Franchise Director

Number of Franchises: 162
Company-Owned Units: 2
Total Units: 164

In Business Since: 1962   **Franchising Since:** 1975

Description of Operation: Pro Golf of America is the franchisor of Pro Golf Discount stores. With Pro Golf, you benefit from our 35 years of experience to give you every opportunity to succeed in the retail golf business. We provide you with instant name recognition, comprehensive training, tremendous buying power, exclusive merchandise program, national programs for advertising, yellow pages ads, and credit cards. We also provide a toll-free 800 number for our franchisees to use for ongoing assistance in their daily operations.

Equity Capital Needed: $200,000-$500,000

Franchise Fee: $24,500-$49,500

Royalty: 2.5-3 percent

Advertising Co-op Fee:

Financial Assistance: None.

Management Assistance: We provide a two-week training program that covers all aspects of the business from staffing the store to ordering and merchandising. We also provide our franchisee with training manuals in each of these areas. We have a toll-free number to put our franchises in touch with an experienced problem solver in any phase of the golf business.

Training Assistance: Training is provided at our corporate offices. It is for 2 weeks, and it covers all major areas required to get the store up and running—from store layout to staffing and ordering of inventories to grand-opening sales.

Shipping, Packaging & Mail Services

Craters & Freighters

7000 E. 47th Avenue Ste. 100
Denver, CO 80216
Web Address: www.cratersandfreighters.com
E-mail Address: franchise@cratersandfreighters.com
Toll-Free Phone: (800) 949-9931
Phone: (303) 399-8190
Fax: (303) 393-7644
Contact: Director of Franchise Development

Number of Franchises: 39
Company-Owned Units: 1
Total Units: 40

In Business Since: 1990   **Franchising Since:** 1991

Description of Operation: As "Specialty Freight Handlers," Craters & Freighters is the best niched concept in the packaging and shipping industry. We're the exclusive source for reliable, affordable specialty shipping services for large, fragile, and valuable pieces. We provide high demand crating and shipping with ironclad insurance to a well defined target market of loyal, upscale clientele. Service your large exclusive territory from low overhead warehouse space. We are the Picasso of the shipping industry!

Equity Capital Needed: $76,000

Franchise Fee: $24,800

Royalty: 5 percent of gross revenues

Advertising Co-op Fee: Yes. 1 percent of gross revenue

Financial Assistance: Third party financing assistance available.

Management Assistance: Previous management or business ownership is beneficial.

Training Assistance: Seven comprehensive days of training in Denver cover all aspects of crating, shipping, marketing, record keeping, and business management.

Parcel Plus, Inc.

2661 Riva Rd., Bldg. 1000, Ste. 1022
Annapolis, MD 21401
Web Address: www.parcelplus.com
E-mail Address: franchise@corp.parelplus.com
Toll-Free Phone: (800) 662-5553
Phone: (410) 266-3200
Fax: (410) 226-3266
Contact: Director of Sales & Marketing

Number of Franchises: 126
Company-Owned Units: 0
Total Units: 126

In Business Since: 1986   **Franchising Since:** 1988

Description of Operation: Shipping, packaging, and business support services for both businesses and consumers.

Equity Capital Needed: $50,000

Franchise Fee: $21,500

Royalty: 4 percent of gross sales

Advertising Co-op Fee: 1 percent

Financial Assistance: Indirect financing is available through several independent funding sources.

Management Assistance: Training, ongoing support, and a mentor program.

Training Assistance: One week Business Orientation, one week of Cargo Training, minimum two weeks in store, home study, and first week of opening with trainer present. No training fees.

Shoe Repair & Care

Hakky Instant Shoe Repair

1739 Sands Pl., Ste. F
Marietta, GA 30067
Toll-Free Phone:
Phone: (770) 956-8651
Fax: (770) 951-0355
Contact: Executive Manager

Number of Franchises: 80
Company-Owned Units: 0
Total Units: 80

In Business Since: 1983   **Franchising Since:** 1989

Description of Operation: European, instant shoe repair.

Equity Capital Needed: $15,000 and up

Franchise Fee: $9,000-$12,000

Royalty: 4 percent

Advertising Co-op Fee:

Financial Assistance: We will help gain financial assistance with SBA loans and leasing on equipment.

Management Assistance: We provide mall reports, sales tax reports, and various additional reports required by local, city, state governments, full-time marketing director, inventory control and machinery maintenance assistance.

Training Assistance: We offer an initial 3 weeks of training in the training center. Grand opening support in store. Ongoing support with materials and machinery. A quarterly newsletter offers support with customer service and merchandising assistance.

Heel Quik/Sew Quik

1730 Cumberland Point Dr. Ste. 5
Marietta, GA 30067
E-mail Address: hqcorp@bellsouth.net
Toll-Free Phone: (800) 255-8145
Phone: (770) 951-9440
Fax: (770) 933-8268
Contact: President

Number of Franchises: 675
Company-Owned Units: 2
Total Units: 677

In Business Since: 1984   **Franchising Since:** 1985

Description of Operation: Heel/Sew Quik! is instant shoe repair, clothing alterations, and monogramming franchise.

Equity Capital Needed: $6,000-$138,000 includes franchise fee

Franchise Fee: $2,500-$17,500

Royalty: 4 percent

Advertising Co-op Fee:

Financial Assistance: We have several leasing companies that will work with new franchisees. We also have put together a formal SBA or business loan package.

Management Assistance: 2 weeks of training at our international training center in Atlanta, GA; store opening coordination and support via toll-free 800 numbers and field support.

Training Assistance: Training is done at our training facility for 2 intensive weeks. Video courses are also presented, following training in the field, along with manuals. Assistance in the field is provided during opening and on an ongoing basis.

Sign Products

FastSigns

2550 Midway Rd., Ste. 150
Carrollton, TX 75006-2366
Web Address: www.fastsigns.com
Toll-Free Phone: (800) 827-7446
Phone: (972) 447-0777
Fax: (972) 248-8201
Contact: Director of Franchise Development

Number of Franchises: 200
Company-Owned Units: 1
Total Units: 201

In Business Since: 1985   **Franchising Since:** 1986

Description of Operation: Number one business to business franchise. Success '93; number one sign franchise, Entrepreneur '90,'91, '92, '93, '94; ranked among the *Inc.* magazine list of the 500 fastest-growing private companies for the past three years. Founder of computer-generated quick-sign industry. Retail stores produce signs and graphics for business; unique systems include fully-documented operating procedures, order-based PO's with marketing support, proven sales and marketing technique and national accounts programs.

Equity Capital Needed: $30,000

Franchise Fee: $20,000

Royalty: 6 percent

Advertising Co-op Fee:

Financial Assistance: Qualified franchisees may apply for SBA loans. FastSigns also has third-party financing available to qualified franchisees.

Management Assistance: Comprehensive training in financial management, operations management and marketing. Complete training manuals for every aspect of the business. Experienced field representatives provide on-site consultation in every area of the business.

Training Assistance: An intensive 3 weeks of training covers complete FastSigns business system. No sign

experience is needed. Sales and marketing helpful. Comprehensive support includes site selection, store design, financing assistance, grand opening marketing package, on-site opening assistance, ongoing store visits, toll-free hotline, and more.

Signs & More In 24

1739 St. Marys Ave.
Parkersburg, WV 26101
Web Address: www.signs-and-more.com
E-mail Address: signsmore@citynet.net
Toll-Free Phone: (800) 358-2358
Phone: (304) 422-7446
Fax: (304) 422-7449
Contact: President

Number of Franchises: 7
Company-Owned Units: 2
Total Units: 9

In Business Since: 1990   **Franchising Since:** 1992

Description of Operation: 24-hour sign franchise, offering all types of signs in 24 hours in a well-decorated retail store. In addition, custom-made residential and commercial awnings are offered, as well as flags, electrical, and neon signage. Our variety allows for higher sales than similar companies and a total signage mixture.

Equity Capital Needed: $45,000-$99,000

Franchise Fee: $13,000

Royalty: 3-6 percent

Advertising Co-op Fee:

Financial Assistance: We help the potential franchisee prepare the business plans and marketing studies and help in finding the proper lending situations.

Management Assistance: Signs and More in 24 provides 1 week of on-site assistance after opening, as well as 1 week of outside selling, along with 2-3 weeks of training at our headquarters. An 800 number assistance hotline, constant news and product updates, along with operations, marketing, pricing, and vendor manuals. In addition, on-site visits are available and a monthly newsletter, accounting and advertising systems are also provided.

Training Assistance: Same as above.

Signs By Tomorrow

6460 Dobbin Rd.
Columbia, MD 21045
E-mail Address: sbtusa@aol.com
Toll-Free Phone: (800) 765-7446
Phone: (410) 992-7192
Fax: (410) 992-7675
Contact: Director of Franchise Development

Number of Franchises: 21
Company-Owned Units: 1
Total Units: 22

In Business Since: 1986 **Franchising Since:** 1988

Description of Operation: One day computer-based sign shops. Signs By Tomorrow stores produce signs and graphics for virtually all sizes of businesses. The franchisee's role is to lead the sales and administrative areas in servicing a business-to-business clientele during regular working hours.

Equity Capital Needed: $85,000-$95,000

Franchise Fee: $17,500

Royalty: 5-3 percent

Advertising Co-op Fee:

Financial Assistance: Equipment leasing plan is available.

Management Assistance: Signs By Tomorrow offers complete initial training and an ongoing support program.

Training Assistance: We offer 4 weeks of training-1 week at SBT headquarters and 2 weeks at the franchisee's location.

Signs First

813 Ridge Lake Blvd., Ste. 390
Memphis, TN 38120
Toll-Free Phone: (800) 852-2163
Phone: (901) 682-2264
Fax: (901) 682-2476
Contact:

Number of Franchises: 32
Company-Owned Units: 2
Total Units: 34

In Business Since: 1966 **Franchising Since:** 1989

Description of Operation: Retail computerized sign store with a strong showroom design and service focus. Serving retail, professional, and commercial businesses with temporary and permanent signs on a cash and carry basis. We offer the only franchise with over 25 years of experience in the sign industry.

Equity Capital Needed: $20,000

Franchise Fee: $10,000-15,000

Royalty: 6 percent

Advertising Co-op Fee: None

Financial Assistance: Data not provided

Management Assistance: Three-phase training program; on-site assistance; operations manuals; toll-free phone assistance; regional seminars; radio, TV, and print materials available; key account assistance; and proven systems and procedures.

Training Assistance: Phase I Training—3 weeks at franchise headquarters. Phase II & III Training—continuing education at franchisee's location.

Signs Now

4900 Manatee Ave. W. Ste. 201
Brandenton, FL 34209
Web Address: www.signsnow.com
E-mail Address: terry@signsnow.com
Toll-Free Phone: (800) 356-3373
Phone: (941) 747-7747
Fax: (941) 747-5074
Contact: President

Number of Franchises: 295
Company-Owned Units: 0
Total Units: 295

In Business Since: 1985 **Franchising Since:** 1986

Description of Operation: Computerized one-day sign shop, creating signs and graphics for business and retail.

Equity Capital Needed: $53,500-$120,300

Franchise Fee: $19,800 included in price

Royalty: 5 percent

Advertising Co-op Fee:

Financial Assistance: Equipment leasing is available. Third party and SBA.

Management Assistance: We provide 2-4 weeks of training in a regional operating store. The complete corporate staff is trained in sign store operations. Twenty regional managers in the field to assist.

Training Assistance: Training includes 2-4 weeks in a regional operating store, 3-7 days on equipment and 1 week with regional manager in franchise store.

Speedy Sign-A-Rama, USA

1601 Belvedere Rd. Ste. 403 E.
West Palm Beach, FL 33406
Web Address: www.signarama.com
E-mail Address: signinfo@signarama.com
Toll-Free Phone: (800) 776-8105
Phone: (407) 640-5570
Fax: (407) 640-5580
Contact: Vice President

Number of Franchises: 150
Company-Owned Units: 0
Total Units: 150

In Business Since: 1986 **Franchising Since:** 1987

Description of Operation: Full-service retail computerized sign franchise, using the latest in computer software technology to produce custom signage quickly and inexpensively. No experience necessary. Full company training. A two-week in-house training course with local back-up and support is provided on an ongoing basis.

Equity Capital Needed: $35,000-$75,000

Franchise Fee: $29,500

Royalty: 6 percent

Advertising Co-op Fee:

Financial Assistance: The company provides financing for qualified applicants, as well as various programs to help the franchisee get started.

Management Assistance: After an intensive two-week training course at national headquarters, assistance is provided on a local basis. This assistance includes complete support in all phases of running the franchise—from management to hiring to training personnel.

Training Assistance: Training is a two-week program that completely covers all phases of our franchise, from marketing techniques to complete training. Training is part of the franchise fee.

Tools and Hardware

U. S. Rooter

17025 Batesville Pike Rd.
North Little Rock, AR 72120
Web Address:
E-mail Address:
Toll-Free Phone:
Phone: (501) 835-5020
Fax:
Contact: Secretary/Treasurer

Number of Franchises: 3
Company-Owned Units: 0
Total Units: 3

In Business Since: 1965   **Franchising Since:** 1969

Description of Operation: We furnish patented sewer and drain cleaning equipment, a registered name and trademark, instruction and training, as well as help in any phase of the business to get the franchisee started in a business of his/her own.

Equity Capital Needed: $5,000-$75,000

Franchise Fee: $20,000-$25,000

Royalty: Flat fee

Advertising Co-op Fee:

Financial Assistance: There is no financial assistance.

Management Assistance: Using our years of experience, we will instruct the new franchisee, using an instruction booklet and verbal communications.

Training Assistance: We provide a two-week training period to train the franchisee or whomever he/she chooses for us to train. Longer period, if required.

Wholesale Operations

Atlantic Mower Parts Supplies, Inc.
13421 S.W. 14 Pl.
Ft. Lauderdale, FL 33325
Toll-Free Phone:

Phone: (954) 474-4942
Fax: (954) 475-0414
Contact: President

Number of Franchises: 14
Company-Owned Units: 0
Total Units: 14

In Business Since: 1971   **Franchising Since:** 1985

Description of Operation: Outdoor power equipment after-market parts (small engine, chain saw, lawn mower, snow blower, and more.)

Equity Capital Needed: $45,000

Franchise Fee: $15,900

Royalty: 5 percent of retail sales

Advertising Co-op Fee: None

Financial Assistance:

Management Assistance: You will also receive periodic communication.

Training Assistance: One week training program in Ft. Lauderdale and addition to your initial training an operations specialist will work with your unit before opening.

Chemstation

3400 Encrete Ln.
Dayton, OH 45439
Toll-Free Phone:
Phone: (937) 294-8265
Fax: (937) 294-5360
Contact: Director of Operations

Number of Franchises: 23
Company-Owned Units: 2
Total Units: 25

In Business Since: 1965   **Franchising Since:** 1984

Description of Operation: Manufacture and distribute detergents in bulk.

Equity Capital Needed: $250,000

Franchise Fee: $20,000

Royalty: 4 percent

Advertising Co-op Fee:

Financial Assistance: None.

Management Assistance: Complete training manuals, as well as operations manual. Managerial support is provided on an ongoing basis.

Training Assistance: We provide an extensive one-week training period at the home office in Dayton, OH. Sales, operations and administration training are ongoing.

Tempaco, Inc.

1701 Alden Road
Orlando, FL 32854-7667
Web Address: www.tempaco.com
E-mail Address: info@tempaco.com

Toll-Free Phone: (800) 868-7667
Phone: (407) 898-3456
Fax: (407) 898-7316
Contact: President

Number of Franchises: 16
Company-Owned Units: 5
Total Units: 21

In Business Since: 1946 **Franchising Since:** 1972

Description of Operation: Tempaco Inc. is a well established, full line stocking wholesale distributor of controls and accessories throughout the southeastern USA. Customer base includes propane and natural gas companies, schools, and governmental agencies, manufacturers, industrial operations, hospitals, and repair dealers. Franchises are given protected territories and certain backup assistance. Franchise candidates are screened for certain capabilities before serious consideration. Franchises not available in certain states.

Equity Capital Needed: $100,000

Franchise Fee: $25,000 plus

Royalty: 4 percent of net sales

Advertising Co-op Fee: None

Financial Assistance: Consulting only.

Management Assistance: Two week basic training at headquarters, plus one week equivalent field training. Plus advisory and consulting services.

Training Assistance: Two week basic training at headquarters, plus one week equivalent field training.

Miscellaneous—General

A Wonderful Wedding Franchising, Inc.

2011-B Bee's Ferry Road
Charleston, SC 29414
Web Address: www.awonderfulwedding.com
E-mail Address: krt@awonderfulwedding.com
Toll-Free Phone: (800) 661-9135
Phone: (803) 556-1500
Fax: (803) 769-0269
Contact: President

Number of Franchises: 0
Company-Owned Units: 1
Total Units: 1

In Business Since: 1993 **Franchising Since:** 1997

Description of Operation: A Wonderful Wedding offers qualified franchisees the opportunity to own an exciting home-based business in the $33 billion wedding industry. Franchisees publish a semi-annual bridal guide and produce an annual bridal show in their local market. The bridal guide and show are two effective directly targeted advertising mediums for wedding professionals. Their effectiveness results in a high customer retention rate and a steady revenue stream for our franchisees. A Wonderful Wedding presents a wonderful opportunity for those individuals who are people-oriented and want to use their creativity and marketing skills.

Equity Capital Needed: $31,450-$45,400

Franchise Fee: $20,000

Royalty: 10 percent of gross revenues

Advertising Co-op Fee: None

Financial Assistance: Not available

Management Assistance: A management team with 16 years of experience in the wedding industry and with strengths in all facets of running a business: administration, sales, marketing, daily operations, accounting, market research, public relations, and planning. This management team offers the ongoing day-to-day support to help make all of our franchisees successful.

Training Assistance: Initial training consists of ten days at the corporate office, covering all aspects of operating business including on-the-job sales training. Franchisee also receives five days of training in their market. Comprehensive Operating Manuals, along with day-to-day support.

Agway

P.O. Box 4746
Syracuse, NY 13221
Web Address: www.agway.com
Toll-Free Phone:
Phone: (315) 449-7649
Fax: (315) 461-2253
Contact: Vice President of Franchise Operations

Number of Franchises: 320
Company-Owned Units: 116
Total Units: 436

In Business Since: 1964 **Franchising Since:** 1964

Description of Operation: Agway is a co-operative owned by farmer-members in twelve Northeastern states. Agway produces and markets crop needs and services, dairy and livestock feeds, farm related products, pet foods and supplies, and yard and garden products. Its internal and external subsidiaries are involved in food processing and marketing, energy products and lease financing.

Equity Capital Needed: $200,000-$600,000

Franchise Fee: $25,000

Royalty: 3-5 percent

Advertising Co-op Fee:

Financial Assistance: Third-party financing available.

Management Assistance: A four-week training program includes managerial assistance, as well as training from a regional manager.

Training Assistance: A four-day operational and product knowledge training program. Set up training and other training programs are ongoing.

Alterations Express

850 McKay Ct.
Youngstown, OH 44512
Toll-Free Phone: (800) 221-1198
Phone: (330) 629-9466
Fax: (330) 629-9465
Contact:

Number of Franchises: 3
Company-Owned Units: 3
Total Units: 6

In Business Since: 1990   **Franchising Since:** 1994

Description of Operation: Quality clothing alterations at reasonable prices and fast service.

Equity Capital Needed: Negotiable.

Franchise Fee: $5,000-$10,000

Royalty: 4 percent

Advertising Co-op Fee:

Financial Assistance: Data not available.

Management Assistance: We have start-up manuals for a complete turnkey operation, as well as marketing and advertising manuals. Our management manuals include weekly production, weekly budgeting, supply ordering and goal setting, plus our ongoing support.

Training Assistance: We begin every market with a talent search. We provide guidelines for management and assist them with the evaluation of prospective employees.

Armoloy Corporation, The

1325 Sycamore Rd.
DeKalb, IL 60115
Web Address: www.armoloycorp.com
E-mail Address: armoloy@tbcnet.com
Toll-Free Phone:
Phone: (815) 758-6657
Fax: (815) 758-0268
Contact: President

Number of Franchises: 10
Company-Owned Units: 2
Total Units: 12

In Business Since: 1957   **Franchising Since:** 1978

Description of Operation: License of precision, proprietary chromium alloy coating for industry. The Armology process creates a thin, dense modular chromium (NTDC) coating with a 72Rc surface hardness; excellent friction-reduction lubricity characteristics; superior corrosion-resistant properties; and virtually no size changes to coated parts.

Equity Capital Needed: $300,000-$400,000

Franchise Fee: $50,000 minimum

Royalty: 7 percent

Advertising Co-op Fee:

Financial Assistance: No direct financing. We will work to create payment schedules where required.

Management Assistance: All training provided to key personnel. The sales training program takes 2-4 weeks. Processing training takes 4-6 weeks. All training is done in the Dekalb, IL corporate facility. The Armoloy Corporation works directly with the licensee during the plant development and the first operating year.

Training Assistance: Same as above.

Bevinco Bar Systems

235 Yorkland Blvd. Ste. 409
Toronto, ON M2J 4Y8
Web Address: www.bevinco.com
E-mail Address: info@bevinco.com
Toll-Free Phone: (888) 238-4620
Phone: (416) 490-6266
Fax: (416) 490-6899
Contact: President

Number of Franchises: 130
Company-Owned Units: 1
Total Units: 131

In Business Since: 1987   **Franchising Since:** 1990

Description of Operation: Liquor inventory control service for licensed bars and restaurants. Inventory stock-taking is done by weighing the open bottles and kegs on our computerized system and counting all full bottles. Sales from the cash register are then entered into the system, producing detailed reports highlighting any and all shrinkage problems to the owner. The service is done on an ongoing, weekly basis, creating a terrific cash flow with only a few accounts.

Equity Capital Needed: $20,00-$30,000

Franchise Fee: $22,500

Royalty: $15 per audit

Advertising Co-op Fee:

Financial Assistance: Third-party leasing on equipment is available.

Management Assistance: Area master franchisees and franchisor are available for ongoing hotline support, seminars, and training sessions. Quarterly software enhancement updates are provided at no additional cost.

Training Assistance: 5 days of classroom training and 5 days of on-site training are provided.

Calculated Couples

4839 E. Greenway Rd.
Scottsdale, AZ 85254
E-mail Address: lovedoctor@juno.com

Toll-Free Phone: (800) 443-2824
Phone: (602) 230-4172
Fax:
Contact: President

Number of Franchises: 9
Company-Owned Units: 6
Total Units: 15

In Business Since: 1983   **Franchising Since:** 1989

Description of Operation: All cash singles business. The 90's way for singles to meet. No dues, nothing to join, overnight results. A fun full or part-time business.

Equity Capital Needed: Not applicable

Franchise Fee: $4,995

Royalty: None

Advertising Co-op Fee: None

Financial Assistance: None

Management Assistance: Toll-free help line, training.

Training Assistance: Training manuals and optional on-site training.

Crown Trophy

1 Odell Plaza
Yonkers, NY 10701
Web Address: www.crowntrophy.com
E-mail Address: crowninfo@crowntrophy.com
Toll-Free Phone: (800) 227-1557
Phone: (914) 964-8366
Fax: (914) 963-4841
Contact: Vice President of Franchise Operations

Number of Franchises: 50
Company-Owned Units: 1
Total Units: 51

In Business Since: 1978   **Franchising Since:** 1986

Description of Operation: Crown Trophy is a rapidly-growing awards business. You assemble, engrave, and mass produce awards, selling at discounted prices to many different markets-schools, organizations, businesses, leagues, and so on.

Equity Capital Needed: $60,000-$90,000

Franchise Fee: $20,000

Royalty: 5 percent

Advertising Co-op Fee:

Financial Assistance: None.

Management Assistance: The contents of training will include sales and marketing techniques, ordering techniques, business practices, bookkeeping, computer training, and instruction in the use of equipment.

Training Assistance: Initial training for 2 weeks at corporate office and 1 week of on-site training.

Fast-Fix Jewelry Repairs

1750 N. Florida Mango Rd. Ste. 103
West Palm Beach, FL 33409
Web Address: www.fastfix.com
E-mail Address: fastfix@bellsouth.net
Toll-Free Phone: (800) 359-0407
Phone: (561) 478-5292
Fax: (561) 478-5291
Contact: Executive VP Franchise Development

Number of Franchises: 78
Company-Owned Units: 2
Total Units: 80

In Business Since: 1984   **Franchising Since:** 1987

Description of Operation: Jewelry and watch repairs while you wait. Located in regional malls throughout the country.

Equity Capital Needed: $90,000 includes franchise fee

Franchise Fee: $25,000

Royalty: 5 percent

Advertising Co-op Fee:

Financial Assistance: Third party financial assistance available.

Management Assistance: Home office personnel are available to assist in completing forms and setting up record keeping, ongoing support, annual convention, and regional meetings.

Training Assistance: On-site training and ongoing support.

Homesteader, The

129 Concord St., Ste. 30
Framingham, MA 01703
Web Address: www.homesteader.com
E-mail Address: homestea@tiac.net
Toll-Free Phone: (800) 941-9907
Phone:
Fax:
Contact: Vice President

Number of Franchises: 10
Company-Owned Units: 8
Total Units: 18

In Business Since: 1989   **Franchising Since:** 1993

Description of Operation: Publish a local edition of the Homesteader, the publication for new homeowners. Sell advertising to local businesses, work with local writers and vendors, and benefit from franchisor's training and monthly editorial packages. This low-cost, high income potential franchise is ideal for anyone with sales, publishing, or business background.

Equity Capital Needed: $8,000-$22,000

Franchise Fee: $5,000

Royalty: 10 percent monthly   **Advertising Co-op Fee:**

Financial Assistance: None

Management Assistance: Extensive operations manual and free telephone consultation.

Training Assistance: Classroom training for 2 days.

Homewatch

2865 S. Colorado Blvd.
Denver, CO 80222
Web Address: www.homewatch-iwtl.com
E-mail Address: hwcorp@aol.com
Toll-Free Phone: (800) 777-9770
Phone: (303) 758-7290
Fax: (303) 758-1724
Contact: President

Number of Franchises: 26
Company-Owned Units: 4
Total Units: 30

In Business Since: 1973   **Franchising Since:** 1986

Description of Operation: Total home services. Pet and home services, while people are away on business or vacation. Elderly services non-medical assistance for the elderly living in their own homes. Maintenance, repair, and total remodeling services.

Equity Capital Needed: Care-$48,500 handyman-$2,500 pet/household-$4,950

Franchise Fee: Care-$10,000 handyman-$10,000 pet-$5,000

Royalty: 5 percent

Advertising Co-op Fee:

Financial Assistance: None.

Management Assistance: Monthly calls, 800 number, newsletters, quarterly and all-service newsletter, videos on services and training, development of national accounts, advertising blitz at grand opening, national conventions, and computer updates and faxes.

Training Assistance: Care service—1 week; handyman—4 days; pet—2 days.

International Loss Prevention Systems

1350 E. 4th Ave.
Vancouver, BC V5N 1J5
Toll-Free Phone:
Phone: (604) 255-5000
Fax: (604) 254-2575
Contact: President

Number of Franchises: 28
Company-Owned Units: 2
Total Units: 30

In Business Since: 1987   **Franchising Since:** 1988

Description of Operation: Manufacturer and exporter of shoplifting and employee theft prevention systems.

Equity Capital Needed: $25,000

Franchise Fee: $5,000

Royalty: 1 percent

Advertising Co-op Fee:

Financial Assistance: Up to 50 percent of start up costs can be financed. The company will carry these costs.

Management Assistance: The company supports the franchisees in the field and with regular on-site visits.

Training Assistance: Training for the new franchisee is approximately 1 week in the head office in Vancouver, BC.

ISU International

100 Pine St., #1700
San Francisco, CA 94111
Toll-Free Phone:
Phone: (415) 788-9810
Fax: (415) 397-5530
Contact:

Number of Franchises: 85
Company-Owned Units: 0
Total Units: 85

In Business Since: 1979   **Franchising Since:** 1980

Description of Operation: Conversion franchises for independent insurance agencies.

Equity Capital Needed: Not applicable.

Franchise Fee: $12,500

Royalty: Flat fee plus 3 percent.

Advertising Co-op Fee:

Financial Assistance: None.

Management Assistance: Regional office staffs.

Training Assistance: 3 days for new franchisee principals; 5 days for CSR's and producers in agencies.

Knockout Pest Control

1009 Front St.
Uniondale, NY 11553
Web Address: www.knockoutpest.com
Toll-Free Phone: (800) 244-7378
Phone: (516) 489-7817
Fax: (516) 489-4348
Contact: President

Number of Franchises: 2
Company-Owned Units: 1
Total Units: 3

In Business Since: 1975   **Franchising Since:** 1993

Description of Operation: Pest control services.

Equity Capital Needed: $25,000

Franchise Fee: $15,000

Royalty: 10 percent

Advertising Co-op Fee:

Financial Assistance: None.

Management Assistance: Complete marketing and management assistance.

Training Assistance: Initial and ongoing training on a regular basis.

Magis Fund Raising Specialists

845 Heathermoor Ln. Ste. 961
Perrysburg, OH 43551
Toll-Free Phone:
Phone: (419) 244-6711
Fax: (419) 244-4791
Contact: President

Number of Franchises: 1
Company-Owned Units: 1
Total Units: 2

In Business Since: 1991   **Franchising Since:** 1991

Description of Operation: Magis provides full-service fund raising, financial development, marketing, and public relations services to all non-profit organizations. Magis conducts major pledge campaigns for new facilities, increases annual giving by 20 percent or more, builds endowments of $1 million or more, conducts feasibility studies, fundraising audits, personnel searches, writes grant proposals, trains leadership, conducts seminars and workshops, strategic planning, video presentations, and newsletters.

Equity Capital Needed: $28,500-$52,000

Franchise Fee: $7,500

Royalty: 8 percent or $200 per month minimum

Advertising Co-op Fee:

Financial Assistance: Leased computer hardware, software and office equipment may be financed over sixty payments. Very little capital is needed, as the business can be conducted from your home or added to an existing business with an office already established.

Management Assistance: Daily back-up and support. A sales and marketing system. Expertise in all areas of fundraising and development. Whether $5,000 or $50 million is needed, the Magis network can meet the client's fundraising needs. New products and services are constantly tested and offered.

Training Assistance: 1 week of correspondence of preliminary materials provided for at-home study. A second week at Magis' headquarters, where all systems are taught. A third week at your location. Ongoing contact by phone, fax and regular regional seminars. We are looking for people who wish to serve local non-profit community groups and organizations.

Mr. Electric Corp.

1020 N. University Parks Dr.
Waco, TX 76707
Web Address: www.dwyergroup.com/mrelec

E-mail Address: Rgoertz@dwyergroup.com
Toll-Free Phone: (800) 805-0575
Phone: (254) 745-2440
Fax: (254) 745-2546
Contact: Chief Operating Officer

Number of Franchises: 52
Company-Owned Units: 0
Total Units: 52

In Business Since: 1994   **Franchising Since:** 1994

Description of Operation: Mr. Electric is the only franchise system of electrical contractors servicing the residential and light commercial sector. Mr. Electric offers extensive business and systems training, computerization, marketing, and advertising programs. Regional and national conferences, ongoing field and phone support, with locations both nationally as well as internationally.

Equity Capital Needed: $25,000 minimum

Franchise Fee: $15,000 per 100,000 population

Royalty: Fluctuating (3-6 percent) of gross weekly sales

Advertising Co-op Fee: None

Financial Assistance: Internal financing on franchise fee-50 percent down, 60 months at 12 percent on approval. Third party financing on franchise fee-30 percent down.

Management Assistance: Field support ongoing. Toll-free phone support ongoing. Assist in opening.

Training Assistance: Basic training, quarterly regional meetings, and an annual convention.

Property Damage Appraisers

6100 S.W. Building Ste. 200
Fort Worth, TX 76109
Toll-Free Phone: (800) 749-7324
Phone: (817) 731-5555
Fax: (817) 731-5550
Contact: Director of Training & Development

Number of Franchises: 262
Company-Owned Units: 0
Total Units: 262

In Business Since: 1963   **Franchising Since:** 1963

Description of Operation: The industry's largest franchised appraising company. National marketing support, a computerized office management system, training, and ongoing management assistance are provided. Automobile damage appraising experience is a prerequisite. PDA provides automobile and property appraisal services for insurance companies and the self-insured.

Equity Capital Needed: $9,250-$23,450

Franchise Fee: $0

Royalty: 15 percent

Advertising Co-op Fee:

Financial Assistance: Not available.

Management Assistance: Perpetual assistance is provided as needed, by regional managers.

Training Assistance: Operational training is on site-4 days in duration and 1 week at corporate office. A comprehensive operations manual and use guide for a computerized management system is provided.

Rich Plan Corporation

4981 Commercial Dr.
Yorkville, NY 13495
Toll-Free Phone: (800) 243-1358
Phone: (315) 736-0851
Fax: (315) 736-7597
Contact: Executive Vice President

Number of Franchises: 20
Company-Owned Units: 0
Total Units: 20

In Business Since: 1946   **Franchising Since:** 1952

Description of Operation: Franchised dealers operate a direct-to-the-home food service and appliance sales franchise under name of Rich Plan. Each franchisee provides customers with various food analysis services and offers a line of high-quality, pre-packaged frozen food. Items are ordered from a price list, food guide, or menu planner and are delivered directly to the customer's home. Advertising is mainly direct referrals.

Equity Capital Needed: $100,000

Franchise Fee: $10,000

Royalty: $250 per month or $10 per net new customers

Advertising Co-op Fee:

Financial Assistance: None.

Management Assistance: Direct on-site managerial assistance is not provided. New franchisees are provided with monthly sales reports, a bi-monthly newsletter, and a toll-free 800 number telephone access to staff for specific questions.

Training Assistance: New franchisees are encouraged to visit the national office in Utica, NY for dealer training with respect to operating a home food service business, sales techniques, dealership organization, and financing practices. Training is also available at the other existing franchisee locations.

Sport It

4196 Corporate Square
Naples, FL 33942
Web Address: www.sportit.com
Toll-Free Phone: (800) 467-8953
Phone: (813) 643-6811
Fax: (813) 643-6811
Contact: Marketing Director

Number of Franchises: 456
Company-Owned Units: 0
Total Units: 456

In Business Since: 1984   **Franchising Since:** 1984

Description of Operation: Dealers sell competitively-priced, brand-name athletic equipment from their homes. Dealers can choose from 6 selling opportunities: outside sales, fund raising, mail order, home party plan, rep group, and catalog retail store.

Equity Capital Needed: $1,500+

Franchise Fee: $1,500

Royalty: $25 per month

Advertising Co-op Fee:

Financial Assistance: None.

Management Assistance: We provide newsletters, free consultation, service training seminars, conventions, product knowledge, market analysis, competitive pricing, business management, introduction of special programs, central order processing, and so on.

Training Assistance: Same as above.

Sports Section, The

3871 Lakefield Dr., Ste. 100
Suwanee, GA 30024
Web Address: sports-section.com
E-mail Address: larry@office.sports-section.com
Toll-Free Phone: (800) 321-9127
Phone: (770) 622-4900
Fax: (770) 622-4949
Contact: National Director, Franchise Development

Number of Franchises: 135
Company-Owned Units: 2
Total Units: 137

In Business Since: 1983   **Franchising Since:** 1985

Description of Operation: T.S.S. franchisees market a full line of photo related products to youth organizations including all individual and team oriented sports, dance, karate, pre-schools, and so on. All order processing, film development. and packaging is done at T.S.S. headquarters. Low-overhead, cash up front business. Can be operated from your home or commercial office—full or part-time. Exclusive, protected territories. Potential to earn executive level income. No photography experience required.

Equity Capital Needed: Varies

Franchise Fee: $9,900 and up depending on territory

Royalty: 0 percent

Advertising Co-op Fee: Data not provided

Financial Assistance: Third party financing for equipment package.

Management Assistance: T.S.S. provides initial business start-up, market development, and ongoing support in all areas of the operation of your franchise.

Training Assistance: Franchisees are provided up to 3 days of sales/marketing/photography training. Training sessions are provided at the franchisee's location. Additional training is available at T.S.S. seminars and conventions.

TravelCenters of America

24601 Center Ridge Road, Ste. 200
Westlake, OH 44145
Web Address: www.tatravelcenters.com
Toll-Free Phone: (800) 872-7024
Phone: (440) 808-9100
Fax: (440) 808-4458
Contact: Vice President of Franchising

Number of Franchises: 44
Company-Owned Units: 84
Total Units: 128

In Business Since: 1965   **Franchising Since:** 1980

Description of Operation: Full-service interstate highway travel centers and truckstops.

Equity Capital Needed: $250,000-$9,000,000

Franchise Fee: $100,000

Royalty: 3.75 percent of non-fuel sales

Advertising Co-op Fee: 6 percent of non-fuel sales

Financial Assistance: No direct financing is provided. However, we will assist in developing lender presentations and making presentations for approved projects.

Management Assistance: We provide classroom and on-site training. An experienced manager is at new franchised site before, during, and after opening.

Training Assistance: Training consists of on-site training at other established locations, classroom training at our dedicated training centers, and training at the new franchisee's site.

United Consumers Club

8450 Broadway
Merrillville, IN 46410
Web Address: www.shopucc.com
Toll-Free Phone: (800) 827-6400
Phone: (219) 736-1100
Fax: (219) 755-6208
Contact: Vice President of Franchise Development

Number of Franchises: 81
Company-Owned Units: 8
Total Units: 89

In Business Since: 1971   **Franchising Since:** 1972

Description of Operation: Private consumer buying service. Members buy at a franchised showroom, directly from the manufacturers, without any retail profit mark-up, saving up to 50 percent compared to store sales prices.

UCC is one of America's most profitable franchises and offers an excellent return on investment.

Equity Capital Needed: Data not available.

Franchise Fee: $55,000

Royalty: 22 percent

Advertising Co-op Fee:

Financial Assistance: Data not available.

Management Assistance: We provide regularly updated, comprehensive operations manual, telephone access to 130 specialists at home office. Ten-person field staff, monthly newsletters, customized audio and video tapes, and quarterly meetings and awards programs.

Training Assistance: Training consists of an intensive four-week training program at the home office, followed by on-the-job training at an established club. Additional training at new franchisee's location for entire staff when club opens.

Video Data Services

3136 Winton Rd. S. Ste. 304
Rochester, NY 14623
Web Address:
E-mail Address:
Toll-Free Phone: (800) 836-9461
Phone: (716) 424-5320
Fax: (716) 424-5324
Contact: President

Number of Franchises: 268
Company-Owned Units: 1
Total Units: 269

In Business Since: 1981   **Franchising Since:** 1982

Description of Operation: Video, photography, and film-to-tape transfers, weddings, other social occasions, promotional and training videos, legal depositions, video editing, and special effects. We are the only franchisor to offer a 100 percent money-back guarantee, even after training.

Equity Capital Needed: $21,950

Franchise Fee: $19,950

Royalty: $750 annually

Advertising Co-op Fee:

Financial Assistance: None.

Management Assistance: We provide advertising, marketing, public relations, and management consulting via newsletters, phone and an annual convention.

Training Assistance: We offer 2 weeks of pre-classroom training and 3 days of classroom training in Rochester, NY or San Diego, CA.

CONTACT INFORMATION FOR THE U.S. SMALL BUSINESS ADMINISTRATION

The SBA has a number of programs and services available. They include training and educational programs, advisory services, publications, financial programs and contract assistance. The Agency also offers specialized programs for women business owners, minorities, veterans, international trade and rural development.

The SBA has offices located around the country. This appendix provides a directory to help you find the one nearest you. You can also call the Small Business Answer Desk at 1-800-U ASK SBA.

All SBA's programs and services are extended to the public on a nondiscriminatory basis.

U.S. Small Business Administration
409 3rd St., SW Suite 7000
Washington, DC 20416
FAX 202/205-7064
202/205-6600

Aida Alvarez, Administrator	202/205-6605
Ginger Lew, Deputy Administrator	202/205-6605
Jeanne Sadler, Counselor to the Administrator	202/205-6615
Darryl Dennis, Counselor to the Administrator	202/205-6659
Paul Weech, Chief of Staff	202/205-6682
Jeanne Sclater, Acting Associate Deputy Administrator for Economic Development	202/205-6657
John D. Whitmore, Acting Associate Deputy Administrator for Government Contracting and Minority Enterprise Development	202/205-6459
M. Kris Swedin, Assistant Administrator for Congressional and Legislative Affairs	202/205-6700

Regional, District, and Branch Offices by State

OFFICE TYPE	CITY	STATE	ZIP	ADDRESS	PHONE	FAX
Alabama						
District	Birmingham	AL	35203	2121 8th Ave. N.	(205)731-1344	(205)731-1404
Alaska						
District	Anchorage	AK	99513	222 West 8th Avenue	(907)271-4022	(907)271-4545
Arkansas						
District	Little Rock	AR	72202	2120 Riverfront Drive	(501)324-5278	(501)324-5199
Arizona						
District	Phoenix	AZ	85004	2828 N. Central Ave.	(602)640-231	(602)640-2360
California						
Regional	San Francisco	CA	94105	455 Market St., Ste 2200	(415)744-2118	(415)744-2119
District	Fresno	CA	93727	2719 N. Air Fresno Dr., Ste. 200	(209)487-5791	(209)487-5292
District	Glendale	CA	91203	330 N. Brand Blvd.	(818)552-3210	(818)552-3260
District	Sacramento	CA	95814	660 J Street, Ste. 215	(916)498-6410	(916)498-6422
District	San Diego	CA	92101	550 W. C Street	(619)557-7252	(619)557-5894
District	Santa Ana	CA	92701	200 W. Santa Ana Blvd. #700	(714)550-7420	(714)550-0191
District	San Francisco	CA	94105	455 Market St, 6th Fl.	(415)744-6820	(415)744-6812
Colorado						
Regional	Denver	CO	80202	721 19th Street, Ste. 500	(303)844-0500	(303)844-0500
District	Denver	CO	80202	721 19th Street, Ste. 400	(303)844-3984	(303)844-6468
Connecticut						
District	Hartford	CT	06106	330 Main St.	(203)240-4700	(203)240-4659
Delaware						
Branch	Wilmington	DE	19801	824 N. Market St.	(302)573-6294	(302)573-6060
District of Columbia						
District	Washington	DC	20005	1110 Vermont Ave.,N.W.	(202)606-4000	(202)606-4225
Florida						
District	Coral Gables	FL	33146	1320 S. Dixie Hgwy.	(305)536-5521	(305)536-5058
District	Jacksonville	FL	32256	7825 Baymeadows Way	(904)443-1900	(904)443-1980
Georgia						
Regional	Atlanta	GA	30309	1720 Peachtree Rd., NW	(404)347-4999	(404)347-2355
District	Atlanta	GA	30309	1720 Peachtree Rd., NW	(404)347-4749	(404)347-4745
Hawaii						
District	Honolulu	HI	96850	300 Ala Moana Blvd.	(808)541-2990	(808)541-2976
Idaho						
District	Boise	ID	83702	1020 Main Street	(208)334-1696	(208)334-1696
Illinois						
Regional	Chicago	IL	60661	500 W. Madison St.	(312)353-5000	(312)353-3426
District	Chicago	IL	60661	500 W. Madison St.	(312)353-4528	(312)886-5688
Branch	Springfield	IL	62704	511 W. Capitol Ave.	(217)492-4416	(217)492-4867
Indiana						
District	Indianapolis	IN	46204	429 N. Pennsylvania	(317)226-7272	(317)226-7259

OFFICE TYPE	CITY	STATE	ZIP	ADDRESS	PHONE	FAX
Iowa						
District	Cedar Rapids	IA	52401	215 4th Avenue Rd, SE	(319)362-6405	(319)362-7861
District	Des Moines	IA	50309	210 Walnut Street	(515)284-4422	(515)284-4572
Kansas						
District	Wichita	KS	67202	100 East English St.	(316)269-6616	(316)269-6499
Kentucky						
District	Louisville	KY	40202	600 Dr. M.L. King Jr. Pl.	(502)582-5971	(502)582-5009
Louisiana						
District	New Orleans	LA	70130	365 Canal Street	(504)589-6685	(504)589-2339
Maine						
District	Augusta	ME	04330	40 Western Ave.	(207)622-8378	(207)622-8277
Maryland						
District	Baltimore	MD	21201	10 S. Howard St.	(410)962-4392	(410)962-1805
Massachusetts						
Regional	Boston	MA	02222	10 Causeway St.	(617)565-8415	(617)565-8420
District	Boston	MA	02222	10 Causeway St.	(617)565-5590	(617)565-5598
Branch	Springfield	MA	01103	1441 Main St., Ste. 410	(413)785-0268	(413)785-0267
Michigan						
District	Detroit	MI	48226	477 Michigan Ave.	(313)226-6075	(313)226-4769
Branch	Marquette	MI	49855	501 South Front Street	(906)225-1108	(906)225-1109
Minnesota						
District	Minneapolis	MN	55403	100 N. 6th St.	(612)370-2324	(612)370-2303
Mississippi						
Distrtrict	Jackson	MS	39201	101 W. Capitol St.	(601)965-4378	(601)965-4294
Branch	Gulfport	MS	39501	One Bank Of Mississippi, Ste. 203	(228)863-4449	(228)864-0179
Missouri						
Regional	Kansas City	MO	64105	323 W 8th St. Ste. 307	(816)374-6380	(816)374-6339
District	Kansas City	MO	64105	323 W 8th St. Ste. 501	(816)374-6708	(816)374-6759
District	St. Louis	MO	63101	815 Olive Street	(314)539-6600	(314)539-3785
Branch	Springfield	MO	65802	620 S. Glenstone St.	(417)864-7670	(417)864-4108
Montana						
District	Helena	MT	59626	301 South Park	(406)441-1081	(406)441-1090
Nebraska						
District	Omaha	NE	68154	11145 Mill Valley Rd.	(402)221-4691	(402)221-3680
Nevada						
District	Las Vegas	NV	89125	301 East Stewart St.	(702)388-6611	(702)388-6469
New Jersey						
District	Newark	NJ	07102	Two Gateway Ctr, 4th Fl.	(973)645-2434	(973)645-6265
New Hampshire						
District	Concord	NH	03301	143 N. Main St.	(603)225-1400	(603)225-1409

OFFICE TYPE	CITY	STATE	ZIP	ADDRESS	PHONE	FAX
New Mexico						
District	Albuquerque	NM	87102	625 Silver Avenue, SW	(505)766-1870	(505)766-1057
New York						
Regional	New York	NY	10278	26 Federal Plaza	(212)264-1450	(212)264-0038
District	Buffalo	NY	14202	111 West Huron St.	(716)551-4301	(716)551-4418
District	New York	NY	10278	26 Federal Plaza	(212)264-2454	(212)264-7751
District	Syracuse	NY	13202	401 S. Salina St., 5th Fl.	(315)471-9393	(315)471-9288
Branch	Elmira	NY	14901	333 East Water St.	(607)734-8130	(607)733-4656
Branch	Melville	NY	11747	35 Pinelawn Rd.	(516)454-0750	(516)454-0769
Branch	Rochester	NY	14614	100 State St.	(716)263-6700	(716)263-3146
North Carolina						
District	Charlotte	NC	28202	200 N. College St.	(704)344-6563	(704)344-6644
North Dakota						
District	Fargo	ND	58108	657 2nd Ave North	(701)239-5131	(701)239-5645
Ohio						
District	Cleveland	OH	44144	1111 Superior Ave.	(216)522-4180	(216)522-2038
District	Columbus	OH	43215	2 Nationwide Plaza	(614)469-6860	(614)469-2391
Branch	Cincinnati	OH	45202	525 Vine St.	(513)684-2814	(513)684-3251
Oklahoma						
District	Oklahoma City	OK	73102	210 Park Ave. Ste. 1300	(405)231-5521	(405)231-4876
Oregon						
District	Portland	OR	97201	1515 SW Fifth Avenue	(503)326-2682	(503)326-2808
Pennsylvania						
District	King Of Prussia	PA	19406	475 Allendale Rd.	(610)962-3800	(610)962-3795
District	Pittsburgh	PA	15222	1000 Liberty Ave. Federal Bldg. Room 1128	(412)395-6560	(412)395-6562
Branch	Harrisburg	PA	17101	100 Chestnut St.	(717)782-3840	(717)782-4839
Branch	Wilkes-Barre	PA	18701	20 N. Pennsylvania Ave.	(717)826-6497	(717)826-6287
Rhode Island						
District	Providence	RI	02903	380 Westminister Mall	(401)528-4562	(401)528-4539
South Carolina						
District	Columbia	SC	29201	1835 Assembly St.	(803)765-5377	(803)765-5962
South Dakota						
District	Sioux Falls	SD	57102	101 South Main Avenue	(605)330-4231	(605)330-4215
Tennessee						
District	Nashville	TN	37228	50 Vantage Way	(615)736-5881	(615)736-7232
Texas						
Branch	Corpus Christi	TX	78476	606 North Carancahua	(512)888-3331	(512)888-3418
Regional	Dallas/Ft.Worth	TX	76155	4300 Amon Carter Blvd.	(817)885-6581	(817)885-6588
District	El Paso	TX	79935	10737 Gateway West	(915)540-5676	(915)540-5636
District	Dallas/Ft.Worth	TX	76155	4300 Amon Carter Blvd.	(817)885-6500	(817)885-6516
District	Harlingen	TX	78550	222 East Van Buren St.	(956)427-8625	(956)427-8537
District	Houston	TX	77074	9301 Southwest Freeway	(713)773-6500	(713)773-6550

OFFICE TYPE	CITY	STATE	ZIP	ADDRESS	PHONE	FAX
Texas (*Continued*)						
District	Lubbock	TX	79401	1611 Tenth Street	(806)472-7462	(806)472-7487
District	San Antonio	TX	78206	727 E. Durango	(210)472-5900	(210)472-5937
Utah						
District	Salt Lake City	UT	84138	125 South State St.	(801)524-5800	(801)524-4160
Vermont						
District	Montpelier	VT	05602	87 State St.	(802)828-4422	(802)828-4485
Virginia						
District	Richmond	VA	23229	1504 Santa Rosa Rd. Dale Bldg Ste 200	(804)771-2400	(804)771-8018
Washington						
Regional	Seattle	WA	98101	1200 6th Ave. Ste. 1805	(206)553-5676	(206)553-2872
District	Seattle	WA	98101	1200 6th Ave. Ste. 1700	(206)553-7310	(206)553-7099
District	Spokane	WA	99204	West 601 First Ave.	(509)353-2800	(509)353-2829
West Virginia						
District	Clarksburg	WV	26301	168 W. Main St.	(304)623-5631	(304)623-0023
Branch	Charleston	WV	25301	405 Capitol St., Ste. 412	(304)347-5220	(304)347-5350
Wisconsin						
District	Madison	WI	53703	212 E. Washington Ave.	(608)264-5261	(608)264-5541
Branch	Milwaukee	WI	53203	310 W. Wisconsin Ave.	(414)297-3941	(414)297-1377
Wyoming						
District	Casper	WY	82602	100 East B St., Rm. 4001, Box 2839	(307)261-6500	(307)261-6535
Guam						
Branch	Mongmong	GU	96927	400 Route 8, Ste. 302	(671)472-7277	(671)472-7365
Puerto Rico						
District	Hato Rey	PR	00918	252 Ponce De Leon Ave.	(809)766-5572	(809)766-5309
Virgin Islands						
District	St. Croix	VI	00820	3013 Golden Rock	(809)778-5380	(809)778-1102
District	St. Thomas	VI	00802	3800 Crown Bay	(809)774-8530	(809)776-2312

DIRECTORY OF SMALL BUSINESS DEVELOPMENT CENTERS

This appendix provides information about the Small Business Development Center (SBDC) program and a directory of the almost 1,000 centers throughout the United States and its territories. These centers provide an ideal place to obtain information about starting a business or franchise.

An Introduction to SBDCs

The U.S. Small Business Administration administers the Small Business Development Center Program to provide management assistance to current and prospective small business owners. SBDCs offer one-stop assistance to small businesses by providing a wide variety of information and guidance in central and easily accessible branch locations. The program is a cooperative effort of the private sector, the educational community, and federal, state and local governments. It enhances economic development by providing small businesses with management and technical assistance.

There are now 57 small business development centers—one in every state (Texas has four), the District of Columbia, Puerto Rico, the U.S. Virgin Islands and Guam—with a network of more than 1,000 service locations. Ineach state there is a lead organization that sponsors the SBDC and manages the program. The lead organization coordinates program services offered to small businesses through a network of subcenters and satellite locations in each state. Subcenters are located at colleges, universities, community colleges, vocational schools, chambers of commerce and economic-development corporations.

SBDC assistance is tailored to the local community and the needs of individual clients. Each center develops services in cooperation with local SBA district offices to ensure statewide coordination with other available resources.

Each center has a director, staff members, volunteers, and part-time personnel. Qualified individuals recruited from professional and trade associations, the legal and banking communities, academia, chambers of commerce and SCORE (the Service Corps of Retired Executives) are among those who donate their services.

SBDCs also use paid consultants, consulting engineers and testing laboratories from the private sector to help clients who need specialized expertise.

What the Program Does

The SBDC Program is designed to deliver up-to-date counseling, training and technical assistance in all aspects of small business management. SBDC services include, but are not limited to, assisting small businesses with financial, marketing, produc-tion, organization, engineering and technical prob-lems, and feasibility studies. Special SBDC programs and economic development activities include interna-tional-trade assistance, technical assistance, procure-ment assistance, venture-capital formation, and rural development.

The SBDCs also make special efforts to reach socially and economically disadvantaged groups, veterans, women and the disabled. Assistance is provided to both current and potential small business owners.

SBDCs also provide assistance to small businesses applying for Small Business Innovation and Research grants from federal agencies.

Eligibility

SBDC assistance is available to anyone interested in starting or expanding a small business who cannot afford the services of a private consultant.

Directory of Small Business Development Centers

This directory is organized into centers that service states and territories. There may be centers listed for one state that are located in another. This is because those Centers service areas in both their state of residence and a nearby state. Information in this directory was released by the SBA in March 1998.

Alabama

Alabama Small Business Development Consortium
UNIVERSITY OF ALABAMA AT BIRMINGHAM—Lead Center
Mr. John Sandefur, State Director   (205) 934-7260
Medical Towers Building   Fax: (205) 934-7645
1717 Eleventh Avenue South, Suite 419
Birmingham, AL 35294-4410
E-mail: sandefur@uab.edu

Alabama Small Business Development Center
Mr. Ernie Gauld, Associate State Director   (205) 934-7260
1717 Eleventh Avenue South,   Fax: (205) 934-7645
    Suite 419
Birmingham, AL 35294-4410
E-mail: Ernieg@asbdc.asbdc.uab.edu

Alabama International Trade Center—Specialized Center
Small Business Development Center
Mr. Brian Davis, Director   (205) 348-7621
University of Alabama   Fax: (205) 348-6974
Bidgood Hall, Room 201
Tuscaloosa, AL 35487-0396
E-mail: aitc@aitc.cba.ua.edu

Alabama Small Business Procurement System—Specialized Center
Small Business Development Consortium
Mr. Charles Hopson, Procurement Director (205) 934-7260
University of Alabama at Birmingham   Fax: (205) 934-7645

1717 Eleventh Avenue South, Suite 419
Birmingham, AL 35294-4410
E-mail: charlesh@asbdc.asbdc.uab.edu

Alabama State University#
Small Business Development Center
Mr. Lorenzo Patrick, Director   (334) 229-4138
915 South Jackson Street   Fax: (334) 265-9144
Montgomery, AL 36195
E-mail: lpatrick@asunet.alasu.edu

Auburn University
Small Business Development Center
Mr. Devron Veasley, Director   (334) 844-4220
108 College of Business   Fax: (334) 844-4268
Auburn, AL 36849-5243
E-mail: veasley@business.auburn.edu

Jacksonville State University
Small Business Development Center
Mr. Pat W. Shaddix, Director   (205) 782-5271
114 Merrill Hall   Fax: (205) 782-5179
700 Pelham Road North
Jacksonville, AL 36265
E-mail: sbdc@jsucc.jsu.edu

University of West Alabama
Small Business Development Center
Mr. Paul Garner, Director   (205) 652-3665
Station 35   Fax: (205) 652-3516
Livingston, AL 35470

North East Alabama Regional
Small Business Development Center
Mr. David Taylor, Director   (205) 535-2061
Alabama A&M University and the   Fax: (205) 535-2050
University of Alabama at Huntsville
P.O. Box 168
225 Church Street, N.W.
Huntsville, AL 35804-0168
E-mail: dtaylor@hsv.chamber.org

Troy State University
Small Business Development Center
Ms. Janet Kervin, Director   (334) 670-3771
102 Bibb Graves   Fax: (334) 670-3636
Troy, AL 36082-0001
E-mail: jkervin@trojan.troyst.edu

University of Alabama
Small Business Development Center
Mr. Paavo Hanninen, Director   (205) 348-7011
P.O. Box 870397   Fax: (205) 348-9644
Bidgood Hall, Room 250
Tuscaloosa, AL 35487-0397
E-mail: phaninen@ualvm.ua.edu

University of Alabama at Birmingham
Small Business Development Center
Ms. Brenda Walker, Director   (205) 934-6760
1601 11th Avenue South   Fax: (205) 934-0538
Birmingham, AL 35294-2180

University of North Alabama
Small Business Development Center
Dr. Kerry Gatlin, Director   (205) 765-4629
Box 5248, Keller Hall   Fax: (205) 765-4813
Florence, AL 35632-0001

University of South Alabama
Small Business Development Center
Mr. Thomas Tucker, Director   (334) 460-6004
College of Business, Room 8   Fax: (334) 460-6246
Mobile, AL 36688
E-mail: btbrown@jaguar1.usouthal.edu

Alaska

Alaska Small Business Development Center
UNIVERSITY OF ALASKA ANCHORAGE—Lead Center
Ms. Jan Fredericks, State Director   (907) 274-7232
430 West Seventh Avenue, Suite 110 Fax: (907) 274-9524
Anchorage, AK 99501

Kenai Peninsula
Small Business Development Center
Mr. Clyde Johnson, Director   (907) 283-3335
P.O. Box 3029   Fax: (907) 283-3913
Kenai, AK 99611

Mat-Su Borough
Small Business Development Center
Ms. Marian Romano, Director   (907) 373-7232
1801 Parks Highway, Suite C-18   Fax: (907) 373-2560
Wasilla, AK 99654

Southeast Alaska
Small Business Development Center
Mr. Charles Northrip, Director   (907) 463-3789
400 Willoughby Street, Suite 211   Fax: (907) 463-3929
Juneau, AK 99801

University of Alaska
Small Business Development Center
Mr. Vern Craig, Director   (907) 274-7232
Rural Outreach Program   Fax: (907) 274-9524
430 West Seventh Avenue, Suite 110
Anchorage, AK 99501

University of Alaska Anchorage
Small Business Development Center
Ms. Jean Wall, Director   (907) 274-7232
430 West Seventh Avenue, Suite 10   Fax: (907) 274-9524
Anchorage, AK 99501

University of Alaska Fairbanks
Small Business Development Center
Ms. Laurie Henderson, Director   (907) 456-1701
510 Second Avenue, Suite 101   Fax: (907) 456-1873
Fairbanks, AK 99701

Arizona

Arizona Small Business Development Center Network
MARICOPA COUNTY COMMUNITY COLLEGES—Lead
Center
Small Business Development Center
Mr. Michael York, State Director   (602) 731-8722
2411 West 14th Street, Suite 132   Fax: (602) 731-8729
Tempe, AZ 85281
E-mail: york@maricopa.edu

Arizona Western College
Small Business Development Center
Mr. John Lundin, Director   (520) 341-1650
281 West 24th Street, #152   Fax: (520) 726-2636
Yuma, AZ 85364

Central Arizona College
Pinal County
Small Business Development Center
Ms. Carol Giordano, Director   (520) 426-4341
8470 North Overfield Road   Fax: (520) 426-4284
Coolidge, AZ 85228

Cochise College
Small Business Development Center
Ms. Debbie Elver, Director   (520) 515-5443
901 North Colombo, Room 411   Fax: (520) 515-5478
Sierra Vista, AZ 85635

Coconino County Community College
Small Business Development Center
Mr. Mike Lainoff, Director   (520) 526-5072
3000 North 4th Street, Suite 25   Fax: (520) 526-8693
Flagstaff, AZ 86004

Eastern Arizona College/Thatcher
Small Business Development Center
Mr. Frank Granberg, Director   (520) 428-8590
622 College Avenue   Fax: (520) 526-8693
Thatcher, AZ 85552-0769

Mohave Community College
Small Business Development Center
Ms. Jenn Miles, Director   (520) 757-0894
1971 Jagerson Avenue   Fax: (520) 757-0836
Kingman, AZ 86401

Northland Pioneer College
Small Business Development Center
Mr. Joel Eittreim, Director   (520) 537-2976
P.O. Box 610   Fax: (520) 524-2227
Holbrook, AZ 86025

Pima Community College
Small Business Development and
 Training Center
Ms. Linda Andrews, Director   (520) 748-4906
4905-A East Broadway, Ste. 101   Fax: (520) 748-4585
Tucson, AZ 85709

Maricopa Community Colleges
Small Business Development Center   (602) 230-7308
702 East Osborn Road, Ste. 150   Fax: (602) 230-7989
Phoenix, AZ 85014

Yavapai College
Small Business Development Center
Mr. Richard Senopole, Director   (520) 757-0894
117 East Gurley Street, Suite 206   Fax: (520) 778-3109
East Building
Prescott, AZ 86301

Arkansas

Arkansas Small Business Development Center
UNIVERSITY OF ARKANSAS AT LITTLE ROCK—Lead
Center
Ms. Janet Nye, State Director   (501) 324-9043
Little Rock Technology Center Building Fax: (501) 324-9049
100 South Main, Suite 401
Little Rock, AR 72201

Arkansas State University
Small Business Development Center
Mr. Herb Lawrence, Director   (501) 972-3517
P.O Box 2650   Fax: (501) 972-3868
State University, AR 72467

Henderson State University
Small Business Development Center
Mr. Bill Akin, Director   (501) 230-5224
P.O. Box 7624   Fax: (501) 230-5236
Arkadelphia, AR 71923

Harrison Regional Office
Small Business Development Center
Mr. Bob Penquite, Business Specialist   (501) 741-8009
818 Highway 62-65-412 North 72601   Fax: (501) 741-1905
P.O. Box 190
Harrison, AR 72601-0190

Southeast Arkansas Regional Office
Small Business Development Center
Ms. Audrey Long, Business Specialist   (501) 536-0654
Enterprise Center III   Fax: (501) 536-7713
400 Main, Suite 117
Pine Bluff, AR 71601

Magnolia Regional Office
Small Business Development Center
Mr. Lairie Kincaid, Business Specialist   (501) 234-4030
600 Bessie, P.O. Box 767   Fax: (501) 234-0135
Magnolia, AR 71753

Stuttgart Arkansas Regional Office
Small Business Development Center
Mr. Larry Lefler, Business Specialist   (501) 673-8707
301 South Grand, Suite 101   Fax: (501) 673-8707
P.O. Box 289
Stuttgart, AR 72160

University of Arkansas at Fayetteville
Small Business Development Center
Ms. Jimmie Wilkins, Director   (501) 575-5148
College of Business—BA 106   Fax: (501) 575-4013
Fayetteville, AR 72701

University of Arkansas at Little Rock
Small Business Development Center
Mr. John Harrison, Business Specialist   (501) 324-9043
100 South Main, Suite 401   Fax: (501) 324-9049
Little Rock, AR 72201

West Arkansas Regional Office
Small Business Development Center
Ms. Vonnelle Vanzant, Business Specialist   (501) 785-1376
1109 South 16th Street   Fax: (501) 785-1964
P.O. Box 2067
Fort Smith, AR 72901-2067

West Central Arkansas Regional Office
Small Business Development Center
Mr. Richard Evans, Business Specialist   (501) 624-5448
835 Central Avenue, Box 402-D   Fax: (501) 624-6632
Hot Springs, AR 71901

West Memphis Regional Office
Small Business Development Center
Mr. Ronny Brothers, Business Consultant   (501) 733-6767
Mid-South Community College
2000 West Broadway
P.O. Box 2067
West Memphis, AR 72303-2067

California

California Small Business Development Center
CALIFORNIA TRADE AND COMMERCE AGENCY—Lead
Center   (800) 303-6600
Ms. Kim Neri, State Director   (916) 324-5068
801 K Street, Suite 1700   Fax: (916) 322-5084
Sacramento, CA 95814
Web site: http://commerce.ca.gov/small

Alpine Chamber of Commerce & Visitor Authority
3 Webster Street   (530) 694-2475
P.O. Box 265   Fax: (530) 694-2478
Markleeville, CA 96120

Amador County SBDC Outreach Center
1500 S. Highway 49   (209) 223-0351
P.O. Box 1077   Fax: (209) 223-2261
Jackson, CA 95642

Cascade Small Business Development Center
Ms. Carole Enmark, Director   (916) 225-2770
737 Auditorium Drive, Suite A   Fax: (916) 225-2769
Redding, CA 96001
E-mail: cenmark@awwsome.com

Central California SBDC   (800) 974-0664
Mr. Dennis Winans, Director   (209) 275-1223
3419 West Shaw Avenue, Suite 102 Fax: (209) 275-1499
Fresno, CA 93711
E-mail: sbdc@abrillo.cc.ca.us
Web site: http://www.ccsbdc.org

Central California/Visalia Satellite
Small Business Development Center
Mr. Randy Mason, Manager   (209) 625-3051
430 W. Caldwell Avenue, Suite D Fax: (209) 625-3053
Visalia, CA 93277
E-mail: wendim@csufresno.edu

Central Coast Small Business Development Center
Ms. Teresa Thomae, Director   (408) 479-6136
6500 Soquel Drive   Fax: (408) 479-6166
Aptos, CA 95003
E-mail: sbdc@cabrillo.cc.ca.us

Coachella Valley/Palm Springs Satellite
Small Business Development Center
Mr. Brad Mix, Office Manager   (619) 864-1311
500 S. Palm Canyon Drive, Suite 222 Fax: (619) 864-1319
Palm Springs, CA 92264

Colusa County SBDC
144 Market Street   (916) 458-5881
Colusa, CA 95932   Fax: (916) 458-0335

Contra Costa Small Business Development Center
Ms. Rita Hayes, Interim Director   (510) 646-5377
2425 Bisso Lane, Suite 200   Fax: (510) 646-5299
Concord, CA 94520
E-mail: rhays@pic.co.contra-costa.ca.us

East Bay Small Business Development Center
Mr. Faheem Hameed, Director   (510) 893-4114
519 17th Street, Suite 210   Fax: (510) 893-5532
Oakland, CA 94612
E-mail: sbdc@peralta.cc.ca.us

South Central Los Angeles Small Business Development
Center
Cope Norcross, Manager
3650 Martin Luther King Jr. Blvd. Suite 246 (213) 290-2832
Los Angeles, CA 90008   Fax: (213) 290-7190
E-mail: sbdcla@ibm.net

Eastern Los Angeles County
Small Business Development Center
Ms. Toni Valdez, Director   (909) 629-2247
375 South Main Street, Suite 101 Fax: (909) 629-8310
Pomona, CA 91766

Export Small Business Development Center
El Monte Outreach Center
Mr. Charles Blythe, Manager   (818) 459-4111
10501 Valley Blvd., Ste. 106   Fax: (818) 443-0463
El Monte, CA 91731
E-mail: info@exportsbdc.org

Export SBDC of Southern California
Ms. Gladys Moreau, Director
222 North Sepulveda, Ste. 1690   (310) 606-0166
El Segundo, CA 90245   Fax: (310) 606-0155
E-mail: info@exportsbdc.org
Web site: http://www.exportsbdc.org

Export SBDC Satellite Center
Ms. Heather Wicka, Manager   (805) 644-6191
5700 Ralston St., Ste. 310   Fax: (805) 658-2252
Ventura, CA 93003

Gavilan College Small Business Development Center
Mr. Peter Graff, Director   (408) 847-0373
7436 Monterey Street   Fax: (408) 847-0393
Gilroy, CA 95020
E-mail: l.nolan@gilroy.com
Web site: http://gilroy.com/sbdc/sbdc.html

Gold Coast Small Business Development Center
Mr. Joe Huggins, Manager   (805) 658-2688
5700 Ralston St., Ste. 310   Fax: (805) 658-2252
Ventura, CA 93003
E-mail: GCsbdc@aol.com

Greater Sacramento
Small Business Development Center
Ms. Cynthia Steimle, Director   (916) 563-3210
1410 Ethan Way   Fax: (916) 563-3266
Sacramento, CA 95825
E-mail: steimlc@mail.do.losrios.cc.ca.us
Web site: http://www.losrios.cc.ca.us/oeed/sbdc/sbdc.htm

Greater San Diego Chamber of Commerce
Small Business Development Center
Mr. Hal Lefkowitz, Director   (619) 453-9388
4275 Executive Square, Suite 920   Fax: (619) 450-1997
La Jolla, CA 92037
E-mail: sbdc@smallbiz.org
Web site: http://www.smallbiz.org

High Desert/Victorville Satellite
Small Business Development Center
Ms. Janice Harbaugh, Office Manager   (619) 951-1592
15490 Civic Drive, Suite 102   Fax: (619) 951-8929
Victorville, CA 92392

Imperial Valley Satellite
Small Business Development Center
Town & Country Shopping Center   (619) 312-9800
Ms. Debbie Trujillo, Satellite Manager Fax: (619) 312-9838
301 N. Imperial Avenue, Suite B
El Centro, CA 92243
E-mail: ivsbdc@quix.net

Inland Empire Small Business Development Center
Mr. Michael Roessler, Interim Director (800) 750-2353
1157 Spruce Street   (909) 781-2345
Riverside, CA 92507   Fax: (909) 781-2353
E-mail: sbdc@winriverside.org
Web site: http://www.iesbdc.org

Inland Empire Business Incubator
Mr. Chuck Eason, Incubator Manager   (909) 382-0065
155 S. Memorial Drive   Fax: (909) 382-8543
Norton Air Force Base, CA 92509

International Trade Center—Specialized Center
Small Business Development Center
Ms. Mary Wylie, Director   (619) 482-6391
Southwestern College   Fax: (619) 482-6402
900 Otay Lakes Road, Bldg. 1600
Chula Vista, CA 91910
Web site: http://www.sbditc.org

Napa Valley College
Small Business Development Center
Mr. Chuck Eason, Director   (707) 253-3210
1556 First Street, Suite 103   Fax: (707) 253-3068
Napa, CA 94559
E-mail: charles.eason@usa.net

North Coast Small Business Development Center
Ms. Fran Clark, Director   (707) 464-2168
207 Price Mall, Suite 500   Fax: (707) 465-6008
Crescent City, CA 95531
E-mail: fransbdc@northcoast.com

North Coast/Satellite Center
Small Business Development Center
Ms. Fran Clark, Director   (707) 445-9720
520 E Street   Fax: (707) 445-9652
Eureka, CA 95501
E-mail: fransbdc@northcoast.com

North Los Angeles
Small Business Development Center
Ms. Wilma Berglund, Interim Director   (818) 907-9922
4717 Van Nuys Blvd., Suite 201   Fax: (818) 907-9890
Van Nuys, CA 91403
E-mail: VNsbdc@aol.com

Orange County Small Business Development Center
Mr. Gregory Kishel, Director   (714) 647-1172
901 East Santa Ana Boulevard   Fax: (714) 835-9008
Suite 101
Santa Ana, CA 92701
E-mail: gkishel@pacbell.net

Pasadena Small Business Development Center
Mr. David Ryal, Manager   (818) 552-3254
330 N. Brand, Suite 190   Fax: (818) 398-3059
Glendale, CA 91203

Redwood Empire Small Business Development Center
Mr. Jim Burke, Interim Director   (707) 524-1770
520 Mendocino Avenue, Suite 210   Fax: (707) 524-1772
Santa Rosa, CA 95401
E-mail: burke@wco.com
Web site: http://www.santarosa.edu/sbdc

San Francisco Small Business Development Center
Mr. Tim Sprinkles, Director   (415) 561-1890
711 Van Ness Ave., Suite. 305   Fax: (415) 561-1894
San Francisco, CA 94102
E-mail: sfsbdc@ziplink.net

San Joaquin Delta College
Small Business Development Center
Ms. Gillian Murphy, Director   (209) 943-5089
445 North San Joaquin Street   Fax: (209) 943-8325
Stockton, CA 95202
E-mail: gmurphy@sjdccd.cc.ca.us
Web site: http://www.inreach.com/sbdc

Sierra College
Small Business Development Center
Ms. Mary Wollesen, Director   (916) 885-5488
560 Wall Street, Suite J   Fax: (916) 823-2831
Auburn, CA 95603
E-mail: smallbuz@sierra.campus.mci.net

Silicon Valley Small Business Development Center
Mr. Elza Minor, Director   (408) 736-0680
298 S. Sunnyvale Ave., Ste. 204   Fax: (408) 736-0679
Sunnyvale, CA 94086
E-mail: Rebecca@siliconvalley-sbdc.org
Web site: http://www.siliconvalley-sbdc.org

Solano County Small Business Development Center
Ms. Beth Pratt, Director   (707) 864-3382
424 Executive Court North, Suite C Fax: (707) 864-8025
Suisun, CA 94585
E-mail: epratt@solano.cc.ca.us

Southwest Los Angeles County
Small Business Development Center
Ms. Susan Hunter, Director   (310) 787-6466
21221 Western Avenue, Suite 110   Fax: (310) 782-8607
Torrance, CA 90501

Westside SBDC
Small Business Development Center
Mr. Ken Davis, Administrative Assistant   (310) 398-8883
3233 Donald Douglas Loop South,   Fax: (310) 398-3024
   Suite C
Santa Monica, CA 90405

Yuba College Lake County SBDC
Mr. George McQueen, Director   (707) 263-0330
P.O. Box 1566   Fax: (707) 263-8516
Lakeport, CA 95453
E-mail: 4833@sshare.com

Yuba/Sutter Satellite SBDC
429 10th Street   (916) 749-0153
P.O. Box 262 (mailing)   Fax: (916) 749-0152
Marysville, CA 95901

Valley Sierra Small Business Development Center
Mr. Kelly Bearden, Director   (209) 521-6177
1012 Eleventh Street, Suite 400   Fax: (209) 521-9373
Modesto, CA 95354
E-mail: bearden@scedco.org

Valley Sierra/Merced
Small Business Development Center Satellite
Mr. Nick Stavrianoudakis,
   Satellite Manager   (209) 725-3800
1632 N Street   Fax: (209) 383-4959
Merced, CA 95340
E-mail: sbdc@cell2000.net

Weill Institute Small Business Development Center
Mr. Jeffrey Johnson, Director   (805) 322-5881
1706 Chester Ave., Ste. 200   Fax: (805) 322-5663
Bakersfield, CA 93301
E-mail: weill@lightspeed.net

West Company coast Office
Small Business Development Center   (707) 964-7571
306 Redwood Avenue   Fax: (707) 964-7571
Fort Bragg, CA 95437

West Company Small Business Development Center
Ms. Sheilah Rogers, Executive Director   (707) 468-3553
367 N. State St., Ste. 201   Fax: (707) 468-3555
Ukiah, CA 95482

Colorado

Colorado Small Business Development Center
OFFICE OF BUSINESS DEVELOPMENT—Lead Center
Cec Ortiz, State Director   (303) 892-3840
1625 Broadway, Suite 1710   Fax: (303) 892-3848
Denver, CO 80202
E-mail: sbdclcl@attmail.com
Web site: http://www.state.co.us/gov_dir/obd/sbdc.htm

Adams State College
Small Business Development Center
Ms. Mary Hoffman, Director   (719) 589-7372
Alamosa, CO 81102   Fax: (719) 589-7603
E-mail: mchoffma@adams.edu

Aims Community College
Small Business Development Center
Mr. Ronald Anderson, Director   (970) 352-3661
Greeley/Weld Chamber of Commerce   Fax: (970) 352-3572
902 7th Avenue
Greeley, CO 80631
E-mail: aimcc@attmail.com

Colorado Mountain College
Small Business Development Center
Ms. Alisa Zimmerman, Director   1-800-621-1647
215 Ninth Street   (970) 928-0120
Glenwood Springs, CO 81601   Fax: (970) 947-8385
E-mail: lwiltse@coloradomtn.edu

Colorado Northwestern Community College
Small Business Development Center
Mr. Ken Farmer, Director   (970) 824-7078
50 College Drive   Fax: (970) 824-1134
Craig, CO 81625
E-mail: cnwcc@attmail.com

Community College of Aurora—Specialized Center
Small Business Development Center
Mr. Randy Johnson, Director   (303) 341-4849
9905 East Colfax Avenue   Fax: (303) 361-2953
Aurora, CO 80010-2119
E-mail: asbdc@henge.com

Community College of Denver—Specialized Center
Small Business Development Center
Ms. Tamela Lee, Director   (303) 620-8076
Metro Denver Chamber of Commerce   Fax: (303) 534-3200
1445 Market Street
Denver, CO 80202
E-mail: ccd@attmail.com

Delta Montrose Vocational School
Small Business Development Center
Mr. Bob Marshall, Director   (970) 874-8772
1765 US Highway 50   Fax: (970) 874-8796
Delta, CO 81416
E-mail: dmvs@attmail.com

Douglas County SBDC
Castle Rock Chamber of Commerce
Dennie Kamlet   (303) 814-0936
P.O. Box 282   Fax: (303) 688-2688
420 Jerry Street
Castle Rock, CO 80104

Fort Lewis College
Small Business Development Center
Mr. Jim Reser, Director   (970) 247-7009
1000 Rim Dr., 126-G Hesperus Hall   Fax: (970) 247-7623
Durango, CO 81301-3999
E-mail: RESER_J@fortlewis.Edu
Web site: http://www.fortlewis.edu/soba/sbdc

Front Range Community College/Ft. Collins—Specialized
Center
Small Business Development Center
Mr. Frank Pryor, Director   (970) 498-9295
125 South Howes Street, Suite 150   Fax: (970) 221-2811
Key Tower Building
Fort Collins, CO 80526
E-mail: ftcsbdc@attmail.com

Boulder SBDC
Small Business Development Center
Ms. Marilynn Force, Director   (303) 442-1475
Boulder Chamber of Commerce   Fax: (303) 938-8837
2440 Pearl Street
Boulder, CO 80302
E-mail: marilynn@chamber.boulder.co.us

Front Range Community College—Specialized Center
Small Business Development Center
Mr. Joe Pariseau, Associate Director   (303) 460-1032
3645 West 112th Avenue   Fax: (303) 469-7143
Westminster, CO 80030
E-mail: fr_henry@cccs.ccoes.edu

Lamar Community College
Small Business Development Center
Mr. Dan Minor, Director   (719) 336-8141
2400 S. Main   Fax: (719) 336-2448
Lamar, CO 81052
E-mail: lcc@attmail.com

Mesa State Community College
Small Business Development Center
Western Colorado Business Development Corp.
Ms. Julie Morey, Director   (970) 243-5242
304 W. Main Street   Fax: (970) 241-0771
Grand Junction, CO 81505-1606
E-mail: mesastate@attmail.com

Morgan Community College
Small Business Development Center
Mr. Dan Simon, Director   (970) 867-3351
300 Main Street   Fax: (970) 867-3352
Fort Morgan, CO 80701
E-mail: comcc@attmail.com

University of Colorado at Colorado Springs
Small Business Development Center
Ms. Iris Clark, Director   (719) 592-1894
CITTI Building   Fax: (719) 533-0545
1420 Austin Bluffs Pkwy.
Colorado Springs, CO 80933
E-mail: sbdc@uccs.edu

Pueblo Community College
Small Business Development Center
Ms. Rita Friberg, Director   (719) 549-3224
900 West Orman Avenue   Fax: (719) 549-3139
Pueblo, CO 81004
E-mail: friberg@pcc.cccoes.edu

Pueblo Community College/Canon City
Small Business Development Center
Canon City Chamber of Commerce
(Vacant), Director   (719) 275-5335
3080 E. Main   Fax: (719) 269-7334
Canon City, CO 81212
E-mail: canonsbdc@attmail.com

Red Rocks Community College—Specialized Center
Small Business Development Center
Ms. Jayne Reiter, Director   (303) 277-1840
1726 Cole Blvd., Bldg 22, Ste. 310   Fax: (303) 277-1899
Golden, CO 80401
E-mail: sbdcrrcc@rmii.com

Trinidad State Junior College
Small Business Development Center
Mr. Dennis O'Connor, Director   (719) 846-5644
136 West Main Street   Fax: (719) 846-4550
Trinidad, CO 81082
E-mail: tsjc@attmail.com

Connecticut

Connecticut Small Business Development Center
UNIVERSITY OF CONNECTICUT—Lead Center
Mr. Dennis Gruell, State Director   (860) 486-4135
Mr. Sotiris Malas, MIS Manager   Fax: (860) 486-1576
School of Business Administration
2 Bourn Place, U-94
Storrs, CT 06269-5094
E-mail: Questions@ct.sbdc.uconn.edu

Bridgeport Regional Business Council
Small Business Development Center
Mr. Juan Scott, Regional Director   (203) 330-4813
10 Middle Street, 14th Floor   Fax: (203) 366-0105
Bridgeport, CT 06604-4229
E-mail: Bridgeport@ct.sbdc.uconn.edu

Eastern Connecticut State University
Small Business Development Center
 (Monday, Wednesday and Friday)
Mr. Richard Cheney, Counsellor   (860) 465-5349
83 Windham Street   Fax: (860) 465-5143
Williamantic, CT 06226-2295
E-mail: Williamantic@ct.sbdc.uconn.edu

Greater New Haven Chamber of Commerce
Small Business Development Center   (203) 782-4390
Mr. Pete Rivera, Regional Director   ext. 190
900 Chapel Street, 10th Floor   Fax: (203) 787-4329

New Haven, CT 06510-2009
E-mail: NewHaven@ct.sbdc.uconn.edu

Middlesex County Chamber of Commerce
Small Business Development Center
Mr. John Serignese, Counsellor   (860) 344-2158
393 Main Street   Fax: (860) 346-1043
Middletown, CT 06457
E-mail: Middletown@ct.sbdc.uconn.edu

Quinebaug Valley Community & Technical College
Small Business Development Center
 (Tuesday and Thursday)
Mr. Roger Doty, Counsellor   (860) 774-1133
742 Upper Maple Street   Fax: (860) 774-6737
Danielson, CT 06239-1440
E-mail: Danielson@ct.sbdc.uconn.edu

Naugatuck Valley Development Corp.
Small Business Development Center
Ms. Ilene Oppenheim, Director   (203) 757-8937
100 Grand Street, 3rd Floor   Fax: (203) 756-9077
Waterbury, CT 06702
E-mail: Waterbury@ct.sbdc.uconn.edu

Southwestern Area Commerce and
 Industry Association (SACIA)
Small Business Development Center
Mr. Harvey Blomberg, Regional Director   (203) 359-3220
One Landmark Square   ext. 302
Stamford, CT 06901   Fax: (203) 967-8294
E-mail: Stamford@ct.sbdc.uconn.edu

University of Connecticut
Small Business Development Center
Mr. Ben Chepovsky, Counsellor   (860) 570-9109
1800 Asylum Avenue   Fax: (860) 570-9107
West Hartford, CT 06117-2659
E-mail: WestHartford@ct.sbdc.uconn.edu

University of Connecticut
Small Business Development Center
Ms. Louise Kahler, Counsellor   (860) 405-9002
Administration Building, Room 300   Fax: (860) 405-9041
1084 Shennecossett Road
Groton, CT 06340-6097
E-mail: Groton@ct.sbdc.uconn.edu

The Greater Danbury Chamber of Commerce
Small Business Development Center   (203) 743-5565
72 West Street
Danbury, CT 06810
E-mail: Danbury@ct.sbdc.uconn.edu

Delaware

Delaware Small Business Development Center
UNIVERSITY OF DELAWARE—Lead Center
Mr. Clinton Tymes, State Director   (302) 831-1555
Purnell Hall—Suite 005   Fax: (302) 831-1423
Newark, DE 19716-2711

Delaware State University
Small Business Development Center
Mr. Jim Crisfield, Director   (302) 678-1555
School of Business Economics   Fax: (302) 739-2333
1200 North Dupont Highway
Dover, DE 19901

Delaware Technical and Community College
Small Business Development Center
Mr. William F. Pfaff, Director   (302) 856-1555
Industrial Training Building   Fax: (302) 856-5779
P.O. Box 610
Georgetown, DE 19947

District Of Columbia Vicinity

HOWARD UNIVERSITY—Lead Center
Small Business Development Center
Edith McCloud, Director   (202) 806-1550
2600 6th Street, NW, Room 128   Fax: (202) 806-1777
Washington, DC 20059

Central Region Sub-Center
Howard University Center for Urban Progress
Frank Reeves Municipal Center
Jose Hernandez, Director   (202) 939-3018
14th and U Streets, NW, 2nd Floor   Fax: (202) 673-4557
Washington, DC 20001

Southwest Region Sub-Center
Small Business Development Center
Friendship House Associates/Southern University
Elise Ashby, Acting Director   (202) 547-7944
921 Pennsylvania Avenue, SE   Fax: (202) 546-3080
Washington, D.C. 20003

George Washington University
 National Law Center Sub-Center
Small Business Legal Clinic
Professor Susan Jones, Director   (202) 994-7463
2000 G Street, NW, Suite 200   Fax: (202) 994-4946
Washington, DC 20052

Virginia:

Northern Virginia SBDC
Attention: Jody Keenan   (703) 277-7700
4301 University Drive, Suite 200   Fax: (703) 277-7722
Fairfax, VA 22030

Arlington SBDC
GMU Arlington Campus   (703) 993-8129
Paul Hall, Director
4001 N. Fairfax Drive, Suite 450
Arlington, VA 22001

Northern Virginia SBDC—Loudoun Information
Ted London, Director   (703) 430-7222
207 Holly Avenue, Suite 214
Sterling, VA 20146

Alexandria SBDC
Bill Regan   (703) 299-9146
1055 N. Fairfax Street   Fax: (703) 549-6578
Suite 204
Alexandria, VA 22314
E-mail: wregan@erols.com

Maryland:

Maryland Small Business Development Center
Center for Business and Industry   (301) 386-5600
Attention: James McGinnis
Meena Kerns
9200 Basil Court
Suite 200
Springdale, MD 20774

Montgomery County Office of Economic Development
Attention: Linda Miller   (301) 217-2345
101 Monroe Street, 15th Floor   Fax: (301) 217-2045
Rockville, MD 20850

SBDC Lead Center—Lead Center
Attention: James N. Graham, Director   (301) 403-8300
7100 Baltimore Avenue, Suite 401
College Park, MD 20740-3627

State Economic Development Agencies:

DC: Economic Development Office of the Mayor
441 4th Street, NW, Suite 1140 North   (202) 727-6365
Washington, DC 20001   Fax: (202) 727-6703

MD: Department of Business & Economic Development
217 E. Redwood Street   (410) 333-6901
Baltimore, MD 21202-3316

VA: Department of Economic Development
901 E. Byrd Street   (804) 371-8106
Richmond, VA 23219-4069

Florida

Florida Small Business Development Center
UNIVERSITY OF WEST FLORIDA—Lead Center
(800) 644-SBDC
Mr. Jerry Cartwright, State Director   (904) 444-2060
19 West Garden Street, Suite 300   Fax: (904) 444-2070
Pensacola, FL 32501

Central Florida Development Council
Small Business Development Center
Ms. Marcela Stanislaus, Vice President   (941) 534-4370
600 N. Broadway, Suite 300   Fax: (941) 533-1247
Bartow, FL 33830

Daytona Beach Community College
Small Business Development Center
Ms. Brenda Thomas-Ramos, Director   (904) 947-5463
1200 W. International Speedway Blvd.   Fax: (904) 254-4465
Daytona Beach, FL 32114

Indian River Community College
Small Business Development Center
Ms. Marsha L. Thompson, Director   (561) 462-4756
3209 Virginia Avenue, Room 114   Fax: (561) 462-4796
Ft. Pierce, FL 34981-5599

Small Business Development Center
Mr. Philip R. Geist, Area Director   (352) 622-8763
110 E. Silver Springs Boulevard   Fax: (352) 351-1031
Ocala, FL 34470-6613
E-mail: sbdcoca@mercury.net

Brevard Community College
Small Business Development Center
Ms. Victoria Peake, Manager   (407) 632-1111
3865 North Wickham Road, CM 207   Ext. 33201
Melbourne, FL 32935   Fax: (407) 634-3721

Florida Gulf Coast University
Small Business Development Center
College of Business   (941) 590-7316
The Midway Center   Fax: (941) 590-1010
17595 South Tamiami Trail, Suite 200
Fort Myers, FL 33908-4500

Florida A & M University#
Small Business Development Center
Ms. Patricia McGowan, Director   (904) 599-3407
1157 East Tennessee Street   Fax: (904) 561-2049
Tallahassee, FL 32308

Florida Atlantic University
Small Business Development Center
Ms. Nancy Young, Director   (561) 362-5620
P.O. Box 3091—Building T9   Fax: (561) 362-5623
Boca Raton, FL 33431

Florida Atlantic University
Small Business Development Center
Mr. Marty Zients, Manager   (954) 771-6520
Commercial Campus   Fax: (954) 351-4120
1515 West Commercial Blvd., Room 11
Fort Lauderdale, FL 33309

Florida International University
Small Business Development Center
Mr. Marvin Nesbit, Regional Director   (305) 348-2272
Trailer MO1—Tamiami Campus   Fax: (305) 348-2965
Miami, FL 33199

Florida International University
Small Business Development Center
Mr. Royland Jarrett, Regional Manager   (305) 919-5790
North Miami Campus   Fax: (305) 919-5792
Academic Building #1, Room 350
NE 151 and Biscayne Boulevard
Miami, FL 33181

Gulf Coast Community College
Small Business Development Center
Mr. Doug Davis, Director   (904) 271-1108
2500 Minnesota Avenue   Fax: (904) 271-1109
Lynn Haven, FL 32444

Miami Dade Community College
Small Business Development Center
Mr. Frederick Bonneau, Director   (305) 237-1906
6300 NW Seventh Avenue   Fax: (305) 237-1908
Miami, FL 33150

Procurement Technical Assistance Program—Specialized Center
University of West Florida
UFW Downtown Center
Small Business Development Center
Ms. Martha Cobb, Interim Director   (904) 470-4980
19 West Garden Street, Suite 302   Fax: (904) 470-4987
Pensacola, FL 32514-5750

Seminole Community College
Small Business Development Centers
Mr. Wayne Hardy, Regional Manager   (407) 328-4722
100 Weldon Boulevard, Building R   ext. 3341
Sanford, FL 32773   Fax: (407) 330-4489

Small Business Development Center
Mr. Bill Stensgaard, Regional Manager   (352) 377-5621
505 NW Second Avenue, Suite D   Fax: (352) 377-0288
P.O. Box 2518
Gainesville, FL 32602-2518

Okaloosa-Walton Community College
University of West Florida
Small Business Development Center
Mr. Walter Craft, Manager   (904) 863-6543
1170 Martin Luther King, Jr. Blvd.   Fax: (904) 863-6564
Fort Walton Beach, FL 32547

Small Business Development Center
Mr. William Healy, Regional Manager   (954) 987-0100
46 SW First Avenue   Fax: (954) 987-0106
Dania, FL 33304

Special Services—Specialized Center
University of South Florida
Mr. Al Othmer, Program Manager (Energy)
Mr. Dick Hardesty, Program Manager (DOD)
College of Business Administration   (813) 974-4371
4202 East Fowler Avenue, BSN 3403   Fax: (813) 974-5020
Tampa, FL 33620   (Call First)

University of Central Florida
Small Business Development Center
Mr. Al Polfer, Director   (407) 823-5554
CBA Suite 309   Fax: (407) 823-3073
P.O. Box 161530
Orlando, FL 32816-1530

University of North Florida
Small Business Development Center
Dr. Lowell Salter, Director   (904) 646-2476
College of Business   Fax: (904) 646-2567
Building 11, Room 2163
4567 St. John's Bluff Road, South
Jacksonville, FL 32216

University of South Florida
Small Business Development Center
Ms. Irene Hurst, Interim Director   (813) 554-2341
1111 North Westshore Drive,   Fax: (813) 554-2356
  Annex B
Tampa, FL 33607

Georgia

Georgia Small Business Development Center
UNIVERSITY OF GEORGIA—Lead Center
Mr. Hank Logan, State Director   (706) 542-6762
Chicopee Complex   Fax: (706) 542-6776
1180 East Broad Street
Athens, GA 30602-5412
E-mail: sbdcdir@uga.cc.uga.edu

NORTHEAST GEORGIA DISTRICT
Small Business Development Center
Mr. Harold Roberts, Asst. State Director   (706) 542-7436
Ms. Nancy Staton, Area Director   Fax: (706) 542-6803
University of Georgia
Chicopee Complex
1180 East Broad Street
Athens, GA 30602-5412
E-mail: nancys@uga.cc.uga.edu

Augusta Small Business Development Center
Mr. Jeff Sanford, Area Director   (706) 737-1790
1054 Claussen Road, Suite 301   Fax: (706) 731-7937
Augusta, GA 30907-3215
E-mail: sdbcaug@uga.cc.uga.edu

Decatur Small Business Development Center
Mr. Eric Bonaparte, Area Director   (404) 373-6930
DeKalb Chamber of Commerce   Fax: (404) 687-9684
750 Commerce Drive
Decatur, GA 30030-2622
E-mail: sbdcdec@uga.cc.uga.edu

Gainesville Small Business Development Center
Mr. Ron Simmons, Area Director   (770) 531-5681
500 Jesse Jewel Parkway, Suite 304   Fax: (770) 531-5684
Gainesville, GA 30501-3773
E-mail: sbdcgain@uga.cc.uga.edu

Clayton College and State University
Small Business Development Center
Mr. Bernie Meineke, Area Director   (770) 961-3440
P.O. Box 285   Fax: (770) 961-3428
Morrow, GA 30260
E-mail: sbdcmorr@uga.cc.uga.edu

Floyd College Small Business Development Center
Mr. Drew Tonsmeire, Area Director   (706) 295-6326
P.O. Box 1864   Fax: (706) 295-6732
Rome, GA 30162-1864
E-mail: sbdcrome@uga.cc.uga.edu

Georgia State University
Small Business Development Center
Mr. Lee Quarterman, Area Director   (404) 651-3550
University Plaza, Box 874   Fax: (404) 651-1035
Atlanta, GA 30303-3083
E-mail: sbdcatl@uga.cc.uga.edu

Kennesaw State University
Small Business Development Center
Ms. Carlotta Roberts, Area Director   (770) 423-6450
1000 Chastain Road   Fax: (770) 423-6564
Kennesaw, GA 30144-5591
E-mail: sbdcmar@uga.cc.uga.edu

SOUTHEAST GEORGIA DISTRICT
Small Business Development Center
Mr. Wendell Perkins, Area Director   (912) 751-6596
    (Interim)   Fax: (912) 751-6607
Ms. Denise Ricketson, Area Director
P.O. Box 13212
Macon, GA 31208-3212
or
401 Cherry Street, Suite 701
Macon, GA 31201
E-mail: sbdcmac@uga.cc.uga.edu

Brunswick Small Business Development Center
Mr. David Lewis, Area Director   (912) 264-7343
1107 Fountain Lake Drive   Fax: (912) 262-3095
Brunswick, GA 31525-3039
E-mail: sbdcbrun@uga.cc.uga.edu

Savannah Small Business Development Center
Lynn Vos, Area Director   (912) 356-2755
450 Mall Boulevard, Suite H   Fax: (912) 353-3033
Savannah, GA 31406-4824
E-mail: sbdcsav@uga.cc.uga.edu

Statesboro Small Business Development Center
Mr. Mark Davis, Area Director   (912) 681-5194
Landrum Center Box 8156   Fax: (912) 681-0648
Statesboro, GA 30460-8156
or
College of Business Admin., Room 2200
Statesboro, GA 30460
E-mail: sbdcstat@uga.cc.uga.edu

Warner Robbins Small Business Development Center
Mr. David Mills, Asst. Director for Economic Development
Research
151 Osigian Boulevard   (912) 953-9356
Warner Robbins, GA 31088   Fax: (912) 953-9376
E-mail: sbdcwr@uga.cc.uga.edu

SOUTHWEST GEORGIA DISTRICT
Small Business Development Center
Ms. Sue Ford, Asst. State Director   (912) 430-4303
230 South Jackson Street, Suite 333   Fax: (912) 430-3933
Albany, GA 31701-2885
E-mail: sbdcal@uga.cc.uga.edu

Columbus Small Business Development Center
Mr. Jerry Copeland, Area Director   (706) 649-7433
928 45th Street, North Building   Fax: (706) 649-1928
Room 202
Columbus, GA 31904-6572
E-mail: sbdccolu@uga.cc.uga.edu

Valdosta Small Business Development Center
Ms. Suzanne Barnett, Area Director
Valdosta State University   (912) 245-3738
College of Business Administration   Fax: (912) 245-3741
Thaxton Hall
Valdosta, GA 31698-0065
E-mail: sbdcval@uga.cc.uga.edu

Dalton Small Business Development Center
Mr. Mike Doyle, Area Director
Technical Building, Room 112
213 North College Drive   (706) 272-2707
Dalton, GA 30720-3745   Fax: (706) 272-2701
E-mail: sbdcdal@uga.cc.uga.edu

LaGrange Small Business Development Center
601 Broad Street   (706) 812-7353
LaGrange, GA 30240-2955   Fax: (706) 845-0391

Norcross Small Business Development Center
Mr. Robert Andoh, Area Director
Oakbrook Plaza   (770) 806-2124
1770 Indian Trail Road, Suite 410   Fax: (770) 806-2129
Norcross, GA 30093
E-mail: sbdclaw@uga.cc.uga.edu

Carrollton Small Business Development Center
State University of West Georgia   (770) 838-3082
Cobb Hall   Fax: (770) 838-3083
Carrollton, GA 30118-3030

Guam

Guam Small Business Development Center
UNIVERSITY OF GUAM—Lead Center
Dr. Stephen L. Marder, Executive Director   (671) 735-2590
P.O. Box 5061
UOG Station, Mangilao,   Fax: (671) 734-2002
Guam, USA 96923

Hawaii

Hawaii Small Business Development Center
UNIVERSITY OF HAWAII AT HILO—Lead Center
Mr. Darryl Mleynek, State Director   (808) 974-7515
200 West Kawili Street   Fax: (808) 974-7683
Hilo, HI 96720-4091
E-mail: darrylm@interpac.net

Kaua'i Community College
Small Business Development Center
Mr. Randy Gingras, Center Director   (808) 246-1748
Kaua'i County   Fax: (808) 245-5102
3-1901 Kaumualii Highway
Lihue, HI 96766-9591
E-mail: randyg@aloha.net

Maui Community College
Maui County Small Business Development Center
Mr. David B. Fisher, Center Director   (808) 875-2402
Maui Research and Technology Center Fax: (808) 875-2452
590 Lipoa Parkway
Kihei, HI 96753-6900
E-mail: dfisher@maui.com

University of Hawaii at Hilo
Hawaii County
Small Business Development Center
Ms. Rebecca Winters, Center Director   (808) 969-1814
200 West Kawili Street   Fax: (808) 969-7669
Hilo, HI 96720-4091
E-mail: winters@interpac.net

University of Hawaii at West Oahu
Honolulu County
Small Business Development Center
Ms. Laura Noda, Center Director   (808) 522-8131
1111 Bishop Street, Suite 204   Fax: (808) 522-8135
Honolulu, HI 96813
E-mail: lnoda@aloha.net

Maui Community College
Maui Research & Technology Center
Business Research Library (BRL)   (808) 875-2400
590 Lipoa Parkway, Suite 128   Fax: (808) 875-2452
Kihei, HI 96753-6900

Leeward Satellite
Small Business Development Center
Mr. Michael Keltos, Consultant   (808) 671-8837
94-229 Waipahu Depot Road, Suite 402 Fax: (808) 671-0476
Waipahu, HI 96797

Idaho

Idaho Small Business Development Center
BOISE STATE UNIVERSITY—Lead Center
Mr. James Hogge, State Director   1-800-225-3815
College of Business   (In Idaho)
1910 University Drive   (208) 385-1640
Boise, ID 83725   Fax: (208) 385-3877
E-mail: jhogge@bsu.idbsu.edu
Web site: http://www.idbsu.edu/isbdc

Boise State University
Small Business Development Center
Mr. Robert Shepard, Regional Director   1-800-225-3815
1910 University Drive   (In Idaho)
Boise, ID 83725   (208) 385-3875
E-mail: bshepard@bsu.idbsu.edu   Fax: (208) 385-3877

College of Southern Idaho
Small Business Development Center
Ms. Cindy Bond, Regional Director   (208) 733-9554
315 Falls Avenue   Ext. 2450
P.O. Box 1238   Fax: (208) 733-9316
Twin Falls, ID 83303-1238
E-mail: cbond@evergreen2.csi.cc.id.us
Web site: http://www.csi.cc.id.us/Support/ISBDC/ISBDC.htm

Idaho State University
Small Business Development Center   (800) 232-4921
Mr. Paul Cox, Regional Director   (208) 232-4921
1651 Alvin Ricken Drive   Fax: (208) 233-0268
Pocatello, ID 83201
E-mail: coxpaul@isu.edu

Idaho State University
Small Business Development Center   (800) 658-3829
Ms. Betty Capps, Regional Director   (208) 523-1087
2300 North Yellowstone   Fax: (208) 523-1049
Idaho Falls, ID 83401
E-mail: cappmary@fs.isu.edu

Lewis-Clark State College
Small Business Development Center   (800) 933-5272
Ms. Helen LeBoeuf-Binninger,   (208) 799-2465
Regional Director
500 Eighth Avenue   Fax: (208) 799-2878
Lewiston, ID 83501
E-mail: hleboeuf@lcsc.edu

North Idaho College
Small Business Development Center
Mr. John Lynn, Regional Director   (208) 769-3444
525 West Clearwater Loop   Fax: (208) 769-3223
Post Falls, ID 83854
E-mail: jalynn@nic.edu

Idaho Small Business Development Center
Mr. Larry Smith, Associate Business   (208) 634-2883
    Consultant
P.O. Box 1901
McCall, ID 83638

Idaho Small Business Development Center
Mr. Ben Dicus, Associate Business   (208) 467-5707
    Consultant
Caldwell County Center
2407 Caldwell Blvd.
Nampa, Idaho 83651
E-mail: bdicus@bsu.idbsu.edu

Eastern Oregon State College
Small Business Development Center   (541) 962-3391
Mr. John Prosnick, Jr.
1410 L. Avenue
La Grande, Oregon 97850

Treasure Valley Community College
Small Business Development Center   (541) 889-6493
Ms. Kathy Simko   Ext. 356
650 College Blvd.
Ontario, Oregon 97914

Illinois

Illinois Small Business Development Center
DEPARTMENT OF COMMERCE & COMMUNITY AFFAIRS—
Lead Center
Mr. Jeff Mitchell, State Director   (217) 524-5856
620 East Adams Street, Third Floor   (217) 524-0171
Springfield, IL 62701   Fax: (217) 785-6328

Asian American Alliance
Small Business Development Center
Mr. Joon H. Lee, Director   (773) 202-0600
6246 North Pulaski Road, Suite 101   Fax: (773) 202-1007
Chicago, IL 60646

Back of the Yards Neighborhood Council
Small Business Development Center
Mr. Bill Przybylski   (773) 523-4419
1751 West 47th Street   Fax: (773) 254-3525
Chicago, IL 60609

Black Hawk College Small Business Development Center
Ms. Donna Scalf, Director   (309) 755-2200
301 42nd Avenue   Ext. 211
East Moline, IL 61244   Fax: (309) 755-9847

Bradley University Small Business Development Center
Mr. Roger Luman, Director   (309) 677-3075
141 North Jobst Hall, First Floor   Fax: (309) 677-3386
Peoria, IL 61625

College of DuPage Small Business Development Center
Mr. David Gay, Director   (630) 942-2771
425 22nd Street   Fax: (630) 942-3789
Glen Ellyn, IL 61832

College of Lake County
Small Business Development Center   (847) 223-3633
19351 West Washington Street   Fax: (847) 223-9371
Grayslake, IL 60030

Cooperative Extension Service
Small Business Development Center
Mr. Rick Russell, Director   (217) 875-8284
985 West Pershing Road, Suite F-4   Fax: (217) 875-8288
Decatur, IL 62526

Danville Area Community College
Small Business Development Center
Mr. Ed Adrain, Director   (217) 442-7232
28 West North Street   Fax: (217) 442-6228
Danville, IL 61832

Department of Commerce and Community
Affairs—James R. Thompson Center
Small Business Development Center
Mr. Carson Gallagher, Director   (312) 814-6111
100 West Randolph, Suite 3-400   Fax: (312) 814-2807
Chicago, IL 60601

Department of Commerce and Community
Affairs—State Office Building
Small Business Development Center
Mr. Robert Ahart   (618) 583-2270
10 Collinsville   Fax: (618) 583-2274
East St. Louis, IL 62201

Eighteenth St. Development Corporation
Small Business Development Center
Ms. Maria Munoz, Director   (312) 733-2270
1839 South Carpenter   Fax: (312) 733-7315
Chicago, IL 60608

Elgin Community College
Small Business Development Center
Mr. Craig Fowler, Director   (847) 888-7488
1700 Spartan Drive   Fax: (847) 931-3911
Elgin, IL 60123

Evanston Business and Technology Center
Small Business Development Center
Mr. Rick Holbrook, Director   (847) 866-1817
1840 Oak Avenue   Fax: (847) 866-1808
Evanston, IL 60201-3670

Governors State University
Small Business Development Center
Ms. Christine Cochrane, Director   (708) 534-4929
College of Business, Room C-3305   Fax: (708) 534-8457
University Park, IL 60466

Greater North Pulaski Development Corporation
Small Business Development Center
Mr. Paul Petersen, Director   (773) 384-2262
4054 West North Avenue   Fax: (773) 384-3850
Chicago, IL 60639

Illinois Eastern Community College
Small Business Development Center
Ms. Debbie Chillson, Director   (618) 395-3011
401 East Main Street   Fax: (618) 395-1922
Olney, IL 62450

Illinois Valley Community College
Small Business Development Center
Mr. Boyd Palmer, Director   (815) 223-1740
815 North Orlando Smith Ave.,   Fax: (815) 224-3033
   Bldg. 11
Oglesby, IL 61348

Industrial Council of NW Chicago
Small Business Development Center
Mr. Melvin Eiland, Director   (312) 421-3941
2023 West Carroll   Fax: (312) 421-1871
Chicago, IL 60612

Joliet Junior College
Small Business Development Center
Ms. Denise Mikulski, Director   (815) 727-6544
Renaissance Center, Room 312   Ext. 1321
214 North Ottawa Street   Fax: (815) 722-1895
Joliet, IL 60431

Kankakee Community College
Small Business Development Center
Kelly Berry   (815) 933-0376
P.O. Box 888   Fax: (815) 933-0217
River Road
Kankakee, IL 60901

Kaskaskia College Small Business Development Center
Mr. Richard McCullum, Director   (618) 532-2049
27210 College Road   Fax: (618) 532-4983
Centralia, IL 62801

Latin American Chamber of Commerce
Small Business Development Center
Mr. Arturo Venecia, Director   (773) 252-5211
2539 North Kedzie, Suite 11   Fax: (773) 252-7065
Chicago, IL 60647

Lewis and Clark Community College
Small Business Development Center
Mr. Bob Duane, Director   (618) 466-3411
5800 Godfrey Road   Fax: (618) 466-0810
Godfrey, IL 62035

Lincoln Land Community College
Small Business Development Center
Ms. Frieda Schreck, Director   (217) 789-1017
100 North Eleventh Street   Fax: (217) 789-0958
Springfield, IL 62703

Maple City Business & Technology Center
Small Business Development Center
Ms. Carol Cook, Director   (309) 734-4664
620 South Main Street   Fax: (309) 734-8579
Monmouth, IL 61462-2688

McHenry County College
Small Business Development Center
Ms. Susan Whitfield, Director (815) 455-6098
8900 U.S. Highway 14 Fax: (815) 455-9319
Crystal Lake, IL 60012-2761

Moraine Valley College
Small Business Development Center
Ms. Hilary Gereg, Director (708) 974-5469
10900 South 88th Avenue Fax: (708) 974-0078
Palos Hills, IL 60465

North Business and Industrial Council (NORBIC)
Small Business Development Center
Mr. Tom Kamykowski, Director (773) 588-5855
2500 West Bradley Place Fax: (773) 588-0734
Chicago, IL 60618

Rend Lake College Small Business
   Development Center (618) 437-5321
Ms. Lisa Payne, Director ext. 335
Route #1 Fax: (618) 437-5677
Ina, IL 62846 ext. 385

Rock Valley College Small Business Development Center
Ms. Beverly Kingsley, Director (815) 968-4087
1220 Rock Street Fax: (815) 968-4157
Rockford, IL 61110-1437

Sauk Valley Community College
Small Business Development Center
Mr. John Nelson, Director (815) 288-5511
173 Illinois Route #2 Fax: (815) 288-5958
Dixon, IL 61021-9110

Shawnee Community College
Small Business Development Center
Mr. Donald Denny, Director (618) 634-9618
Shawnee College Road Fax: (618) 634-9028
Ullin, IL 62992

Southeastern Illinois College
Small Business Development Center
Ms. Becky Williams, Director (618) 252-5001
303 S. Commercial Street Fax: (618) 252-0210
Harrisburg, IL 62946-2125

Southern Illinois University at Carbondale
Small Business Development Center
Mr. Dennis Cody, Director (618) 536-2424
Carbondale, IL 62901-6702 Fax: (618) 453-5040

Southern Illinois University at Edwardsville
Small Business Development Center
Mr. Alan Hauff, Director (618) 692-2929
Campus Box 1107 Fax: (618) 692-2647
Edwardsville, IL 62026

Triton College
Small Business Development Center
Lon Bancroft (708) 456-0300
2000 Fifth Avenue Ext. 246
River Grove, IL 60171 Fax: (708) 583-3118

Waubonsee Community College
Small Business Development Center
Mr. Mike O'Kelley, Director (630) 801-7900
Aurora Campus, 5 East Galena Blvd.
Aurora, IL 60506 Fax: (630) 892-4668

Western Illinois University
Small Business Development Center
Mr. Dan Voorhis, Director (309) 298-2211
214 Seal Hall Fax: (309) 298-2520
Macomb, IL 61455

Women's Business Development Center
Small Business Development Center
Ms. Joyce Wade (312) 853-3477
8 South Michigan, Suite 400 Fax: (312) 853-0145
Chicago, IL 60603

Apparel Industry Board
Small Business Development Center
Ms. Nancy Berman
350 N. Orleans, Suite 1047 (312) 836-1041
Chicago, IL 60654

Midwest Chicago Avenue Business Association
Small Business Development Center
Ms. Sonja Davis (773) 826-4055
3709 West Chicago Avenue Fax: (773) 826-7375
Chicago, IL 60651

University of Illinois at Chicago
Small Business Development Center
CUB 601 S. Morgan (773) 996-4057
2231 UH M/C 075 Fax: (773) 996-4567
Chicago, IL 60607

Illinois Easter Seal Society
Small Business Development Center
Mr. Tom Berkshire (217) 525-0398
2715 South 4th Street Fax: (217) 525-0442
Springfield, IL 62703

Indiana

BLOOMINGTON AREA
Small Business Development Center
Mr. David Miller, Director (812) 339-8937
216 West Allen Street Fax: (812) 335-7352
Bloomington, IN 47403

COLUMBUS REGIONAL
Small Business Development Center
Mr. Jack Hess, Director   (812) 372-6480
4920 North Warren Drive   Fax: (812) 372-0228
Columbus, IN 47203

EAST CENTRAL INDIANA
Small Business Development Center
Ms. Barbara Armstrong, Director   (765) 284-8144
401 South High Street   Fax: (765) 751-9151
Muncie, IN 47305

GREATER LAFAYETTE AREA
Small Business Development Center
Ms. Susan Davis, Director   (765) 742-2394
122 North Third   Fax: (765) 742-6276
Lafayette, IN 47901-0311

TERRE HAUTE AREA
Small Business Development Center
Mr. William Minnis, Director   (812) 237-7676
ISU School of Business, Room 510 Fax: (812) 237-7675
Terre Haute, IN 47809

INDIANAPOLIS REGIONAL
Small Business Development Center
Mr. Glenn Dunlap, Director   (317) 261-3030
342 North Senate Avenue   Fax: (317) 261-3053
Indianapolis, IN 46204

KOKOMO/HOWARD COUNTY
Small Business Development Center
Mr. Kim Moyers, Director   (765) 457-7922
106 North Washington   Fax: (765) 452-4564
Kokomo, IN 46901

NORTHEAST INDIANA
Small Business Development Center
Mr. A. V. Fleming, Director   (219) 426-0040
1830 Wayne Trace   Fax: (219) 424-0024
Fort Wayne, IN 46803

NORTHWEST INDIANA
Small Business Development Center
Mr. Mark McLaughlin, Director   (219) 762-1696
6100 Southport Road   Fax: (219) 763-2653
Portage, IN 46368

RICHMOND/WAYNE COUNTY
Small Business Development Center
Mr. Cliff Fry, Director   (765) 962-2887
33 South Seventh Street, Suite 200 Fax: (765) 966-0882
Richmond, IN 47374

SOUTH BEND AREA
Small Business Development Center
Ms. Carolyn Anderson, Director   (219) 282-4350
300 North Michigan   Fax: (219) 236-1056
South Bend, IN 46601

SOUTHERN INDIANA
Small Business Development Center
Ms. Gretchen Mahaffey, Director   (812) 945-0266
4100 Charleston Road   Fax: (812) 948-4664
New Albany, IN 47150

SOUTHEASTERN INDIANA
Small Business Development Center
Ms. Rose Marie Roberts, Director   (812) 265-3127
975 Industrial Drive   Fax: (812) 265-5544
Madison, IN 47250

SOUTHWESTERN INDIANA
Small Business Development Center
Mr. Kate Northrup, Director   (812) 425-7232
100 N.W. Second Street, Suite 200 Fax: (812) 421-5883
Evansville, IN 47708

Iowa

Iowa Small Business Development Center
IOWA STATE UNIVERSITY—Lead Center
Mr. Ronald Manning, State Director   (800) 373-7232
College of Business Administration   (515) 292-6351
137 Lynn Avenue   Fax: (515) 292-0020
Ames, IA 50014
E-mail: rmanning@iastate.edu
Web site: http://www.iowasbdc.org/staff.html

DMACC Small Business Development Center
Ms. Lori Harmening-Webb, Director   (712) 563-2623
Circle West Incubator   Fax: (712) 563-2301
P.O. Box 204
Audubon, IA 50025
E-mail: 76756.136@compuserve.com

Drake University
Small Business Development Center
Mr. Benjamin Swartz, Director   (515) 271-2655
Drake Business Center   Fax: (515) 271-1899
2507 University Avenue
Des Moines, IA 50311-4505
E-mail: 76756.141@compuserve.com

Eastern Iowa Community College
Small Business Development Center
Mr. Jon Ryan, Director   (319) 336-3440
314 West Second Street   Fax: (319) 336-3494
Davenport, IA 52801
E-mail: 76756.143@compuserve.com

Indian Hills Community College
Small Business Development Center
Mr. Bryan Ziegler, Director   (515) 683-5127
525 Grandview Avenue   Fax: (515) 683-5263
Ottumwa, IA 52501
E-mail: 76756.145@compuserve.com

Iowa Central Community College
Small Business Development Center   (800) 362-2793
Mr. Todd Madson, Director   (515) 576-5090
900 Central Avenue, Suite 4   Fax: (515) 576-0826
Fort Dodge, IA 50501
E-mail: 76756.146@compuserve.com

Iowa Lakes Community College
Small Business Development Center
Mr. John Beneke, Director   (712) 262-4213
1900 North Grand Avenue, Suite 8   Fax: (712) 262-4047
Spencer, IA 51301
E-mail: sbdcjb@rconnect.com

Iowa State University
Small Business Development Center
Mr. Steve Carter, Director
2501 North Loop Drive, Bldg. 1, Suite 615   (515) 296-7828
Ames, IA 50010-8283   Fax: (515) 296-6714
E-mail: stc@iastate.edu

Iowa Western Community College
Small Business Development Center
Mr. Ronald Helms, Director   (712) 325-3260
2700 College Road, Box 4C   Fax: (712) 325-3408
Council Bluffs, IA 51502
E-mail: 76756.155@compuserve.com

Kirkwood Community College
Small Business Development Center
Mr. Steve Sprague, Director   (319) 377-8256
2901 Tenth Avenue   Fax: (319) 377-5667
Marion, IA 52302
E-mail: 104702.2376@compuserve.com

North Iowa Area Community College
Small Business Development Center
Mr. Richard Petersen, Director   (515) 422-4342
500 College Drive   Fax: (515) 422-4129
Mason City, IA 50401
E-mail: peterric@niacc.cc.ia.us

Northeast Iowa Small Business Development Center
Mr. Charles Tonn, Director   (319) 588-3350
770 Town Clock Plaza   Fax: (319) 557-1591
Dubuque, IA 52001
E-mail: 76756.161@compuserve.com

Southeastern Community College
Small Business Development Center   (800) 828-7322
Ms. Deb Dalziel, Director   (319) 752-2731
Drawer F   Ext. 103
West Burlington, IA 52655   Fax: (319) 752-3407
E-mail: 76756.164@compuserve.com

Southwestern Community College
Small Business Development Center
Robin Beech Travis, Director   (515) 782-4161
1501 West Townline Road   Fax: (515) 782-3312
Creston, IA 50801
E-mail: 103063.3634@compuserve.com

University of Iowa
Small Business Development Center
Mr. Paul Heath, Director
Ms. Kathryn Kurth, Associate Director
108 Pappajohn, Bus. Admin. Bldg.   (319) 335-3742
Suite S-160   Fax: (319) 353-2445
Iowa City, IA 52242-1000
E-mail: paul-heath@uiowa.edu
E-mail: kathryn-kurth@uiowa.edu

University of Northern Iowa
Small Business Development Center
Mr. Lyle Bowlin, Director   (319) 273-2696
Ms. Maureen Collins-Williams, Assoicate   (888) 237-8124
     Director   Fax: (319) 236-8240
200 E. 4th Street
Waterloo, IA 50703
E-mail: lyle.bowlin@uni.edu
E-mail: maureen.collins-williams@uni.edu
Web site: http://www.esd.uni.edu/sbdc

Western Iowa Tech Community College
Small Business Development Center
Mr. Dennis Bogenrief, Director   (800) 352-4649
4647 Stone Avenue, P.O. Box 5199   (712) 274-6418
Sioux City, IA 51102-5199   Fax: (712) 274-6429
E-mail: 76756.171@compuserve.com

Kansas

Kansas Small Business Development Center
WICHITA STATE UNIVERSITY—Lead Center
Ms. Joann Ard, Regional Director   (316) 978-3193
1845 Fairmont   Fax: (316) 978-3647
Wichita, KS 67260

Emporia State University
Small Business Development Center
Ms. Lisa Brumbaugh, Regional Director   (316) 342-7162
130 Cremer Hall   Fax: (316) 341-5418
Emporia, KS 66801

Fort Hays State University
Small Business Development Center
Ms. Clare Gustin, Regional Director   (913) 628-6786
109 W. 10th Street   Fax: (913) 628-0533
Hays, KS 67601

Colby Community College
Small Business Development Center
Mr. Robert Selby, Director   (913) 462-3984
1255 South Range   Ext. 239
Colby, KS 67701   Fax: (913) 462-8315

Garden City Community College
Small Business Development Center
Mr. Bill Sander, Regional Director   (316) 276-9632
801 Campus Drive   Fax: (316) 276-9630
Garden City, KS 67846

Dodge City Community College
Small Business Development Center
Vacant   (316) 227-9247
2501 North 14th Avenue   Fax: (316) 227-9200
Dodge City, KS 67801

Seward County Community College
Small Business Development Center
Mr. Dale Reed, Director   (316) 624-1951
1801 North Kansas   Ext. 150
Liberal, KS 67901   Fax: (316) 624-0637

Johnson County Community College
Small Business Development Center
Ms. Kathy Nadlman, Regional Director   (913) 469-3878
CEC Building, Room 223   Fax: (913) 469-4415
Overland Park, KS 66210-1299

Kansas City Kansas Community College
Small Business Development Center
Ms. Sue Courtney   (913) 596-9659
7250 State Avenue   Fax: (913) 596-9663
Kansas City, KS 66112

Kansas State University
Small Business Development Center
Mr. Fred Rice, Regional Director   (913) 532-5529
2323 Anderson Avenue, Suite 100   Fax: (913) 532-5827
Manhattan, KS 66502-2947

Salina College of Technology
Small Business Development Center
Vacant   (913) 826-2616
Kansas State University   Fax: (913) 826-2630
2409 Scanlan Avenue
Salina, KS 67401

Pittsburg State University
Small Business Development Center
Ms. Kathryn Richard, Regional Director   (316) 235-4920
Shirk Hall   Fax: (316) 232-4919
Pittsburg, KS 66762

Allen County Community College
Small Business Development Center
Ms. Susan Thompson, Director   (316) 365-5116
1801 North Cottonwood   Fax: (316) 365-3284
Iola, KS 66749

Coffeyville Community College
Small Business Development Center
Mr. Charles Shaver, Director   (316) 251-7700
11th and Willow Streets   Fax: (316) 252-7098
Coffeyville, KS 67337-5064

Fort Scott Community College
Small Business Development Center
Mr. Steve Pammenter, Director   (316) 223-2700
2108 South Horton   Fax: (316) 223-6530
Fort Scott, KS 66701

Independence Community College
Small Business Development Center
Mr. Preston Haddan, Director   (316) 332-1420
College Avenue and Brookside   Fax: (316) 331-5344
P.O. Box 708
Independence, KS 67301

Labette Community College
Small Business Development Center
Mr. Mark Turnbull, Director   (316) 421-6700
200 South 14th   Fax: (316) 421-0921
Parsons, KS 67357

Neosho County Community College
Small Business Development Center
Vacant   (316) 431-2820
1000 South Allen   Ext. 219
Chanute, KS 66720   Fax: (316) 431-0082

University of Kansas
Small Business Development Center
Ms. Randee Brady, Regional Director   (913) 843-8844
734 Vermont Street, Suite 104   Fax: (913) 843-8878
Lawrence, KS 66044

Washburn University
Small Business Development Center
Mr. Dan Kingman, Regional Director   (913) 231-1010
101 Henderson Learning Center   Ext. 1305
Topeka, KS 66621   Fax: (913) 231-1063

Hutchinson Community College
Small Business Development Center
Mr. Clark Jacobs, Director (316) 665-4950
815 North Walnut, Suite 225 Fax: (316) 665-8354
Hutchinson, KS 67501

Pratt Community College
Small Business Development Center
Vacant (316) 672-5641
Highway 61 Fax: (316) 672-5288
Pratt, KS 67124

Kentucky

Kentucky Small Business Development Center
UNIVERSITY OF KENTUCKY—Lead Center
Ms. Janet S. Holloway, State Director (606) 257-7668
Center for Business Development Fax: (606) 323-1907
225 C.M. Gatton Business and Economics Building
Lexington, KY 40506-0034

Bellarmine College
Small Business Development Center
Mr. Thomas Daley, Director (502) 574-4770
School of Business Fax: (502) 574-4771
600 West Main Street, Suite 219
Louisville, KY 40202

Eastern Kentucky University
South Central Small Business Development Center
Mr. Donald R. Snyder, Director (606) 677-6120
2292 S. Hwy. 27, Suite 260 Fax: (606) 677-6083
Somerset, KY 42501

Morehead State University
Small Business Development Center
Mr. Wilson Grier, District Director (606) 783-2895
CB 309, UPO 2479 Fax: (606) 783-5020
Morehead, KY 40351

Morehead State University/Ashland
Boyd-Greenup County Chamber of Commerce
Ms. Kimberly A. Jenkins, Director (606) 329-8011
1401 Winchester Ave., Suite 305 Fax: (606) 324-4570
Ashland, KY 41101

Morehead State University/Pikeville
Small Business Development Center
Mr. Michael Morley, Director (606) 432-5848
Justice Office Bldg. Fax: (606) 432-8924
Route 7, 110 Village Street
Pikeville, KY 41501

Murray State University
Small Business Development Center
Ms. Rosemary Miller, Director (502) 762-2856
P.O. Box 9 Fax: (502) 762-3049
Murray, KY 42071

Murray State University/Hopkinsville
Small Business Development Center
Mr. Michael Cartner, Director (502) 889-8666
300 Hammond Drive Fax: (502) 886-3211
Hopkinsville, KY 42240

Murray State University/Owensboro
Small Business Development Center
Mr. Mickey Johnson, District Director (502) 926-8085
3860 U.S. Highway 60 West Fax: (502) 684-0714
Owensboro, KY 42301

Northern Kentucky University
Small Business Development Center
Mr. Sutton Landry, Director (606) 572-6524
BEP Center 463 Fax: (606) 572-6177
Highland Heights, KY 41099-0506

Southeast Community College
Small Business Development Center
Ms. Kathleen Moats, Director (606) 242-2145 x 2021
1300 Chichester Avenue Fax: (606) 242-4514
Middlesboro, KY 40965-2265

University of Kentucky/Lexington
Small Business Development Center
Ms. Marge Berge, Program Coordinator (606) 257-7666
c/o Downtown Public Library Fax: (606) 257-1751
140 E. Main Street
Lexington, KY 40507-1376

University of Kentucky
Small Business Development Center
Ms. Lou Ann Allen, Director (502) 765-6737
133 West Dixie Avenue Fax: (502) 769-5095
Elizabethtown, KY 42701

University of Louisville—Specialized Center
Small Business Development Center
Mr. Lou Dickie, Director (502) 852-7854
Center for Entrepreneurship & Technology Fax: (502) 852-8573
Room 122 Burhans Hall, Shelby Campus
Louisville, KY 40292

Western Kentucky University
Small Business Development Center
Mr. Richard S. Horn, Director (502) 745-1905
2355 Nashville Rd. Fax: (502) 745-1931
Bowling Green, KY 42101

Louisiana
Louisiana Small Business Development Center
NORTHEAST LOUISIANA UNIVERSITY—Lead Center
Dr. John Baker, State Director   (318) 342-5506
College of Business Administration   Fax: (318) 342-5510
Room 2-57
Monroe, LA 71209

Louisiana Electronic Assistance Program—Specialized
Center
Dr. Jerry Wall, Director   (318) 342-1215
Northeast Louisiana University   Fax: (318) 342-1209
College of Business Administration
Monroe, LA 71209

Louisiana International Trade Center—Specialized Center
Small Business Development Center
Mr. Ruperto Chavarri, Director   (504) 568-8222
World Trade Center, Suite 2926   Fax: (504) 568-8228
2 Canal Street
New Orleans, LA 70130

Louisiana State University at Shreveport
Small Business Development Center
Ms. Peggy K. Connor   (318) 797-5144
College of Business Administration   Fax: (318) 797-5208
One University Drive
Shreveport, LA 71115
E-mail: pconnor@pilot.lsus.edu

Louisiana Tech University
Small Business Development Center
Tracey Jeffers, Director   (318) 257-3537
College of Business Administration   Fax: (318) 257-4253
Box 10318, Tech Station
Ruston, LA 71271-0046

Loyola University
Small Business Development Center
Mr. Ronald Schroeder, Director   (504) 865-3474
College of Business Administration   Fax: (504) 865-3496
Box 134
New Orleans, LA 70118

McNeese State University
Small Business Development Center
Mr. Paul Arnold, Director   (318) 475-5529
College of Business Administration   Fax: (318) 475-5012
Lake Charles, LA 70609

Nicholls State University
Small Business Development Center
Mr. Weston Hull, Director   (504) 448-4242
College of Business Administration   Fax: (504) 448-4922
P.O. Box 2015
Thibodaux, LA 70310

Northeast Louisiana University
Small Business Development Center
Dr. Paul Dunn, Director   (318) 342-1224
College of Business Administration   Fax: (318) 342-1209
Monroe, LA 71209

Northwestern State University
Small Business Development Center
Ms. Mary Lynn Wilkerson, Director   (318) 357-5611
College of Business Administration   Fax: (318) 357-6810
Natchitoches, LA 71497

Small Business Development Center
Ms. Kathey Hunter, Consultant   (318) 484-2123
Hibernia National Bank Building   Fax: (318) 484-2126
Suite 510
934 Third Street
Alexandria, LA 71301

Southeastern Louisiana University
Small Business Development Center
Mr. William Joubert, Director   (504) 549-3831
College of Business Administration   Fax: (504) 549-2127
Box 522, SLU Station
Hammond, LA 70402

Southern University
Capital Small Business Development Center
Mr. Gregory Spann, Director   (504) 922-0998
9613 Interline Avenue   Fax: (504) 922-0999
Baton Rouge, LA 70809   (Call First)

Southern University at New Orleans#
Small Business Development Center
Mr. Jon Johnson, Director   (504) 286-5308
College of Business Administration   Fax: (504) 286-5131
New Orleans, LA 70126

University of New Orleans
Small Business Development Center
Ms. Norma Grace, Director   (504) 539-9292
1600 Canal Street, Suite 620   Fax: (504) 539-9205
New Orleans, LA 70112

University of Southwestern Louisiana
Acadiana Small Business Development Center
Ms. Kim Spence, Director   (318) 262-5344
College of Business Administration   Fax: (318) 262-5296
Box 43732
Lafayette, LA 70504

Maine

Maine Small Business Development Center
UNIVERSITY OF SOUTHERN MAINE—Lead Center
Mr. Charles Davis, Director   (207) 780-4420
15 Surrenden Street   Fax: (207) 780-4810
Portland, ME 04103
E-mail: msbdc@portland.maine.edu
Home Page: http://www.usm.maine.edu/~sbdc

Androscoggin Valley Council of Governments (AVCOG)
Small Business Development Center
Ms. Jane Mickeriz, Counselor   (207) 783-9186
125 Manley Road   Fax: (207) 783-5211
Auburn, ME 04210

South Paris Satellite
Small Business Development Center
By appointment—Contact Auburn Office   (207) 783-9186
166 Main Street   Fax: (207) 783-5211
South Paris, ME 04281

Wilton
Small Business Development Center
By appointment—Contact Auburn Office   (207) 783-9186
Robinhood Plaza   Fax: (207) 783-5211
Route 2 & 4
East Wilton, ME 04234

Rumford
By appointment—Contact Auburn Office   (207) 783-9186
River Valley Growth Council   Fax: (207) 783-5211
Hotel Harris Building
23 Hartford Street
Rumford, ME 04276

Lewiston
(Mon. & Thurs.)—Contact Auburn Office   (207) 783-9186
Business Information Center (BIC)   Fax: (207) 783-5211
Bates Mill Complex
35 Canal Street
Lewiston, ME 04240

Coastal Enterprises Incorporated
Small Business Development Center
Mr. James Burbank II, Subcenter Director   (207) 882-4340
Water Street   Fax: (207) 882-4456
P.O. Box 268
Wiscasset, ME 04578

Coastal Enterprises Incorporated
Small Business Development Center
Mr. W. Bradshaw Swanson, Counselor   (207) 621-0245
Tues., Wed., Thurs. (by appointment)   Fax: (207) 622-9739
Weston Building
7 North Chestnut Street
Augusta, ME 04330

Brunswick Satellite Small Business Development Center
By appointment—Contact Wiscasset Office   (207) 882-4340
Midcoast Council for Business   Fax: (207) 882-4456
  Development
8 Lincoln Street
Brunswick, ME 04011

Rockland Satellite Small Business Development Center
Wednesdays—Contact Wiscasset Office   (207) 882-4340
Key Bank of Maine   Fax: (207) 882-4456
331 Main Street
Rockland, ME 04841

Skowhegan Satellite Small Business Development Center
By appointment—Contact Augusta Office   (207) 621-0245
Skowhegan Cooperative Extension Service Fax: (207) 622-9739
Norridgewock Avenue
Skowhegan, ME 04976

Waterville Satellite Small Business Development Center
Tuesday and Friday—by appointment   (207) 621-0245
Contact Augusta Office   Fax: (207) 622-9739
Thomas College
Administration Building—Library
180 West River Road
Waterville, ME 04901

Eastern Maine Development Corporation
Small Business Development Center
Mr. Ron Loyd, Subcenter Director   (800) 339-6389
One Cumberland Place, Suite 300   (In Maine)
P.O. Box 2579   (207) 942-6389
Bangor, ME 04402-2579   Fax: (207) 942-3548

Belfast Satellite Small Business Development Center
By appointment—Contact Bangor Office   (800) 339-6389
Waldo County Development Corporation   (In Maine)
67 Church Street   (207) 942-6389
Belfast, ME 04915   Fax: (207) 942-3548

Dover-Foxcroft Satellite   (800) 339-6389
Small Business Development Center   (In Maine)
By appointment—Contact Bangor Office   (207) 942-6389
On-site—at client's place of business Fax: (207) 942-3548

East Millinocket Satellite
Small Business Development Center
By appointment—Contact Bangor Office   (207) 746-5338
Katahdin Regional Development   Fax: (207) 746-9535
  Corporation
58 Main Street
East Millinocket, ME 04430

Machias Satellite (Fridays)
Small Business Development Center
Ms. Diane Tilton, Counselor (207) 255-0983
Sunrise County Economic Council (207) 454-2430
Washington County Regional Planning
    Commission   (Calais Area)
63 Main Street, P.O. Box 679
Machias, ME 04654

Northern Maine Development Commission
Small Business Development Center
Mr. Rodney Thompson, Subcenter Director (800) 427-8736
2 South Main Street (In Maine)
P.O. Box 779 (207) 498-8736
Caribou, ME 04736 Fax: (207) 493-3108

Houlton Satellite Small Business Development Center
One day biweekly—by appointment—Contact Caribou (In
Maine)
Superior Court House (800) 427-8736
Court Street (207) 498-8736
Houlton, ME 04730 Fax: (207) 493-3108

Fort Kent Satellite Small Business Development Center
One day biweekly—by appointment (207) 498-8736
Aroostook County Registry of Deeds
Contact Caribou Office (800) 427-8736
Corner of Elm and Hall Streets (In Maine)
Fort Kent, ME 04743 Fax: (207) 493-3108

Southern Maine Regional Planning Commission
Small Business Development Center
Mr. Joseph Vitko, Subcenter Director (207) 324-0316
255 Main Street Fax: (207) 324-2958
P.O. Box Q
Sanford, ME 04073

York Satellite Small Business Development Center
First Wednesday of the month -
 Contact Sanford Office (207) 363-4422
York Chamber of Commerce Fax: (207) 324-2958
449 Route One
York, ME 03909

University of Southern Maine
Small Business Development Center
Mr. John Entwistle, Subcenter Director (207) 780-4949
15 Surrenden Street Fax: (207) 780-4810
Portland, ME 04103
 MAILING ADDRESS:
 96 Falmouth Street
 P.O. Box 9300
 Portland, ME 04104-9300
E-mail: msbdc@portland.maine.edu

Saco Satellite Small Business Development Center
Mr. Frederick Aiello, Counselor, Fridays (207) 282-1567
Biddeford-Saco Fax: (207) 282-3149
Chamber of Commerce and Industry
110 Main Street
Saco, ME 04072

Maryland

Maryland Small Business Development Center
Mr. James N. Graham, State Director
7100 Baltimore Ave., Suite 401 (301) 403-8300
College Park, MD 20740 Fax: (301) 403-8303
E-mail: jgraham@mbs.umd.edu
Web site: http://www.mbs.umd.edu/sbdc

CENTRAL MARYLAND
Small Business Development Center
Ms. Sonia Stockton, Executive Director (410) 659-1930
Towson State University Fax: (410) 659-1939
Small Business Resource Center
3 West Baltimore Street
Baltimore, MD 21201

EASTERN SHORE
Small Business Development Center
Mr. Marty Green, Executive Director 1-800-999-SBDC
Salisbury State University (410) 546-4325
Power Professional Bldg., Suite 170 Fax: (410) 548-5389
Salisbury, MD 21801

WESTERN MARYLAND
Small Business Development Center
Mr. Sam LaManna, Executive Director 1-800-457-SBDC
Three Commerce Drive (301) 724-6716
Cumberland, MD 21502 Fax: (301) 777-7504

Southern Maryland
Small Business Development Center
Ms. Betsy Cooksey, Executive Director 1-800-762-SBDC
Charles County Community College (301) 934-7583
P.O. Box 910 Fax: (301) 934-7681
Mitchell Road
LaPlata, MD 20646-0910
Web site: http://www.eaglenet.com/tree1/SBDC

Massachusetts

Massachusetts Small Business Development Center
UNIVERSITY OF MASSACHUSETTS—Lead Center
Mr. John Ciccarelli, State Director (413) 545-6301
205 School of Management Fax: (413) 545-1273
Amherst, MA 01003

Boston College Small Business Development Center
Dr. Jack McKiernan, Regional Director   (617) 552-4091
Metro Boston Regional Office   Fax: (617) 552-2730
142 Beacon Street
Chestnut Hill, MA 02167

Capital Formation Service-Statewide—Specialized Center
Small Business Development Center
Mr. Don Rielly, Director   (617) 552-4091
Boston College-Coordinating Site   Fax: (617) 552-2730
142 Beacon Street
Chestnut Hill, MA 02167

Clark University Small Business Development Center
Mr. Laurence Marsh, Director   (617) 793-7615
Central Region   Fax: (617) 793-8890
950 Main Street, Dana Commons
Worcester, MA 01610

Massachusetts Export Center—Specialized Center
Small Business Development Center
Ms. Paula Murphy, Director   1-800-478-4133
World Trade Center, Suite 315   Fax: (617) 478-4135
Boston, MA 02210

Minority Business Assistance Center—Specialized Center
Small Business Development Center
Mr. Hank Turner, Director   (617) 287-7750
University of Massachusetts Boston   Fax: (617) 287-7725
College of Management, Fifth Floor
Boston, MA 02125-3393

Salem State College
Small Business Development Center
Mr. Frederick Young, Director   (508) 741-6343
197 Essex Street   Fax: (508) 741-6345
Salem, MA 01970

University of Massachusetts/Dartmouth
Southeastern Region Small Business Development Center
Mr. Clyde L. Mitchell, Regional Director   (508) 673-9783
200 Pocasset Street—P.O. Box 2785   Fax: (508) 674-1929
Fall River, MA 02722

University of Massachusetts
Western Region Small Business Development Center
Ms. Dianne Fuller Doherty, Director   (413) 737-6712
101 State Street, Suite 424   Fax: (413) 737-2312
Springfield, MA 01103

Michigan

Michigan Small Business Development Center
WAYNE STATE UNIVERSITY—Lead Center
Mr. Ronald R. Hall, State Director   (313) 964-1798
2727 Second Avenue, Suite 107   Fax: (313) 964-3648
Detroit, MI 48201   Fax: (313) 964-4164

MAILING ADDRESS:
Michigan Small Business Development Center
2727 Second Avenue
Detroit, MI 48201
E-mail: ron@misbdc.wayne.edu
Web site: http://bizserve.com/sbdc

Albion economic Development Corporation
Small Business Development Center   (517) 629-3926
941 Austin Avenue, P.O. Box 725   Fax: (517) 629-3929
Albion, MI 49224

Allegan County Economic Development Alliance
Small Business Development Center
Mr. Chuck Birr, Director   (616) 673-8442
2891 116th Ave., M-222 East   Fax: (616) 650-8042
P.O. Box 2777
Allegan, MI 49010
E-mail: aceda@accn.org

Alpena Community College
Small Business Development Center
Mr. Carl Bourdelais, Regional Director   (517) 356-9021
666 Johnson Street   ext. 296
Alpena, MI 49707   Fax: (517) 354-7507
E-mail: bourdelc@alpena.cc.mi.us

Alpena Community College
Small Business Development Center
Huron Shores Campus
Mr. Dave Wentworth, Director   (517) 739-1445
5800 Skeel Avenue   Fax: (517) 739-1161
Oscoda, MI 48750

Ann Arbor Center for Independent Living
Small Business Development Center
Mr. Edward Wollmann, Director   (313) 971-0277
2568 Packard Road   Fax: (313) 971-0826
Ann Arbor, MI 48104-6831
E-mail: edwoll@provide.net

Arenac County Extension Service
Small Business Development Center
Mr. Ken Kernstock, Director   (5170 846-4111
County Building
P.O. Box 745
Standish, MI 48658
E-mail: arenac@msue.msu.edu

Association of Commerce and Industry
Small Business Development Center
Ms. Karen K. Benson, Director   (616) 846-3153
One South Harbor Avenue   Fax: (616) 842-0379
P.O. Box 509
Grand Haven, MI 49417
E-mail: acisbdc@hotmail.com

Battle Creek Area Chamber of Commerce
Small Business Development Center
Mr. Kevin R. Wells, Director
4 Riverwalk Center   (616) 962-8996
34 West Jackson, Suite A, Lower Level   Fax: (616) 962-3692
Battle Creek, MI 49017
E-mail: bizstore@net-link.net

Bay Area Chamber of Commerce
Small Business Development Center
Ms. Shirley Roberts, Director
901 Saginaw   (517) 893-4567
Bay City, MI 48708   Fax: (517) 893-7016

Branch County Economic Growth Alliance
Small Business Development Center
Ms. Colleen Knight, Interim Director   (517) 278-4146
20 Division Street   Fax: (517) 278-8369
Coldwater, MI 49036
E-mail: bcega@orion.branch-co.lib.mi.us

Buchanan Chamber of Commerce
Small Business Development Center
Ms. Joni Tumbleson, Director
119 Main Street   (616) 695-3291
Buchanan, MI 49107   Fax: (616) 695-4250

Central Michigan University
Small Business Development Center
Mr. Charles Fitzpatrick, Regional Director   (517) 774-3270
256 Applied Business Studies   Fax: (517) 774-2372
  Complex
Mt. Pleasant, MI 48859
E-mail: 34ntjen@cmuvm.csv.cmich.edu

Community Capital Development Corporation
Small Business Development Center
Mr. Kim D. Yarber, Regional Director   (810) 239-5847
711 North Saginaw, Suite 123   Fax: (810) 239-5575
Walter Reuther Center
Flint, MI 48503
E-mail: ccdc@bizserve.com

Downriver Community Conference
Small Business Development Center
Ms. Paula Boase, Director   (313) 281-0700 x 190
15100 Northline Road   Fax: (313) 281-3418
Southgate, MI 48195
E-mail: pboase@bizserve.com

Livingston County EDC
Mr. Dennis Whitney, Director   (810) 227-3556
131 South Hyne Street   Fax: (810) 227-3080
Brighton, MI 48116
E-mail: livibusi@bizserve.com

First Step, Incorporated
Small Business Development Center
Mr. David Gillis, Regional Director   (906) 786-9234
2415 Fourteenth Avenue, South   Fax: (906) 786-4442
Escanaba, MI 49829
E-mail: cuppad@up.net

Grand Valley State University
Ms. Carol Lopucki, Regional Director   (616) 771-6693
301 West Fulton, Room 718S   Fax: (616) 458-3872
Eberhard Center
Grand Rapids, MI 49504
E-mail: lopuckic@gvsu.edu

Gratiot Area Chamber of Commerce
Small Business Development Center
Ms. Sherri O. Graham, Director   (517) 463-5525
110 West Superior Street   Fax: (517) 463-6588
P.O. Box 516
Alma, MI 48801-0516

Greater Gratiot Development, Inc.
Small Business Development Center
Mr. Don Schurr, Director   (517) 875-2083
136 South Main   Fax: (517) 875-2990
Ithaca, MI 48847
E-mail: don.schurr@gratiot.com

Greater Niles Economic Development Foundation
Small Business Development Center
Ms. Sharon Witt, Director   (616) 683-1833
1105 North Front Street   Fax: (616) 683-7515
Niles, MI 49120

Greater South Haven Chamber of Commerce
Small Business Development Center
Mr. Larry King, Director   (616) 637-5171
300 Broadway   Fax: (616) 639-1570
South Haven, MI 49090
E-mail: cofc@southhavenmi.com

Harbor County Chamber of Commerce
Small Business Development Center
Ms. Peggy Klute, Office Manager   (616) 469-5409
530 South Whittaker Street, #5   Fax: (616) 469-2257
New Buffalo, MI 49117
E-mail: hccc@hc.cns.net

Hastings Industrial Incubator
Small Business Development Center
Mr. Joe Rahn, Director   (616) 948-2305
1035 East State Street   Fax: (616) 948-2947
Hastings, MI 49058
E-mail: edohast.im4u.net

Huron County Economic Development Corp.
Small Business Development Center
Mr. Carl Osentoski, Director   (517) 269-6431
Huron County Bldg., Room 303   Fax: (517) 269-7221
250 East Huron Avenue
Bad Axe, MI 48413
E-mail: cjo@avci.net

Jackson Small Business Development Center
Mr. Duane K. Miller, Director   (517) 787-0442
414 North Jackson Street   Fax: (517) 787-3960
Jackson, MI 49201
E-mail: jbdc@jacksonmi.com

Kalamazoo College
Small Business Development Center
Mr. Carl R. Shook, Regional Director   (616) 337-7350
Stryker Center for Management   Fax: (616) 337-7415
  Studies
1327 Academy Street
Kalamazoo, MI 49006-3200
E-mail: sbdc@kzoo.edu

Kirtland Community College
Small Business Development Center
Mr. John Loiacano, Director   (517) 275-5121 ext. 297
10775 North Street Helen Road   Fax: (517) 275-8745
Roscommon, MI 48653
E-mail: loiacanj@k2.kirtland.cc.mi.us

Lake Michigan College
Small Business and International Business Center
Mr. Milt Richter, Director   (616) 927-8179
Corporation and Community   Fax: (616) 927-8103
  Development Div.
2755 East Napier
Benton Harbor, MI 49022-1899
E-mail: richter@raptor.lmc.cc.mi.us

Lansing Community College
Small Business Development Center
Mr. Deleski (Dee) Smith, Regional Director   (517) 483-1921
Continental Building   Fax: (517) 483-9803
333 North Washington Square
P.O. Box 40010
Lansing, MI 48901-7210
E-mail: ds1921@lois.lansing.cc.mi.us

Lapeer Development Corporation
Small Business Development Center
Ms. Patricia Lucas Crawford, Director   (810) 667-0080
449 McCormick Drive   Fax: (810) 667-3541
Lapeer, MI 48446
E-mail: ldc@tir.com

Lawrence Technological University
c/o Division of Continuing Education
Small Business Development Center for Oakland County
Mr. Daniel Belknap, Regional Dirctor   (248) 204-4056
21000 West Ten Mile Road   Fax: (248) 204-4016
Southfield, MI 48075-1058
E-mail: belknap@bizserve.com

Lenawee County Chamber of Commerce
Small Business Development Center
Ms. Sally Pinchock, Director   (517) 266-1488
202 North Main Street, Suite A   (517) 263-6065
Adrian, MI 49221
E-mail: spin@orchard.washtenaw.cc.mi.us

Macomb Community College
Center for Continuing Education
Small Business Development Center
Dr. Donald Amboyer, Director   (810) 296-3516
32101 Caroline   Fax: (810) 293-0427
Fraser, MI 48026
E-mail: ambo01d@macomb.cc.mi.us

Macomb County Business Assistance Center
Small Business Development Center
Mr. Donald Morandini, Director   (810) 469-5118
115 South Groesbeck Highway   Fax: (810) 469-6787
Mt. Clemens, MI 48043
E-mail: bacmac@bizserve.com

Michigan Manufacturing Technology Center
Small Business Development Center
Mr. William Loomis, Director   (313) 769-4110
2901 Hubbard Road   Fax: (313) 769-4064
P.O. Box 1485
Ann Arbor, MI 48106-1485
E-mail: wrl@iti.org

Midland Chamber of Commerce
Small Business Development Center
Ms. Christine Greve, Director   (517) 839-9901
300 Rodd Street   Fax: (517) 835-3701
Midland, MI 48640
E-mail: chamber@macc.org

Monroe County Industrial Development Corporation
Small Business Development Center
Ms. Dani Topolski, Director   (313) 243-5947
111 Conant Avenue   Fax: (313) 242-0009
Monroe, MI 48161
E-mail: mcidc@ic.net

Muskegon Economic Growth Alliance
Small Business Development Center
Mr. Mert Johnson, Director   (616) 722-3751
230 Terrace Plaza, P.O. Box 1087   Fax: (616) 728-7251
Muskegon, MI 49443-1087

North Central Michigan College
Attn: IBIT
Small Business Development Center
Mr. Tom Nathe, Director   (616) 348-6600
1515 Howard Street   Fax: (616) 348-6630
Petoskey, MI 49770
E-mail: tnath@sunny.ncmc.cc.mi.us

Northern Lakes Economic Alliance
Small Business Development Center
Mr. Thomas Johnson, Director   (616) 582-6482
1048 East Main Street   Fax: (616) 582-3213
P.O. Box 8
Boyne City, MI 49712-0008
E-mail: johnsoth@msue.msu.edu

Northwest Michigan Council of Governments
Small Business Development Center
Mr. Richard Beldin, Director   (616) 929-5000
2200 Dendrinos Drive   Fax: (616) 929-5017
P.O. Box 506
Traverse City, MI 49685-0506
E-mail: dbeldin@nwm.cog.mi.us

Northwestern Michigan College
Small Business Development Center
Ms. Cheryl Throop, Director   (616) 922-1717
Center for Business and Industry   Fax: (616) 922-1722
1701 East Front Street
Traverse City, MI 49686
E-mail: cthroop@nmc.edu

Oceana County Economic Development Corporation
Small Business Development Center
Mr. Charles Persenaire, Director   (616) 873-7141
100 State Street   Fax: (616) 873-5914
P.O. Box 168
Hart, MI 49420-0168

Oakland County—MSU Extension
Small Business Development Center
Mr. Wayne Nierman, Director   (810) 858-0880
Executive Office Building   Fax: (810) 858-1477
1200 North Telegraph Road, Department 416
Pontiac, MI 48341
E-mail: niermanw@msue.msu.edu

Ottawa County Economic Development Office, Inc.
Small Business Development Center
Mr. Ken Rizzio, Director   (616) 892-4120
6676 Lake Michigan Drive   Fax: (616) 895-6670
P.O. Box 539
Allendale, MI 49401-0539
E-mail: krizzio@altelco.net

Wayne State University
Small Business Development Center
Mr. B. Kevin Lauderdale, Regional Director   (313) 577-4850
2727 Second Avenue, Suite 121   Fax: (313) 577-8933
Detroit, MI 48201
E-mail: lauderk@bizserve.com

Saginaw County Chamber of Commerce
Small Business Development Center
Mr. James Bockelman, Director   (517) 752-7161
901 South Washington Avenue   Fax: (517) 752-9055
Saginaw, MI 48601
E-mail: jroe@voyager.net

Saginaw Future Inc.
Small Business Development Center
Mr. Matthew F. Hufnagel, Director   (517) 754-8222
301 East Genesee, 3rd Floor   Fax: (517) 754-1715
Saginaw, MI 48607
E-mail: matthuf@bizserve.com

Saginaw Valley State University
Small Business Development Center
Mr. Charles B. Curtiss, Jr.,   (517) 791-7746
  Interim Regional Dir.
Business & Industrial Dev. Institute   Fax: (517) 249-1955
7400 Bay Road, Wickes 387
University Center, MI 48710

Southwestern Michigan College
58900 Cherry Grove Road   (616) 782-1277
Dowagiac, MI 49047   Fax: (616) 782-1382

St. Clair County IDC
Small Business Development Center
Mr. Todd Brian, Director   (810) 982-9511
800 Military Street, Suite 320   Fax: (810) 982-9531
Port Huron, MI 48060-5015

Sterling Heights Area Chamber of Commerce
Small Business Development Center
Ms. Lillian Adams, Director   (810) 731-5400
12900 Hall Road, Suite 110   Fax: (810) 731-3521
Sterling Heights, MI 48313
E-mail: suscc.com

The Right Place
Small Business Development Center
Mr. Raymond De Winkle, Director   (616) 771-0571
820 Monroe Avenue NW, Suite 350   Fax: (616) 458-3768
Grand Rapids, MI 49503-1423
E-mail: dewinkler@rightplace.org

Traverse Bay Economic Development Corp.
Small Business Development Center
Mr. Charles Blankenship, Regional Director (616) 946-1596
202 East Grandview Parkway   Fax: (616) 946-2565
P.O. Box 387
Traverse City, MI 49685-0387
E-mail: chamber@gtii.com

Traverse City Area Chamber of Commerce
Small Business Development Center
Mr. Matthew Meadors, Director and   (616) 947-5075
   Vice-President   Fax: (616) 946-2565
202 East Grandview Parkway
P.O. Box 387
Traverse City, MI 49684
E-mail: chamber@gtii.com

Tuscola County Economic Development Corporation
Small Business Development Center
Mr. James McLoskey, Director   (517) 673-2849
194 North State Street, Suite 200   Fax: (517) 673-2517
Caro, MI 48723

University of Detroit—Mercy
Small Business Development Center
College of Business Administration
Dr. Ram Kesavan, Director   (313) 993-1115
Commerce & Finance Bldg., Room 105 Fax: (313) 993-1052
4001 West McNichols
P.O. Box 19900
Detroit, MI 48219-0900
E-mail: kesavar@udmercy.edu

Warren, Center Line, Sterling Heights
Chamber of Commerce
Small Business Development Center
Ms. Jan Masi, Director   (810) 751-3939
30500 Van Dyke, Suite 118   Fax: (810) 751-3995
Warren, MI 48093
E-mail: janetmorris@chambercom.com

Washtenaw Community College
Small Business Development Center
Mr. Baldomero Garcia, Regional Director   (313) 944-1016
740 Woodland Drive   Fax: (313) 944-0165
Saline, MI 48176
E-mail: dstotz@orchard.washtenaw.cc.mi.us

West Shore Community College
Small Business Development Center
Mr. Mark Bergstrom, Director   (616) 845-6211
Business & Industrial Dev. Institute Fax: (616) 845-0207
3000 North Stiles Road
P.O. Box 277
Scottville, MI 49454-0277
E-mail: bergstr@westshore.cc.mi.us

Women's Christian Association of Berrien County
Small Business Development Center
Ms. Suzanne Thursby, Director   (616) 983-4453
508 Pleasant Street   Fax: (616) 983-4564
St. Joseph, MI 49058

Minnesota

Minnesota Small Business Development Center
MINNESOTA DEPARTMENT OF TRADE AND ECONOMIC
DEVELOPMENT—Lead Center
Ms. Mary Kruger, State Director   (612) 297-5773
500 Metro Square   Fax: (612) 296-1290
121 Seventh Place East
St. Paul, MN 55101-2146
E-mail: mary.kruger@state.mn.us

Central Lakes College
Small Business Development Center
Ms. Pamela Thomsen, Director   (218) 825-2028
501 West College Drive   Fax: (218) 825-2053
Brainerd, MN 56401

Century College
Small Business Development Center   (612) 773-1794
3300 Century Avenue, N., Suite 230-H Fax: (612) 779-5802
White Bear Lake, MN 55110-1894

Dakota County Technical College
Small Business Development Center
Mr. Tom Trutna, Director   (612) 423-8262
1300 145th Street East   Fax: (612) 423-8761
Rosemount, MN 55068
E-mail: ttrut@dak.tec.mn.us

Hibbing Community College
Small Business Development Center
Mr. Jim Antilla, Director   (218) 262-6703
1515 East 25th Street   Fax: (218) 262-6717
Hibbing, MN 55746
E-mail: j.antilla@hi.cc.mn.us

Itasca Development Corporation
Small Business Development Center
Mr. Kirk Bustrom, Director   (218) 327-2241
19 NE Third Street   Fax: (218) 327-2242
Grand Rapids, MN 55744
E-mail: idsbdc@uslink.net

Minnesota Project Innovation—Specialized Center
Small Business Development Center
Ms. Pat Dillon, Director   (612) 347-6751
111 Third Avenue South, Suite 100 Fax: (612) 338-3483
Minneapolis, MN 55401
E-mail: pdillon@mpi.org

Minnesota Technology, Inc.
Small Business Development Center   (218) 741-4241
Olcott Plaza Bldg.   Fax: (218) 741-4249
820 North 9th Street
Virginia, MN 55792
E-mail: cchrist1@d.umn.edu

Moorhead State University
Small Business Development Center
Mr. Len Sliwoski, Director   (218) 236-2289
MSU Box 303   Fax: (218) 236-2280
1104 Seventh Avenue South
Moorhead, MN 56563

Normandale Community College
Small Business Development Center
Mr. Scott Harding, Director   (612) 832-6398
9700 France Avenue South   Fax: (612) 832-6352
Bloomington, MN 55431

North Shore Business Ent. Center
Small Business Development Center
Mr. Allen Jackson, Director   (218) 834-3494
5 Fairgrounds Road, P.O. Box 248   Fax: (218) 834-5074
Two Harbors, MN 55616
E-mail: ajackso2@d.umn.edu

Northwest Technical College
Small Business Development Center
Ms. Susan Kozojed, Director   (218) 755-4286
905 Grant Avenue, SE   Fax: (218) 755-4289
Bemidji, MN 56601

Owatonna Incubator, Inc.
Small Business Development Center
Mr. Ken Henrickson, Director   (507) 451-0517
560 Dunnell Drive, Suite #203   Fax: (507) 455-2788
P.O. Box 505
Owatonna, MN 55060

Pine Technical College
Small Business Development Center
Mr. John Sparling, Director   (320) 629-7340
1100 Fourth Street   Fax: (320) 629-7603
Pine City, MN 55063

Rainy River Community College
Small Business Development Center
Mr. Tom West, Director   (218) 285-2255
1501 Highway 71   Fax: (218) 285-2239
International Falls, MN 56649

Region Nine Development Commission
Small Business Development Center
Ms. Jill Miller, Director   (507) 389-8863
410 Jackson Street   Fax: (507) 387-7105
P.O. Box 3367
Mankato, MN 56002-3367
E-mail: jillm@rndc.mankato.mn.us

Small Business Administration
Mr. Michael J. Lyons, SBDC Project Officer
610-C Butler Square   (612) 370-2343
100 North Sixth Street   Fax: (612) 370-2303
Minneapolis, MN 55403
E-mail: michael.lyons@sba.gov

Southeast MN Development Corp.
Small Business Development Center
Mr. Terry Erickson, Director   (507) 864-7557
111 West Jessie Street   Fax: (507) 864-2091
P.O. Box 684
Rushford, MN 55971

Southwest State University
Small Business Development Center
Mr. Jack Hawk, Director   (507) 537-7386
Science & Technology Resource   Fax: (507) 537-6094
  Center
1501 State Street—ST 105
Marshall, MN 56258
E-mail: hawk@ssu.southwest.msus.edu

St. Cloud State University
Small Business Development Center
Ms. Dawn Jensen-Regnier, Director   (320) 255-4842
720 4th Avenue South   Fax: (320) 255-4957
St. Cloud, MN 56301

Rochester Community & Technical College
Small Business Development Center
Ms. Michelle Pyfferoen, Director   (507) 285-7425
Riverland Hall   Fax: (507) 285-7110
851 30th Avenue, SE
Rochester, MN 55904
E-mail: mpyffero@ucrpo.roch.edu

University of Minnesota at Duluth
Small Business Development Center
Ms. Lee Jensen, Director   (218) 726-8758
150 School of Bus. & Economics   Fax: (218) 726-6338
10 University Drive
Duluth, MN 55812-2496
E-mail: ljensen@d.umn.edu

University of St. Thomas
Small Business Development Center
Mr. Gregg Schneider, Director   (612) 962-4505
1000 La Salle Avenue   Fax: (612) 962-4410
Suite MPL 100
Minneapolis, MN 55403
E-mail: gwschneider@stthomas.edu

Vermillion Community College
Small Business Development Center
Mr. Allen Jackson, Director   (218) 365-7295
1900 E. Camp St., Room NS110
Ely, MN 55731
E-mail: ajackso2@d.umn.edu

Mississippi

Mississippi Small Business Development Center
UNIVERSITY OF MISSISSIPPI—Lead Center
Mr. Raleigh Byars, State Director   (601) 232-5001
Old Chemistry Building, Suite 216   Fax: (601) 232-5650
University, MS 38677
E-mail: rbyars@olemiss.edu

Alcorn State University#
Small Business Development Center
Ms. Sharon Witty, Director   (601) 877-6684
P.O. Box 90   Fax: (601) 877-6256
1000 ASU Drive
Lorman, MS 39096-9402

Co-Lin Community College
Small Business Development Center
Mr. Bob D. Russ, Director   (601) 445-5254
11 Co-Lin Circle   Fax: (601) 446-1221
Natchez, MS 39120
E-mail: RobertR@natl.colin.cc.ms.us

Delta State University
Small Business Development Center
Mr. David Holman, Director   (601) 846-4236
P.O. Box 3235 DSU   Fax: (601) 846-4235
Whitfield Gymnasium Building, Suite 105
Cleveland, MS 38733
E-mail: sbdc@dsu.deltast.edu

East Central Community College
Small Business Development Center
Mr. Ronald Westbrook, Director   (601) 635-2111
P.O. Box 129   ext.297
275 Broad Street   Fax: (601) 635-4031
Decatur, MS 39327

International Trade Center—Specialized Center
Small Business Development Center
Ms. Marquerite Wall, Director   (601) 857-3536
Hinds Community College   Fax: (601) 857-3474
P.O. Box 1170
1500 Raymond Lake Road, 2nd Floor
Raymond, MS 39154
E-mail: hccrcu2@teclink.net

Holmes Community College
Small Business Development Center
Mr. John Deddens, Director   (601) 853-0827
413 West Ridgeland Avenue   Fax: (601) 853-0844
Ridgeland, MS 39157

Itawamba Community College
Small Business Development Center
Mr. Rex Hollingsworth, Director   (601) 680-8515
2176 South Eason Boulevard   Fax: (601) 680-8547
Tupelo, MS 38801
E-mail: iccsbdc@ebicom.net

Jackson State University#
Small Business Development Center
Mr. Henry Thomas, Director   (601) 968-2795
Suite 2A-1, Jackson Enterprise Center   Fax: (601) 968-2796
931 Highway 80 West, Unit 43
Jackson, MS 39204
E-mail: hthomas@ccaix.jsums.edu

Jones Junior College
Small Business Development Center
Mr. Gary Suddith, Director   (601) 477-4165
900 Court Street   Fax: (601) 477-4166
Ellisville, MS 39437
E-mail: crc@jcjc.cc.ms.us

Meridian Community College
Small Business Development Center
Mr. W. Mac Hodges, Director   (601) 482-7445
910 Highway 19 North   Fax: (601) 482-5803
Meridian, MS 39307
E-mail: mhodges@mcc.cc.ms.us

Mississippi Contract Procurement Center
Small Business Development Center
Mr. Richard Speights, Executive Director   (601) 396-1288
1636 Popps Ferry Road, Suite 229   Fax: (601) 396-2520
Biloxi, MS 39532
E-mail: mprogoff@aol.com

Mississippi Delta Community College
Small Business Development Center
Mr. Chuck Herring, Director   (601) 378-8183
P.O. Box 5607   Fax: (601) 378-5349
1656 E. Union
Greenville, MS 38704-5607
E-mail: mdccsbdc@tecinfo.com

Mississippi Gulf Coast Community College
Small Business Development Center
Ms. Janice Mabry, Director   (601) 497-7723
Jackson County Campus   Fax: (601) 497-7788
P.O. Box 100
Gautier, MS 39553

Mississippi State University
Small Business Development Center
Mr. Sonny Fisher, Director   (601) 325-8684
P.O. Drawer 5288   Fax: (601) 325-4016
#1 Research Blvd., Suite 201
Mississippi State, MS 39762
E-mail: sfisher@cobilan.msstate.edu

Mississippi Valley State University
Affiliate Small Business Development Center
Dr. Jim Breyley, Director   (601) 254-3601
Itta Bena, MS 38941   Fax: (601) 254-3600

Northeast Mississippi Community College
Small Business Development Center
Mr. Kenny Holt, Director (601) 720-7448
Cunningham Boulevard Fax: (601) 720-7464
Holliday Hall, Second Floor
Booneville, MS 38829
E-mail: kholt@necc.cc.ms.us

Northwest Mississippi Community College
Small Business Development Center
Mr. Jody Dunning, Director (601) 342-7648
DeSoto Center Fax: (601) 342-7648
5197 W. E. Ross Parkway, RM 208
Southaven, MS 38671
E-mail: smbusdev@nwcc.cc.ms.us

Pearl River Community College
Small Business Development Center
Ms. Heidi McDuffie, Director (601) 554-9133
5448 U.S. Highway 49 South Fax: (601) 554-9149
Hattiesburg, MS 39401

Southwest Mississippi Community College
Small Business Development Center
Ms. Kathryn "Sissy" Whittington, Director (601) 276-3890
College Drive Fax: (601) 276-3883
Summit, MS 39666

University of Mississippi
Small Business Development Center
Mr. Michael Vanderlip, Director (601) 234-2120
Room 1082, N.C.P.A. Fax: (601) 232-1220
University, MS 38677
E-mail: sbdc@olemiss.edu

University of Southern Mississippi
Small Business Development Center
Ms. Lucy Betcher, Director (601) 865-4578
136 Beach Park Place Fax: (601) 865-4581
Long Beach, MS 39560
E-mail: lbetcher@medea.gp.usm.edu

Missouri

Missouri Small Business Development Center
UNIVERSITY OF MISSOURI—Lead Center
Mr. Max E. Summers, State Director (573) 882-0344
300 University Place Fax: (573) 884-4297
Columbia, MO 65211

Center for Technology Transfer and Economic
Development—Specialized Center
Small Business Development Center
Mr. Fred Goss, Director (573) 341-4559
University of Missouri at Rolla Fax: (573) 341-4922
Room 104, Bldg. 1, Nagogami Terrace
Rolla, MO 65401-0249

Central Missouri State University
Small Business Development Center
Vacant (816) 543-4402
Grinstead #75 Fax: (816) 747-1653
Warrensburg, MO 64093-5037

Chillicothe City Hall
Small Business Development Center
Mr. Brian Olson, Director (816) 646-6920
715 Washington Fax: (816) 646-6811
Chillicothe, MO 64601

Mineral Area College
Small Business Development Center
Mr. Eugene Cherry, Director (573) 431-4593
P.O. Box 1000 Ext. 283
Flat River, MO 63601 Fax: (573) 431-6807

Missouri Southern State College
Small Business Development Center
Mr. Jim Krudwig, Director (417) 625-9313
#107 Matthews Hall Fax: (417) 625-9782
3950 Newman Road
Joplin, MO 64801-1595

Truman State University
Small Business Development Center
Mr. Glen Giboney, Director (816) 785-4307
207 East Patterson Fax: (816) 785-4181
Kirksville, MO 63501

Northwest Missouri State University
Small Business Development Center
Mr. Brad Anderson, Director (816) 562-1701
423 North Market Street Fax: (816) 582-3071
Maryville, MO 64468

Rockhurst College
Small Business Development Center
Ms. Rhonda Gerke, Director (816) 501-4572
1100 Rockhurst Road Fax: (816) 501-4646
Kansas City, MO 64110-2599

Southeast Missouri State University
Small Business Development Center
Mr. Frank "Buz" Sutherland, Director (573) 290-5965
222 North Pacific Fax: (573) 651-5005
Cape Girardeau, MO 63701 (Call First)

Southwest Missouri State University
Small Business Development Center
Ms. Jane Peterson, Director (417) 836-5685
Center for Business Research Fax: (417) 836-6337
901 South National, Box 88
Springfield, MO 65804-0089

St. Louis University
Small Business State University
Ms. Virginia Campbell, Director (314) 977-7232
3750 Lindell Boulevard Fax: (314) 977-7241
Saint Louis, MO 63108

Technology Development Center—Specialized Center
Small Business Development Center
Mr. Wes Savage, Assistant Director (816) 543-4402
Central Missouri State University Fax: (816) 543-8159
Grinstead #9
Warrensburg, MO 64093-5037

University Extension Small Business Development Center
Dr. Tom Henderson, Director (573) 882-4142
Business and Industrial Specialists Fax: (573) 882-2595
821 Clark Hall
Columbia, MO 65211

University of Missouri at Columbia
Small Business Development Center
Mr. Frank Siebert, Director (573) 882-9931
1800 University Place Fax: (573) 882-6156
Columbia, MO 65211

University of Missouri at Rolla
Small Business Development Center
Mr. Robert Laney, Director (314) 341-4561
223 Engineering Management Building Fax: (314) 341-2071
Rolla, MO 65401-0249

Montana

Montana Small Business Development Center
MONTANA DEPARTMENT OF COMMERCE—Lead Center
Mr. Ralph Kloser, State Director (406) 444-4780
1424 Ninth Avenue Fax: (406) 444-1872
Helena, MT 59620

Bear Paw Development Corporation
Small Business Development Center
Mr. Randy Hanson, Director (406) 265-9226
48 2nd Avenue Fax: (406) 265-5602
P.O. Box 170
Havre, MT 59501

Flathead Valley Community College
Small Business Development Center
Vacant, Director (406) 756-3833
218 Main/PO Box 8300 Fax: (406) 756-3815
Kalispell, MT 59901

Gallatin Development Corporation
Small Business Development Center
Ms. Michele DuBose, Director (406) 587-3113
222 East Main, Suite 102 Fax: (406) 587-9565
Bozeman, MT 59715
E-mail: mdubose@bozeman.org

Montana Tradepost Authority
Small Business Development Center
Mr. Tom McKerlick, Director (406) 256-6875
2722 Third Ave. North, Suite 300 W Fax: (406) 256-6877
Billings, MT 59101-1931

Southwest Montana Service Center
Small Business Development Center
Mr. John Donovan, Director (406) 782-7333
305 West Mercury, Suite 211 Fax: (406) 782-9675
Butte, MT 59701

Montana Community Development Corporation
Small Business Development Center
Mr. Bret George, Director (406) 728-9234
127 North Higgins, Third Floor Fax: (406) 721-4584
Missoula, MT 59802

High Plains Development Authority
Small Business Development Center
Ms. Susie David, Director (406) 454-1934
P.O. Box 2568 Fax: (406) 454-2995
710 1st Avenue North
Great Falls, MT 59403

Missouri Valley Development Corp.
Small Business Development Center
Ms. Laura McPherson, Director (406) 482-5024
220 3rd Avenue S, #D Fax: (406) 653-1844
Wolf Point, MT 59201

Nebraska

Nebraska Small Business Development Center
UNIVERSITY OF NEBRASKA AT OMAHA—Lead Center
Mr. Robert Bernier, State Director (402) 554-2521
60th & Dodge Streets Fax: (402) 554-3747
CBA Room 407
Omaha, NE 68182-0248

Chadron State College
Small Business Development Center
Mr. Cliff Hanson, Director (308) 432-6282
Administration Building Fax: (308) 432-6430
Chadron, NE 69337
E-mail: chanson@cscl.csc.edu

Mid-Plains Community College
Small Business Development Center
Mr. Dean Kurth, Director (308) 635-7513
416 North Jeffers, Room 26
North Platte, NE 69101

Omaha Business & Technology Center—Specialized Center
Small Business Development Center
Mr. Tom McCabe, Director (402) 595-3511
2505 North 24th Street, Suite 101 Fax: (402) 595-3524
Omaha, NE 68110

Peru State College
Small Business Development Center
Mr. David Ruenholl, Director   (402) 872-2274
T.J. Majors Hall, Room 248   Fax: (402) 872-2422
Peru, NE 68421

Scottsbluff Small Business Development Center
Ms. Ingrid Battershell, Director   (308) 635-7513
Nebraska Public Power Building   Fax: (308) 635-6596
1721 Broadway, Room 400
Scottsbluff, NE 69361

University of Nebraska at Kearney
Small Business Development Center
Ms. Kay Payne, Director   (308) 865-8344
Welch Hall, 19th and College Drive   Fax: (308) 865-8153
Kearney, NE 68849-3035

University of Nebraska at Lincoln
Small Business Development Center
Ms. Irene Cherhoniak, Director   (402) 472-3358
1135 M Street, Suite #200   Fax: (402) 472-0328
Lincoln, NE 68508

University of Nebraska at Omaha
Small Business Development Center
Ms. Jeanne Eibes, Director   (402) 595-2381
Peter Kiewit Conference Center   Fax: (402) 595-2385
1313 Farnam-on-the-Mall, Suite 132
Omaha, NE 68182-0248

Wayne State College
Small Business Development Center
Ms. Loren Kucera, Director   (402) 375-7575
Gardner Hall   Fax: (402) 375-7574
1111 Main Street
Wayne, NE 68787

Nevada

Nevada Small Business Development Center
UNIVERSITY OF NEVADA RENO—Lead Center
Mr. Sam Males, State Director   (702) 784-1717
College of Business Administration/032   Fax: (702) 784-4337
Business Bldg., Room 411
Reno, NV 89557-0100

Carson City Chamber of Commerce
Small Business Development Center
Mr. Larry Osborne, Executive Director   (702) 882-1565
1900 South Carson Street, #100   Fax: (702) 882-4179
Carson City, NV 89702

Small Business Development Center
Ms. Sharolyn Craft, Dirctor   (702) 734-7575
3270 Howard Hughes Parkway,   Fax: (702) 734-7633
Suite 130
Las Vegas, NV 89109

Great Basin College
Small Business Development Center
Mr. John Pryor, Director   (702) 753-2205
1500 College Parkway   Fax: (702) 753-2242
Elko, NV 89801

Small Business Development Center
Ms. Janis Stevenson, Business Dev.   (702) 399-6300
   Specialist   Fax: (702) 399-6301
19 West Brooks Avenue
North Las Vegas, NV 89030

Tri-County Development Authority
Small Business Development Center
Ms. Teri Williams, Director   (702) 623-5777
P.O. Box 820   Fax: (702) 623-5999
Winnemucca, NV 89446

Business Environmental Program
Nevada Small Business Development Center
Sierra Pacific Power Company   (702) 689-6688
6100 Neil Road, Suite 400   Fax: (702) 689-6689
Reno, NV 89511

New Hampshire

New Hampshire Small Business Development Center
UNIVERSITY OF NEW HAMPSHIRE—Lead Center
Ms. Mary Collins, State Director   (603) 862-2200
108 McConnell Hall   Fax: (603) 862-4876
Durham, NH 03824-3593

Office of Economic Initiatives
Small Business Development Center
Ms. Amy Jennings, Director   (603) 624-2000
1000 Elm Street, 12th Floor   Fax: (603) 647-4410
Manchester, NH 03101

Small Business Development Center
Ms. Judy Orfao, Acting Regional Manager   (603) 886-1233
Center for Economic Development   Fax: (603) 598-1164
One Indiana Head Plaza, Suite 510
Nashua, NH 03060

Small Business Development Center
Mr. Gary Cloutier, Regional Manager   (603) 358-2602
Blake House   Fax: (603) 358-2612
Keene State College
Keene, NH 03431

Small Business Development Center
Ms. Janice Kitchen, Regional Manager   (603) 535-2523
Outreach Center, MSC#24A   Fax: (603) 535-2850
Plymouth State College
Plymouth, NH 03264

Small Business Development Center
Mr. Bob Ebberson, Regional Manager   (603) 624-2000
1000 Elm Street, 12th Floor   Fax: (603) 647-4410
Manchester, NH 03101

Small Business Development Center
Ms. Elizabeth Ward, Regional Manager   (603) 444-1053
120 Main Street   Fax: (603) 444-5463
Littleton, NH 03561

Small Business Development Center
Ms. Jeanine DiMario, Regional Manager   (603) 330-1929
Chamber of Commerce, Suite 3A   Fax: (603) 330-1948
18 S. Main Street
Rochester, NH 03867

New Jersey

New Jersey Small Business Development Center
RUTGERS UNIVERSITY—Lead Center
Ms. Brenda B. Hopper, State Director   (973) 353-5950
49 Bleeker Street   Fax: (973) 353-1110
Third Floor, Ackerson Hall
Newark, NJ 07102
E-mail: bhopper@andromeda.rutgers.edu

Bergen County Community College
Small Business Development Center
Ms. Melody Irvin, Director   (201) 447-7841
400 Paramus Road, Room A328   Fax: (201) 447-9405
Paramus, NJ 07652
E-mail: mirvin@pilot.njin.net

Brookdale Community College
Small Business Development Center
Mr. Bill Nunnally, Co-Director   (908) 842-8685
Mr. Larry Novick, Co-Director   Fax: (908) 842-0203
Newman Springs Road
Lincroft, NJ 07738
E-mail: lnovick@brookdale.cc.nj.us

Greater Atlantic City Chamber of Commerce
Small Business Development Center
Mr. William R. McGinley, Director   (609) 345-5600
1125 Atlantic Avenue   Fax: (609) 345-1666
Atlantic City, NJ 08401

Kean College Small Business Development Center
Ms. Mira Kostak, Director   (908) 527-2946
East Campus, Room 242   Fax: (908) 527-2960
Union, NJ 07083

Mercer County Community College
Small Business Development Center
West Windsor Campus
Mr. Herbert Spiegel, Director   (609) 586-4800
1200 Old Trenton Road   Ext. 469
P.O. Box B   Fax: (609) 890-6338
Trenton, NJ 08690
E-mail: hss@mccc.edu

Rutgers University
Small Business Development Center
Mr. Leroy A. Johnson, Director   (201) 648-5950
180 University Avenue, 3rd Floor   Fax: (201) 648-1175
Third Floor, Ackerson Hall
Newark, NJ 07102
E-mail: leroyj@andromeda.rutgers.edu

Rutgers University/Camden
Small Business Development Center
Ms. Patricia Peacock, Ed.D., Director   (609) 225-6221
Schools of Business   Fax: (609) 225-6621
227 Penn Street, 3rd Floor, Room 334
Camden, NJ 08102
E-mail: ppeacock@camden.rutgers.edu

Warren County Community College
Small Business Development Center
Mr. James H. Smith, Director   (908) 689-9620
475 Route 57 West   Fax: (908) 689-2247
Washington, NJ 07882-9605
E-mail: smith@mail.warren.cc.nj.us

Paterson Small Business Development Center
Mr. Joseph M. Bair, Director   (201) 754-8695
131 Ellison Street
Paterson, NJ 07505
E-mail: jbair@andromeda.rutgers.edu

New Mexico

New Mexico Small Business Development Center
SANTA FE COMMUNITY COLLEGE—Lead Center
Mr. J. Roy Miller, State Director   1-800-281-SBDC
6401 Richards Avenue   (505) 438-1362
Santa Fe, NM 87505   Fax: (505) 471-9469

Albuquerque Technical Vocational Institute
Small Business Development Center
Mr. Ray Garcia, Director   (505) 272-7980
801 University SE, Suite 300   Fax: (505) 224-4251
Albuquerque, NM 87106
MAILING ADDRESS:
 525 Buena Vista, SE
 Albuquerque, NM 87106

Clovis Community College
Small Business Development Center
Ms. Sandra Taylor-Smith, Director   (505) 769-4136
417 Schepps Boulevard   Fax: (505) 769-4190
Clovis, NM 88101

Dona Ana Branch Community College
Small Business Development Center
Mr. Terry Sullivan, Director   (505) 527-7540
3400 South Espina Street   Fax: (505) 527-7515
Box 30001, Department 3DA
Las Cruces, NM 88033-0001

Eastern New Mexico University
Small Business Development Center
Mr. Eugene D. Simmons, Director   (505) 624-7133
57 University Avenue   Fax: (505) 624-7132
P.O. Box 6000
Roswell, NM 88201-6000

Luna Vocational Technical Institute
Small Business Development Center
Mr. Don Bustos, Director   (505) 454-2595
Luna Campus, P.O. Box 1510   Fax: (505) 454-2518
Las Vegas, NM 87701

Mesa Technical College
Small Business Development Center
Mr. Richard Spooner, Director   (505) 461-4413
P.O. Box 1143   Fax: (505) 461-1901
911 South 10th
Tucumcari, NM 88401

New Mexico Junior College
Small Business Development Center
Mr. Don Leach, Director   (505) 392-4510
5317 Lovington Highway   Fax: (505) 392-2526
Hobbs, NM 88240

New Mexico State University/Alamogordo
Small Business Development Center
Mr. Dwight Harp, Director   (505) 434-5272
2230 Lawrence   Fax: (505) 434-1432
Alamogordo, NM 88310   (Call First)

New Mexico State University/Carlsbad
Small Business Development Center
Mr. Larry Coalson, Director   (505) 887-6562
P.O. Box 1090   Fax: (505) 885-0818
301 S. Canal
Carlsbad, NM 88220

New Mexico State University/Grants
Small Business Development Center
Mr. Clemente Sanchez, Director   (505) 287-8221
709 East Roosevelt Avenue   Fax: (505) 287-2125
Grants, NM 87020

Northern New Mexico Community College
Small Business Development Center
Mr. Darien Cabral, Director   (505) 747-2236
1002 North Onate Street   Fax: (505) 747-2180
Espanola, NM 87532

San Juan College
Small Business Development Center
Mr. Calvin A. Tingey, Director   (505) 599-0528
4601 College Blvd.   Fax: (505) 325-3964
Farmington, NM 87402

Santa Fe Community College
Small Business Development Center
Ms. Monica Montoya, Director   (505) 438-1343
6401 Richards Avenue   Fax: (505) 471-9469
Santa Fe, NM 87505

South Valley Small Business Development Center
Mr. Steven Becerra, Director   (505) 248-0132
700 4th Street, SW, Suite A   Fax: (505) 248-0127
Albuquerque, NM 87102

University of New Mexico/Gallup
Small Business Development Center
Ms. Elsie Sanchez, Director   (505) 722-2220
P.O. Box 1395   Fax: (505) 863-6006
103 W. Highway 66
Gallup, NM 87301

University of New Mexico/Los Alamos
Small Business Development Center
Mr. Jay Weschler, Acting Director   (505) 662-0001
901 18th Street, #11800   Fax: (505) 662-0099
P.O. Box 715
Los Alamos, NM 87544

University of New Mexico/Valencia
Small Business Development Center
Mr. David Ashley, Director   (505) 925-8980
280 La Entrada   Fax: (505) 925-8981
Los Lunas, NM 87031
E-mail: dashley@unm.edu
Web site: http://www.unm.edu/~vcsbdc/

Western New Mexico University
Small Business Development Center
Ms. Linda Kay Jones, Director   (505) 538-6320
P. O. Box 2672   Fax: (505) 538-6341
Silver City, NM 88062

New York

New York Small Business Development Centers
STATE UNIVERSITY OF NEW YORK (SUNY)—Lead Center
Mr. James L. King, State Director   1-800-732-SBDC
SUNY Plaza, S-523   (518) 443-5398
Albany, NY 12246   Fax: (518) 465-4992
E-mail: kingjl@cc.sunycentral.edu

Bronx Community College
Small Business Development Center
Mr. Eugene Williams, Director   (718) 563-3570
McCracken Hall, Room 14   Fax: (718) 563-3572
West 181st Street & University Ave.
Bronx, NY 10453

Bronx Outreach Center
Contact Bronx Community College
Small Business Development Center   (718) 563-9204
Con Edison
560 Cortlandt Ave.
Bronx, NY 10451

Clinton Community College
Small Business Development Center
Ms. Merry Gwynn, Coordinator   (518) 562-4260
Lake Shore Road, Route 9 South   Fax: (518) 563-9759
136 Clinton Point Drive
Plattsburgh, NY 12901

College of Staten Island
Small Business Development Center
Dr. Ronald Sheppard, Acting Director   (718) 982-2560
2800 Victory Blvd.   Fax: (718) 982-2323
Building 1A, Room 211
Staten Island, NY 10314-9806

Corning Community College
Small Business Development Center
Ms. Bonnie Gestwicki, Director   (607) 962-9461
24 Denison Parkway West   Fax: (607) 936-6642
Corning, NY 14830

Jamestown Community College
Small Business Development Center
Ms. Irene Dobies, Director   1-800-522-7232
P.O. Box 20   (716) 665-5754
Jamestown, NY 14702-0020   Fax: (716) 665-6733

Jefferson Community College
Small Business Development Center
Mr. John F. Tanner, Director   (315) 782-9262
Coffeen Street   Fax: (315) 782-0901
Watertown, NY 13601

Canton Outreach Center
Small Business Development Center
Contact Jefferson Community College   (315) 386-7312
SUNY Canton   Fax: (315) 386-7945
Canton, NY 12617

Kingsborough Community College
Small Business Development Center
Mr. Edward O'Brien, Director   (718) 368-4619
2001 Oriental Boulevard   Fax: (718) 368-4629
Bldg. T4, Room 4204
Brooklyn, NY 11235

Downtown Brooklyn Outreach Center
Small Business Development Center
Contact Kingsborough Community College (718) 260-9783
395 Flatbush Ave. Extension Room 413   Fax: (718) 260-9797
Brooklyn, NY 11201

Manufacturing Field Office—Specialized Center
Small Business Development Center
Mr. Bill Brigham, Acting Director   (518) 286-1014
Rensselaer Technology Park   Fax: (518) 286-1006
385 Jordan Road
Troy, NY 12180-7602

Niagara Community College at Sanborn
Small Business Development Center
Mr. Richard Gorko, Director   (716) 693-1910
3111 Saunders Settlement Road   Fax: (716) 731-3595
Sanborn, NY 14132

Geneseo Outreach Center
Small Business Development Center
Mr. Charles VanArsdale, Director
Contact Niagara Community College   (716) 245-5429
SUNY Geneseo   Fax: (716) 245-5430
One College Circle
South Hall #111
Geneseo, NY 14454-1485

Niagara Falls Satellite Office
Small Business Development Center
Contact Niagara Community College   (716) 285-4793
Carborundum Center   Fax: (716) 285-4797
345 Third Street
Niagara Falls, NY 14303-1117

Onondaga Community College
Small Business Development Center
Mr. Robert Varney, Director   (315) 498-6070
Excell Building, Room 108   Fax: (315) 492-3704
4969 Onondaga Road
Syracuse, NY 13215-1944

State University of New York at Oswego
Small Business Development Center
Contact Onondaga Community College   (315) 343-1545
Oswego Outreach Center   Fax: (315) 343-1546
Operation Oswego County
44 West Bridge Street
Oswego, NY 13126

Pace University Small Business Development Center
Mr. Ira Davidson, Director   (212) 346-1900
One Pace Plaza, Room W483   Fax: (212) 346-1613
New York, NY 10038

Baruch College
Small Business Development Center
Ms. Cheryl Fenton, Director   (212) 802-6620
360 Park Avenue South, Room 1101   Fax: (212) 802-6613
New York, NY 10010

Baruch College Mid-Town Outreach Center
Small Business Development Center
Mr. Barrie Phillip, Coordinator   (212) 802-6620
360 Park Avenue South, Room 1101   Fax: (212) 802-6613
New York, NY 10010

East Harlem Outreach Center
Small Business Development Center
Mr. Anthony Sanchez, Coordinator   (212) 346-1900
145 East 116th Street, Third Floor   Fax: (212) 534-4576
New York, NY 10029

Central Harlem Outreach Center
Small Business Development Center
Mr. Anthony Sanchez, Coordinator   (212) 346-1900
163 West 125th Street, Room 1307   Fax: (212) 534-4576
New York, NY 10027

Rockland Community College
Small Business Development Center
Mr. Thomas J. Morley, Director   (914) 356-0370
145 College Road   Fax: (914) 356-0381
Suffern, NY 10901-3620

Mercy College Outreach Center
Small Business Development Center
Mr. Tom Milton, Coordinator   (914) 674-7485
555 Broadway   Fax: (914) 693-4996
Dobbs Ferry, NY 10522-1189

Small Business Resource Center
Small Business Development Center Outreach
Ms. Maria Circosta, Coordinator   (914) 644-4116
222 Bloomingdale Road, Third Floor   Fax: (914) 644-2184
White Plains, NY 10605-1500

SUNY at Stony Brook
Small Business Development Center
Ms. Judith McEvoy, Director   (516) 632-9070
Harriman Hall, Room 109   Fax: (516) 632-7176
Stony Brook, NY 11794-3775

Long Island University at Southhampton
Small Business Development Center
Contact SUNY at Stony Brook   (516) 287-0059
Southampton Outreach Center   (516) 287-0071
Abney Peak, Montauk Highway   Fax: (516) 287-8287
Southampton, NY 11968

Sulfolk County Community College
Riverhead Outreach Center
Small Business Development Center
Contact SUNY at Stony Brook   (516) 369-1409
Rochester Outreach Center   (516) 369-1507
Riverhead, NY 11901   Fax: (516) 369-3255

State University College at Buffalo
Bacon Hall 117
Small Business Development Center
Ms. Susan McCartney, Director   (716) 878-4030
1300 Elmwood Avenue   Fax: (716) 878-4067
Buffalo, NY 14222

State University College of Technology at Farmingdale
Small Business Development Center
Mr. Joseph Schwartz, Director   (516) 420-2765
Campus Commons   Fax: (516) 293-5343
Farmingdale, NY 11735

Hempstead Outreach Center
Small Business Development Center   (516) 564-1895
Contact State University College of Technology   (516) 564-8672
269 Fulton Avenue   Fax: (516) 481-4938
Hempstead, NY 11550

State University Institute of Technology at Utica/Rome
Small Business Development Center
Mr. David Mallen, Director   (315) 792-7546
P.O. Box 3050   Fax: (315) 792-7554
Utica, NY 13504-3050

State University of New York at Albany
Small Business Development Center
Mr. Peter George III, Director   (518) 442-5577
Draper Hall, Room 107   Fax: (518) 442-5582
135 Western Avenue
Albany, NY 12222

Cobleskill Outreach Center
Small Business Development Center
Contact SUNY at Albany   (518) 234-5528
SUNY Cobleskill   Fax: (518) 234-5272
Warner Hall, Room 218
Cobleskill, NY 12043

Binghamton University
Small Business Development Center
Ms. Joanne Bauman, Director   (607) 777-4024
P.O. Box 6000   Fax: (607) 777-4029
Binghamton, NY 13902-6000
E-mail: sbdcbu@spectra.net

State University of New York
Small Business Development Center
Mr. Wilfred Bordeau, Director   (716) 637-6660
74 North Main Street   Fax: (716) 637-2102
Brockport, NY 14420

Geneva Outreach Center
Small Business Development Center
Ms. Sandy Bordeau, Administrative Director (315) 781-1253
122 North Genesee Street
Geneva, NY 14456

Small Business Development Center
Contact SUNY at Brockport   (716) 232-7310
State University at Brockport   Fax: (716) 637-2182
Temple Building
14 Franklin Street, Suite 200
Rochester, NY 14604

Small Business Development Center
Ms. Patricia LaSusa, Director   (914) 339-0025
One Development Court   Fax: (914) 339-1631
Kingston, NY 12401

Marist College Outreach Center
Small Business Development Center
Contact Kingston SBDC   (914) 897-2607
Fishkill Extension Center   Fax: (914) 897-4653
2600 Route 9, Unit 90
Fishkill, NY 12524-2001

York College/The City University of New York
Small Business Development Center
Mr. James A. Heyliger   (718) 262-2880
Science Building, Room 107   Fax: (718) 262-2881
94-50 159th Street
Jamaica, NY 11451

North Carolina

North Carolina Small Business Development Center
UNIVERSITY OF NORTH CAROLINA—Lead Center
Mr. Scott R. Daugherty, Executive   1-800-2580-UNC
  Director   (919) 715-7272
333 Fayetteville Street Mall, #1150 Fax: (919) 715-7777
Raleigh, NC 27601-1742

Appalachian State University Northwestern Region
Small Business Development Center
Mr. Bill Parrish, Director   (704) 262-2492
Walker College of Business   Fax: (704) 262-2027
2125 Raley Hall
Boone, NC 28608

Catawba Valley Region
Small Business Development Center
Mr. Blair Abee, Director   (704) 345-1110
514 Highway 321 NW, Suite A   Fax: (704) 326-9117
Hickory, NC 28601-4738

East Carolina University Eastern Region
Small Business Development Center
Mr. Walter Fitts, Director   (919) 328-6157
300 East First Street, Willis Bldg. Fax: (919) 328-6992
Greenville, NC 27858-4353

Elizabeth City State University#
Northeast Region Small Business Development Center
Ms. Wauna Dooms, Director   (919) 335-3247
1704 Weeksville Road   Fax: (919) 335-3648
P.O. Box 874
Elizabeth City, NC 27909

Fayetteville State University#
Cape Fear Region Small Business Development Center
Dr. Sid Gautam, Director   (910) 486-1727
Continuing Education Center   Fax: (910) 486-1949
P.O. Box 1334
Fayetteville, NC 28302
FOR FED EX DELIVERY:
  Fayetteville State University
  1200 Murchison Road
  Fayetteville, NC 28301

North Carolina A&T State University#
Northeast Piedmont Region
Small Business Development Center
Ms. Cynthia Clemons, Director   (910) 334-7005
CH Moore Agricultural Research   Fax: (910) 334-7073
  Center
1601 East Market Street
P.O. Box D-22
Greensboro, NC 27411

North Carolina State University Capital Region
Small Business Development Center
Mr. Mike Seibert, Director   (919) 715-0520
MCI Small Business Resource Center Fax: (919) 715-0518
800 1/2 South Salisbury Street
Raleigh, NC 27601

University of North Carolina at Chapel Hill
Central Carolina Region
Small Business Development Center
Mr. Dan Parks, Director   (919) 962-0389
608 Airport Road, Suite B   Fax: (919) 962-3291
Chapel Hill, NC 27514

University of North Carolina at Charlotte
Southern Piedmont Region
Small Business Development Center
Mr. George McAllister, Director   (704) 548-1090
The Ben Craig Center   Fax: (704) 548-9050
8701 Mallard Creek Road
Charlotte, NC 28262

University of North Carolina at Wilmington
Southeastern Region Small Business Development Center
Dr. Warren Gulko, Director   (910) 962-3744
601 South College Road   Fax: (910) 962-3014
Wilmington, NC 28403

Western Carolina University Western Region
Small Business Development Center
Mr. Allan Steinberg, Director   (704) 227-7494
Center for Improving Mountain Living   Fax: (704) 227-7422
Bird Building
Cullowhee, NC 28723

Winston-Salem State University#
Northwest Piedmont Region
Small Business Development Center
Vacant, Director   (910) 750-2030
P.O. Box 19483   Fax: (910) 750-2031
Winston-Salem, NC 27110
FOR FED EX DELIVERY:
   Winston-Salem State University
   Albert Anderson Center, Room 118
   MLK & Reynolds Park Road
   Winston-Salem, NC 27110

Pembroke State University
Small Business Development Center
Ms. Cammie Flurry, Assistant Director   (910) 521-6611
P.O. Box 1510   Fax: (910) 521-6550
Pembroke, NC 28372-1510
FOR FED EX DELIVERY:
   1 University Drive

North Carolina Wesleyan College
Small Business Development Center
Mr. Michael Twiddy   (919) 985-5130
3400 North Wesleyan Boulevard   Fax: (919) 977-3701
Rocky Mount, NC 27804
(only there on certain days,
  call Elizabeth City first)

North Dakota

North Dakota Small Business Development Center
UNIVERSITY OF NORTH DAKOTA—
   Lead Center   1-800-445-7232
Mr. Walter "Wally" Kearns, State Director   (701) 777-3700
118 Gamble Hall, UND   Fax: (701) 777-3225
Box 7308
Grand Forks, ND 58202-7308

Bismarck Regional Small Business Development Center
Mr. Jan Peterson, Regional Director   (701) 223-8583
400 East Broadway, Suite 416   Fax: (701) 250-4799
Bismarck, ND 58501

Dickinson Regional Small Business Development Center
Mr. Bryan Vendsel, Regional Director   (701) 227-2096
314 Third Avenue West, Drawer L   Fax: (701) 225-5116
Dickinson, ND 58602

Fargo Regional Small Business Development Center
Mr. Jon Grinager, Regional Director   (701) 237-0986
P.O. Box 1309   Fax: (701) 237-9734
657 Second Avenue North, Room 219
Fargo, ND 58108-1309

Grand Forks Regional Small Business Development Center
Mr. Gordon Snyder, Regional Director   (701) 772-8502
202 North Third Street, Suite 200   Fax: (701) 772-9238
Grand Forks, ND 58203

Minot Regional Small Business Development Center
Mr. Brian Argabright, Regional Director   (701) 852-8861
900 North Broadway, Suite 300   Fax: (701) 858-3831
Minot, ND 58703

Devils Lake Outreach Center
Mr. Gordon Snyder, Regional Director   1-800-445-7232
417 Fifth Street
Devils Lake, ND 58301

Grafton Outreach Center
Mr. Gordon Snyder, Regional Director   1-800-445-7232
Red River Regional Planning Council
P.O. Box 633
Grafton, ND 58237

Procurement Assistance Center
P.O. Box 1309   (701) 237-9678
657 Second Avenue North, Room 219   Fax: (701) 237-9734
Fargo, ND 58107-1309

Jamestown Outreach Center
Mr. Jon Grinager, Regional Director   (701) 252-9243
210 Tenth Street Southeast   Fax: (701) 251-2488
P.O. Box 1530   Fax: (701) 252-4837
Jamestown, ND 58402

Williston Outreach Center
Mr. Bryan Vendsel, Regional Director   1-800 445-7232
Tri-County Economic Development
P.O. Box 2047
Williston, ND 58801

Ohio

Ohio Small Business Development Center
DEPARTMENT OF DEVELOPMENT—Lead Center
Ms. Holly I. Schick, State Director   (614) 466-2711
77 South High Street, 28th Floor   Fax: (614) 466-0829
Columbus, OH 43215-6108

Akron Regional Development Board
Small Business Development Center
Mr. Charles Smith, Director   (216) 379-3170
One Cascade Plaza, 8th Floor   Fax: (216) 379-3164
Akron, OH 44308-1192

Ashtabula County Economic Development Council, Inc.
Small Business Development Center
Ms. Sarah Bogardus, Director   (216) 576-9134
36 West Walnut Street   Fax: (216) 576-5003
Jefferson, OH 44047

CAMP/NOM SBDC
Northern Ohio Manufacturing SBDC
Robert Schauer, Manager
Prospect Park Building   (216) 432-5364
4600 Prospect Avenue   Fax: (216) 361-2900
Cleveland, OH 44103-4314

Clermont County Area
Small Business Development Center
Mr. Dennis Begue, Director   (513) 753-7141
Clermont County Chamber of Commerce   Fax: (513) 753-7146
4440 Glen Este-Withamsville Road
Cincinnati, OH 45245

Dayton Area Chamber of Commerce
Small Business Development Center
Mr. Harry Bumgarner, Director   (513) 226-8239
Chamber Plaza—5th and Main Streets   Fax: (513) 226-8254
Dayton, OH 45402-2400

EMTEC/Southern Area Manufacturing
Small Business Development Center
Mr. Harry Bumgarner, Director   (513) 258-6180
3155 Research Park, Suite 206   Fax: (513) 258-6189
Kettering, OH 45420

Enterprise Center/OSU/OCES
Small Business Development Center
Mr. Bill Grunkemeyer, Interim Director   (513) 393-9599
129 East Main Street   Fax: (513) 393-8159
Hillsboro, OH 45133

Enterprise Development Corporation
Small Business Development Center
Ms. Karen Patton, Director   (614) 592-1188
900 East State Street   Fax: (614) 593-8283
Athens, OH 45701

Greater Cleveland Growth Association
Small Business Development Center
Ms. Ann Hach, Director   (216) 621-3300
200 Tower City Center/50 Public   Fax: (216) 621-4617
   Square
Cleveland, OH 44113-2291

Hamilton County Development Company
Small Business Development Center
Ms. Danielle K. Remmy, Director   (513) 632-8292
1776 Mentor Avenue   Fax: (513) 351-0610
Cincinnati, OH 45212-3597
E-mail: HCDCSBDC@AOL.COM

Heart of Ohio Marion Area Chamber of Commerce
Small Business Development Center
Ms. Lynn Lovell, Director   (614) 387-0188
206 South Prospect Street   Fax: (614) 387-7722
Marion, OH 43302

Kent State University/Salem Campus
Small Business Development Center
Deanne Taylor, Director   (216) 332-0361
2491 State Route 45 South   Fax: (216) 332-9256
Salem, OH 44460

Kent State University/Stark Campus
Small Business Development Center
Ms. Amy DeGeorge, Coordinator   (216) 499-9600
6000 Frank Avenue N.W.   Fax: (216) 494-6121
Canton, OH 44720

Kent State University Partnership
Kent-Portage SBDC
Ms. Linda Yost, Director
Kent State University   (216) 672-2772
College of Business Administration   ext 254
Room 300A   Fax: (216) 672-2448
Kent, Ohio 44242

Lake County Economic Development Center
Small Business Development Center
Ms. Catherine C. Haworth, Director   (216) 951-1290
Lakeland Community College   Fax: (216) 951-7336
7750 Clocktower Drive
Kirkland, OH 44094

Lawrence County Chamber of Commerce
SE Small Business Development Center
Ms. Lou-Ann Walden, Director   (614) 894-3838
U.S. Route 52 & Solida Road   Fax: (614) 894-3836
P.O. Box 488
Southpoint, OH 45680

Lima Technical College
Small Business Development Center
Mr. Gerald J. Biedenharn, Director   (419) 229-5320
West Central Office   Fax: (419) 229-5424
545 West Market Street, Suite 305
Lima, OH 45801-4717

Lorain County Chamber of Commerce
Small Business Development Center
Mr. Dennis Jones, Director   (216) 233-6500
6100 South Broadway   Fax: (216) 246-4050
Lorain, OH 44053

Marietta College
Small Business Development Center
Mr. Emerson Shimp, Director   (614) 376-4832
213 Fourth Street, 2nd Floor   Fax: (614) 376-4901
Marietta, OH 45750

Mid-Ohio Small Business Development Center
Ms. Barbara Harmony, Director   (800) 366-7232
246 East Fourth Street   Fax: (419) 522-6811
P.O. Box 1208
Mansfield, OH 44901

North Central Small Business Development Center
Fremont Office   (419) 334-8400
Terra Community College   ext 255
Mr. Joe Wilson, Director   (800) 825-2431
2830 Napoleon Road   Fax: (419) 334-9414
Fremont, OH 43420

Private Industry Council
Northwest Small Business Development Center
Mr. Don Wright, Director   (419) 784-3777
1935 East Second Street, Suite D   Fax: (419) 782-4649
Defiance, OH 43512

SBDC—Southeast Ohio
Small Business Development Center
Ohio University
Enterprise and Technology Bldg.
Ms. Debra McBride, Director   (614) 593-1797
20 East Circle Drive, Suite 190   Fax: (614) 593-1795
Athens, OH 45701

Shawnee State University
Small Business Development Center
Mr. Patrick Dengel, Director   (614) 355-2274
940 Second St., Rm. 008 Massie Hall   Fax: (614) 355-2598
Portsmouth, OH 45662-4344

Southeast Small Business Development Center
Ms. Lou-Ann Walden, Director
Lawrence County Chamber of Commerce
U.S. Route 52 & Solida Rd.   (614) 894-3838
P.O. Box 488   Fax: (614) 894-3836
South Point, OH 45680

Springfield Small Business Development Center, Inc.
Mr. Rafeal Underwood, Executive Director   (513) 322-7821
300 East Auburn Avenue   Fax: (513) 322-7874
Springfield, OH 45505

Toledo Small Business Development Center
Ms. Linda Fayerweather, Director   (419) 243-8191
300 Madison Avenue   Fax: (419) 241-8302
Enterprise Suite 200
Toledo, OH 43604-1575

Tuscarawas Small Business Development Center
Mr. Tom Farbizo, Director   (216) 339-3391
Kent State University   Ext. 279
300 University Drive, NE   Fax: (216) 339-2637
New Philadelphia, OH 44663-9447

University of Cincinnati
Small Business Development Center
Mr. Bill Fioretti, Director   (513) 948-2082
1275 Section Road   Fax: (513) 948-2007
Cincinnati, OH 45237-2615

Upper Valley Joint Vocational School
Small Business Development Center
Mr. Jon Heffner, Acting Director   (800) 589-6963
8811 Career Drive, North County Rd. 25A   (513) 778-8419
Piqua, OH 45356   Fax: (513) 778-9237

Wright State University/Dayton Satellite
Small Business Development Center
Ms. Marsha Adams, Director   (513) 873-3503
Center for Small Business Assistance   Fax: (513) 873-3545
College of Business, 120 Rike Hall
Dayton, OH 45433

Wright State University/Lake Campus
Small Business Development Center
Dr. Tom Knapke, Director   (800) 237-1477
West Central Office   (419) 586-0355
7600 State Route 703   Fax: (419) 586-0358
Celina, OH 45882

Youngstown State University
Small Business Development Center
Ms. Patricia Veisz, Manager   (216) 746-3350
Cushwa Center for Business   Fax: (216) 746-3324
   Development
241 Federal Plaza
Youngstown, OH 44503

Zanesville Area Chamber of Commerce
Mid East Small Business Development Center
Ms. Bonnie J. Winnett, Director   (614) 452-4868
217 North Fifth Street   Fax: (614) 454-2963
Zanesville, OH 43701

Oklahoma

Oklahoma Small Business Development Center
SOUTHEASTERN OKLAHOMA STATE UNIVERSITY—Lead
Center
Dr. Grady Pennington, State Director   1-800-522-6154
517 University   (580) 924-0277
Station A, Box 2584   Fax: (580) 920-7471
Durant, OK 74701
E-mail: gpennington@sosu.edu

AmQuest Bank, N.A.
Small Business Development Center
Mr. James C. Elliott, Business Dev. Specialist   (580) 248-4946
601 SW "D," Suite 209   Fax: (580) 248-4946
Lawton, OK 73501

Carl Albert College
Small Business Development Center
Mr. Dean Qualls, Director (918) 647-4019
1507 South McKenna Fax: (918) 647-1218
Poteau, OK 74953
E-mail: dqualls@casc.cc.ok.us

East Central University
Small Business Development Center
Mr. Frank Vater, Director (580) 436-3190
1036 East Tenth Fax: (580) 436-3190
Ada, OK 74820
E-mail: osbdcecu@chickasaw.com

Langston University Minority Assistance Center—
Specialized Center
Small Business Development Center
Mr. Robert Allen, Director (405) 466-3256
Highway 33 East Fax: (405) 466-2909
Langston, OK 73050

NE Oklahoma A & M
Small Business Development Center
Mr. Hugh Simon, Bus. Dev. Specialist (918) 540-0575
215 I Street, NE Fax: (918) 540-0575
Miami, OK 74354
E-mail: hsimon@neoam.cc.ok.us

Northeastern Oklahoma State University
Small Business Development Center
Ms. Danielle Coursey, Bus. Dev. Specialist (918) 458-0802
Tahlequah, OK 74464 Fax: (918) 458-2105
E-mail: meigs@cherokee.nsuok.edu

Northwestern Oklahoma State University
Small Business Development Center
Mr. Guy Forell, Director (580) 327-8608
709 Oklahoma Blvd. Fax: (580) 327-0560
Alva, OK 73717
E-mail: gvfore@ranger2.nwalva.edu

Phillips University
Small Business Development Center
Mr. Bill Gregory, Coordinator (580) 242-7989
100 South University Avenue Fax: (580) 237-1607
Enid, OK 73701
E-mail: b9finger@enid.com

Rose State College Procurement Specialty Center—
Specialized Center
Small Business Development Center
Ms. Judy Robbins, Director (405) 733-7348
6420 Southeast 15th Street Fax: (405) 733-7495
Midwest City, OK 73110
E-mail: jrobbins@ms.rose.cc.ok.us

Southeastern Oklahoma State University
Small Business Development Center
Ms. Claire Livingston, Director (580) 924-0277
517 University Fax: (580) 920-7471
Durant, OK 74701
E-mail: clivingston@sosu.edu

Southwestern Oklahoma State University
Small Business Development Center
Mr. Chuck Felz, Director (580) 774-1040
100 Campus Drive Fax: (580) 774-7091
Weatherford, OK 73096
E-mail: sbdcswsu@brightok.net

Tulsa State Office Building
Small Business Development Center
Mr. Jeff Horvath, Director (918) 583-2600
616 South Boston Fax: (918) 599-6173
Tulsa, OK 74119
E-mail: jeffhorvath@tulsachamber.com

University of Central Oklahoma
Small Business Development Center
Ms. Susan Urbach, Director (405) 232-1968
115 Park Ave. Fax: (405) 232-1967
P.O. Box 1439
Oklahoma City, OK 73101-1439
E-mail: surbach@aix1.ucok.edu

Oregon

Oregon Small Business Development Center
LANE COMMUNITY COLLEGE—Lead Center
Dr. Sandy Cutler, State Director (541) 726-2250
44 West Broadway, Suite 501 Fax: (541) 345-6006
Eugene, OR 97401-3021
E-mail: cutlers@lanecc.edu

Blue Mountain Community College
Small Business Development Center
Mr. Gerald Wood, Director (541) 276-6233
37 SE Dorion Fax: (541) 276-6819
Pendleton, OR 97801
E-mail: jerry_wood@ortel.org

Central Oregon Community College
Small Business Development Center
Mr. Bob Newhart, Director (541) 383-7290
2600 NW College Way Fax: (541) 383-3445
Bend, OR 97701
E-mail: BDC@cocc.edu

Chemeketa Community College
Small Business Development Center
Mr. Tom Nelson, Director (503) 399-5088
365 Ferry Street SE Fax: (503) 581-6017
Salem, OR 97301
E-mail: nelt@chemek.cc.or.us

Clackamas Community College
Small Business Development Center
Ms. Jan Stennick, Director   (503) 656-4447
7616 SE Harmony Road   Fax: (503) 652-0389
Milwaukee, OR 97222
E-mail: jans@clackamas.cc.or.us

Clatstop Community College
Small Business Development Center
Mr. Paul Mallonee, Interim Director   (503) 738-3347
1761 N Holladay Drive   Fax: (503) 738-7843
Seaside, OR 97138

Columbia Gorge Community College
Small Business Development Center
Mr. Bob Cole, Director   (541) 298-3118
400 E. Scenic Drive, Suite 257   Fax: (503) 298-3119
The Dalles, OR 97058

Eastern Oregon State College
Small Business Development Center
Mr. John Prosnik, Jr., Director   (541) 962-3391
1410 L Avenue   Fax: (541) 962-3668
LaGrande, OR 97850
E-mail: prosnij@eosc.osshe.edu

International Trade Program—Specialized Center
Small Business Development Center
Mr. Tom Niland, Director   (503) 274-7482
Portland Community College   Fax: (503) 228-6350
121 SW Salmon Street, Suite 210
Portland, OR 97204
E-mail: tniland@pcc.edu
E-mail: tniland@ortel.com

Lane Community College
Small Business Development Center
Ms. Jane Scheidecker, Director   (541) 726-2255
1059 Williamette Street   Fax: (541) 686-0096
Eugene, OR 97401
E-mail: scheideckerj@lanecc.edu

Linn-Benton Community College
Small Business Development Center
Mr. Dennis Sargent, Director   (541) 917-4923
6500 SW Pacific Boulevard   Fax: (541) 917-4445
Albany, OR 97321
E-mail: Sargend@Peak.org
E-mail: sargend@gw.lbcc.cc.or.us

Mount Hood Community College
Small Business Development Center
Ms. Billi Jo Schmuck, Acting Director   (503) 667-7658
323 NE Roberts Street   Fax: (503) 666-1140
Gresham, OR 97030

Oregon Institute of Technology
Small Business Development Center
Ms. Jamie Albert, Director   (541) 885-1760
3201 Campus Drive, South 314   Fax: (541) 885-1855
Klamath Falls, OR 97601
E-mail: ALBERTJ@oit.osshe.edu

Oregon Coast Community College
Small Business Development Center   (541) 765-2515
Mr. Guy Faust, Director   (541) 994-4166
4157 NW Highway 101, Suite 123   Fax: (541) 996-4958
P.O. Box 419   (541) 265-2283
Lincoln City, OR 97367   ext. 122
Newport Office   Fax: (541) 265-3520

Portland Community College
Small Business Development Center
Mr. Robert Keyser, Director   (503) 978-5080
Montgomery Park, Suite 499   Fax: (503) 222-2570
2701 NW Vaughn Street
Portland, OR 97210

Rogue Community College
Small Business Development Center
Mr. Lee Merritt, Director   (541) 471-3515
214 SW Fourth Street   Fax: (541) 471-3589
Grants Pass, OR 97526
E-mail: sbdclee@MAGICK.NET

Southern Oregon State College/Medford
Small Business Development Center
Ms. Liz Shelby, Director   (541) 772-3478
Regional Services Institute   Fax: (541) 734-4813
332 West Sixth Street
Medford, OR 97501
E-mail: Shelby@wpo.sosc.osshe.edu

Southwestern Oregon Community College
Small Business Development Center
Mr. Jon Richards, Director   (541) 888-7100
2110 Newmark Avenue   Fax: (541) 888-7113
Coos Bay, OR 97420
E-mail: jrichards@ortel.org

Tillamook Bay Community College
Small Business Development Center
Ms. Kathy Wilkes, Director   (503) 842-2551
401 B Main Street   Fax: (503) 842-2555
Tillamook, OR 97141

Treasure Valley Community College
Small Business Development Center
Ms. Kathy Simko, Director   (541) 889-2617
88 SW Third Avenue   Fax: (541) 889-8331
Ontario, OR 97914
E-mail: simko@Mailman.tvcc.cc.or.us

Umpqua Community College
Small Business Development Center
Mr. Terry Swagerty, Director   (541) 672-2535
744 SE Rose   Fax: (541) 672-3679
Roseburg, OR 97470
E-mail: swagert@rosenet.net

Pennsylvania

Pennsylvania Small Business Development Center
UNIVERSITY OF PENNSYLVANIA—Lead Center
Mr. Gregory L. Higgins, Jr., State Director   (215) 898-1219
The Wharton School   Fax: (215) 573-2135
Vance Hall, 4th Floor
3733 Spruce Street
Philadelphia, PA 19104-6374
E-mail: pasbdc@wharton.upenn.edu
Web site: http://www.libertynet.org/pasbdc

Bucknell University
Small Business Development Center
Product Development Specialty Center
Dr. Charles Knisely, Director   (717) 524-1249
126 Dana Engineering Building   Fax: (717) 524-1768
Lewisburg, PA 17837
E-mail: SBDC@coral.bucknell.edu
Web site: http://www.bucknell.edu/~sbdc

Clarion University of Pennsylvania
Small Business Development Center
Dr. Woodrow Yeaney, Director   (814) 226-2060
102 Dana Still Building   Fax: (814) 226-2636
Clarion, PA 16214
Web site: http://www.libertynet.org/pasbdc/clarion

Duquesne University
Small Business Development Center
Dr. Mary T. McKinney, Director   (412) 396-6233
Rockwell Hall, Room 10 Concourse   Fax: (412) 396-5884
600 Forbes Avenue
Pittsburgh, PA 15282
E-mail: duqsbdc@duq.edu
Web site: http://www.duq.edu/SBDC/index2.html

Gannon University
Small Business Development Center
Mr. Ernie Post, Director   (814) 871-7714
A.J. Palumbo Academic Center   Fax: (814) 871-7383
University Square
Erie, PA 16541
Web site: http://www.libertynet.org/pasbdc/gannon

Indiana University
Small Business Development Center   (412) 357-7915
208 Eberly College of Business   Fax: (412) 357-5985
Indiana, PA 15705-1071

Kutztown University
Small Business Development Center   (717) 720-4230
2986 North Second Street   Fax: (717) 720-4262
Harrisburg, PA 17110
Web site: http://www.libertynet.org/pasbdc/kutztown

Lehigh University
Small Business Development Center
Mr. Larry Strain, Director   (610) 758-3980
Rauch Business Center #37   Fax: (610) 758-5205
621 Taylor Street
Bethlehem, PA 18015
Web site: http://www.lehigh.edu/~insbdc

Pennsylvania State University
Small Business Development Center   (814) 865-0427
Ms. Donna Holmes, Director   Fax: (814) 865-5909
117 Technology Center
University Park, PA 16827

Saint Vincent College
Small Business Development Center
Mr. Jack Fabean, Director   (412) 537-4572
Alfred Hall, Fourth Floor   Fax: (412) 537-0919
300 Fraser Purchase Road
Latrobe, PA 15650
Web site: http://www.libertynet.org/pasbdc/vincent

St. Francis College
Small Business Development Center
Mr. Edward Huttenhower, Director   (814) 472-3200
Business Resource Center   Fax: (814) 472-3202
Loretto, PA 15940
Web site: http://www.libertynet.org/pasbdc/francis

Temple University
Small Business Development Center
Ms. Geraldine Perkins, Director   (215) 204-7282
1510 Cecil B. Moore Avenue   Fax: (215) 204-4554
Philadelphia, PA 19121
Web site: http://www.temple.edu/department/SBDC

University of Pittsburgh
Small Business Development Center
Ms. Ann Dugan, Director   (412) 648-1544
208 Bellefield Hall   Fax: (412) 648-1636
315 South Bellefield Avenue
Pittsburgh, PA 15213
E-mail: sbdc+@pitt.edu
Web site: http://www.pitt.edu/~sbdc

University of Pennsylvania
Small Business Development Center
Mr. Paul Morin, Director   (215) 898-4861
The Wharton School   Fax: (215) 898-1063
409 Vance Hall
3733 Spruce Street
Philadelphia, PA 19104-6374
Web site: http://www.libertynet.org/pasbdc/wharton

University of Scranton
Small Business Development Center   (800) 829-7232
Ms. Elaine M. Tweedy, Director   (717) 941-7588
St. Thomas Hall, Room 588   Fax: (717) 941-4053
Scranton, PA 18510-4639
Web site: http://www.libertynet.org/pasbdc/scranton

West Chester University
Small Business Development Center   (610) 436-2162
Mr. Bob Scanlon, Director   Fax: (610) 436-2577
211 Carter Drive
West Chester, PA 19383

Wilkes University
Small Business Development Center
Dr. Jeffrey Ross Alves, Director   (717) 408-4340
Hollenbeck Hall   Fax: (717) 824-2245
192 South Franklin Street
Wilkes-Barre, PA 18766-0001
E-mail: sbdc@wilkes1.wilkes.edu
Web site: wilkes1.wilkes.edu/~sbdc

Puerto Rico

Puerto Rico Small Business Development Center
Edificio Union Plaza, Suite 701
Carmen Marti, Executive Director   (787) 763-6811
416 Ponce De Leon Avenue   Fax: (787) 763-4629
Hato Rey, PR 00918
E-mail: cmarti@ns.inter.edu

Arecibo Regional Center
Inter American University Arecibo Campus
Ms. Wanda Vega Rosado, Regional   (787) 878-5475
   Director   ext. 2236
P.O. Box 4050   Fax: (787) 880-1624
Arecibo, PR 00614
E-mail: wanvega@ns.inter.edu

Fajardo Regional Center
Inter American University Fajardo Campus
Ms. Joy C. Vilardi de Camacho, Regional   (787) 863-2390
   Director   ext. 2219
P.O. Box 70003   Fax: (787) 860-3470
Fajardo, PR 00738
E-mail: jvilardi@ns.inter.edu

Ponce Regional Center
Inter American University Ponce Campus
Mr. Carlos Maldonado, Regional   (787) 284-1912
   Director   ext. 2023
Carr.#1, Km. 123.2   Fax: (787) 841-0103
Mercedita, PR 00715
E-mail: carmaldo@ns.inter.edu

San German Regional Center
Inter American University San German Campus
Mr. Luis E. Valderrama, Regional Director   (787) 264-1912
P.O. Box 5100   ext. 7715
San German, PR 00683   Fax: (787) 892-6350
E-mail: lvalderr@ns.inter.edu

San Juan Regional Center
Dr. Mario Sverdlik, Regional Director
Union Plaza Building, Suite 701   (787) 763-5108
416 Ponce de Leon Avenue   Fax: (787) 763-4629
Hato Rey, PR 00918
E-mail: msverdik@ns.inter.edu

Rhode Island

Bryant College—Lead Center
Small Business Development Center
Douglas H. Jobling, State Director   (401) 232-6111
1150 Douglas Pike   Fax: (401) 232-6933
Smithfield, RI 02917-1284

Northern RI Chamber of Commerce   (401) 334-1000
Sheila Hoogeboom, Case Manager   ext. 113
6 Blackstone Valley Place, Suite 105   Fax: (401) 334-1009
Lincoln, Rl 02865-1105

South County Office
Liz Kroll, Case Manager
South County RISBDC, QP/D Industrial Park   (401) 294-1227
35 Belver Avenue # 212   Fax: (401) 294-6897
N. Kingstown, Rl 02852-7556

Greater Providence Chamber of Commerce
Erwin Robinson, Program Manager
Bryant College RISBDC   (401) 831-1330
30 Exchange Terrace 4th floor   Fax: (401) 274-5410
Providence, RI 02903-1793

East Bay Office
Sam Carr, Case Manager
East Bay RISBDC
Newport County Chamber of Commerce   (401) 849-6900
45 Valley Road   Fax: (401) 849-5848
Middletown, Rl 02842-6377

Central RI Chamber of Commerce
Thomas J. Moakley, Case Manager   (401) 732-1100
3288 Post Road   Fax: (401) 732-1107
Warwick, RI 02886-7151

NYNEX Telecommunications Center
Kate Dolan, Managing Director
Bryant College Koffler Technology Center   (401) 232-0220
1150 Douglas Pike   Fax: (401) 232-0242
Smithfield, Rl 02917-1284

Enterprise Community RISBDC/BIC
Jaime Aguayo/Ann-Marie Marshall   (401) 272-1083
550 Broad Street   Fax: (401) 272-1186
Providence, Rl 02905-1445

R.I. Department of Transportation
O.J. Silas, Program Manager
RIDOT/SBDC Supportive Services Program (401) 277-4576
2 Capitol Hill, Room 106   Fax: (401) 277-6168
Providence, Rl 02903-1111

Export Assistance Center
Raymond Fogarty, Director
Bryant College EAC   (401) 232-6407
1150 Douglas Pike   Fax: (401) 232-6416
Smithfield, Rl 02917-1284

Bristol County Chamber of Commerce
Sam Carr, Case Manager   (401) 245-0750
PO Box 250   Fax: (401) 245-0110
Warren, Rl 02885-0250

Entrepreneurship Training Program
Bryant College
Cheryl Faria, Assistant Director
Dennis McCarthy, Program Manager   (401) 232-6115
1150 Douglas Pike   Fax: (401) 232-6933
Smithfield, RI 02917-1284

South Carolina

South Carolina Small Business Development Center
UNIVERSITY OF SOUTH CAROLINA—Lead Center
Mr. John Lenti, State Director   (803) 777-4907
College of Business Administration   Fax: (803) 777-4403
Hipp Building
1710 College Street
Columbia, SC 29208
E-mail: lenti@darla.badm.sc.edu

University of South Carolina—Aiken
Small Business Development Center
Vacant, Area Manager   (803) 641-3646
171 University Parkway, Suite 100   Fax: (803) 641-3647
School of Business
Aiken, SC 29801
E-mail: BillieW@Aiken.sc.edu

Charleston Small Business Development Center
Mr. Bill R. Pointer, Area Manager   (803) 740-6160
5900 Core Drive, Suite 104   Fax: (803) 740-1607
North Charleston, SC 29406
E-mail: Pointer@infoave.net

Clemson Regional Small Business Development Center
Ms. Rebecca Hobart, Regional Director   (864) 656-3227
Ms. Jill Burroughs, Area Manager   Fax: (864) 656-4869
Clemson University
College of Business & Public Affairs

425 Sirrine Hall
Clemson, SC 29634-1392
E-mail: HobartR@clemson.edu
E-mail: JillB@clemson.edu

Conway Small Business Development Center
Ms. Nancy Robinson, Area Manager   (803) 349-2170
Coastal Carolina University   Fax: (803) 349-2455
School of Business Administration
Wall Building, Suite 111, P.O. Box 261954
Conway, SC 29528-6054
E-mail: Robinson@coastal.edu

Florence Darlington Technical College
Small Business Development Center
Mr. David Raines, Area Manager   (803) 661-8256
P.O. Box 100548   Fax: (803) 661-8041
Florence, SC 29501-0548
E-mail: RainesD@A1.flo.tec.sc.us

Greenville Small Business Development Center
Ms. Susan Dunlap, Area Manager   (864) 250-8894
University Center   Fax: (803) 250-8897
216 S. Pleasantburg Drive, Room 140
Greenville, SC 29607
E-mail: Sdunlap@clemson.edu

South Carolina State University#
Small Business Development Center
Mr. John W. Gadson, Regional Director   (803) 536-8445
Mr. Francis Heape, Area Manager   Fax: (803) 536-8066
School of Business; Algernon S. Belcher Hall
300 College Street, Campus Box 7176
Orangeburg, SC 29117
E-mail: Jgadson@scsu.edu
E-mail: Fheape@scsu.edu

University of South Carolina
Small Business Development Center
Mr. James L. Brazell, Regional Director
Vacant, Area Manager   (803) 777-5118
College of Business Administration   Fax: (803) 777-4403
Columbia, SC 29208-9980
E-mail: Brazell@darla.badm.sc.edu

University of South Carolina/Beaufort
Small Business Development Center
Mr. Martin Goodman, Area Manager   (803) 521-4143
801 Carteret Street   Fax: (803) 521-4142
Beaufort, SC 29902
E-mail: Goodman@hargray.com

University of South Carolina/Hilton Head
Small Business Development Center
Pat Cameron, Consultant   (803) 785-3995
1 College Center Drive   Fax: (803) 785-3995
Hilton Head Island, SC 29928
E-mail: Cameron@hargray.com

©JIST Works, Inc., Indianapolis, IN 46202

Upper Savannah Council of Government
Small Business Development Center
Mr. George Long, Area Manager   (864) 941-8071
SBDC Exchange Bldg.   Fax: (864) 941-8090
222 Phoenix Street, P.O. Box 1366
Greenwood, SC 29648
E-mail: Glong@emeraldis.com

Winthrop University
Small Business Development Center
Mr. Nate Barber, Regional Director
Ms. Dianne Hockett, Area Manager   (803) 323-2283
School of Business Administration   Fax: (803) 323-4281
118 Thurmond Building
Rock Hill, SC 29733
E-mail: BarberN@winthrop.edu
E-mail: HockettD@winthrop.edu

University of South Carolina—Sumter
Small Business Development Center
Lee Eron, Consultant   (803) 775-6341
200 Miller Road   Fax: (803) 775-2180
Sumter, SC 29150-2498
E-mail: Leron@uscsumter.uscsu.sc.edu

Small Business Development Center
Williamsburg Enteprise Community
Ms. Nicole Singleton, Area Manager   (803) 354-9070
P.O. Box 428   Fax: (803) 354-3252
128 Mill Street
Kingstree, SC 29556
E-mail: nsinglet@webplanets.com

Spartanburg Small Business Development Center
Mr. David Tinsley, Area Manager   (864) 250-8894
University Center   Fax: (864) 250-8897
216 S. Pleasantburg Drive, Room 140
Greenville, SC 29607
E-mail: Dtinsle@clemson.edu

South Dakota

South Dakota Small Business Development Center
UNIVERSITY OF SOUTH DAKOTA—Lead Center
Mr. Robert E. Ashley, Jr., State Director   (605) 677-5498
School of Business   Fax: (605) 677-5272
414 East Clark Street
Vermillion, SD 57069-2390
E-mail: rashley@iw.net

Northeast Region Small Business Development Center
Ms. Belinda G. Engelhart, Regional Director (605) 626-2565
620 15th Avenue SE   Fax: (605) 626-2667
Aberdeen, SD 57401

Sioux Falls Region
Small Business Development Center
Mr. Wade D. Druin, Regional Director   (605) 367-5757
405 S. Third Avenue, Suite 101   Fax: (605) 367-5755
Sioux Falls, SD 57104

Sioux Falls Region
Small Business Development Center
Mr. Matthew D. Johnson,   (605) 367-5757
  Assistant State Director
405 S. Third Avenue, Suite 101   Fax: (605) 367-5755
Sioux Falls, SD 57104
E-mail: mdjohnso@sundance.usd.edu

Western Region Small Business Development Center
Ms. Valerie S. Simpson, Regional Director   (605) 394-5311
444 North Mt. Rushmore, Suite 208   Fax: (605) 394-6140
Rapid City, SD 57701

Tennessee

Tennessee Small Business Development Center
UNIVERSITY OF MEMPHIS—Lead Center
Dr. Kenneth J. Burns, State Director   (901) 678-2500
South Campus (Getwell Road)   Fax: (901) 678-4072
Building #1
Memphis, TN 38152-0001

Austin Peay State University
Small Business Development Center
Mr. John Volker, Director   (615) 648-7764
College of Business   Fax: (615) 648-6316
Clarksville, TN 37044-0001

Chattanooga State Technical Community College
Small Business Development Center
Ms. Donna Marsh,   (423) 752-1774
  Small Business Specialist   Fax: (423) 752-1925
100 Cherokee Blvd., Suite 202
Chattanooga, TN 37405-3878

Cleveland State Community College
Small Business Development Center
Mr. Don Geren, Director   (423) 478-6247
Adkisson Drive   Fax: (423) 478-6251
P.O. Box 3570
Cleveland, TN 37320-3570

Dyersburg State Community College
Small Business Development Center
Mr. Bob Wylie, Senior Business Specialist   (901) 286-3201
Office of Extension Services   Fax: (901) 286-3271
1510 Lake Road
Dyersburg, TN 38024-2450

East Tennessee State University
Small Business Development Center
Mr. Bob Justice, Director   (423) 439-5630
College of Business   Fax: (423) 439-7080
P.O. 70698
Johnson City, TN 37614-0698

East Tennessee State University
Small Business Development Center
Mr. Rob Lytle, Business Counselor   (423) 392-8017
Kingsport University Center   Fax: (423) 392-8017
1501 University Boulevard
Kingsport, TN 37660-8488

Four Lakes Regional Industrial Development Authority
Small Business Development Center
Ms. Dorothy Vaden, Small Business   (615) 374-9521
  Specialist   Fax: (615) 374-4608
P.O. Box 63
Hartsville, TN 37074-0063

International Trade Center—Specialized Center
Small Business Development Center
Mr. Richard Vogler, IT Specialist   (423) 637-4283
301 East Church Avenue   Fax: (423) 523-2071
Knoxville, TN 37915-2572

International Trade Center—Specialized Center
Small Business Development Center
Mr. Philip Johnson, Director   (901) 678-4174
University of Memphis   Fax: (901) 678-4072
Memphis, TN 38152-0001

Jackson State Community College
Small Business Development Center
Mr. David L. Brown, Business Counselor   (901) 424-5389
2046 North Parkway Street   Fax: (901) 425-2647
Jackson, TN 38305-3797

Middle Tennessee State University
Small Business Development Center
Mr. Patrick Geho, Director   (615) 898-2745
Rutherford County Chamber of   Fax: (615) 893-7089
  Commerce Bldg.
501 Memorial Blvd.
Murfreesboro, TN 37129-0001

Pellissippi State Technical Community College
Small Business Development Center
Ms. Teri Brahams, Director   (423) 525-0277
Chamber of Commerce   Fax: (423) 971-4439
301 East Church Avenue
Knoxville, TN 37915-2572

Small Business Development Center
Mr. Eugene Osekowsky, Business Specialist   (615) 898-2745
P.O. Box 8069   Fax: (615) 893-7089
Columbia, TN 38402

Southeast Tennessee Development District
Small Business Development Center
Ms. Sherri E. Bishop, Business Specialist   (423) 266-5781
P.O. Box 4757   Fax: (423) 267-7705
25 Cherokee Blvd.
Chattanooga, TN 37405-0757

Tennessee State University#
Small Business Development Center
Mr. Billy E. Lowe, Director   (615) 963-7179
College of Business   Fax: (615) 963-7160
330 Tenth Avenue North
Nashville, TN 37203-3401

University of Memphis
Small Business Development Center
Mr. Earnest Lacey, Director   (901) 527-1041
320 South Dudley Street   Fax: (901) 527-1047
Memphis, TN 38104-3206

Walters State Community College
Small Business Development Center
Mr. Jack Tucker, Director   (423) 585-2675
500 South Davy Crockett Parkway   Fax: (423) 585-2679
Morristown, TN 37813-6889

Tennessee Small Business Development Center
Mr. Dan Collier, Business Specialist   (423) 483-2668
Technology 2020 Office   Fax: (423) 220-2030
1020 Commerce Park Drive
Oak Ridge, TN 37830-8026

Tennessee Small Business Development Center
Dr. Paul Jennings, Director   (901) 678-4057
Technology and Energy Services   Fax: (901) 678-4072
The University of Memphis
Memphis, TN 38152-0001

Texas

North Texas Small Business Development Center
DALLAS COUNTY COMMUNITY COLLEGE—Lead Center
Ms. Liz Klimback, Regional Director   (800) 350-7232
1402 Corinth Street   (214) 860-5835
Dallas, TX 75215   Fax: (214) 860-5813

Best Southwest Small Business Development Center
Mr. Neil Small, Director   (800) 317-7232
214 South Main, Suite 102A   (972) 709-5878
Duncanville, TX 75116   Fax: (972) 709-6089

Center for Government Contracting/Technology Assistance Center
Small Business Development Center
Mr. Gerald Chandler, Director   (800) 348-7232
1402 Corinth Street   (214) 860-5841
Dallas, TX 75215   Fax: (214) 860-5881

Courtyard Center for Professional and Economic Development
Small Business Development Center
Ms. Chris Jones, Director (972) 985-3770
4800 Preston Park Boulevard Fax: (972) 985-3775
Suite A126/Box 15
Plano, TX 75093

Dallas County Community College
Small Business Development Center
Mr. Earnest Castillo, Director (214) 860-5850
1402 Corinth Street Fax: (214) 860-5881
Dallas, TX 75215

Grayson County College
Small Business Development Center
Ms. Karen Stidham, Director (800) 316-7232
6101 Grayson Drive (903) 463-8787
Denison, TX 75020 Fax: (903) 463-5437

Bonham Satellite Small Business Development Center
Mr. Darroll Martin, Coordinator (903) 583-7565
Sam Rayburn Library Fax: (903) 583-6706
1201 E. 9th St., Bldg. 2
Bonham, TX 75418

International Assistance Center—Specialized Center
Small Business Development Center
Ms. Beth Huddleston, Director (800) 337-7232
World Trade Center, Suite #150 (214) 747-1300
2050 Stemmons Freeway Fax: (214) 748-5774
P.O. Box 58299
Dallas, TX 75258

Kilgore College Small Business Development Center
Mr. Brad Bunt, Director (800) 338-7232
Triple Creek Shopping Plaza (903) 757-5857
110 Triple Creek Drive, Suite #70 Fax: (903) 753-7920
Longview, TX 75601

McLennan Community College
Small Business Development Center
Ms. Lu Billings, Director (800) 349-7232
401 Franklin (254) 714-0077
Waco, TX 76701 Fax: (254) 714-1668

Navarro Small Business Development Center
Mr. Leon Allard, Director (800) 320-7232
120 North 12th Street (903) 874-0658
Corsicana, TX 75110 Fax: (903) 874-4187

North Central Texas College
Small Business Development Center
Ms. Cathy Keeler, Director (800) 351-7232
1525 West California (254) 668-4220
Gainesville, TX 76240 Fax: (254) 668-6049

Denton Satellite Small Business Development Center
Ms. Carolyn Birkhead, Coordinator (254) 380-1849
P.O. Drawer P Fax: (254) 382-0040
Denton, TX 76201

Northeast/Texarkana Small Business Development Center
Mr. Bob Wall, Director (800) 357-7232
P.O. Box 1307 (903) 572-1911
Mt. Pleasant, TX 75455 Fax: (903) 572-0598
Web site: http://www.bizcoach.org

Paris Junior College
Small Business Development Center
Ms. Pat Bell, Director (903) 784-1802
2400 Clarksville Street Fax: (903) 784-1801
Paris, TX 75460

Tarrant County Junior College
Small Business Development Center
Mr. David Edmonds, Director (817) 871-6028
7917 Highway 80 West Fax: (817) 871-0031
Ft. Worth, TX 76102
MAILING ADDRESS:
 1500 Houston Street, Room 163
 Ft. Worth, TX 76102

Small Business Development Center for Enterprise Excellence
Ms. Jo-An Weddle, Director (817) 272-5930
7300 Jack Newell Boulevard, South Fax: (817) 272-5952
Fort Worth, TX 76118

Trinity Valley Community College
Small Business Development Center
Ms. Judy Loden, Director (800) 335-7232
500 South Prairieville (903) 675-7403
Athens, TX 75751 Fax: (903) 675-5199

Tyler Junior College
Small Business Development Center
Mr. Frank Viso, Director (903) 510-2975
1530 South SW Loop 323, Suite 100 Fax: (903) 510-2978
Tyler, TX 75701

Texas Gulf Coast Small Business Development Center
UNIVERSITY OF HOUSTON—Lead Center
Dr. Elizabeth Gatewood, Executive Director (713) 752-8444
1100 Louisiana, Suite 500 Fax: (713) 756-1500
Houston, TX 77002

Angelina Community College
Small Business Development Center
Mr. Brian McClain, Director (409) 639-1887
P.O. Box 1768 Fax: (409) 639-3863
Lufkin, TX 75902

Blinn College
Small Business Development Center
Ms. Phillis Nelson, Director   (409) 830-4137
902 College Avenue   Fax: (409) 830-4135
Brenham, TX 77833

Bryan College Station
Small Business Development Center
Mr. Sam Harwell, Director   (409) 260-5222
4001 East 29th Street, Suite 175   Fax: (409) 260-5229
Bryan, TX 77805
MAILING ADDRESS:
  P.O. Box 3695
  Bryan, TX 77805-3695
Web site: http://www.bvsbdc.org

Brazosport College Small Business Development Center
Ms. Patricia Leyendecker, Director   (409) 266-3380
500 College Drive   Fax: (409) 266-3482
Lake Jackson, TX 77566

College of the Mainland   (409)-938-1211
Small Business Development Center   ext. 494
Ms. Elizabeth Boudreau, Director   (281) 280-3991
1200 Amburn Road   ext. 494
Texas City, TX 77591   Fax: (409) 938-7578

Galveston College Small Business Development Center
Ms. Georgette Peterson, Director   (409) 740-7380
5001 Avenue U   Fax: (409) 740-7381
Galveston, TX 77550
MAILING ADDRESS:
  4015 Avenue Q
  Galveston, TX 77550

Houston Community College System
Small Business Development Center
Mr. Joe Harper, Director   (281) 933-7932
10405 Stancliff, Suite 100   Fax: (281) 568-3690
Houston, TX 77099

UH International Trade Center—Specialized Center
Small Business Development Center
Mr. Carlos Lopez, Director   (713) 752-8404
University of Houston   Fax: (713) 756-1515
1100 Louisiana, Suite 500
Houston, TX 77002

Lamar University
Small Business Development Center
Mr. Gene Arnold, Director   (409) 880-2367
855 Florida Avenue   Fax: (409) 880-2201
Beaumont, TX 77705

Lee College Small Business Development Center
Mr. Tommy Hathaway, Director   (281) 425-6309
200 Lee Drive   Fax: (281) 425-6307
Rundell Hall
Baytown, TX 77522-0818
MAILING ADDRESS:
  P.O. Box 818
  Baytown, TX 77522-0818

North Harris Montgomery County College District
Small Business Development Center
Ms. Kay Hamilton, Director   (281) 933-7932
250 North Sam Houston Parkway East   Fax: (281) 591-9374
Houston, TX 77060

Sam Houston State University
Small Business Development Center
Mr. Bob Barragan, Director   (409) 294-3737
843 South Sam Houston Avenue   Fax: (409) 294-3738
Huntsville, TX 77341
MAILING ADDRESS:
  P.O. Box 2058
  Huntsville, TX 77341-2058

UH Texas Information Procurement Service—Specialized
Center
University of Houston
Small Business Development Center
Ms. Jacqueline Taylor, Director   (800) 252-7232
1100 Louisiana, Suite 500   (713) 752-8477
Houston, TX 77002   Fax: (713) 756-1515

Wharton County Junior College
Small Business Development Center
Mr. Lynn Polson, Director   (409) 532-0604
Administration Building, Room 102   Fax: (409) 532-2410
911 Boling Highway
Wharton, TX 77488-0080

Northwestern Texas Small Business Development Center
TEXAS TECH UNIVERSITY—Lead Center
Mr. Craig Bean, Regional Director   (806) 745-3973
Spectrum Plaza   Fax: (806) 745-6207
2579 South Loop 289, Suite 114
Lubbock, TX 79423
E-mail: odbea@ttacs.ttu.edu

Abilene Christian University
Caruth Small Business Development Center
Ms. Judy Wilhelm, Director   (915) 670-0300
College of Business Administration   Fax: (915) 670-0311
648 East Highway 80
Abilene, TX 79601

Midwestern State University
Small Business Development Center
Mr. Tim Thomas, Director   (817) 689-4373
3410 Taft Boulevard   Fax: (817) 689-4374
Wichita Falls, TX 76308

Tarleton State University
Small Business Development Center
Mr. Rusty Freed, Director   (817) 689-4373
College of Business Administration   Fax: (817) 689-4374
Box T-0650
Stephenville, TX 76402

Texas Tech University
Small Business Development Center
Mr. Steve Anderson, Director   (806) 745-1637
Spectrum Plaza   Fax: (806) 745-6717
2579 South Loop 289, Suite 210
Lubbock, TX 79423

University of Texas/Permian Basin
Small Business Development Center
Mr. Karl Painter, Director   (915) 552-2455
4901 East University   Fax: (915) 552-2433
Odessa, TX 79762

West Texas A&M University
Small Business Development Center
Mr. Don Taylor, Director   (806) 372-5151
T. Boone Pickens School of Business   Fax: (806) 372-5261
1800 South Washington, Suite 209
Amarillo, TX 79102

South Texas Border Small Business Development Center
UNIVERSITY OF TEXAS AT SAN ANTONIO DOWNTOWN—
Lead Center
Mr. Robert McKinley, Regional Director   (210) 458-2450
USTA Downtown   Fax: (210) 458-2464
1222 North Main, Suite 450
San Antonio, TX 78212
E-mail: rmckinley@utsa.edu

Angelo State University
Small Business Development Center
Ms. Patti Warrington, Director   (915) 942-2098
2610 West Avenue N   Fax: (915) 942-2096
Campus Box 10910
San Angelo, TX 76909

Greater Corpus Christi Business Alliance
Small Business Development Center
Mr. Oscar Martinez, Director   (512) 881-1847
1201 North Shoreline   Fax: (512) 882-4256
Corpus Christi, TX 78403

El Paso Community College
Small Business Development Center
Mr. Roque R. Segura, Director   (915) 534-3410
103 Montana Avenue, Suite 202   Fax: (915) 534-4625
El Paso, TX 79902-3929

International Trade Center—Specialized Center
University of Texas at San Antonio
Small Business Development Center
Ms. Sara Jackson, Director   (210) 458-2470
1222 North Main, Suite 450   Fax: (210) 458-2464
San Antonio, TX 78212

Kingsville Chamber of Commerce
Small Business Development Center
Ms. Elizabeth Soliz, Director   (512) 595-5088
635 East King   Fax: (512) 592-0866
Kingsville, TX 78363

Laredo Development Foundation
Small Business Development Center
Mr. David Puig, Director   (210) 722-0563
616 Leal Street   Fax: (210) 722-6247
Laredo, TX 78041

Lower Colorado River Authority
Small Business Development Center
Mr. Larry Lucero, Director   (512) 473-3510
3700 Lake Austin Boulevard   Fax: (512) 473-3285
Jack Miller Bldg Mail Stop M104
Austin, TX 78767

Middle Rio Grande Development Council
Small Business Development Center
Mr. Mario Riojas, Director   (210) 278-2527
209 North Getty Street   Fax: (210) 278-2929
Uvalde, TX 78801

Sul Ross State University
Small Business Development Center
Mr. Michael Levine, Director   (915) 837-8694
P.O. Box C-47, Room 319   Fax: (915) 837-8104
Alpine, TX 79832

Technology Center—Specialized Center
Small Business Development Center
Ms. Judith Ingalls, Director   (210) 458-2458
University of Texas at San Antonio   Fax: (210) 458-2464
1222 North Main, Suite 450
San Antonio, TX 78212

University of Houston-Victoria
Small Business Development Center
Ms. Carole Parks, Director   (512) 575-8944
700 Main Center, Suite 102   Fax: (512) 575-8852
Victoria, TX 79901
E-mail: parks@jade.vic.uh.edu

University of Texas-Pan American
Small Business Development Center
Mr. Juan Garcia, Director   (210) 316-2610
1201 West University   Fax: (210) 316-2612
Edinburg, TX 78539-2999

University of Texas at San Antonio Downtown
Small Business Development Center
Mr. Morrison Woods, Director   (210) 458-2460
1222 North Main, Suite 450   Fax: (210) 458-2464
San Antonio, TX 78212

Lower Colorado River Authority Coastal Plains
Small business Development Center
Ms. Lynn Polson, Director   (409) 532-1007
301 West Milam   Fax: (409) 532-0056
Wharton, TX 77488
Mailing Address:
 P.O. Box 148
 Wharton, TX 77488

Middle Rio Grande Development Council
Small Business Development Center
Mr. Patrick Gibbons, Director   (210) 278-2527
209 North Getty Street   Fax: (210) 278-2929
Uvalde, TX 78801

Utah

Lead Center
Small Business Development Center
Salt Lake Community College
Mr. Mike Finnerty, State Director   (801) 957-3480
1623 South State Street   Fax: (801) 957-3489
Salt Lake City, UT 84115
E-mail: FinnerMi@slcc.edu

South City Center (Salt Lake City)
Small Business Development Center
Salt Lake Community College
Ms. Pamela Hunt, Regional Director   (801) 957-3480
1623 South State Street   Fax: (801) 957-3489
Salt Lake City, UT 84115
E-mail: HuntPa@slcc.edu

Price Center
South Eastern Utah AOG
Small Business Development Center
Mr. Dennis Rigby, Regional Director   (801) 637-5444
P.O. Box 1106   Fax: (801) 637-4102
Price, UT 84501
E-mail: drigby@seuaognet.seuaog.dst.ut.us

St. George Center
Dixie College Small Business Development Center
Ms. Jill Ellis, Regional Director   (801) 652-7751
225 South 700 East   Fax: (801) 652-7870
St. George, UT 84770
E-mail: ellissj@dixie.edu

Ephraim Center
Snow College Small Business Development Center
Mr. Russell Johnson, Regional Director   (801) 283-6890
345 West 100 North   Fax: (801) 283-6913
Ephraim, UT 84627
E-mail: russel_johnson@snow.edu

Cedar City Center
Southern Utah University
Small Business Development Center
Mr. Derek Snow, Regional Director   (801) 586-5400
351 West Center   Fax: (801) 586-5493
Cedar City, UT 84720
E-mail: snow@suu.edu

Roosevelt/Vernal Center
Utah State University Extension Office
Small Business Development Center
Regional Director, Vacant   (801) 722-2294
987 East Lagoon Street   Fax: (801) 722-5804
Roosevelt, UT 84066

Logan Center
Utah State University
Small Business Development Center
Mr. Franklin C. Prante, Regional Director   (801) 797-2277
East Campus Building, Room 24   Fax: (801) 797-3317
Logan, UT 84322-8330
E-mail: fprante@ext.usu.edu

Orem/Provo Center
Utah Valley State College
Small Business Development Center
Mr. Charles Cozzens, Regional Director   (801) 222-8230
800 West 1200 South   Fax: (801) 225-1229
Orem, UT 84058
E-mail: Cozzench@uvsc.edu

Ogden Center
Weber State University
Small Business Development Center
Mr. Bruce Davis, Regional Director   (801) 626-7232
College of Business and Economics   Fax: (801) 626-7423
Ogden, UT 84720
E-mail: BrDavis@weber.edu

Blanding/Moab/Monticello Center
Small Business Development Center
Mr. Bill Olderog, Regional Director
College of Eastern Utah   (801) 678-2201
639 West 100 South   ext. 130
Blanding, UT 84511

Sandy Center
Small Business Development Center
Salt Lake Community College
Mr. Barry Bartlett, Regional Director   (801) 255-5878
8811 South 700 East   Fax: (801) 255-6393
Sandy, UT 84070
E-mail: BartleBa@slcc.edu

Vermont

Vermont Small Business Development Center
VERMONT TECHNICAL COLLEGE—Lead Center
Mr. Donald L. Kelpinski, State Director   (800) 464-SBDC
P.O. Box 422   (802) 728-9101
Randolph Center, VT 05060-0422   Fax: (802) 728-3026
E-mail: dkelpins@vtc.vsc.edu

Addison County Economic Development Corp.
Small Business Development Center
Mr. James B. Stewart, Executive Director   (802) 388-7953
RD #4, Box 1309 A   Fax: (802) 388-0119
Middlebury, VT 05753
E-mail: acedc@sover.net

Bennington County Industrial Corporation
Small Business Development Center
Mr. Lance Matteson, Executive Director   (802) 442-8975
P.O. Box 357   Fax: (802) 447-1101
No. Bennington, VT 05257-0357
E-mail: lance@bcic.org

Brattleboro Development Credit Corporation
Small Business Development Center
Mr. William McGrath, Executive V.P.   (802) 257-7731
72 Cotton Mill Hill   Fax: (802) 257-0294
Brattleboro, VT 05301-1177
E-mail: bdcc@sover.net

Central Vermont Economic Development Corporation
Small Business Development Center
Mr. Richard Angney, Executive Director   (802) 223-4654
P.O. Box 1439   Fax: (802) 223-4655
Montpelier, VT 05601-1439
E-mail: cvedc@plainfield.bypass.com

Franklin County Industrial Development Corporation
Small Business Development Center
Mr. Timothy J. Soule, Executive Director   (802) 524-2194
P.O. Box 1099   Fax: (802) 524-6793
St. Albans, VT 05478-1099
E-mail: fcidc@together.net

Greater Burlington Industrial Corporation
Northwest Vermont Small Business Development Center—
Specialized Center
Mr. Thomas D. Schroeder, SBDC Specialist   (802) 658-9228
Mr. Norbert Lavigne, President   Fax: (802) 860-1899

P.O. Box 786
Burlington, VT 05402-0786
E-mail: gbic@vermont.org

Green Mountain Economic Development Corporation
Central Vermont Small Business Development Center—
Specialized Center
Mr. Jim Saudade, Executive Director
Ms. Lenae Quillen-Blume, SBDC Specialist   (802) 295-3710
P.O. Box 246   Fax: (802) 295-3779
White River Jct., VT 05001-0246
E-mail: gmedc@aol.com

Lake Champlain Islands Chamber of Commerce
Small Business Development Center
Ms. Barbara Mooney, Executive Director   (802) 372-5683
P.O. Box 213   Fax: (802) 372-3205
North Hero, VT 05474-0213
E-mail: ilandfun@together.net

Lamoille Economic Development Corporation
Small Business Development Center
Mr. John Sullivan, Executive Director   (802) 888-5640
P.O. Box 455   Fax: (802) 888-7612
Morrisville, VT 05661-0455
E-mail: ledc@together.net

Northeastern Vermont Development Assn.
Northeastern Vermont Small Business Development
Center—Specialized Center
Mr. Joseph P. Wynne, SBDC Specialist   (802) 748-1014
Mr. Charles E. Carter, Executive   Fax: (802) 748-1223
  Director
P.O. Box 630
St. Johnsbury, VT 05819-0630
E-mail: nvda@plainfield.bypass.com

Rutland Economic Development Corporation
Southwestern Vermont Small Business Development
Center—Specialized Center
Ms. Wendy Wilton, SBDC Specialist   (802) 773-9147
Mr. David O'Brien, Executive Director   Fax: (802) 773-2772
256 North Main Street
Rutland, VT 05701
E-mail: wwilton@vtc.vsc.edu

Springfield Regional Development Corporation
Southeastern Vermont Small Business Development
Center—Specialized Center
Mr. Steve Casabona, SBDC Specialist   (802) 885-2071
Ms. Pat Moulton-Powden, Executive   Fax: (802) 885-3027
  Director
P.O. Box 58
Springfield, VT 05156-0058
E-mail: srdc@sover.net

Virgin Islands

Virgin Islands Small Business Development Center
UNIVERSITY OF THE VIRGIN ISLANDS—Lead Center
Mr. Chester Williams, Director   (809) 776-3206
8000 Nisky Center, Suite 202   Fax: (809) 775-3756
Charlotte Amalie
St. Thomas, U.S. Virgin Islands 00802-5804

University of the Virgin Islands
Small Business Development Center
Mr. Ian Hodge, Director   (809) 778-8270
United Shopping Plaza   Fax: (809) 778-7629
Suite #5, Sion Farm
St. Croix, U.S. Virgin Islands 00820-4487

Virginia

Virginia Small Business Development Center
Commonwealth of Virginia
DEPARTMENT OF ECONOMIC DEVELOPMENT—Lead
Center
Mr. Robert D. Wilburn, State Director   (804) 371-8253
901 East Byrd Street, Suite 1400   Fax: (804) 225-3384
Richmond, VA 23219
E-mail: rwilburn@dba.state.va.us

Regional Chamber Small Business Development Center
Mr. Doug Murray, Director   (540) 983-0717
212 S. Jefferson Street, Mez. level   Fax: (540) 983-0723
Roanoke, VA 24011
E-mail: djmr@roanoke.infi.net

Capital Area Small Business
  Development Center   (804) 648-7838
Mr. Taylor Cousins, Executive Director   1-800-646-SBDC
1 N. Fifth St., Suite 510   Fax: (804) 648-7849
Richmond, VA 23219
E-mail: pwinter@richmond.infi.net

Central Virginia Small Business Development Center
Mr. Robert A. Hamilton, Jr., Director   (804) 295-8198
918 Emmet Street North, Suite 200   Fax: (804) 295-7066
Charlottesville, VA 22903
E-mail: Hamilton@sbdc.acs.virginia.edu

Dr. William E. S. Flory Small Business Development
  Center
Ms. Linda Decker, Director   (703) 335-2500
10311 Sudley Manor Drive   Fax: (703) 335-1700
Manassas, VA 22109-2962
E-mail: florysbdc@aol.com

James Madison University Small Business Development
Center
Ms. Karen Wigginton, Director   (540) 568-3227
JMU College of Business   Fax: (540) 568-3106
Zane Showker Hall—Room 527
Harrisonburg, VA 22807
E-mail: vancesn@jmu.edu

Longwood College Small Business Development Center
Mr. Gerald L. Hughes, Jr., Director   (804) 395-2086
515 Main Street   Fax: (804) 395-2359
Farmville, VA 23909
E-mail: jhughes@longwood.lwc.edu

South Boston Small Business Development Center
  of the Longwood SBDC
Mr. Vincent Decker, Director   (804) 575-0044
515 Broad Street   Fax: (804) 572-1762
P.O. Box 1116
South Boston, VA 24592

Lord Fairfax Small Business Development Center
Lord Fairfax Community College
Mr. Robert Crosen, Director   (540) 869-6649
P.O. Box 47, 173 Skirmisher Lane   Fax: (540) 868-7002
Middletown, VA 22645
E-mail: lfcrosr@lf.cc.va.us

Lynchburg Regional Small Business Development Center
Mr. Barry Lyons, Director   1-800-876-7232
147 Mill Ridge Road   (804) 582-6170
Lynchburg, VA 24502   Fax: (804) 582-6169
E-mail: lrsbdc@aol.com

Mountain Empire Community College
Small Business Development Center
Mr. Tim Blankenbecler, Director   (540) 523-6529
Drawer 700, Route 23 South   Fax: (540) 523-8139
Big Stone Gap, VA 24219
E-mail: meblant@me.cc.va.us

Northern Virginia Small Business Development Center
Small Business Development Center
Ms. Julie Janoski, Director
4031 University Drive, Suite 200   (703) 277-7700
Fairfax, VA 22030-3409   Fax: (703) 277-7722
E-mail: jjanoski@gmu.edu

Arlington Small Business Development Center
  of the Northern VA SBDC Network
Mr. Paul Hall, Director   (703) 993-8129
GMU Arlington Campus   Fax: (703) 993-8130
4001 North Fairfax Drive, Suite 400
Arlington, VA 22001
E-mail: phall@gmu.edu

Loudoun County Small Business Development Center
 of the Northern VA SBDC Network
Mr. Ted London, Director   (703) 430-7222
207 E. Holly Ave., Suite 214   Fax: (703) 430-7258
Sterling, VA 20164
E-mail: tedlondon@aol.com

Rappahannock Region Small Business Development Center
Mr. Jeff Sneddon, Director   (540) 654-1060
1301 College Avenue   Fax: (540) 654-1070
Seacobeck Hall
Fredericksburg, VA 22401
E-mail: jsneddon@mwcgw.mwc.edu

Warsaw Small Business Development Center
 of the Rappahannock Region SBDC
Mr. John Clickener, Director   (804) 333-0286
P.O. Box 490   1-800-524-8915
5559 West Richmond Road   Fax: (804) 333-0187
Warsaw, VA 22572
E-mail: sbdcwarsaw@sylvaninfo.net

Small Business Development Center of Hampton Roads, Inc.
Mr. William J. Holloran, Jr., Executive   (757) 825-2957
 Director   Fax: (757) 825-2960
525 Butler Farm Road, Suite 102
Hampton, VA 23666
E-mail: bhollora@chespo.hrccva.com

Southwest Virginia Small Business Development Center
Southwest Virginia Community College
Mr. Jim Boyd, Director   (540) 964-7345
P.O. Box SVCC, Route 19   Fax: (540) 964-5788
Richlands, VA 24641
E-Mail: jim_boyd@sw.cc.va.us

Wytheville Small Business Development Center
Wytheville Community College
Mr. Rob Edwards, Director   1-800-468-1195
1000 East Main Street   ext. 4798
Wytheville, VA 24382   (540) 223-4798
E-mail: redwards@naxs.com   Fax: (540) 223-4778

Virginia Highlands Small Business Development Center
Mr. Jim Tilley, Director   (540) 676-5615
P.O. Box 828, Route 372   Fax: (540) 628-7576
 off Route 140
Abingdon, VA 24212
E-mail: vhtillj%vccscent.bitnet@vtbit.cc.vt.edu

Alexandria Small Business Development Center
Alexandria Graduate Education Center   (703) 299-9146
Mr. Bill Reagan, Director   Fax: (703) 299-0295
1775-B Duke Street
Alexandria, VA 22314
E-mail: bill@agec.dup.gwu.edu

Tri-Cities Small Business Development Center
 of the Capital Area SBDC
Ms. Kathryn Culbertson, Director   (804) 643-7232
325 Washington Street
Petersburg, VA 23804
E-mail: kgbus@sprynet.com

Eastern Shore Office
 of the SBDC of Hampton Roads, Inc.
Small Business Development Center
Ms. Susan Tyler, Business Analyst   (757) 442-7179
P.O. Box 395   Fax: (757) 442-7181
Belle Haven, VA 23306

Martinsville Small Business Development Center
 of the Longwood SBDC
Mr. Ken Copeland, Director   (540) 632-4462
115 Broad Street   Fax: (540) 632-5059
P.O. Box 709
Martinsville, VA 24114

South Fairfax Business Resource Center
 of the Northern VA SBDC Network
Ms. Gwendolyn Reape   (703) 768-1440
6911 Richmond Highway, Suite 290   Fax: (703) 768-0547
Alexandria, VA 22306

Radford University—New River Valley SBDC
Mr. David O. Shanks, Director   (540) 831-6056
600-H Norwood Street   Fax: (540) 831-6057
Radford, VA 24141
E-mail: dshanks@runet.edu

Washington

Washington State Small Business Development Center
WASHINGTON STATE UNIVERSITY—Lead Center
Ms. Carol Reisenberg, Acting State Director   (509) 335-1576
College of Business and Economics   Fax: (509) 335-0949
501 Johnson Tower
Pullman, WA 99164-4851

Bellevue Community College
Small Business Development Center
Mr. Bill Huenefeld, BDS   (206) 643-2888
300 Landerholm Circle SE   Fax: (206) 649-3113
Bellevue, WA 98007-6484

Centralia College Small Business Development Center
Mr. Don Hays, BDS   (360) 736-9391
600 West Locust Street   (360) 753-3404
Centralia, WA 98036

Edmonds Community College
Small Business Development Center
Mr. Jack Wicks, BDS   (206) 640-1435
6600 196th Street, SW   Fax: (206) 640-1532
Lynwood, WA 98036

North Seattle Community College
Small Business Development Center
U.S. Export Assistance Center
Ms. Ann Tamura, IT Specialist   (206) 553-5615
2001 Sixth Ave., Suite 650
Seattle, WA 98121

Mt. Vernon Skagit Valley College
Small Business Development Center
Mr. Peter Stroosma, BDS   (360) 428-1282
2405 College Way   Fax: (360) 336-6116
Mt. Vernon, WA 98273

Tacoma Small Business Development Center
Mr. Neil Delisanti, BDS   (206) 272-7232
950 Pacific Avenue, Suite 300   Fax: (206) 597-7305
P.O. Box 1933
Tacoma, WA 98401-1933

Seattle Small Business Development Center
Mr. Bill Jacobs, BDS   (206) 464-5450
180 Nickerson, Suite 207   Fax: (206) 464-6357
Seattle, WA 98109

South Puget Sound Community College
Small Business Development Center
Mr. Douglas Hammel, BDS   (360) 753-5616
721 Columbia Street, SW   Fax: (360) 586-5493
Olympia, WA 98501

South Seattle Community College
Small Business Development Center
Ms. Ruth Ann Halford, BDS   (206) 764-5375
Duwamish Industrial Educational   Fax: (206) 764-5838
  Center
6770 East Marginal Way South
Seattle, WA 98108-3405

Bellingham Western Washington University
Small Business Development Center
Mr. Lynn Trzynka, BDS   (360) 650-3899
College of Business and Economics   Fax: (360) 650-4844
308 Parks Hall
Bellingham, WA 98225-9073

Aberdeen/Grays Harbor College
Small Business Development Center   (360) 538-4021
1620 Edward P. Smith Drive
Aberdeen, WA 98520

Clallam County EDC
102 East Front Street   (360) 457-7793
P.O. Box 1085
Port Angeles, WA 98362

Whatcom Community College
Small Business Development Center   (360) 676-2170
237 West Kellogg Road
Bellingham, WA 98226

West Virginia

West Virginia Small Business Development Center
WEST VIRGINIA DEVELOPMENT OFFICE—Lead Center
Dr. Hazel Kroesser Palmer, State Director   (304) 558-2960
950 Kanawha Boulevard East,   Fax: (304) 558-0127
  2nd Floor
Charleston, WV 25301
E-mail: palmeh@mail.wvnet.edu

College of West Virginia
Small Business Development Center   (800) 766-4556
Mr. Tom Hardiman, Program Manager   (304) 255-4022
306 South Kanawha Street   Fax: (304) 252-9584
P.O. Box AG
Beckley, WV 25802
E-mail: sbdc@cwv.edu

Elkins Satellite Small Business Development Center
Mr. James Martin, Business Analyst   (304) 637-7205
10 Eleventh Street, Suite One   Fax: (304) 637-4902
Elkins, WV 26241
E-mail: jrjm@access.mountain.net

Fairmont State College
Small Business Development Center
Mr. Jack Kirby, Program Manager   (304) 367-2712
1000 Technology Drive, Suite 1120   Fax: (304) 367-2717
Fairmont, WV 26554
E-mail: jrkl@fscvax.wvnet.edu

Charleston Sub-Center
Small Business Development Center
Mr. Bob Henrich, Business Specialist   (304) 558-2960
950 Kanawha Boulevard East, 2nd Floor Fax: (304) 558-0127
Charleston, WV 25301
E-mail: bobh@wvdo.org

Marshall University
Small Business Development Center
Ms. Edna McClain, Program Manager   (304) 696-6246
1050 Fourth Avenue   Fax: (304) 696-4835
Huntington, WV 25755-2126
E-mail: emcclain@murc.marshall.edu

Shepherd College
Small Business Development Center
Gardiner Hall
Mr. Fred Baer, Program Manager   (304) 876-5261
Shepherdstown, WV 25443   Fax: (304) 876-5467
E-mail: fbaer@shepherd.wvnet.edu

Southern WV Community College
Small Business Development Center   (304) 792-7098
Mr. Larry Salyers, Program Manage   ext. 118
P.O. Box 2900   Fax: (304) 792-7056
Mt. Gay, WV 25637
E-mail: larrys@southern.wvnet.edu

West Virginia Institute of Technology
Small Business Development Center
Mr. James Epling, Program Manager   (304) 465-1434
912 East Main Street   Fax: (304) 465-8680
Oak Hill, WV 25901
E-mail: jeepli@wvit.wvnet.edu

West Virginia Northern Community College
Small Business Development Center
Mr. Ron Trevellini, Program Manager   (304) 233-5900
College Square   ext. 4206
Wheeling, WV 26003   Fax: (304) 232-0965
E-mail: rtrevellini@nccvax.wvnet.edu

West Virginia University
Small Business Development Center
Ms. Sharon Stratton, Business Development Spec.   (304) 293-5839
439 B&E Building   Fax: (304) 293-8905
P.O. Box 6025
Morgantown, WV 26506
E-mail: stratton@wvubel.be.wvu.edu

West Virginia University at Parkersburg
Small Business Development Center
Mr. Greg Hill, Program Manager   (304) 424-8277
Route 5, Box 167-A   Fax: (304) 424-8266
Parkersburg, WV 26101
E-mail: ghill@alpha.wvup.wvnet.edu

Wisconsin

Wisconsin Small Business Development Center
UNIVERSITY OF WISCONSIN
Ms. Erica McIntire, State Director   (608) 263-7794
432 North Lake Street, Room 423   Fax: (608) 262-3878
Madison, WI 53706

University of Wisconsin at Eau Claire
Small Business Development Center
Mr. Kevin Jones, Director   (715) 836-5811
P.O. Box 4004   Fax: (715) 836-5263
Eau Claire, WI 54702-4004

University of Wisconsin at Green Bay
Small Business Development Center
Jan Thornton, Director   (920) 465-2089
Wood Hall, Suite 460   Fax: (920) 465-2552
Green Bay, WI 54311-7001

University of Wisconsin at Parkside
Small Business Development Center
Ms. Ester Letvin   (414) 595-2208
284 Tallent Hall   Fax: (414) 595-2513
Kenosha, WI 53141

University of Wisconsin at La Crosse
Small Business Development Center
Ms. Jan Gallagher, Director   (608) 785-8782
120 North Hall   Fax: (608) 785-6919
La Crosse, WI 54601

University of Wisconsin at Madison
Small Business Development Center
Mr. Neil Lerner, Director   (608) 263-2221
975 University Avenue   Fax: (608) 263-0818
Madison, WI 53706

University of Wisconsin at Milwaukee
Small Business Development Center
Ms. Lucy Holifield   (414) 227-3240
161 W. Wisconsin Ave., Suite 6000   Fax: (414) 227-3142
Milwaukee, WI 53204

University of Wisconsin at Oshkosh
Small Business Development Center
Mr. John Mozingo, Director   (920) 424-1453
201 Clow Faculty   Fax: (920) 424-7413
800 Algoma Blvd.
Oshkosh, WI 54901

University of Wisconsin at Platteville
Small Business Development Center   (608) 342-1038
Ms. Karen Steindorf, Director   (608) 342-1454
133 Warner Hall
1 University Plaza
Platteville, WI 53818

University of Wisconsin at Stevens Point
Small Business Development Center
Ms. Vicki Lobermeier, Director   (715) 346-3838
103 Old Main Building   Fax: (715) 346-4045
2100 Main Street
Stevens Point, WI 54481

University of Wisconsin at Superior
Small Business Development Center
Loren Erickson, Director   (715) 394-8351
1800 Grand Avenue   Fax: (715) 394-8454
Sundquist Hall
Superior, WI 54880

University of Wisconsin at Whitewater
Small Business Development Center
Ms. Carla Lenk, Director   (414) 472-3217
800 West Main Street   Fax: (414) 472-4863
2000 Carlson Building
Whitewater, WI 53190

Wisconsin Innovation Service Center/Technology—
Specialized Center
Small Business Development Center
Ms. Debra Malewicki, Director   (414) 472-3217
University of Wisconsin at Whitewater Fax: (414) 472-1600
402 McCutchen Hall
Whitewater, WI 53190

Wyoming

Wyoming Small Business Development Center
UNIVERSITY OF WYOMING—Lead Center
Ms. Diane Wolverton, State Director   (800) 348-5194
Mr. Matt Edwards, Asst. to the Director   (307) 766-3505
P.O. Box 3622   Fax: (307) 766-3406
Laramie, WY 82071-3622

Region I Small Business Development Center
Mr. Bill Ellis, Director   (800) 348-5205
P.O. Box 1168   (307) 352-6894
Rock Springs, WY 82902   Fax: (307) 352-6876

Region II Small Business Development Center
Mr. Dwane Heintz, Director   (800) 383-0371
146 South Bent Street   (307) 754-2139
Powell, WY 82435   Fax: (307) 754-0368

Region III Small Business Development Center
Mr. Leonard Holler, Director   (800) 348-5207
111 West Second Street, Suite 502   (307) 234-6683
Casper, WY 82601   Fax: (307) 577-7014

Region IV Small Business Development Center
Ms. Arlene Soto, Regional Director   (800) 348-5208
1400 East College Drive   (307) 632-6141
Cheyenne, WY 82007-3298   Fax: (307) 632-6061

SERVICE CORPS OF RETIRED EXECUTIVES

The Service Corps of Retired Executives (SCORE) is another resource that you can use for business advice and consultation. This appendix contains an explanation of the program and a directory of SCORE offices throughout the United States and its territories.

Introduction to SCORE

Service Corps of Retired Executives (SCORE), is a locally-chartered volunteer organizations funded by SBA, which provide free expert problem-solving assistance to small businesses. Helping American small businesses to prosper has been SCORE's goal since the program began in 1964.

SCORE tries to match counselor experience with client needs and provide one-on-one counseling. SCORE also conducts well-developed pre-business workshops and a variety of business oriented seminars and training sessions.

Quick-Facts on SCORE: 1997

➤ Score Founded: 1964

➤ Women Counselors: 1,500

➤ Number of SCORE Volunteers: 12,600

➤ Locations in U.S.: 700

➤ Counselors with Foreign Trade Experience: 800

➤ Total Number of Clients Served: 4.2 million

Principal Topics of SCORE Workshops

➤ Pre-business Planning

➤ Basic Management Techniques

➤ Marketing & Sales

➤ Women's Business Operations

➤ Financial Management Techniques

➤ Veteran's Business Operations

➤ International Trade

➤ Expansion & Franchising

➤ Employee Rights & Regulations

➤ Taxes & Accounting

SBA Acting SCORE National Program Manager

John Bebris   202/205-6665
Office of Business Education &   FAX/205-7416
   Resource Management, Suite 6200
409 3rd Street, S.W., Washington, DC 20416

National SCORE Office   800/634-0245
Suite 4800   FAX/205-7636
409 3rd Street, S.W., Washington, DC 20416

W. Kenneth Yancey, Jr.,   202/205-6762
   Executive Director
National SCORE President (FY97/98)
   from Region I, Boston
Frederic W. Thomas   202/205-6762

Directory of SCORE Chapters

Alaska

Anchorage SCORE
c/o il SBA/#67
222 W. 8th Avenue
Anchorage, AK 99513-7559

Phone: (907) 271-4022

Alabama

North Alabama SCORE Chapter
c/o UAB Small Business Development Center
901 South 15th Street, Room 201 Fax: (205) 934-0538
Birmingham, AL 35294-4552

Phone: (205) 934-6868

Tuscaloosa SCORE Chapter
c/o Chamber of Commerce of West Alabama
P.O. Box 020410
Tuscaloosa, AL 35402

Phone: (205) 758-7588

Southern Alabama Score Chapter
c/o Mobile Area Chamber of Commerce
P.O. Box 2187
Mobile, AL 36601

Phone: (334) 433-6951

Shoals SCORE Chapter
18 Brannon Court
Florence, AL 35630

Phone: (205) 764-0244

Capitol City SCORE Chapter
c/o Montgomery Chamber of Commerce
600 South Court Street
Montgomery, AL 36104

Phone: (334) 240-6868

Baldwin County SCORE Chapter
c/o Fairhope Chamber of Commerce
327 Fairhope Avenue
Fairhope, AL 36532

Phone: (334) 928-5838

East Alabama SCORE Chapter
c/o Opelika Chamber of Commerce
P.O. Box 2366
Opelika, AL 36803-2366

Phone: (334) 745-4861

Northeast Alabama SCORE Chapter
c/o Calhoun County Chamber of Commerce
P.O. Box 1087
Anniston, AL 36202

Phone: (205) 237-3536

Foley SCORE Office
c/o South Baldwin Chamber of Commerce
P.O. Box 1117
Foley, AL 36536

Phone: (334) 943-1555

Arkansas

Little Rock SCORE
2120 Riverfront Drive
SBA Room 100
Little Rock, AR 72202-1747

Phone: (501) 324-5893
Fax: (501) 324-5199

NW Arkansas SCORE
#4 Glenn Haven Drive
Fort Smith, AR 72901

Phone: (501) 783-3556

Ozark SCORE
c/o Margaret Parrish
1141 Eastwood Drive
Fayetteville, AR 72701

Phone: (501) 442-7619

Garland County SCORE
1412 Airport Rd., B10
Hot Springs, AR 71913

Phone: (501) 321-1700

South Central SCORE
201 N. Jackson Avenue
El Dorado, AR 71730-5803

Phone: (870) 863-6113
Fax: (870) 863-6115

SE Arkansas SCORE
P.O. Box 6866
Pine Bluff, AR 71611

Phone: (870) 535-7189
Fax: (870) 535-1643

Arizona

Phoenix SCORE
2828 N. Central Avenue, #800
Central & One Thomas
Phoenix, AZ 85004

Phone: (602) 640-2329

Tucson SCORE
P.O. BOX 2143
Tucson, AZ 85702

Phone: (520) 670-5008

East Valley SCORE
Federal Building, Room #104
26 N. MacDonald
Mesa, AZ 85201

Phone: (602) 379-3100
Fax: (602) 379-3143

Prescott Arizona SCORE
101 W. Goodwin Street
P.O. Bldg., Suite 307
Prescott, AZ 86303

Phone: (520) 778-7438

Lake Havasu SCORE
P.O Box 2049
Lake Havasu City, AZ 86405

Phone: (520) 453-5951

Flagstaff SCORE
Attn: Barbara Haynes
1 West Rte 66
Flagstaff, AZ 86001

Phone: (520) 556-7333

California

Los Angeles SCORE
330 North Brand Boulevard
Suite 190
Glendale, CA 91203-2304
Phone: (818) 552-3206
Fax: (818) 552-3323

San Francisco SCORE
455 Market Street, 6th Floor
San Francisco, CA 94105
Phone: (415) 744-6827
Fax: (415) 744-6812

Orange Cty SCORE
200 W. Santa Ana Blvd., Suite 700
Santa Ana, CA 92701
Phone: (714) 550-7369
Fax: (714) 550-0191

San Diego SCORE
550 West C Street, Suite 550
San Diego, CA 92101-3500
Phone: (619) 557-7272
Fax: (619) 557-5894

Santa Barbara SCORE
P.O. Box 30291
Santa Barbara, CA 93130
Phone: (805) 563-0084

Ventura SCORE
5700 Ralston Street, Suite 310
Ventura, CA 93001
Phone: (805) 658-2688

Pomona SCORE
c/o Pomona Chamber of Commerce
485 N. Garey Avenue, P.O. Box 1457
Pomona, CA 91769-1457
Phone: (909) 622-1256

Palm Springs SCORE
555 South Palm Canyon, Room A206
Palm Springs, CA 92264
Phone: (760) 320-6682
Fax: (760) 323-9426

Central California SCORE
2719 N. Air Fresno Drive, Suite 200
Fresno, CA 93727-1547
Phone: (209) 487-5605
Fax: (209) 487-5636

Santa Clara Cty SCORE
280 South 1st Street, Room 137
San Jose, CA 95113
Phone: (408) 288-8479
Fax: (408) 535-5541

Sacramento SCORE
660 J Street, Suite 215
Sacramento, CA 95814-2413
Phone: (916) 498-6420
Fax: (916) 498-6422

Santa Rosa SCORE
777 Sonoma Avenue, Room 115E
Santa Rosa, CA 95404
Phone: (707) 571-8342
Fax: (707) 541-0331

Stockton SCORE
401 N. San Joaquin Street, Room 215
Stockton, CA 95202
Phone: (209) 946-6293

Central Coast SCORE
2524 South LaCosta Drive
Santa Maria, CA 93455
Phone: (805) 934-4146

Hemet SCORE
1700 E. Florida Avenue
Hemet, CA 92544-4679
Phone: (909) 652-4390
Fax: (909) 929-8543

East Bay SCORE
519 17th Street
Oakland, CA 94612
Phone: (510) 273-6611
Fax: (510) 273-6015

Shasta SCORE
c/o Cascade SBDC
737 Auditorium Drive
Redding, CA 96099
Phone: (916) 247-8100

Yosemite SCORE
c/o SCEDCO
1012 11th Street, Suite 300
Modesto, CA 95354
Phone: (209) 521-9333

Golden Empire SCORE
1706 Chester Ave., #200
Bakersfield, CA 93301
Phone: (805) 327-4421

Steinbeck-Roecker SCORE
Monterey Peninsula Chamber of Commerce
380 Alvarado
Monterey, CA 93940-1770
Phone: (408) 649-1770

Greater Chico Area SCORE
1324 Mangrove Street, Suite 114
Chico, CA 95926
Phone: (916) 342-8932

Antelope Valley SCORE
445 W. Palmdale Blvd., Ste. N
Palmdale, CA 93551
Phone: (805) 265-7733
Fax: (805) 265-7712

Tuolumne County SCORE
222 S. Shepherd Street
Sonora, CA 95370
Phone: (209) 532-4212

San Luis Obispo SCORE
3566 South Hiquera, #104
San Luis Obispo, CA 93401
Phone: (805) 547-0779

Colorado

Denver SCORE
US Custom's House, 4th Floor
721 19th Street
Denver, CO 80201-0660
Phone: (303) 844-3985
Fax: (303) 844-6490

Pueblo SCORE
c/o Chamber of Commerce
302 N. Santa Fe
Pueblo, CO 81003
Phone: (719) 542-1704
Fax: (719) 542-1624

Grand Junction SCORE
c/o Chamber of Commerce
360 Grand Avenue
Grand Junction, CO 81501

Phone: (970) 242-3214

Colorado Springs SCORE
2 North Cascade Avenue, Suite 110
Colorado Springs, CO 80903

Phone: (719) 636-3074

Connecticut

Fairfield Cty SCORE
24 Belden Avenue, 5th Floor
Norwalk, CT 06850

Phone: (203) 847-7348
Fax: (203) 849-9308

Grtr Hartford Cty SCORE
330 Main Street
Hartford, CT 06106-

Phone: (860) 240-4700

New Haven SCORE
25 Science Park
Bldg. 25, Room 366
New Haven, CT 06511

Phone: (203) 865-7645

Greater Bridgeport SCORE
10 Middle Street, 14th Floor
Bridgeport, CT 06604

Phone: (203) 335-3800
Fax: (203) 366-0105

Old Saybrook SCORE
Old Saybrook Chamber of Commerce
PO Box 625, 146 Main Street
Old Saybrook, CT 06475

Phone: (860) 388-9508

Greater Danbury SCORE
100 Mill Plain Road
Danbury, CT 06811

Phone: (203) 791-3804

District of Columbia

Washington DC SCORE
1110 Vermont Avenue, NW, 9th Floor
PO Box 34346
Washington, DC 20043

Phone: (202) 606-4000
ext. 287
Fax: (202) 606-4225

Delaware

Wilmington SCORE
824 Market Street, Suite 610
Wilmington, DE 19801

Phone: (302) 573-6552
Fax: (302) 573-6092

Florida

Ft. Lauderdale SCORE
299 East Broward Blvd.
Fed. Bldg., Suite 123
Ft. Lauderdale, FL 33301

Phone: (954) 356-7263
Fax: (954) 356-7145

Dade SCORE
1320 South Dixie Hwy., 3rd Floor
Coral Gables, FL 33146

Phone: (305) 536-5521
Fax: (305) 536-5058

Jacksonville SCORE
7825 Baymeadows Way, 100-B
Jacksonville, FL 32256

Phone: (904) 443-1911

Daytona Beach SCORE
921 N. Nova Rd., Ste. A
Holly Hills, FL 32117

Phone: (904) 255-6889
Fax: (904) 255-0229

Suncoast/Pinellas SCORE
Airport Business Center
4707 140th Avenue North, #311
Clearwater, FL 34622

Phone: (813) 532-6800
Fax: (813) 532-6800

Manasota SCORE
2801 Fruitville Road, Suite 280
Sarasota, FL 34237

Phone: (941) 955-1029

Central Florida SCORE
404 North Ingraham Avenue
Lakeland, FL 33801

Phone: (941) 687-4403
Fax: (941) 687-6225

Orlando SCORE
80 N. Hughey Avenue
Room 455, Federal Bldg.
Orlando, FL 32801

Phone: (407) 648-6476
Fax: (407) 648-6425

Hillsborough SCORE
4732 Dale Mabry Highway North, Suite 400
Tampa, FL 33614-6509

Phone: (813) 870-0125

Southwest Florida SCORE
The Renaissance, 8695 College Pkwy., Suites 345 & 346
Fort Myers, FL 33919

Phone: (941) 489-2935

Palm Beach SCORE
500 Australian Avenue South Fax: (561) 833-1712
Suite 100
West Palm Beach, FL 33401

Phone: (561) 833-1672

South Broward SCORE
3475 Sheridian Street, Suite 203
Hollywood, FL 33021

Phone: (954) 966-8415

Treasure Coast SCORE
Professional Center, Suite 2
3220 South US #1
Ft. Pierce, FL 34982

Phone: (561) 489-0548

Charlotte County SCORE
Punta Gorda Professional Center
201 W. Marion Avenue, #211
Punta Gorda, FL 33950

Phone: (941) 575-1818

Space Coast SCORE
Melbourne Professional Complex
1600 Sarno, Suite 205
Melbourne, FL 32935

Phone: (407) 254-2288
Fax: (407) 254-2288

Gainesville SCORE
101 SE 2nd Place, Suite #104
Gainesville, FL 32601

Phone: (352) 375-8278

South Palm Beach SCORE
1050 S. Federal Highway, Suite 132
Delray Beach, FL 33483

Phone: (561) 278-7752
Fax: (561) 278-0288

Lake-Sumter SCORE
First Union National Bank
122 East Main Street
Tavares, FL 32778-3810

Phone: (352) 365-3556

Pasco County SCORE
6014 US Highway 19, Suite 302
New Port Richey, FL 34652

Phone: (813) 842-4638

Ocala SCORE
110 E. Silver Spring Blvd.
Ocala, FL 34470

Phone: (352) 629-5959

Naples of Collier SCORE
Barnett Bank
3285 Tamiami Trail East
Naples, FL 34112

Phone: (941) 417-1280
Fax: (941) 417-1281

Tallahassee SCORE
c/o Leon County Library
200 W. Park Avenue
Tallahassee, FL 32302

Phone: (904) 487-2665

Georgia

Atlanta SCORE
1720 Peachtree Road, NW, 6th Floor
Atlanta, GA 30309
E-mail: scoreatl@mindspring.com
Web site: http://www.scoreatlanta.org

Phone: (404) 347-2442
Fax: (404) 347-1227

Savannah SCORE
111 E. Liberty Street, Suite 103
Savannah, GA 31401

Phone: (912) 652-4335
Fax: (912) 652-4184

Dalton-Whitfield SCORE
P.O. Box 1941
Dalton, GA 30722

Phone: (706) 279-3383

Columbus SCORE
Mr. Ed Stratton
1st Union Bank
101 13th Street
Columbus, GA

Phone: (706) 596-8331

Augusta SCORE
Mr. Kenneth Stinson
106 Pleasant Home Road
LePavillion Center, Suite 2-R
Augusta, GA

Phone: (706) 869-9100

Winterville SCORE
 (Athens metro area)
Mr. Gerald Rucker
340 Weatherly Woods Drive
Winterville, GA 30683

Phone: (706) 548-5968

Hawaii

SCORE of Hawaii, Inc.
130 Merchant Street, Suite 1030
Honolulu HI 96813

Phone: (808) 522-8130
Fax: (808) 522-8135

SCORE of Maui, Inc.
590 E. Lipoa Parkway, Suite 227
Kihei, HI 96753

Phone: (808) 875-2380

Iowa

Des Moines SCORE
Federal Building/ Room 749
210 Walnut Street
Des Moines, IA 50309-2186

Phone: (515) 284-4760

Sioux City SCORE
Federal Building
320 6th Street
Sioux City, IA 51101

Phone: (712) 277-2324

Council Bluffs SCORE
Chamber of Commerce
P.O. Box 1565
Council Bluffs, IA 51502-1565

Phone: (712) 325-1000

Cedar Rapids SCORE
Lattner Building
215 4th Avenue, SE, #200
Cedar Rapids, IA 52401-1806

Phone: (319) 362-6405
Fax: (319) 362-7861

River City SCORE
15 West State Street; PO Box 1128
Mason City, IA 50401

Phone: (515) 423-5724

Waterloo SCORE
Chamber of Commerce
215 East 4th
Waterloo, IA 50703

Phone: (319) 233-8431

Burlington SCORE
Federal Building Room #216
300 N. Main Street
Burlington, IA 52601

Phone: (319) 752-2967
ext.205

Dubuque SCORE
c/o Northeast Iowa Comm College
10250 Sundown Road
Peosta, IA 52068
Phone: (319) 556-5110
ext.249

Fort Dodge SCORE
Federal Building, Room 436
205 South 8th Street
Fort Dodge, IA 50501
Phone: (515) 955-2622

Iowa Lakes SCORE
PO Box 7937; 122 West 5th Street
Spencer, IA 51301
Phone: (712) 262-3059

South Central SCORE
SBDC, Indian Hills Community College
525 Grandview Avenue
Ottumwa, IA 52501
Phone: (515) 683-5127

Iowa City SCORE
210 Federal Building; PO Box 1853
Iowa City, IA 52240-1853
Phone: (319) 338-1662

Central Iowa SCORE
Fisher Community College
709 South Center
Marshalltown, IA 50158
Phone: (515) 753-6645

Southwest Iowa SCORE
Chamber of Commerce
614 W. Sheridan, Box 38
Shenandoah, IA 51601
Phone: (712) 246-3260

Illowa SCORE
Clinton Community College
1000 Lincoln Blvd.
Clinton, IA 52732
Phone: (319) 242-5702

Northeast Iowa SCORE
3404 285th Street
Cresco, IA 52136
Phone: (319) 547-3377

Keokuk SCORE
c/o Keokuk Area Chamber of Commerce
401 Main Street, Pierce Bldg. #1
Keokuk, IA 52632
Phone: (319) 524-5367

Vista SCORE
Storm Lake Chamber of Commerce
119 West 6th Street
Storm Lake, IA 50588
Phone: (712) 732-3780

Idaho

Treasure Valley SCORE
1020 Main Street, #290
Boise, ID 83702
Phone: (208) 334-1696
Fax: (208) 334-9353

Eastern Idaho SCORE
2300 N. Yellowstone, Suite 119
Idaho Falls, ID 83401
Phone: (208) 523-1022
Fax: (208) 528-7127

Illinois

Chicago SCORE
Northwest Atrium Center
500 W. Madison Street, #1250
Chicago IL 60661
Phone: (312) 353-7724
Fax: (312) 886-5688

Peoria SCORE
c/o Peoria Chamber of Commerce
124 SW Adams, Suite 300
Peoria, IL 61602
Phone: (309) 676-0755
Fax: (309) 676-7534

Fox Valley SCORE
40 W. Downer Place
PO Box 277
Aurora, IL 60507
Phone: (630) 897-9214
Fax: (630) 897-7002

Decatur SCORE
Milliken University
1184 W. Main Street
Decatur, IL 62522
Phone: (217) 424-6297
Fax: (217) 424-3993

Southern Illinois SCORE
150 E. Pleasant Hill Road
Box 1
Carbondale, IL 62901
Phone: (618) 453-6654
Fax: (618) 453-5040

Greater Alton SCORE
5800 Godfrey Road
Alden Hall
Godfrey, IL 62035-2466
Phone: (618) 467-2280
Fax: (618) 466-8289

Quad Cities SCORE
c/o Chamber of Commerce
622 19th Street
Moline, IL 61265
Phone: (309) 797-0082
Fax: (309) 757-5435

Quincy Tri-State SCORE
c/o Chamber of Commerce
300 Civic Center Plaza, Suite 245
Quincy, IL 62301
Phone: (217) 222-8093
Fax: (217) 222-3033

Springfield SCORE
511 West Capitol Avenue, Suite 302
Springfield, IL 62704
Phone: (217) 492-4359
Fax: (217) 492-4867

Northern Illinois SCORE
515 North Court Street
Rockford, IL 61103
Phone: (815) 962-0122
Fax: (815) 962-0122

Indiana

Indianapolis SCORE   Phone: (317) 226-7264
429 N. Pennsylvania Street, Suite 100
Indianapolis, IN 46204-1873

Fort Wayne SCORE   Phone: (219) 422-2601
1300 S. Harrison Street   Fax: (219) 422-2601
Fort Wayne, IN 46802

South Bend SCORE   Phone: (219) 282-4350
300 N. Michigan Street
South Bend, IN 46601

Evansville SCORE   Phone: (812) 421-5879
Old Post Office Place
100 NW 2nd Street, #300
Evansville, IN 47708

Gary SCORE   Phone: (219) 882-3918
973 West 6th Avenue, Room 326
Gary, IN 46402

South East Indiana SCORE   Phone: (812) 379-4457
c/o Chamber of Commerce
500 Franklin Street, Box 29
Columbus, IN 47201

Anderson SCORE   Phone: (317) 642-0264
c/o Chamber of Commerce
205 W. 11th, PO Box 469
Anderson, IN 46015

S. Central Indiana SCORE   Phone: (812) 945-0266
4100 Charleston Road
New Albany, IN 47150-9538

Bloomington SCORE   Phone: (812) 335-3744
Star Center
216 West Allen
Bloomington, IN 47403

Kokomo/Howard Co. SCORE   Phone: (765) 457-5301
106 North Washington Street   Fax: (765) 452-4564
Kokomo, IN 46901

Marion/Grant Co SCORE   Phone: (317) 664-5107
215 S. Adams
Marion, IN 46952

Elkhart SCORE   Phone: (219) 293-1531
418 S. Main Street   Fax: (219) 294-1859
PO Box 428
Elkhart, IN 46515

Logansport SCORE   Phone: (219) 753-6388
Logansport County Chamber of Commerce
300 East Broadway, Suite 103
Logansport, IN 46947

Kansas

Wichita SCORE   Phone: (316) 269-6273
SBA/ 100 East English, Suite 510
Wichita, KS 67202

Salina SCORE   Phone: (913) 243-4290
130 W. 18th, PO Box 642
Concordia, KS 66901

Emporia SCORE   Phone: (316) 342-1600
Chamber of Commerce
719 Commercial, PO Box 703
Emporia, KS 66801

Ark Valley SCORE   Phone: (316) 221-1617
Box 314
Winfield, KS 67156

Topeka SCORE   Phone: (913) 231-1010
1700 College
Topeka, KS 66621

Hays SCORE   Phone: (913) 625-6595
c/o Emprise Bank NA
PO Box 400
Hays, KS 67601

Hutchison SCORE   Phone: (316) 665-8468
One East 9th
Hutchison, KS 67501

Southwest Kansas SCORE   Phone: (316) 227-3119
Dodge City Chamber of Commerce
PO Box 939
Dodge City, KS 67801

Golden Belt SCORE   Phone: (316) 792-2401
Chamber of Commerce
1307 Williams
Great Bend, KS 67530

Southeast Kansas SCORE   Phone: (316) 724-6100
PO Box 342
Girard KS 66743

McPherson SCORE   Phone: (316) 241-3303
Chamber of Commerce
306 N. Main
McPherson KS 67460

Kentucky

Louisville SCORE
600 Dr. Martin Luther King Jr. Place
188 Federal Office Bldg.
Louisville, KY 40202
Phone: (502) 582-5976

Paducah SCORE
Federal Office Building
501 Broadway, Room B-36
Paducah, KY 42001
Phone: (502) 442-5685

Lexington SCORE
410 W. Vine St., Suite 290, Civic C
Lexington, KY 40507
Phone: (606) 231-9902
Fax: (606) 253-3190

Elizabethtown SCORE/BITAC Office
600 College Street Road
Elizabethtown, KY 42701
Phone: (502) 737-0324

Bowling Green SCORE Office
PO Box 51
Bowling Green, KY 42102
Phone: (502) 781-3200

Elkton SCORE Office
71 Public Square
Elkton, KY 40220
Phone: (502) 265-9877

Madisonville SCORE Office
257 N. Main Street
Madisonville, KY 42431
Phone: (502) 825-1399

Hopkinsville SCORE Office
Hopkinsville Christian County
    Chamber of Commerce
PO Box 1382
Hopkinsville, KY 42241
Phone: (502) 886-9000

Louisiana

New Orleans SCORE
365 Canal Street, Suite 3100
New Orleans, LA 70130
Phone: (504) 589-2356
Fax: (504) 589-2339

Baton Rouge SCORE
564 Laurel Street
PO Box 3217
Baton Rouge, LA 70801
Phone: (504) 381-7130
Fax: (504) 336-4306

Lake Charles SCORE
120 W. Pujo Street
Lake Charles, LA 70601
Phone: (318) 433-3632

Shreveport SCORE
400 Edwards Street
Shreveport, LA 71101
Phone: (318) 677-2536
Fax: (318) 677-2541

Lafayette SCORE
804 St. Mary Blvd
Laf. C of C/PO Drawer 51307
Lafayette, LA 70505-1307
Phone: (318) 233-2705
Fax: (318) 234-8671

Central Louisiana SCORE
802 Third Street
PO Box 992
Alexandria, LA 71309
Phone: (318) 442-6671

North Shore SCORE
PO Box 1458
Hammond, LA 70404
Phone: (504) 345-4457
Fax: (504) 345-4749

Massachusetts

Boston SCORE
10 Causeway Street, Room 265
Boston, MA 02222-1093
Phone: (617) 565-5591
Fax: (617) 565-5598

Worcester SCORE
33 Waldo Street
Worcester, MA 01608
Phone: (508) 753-2929
Fax: (508) 754-8560

Cape Cod SCORE
270 Communications Way
Independence Park, Suite 5B
Hyannis, MA 02601
Phone: (508) 775-4884

Springfield SCORE
1350 Main Street
Springfield, MA 01103
Phone: (413) 785-0314

NE Massachusetts SCORE
Danvers Savings Bank
1 Conant Street
Danvers, MA 01923
Phone: (508) 777-2200

SE Massachusetts SCORE
60 School Street
Brockton, MA 02401
Phone: (508) 587-2673
Fax: (508) 587-1340

Maryland

Baltimore SCORE
The City Crescent Bldg., 6th Floor
10 South Howard Street
Baltimore, MD 21201
Phone: (410) 962-2233
Fax: (410) 962-1805

Salisbury SCORE
c/o Chamber of Commerce
300 E. Main Street
Salisbury, MD 21801
Phone: (410) 749-0185
Fax: (410) 860-9925

Southern Maryland SCORE
2525 Riva Road, Suite 110
Annapolis, MD 21401
Phone: (410) 266-9553
Fax: (410) 573-0981

Hagerstown SCORE
111 W. Washington Street
Hagerstown, MD 21740

Phone: (301) 739-2015
Fax: (301) 739-1278

Upper Shore SCORE
c/o Talbot Cty Chamber of Commerce
PO Box 1366
Easton, MD 21601

Phone: (410) 822-4606
Fax: (410) 822-7922

Frederick County SCORE
43A South Market Street
Frederick, MD 21701

Phone: (301) 662-8723
Fax: (301) 846-4427

Maine

Portland SCORE
66 Pearl Street, Room 210
Portland, ME 04101

Phone: (207) 772-1147
Fax: (207) 772-5581

Augusta SCORE
40 Western Avenue
Augusta, ME 04330

Phone: (207) 622-8509

Cen & N Arrostock SCORE
NMDC
2 S. Main Street
Caribou, ME 04736

Phone: (207) 498-6562

Bangor SCORE
Husson College, One College Circle
Peabody Hall, Room 229
Bangor, ME 04401

Phone: (207) 941-9707

Lewiston-Auburn SCORE
BIC of Maine-Bates Mill Complex
35 Canal Street
Lewiston, ME 04240-7764

Phone: (207) 782-3708
Fax: (207) 783-7745

Maine Coastal SCORE
Box 1105, Mill Mall
Ellsworth, ME 04605-1105

Phone: (207) 667-5800

Oxford Hills SCORE
166 Main Street
South Paris, ME 04281

Phone: (207) 743-0499

Western Mountains SCORE
c/o Fleet Bank
PO Box 400, 108 Congress Street
Rumford, ME 04276

Phone: (207) 364-3735

Michigan

Detroit SCORE
477 Michigan Avenue
Room 515
Detroit, MI 48226

Phone: (313) 226-7947
Fax: (313) 226-3448

Upper Peninsula SCORE
c/o Chamber of Commerce
2581 I-75 Business Spur
Sault Ste. Marie, MI 49783

Phone: (906) 632-3301

Kalamazoo SCORE
128 North Kalamazoo Mall
Kalamazoo, MI 49007

Phone: (616) 381-5382
Fax: (616) 343-0430

Traverse City SCORE
PO Box 387
202 East Grandview Parkway
Traverse City, MI 49685-0387

Phone: (616) 947-5075

Petoskey SCORE
401 E. Mitchell
Petoskey, MI 49770

Phone: (616) 347-4150

Minnesota

Minneapolis SCORE
5217 Wayzata Blvd
North Plaza Bldg, Suite 51
Minneapolis, MN 55416

Phone: (612) 591-0539
Fax: (612) 544-0436

SW Minnesota SCORE
Box 999, 112 Riverfront Street
Mankato, MN 56001

Phone: (507) 345-4519
Fax: (507) 345-4451

St. Paul SCORE
Lowry Professional Building
350 St. Peter Street, #295
St. Paul, MN 55102

Phone: (612) 223-5010
Fax: (612) 223-5048

SE Minnesota SCORE
Rochester Chamber of Commerce
220 S. Broadway, Suite 100
Rochester, MN 55901

Phone: (507) 288-1122
Fax: (507) 282-8960

Central Area SCORE
1527 Northway Drive
St. Cloud, MN 56303

Phone: (320) 240-1332
Fax: (320) 255-9050

South Metro SCORE
101 West Burnsvile Pkwy #150
Burnsville, MN 55337

Phone: (612) 898-5645
Fax: (612) 435-6972

Duluth SCORE
4879 Adrian Lane
Hermantown, MN 55811

Phone: (218) 723-2701
Fax: (218) 723-2712

Missouri

Kansas City SCORE
323 W. 8th Street, Suite 104
Kansas City, MO 64105

Phone: (816) 374-6675
Fax: (816) 374-6759

St. Louis SCORE
815 Olive Street, Room 242
St. Louis, MO 63101-1569
Phone: (314) 539-6970
Fax: (314) 539-3785

Springfield SCORE
620 S. Glenstone, #110
Springfield, MO 65802-3200
Phone: (417) 864-7670
Fax: (417) 864-4108

Tri-Lakes SCORE
c/o Dwayne Shoemaker
PO Box 1148
Kimberling City, MO 65686
Phone: (417) 739-3041

SE Missouri SCORE
Route 1, Box 280
Neelyville, MO 63954
Phone: (573) 989-3577

Mexico SCORE
c/o Dennis Dexter
531 Fox Pointe Drive
St. Charles, MO 63304
Phone: (314) 928-6153

Mid Missouri SCORE
c/o Milo Dahl
1705 Halsted Court
Columbia, MO 65203
Phone: (573) 874-1132

St. Joseph SCORE
Chamber of Commerce
3003 Frederick Avenue
St. Joseph, MO 64506
Phone: (816) 232-4461

Ozark-Gateway SCORE
1102 Oak Hill Road
Cuba, MO 65453
Phone: (573) 885-4954

Lewis & Clark SCORE
425 Spencer Road
St. Peters, MO 63376
Phone: (314) 928-2900
Fax: (314) 928-2900

Poplar Bluff Area SCORE
c/o James W. Carson, Chair
Route 1, Box 280
Neelyville, MO 63954
Phone: (573) 989-3577

Lake Ozark SCORE
Univ. Extension, P.O. Box 1405
113 Kansas Street
Camdenton, MO 65020
Phone: (573) 346-2644
Fax: (573) 346-2694

Mississippi

Gulfcoast SCORE
One Government Plaza
2909 13th Street, Suite 203
Gulfport, MS 39501
Phone: (601) 863-4449

Jackson SCORE
First jackson Ctr, Ste. 400
101 W. Capitol Street
Jackson, MS 39201
Phone: (601) 965-4378

Delta SCORE
Greenville Chamber/915 Washington A
P.O. Box 933
Greenville, MS 38701
Phone: (601) 378-3141

Montana

Great Falls SCORE
710 1st Avenue North
P.O. Box 2127
Great Falls, MT 59403
Phone: (406) 761-4434
Fax: (406) 761-6129

Missoula SCORE 0259
802 Normans Lane
P.O. Box 632
Missoula, MT 59803
Phone: (406) 327-8806

Butte SCORE
100 George Street
Butte, MT 59701
Phone: (406) 723-3177
Fax: (406) 723-1215

Bozeman SCORE
2905 East Main Street
Bozeman, MT 59715
Phone: (406) 586-5421
Fax: (406) 586-8286

Helena SCORE
301 South Park/Federal Bldg
Helena, MT 59626-0054
Phone: (406) 441-1081
Fax: (406) 441-1090

Billings SCORE
815 S. 27th Street
P.O. Box 31177
Billings, MT 59101
Phone: (406) 245-4111
Fax: (406) 245-7333

Kalispell SCORE
2 Main Street
Kalispell MT 59901
Phone: (406) 756-5271
Fax: (406) 752-6665

Havre SCORE
518 1st Street
Havre, MT 59501
Phone: (406) 265-4383

North Carolina

Charlotte SCORE
200 N. College Street, Suite A2015
Charlotte, NC 28202-2173
Phone: (704) 344-6576
Fax: (704) 344-6769

Raleigh SCORE
Federal Century Bldg.
300 Fayetteville Street Mall; PO Box 406
Raleigh, NC 27602
Phone: (919) 856-4739
Fax: (919) 856-4183

Asheville SCORE
Federal Building, Room 259
151 Patton
Asheville, NC 28801-5007

Phone: (704) 271-4786
Fax: (704) 271-4009

Hendersonville SCORE
Federal Bldg., Room 108
West 4th Avenue & Church Street
Hendersonville, NC 28792

Phone: (704) 693-8702

Greensboro SCORE
400 W. Market Street, Suite 410
Greensboro, NC 27401-2241

Phone: (910) 333-5399

Wilmington SCORE
Alton Lennon Fed. Bldg.
2 Princess Street, Suite 103
Wilmington, NC 28401-3958

Phone: (910) 815-4576
Fax: (910) 815-4576

High Point SCORE
High Point Chamber of Commerce
1101 N. Main Street
High Point, NC 27262

Phone: (910) 882-8625
Fax: (910) 889-9499

Unifour SCORE
Catawba County Community College
470 Highway Ex-70 SW
Hickory, NC 28601

Phone: (704) 328-6111
Fax: (704) 328-1175

Durham SCORE
NC Mutual Plaza
411 W. Chapel Hill Street
Durham, NC 27707

Phone: (919) 541-2171

Sandhills Area SCORE
c/o Sand Hills Area C of C
1480 Hwy 15-501/PO Box 458
Southern Pines, NC 28387

Phone: (910) 692-3926
Fax: (910) 692-0619

Chapel Hill SCORE
c/o Chapel Hill/Carboro C of C
104 S. Estes Drive, PO Box 2897
Chapel Hill, NC 27515

Phone: (919) 967-7075
Fax: (919) 968-6874

Outer Banks SCORE
Outer Banks Chamber of Commerce
PO Box 1757
Kill Devil Hills, NC 27948

Phone: (919) 261-1094
Fax: (919) 441-0338

Down East SCORE
Neuse River Council of Governments
312 Tryon Palace Drive, Suite 6
New Bern, NC 28560

Phone: (919) 633-6688
Fax: (919) 633-9608

North Dakota

Fargo SCORE
PO Box 3086; 657 2nd Avenue, Room 225
Fargo, ND 58108-3083

Phone: (701) 239-5677

Minot SCORE
PO Box 507
Minot, ND 58702-0507

Phone: (701) 852-6883
Fax: (701) 852-6905

Upper Red River SCORE
4300 Technology Dr., PO Box 8372
Grand Forks, ND 58202-8372

Phone: (701) 777-3051

Bismarck-Mandan SCORE
PO Box 5509
Bismarck, ND 58502-5509

Phone: (701) 250-4303

Nebraska

Lincoln SCORE
8800 East O Street
Lincoln, NE 68520

Phone: (402) 437-2409

Omaha SCORE
11145 Mill Valley Road
Omaha, NE 68154

Phone: (402) 221-3606
Fax: (402) 221-3680

Norfolk SCORE
504 Pierce Street
Norfolk, NE 68701

Phone: (402) 371-0940

Columbus SCORE
c/o Wayne R. Davy
41 Stires Lake
Columbus, NE 68601

Phone: (402) 564-2769

North Platte SCORE
414 E. 16th Street
Cozad, NE 69130

Phone: (308) 784-2590

Hastings SCORE
c/o James Svoboda
1338 West 12th Street
Hastings, NE 68901

Phone: (402) 463-5818

Panhandle SCORE
c/o Marvin Harms
150549 CR 30
Minatare, NE 69356

Phone: (308) 632-2133

Fremont SCORE
Chamber of Commerce
92 West 5th Street
Fremont, NE 68025

Phone: (402) 721-2641

New Hampshire

Lakes Region SCORE   Phone: (603) 524-9168
67 Water Street, Suite 105
Laconia, NH 03246

Upper Valley SCORE   Phone: (603) 448-3491
Citizens Bank Bldg.
20 W. Park Street, 316 First
Lebanon, NH 03766

Seacoast SCORE   Phone: (603) 433-0575
195 Commerce Way, Unit A
Portsmouth, NH 03801-3251

Merrimack Valley SCORE   Phone: (603) 666-7561
275 Chestnut Street,   Fax: (603) 666-7925
    Room 618
Manchester, NH 03103

Monadnock SCORE   Phone: (603) 352-0320
34 Mechanic Street
Keene, NH 03431-3421

Concord SCORE   Phone: (603) 225-1400
143 N Main Street, Room 202A
Concord, NH 03301

Mt. Washington Va SCORE   Phone: (603) 383-0800
PO Box 1066
Conway, NH 03818

New Jersey

Somerset SCORE   Phone: (908) 218-8874
Paritan Valley Comm College;
    Box 3300
Somerville, NJ 08876

Newark SCORE   Phone: (201) 645-3982
2 Gateway Center, 4th Floor   Fax: (201) 645-2375
Newark, NJ 07102

North West SCORE   Phone: (201) 209-8525
c/o Bob Kopchains, Chair
25 Tannery Hill Drive
Hamburg, NJ 07419

Monmouth SCORE   Phone: (908) 224-2573
Brookdale Comm Coll Career Service
765 Newman Springs Road
Lincroft, NJ 07738

Bergen Cty SCORE   Phone: (201) 599-6090
327 E. Ridgewood Avenue
Paramus, NJ 07652

Ocean County SCORE   Phone: (908) 505-6033
33 Washington Street
Toms River, NJ 08754

S New Jersey SCORE   Phone: (609) 486-3421
c/o United Jersey Bank
4900 Rte. 70
Pennsauken, NJ 08109

Greater Princeton SCORE   Phone: (609) 520-1776
216 Rockingham Row   Fax: (609) 520-9107
Princeton Forrestal Village
Princeton, NJ 08540

New Mexico

Albuquerque SCORE   Phone: (505) 766-1900
Silver Square, Suite 330   Fax: (505) 766-1833
625 Silver Avenue, SW
Albuquerque, NM 87102

Roswell SCORE   Phone: (505) 625-2112
Federal Building, Room 237   Fax: (505) 623-2545
Roswell, NM 88201

Santa Fe SCORE   Phone: (505) 988-6302
Montoya Federal Building   Fax: (505) 988-6300
120 Federal Place, Rm. 307
Santa Fe, NM 87501

Las Cruces SCORE   Phone: (505) 523-5627
Loretto Towne Center
505 S. Main Street, Ste. 125
Las Cruces, NM 88001

Nevada

Las Vegas SCORE   Phone: (702) 388-6104
301 E. Stewart; Box 7527
Las Vegas, NV 89125

Northern Nevada SCORE   Phone: (702) 784-4436
SBDC   Fax: (702) 784-4337
College of Bus. Adm./U of Nevada
Reno, NV 89557-0100

New York

Rochester SCORE   Phone: (716) 263-6473
601 Keating Federal Building   Fax: (716) 263-3146
100 State Street, Room 410
Rochester, NY 14614

Buffalo SCORE   Phone: (716) 551-4301
Federal Building, Room 1311
111 West Huron Street
Buffalo, NY 14202
Web site: http://www2.pcom.net/score/buf45.html

Dutchess SCORE
c/o Chamber of Commerce
110 Main Street
Poughkeepsie, NY 12601

Phone: (914) 454-1700

Syracuse SCORE
100 S. Clinton Street, Room 1073
Syracuse, NY 13260

Phone: (315) 448-0422

Northeast SCORE
Albany College Chamber of Commerce
1 Computer Drive South
Albany, NY 12205

Phone: (518) 446-1118
Fax: (518) 446-1228

Watertown SCORE
518 Davidson Street
Watertown, NY 13601

Phone: (315) 788-1200
Fax: (315) 788-8251

Utica SCORE
SUNY Institute of Technology
PO Box 3050
Utica, NY 13504-3050

Phone: (315) 792-7553

Auburn SCORE
c/o Chamber of Commerce
30 South Street, POB 675
Auburn, NY 13021

Phone: (315) 252-7291

S Tier Binghamton SCORE
49 Court St., PO Box 995
Metro Center/2nd Floor
Binghamton, NY 13902

Phone: (607) 772-8860

Brookhaven SCORE
96 Jerome Drive
Farmingdale, NY 11735

Phone: (516) 451-6563

Westchester SCORE
350 Main Street
White Plains, NY 10601

Phone: (914) 948-3907
Fax: (914) 948-4645

Chemung SCORE
c/o SBA
333 East Water Street, 4th Floor
Elmira, NY 14901

Phone: (607) 734-3358

Huntington Area SCORE
c/o Chamber of Commerce
151 W. Carver Street
Huntington, NY 11743

Phone: (516) 423-6100

Tompkins County SCORE
c/o Tompkins Chamber of Commerce
904 E. Shore Drive
Ithaca, NY 14850

Phone: (607) 273-7080

Orange County SCORE
Orange Cty Chamber of Commerce
40 Matthews Street
Goshen, NY 10924

Phone: (914) 294-8080
Fax: (914) 294-6121

Staten Island SCORE
c/o Chamber of Commerce
130 Bay Street
Staten Island, NY 10301

Phone: (718) 727-1221

Ulster SCORE
Ulster Cty Comm College
Clinton Bldg., Room 107
Stone Ridge, NY 12484

Phone: (914) 687-5035
Fax: (914) 687-5015

Queens County SCORE
120-55 Queens Blvd., Room 333
Queens Borough Hall
Kew Gardens, NY 11424

Phone: (718) 263-8961
Fax: (718) 263-9032

Suffolk SCORE
6 Quantuck Bay Road
West Hampton Beach, NY 11978

Phone: (516) 288-6340
Fax: (516) 288-5715

New York SCORE
26 Federal Plaza
Room 3100
New York, NY 10278

Phone: (212) 264-4507
Fax: (212) 264-4963

Nassau County SCORE
Dept of Commerce & Ind.
400 County Seat Drive, #140
Mineola, NY 11501

Phone: (516) 571-3303

Ohio

Columbus SCORE
2 Nationwide Plaza
Suite 1400
Columbus, OH 43215-2542

Phone: (614) 469-2357

Cleveland SCORE
1100 Superior Avenue
Suite 620, Eaton Center
Cleveland, OH 44114-2507

Phone: (216) 522-4194
Fax: (216) 522-4844

Cincinnati SCORE
525 Vine Street
Ameritrust Bldg., Room 850
Cincinnati, OH 45202

Phone: (513) 684-2812
Fax: (513) 684-3251

Toledo SCORE
1946 N. 13th St., Ste. 367
Toledo, OH 43624

Phone: (419) 259-7598

Akron SCORE
c/o Regional Dev. Board
One Cascade Plaza, 7th Floor
Akron, OH 44308
Phone: (330) 379-3163
Fax: (330) 379-3164

Dayton SCORE
Federal Building, Room 505
200 W. 2nd Street
Dayton, OH 45402-1430
Phone: (513) 225-2887
Fax: (513) 225-7667

Youngstown SCORE
306 Williamson Hall
Youngstown University
Youngstown, OH 44555
Phone: (330) 746-2687

Mansfield SCORE
Chamber of Commerce
55 N. Mulberry Street
Mansfield, OH 44902
Phone: (419) 522-3211

Licking County SCORE
50 West Locust Street
Newark, OH 43055
Phone: (614) 345-7458

Canton SCORE
116 Cleveland Avenue, NW, Suite 601
Canton, OH 44702-1720
Phone: (330) 453-6047

Heart of Ohio SCORE
377 West Liberty Street
Wooster, OH 44691
Phone: (330) 262-5735
Fax: (330) 262-5745

Oklahoma

Tulsa SCORE
Chamber of Commerce
616 S. Boston, Suite 406
Tulsa, OK 74119
Phone: (918) 581-7462
Fax: (918) 581-6908

Oklahoma City SCORE
c/o SBA, Oklahoma Tower Bldg.
210 Park Avenue, #1300
Oklahoma City, OK 73102
Phone: (405) 231-5163
Fax: (405) 231-4876

Lawton SCORE
4500 W. Lee Blvd.
Bldg. 100, Suite 107
Lawton, OK 73505
Phone: (405) 353-8727
Fax: (405) 250-5677

NE Oklahoma SCORE
201 S. Main
Grove, OK 74344
Phone: (918) 786-6284
Fax: (918) 786-9841

Ardmore SCORE
P.O. Box 1585
Ardmore, OK 73402-1585
Phone: (405) 223-7765

Oregon

Portland SCORE
1515 SW Fifth Avenue, Suite 1050
Portland, OR 97201-5494
E-mail: pgrl34a@prodigy.com
Phone: (503) 326-3441
Fax: (503) 326-2501

Southern Oregon SCORE
132 W. Main; PO Box 969
Medford, OR 97501-0969
E-mail: pgrl34f@prodigy.com
Phone: (541) 776-4220

Willamette SCORE
c/o Chamber of Commerce
1401 Willamette Street; PO Box 1107
Eugene, OR 97401-1107
E-mail: pgrl34e@prodigy.com
Phone: (541) 465-6600
Fax: (541) 484-4942

Salem SCORE
PO Box 4024
Salem, OR 97302-4024
E-mail: pgrl34d@prodigy.com
Phone: (503) 370-2896

Bend SCORE
c/o Bend Chamber of Commerce
63085 North Highway 97
Bend, OR 97701
Phone: (541) 382-3221

Pennsylvania

Pittsburgh SCORE
1000 Liberty Avenue, Room 1122
Pittsburgh, PA 15222
Phone: (412) 395-6560
Fax: (412) 395-6562

Reading SCORE
c/o Chamber of Commerce
645 Penn Street
Reading, PA 19601
Phone: (610) 376-6766

Lancaster SCORE
118 West Chestnut Street
Lancaster, PA 17603
Phone: (717) 397-3092

Harrisburg SCORE
4211 Trindle Road
Camp Hill, PA 17011
Phone: (717) 761-4304
Fax: (717) 761-4315

Philadelphia SCORE
1315 Walnut Street, Suite 500
Philadelphia, PA 19107
Phone: (215) 790-5050
Fax: (215) 790-5016

Lehigh Valley SCORE
Rauch Bldg 37/Lehigh University
621 Taylor Street
Bethlehem, PA 18015
Phone: (610) 758-4496
Fax: (610) 758-5205

Erie SCORE
120 West 9th Street
Erie, PA 16501

Phone: (814) 871-5650

North Central PA SCORE
Federal Building, Room 304
240 W. 3rd Street, PO Box 725
Williamsport, PA 17703

Phone: (717) 322-3720
Fax: (717) 322-1607

Scranton SCORE
Kane Professional Bldg.
116 N. Washington Ave., Ste. 2H
Scranton, PA 18503

Phone: (717) 347-4611

Wilkes-Barre SCORE
20 N. Pennsylvania Avenue
Wilkes-Barre, PA 18702

Phone: (717) 826-6502

York SCORE
Cyber Center
1600 Pennsylvania Avenue
York, PA 17404

Phone: (717) 845-8830
Fax: (717) 854-9333

Uniontown SCORE
POB 2065 DTS, Pittsburg Street
Federal Building
Uniontown, PA 15401

Phone: (412) 437-4222

Mon-Valley SCORE
435 Donner Avenue
Monessen. PA 15062

Phone: (412) 684-4277

E. Montgomery Cty SCORE
Baederwood Shopping Center
1653 The Fairways, Ste. 204
Jenkintown, PA 19046

Phone: (215) 885-3027

Cumberland Valley SCORE
Chambersburg Chamber of Commerce
75 S. Second Street
Chambersburg, PA 17201

Phone: (717) 264-2935

Monroe-Stroudsbrg SCORE
556 Main Street
Stroudsburg, PA 18301

Phone: (717) 421-4433

Chester County SCORE
Gov't Svc Center
Suite 281, 601 Westtown Rd.
West Chester, PA 19382-4538

Phone: (610) 344-6910
Fax: (610) 793-2780

Westmoreland Co. SCORE
St. Vincent College
300 Fraser Purchase Road
Latrobe, PA 15650-2690

Phone: (412) 539-7505

Bucks County SCORE
c/o Chamber of Commerce
409 Hood Boulevard
Fairless Hills, PA 19030

Phone: (215) 943-8850
Fax: (215) 943-7404

Altoona-Blair SCORE
c/o Altoona-Blair Chamber of Commerce
1212 12th Avenue
Altoona, PA 16601-3493

Phone: (814) 943-8151

Warren County SCORE
Warren County Chamber of Commerce
PO Box 942, 315 Second Ave.
Warren, PA 16365

Phone: (814) 723-9017

Tri-County SCORE
238 High Street
Pottstown, PA 19464

Phone: (610) 327-2673

Central PA SCORE
200 Innovation Blvd
#242-B
State College, PA 16803

Phone: (814) 234-9415
Fax: (814) 238-9686

Puerto Rico and Virgin Islands

PR & VI SCORE
Citibank Towers Plaza
252 Ponce de Leon Ave., 2nd Floor
San Juan, PR 00918-2041

Phone: (809) 766-5001

Rhode Island

JGE Knight SCORE
380 Westminster Street
Providence, RI 02903

Phone: (401) 528-4571
Fax: (401) 528-4539

South Carolina

Midlands SCORE
Strom Thurmond Bldg.
1835 Assembly Street, Rm. 358
Columbia, SC 29201

Phone: (803) 765-5131
Fax: (803) 765-5962

Piedmont SCORE
Federal Bldg., Room B-02
300 E. Washington Street
Greenville, SC 29601

Phone: (864) 271-3638

Coastal SCORE
284 King Street
Charleston, SC 29401

Phone: (803) 727-4778
Fax: (803) 853-2529

Grand Strand SCORE
P.O. Box 2468
Myrtle Beach, SC 29578

Phone: (803) 918-1079

South Dakota

Sioux Falls SCORE Phone: (605) 330-4231
First Financial Center
110 South Phillips Ave., Ste. 200
Sioux Falls, SD 57102-1109

Rapid City SCORE Phone: (605) 394-5311
444 Mt. Rushmore Road, #209
Rapid City, SD 57701

Tennessee

Memphis SCORE Phone: (901) 544-3588
Federal Building
167 N. Main Street, Suite 390
Memphis, TN 38103

Nashville SCORE Phone: (615) 736-7621
50 Vantage Way, Suite 201 Fax: (615) 736-7232
Nashville, TN 37228-1500

Chattanooga SCORE Phone: (423) 752-5190
Federal Building Fax: (423) 752-5335
900 Georgia Ave., Rm. 26
Chattanooga, TN 37402

Greater Knoxville SCORE Phone: (423) 545-4203
Farragot Bldg
530 South Gay Street, Suite 224
Knoxville, TN 37902

Jackson SCORE Phone: (901) 423-2200
c/o Chamber of Commerce
PO Box 1904, 194 Auditorium Street
Jackson, TN 38302

Kingsport SCORE Phone: (423) 392-8805
c/o Chamber of Commerce
151 East Main Street
Kingsport, TN 37662

NE Tennessee SCORE Phone: (423) 929-7686
1st Tennessee Bank Bldg Fax: (423) 461-8052
2710 S. Roan Street, Ste. 584
Johnson City, TN 37601

Texas

Dallas SCORE Phone: (214) 828-2471
Comerica Bank-Second Floor Fax: (214) 828-2803
6260 E. Mockingbird
Dallas, TX 75214-2619

Houston SCORE Phone: (713) 773-6565
9301 Southwest Freeway, Suite 550 Fax: (713) 773-6550
Houston, TX 77074

Fort Worth SCORE Phone: (817) 871-6002
100 East 15th Street #24 Fax: (817) 871-6031
Ft. Worth, TX 76102

San Antonio SCORE Phone: (210) 472-5931
c/o SBA, Federal Building Fax: (210) 472-5935
727 E. Durango, Room #A527
San Antonio, TX 78206

L Rio Grande Vly SCORE Phone: (210) 427-8533
222 E. Van Buren, Suite 500 Fax: (210) 427-8537
Harlingen, TX 78550

Corpus Christi SCORE Phone: (512) 888-4322
651 Upper North Broadway, Fax: (512) 888-3418
 Suite 654
Corpus Christi, TX 78477

El Paso SCORE Phone: (915) 534-0541
10737 Gateway West, Suite 320 Fax: (915) 540-5155
El Paso, TX 79935

Lubbock SCORE Phone: (806) 472-7462
1611 10th Street, Suite 200 Fax: (806) 472-7487
Lubbock, TX 79401

Abilene SCORE Phone: (915) 677-1857
2106 Federal Post Office & Court
Abilene, TX 79601

Austin SCORE Phone: (512) 442-7235
2501 S. Congress Fax: (512) 442-7528
Austin, TX 78701

East Texas SCORE Phone: (903) 510-2975
RTDC
1530 SSW Loop 323, Ste. 100
Tyler, TX 75701

Texarkana SCORE Phone: (903) 792-7191
P.O. Box 1468 Fax: (903) 793-4304
Texarkana, TX 75504

Waco SCORE Phone: (254) 754-8898
401 Franklin Avenue Fax: (254) 756-0776
Waco, TX 76701

Brazos Valley SCORE Phone: (409) 776-8876
Norwest Bank Building
3000 Briarcrest, Suite 302
Bryan, TX 77802

Wichita Falls SCORE Phone: (817) 723-2741
Hamilton Building; PO Box 1860
Wichita Falls, TX 76307

Golden Triangle SCORE
P.O. Box 3150
Beaumont, TX 77704

Phone: (409) 838-6581
Fax: (409) 833-6718

Utah

Salt Lake SCORE
169 E. 100 South
Salt Lake City, UT 84111

Phone: (801) 364-1331
Fax: (801) 364-1310

Ogden SCORE
324 25th Street 6104
Ogden, UT 84401

Phone: (801) 625-5712

Central Utah SCORE
1275 N. University, Suite 8
Provo, UT 84604

Phone: (801) 373-5300

Southern Utah SCORE
c/o Dixie College
225 S. 700 East
St. George, UT 84770

Phone: (801) 652-7741

Northern Utah SCORE
c/o Cache Valley Chamber of Commerce
160 N. Main
Logan, UT 84123

Phone: (801) 752-2161

Virginia

Richmond SCORE
1504 Santa Rosa Road
Dale Building, Ste. 200
Richmond, VA 23229

Phone: (804) 771-2400
Fax: (804) 771-8018

Roanoke SCORE
250 Franklin Road
Federal Building, Room 716
Roanoke, VA 24011

Phone: (540) 857-2834
Fax: (540) 857-2043

Hampton Roads SCORE
Federal Building, Room 737
200 Granby Street
Norfolk, VA 23510

Phone: (757) 441-3733
Fax: (757) 441-3733

Peninsula SCORE
c/o Peninsula Chamber of Commerce
PO Box 7269, 6 Manhattan Square
Hampton, VA 23666

Phone: (804) 766-2000

Bristol SCORE
20 Volunteer Parkway
PO Box 519
Bristol, VA 24203

Phone: (423) 989-4850

Shenandoah Valley SCORE
c/o Waynesboro C of C
301 W. Main Street
Waynesboro, VA 22980

Phone: (540) 949-8203

Central Virginia SCORE
918 Emmet Street North, Suite 200
Charlottesville, VA 22903-4878

Phone: (804) 295-6712
Fax: (804) 295-7066

Greater Lynchburg SCORE
Federal Building
1100 Main Street
Lynchburg, VA 24504-1714

Phone: (804) 846-3235

Greater Prince William Co. SCORE
Prince William Chamber of Commerce
4320 Ridgewood Center Drive
Prince William, VA 22192

Phone: (703) 590-5000

Martinsville SCORE
115 Broad Street; PO Box 709
Martinsville, VA 24112-0709

Phone: (540) 632-6401

Williamsburg SCORE
c/o Chamber of Commerce
201 Penniman Road
Williamsburg, VA 23185

Phone: (757) 229-6511

Tri-Cities SCORE
c/o Chamber of Commerce
108 N. Main Street
Hopewell, VA 23860

Phone: (804) 458-5536

Vermont

Montpelier SCORE
c/o SBA; PO Box 605
87 State Street, Room 205
Montpelier, VT 05601

Phone: (802) 828-4422

Champlain Valley SCORE
11 Lincoln Street, Room 106
Winston Prouty Fed. Bldg.
Essex Junction, VT 05452

Phone: (802) 951-6762

Northeast Kingdom SCORE
c/o NCIC/ 20 Main Street;
   PO Box 904
St. Johnsbury, VT 05819

Phone: (802) 748-5101

Marble Valley SCORE
256 N. Main Street
Rutland, VT 05701-2413

Phone: (802) 773-9147

Washington

Seattle SCORE
1200 6th Avenue
Suite 1700
Seattle, WA 98101
Phone: (206) 553-7320
Fax: (206) 553-7044

Spokane SCORE
Business Information Center
1020 W. Riverside Avenue
Spokane, WA 99201
Phone: (509) 353-2820
Fax: (509) 353-2600

Tacoma SCORE
1101 Pacific Avenue
Tacoma, WA 98402
Phone: (206) 274-1288
Fax: (206) 274-1289

Ft. Vancouver SCORE
1200 Ft. Vancouver Way
PO Box 8900
Vancouver, WA 98668
Phone: (360) 992-3241

Mid-Columbia SCORE
c/o SBDC; PO Box 1647
Yakima, WA 98907-1647
Phone: (509) 574-4944
Fax: (509) 574-4943

Bellingham SCORE
Fourth Corner, Economic Dev. Group
PO Box 2803, 1203 Cornwall Ave.
Bellingham, WA 98227
Phone: (360) 676-4255
Fax: (360) 647-9413

Wisconsin

Milwaukee SCORE
310 W. Wisconsin Avenue, #425
Milwaukee, WI 53203
Phone: (414) 297-3942
Fax: (414) 297-1377

Madison SCORE
c/o M & I Bank
7448 Hubbard Avenue
Middleton, WI 53562
Phone: (608) 831-5464

Eau Claire SCORE
Federal Building, Room B11
510 South Barstow Street
Eau Claire, WI 54701
Phone: (715) 834-1573

Fond du Lac SCORE
Fond du Lac Area Association of Commerce
207 North Main Street
Fond du Lac, WI 54935
Phone: (920) 921-9500

Forward Janesville SCORE
51 South Jackson Street
Janesville, WI 53545
Phone: (608) 757-3160

Oshkosh SCORE
120 Jackson Street
Oshkosh, WI 54901
Phone: (920) 424-7700

Fox Cities SCORE
227 S. Walnut Street
PO Box 1855
Appleton, WI 54913
Phone: (920) 734-7101
ext. 24
Fax: (920) 734-7161

La Crosse SCORE
712 Main Street; PO Box 219
La Crosse, WI 54602-0219
Phone: (608) 784-4880

Wausau SCORE
300 Third St., Ste. 200; PO Box 6190
Wausau, WI 54402-6190
Phone: (715) 845-6231

Green Bay SCORE
835 Potts Avenue
Green Bay, WI 54304
Phone: (920) 496-8930
Fax: (920) 496-6009

Central Wisconsin SCORE
1224 Lindberg Avenue
Stevens Point, WI 54481
Phone: (715) 344-7729

Superior SCORE
305 Harborview Parkway
Superior, WI 54880
Phone: (715) 394-7716
Fax: (715) 394-3810

Madison SCORE
212 E. Washington Ave., Rm. 213
Madison, WI 53703
Phone: (608) 264-5508
Fax: (608) 264-5541

West Virginia

Charleston SCORE
1116 Smith Street
Charleston, WV 25301
Phone: (304) 347-5463

Wheeling SCORE
1310 Market Street
Wheeling, WV 26003
Phone: (304) 233-2575

Huntington SCORE
1101 6th Avenue, Suite 220
Huntington, WV 25701-2309
Phone: (304) 523-4092

Monongahela Va SCORE
1000 Technology Drive, Suite 1111
Fairmont, WV 26555
Phone: (304) 363-0486

Wyoming

Casper SCORE
Federal Building Rm 4126
100 East B Street
Casper, WY 82602
Phone: (307) 261-6529
Fax: (307) 261-6530

BIBLIOGRAPHY OF SBA PUBLICATIONS

This appendix contains a bibliography of resources available to aspiring entrepreneurs or small business owners. These resources are published by the Small Business Administration. For more information about SBA publications contact a local SBA office near you or call the Small Business Answer Desk at 1-800-827-5722.

Emerging Business Series

Transferring Management/Family Businesses

Help your family business successfully survive the transfer of ownership from generation to generation. Proper planning is the key. Item # EB01 $3.00

Marketing Strategies for Growing Businesses

Unravel the mystery of marketing—putting the customer first—and discover practical marketing approaches to budgeting, layout and design, copywriting, media analysis, and more. Item # EB02 $3.00

Management Issues for Growing Businesses

Learn to examine the marketplace environment and create employment and profit opportunities that provide growth and financial viability to your business through effective management. Item # EB03 $3.00

Human Resource Management for Growing Businesses

Uncover the characteristics of an effective personnel system and training program. Learn how these functions come together to build employee trust and productivity. Item # EB04 $3.00

Audit Checklist for Growing Businesses

Designed with the small business in mind, this audit checklist helps the entrepreneur conduct a comprehensive search for existing and potential problems and opportunities. Item # EB05 $3.00

Strategic Planning for Growing Businesses

Strategic planning is not just for big business. Learn to effectively match your business' strengths to available opportunities by developing a clear mission statement, goals, and objectives. Item # EB06 $3.00

Financial Management for Growing Businesses

Develop a comprehensive financial plan outlining the assets, debts and current and future profit potential of your business through effective financial management. Item # EB07 $3.00

Financial Management

ABC's of Borrowing

This best-seller tells you what lenders look for and what to expect when borrowing money for your small business. Item # FM01 $2.00

Elementos BASICOS PARA PEDIR DINERO PRESTADO

Esta publicacion le da a conocer lo que los prestatarios buscan y lo que esperan de usted cuando pide dinero prestado para su pequeño negocio. Item # FM01s $2.00

Understanding Cash Flow

The owner/manager is shown how to plan for the movement of cash through the business and thus plan for future requirements. Item # FM04 $2.00

A Venture Capital Primer for Small Business

Learn what venture capital resources are available and how to develop a proposal for obtaining these funds. Item # FM05 $2.00

Budgeting in a Small Service Firm

Learn how to set up and keep sound financial records. Study how to effectively use journals and ledgers and charts to increase profits. Item # FM08 $2.00

Recordkeeping in a Small Business

Need some basic advice on setting up a useful record keeping system? This publication describes how. Item # FM10 $2.00

Pricing Your Products and Services Profitably

Discusses how to price your products profitably, plus various pricing techniques and when to use them. Item # FM13 $2.00

Financing for Small Business

Learn how, when and where to find capital for business needs including step-by-step instructions. Item # FM14 $2.00

Management and Planning

Problems in Managing a Family-Owned Business

Specific problems exist when attempting to make a family-owned business successful. This publication offers suggestions on how to overcome these difficulties. Item # MP3 $2.00

Business Plan for Small Manufacturers

Designed to help an owner/manager of a small manufacturing firm, this publication covers all the basic information necessary to develop an effective business plan. Item # MP04 $2.00

Business Plan for Small Construction Firms

This publication is designed to help an owner/manager of a small construction company pull together the resources to develop a business plan. Item # MP05 $2.00

Planning and Goal Setting for Small Business

Learn proven management techniques to help you plan for success. Item # MP06 $2.00

Business Plan for Retailers

Business plans are essential road maps for success. Learn how to develop a business plan for a retail business. Item # MP09 $2.00

Business Plan for Small Service Firms

Outlines the key points to be included in the business plan of a small service firm. Item # MP11 $2.00

Checklist for Going into Business

This is a must if you're thinking about starting a business. It highlights the important factors you should know in reaching a decision to start your own business. Item # MP12 $2.00

Lista Para Comenzar Su Negocio

Esta publicacion es necesaria si usted esta pensando en comenzar un negocio. Demuestra los factores importantes que usted debebe de conocer antes de tomar la decision de comenzar su propio negocio. Item # MP12s $2.00

How to Get Started with a Small Business Computer

Helps you forecast your computer needs, evaluate the alternatives and select the right computer system for your business. Item # MP14 $2.00

Business Plan for Home-Based Business

Provides a comprehensive approach to developing a business plan for a home-based business. Item # MP15 $2.00

How to Buy or Sell A Business

Learn several techniques for determining the best price to buy or sell a small business. Item # MP16 $2.00

Developing a Strategic Business Plan

This best seller helps you develop a strategic action plan for your small business. Item # MP21 $2.00

Inventory Management

Discusses the purpose of inventory management, types of inventories, record keeping and forecasting inventory levels. Item # MP22 $2.00

Selecting the Legal Structure for Your Business

Discusses the various legal structures that a small business can use in setting up operations. It identifies types of legal structures and the advantages and disadvantages of each. Item # MP25 $2.00

Evaluating Franchise Opportunities

Evaluate franchise opportunities and select the business that's right for you. Item # MP26 $2.00

Small Business Risk Management Guide

This guide can help you strengthen your insurance program by identifying, minimizing and eliminating business risks. Item # MP28 $2.00

Child Day-Care Services

An overview of the industry, including models of day-care operations. Item # MP30 $3.00

Handbook for Small Business

Handy information for getting started in a new publication developed by the SBA's Service Corps of Retired Executives (SCORE). Item # MP31 $3.00

How to Write a Business Plan

What you need to know to write a good plan at the start. It can save your business dow the line. Item # MP32 $3.00

Marketing

Creative Selling: The Competitive Edge

Explains how to use creative selling techniques to increase profits. Item # MT01 $2.00

Marketing for Small Business: An Overview

Provides an overview of marketing concepts and contains an extensive bibliography of sources covering the subject of marketing. Item # MT02 $2.00

Researching Your Market

Learn inexpensive techniques that you can apply to gather facts about your customer base and how to expand it. Item # MT08 $2.00

Selling by Mail Order

Provides basic information on how to run a successful mail order business. Includes information on product selection, pricing, testing, and writing effective advertisements. Item # MT09 $2.00

Advertising

Advertising is critical to the success of any small business. Learn how you can effectively advertise your products and services. Item # MT11 $2.00

Products/Ideas/Inventions

Ideas into Dollars

This publication identifies the main challenges in product development and provides a list of resources to help inventors and innovators take their ideas into the marketplace. Item # PI01 $2.00

Avoiding Patent, Trademark, and Copyright Problems

Learn how to avoid infringing the rights of others and the importance of protecting your own rights. Item # PI02 $2.00

Personnel Management

Employees: How to Find and Pay Them

A business is only as good as the people in it. Learn how to find and hire the right employees. Item # PM02 $2.00

Videotapes

Each VHS videotape below comes complete with a workbook.

Marketing: Winning Customers With A Workable Plan

Take advantage of this easy-to-follow course and develop the marketing plan designed to meet your goals. Developed by two of the country's leading small business marketing experts, this hands-on program offers a step-by-step approach to writing the best possible marketing plan for your business. Item # VT01 $30.00

The Business Plan: Your Road Map to Success

Learn the essentials of developing a business plan that will lead you to capital, growth and profitability. This video teaches you what to include, what to omit, and how to get free help from qualified consultants when developing your business plan. Item # VT02 $30.00

Promotion Solving the Puzzle

Master the components that make a successful promotional campaign; advertising, public relations, direct mail and trade shows. This videotape shows you how to put the pieces together. Learn how to choose the best advertising medium for your needs, and much more. Item # VT03 $30.00

Home-Based Business: A Winning Blueprint

This practical program examines the essentials of operating within a productive and profitable home-based business—from designing your home office and avoiding isolation to networking strategies and building an image that gets you taken seriously. Item # VT04 $30.00

Basics of Exporting

This videotape shows you how to open the doors to international markets. This tape provides information on: getting your goods overseas, payment mechanisms, selling and distributing overseas, international marketing, and sources of financial assistance. Item # VT05 $30.00

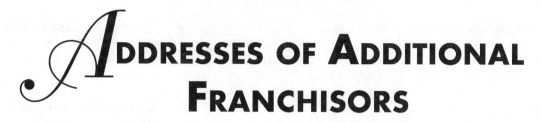

ADDRESSES OF ADDITIONAL FRANCHISORS

Automotive & Truck Services, Parts, Accessories, and Rentals

21st Century Autoalliance™ Inc.
P.O. Box 33863
Kansas City, MO 64120-3863

A.T.L. Motor Max
8334 Veterans Highway
Millersville, MD 21108

Aero Colours
6971 Washington Ave. S.
Minneapolis, MN 55439-1508

All Tune Transmission
8334 Veterans Hwy.
Millersville, MD 21108

Artech Window Tinting & Auto Security
2100 Hwy 360, Ste. 1805
Grand Prarie, TX 75050

Auto Artistry
500 E. North Ave.
Carol Stream, IL 60188

Auto Exam
1901 N. Central Expy., Ste. 220
Richardson, TX 75075

Auto Xtreme Stores
3034 E. 10th St.
Greenville, NC 27858

Automagic Mobile Autobody Repair System
1400 - 400 Burrard St
Vancouver, BC V6C-3G2

Ax Racks
2285 Austell Rd.
Marietta, GA 30060

Brake Centers Of America
35 Old Battery Rd.
Bridgeport, CT 06605

Brake Masters Systems, Inc.
6179 E. Broadway
Tucson, AZ 85711

Bullhide Liner Corporation, The
N. 1000 Argonne Rd., Ste. 120
Spokane, WA 99206

Colors On Parade
5201 Brook Hollow Pkwy., Suite A
Norcross, GA 30071

Colorworks
620 6th Ave. SW
P.O. Box 1796
Aberdeen, SD 57402-1796

Dents Plus
One San Jose Place, #22
Jacksonville, FL 32257

Ding King Franchising Inc., The
1280 Bison Ave., Ste. B-9
Newport Beach, CA 92660

Dr Kar Klean Detail Centres
15687 - 116 Ave.
Edmonton, AB T5M 3W1

Dura-Built Transmissions
777 Campus Commons Rd. #200
Sacramento, CA 95825

Fast Plates
1035 K Street
Lincoln, NE 68508

Fleetbay
P.O. Box 153607
Irving, TX 75015-3607

Gold Finger Inc.
342 W. 200 S., #10
Salt Lake City, UT 84101

Guardian Interlock Systems
110 Marietta Station Walk, Ste. 320
Marietta, GA 30060

House Calls® (Traveling Auto Repair)
2508 Betty St.
Orlando, FL 32803

It's Dents Or Us
7801 W. 63rd. St.
Overland Park, KS 66202

Jet-Black Sealcoating & Repair
9033 Lyndale Ave. S.
Bloomington, MN 55420

Leaverton Auto
827 S. 9th
St. Joseph, MO 64501

Liquid Resins International, Ltd
4295 N. Holly Rd.
Olney, IL 62450

Locationlube
P.O. Box 700
E. Sandwich, MA 02537

Lubemaster
1989 Dundas St. E.
Mississauga, ON M5R 3A6

Mad Hatter Car Care Centers
1235 Styron St.
Charlotte, NC 28203

Mcquik's Oilube
P.O. Box 46
3861 N. Wheeling Ave.
Muncie, IN 47308

Mermaid Car Wash
526 Grand Canyon Dr.
Madison, WI 53719

Ming Auto Beauty Centers
346 E. 100 S.
Salt Lake City, UT 84111

Minit Tune & Brake Auto Centers
398 W. Fifth Ave.
Vancouver, BC V5Y 1J5

Minute Muffler & Brake
1600 3rd Ave. S.
Lethbridge, AB T1J 0L2

Mister Mobile On-Site Oil Changes
5592 61st St. N.
St. Petersburg, FL 33709

Mobile Wheel Refinishing Co.
31337 Walker Rd.
Bay Village, OH 44140

Motorworks Remanufactured Engine Installation Centers
4210 Salem St.
Philadelphia, PA 19124

Mr. Wizard® Glass Tinting Corporation
3368 Tennyson-Lockbox 486
Victoria, BC V8W 2N8

Practical Rent-A-Car
1500 E. Tropicana Ave., Ste. 123
Las Vegas, NV 89119

Prevent-A-Crack Inc.
3116 E. Shea Blvd., #247
Phoenix, AZ 85028

Prompto System, Inc.
13 Scott Dr.
Westbrook, ME 04092

Q Lube Inc.
1385 W. 2200 S.
Salt Lake City, UT 84119

Rennsport
10390 Alpharetta St., S-620
Roswell, GA 30075

Rust Check
1285 Britannia Rd. E.
Mississauga, ON L4W 1C7

Select Auto Leasing
2942 N. 16th St.
Phoenix, AZ 85016-7606

Speedy Vinyl
5468 Dundas St. W., Ste. 551
Toronto, ON M9B 6E3

Stop Brake Shops
13844 Alton Parkway, #132
Irvine, CA 92718

Tire Warehouse
492 Main St.
P.O. Box 486
Keene, NH 03431

Top Value Muffler Shops
36887 Schoolcraft Rd.
Livonia, MI 48150

Transmission USA
4444 W. 147th St.
Midlothian, IL 60445

Truckaline Suspension Centers
1420-B Hillcrest Pkwy.
Altoona, WI 54720

Ugly Duckling Rent-A-Car
2525 E. Camelback Rd., Ste. 510
Phoenix, AZ 85016

Ultra Wash
2335 Naomi St.
Houston, TX 77054

USA Muffler & Brakes
2624 W. Lincoln Hwy.
Merrillville, IN 46410

Victory Lane Quick Oil Change Inc.
2610 W. Liberty, Ste. C
Ann Arbor, MI 48103

Yipes Stripes Inc.
520 Court St.
Dover, DE 19901

Beauty Care and Products & Hair Care

Accent Hair Salon
211 South Main St., Ste. 770
Dayton, OH 45402

Beaux Visages European Skin Care Centers
270 Mount Hope Dr.
Albany, NY 12202

Beneficial Health And Beauty
1780 W. 500 S.
Salt Lake City, UT 84104

City Looks Salons International
300 Industrial Blvd. N.E.
Minneapolis, MN 55413

Com*Plex Skin Fitness Clinics™
393 S. Harlan, Ste. 200
Lakewood, CO 80266

Command Performance
P.O. Box 3000-266
Georgetown, TX 78627

Don Cosa Images
415 1/2 Cedar Ln.
Teaneck, NJ 07666

E-Z Tan
21073 Powerline Rd., #63
Boca Raton, FL 33433

Hair Replacement Centers
12100 Wilshire Blvd., #900
Los Angeles, CA 90025

Hairline Creations Studios
5850-54 W. Montrose Ave.
Chicago, IL 60634

Magicuts
3780 Fourteenth Ave., Ste. 106
Markham, ON L3R 9Y5

Merle Norman Cosmetics
9130 Bellanca Ave.
Los Angeles, CA 90045

Nectar Bath And Body Shop
480 Lepine
Dorval, PQ H9P 2V6

Nectar Skin Care Shops
4164-A Innslake Dr.
Glen Allen, VA 23060

Nu-Concept Body Wrap Inc.
603 Cleveland St.
Elyria, OH 44035

Planet Diva
P.O. Box 3000-266
Georgetown, TX 78627

Pro Image Inc.
563 W. 500 S.
Bountiful, UT 84010

Pro-Cuts
500 Grapevine Hwy., Ste. 400
Hurst, TX 76054-2707

Romay Skin Care Inc.
4201 S. Noland Rd., Ste. F
Independence, MO 64055

Snip N' Clip Haircut Shops
7910 Quivira Rd.
Lenexa, KS 66215

Sunbanque Island Tanning
2533A Yonge St.
Toronto, ON M4P 2H9

Top Of The Line Fragrance Franchise
515 Bath Ave.
Long Branch, NJ 07740

Trade Secret
7201 Metro Blvd.
Minneapolis, MN 55439

Volpe Nails Inc.
1747 Independence Blvd., Ste. E6
Sarasota, FL 34234

We Care Hair
7327 W. 90th St.
Bridgeview, IL 60455

Business Services, Advertising, and Financial Services

ABS Systems
1260 Palmetto Ave., Ste. C
Winter Park, FL 32789

Accountants Inc.
111 Anza Blvd. #400
Burlingame, CA 94010

Ace America's Cash Express
1231 Greenway Dr.
Irving, TX 75038

Advanced Electronic Tax Services
2616 W. 70th Ave.
Shreveport, LA 71108

Adventures In Advertising
2353 130th Ave. N.E., Ste.100
Bellevue, WA 98005

Ag Information Inc.
10407 S. Western Ave.
Chicago, IL 60643

America One Inc.
2214 University Park Dr.
Okemos, MI 48864

Auto Show Magazine
6030 S. Lindbergh
St. Louis, MO 63123

Avalon Coupons Inc.
507 S. Thorton Ave.
Dalton, GA 30720

Business America
2120 Greentree Rd.
Pittsburgh, PA 15220

Business Information International Inc.
The Falls Building
22 N. Front St., Ste. 60
Memphis, TN 38103

Business Opportunities Inc.
466 Arthur Ave.
Shreveport, LA 71105

Business Success Systems Inc.
1408 Biscayne Way
Haslett, MI 48840

Buying & Dining Guide
80 Eighth Ave.
New York, NY 10011

Chances Newspaper
Unit #11 Downtown Heritage Pl.
Orillia, ON L3V 1V4

Chapman Publishing Inc.
222 Lakeview Ave., Ste. 160-116
West Palm Beach, FL 33401

Check Patrol
115 W. Kagy, Ste. G
Bozeman, MT 59715

Checkcare Systems
600 Brookstone Centre Pkwy.
Columbus, GA 31908

Citizens Equality Telecommunications
26A Barnes Park Rd. - N.
Wallingford, CT 06492

Communications Consulting International
1889 Monroe Dr.
Atlanta, GA 30324

Communications World
6025 S. Quebec, Ste. 300
Englewood, CO 80111

Comprehensive Business Services
26722 Plaza Dr.
Mission Viejo, CA 92691

Connect Ad Inc.
1000 W. McNab, Ste. 236
Pompano Beach, FL 33069

Consumer Network Of America
15965 Jeanette
Southfield, MI 48075

Coupon Tabloid International Inc., The
5775 S.W. Jean Rd., #101
Lake Oswego, OR 97035

Debt Doctors Franchising, Inc.
2445 State St., P.O. Box 5357
Lafayette, IN 42903

Dophin Publications Of America
1235 Sunset Grove Rd.
Fallbrook, CA 92028

EBC Office Center
1080 Holcomb Bridge Rd.
Bldg. 100, Ste. 31
Roswell, GA 30076

Enrollment Center®, The
7924 Ivanhoe Ave., Ste. 2
La Jolla, CA 92037

Express Postal Centers
6475 28th St., S.E.
Grand Rapids, MI 49546

Express-It Courier Network
1855 Norman Ave.
Santa Clara, CA 95054-2029

Fax-9
1235 Lake Plaza Dr.
Colorado Springs, CO 80906

Felix Ruslin Direct Response Inc.
8308 S. Kedzie Ave.
Chicago, IL 60652

Full Circle Image
6256 34th Avenue NW
Rochester, MN 55901

Get Lucky Tonight
201 E. Round Grove Rd., Ste. 1618
Lewisville, TX 75067

Great American Coupon Pulications, Inc.
8303 s.w. fRY. #610
Houston, TX 77074

H & R Block Tax Services Inc.
4410 Main St.
Kansas City, MO 64111

Holland Income Tax Inc.
3512 Taylor Blvd.
Louisville, KY 40215

Homes & Land Magazine
1600 Capital Cir., S.W.
Tallahassee, FL 32310

Homesteader Enterprises Inc.
P.O. Box 2824
Framingham, MA 01703

Hq Business Centers
120 Montgomery St., #2350
San Francisco, CA 94104

Impressions On Hold International
6218 S. Lewis, Ste. 116
Tulsa, OK 74136

Information Display Services, Inc.
P.O. Box 7208
Delray Beach, FL 33484-7208

Instafone
3333 S. Congress Ave., Ste. 401
Delray Beach, FL 33445

Insurance Claims Yellow Pages International, Inc.
9420 E. Doubletree Ranch Rd., C-102
Scottsdale, AZ 85258

Interactive Videoconferencing Centers
4807 Rockside Rd., Ste. 400
Independence, OH 44131

Interface Financial Group
4521 PGA Blvd., Ste. 211
Palm Beach Gardens, FL 33418

International Voice Exchange
2323 Foothill Dr.
Salt Lake City, UT 84109

Inviro
P.O. Box 5396
Englewood, CO 80155

Jackson Hewitt Tax Service
4575 Bonney Rd.
Virginia Beach, VA 23462

K & N Mobile Distribution Systems®
4909 Rondo Dr.
Fort Worth, TX 76160

Kingstad Meeting Centers
3800 SW Cedar Hills Blvd., Suite 120
Beaverton, OR 97005

Local Merchant Display Centers
4115 Tiverton Rd.
Randallstown, MD 21133-2019

Look! No-Fault Auto Insurance Agencies Inc.

32630 Cherry Hill
Garden City, MI 48135

M R Communication Consultants Inc.

221 Dufferin St.
Toronto, ON M6K 1R9

Mcgrow Consulting

30 North St.
Hingham, MA 02043-2228

Mister Money - USA Inc.

238 Walnut St.
Ft. Collins, CO 80524

Mobil Ambition U.S.A.

5353 N. Federal Hwy., Ste. 304
Ft. Lauderdale, FL 33308

Money Mailer, Inc.

14271 Corporate Dr.
Garden Grove, CA 92843

National Drive Buy Broadcasting, Inc.

21346 St. Andrews Blvd.
Boca Raton, FL 33434

National Tele-Communications

300 Broadacres Dr.
Bloomfield, NJ 07003

Net$Avings™

2180 SR 434 W. Ste. 1170
Longwood, FL 32779

Next Day Tax Cash

2854 S. Broadway
Englewood, CO 80110

Nexus - Consultants To Management

P.O. Box 1531
Novato, CA 94948

Nix Check Cashing

17019 Kingsview Ave.
Carson, CA 90746

On-Hold International

5650 Breckenridge
Tampa, FL 33610

Paradise Cellular & Paging

6807 Miramar Pkwy.
Miramar, FL 33023

Points For Profit

P.O. Box 2424
La Mesa, CA 91943

Professor Tax Of N.C. Inc.

34 Maxwell St.
Asheville, NC 28801

Q-Pon Book, The

1827 N. Michigan Ave.
Saginaw, MI 48602

Quality Marketing Inc.

6278 N. Federal Hwy., #284
Fort Lauderdale, FL 33308

R & S Public Relations Inc.

400 Skokie Blvd., #200
Northbrook, IL 60062

Ribbon Xchange

7550 River Rd., #14
Delta, BC V4G 1C8

Save-A-Buck™

P.O. Box 290837
Port Orange, FL 32120-0837

Super Coups

180 Bodwell Street
Avon, MA 02322

Supersaver Coupons

80 Eighth Ave. #315
New York, NY 1011

Town Planner

16600 Sprague Rd. #440
Cleveland, OH 44130

Traveltix

1919 S. 40th St., Ste. 202
Lincoln, NE 68506

TV Facts Magazine

Liberty Square
Danvers, MA 01923

TV Times

Box 4554
Chapel Hill, NC 27515

Typing Tigers

P.O. Box 8
San Marcos, TX 78667

U & R Tax Depot

201-1345 Pembina Hwy.
Winnipeg, MB R3T 2B6

Welcome Host Of America Inc.

13953 Perkins Rd.
Baton Rouge, LA 70810-3438

Wizard Of Ads

One Maritime Plaza, Ste. 700
San Francisco, CA 94111

X-Bankers Check Cashing

809 Chapel St.
New Haven, CT 06510

Your Office USA

402 W. Broadway, 4th Floor
San Diego, CA 92101

Carpet & Related Services

America's Carpet Gallery™

P.O. Box 21737
Roanoke, VA 24018

Carpeteria Inc.

25322 Rye Canyon Rd.
Santa Clarita, CA 91355

Color Tile & Carpet

515 Houston
Ft. Worth, TX 76102

Color Your Carpet

2465 Ridgecrest Ave.
Orange Park, FL 32065

Dial-A-Floor

P.O. Box 157
Convent Station, NJ 07961-0157.

Floor Coverings International
5182 Old Dixie Hwy.
Forest Park, GA 30050

Lifestyle Mobil Carpet Showrooms
P.O. Box 3876
Dalton, GA 30721

Children—Services and Products

Baby News
23521 Foley St.
Hayward, CA 94545

Baby Town
1662 Clarkson Rd.
Chesterfield, MO 63017

Compuchild Services Of America, Inc.
406 Rushwood Dr.
Murfreesboro, TN 37130

Computertots
10132 Colvin Run Rd.
Great Falls, VA 22066

Discovery Express
3905 Talmadge Road
Toledo, OH 43606

Gym Rompers Franchise Inc.
1140 City Park Ave.
New Orleans, LA 70119

Gymn' Around (Mobile) Partys / Gymnastics Franchise
705-A-Seminole Dr.
West Columbia, SC 29169

Gymsters® Inc.
6111 Paseo Pueblo Dr.
San Jose, CA 95120-2741

Head Over Heels Franchise System Inc.
2106 Cahaba Rd.
Birmingham, AL 35223

High Touch - High Tech
7908 Wiles Rd.
Coral Springs, FL 33067

J.W. Tumbles® A Childrens Gym
12750 Carmel Country Rd., Ste. 102
San Diego, CA 92130

Kid To Kid
406 W. South Jordan Pkwy., Ste. 160
South Jordan, UT 84095

Little Gym International Inc., The
8180 N. Hayden Blvd., Bldg.D, Ste. 200
Scottsdale, AZ 85258

Little Scientists
P.O. Box 3953
Woodbridge, CT 06525

My Gym Children's Fitness Center
12422 Santa Monica Blvd.
Los Angeles, CA 90025

Once Upon A Child
4200 Dahlberg Dr.
Minneapolis, MN 55422

Pee Wee Workout
34976 Aspenwood Ln.
Willoughby, OH 44094

Pre-Fit Inc.
10340 S. Western Ave.
Chicago, IL 60643

Romparound
215 Rt. 22 E.
GreenBrook, NJ 8812

Safe-T-Child® Program
203 Barsana Ave.
Austin, TX 78737

Sitters Unlimited
23015 Del Lago
Laguna Hills, CA 92653

Tenniskids Inc.
557 21st St.
Manhattan Beach, CA 90266

Toddlin' Time
8084 Station Rd.
Manassas, VA 20111

Tutor Time Child Care Systems Inc.
621 N.W. 53 St., Ste. 450
Boca Raton, FL 33487

Uppy Franchising International, Inc.
601 W. Golf Rd., Ste. 108
Mt. Prospect, IL 60056

USA Baby
857 N. Larch Ave.
Elmhurst, IL 60126

Cleaning, Janitorial, and Maid Services

A-Pro Services
P.O. Box 132
Newfield, NJ 08344

Aerowest And Westair Services
3882 Del Amo Blvd.
Torrance, CA 90503

Brite Site Inc.
4616 W. Fullerton
Chicago, IL 60639-1896

Classy Maids
P.O. Box 160879
Altamonte Springs, FL 32716-0879

Cleaner Option℠
1081 E. Putnam Ave.
Riverside, CT 06878

Cleaning Authority, The
9009 Mendenhall Ct., Ste. G
Columbia, MD 21045

Cleannet, Usa
9861 Broken Land Pkwy.
Columbia, MD 21046

Color Tex Systems Inc.
3555 S. Choctaw
El Reno, OK 73036

Consol Carpet Cleaning Franchise Corporation
P.O. Box 630
Stoughton, MA 02072

Cottage Care
6323 W. 110th St.
Overland Park, KS 66211

Custom Maids
4217 W. 21st
Amarillo, TX 79106

Dririte Inc.
1520 Edgewater Dr., Ste. D
Orlando, FL 32804

International Master Care Janitorial Franchising Inc.
555-6 St., Ste. 327
New Westminster, BC V3L 5H1

Kiwi Carpet Cleaning
4707 140th Ave. N., Ste. 306
Clearwater, FL 34622

Kwik Dry Carpet & Upholstery Cleaning
25665 Caton Farm Rd.
Plainfield, IL 60544

Maid-Rite
815 Office Park Rd., Ste. 9
W. Des Moines, IA 50265

Maidpro
180 Canal St.
Boston, MA 02114

Maids Plus
977 E. Cherry St.
Canal Fulton, OH 44614

Maids-America's Maid Service, The
4820 Dodge St.
Omaha, NE 68132

Master Care Janitorial
#327-555 6th St.
New Westminster, BC V3L 5H1

Mini Maid
819 Pinnacle Place
Marietta, GA 30062-7508

Minimaid/Service Systems Of Canada
192 Shorting Rd.
Scarborough, ON M1S 3S7

National Hygiene Franchise Corp.
950 N. Rand Rd., Ste. 119
Wauconda, IL 60084

Nutech Cleaning Systems
P.O. Box 793
Bountiful, UT 84011-0793

Paul's Restorations
1640 Upper Ottawa St.
Hamilton, ON L8W 3P2

Proforce USA
1950 Old Gallows Rd., Ste. 420
Vienna, VA 22182

Remodeling Contractors & Cleaning Service Inc.
9530 James A. Reed Rd.
Kansas City, MO 64134

Rhinish & Company
P.O. Box 245239
Brooklyn, NY 11224-9993

Service One Janitorial
5104 N.O.B.T., Ste. 224
Orlando, FL 32810

Servpro
575 Airport Blvd.
Gallatin, TN 37066

Sign Washers Inc., The
P.O. Box 1907
Ferndale, WA 98248

Slats Blind Cleaning
3119 Porter Gulch Rd.
Aptos, CA 95003

Sparkle Carpet Cleaning
1222 S. Main Ave.
Scranton, PA 18504

Swisher Maids
6849 Fairview Rd.
Charlotte, NC 28210

Teamworks Cleaning Systems
177 Main St.
Fort Lee, NJ 07024

Tri-Color Carpet Dyeing And Cleaning Co. Llc
3805C Abbott Martin Rd.
Nashville, TN 37215

Computer Services and Products

Advanced Technology Specialists
Rt. 9, Box 534 Hi-Tech Center
Crossville, TN 38555

Computer Doctor
P.O. Box 487
Aberdeen, SD 57402-0487

Computer Renaissance
4200 Dahlberg Dr.
Minneapolis, MN 55422-4837

Cyber Exchange Software & Computers
2686 E. Main St.
St. Charles, IL 60174

Cyberspace Internet
416 Central Ave.
Orange, NJ 07050

First Internet, Inc.
1060 Cordillera, Ste. 101
San Clemente, CA 92673

Firstinternet
1060 Calle Cordillera Suite 101
San Clemente, CA 92673

Laserquipt International Ltd Inc.
10300 Bren Rd. E.
Minnetonka, MN 55343

Rent-A-Computer
246 S. 16th St.
Lincoln, NE 68508

Sky Link Internet Access
30 Greenboro Crescent
Ottawa, ON K1T 1W5

Software City
26 W. Forest Ave.
Englewood, NJ 7631

Sun Computer Services
11500 N. Dale Mabey, Ste. 1415
Tampa, FL 33624

Todays Computer Business Centers
411 Eagleview Blvd.
Exton, PA 19341

UserFriendly Computer Resource Centers
401 Sixth Ave.
New York, NY 10014

Websurf, Inc.
3228 US 64 West
Apex, NC 27502

Construction, Remodeling, Maintenance, and House Inspection

A-1 Concrete Leveling Inc.
2417 Manchester Rd.
Akron, OH 44314

A-1 Homes Inc.
711 Bay Area Blvd., Ste. 517
Webster, TX 77598

ABC+A273 Seamless Siding
3001 Fiechtner Dr.
Fargo, ND 58103

Ace Refinishing
4311 Crystal Lake Drive
Pompano Beach, FL 33064

Brickkicker Home Inspection
1200 Iroquois Dr.
Naperville, IL 60563

Building Services Of America Inc.
11900 W. 87th St., Ste. 135
Lenexa, KS 66215

Canadian Residential Inspection Services Ltd.
P.O. Box 2121
Dartmouth, NS B2W 3Y2

Designer Doors
4810 St. Rt. 7
Burghill, OH 44404

Ever Dry Waterproofing
365 E. Highland Rd.
Macedonia, OH 44056

Grout Grouch
161 Banta Ave.
Garfield, NJ 07026-3601

Handyworks Group, The
11780 Manchester Rd., Ste. 205
St. Louis, MO 63131

Inspectech®
2527 Camino Ramon, Ste. 375
San Ramon, CA 94583

Kitchen Wizards
1020 N. University Parks Dr.
Waco, TX 76707

Kott Koatings Inc.
27161 Burbank St.
Foothill Ranch, CA 92610

Lone Drainer & Pronto!, The
1451 Edinger Ave., Ste. F
Tustin, CA 92680

Marblelife Inc.
6900 Haggerty Rd., Ste. 140
Canton, MI 48187

Nationwide Real Estate Inspectors Service Inc.
134 W. 32nd St., Rm. 501
New York, NY 10001-3201

Newcomer's Inspection Services
8200 Humboldt Ave. S., Ste. 301
Minneapolis, MN 55431

Newcomer's Of America, Property Inspection Services Inc.
210 Wisconsin Ave.
Waukesha, WI 53186

Olga's Kitchen Licensing Inc.
1940 Northwood Dr.
Troy, MI 48084

Perma-Jack Co.
9066 Watson Rd.
St. Louis, MO 63126-2234

Pillar To Post Inc.
14502 N. Dale Mabry Hwy., Ste. 200
Tampa, FL 33618

Potty Doctor Plumbing Service
P.O. Box 1426
Lake Worth, FL 33460-1426

Professional House Doctors Inc.
1406 E. 14th St.
Des Moines, IA 50316

Residential Building Inspectors Inc.
701 Fairway Dr.
Clayton, NC 27520

Roll A Way Storm & Security Shutters
10601 Oak St., N.E.
St. Petersburg, FL 33716

Roto-Static International
6810 Kitimat Rd., Unit 1
Mississauga, ON L4B 3E6

Sealmaster Franchise Group
2520 S. Campbell St.
Sandusky, OH 44870

Super Seamless Steel Siding Of Canada
560 Henderson Dr.
Regina, SK S4N 5X2

Tile Place, The
295 Buck Rd., Ste. 115
Holland, PA 18966

United Energy
3333 Iowa St.
St. Louis, MO 63118

United States Seamless
2001 - 1st Ave. N.
Fargo, ND 58102

Window Coverings International
1280 Bison B9-131
Newport Beach, CA 92660

Window Works
6321 Bury Dr., Ste. 2
Eden Prairie, MN 55346

Wise Cracks
2 Bluewater Rd.
Bedford, NS B4B 1G7

Copying, Printing, Sign Making, and Mail and Packaging

Air Mail Centers
20381 Lake Forest Dr., #B-2
Lake Forest, CA 92630

American Sign Shops
208 Snow Ave.
Raleigh, NC 27603

ASI Sign Systems
3890 West N.W. Hwy., Ste. 102
Dallas, TX 75220

Copycopy Centers
3681 E. Twelve Mile Rd.
Warren, MI 48092

Handle With Care Packaging Store
5675 DTC Blvd., #280
Englewood, CO 80111

Minuteman Press
1640 New Hwy.
Farmingdale, NY 11735

Pack Mart Inc.
13529 U.S. Highway #1
Sebastian, FL 32958

Packaging And Shipping Specialist
3513 103rd St., Ste. 104
Lubbock, TX 79423

Postal Plus Services
6465 Millcreek Dr., Ste. 205
Mississauga, ON L5N 5R3

Printsource Corporation
969 Park Ave.
Cranston, RI 02910

Shipping Connection
1601 Belvedere Rd., Ste. 402E
West Palm Beach, FL 33406

Shipping Dept. Inc., The
5800 Siegen Ln.
Baton Rouge, LA 70809

Sign Express
6 Clarke Circle
Bethel, CT 06801

Sign*A*Rama
1601 Belvedere Rd.
Ste. 402 East
West Palm Beach, FL 33406

Sign-Mobile, Inc.
300 A Commonwealth Dr.
Carol Stream, IL 60188

Sure Graphics
12465-82 Ave.
Surrey, BC V3W 3E8

Sureway Air Express
48-40 34th St.
Long Island City, NY 11101

Unishippers Association Inc.
P.O. Box 9249
Salt Lake City, UT 84109

Wholesale Printing Specialists
210 Andover St.
Wilmington, MA 01887

Yard Cards® Inc.
P.O. Box 618
Teays, WV 25569

Dry Cleaning and Laundry

Champion Cleaners
5117 Hwy. 153
Chattanooga, TN 37343

Dryclean 249
6407 Idlewild Rd.
Charlotte, NC 28212

Dryclean-USA
1875 W. Commercial Blvd., Ste. 140
Ft. Lauderdale, FL 33309

Eagle Cleaners
1750 University Dr., Ste. 111
Coral Springs, FL 33071

Ecomat Cleaners And Laundromats
147 Palmer Ave.
Mamaroneck, NY 10543

Harvey Washbangers®
110 29th Ave. N.
Nashville, TN 37203

Nu-Look 1hr Cleaners
15 S.E. Second Ave.
Deerfield Beach, FL 33441-3999

Soap's Goodtime Laundry
912 Wilson Ave.
Downsview, ON M3K 1E7

Sunday Best!
P.O. Box 7169
Boston, MA 02269

Valet Express
10151 University Blvd., Ste. 224
Orlando, FL i 32817-1981

Education Services and Products

Advanced Sales & Management Courses
927 Eastern Shore Dr.
Salisbury, MD 21801

Berlitz Language Center
400 Alexander Park
Princeton, NJ 08540

Boston Bartenders School Of America
P.O. Box 176
Wilbraham, MA 01095

College Prospects Of America Inc.
12682 College Prospects Dr.
Logan, OH 43138

Compuquest Educational Services
600 Central Ave., Ste. 245
Highland Park, IL 60035

Huntington Learning Centers Inc.
496 Kinderkamack Rd.
Oradell, NJ 07649

John Casablancas Modeling And Career Center
111 E. 22nd St.
New York, NY 10010

John Robert Powers Modeling & Career School
175 Andover St.
Danvers, MA 01923

Knowledge Development Centers Inc.
445 Hutchinson Ave., Ste. 120
Columbus, OH 43235

Krypton Institute
120 N. Wall St., 3rd Floor
Spokane, WA 99205

Kumon Math & Reading Centers
Glenpointe Center E.
2nd Fl. 300 Frank Burr
Teaneck, NJ 07666

Lado International College
2154 Wisconsin Ave. NW
Washington, DC 20007

Learning Authority, The
3001 Executive Dr., #130
Clearwater, FL 34622

National Travel Academy
P.O. Box 42008
St. Petersburg, FL 33742-4008

Oxford Learning Centres Inc.
6465 Millcreek Dr., Ste. 205
Mississauga, ON L5N 5R3

Productivity Point International
15 Salt Creek Ln., #200
Hinsdale, IL 60521

Technokids/Technoplus
461-B27 N. Service Rd. W.
Oakville, ON L6M 2V5

Teller Training Distributors Inc.
P.O. Box 1758
Mercer Island, WA 98040

U-Candu Learning Centres Inc.
3882 Hwy. #7
Markham, ON L3R 1L3

Employment and Staffing Services

Ace Personnel Franchise Corporation
6400 Glenwood
Overland Park, KS 66202

Adia Personnel Services
100 Redwood Shores Pkwy.
Redwood City, CA 94065

Atwork Franchise Inc.
1470 Main St.
White Pine, TN 37890

Basic Needs Home Companion Services
P.O. Box 12672
Lexington, KY 40583-2672

Career Blazers Resume Services
590 Fifth Ave.
New York, NY 10036

Career Blazers Staffing Services
590 Fifth Ave.
New York, NY 10036

Computemp
4401 N. Federal Hwy., Ste. 202
Boca Raton, FL 33431

Dynamic People Inc.
3535 Piedmont Rd.
Atlanta, GA 30305

Fortune Personnel Consultants
1155 Avenue of the Americas
New York, NY 10036

G.A.S. Technical Services Franchising Inc.
6001 Savoy, Ste. 505
Houston, TX 77036

Health Force
177 Crossways Park Dr.
Woodbury, NY 11797

Healthcare Recruiters International
5050 Quorum, Ste. 325
Dallas, TX 75240

Labor World
1144 E. Newport Center
Dearfield Beach, FL 33442

Lawcorps Franchise Corporation
1899 L St., N.W. 5th Floor
Washington, DC 20036

Link Staffing Services
1800 Bering, Ste. 801
Houston, TX 77057

Marshall Group Executive Search Corporation, The
454 Corral de Tierra Road
Salinas, CA 93908

Norrell Temporary Services
3535 Piedmont Rd.
Atlanta, GA 30305

Nurses PRN
9300 S.W. 87 Ave., Ste. 3
Miami, FL 33176

Omniworks!
2465 Ridgecrest Ave.
Orange Park, FL 32065

Personet, The Personnel Network
P.O. Box 4923
Palm Harbor, FL 34685

Pre-Employment Services Inc.
1100 Circle 75 Parkway, Ste. 800
Atlanta, GA 30339

Roth Young Personnel Service Inc.
535 Fifth Ave.
New York, NY 10017

Russoli Temps
295 Buck Rd., Ste. 115
Holland, PA 18966

Smartpeople
4376 Willow Glen
Calabasas, CA 91302

Techstaff, Inc.
11270 W. Park Place
Milwaukee, WI 53224

Telemarketing Temps
55 E. Washington, #915
Chicago, IL 60602

Tempforce
177 Crossways Park Dr.
Woodbury, NY 11797

Temps & Co.
245 Peachtree Center Ave.
Atlanta, GA 30303

Uniforce Staffing Services
415 Crossways Park Dr.
Woodbury, NY 11797

Entertainment, Amusement, Sports, and Related Products

A Corporate A'fair Inc.
1922 Lynn Brook Pl.
Memphis, TN 38116

Action Sports Photos
4526 N.W. First St.
Oklahoma City, OK 73127

Actual Reality International Inc.
8630-53 Ave.
Edmonton, AB T6E 5G2

American Mobile Sound
5266 Hollister, #105
Santa Barbara, CA 93111

Atec Grand Slam U.S.A.
11320 Trade Center Dr., Ste. C
Rancho Cordova, CA 95742

Babbitt Baseball Camps
P.O. Box 431
Burtonsville, MD 20866

Ben Franklin Crafts Inc.
500 E. North Ave.
Carol Stream, IL 60188-2125

Bikers Dream, International
1420 Village Way
Santa Ana, CA 92705

Casey's Sports Zone
1919 S. 40 St., Ste. 202
Lincoln, NE 68506

Cyclepath, The
312 Commissioners Rd. W
London, ON N6J 1Y3

Dek Star Hockey Centers
1106 Reedsdale St.
Pittsburgh, PA 15233

Eclectic Karate Institute
88 Upland Rd.
Plympton, MA 02367

Game Power Headquarters
9990 Global Rd.
Philadelphia, PA 19115

Golf Augusta Pro Shops
3515-A Walton Way Ext.
Augusta, GA 30909

Golf Etc.
712 E. Hwy. 377
Granbury, TX 76048

Great Expectations
125 S. Service Rd.
Jericho, NY 11753

Kkic's Family Martial Arts Centers
P.O. Box 3146
Waco, TX 76707

Lunch Couples Of America
51 Morton St.
Needham, MA 02194

Mandy's Matching Service
6500 Jericho Tpke., Ste. 206A
Commack, NY 11725

Marbles Entertainment
10351 Santa Monica Blvd., Ste. 430
Los Angeles, CA 90025

Party Animals
180 Allen Rd., Ste. 204
Atlanta, GA 30328

Port-A-Pit Food Service System
66740 C.R. 103
Wakarusa, IN 46573

Soccer Post, The
111 Melrose Dr.
New Rochelle, NY 10804

Soundsation Entertainment Services
21515 Chagrin Blvd.
Cleveland, OH 44122-5307

Sports Section, The
3871 Lakefield Dr., Ste. 100
Suwanee, GA 30024

Together Dating Service
161 Worcester Rd., 2nd Fl.
Framingham, MA 01701

Video Galaxy Franchise Inc.
101 West St.
Vernon, CT 06066

Video Gamer
15965 Jeanette
Southfield, MI 48075

Video Thrills Family Entertainment Inc.
125 Rt. 526
Allentown, NJ 08501

Villari's Self Defense Centers
183 Cedar Grove Ln.
Somerset, NJ 08873

Visual Image, The
209 Indiana Ave.
Maryville, TN 37803

Washington Golf Center
2625 Shirlington Rd.
Arlington, VA 22206

Woodworkers Club, The
1919 S. 40th St., Ste. 202
Lincoln, NE 68510

Environmental Services and Products—Including Water Purificaton

Airsopure
15400 Knoll Trail, Ste. 106
Dallas, TX 75248

America's Best Water Treaters Inc.
3808 S. Concord St.
Davenport, IA 52802

American Air Care Inc.
4751 Lydell Rd.
Cheverly, MD 20781

American Lead Consultants Inc.
Three Bala Plaza E.
Bala Cynwyd, PA 19004

Aquacell International
5145 Taravella Rd.
Marrero, LA 70072

Biologix
8503 Mid County Ind. Dr.
St. Louis, MO 63114

Culligan International Company
One Culligan Pkwy.
Northbrook, IL 60062

Ecosmarte Planet Friendly
8033 24th Ave. S.
Bloomington, MN 55425

Pure Water Inc.
3725 Touzalin Ave.
Lincoln, NE 68507

Purified Water To Go
5160 S. Valley View Blvd., Ste. 112
Las Vegas, NV 89118-1778

Tubs To Go
P.O. Box 1132
Edmonds, WA 98020

Florists and Plant

American Wholesale Floral
8601 Georgia Ave., Ste. 905
Silver Spring, MD 20910

Flowerama Of America
3165 W. Airline Hwy.
Waterloo, IA 50703

Jim's Greenery
28 W. Elm St.
West Townsend, MA 01474

Nature Indoors Inc.
3000 Graystone Dr.
Semmes, AL 36575

Roses Only Franchise Inc.
1040 Avenue of the Americas
New York, NY 10018

Food, Beverage, and Convenience Stores

1 Potato 2 Inc.
5640 International Pkwy.
New Hope, MN 55428

6-Twelve Convenient Mart
P.O. Box 86009
Gaithersburg, MD 20886-6009

7-Eleven Stores
2711 N. Haskell Avenue
Dallas, TX 75204

Abbott's Frozen Custard Inc.
4791 Lake Ave.
Rochester, NY 14612

Ahh - Some Gourmet Coffee™
900 Elm St.
Manchester, NH 03101-2007

American Water Ice & Pretzel Co.
240 S. Center Ave.
Leesport, PA 19533

Atlanta Bread Co. International Inc.
115 Davis Cr.
Marietta, GA 30060

Auntie Anne's Hand-Rolled Soft Pretzels
160-A Rte. 41
Gap, PA 17527

Bagel Break Franchising
1915 Old Hunter Trace
Marietta, GA 30062

Bagel Builders Famous Oven Fresh Bagels
1460 Blackwood-Clementon Rd.
Clementon, NJ 08021

Bagel Connection, The
1408 Whalley Ave.
New Haven, CT 06515

Bagel House & Deli
1100 Hooksett Rd.
Hooksett, NH 03106

Bagels Are Forever
P.O. Box 7169
Boston, MA 02269

Bagelz
95 Oak St.
Glastonbury, CT 06033

Bahama Buck's Original Shaved Ice Co.
1741 W. University, #148
Tempe, AZ 85281

Becker Milk Stores
671 Warden Ave.
Scarboro, ON M1L 3Z9

Between Rounds Bagel Deli & Bakery
19 A John Fitch Blvd.
South Windsor, CT 06074

Big City Bagels
151 Kalmus Dr., #C100
Costa Mesa, CA 92626

Big Orange Of Florida Inc.
7700-A W. Fairfield Dr.
Pensacola, FL 32506

Big Sky Bread Company
455 Delta Ave., #204
Cincinnati, OH 45226

Blenz Coffee
300-535 Thurlow St.
Vancouver, BC V6E 3L2

Borvin Beverage Franchise Corp.
1022 King St.
Alexandria, VA 22314

Box Lunch, The
50 Briar Ln.
Wellfleet, MA 02667

Breadsmith Inc.
3510 N. Oakland Ave.
Shorewood, WI 53211

Breadstick Baker, The
947 Paoli Pike
West Chester, PA 19382

Bresler's Ice Cream & Yogurt Shops
3361 Boyington Dr. #160
Carrollton, TX 75006

Brew Thru
P.O. Box 3158
Virginia Beach, VA 23454

Bruster's Old-Fashioned Ice Cream & Yogurt
1445 Market St.
Bridgewater, PA 15009

Candy Bouquet International Inc.
2326 Cantrell Rd.
Little Rock, AR 72202

Candy Express
10480 Little Patuxent Pkwy., Ste. 320
Columbia, MD 21044

Carvel Ice Cream Bakery
20 Batterson Park Rd.
Farmington, CT 06032

Chesapeake Bagel Bakery
6832 Old Dominion Rd., #203
McLean, VA 22101

Cinnamonster
7346 S. Alton Way, #10-A
Englewood, CO 80112

Coffee Beanery Ltd., The
3429 Pierson
Flushing, MI 48433

Coffee News
P.O. Box 8444
Bangor, ME 04402-8444

Coffee Treat
19 Yarn Rd.
Etobicoke, ON M9B 6J6

Coffee Way
123 Rexdale Blvd.
Rexdale, ON M9W 1P3

Country Style Donuts
2 East Beaver Creek, Bldg. #1
Richmond Hill, ON L4B 2N3

Dairy Mart Convenience Stores Inc.
One Vision Dr.
Enfield, CT 06082

Del's Lemonade & Refreshments Inc.
1260 Oaklawn Ave.
Cranston, RI 02920

Different Twist Pretzel Company, The
P.O. Box 334
Bakerstown, PA 15007

Dial & Dine
45 S. Main St., Ste. 109
West Hartford, CT 06107

Dixie Cream Donut Shop
P.O. Box 30130
Bowling Green, KY 42102-5130

Donut Man™, The
9651 13th Ave. N
Minneapolis, MN 55441-5003

Dunkin' Donuts Inc.
14 Pacella Park Dr.
Randolph, MA 02368

Express Mart Convenient Stores
6567 Kinne Rd.
DeWitt, NY 13214

Filterfresh Coffee Service
378 University Ave.
Westwood, MA 02090

First Pie Corporation
100 Ledgewood Pl., Ste. 204
Rockland, MA 02189

Foremost Liquors
4001 W. Devon
Chicago, IL 60646

Freshens Premium Yogurt And Ice Cream
2849 Paces Ferry Rd., Ste. 750
Atlanta, GA 30339

Frozen Fusion Fruit Smoothies
15020 N. 74th St.
Scottsdale, AZ 85260

Fudge Co.
103 Belvedere Ave.
Charlevoix, MI 49720

Gloria Jean's Gourmet Coffees
11480 Commercial Pkwy.
Castroville, CA 95012

Goldberg's New York Bagels
9 Law Dr.
Fairfield, NJ 07006

Good For You!
6 W. 17th Ave.
Vancouver, BC V5Y 1Z4

Gourmet Cup, The
P.O. Box 490
Abbotsford, BC V2S 5Z5

Great American Bagel, The
519 N. Cass Ave.
Westmont, IL 60559

Heavenly Ham
20 Mansell Ct. E., Ste. 500
Roswell, GA 30076

Hot Sam Pretzel Bakery
462 W. Bearcat Drive
Salt Lake City, UT 84115

I Can't Believe It's Yogurt
3361 Boyington, Ste. 160
Carrollton, TX 75006

I.B. Nuts & Fruit Too
1206 N. Bus Loop 70 W
Columbia, MO 65202

Ice Cream And Yogurt Club, The
1580 Highridge Rd.
Boynton Beach, FL 33426

Incredibly Edible Delites
295 Buck Rd., Ste. 115
Holland, PA 18966

Jack's Famous Bagels Inc.
318 N. Milpas St.
Santa Barbara, CA 93103

Jackpot Convenience Stores Inc.
P.O. Box 24447
Seattle, WA 98124

Jakes Take N' Bake Pizza Inc.
620 High St.
San Luis Obispo, CA 93401

Java Joe's
912 Wilson Ave.
North York, ON M3K 1E7

Javahut & Photo Expresso
1050 La Tortuga Dr., Ste. 37
Vista, CA 92083

Jerky Hut
Hamlet Rte. 934
Seaside, OR 97138

Juice Club
17 Chorro, Ste. D
San Luis Obispo, CA 93405

Juice World
1238 Grand Ave.
Arroyo Grande, CA 93420

Karmelkorn
P.O. Box 39286
Minneapolis, MN 55439-0286

Kernels Popcorn
40 Eglinton Ave. E., Ste. 250
Toronto, ON M4P 3A2

Kohr Bros. Frozen Custard
2115 Berkmar Dr.
Charlottesville, VA 22901

Lamar's Donuts
245 S. 84th St., Ste. 210
Lincoln, NE 68510

Larry's Ice Cream & Yogurt Parlours
5361 Boyington Dr., Ste. 160
Carrollton, TX 75006

Le Muffin Plus
675 W. Peachtree St. N.E.
Atlanta, GA 30308

Lil Peach
14 Howard St.
Rockland, MA 02370-1998

Little King Inc.
118Ci11 "I" St.
Omaha, NE 68137

Logan Farms Honey Glazed Hams
10001 Westheimer, #1040
Houston, TX 77042

Love's Yogurt
1830 Techny Ct.
Northbrook, IL 60062

Lox Of Bagels
24412 Hawthorne Blvd.
Torrance, CA 90505

Maison Du Popcorn
188 Washington St.
Norwich, CT 06360

Maxi Broue Brewing Centre Inc.
11720 4th Ave.
Montreal, PQ H1E 5Y2

Mill, The
800 P St.
Lincoln, NE 68508

Mom's Bake At Home Pizza
4457 Main St.
Philadelphia, PA 19128

Morrone's Water Ice & Treat Centers
117 S. 69th St.
Upper Darby, PA 19082

Mountain Man Nut & Fruit Co.
P.O. Box 160
Parker, CO 80134

Mr. Bulky Treats & Gifts
755 W. Big Beaver, Ste. 1600
Troy, MI 48084

Mr. Hero
5755 Granger Rd., 2nd. Floor
Independence, OH 44131

Mrs. Fields Cookies
462 W. Bearcat Dr.
Salt Lake City, UT 84115

Muffin Tin, The
P.O. Box 202
Alden, MI 49612

Nach-O Fast
563 W. 500 S., Ste. 200
Bountiful, UT 84010

New World Coffee & Bagel
379 W. Broadway
New York, NY 10012

Nielsen's Frozen Custard
P.O. Box 731
Bountiful, UT 84010

Oasis Ice Cream & Frozen Yogurt
5712 Sundance
Columbia, MO 65203

Old Fashioned Egg Cream Co., The
4270 N.W. 19th Ave., Ste. D
Pompano Beach, FL 33064

Open Pantry Food Marts Of Wisconsin Inc.
817 S. Main St.
Racine, WI 53403

P.J.'S Coffee & Tea
500 N. Hagan Ave.
New Orleans, LA 70119

Paul Richard's Bagelry
177 Main St., Ste. 103
Fort Lee, NJ 07024

Pennsylvannia Pretzel Co.
177 Main St., Ste. 103
Fort Lee, NJ 07024

Perfect Pretzel, The
4 Garden Rd.
Little Silvir, NJ 07739-1016

Pizza Man "He Delivers"
6930_ Tujunga Ave.
No. Hollywood, CA 91605

Pop's Homemade Water Ice Franchise Corp.
1337 Oregon Ave.
Philadelphia, PA 19148

Port Of Subs
5365 Mae Anne Ave., #A-29
Reno, NV 89523

Poultry King
30 E. Beaver Creek Rd., Ste. 206
Richmond Hill, ON L4B 1J2

Pretzel Mill
8181 Professional Pl., Ste. 130
Landover, MD 20784

Pretzel Time, Inc.
4800 Linglestown Rd., Ste. 202
Harrisburg, PA 17112

Pretzel Twister, The
2706 S. Horseshoe Dr., #112
Naples, FL 34104

Pretzelmaker
1050 17th St., Ste. 1400
Denver, CO 80265

Pretzels Plus Inc.
639 Frederick St.
Hanover, PA 17331

Quizno's Classic Subs
7555 E. Hampden Ave., Ste. 601
Denver, CO 80231

Rally's Hamburger's Inc.
10002 Shelbyville Rd., Ste. 150
Louisville, KY 40223

Rickshaw Chinese Food
1230 El Camino Real, Ste. D4
San Bruno, CA 94066

Sammy's New York Bagels
9 Law Dr.
Fairfield, NJ 07006

Scoopers Ice Cream Inc.
22 Woodrow Ave.
Youngstown, OH 44512

Show Place Ice Cream Parlours
202 Centre St.
Beach Haven, NJ 8008

Smoothie King Franchises Inc.
Xerox Centre 2400 Veterans Blvd., Ste. 110
Kenner, LA 70062

Sobik's Sub Shops
1059 Maitland Center Commons Bl., 2nd Floor
Maitland, FL 32751-7434

Stage Mart
14 Suncook Terr.
Merrimack, NH 03054

Star Mart
10 Universal City Plaza
Universal City, CA 91608

Sweet City
1604 Hilltop W., Ste. 204
Virginia Beach, VA 23451

Takeout Taxi
1175 Herndon Pkwy., Ste. 150
Herndon, VA 22070

Tastee-Freez
48380 Van Dyke
Utica, MI 48317

Tiajuana Taxie® (We Deliver)
2508 Betty St.
Orlando, FL 32803

Total Juice +
1125 E. Glendale Ave.
Phoenix, AZ 85020

Treats
418 Preston St.
Ottawa, ON K1S 4N2

Tropik Sun Fruit & Nut®
37 Sherwood Dr., Ste. 101
Lake Bluff, IL 60044

Uncle Teddys Soft Pretzels & Milk Shakes
307 Delight Meadows Rd.
Reisterstown, MD 21136

Wetzel's Pretzels
65 North Raymond Ave., Ste. 310
Pasadena, CA 91103

Whole Donut, The
894 New Britain Ave.
Hartford, CT 06106

Wok To U Express
3331 Viking Way, Unit 7
Richmond, BC V6V 1X7

Xpresso Drive Thru Cafe Inc.
1424 S. Ward St.
Lakewood, CO 80228

Yogurt & Such
438 Woodbury Rd.
Plainview, NY 11803

Yogurteria
1325 Franklin Ave., Ste. 165
Garden City, NY 11530

Yogurty's Yogurt Discovery
8300 Woodbine Ave., 5th Floor
Markham, ON L3R 9Y7

Franchise Services

Advanced Franchising Worldwide
7100 E. Lincoln Dr., Ste. B-123
Scottsdale, AZ 85253

American Association Of Franchisees And Dealers
P.O. Box 81887
San Diego, CA 92138-1887

American Enterprises Inc.
P.O. Box 2374
Kailua-Kona, HI 96745

American Franchise Partners
1750 Chase Tower
Rochester, NY 14604

Conceptual Edge, The
2102 Business Center Dr., Ste. 130
Irvine, CA 92715

Franchise Associates
2212 Aralia St.
Newport Beach, CA 92660

Franchise Axis
2465 Ridgecrest Ave.
Orange Park, FL 32065

Franchise Brokers Network
3617A Silverside Rd.
Wilmington, DE 19810

Franchise Business International
5310 Zelzah, #305
Encino, CA 91316

Franchise Buyers Advisory Service
51 Morton St.
Needham, MA 02194

Franchise Connection
9237 Ward Parkway, Ste. 300
Kansas City, MO 64114

Franchise Consortium International
245 S. 84th St., Ste. 200
Lincoln, NE 68510

Franchise Developers
1919 S. 40th St., Ste. 202
Lincoln, NE 68506

Franchise Developments, Inc.
4730 Centre Ave.
Pittsburgh, PA 15213

Franchise Finance & Consultants, Inc.
2415 E. Kensington Rd.
Arlington Heights, IL 60004-6658

Franchise Foundations
540 Pacific Ave.
San Francisco, CA 94133

Franchise Law Team
30021 Tomas, Ste. 260
Rancho Santa Margari, CA 92688

Franchise Marketing Inc.
3500 Piedmont Rd., Ste. 725
Atlanta, GA 30305

Franchise Masters
1000 Shelard Pkwy., #320
Minneapolis, MN 55426

Franchise Profiles
2465 Ridgecrest Ave.
Orange Park, FL 32065

Franchise Registration Service
1835 K St. N.W., Ste. 750
Washington, DC 20006

Franchise Sales
1315 S. Villa Ave.
Villa Park, IL 60181

Franchise Search Inc.
431 Carpenter Ave.
Sea Cliff, NY 11579-2102

Franchise Spectrum Inc.
65 Boston Post Rd. W., Ste. 106
Marlboro, MA 01752

Franchise Systems
8001 Irvine Center Dr., Ste. 1500
Irvine, CA 92718

Franchisee Financialine™
P.O. Box 81887
San Diego, CA 92138-1887

Franchisee Legaline™
P.O. Box 81887
San Diego, CA 92138-1887

FranchisInternational Inc.
4730 Centre Ave.
Pittsburgh, PA 15213

Francorp Inc.
20200 Governors Dr.
Olympia Fields, IL 60461

Frannet Of South Florida
2811 NE 46 St.
Lighthouse Point, FL 33064

Future Franchise Development Corp.
105 E. First St., Ste. 203
Hinsdale, IL 60521

Great Western Franchise Consultants
8204 Elmbrook Dr., Ste. 371
Dallas, TX 75247

Grow Biz International Inc.
4200 Dahlberg Dr.
Minneapolis, MN 55422

In Site Franchise Consultants
2400 E. Commercial Blvd., Ste. 808
Ft. Lauderdale, FL 33308

Information Services Inc.
2811 NE 46th St.
Lighthouse Pt., FL 33064

International Flying Colors Franchising Corporation
3720 San Jacinto
Houston, TX 77004

International Franchise Development
26949 Chagrin Blvd., Ste. 304
Cleveland, OH 44122-4230

International Franchise Development Inc.
307 SE 15 Ave.
Pompano Beach, FL 33060

Jacobs And Associates Architects
4141 Blue Lake Cir., Ste. 190
Dallas, TX 75244

National Franchise Associates
3473 Satellite Blvd., Ste. 201
Duluth, GA 30136

National Franchise Consultants
141 Helens Ave., Ste. 200
Highlands, NC 28741

National Franchise Sales
7699 9th St., Ste. 104
Buena Park, CA 90621

Nationwide Franchise Marketing Services
10824 Stone Canyon Rd., Ste. 2341
Dallas, TX 75230

Network Franchising International
1 Concorde Gate, Ste. 201
Toronto, ON M3C 3N6

PACECO Franchise Services
1301 Main
Duncan, OK 73533

Sales Dynamics Inc.
One Cherry Hill, Ste. 300
Cherry Hill, NJ 08002

Seller Direct Inc.
1954 First St. #161
Highland Park, IL 60035

Transmedia
11900 Biscayne Blvd.
North Miami, FL 33181

World Franchise Consultants
25820 Southfield Rd., Ste. 201
Southfield, MI 48075

World Inspection Network
2701 First Ave., Ste. 340
Seattle, WA 98121-1123

Writers' Bloc, The
666 Baker St., Ste. 269
Costa Mesa, CA 92626-4407

Health Services and Products and Fitness Centers

American Alternative Hospitals
18002 Luika Rd.
Apple Valley, CA 92307

Americare/Dental Centers U.S.A.
3233 W. Peoria Ave., Ste. 112
Phoenix, AZ 85029

ATC Health Care Services Inc.
1983 Marcus Ave.
Lake Success, NY 11042

Better Back® Store, The
7936 E. Arapahoe Ct., #2100
Englewood, CO 80112

Bunnies "Fresh Juice Smoothie Bar" Health Products
P.O. Box 880
Mandeville, LA 70470

Diet Workshop
50 Cummings Park
Woburn, MA 01801-2123

Fastserv® Medical
9523 Alta Mesa Rd.
Wilton, CA 95693

First Optometry Eye Care Centers Inc.
32600 Gratiot Ave.
Roseville, MI 48066-1126

Firstat Nursing Services
801 Village Blvd., Ste. 303
West Palm Beach, FL 33409

Fit America
2101 W. Commercial Blvd., Ste. 5500
Ft. Lauderdale, FL 33309

Fitness On Wheels Inc.
1185 S. Milwaukee
Denver, CO 80210

Happy & Healthy Products Inc.
1600 S. Dixie Hwy., Ste. 2AB
Boca Raton, FL 33432

Health Clubs of America
2400 E. Commercial Blvd., Ste. 808
Ft. Lauderdale, FL 33308

Home Instead Senior Care
1104 S. 76th Ave., Ste. A
Omaha, NE 68124

Inches-A-Weigh Weight Loss Center
P.O. Box 59346
Birmingham, AL 35259

Interim Health Care
2050 Spectrum Blvd.
Ft. Lauderdale, FL 33309

Jazzercise
2808 Roosevelt St.
Carlsbad, CA 92008

Jenny Craig Personal Weight Management
445 Marine View Ave., #300
Del Mar, CA 92014

Lady Of America
2400 E. Commercial Blvd., #808
Ft. Lauderdale, FL 33308

Miracle-Ear
4101 Dahlberg Dr.
Minneapolis, MN 55422

Mirage Tanning
15965 Jeanette
Southfield, MI 48075

Nuvision Optical
P.O. Box 2600
Flint, MI 48501

Pearle Vision
2534 Royal Ln.
Dallas, TX 75229

Physicians Weight Loss Centers Of America Inc.
395 Springside Dr.
Akron, OH 44333-2496

Reading Glasses To Go
9131 King Arthur Dr.
Dallas, TX 75247

Serenity Cove Health & Nutrition Centers
267 N. Cedar
Abilene, KS 67410

Staff Builders Home Health Care
1983 Marcus Ave.
Lake Success, NY 11042

Sterling Optical
1500 Hempstead Tpke
East Meadow, NY 11554

Women's Health Boutique
12715 Telge Rd.
Cypress, TX 77429

Household Furnishing, Products, and Services

A Shade Better Inc.
3615 Superior
Cleveland, OH 44114

Alliance Security Systems Inc.
5-140 McGovern Dr.
Cambridge, ON N3H 4R7

Blue Magic Pool Service
2496 W. Shore Rd.
Warwick, RI 02886

Closettec
55 Providence Hwy.
Norwood, MA 02062

Consign & Design Furnishings
1826 W. Broadway Rd., Ste. 3
Mesa, AZ 85202

Decorating Den
7910 Woodmont Ave., Ste. 200
Bethesda, MD 20814

Dip 'N Strip Inc.
2141 S. Platte River Dr.
Denver, CO 80223

Drapery Works System Ltd., The
4640 Western Ave.
Lisle, IL 60532

Energy Wise Inc.
342 Neva St.
Sebastopol, CA 95472-3664

Express Electric International Inc.
5 Walnut St.
Red Bank, NJ 07701

Furniture Weekend
21 W. Main St.
Malone, NY 12953

Guardsman Woodpro
4999 36th St. S.E.
Grand Rapids, MI 49512

Handi-Man Pro-Tem
214 N. Main St., #202
Natick, MA 01760-1131

Hometec Handyman Services Inc.
6300-138 Creedmoor Rd., Ste. 415
Raleigh, NC 27612

House Doctors Handyman Service
4010 Executive Park Dr., Ste. 100
Cincinnati, OH 45241

Independent Lighting Franchise Corporation
873 Seahawk Cir.
Virginia Beach, VA 23452

Mountain Comfort Furnishings
Box 767
Frisco, CO 80443

Mr. Rooter
1020 N. University Parks Dr.
Waco, TX 76707

Naked Furniture
P.O. Box F
Clarks Summit, PA 18411

Nature Tech
900 Hyde Park Rd.
London, ON N6A 4B7

Planet Earth Recycling
P.O.Box 65311
Philadelphia, PA 19155-5311

Thee Chimney Sweep Inc.
36 Vernon Rd., N.E.
Rome, GA 30165

Windowstyles By Decorating Den
7910 Woodmont Ave., Ste. 200
Bethesda, MD 20814

Hotel and Motels

Budgetel Inn
250 E. Wisconsin Ave.
Milwaukee, WI 53202

Clarion Hotels, Resorts And Carriage House Inns
10750 Columbia Pike
Silver Spring, MD 20901

Clubhouse Inns
11230 College Blvd., Ste. 130
Overland Park, KS 66210

Comfort Inns & Comfort Suites
10750 Columbia Pike
Silver Spring, MD 20901

Econo Lodge
10750 Columbia Pike
Silver Spring, MD 20901

Friendship Inns
10750 Columbia Pike
Silver Spring, MD 20901

Mainstay Suites
10750 Columbia Pike
Silver Spring, MD 20901

Quality Inns, Hotels And Suites
10750 Columbia Pike
Silver Spring, MD 20901

Rodeway Inn
10750 Columbia Pike
Silver Spring, MD 20901

Sheraton Inns Inc.
60 State St.
Boston, MA 02109

Sleep Inn
10750 Columbia Pike
Silver Spring, MD 20901

Travelodge, Thriftlodge
1973 Friendship Dr.
El Cajon, CA 92020

Lawn and Garden Products

Greenland Irrigation
150 Ambleside Dr.
London, ON N6G 4R1

Mr Trees
343 San Anselmo Ave.
San Anselmo, CA 94960

Naturalawn® Of America Inc.
141 W. Patrick St.
Frederick, MD 21701

Sharp-N-Lube
3245 St. Rt. 589
CassTown, OH 45312

Super Lawns
Box 5677
Rockville, MD 20855

U.S. Lawns Inc.
369 Mears Blvd.
Oldsmar, FL 34677

Miscellaneous Products and Services

Ad Show Network
3753 Howard Hughes Parkway, #200
Las Vegas, NV 89109

Advanced Business Concepts
145 N. Second Ave. #5
Oakdale, CA 95361

Advisor One
1097-C Irongate Ln.
Columbus, OH 43213

After/Marketing USA Inc.
P.O. Box 2616
Worcester, MA 01613-2616

Air Brook Limousine Inc.
Box 123
Rochelle Park, NJ 07662

Airchek Inc.
P.O. Box 430905
Miami, FL 33243

Allerclean Inc.
6400 Blackhorse Pike
Egg Harbor Township, NJ 08234

Always Open
15201 w. 101st Ave.
Dyer, IN 46311

American United Capital
3915 Mission Ave., Ste. 7414
Oceanside, CA 92054

Automated Mailmen Inc.
222 Munson Rd.
Wolcott, CT 06716-9801

Bladerunner Mobile Sharpening Systems
6431 Orr Rd.
Charlotte, NC 28213

Bridal Accents
38 Pond St., Ste. 104
Franklin, MA 02038

Bride's Day Magazine

750 Hamburg Tpk., #208
Pompton Lakes, NJ 07442

Celtic Craft

8456 E. 23rd St.
Tucson, AZ 85710

Center Court Concierge

76-947 Desi Dr.
Indian Wells, CA 92210

Central Mercantile Collection Service

822 E. Grand River
Brighton, MI 48116

Central Park USA Inc.

300 High St.
Chattanooga, TN 37403

Community Graphics

3495 Winton Place, Bldg. A #4
Rochester, NY 14623

Electric Medic

400 Northlake Dr., Ste. 200
Peachtree City, GA 30269

Embroid It!

10859 Shady Trail Ste. 102
Dallas, TX 75220

Fiesta Cartoon Maps, Inc.

942 N. Orlando
Mesa, AZ 85205

Four Seasons Graphics

4260 Ft. Henry Dr.
Kingsport, TN 37663

Framing Experience

1800 Appleby Line
Burlington, ON L7L 6A1.

Identification Services Of Canada Inc.

150 Clark Blvd., Ste. 238
Brampton, ON L6T 4Y8

Military Rent-All Inc.

10351 Santa Monica Blvd., Ste. 430
Los Angeles, CA 90025

Millicare Environmental Services

201 Lukken Industrial Dr. W.
LaGrange, GA 30240

Minuteman Moving & Storage Inc.

3259 Alden Starnes Rd.
Granite Falls, NC 28630

Mobility Centers Inc.

6693 Dixie Hwy.
Bridgeport, MI 48722

One Hour Motophoto & Portrait Studio®

4444 Lake Center Dr.
Dayton, OH 45426

Proshred Security

2200 Lakeshore Blvd. W., #102
Toronto, ON M8V 1A4

Royal Apples Inc.

1500 E. Beltline SE, Ste. 160
Grand Rapids, MI 49506

Special Delivery Photos

P.O. Box 34905
Bartlett, TN 38134

Two Men And A Truck

1915 E. Michigan Ave.
Lansing, MI 48912

Video Quiklab

2121 W. Oakland Park Blvd.
Fort Lauderdale, FL 33311

Wash On Wheels

5401 S. Bryant Ave.
Stanford, FL 32773

Pet Care, Sales, and Supplies

Canusa (Brant) Pet Products

175 Ashgrove Ave.
Brantford, ON N3R 7C6

Critter Care Of America

8261 Summa #F
Baton Rouge, LA 70809

Haynes Pet Centre

10515 Wynbridge Dr.
Alpharetta, GA 30202

Laund-Ur-Mutt

8854 S. Edgewood St.
Highlands Ranch, CO 80126

Pet Nanny Of America Inc.

340 Morgan Ln.
Lansing, MI 48912

Pet Paradise Inc.

Box 3400
Markham, ON L3R 6G7

Potts Doggie Shop

16305 San Carlos Blvd.
Ft. Myers, FL 33908

Ryan's Pet Food

6315 Kestrel Rd.
Mississauga, ON L5T 1Z4

Shake-A-Paw Puppy Stores

177 Main St., Ste. 103
Fort Lee, NJ 07024

Protective Serivces

Dynamark Security Centers Inc.

19833 Leitersburg Pike
Hagerstown, MD 21742

Fire Defense Centers

3919 Morton St.
Jacksonville, FL 32217

Firemaster

520 Broadway, Ste. 650
Santa Monica, CA 90401

Sonitrol Corporation

1800 Diagonal Rd., Ste. 180
Alexandria, VA 22314

Real Estate Services

Apartment Search International

7900 Xerxes Ave. S., Ste. 2250
Bloomington, MN 55431

Better Lifestyles

P.O. Box 540912
Flushing, NY 11354

Boni Franchise Real Estate

2455 N. 54th St.
Philadelphia, PA 19131

Castles Unlimited Of Boston, Inc.

837 Beacon St.
Newton Centre, MA 02159

Coldwell Banker Residential Affiliates Inc.

27271 Las Ramblas, #132
Mission Viejo, CA 92691

Electronic Realty Associates

P.O. Box 2974
Shawnee Mission, KS 66201

Home Inc. - For Sale By Owner -

6348 Palmas Bay Cir.
Port Orange, FL 32127

Homestock United States Real Estate

25 Burlington Mall Rd., Ste. 300
Burlington, MA 01803

Joseph J. Murphy Realty Inc.

P.O. Box 525
Saddle River, NJ 07458

Realty Executives

4427 N. 36th St., #100
Phoenix, AZ 85018

Sale By Owner Systems

8450 Hickman, #11
Des Moines, IA 50325

TPMC Realty Services Group

2741 Beltline, Ste. 106
Carrollton, TX 75006

Restaurants

Anntony's Caribbean Cafe

P.O. Box 3030
Charlotte, NC 28217

Bain's Deli

1000 South Ave.
Staten Island, NY 10314

Baldinos Giant Jersey Subs

760 Elaine St.
Hinesville, GA 31313

Bennigan's

12404 Park Central Dr.
Dallas, TX 75251

Big Town Hero Sandwiches

412 S.W. 2nd
Portland, OR 97204

Blimpie

1775 The Exchange, Ste. 600
Atlanta, GA 30339

Blommer's Ice Cream & Sam's Subs

5900 N. Port Washington Rd.
Milwaukee, WI 53217

Bonanza

12404 Park Central Dr.
Dallas, TX 75251

Bonjour Bagel Cafe

2064 W. Avenue J #137
Lancaster, CA 93536-5913

Boston Beanery Restaurant And Tavern

P.O. Box 4385
Morgantown, WV 26504-4385

Boston Pizza

200-5500 Parkwood Way
Richmond, BC V6V 2M4

Boxies Cafe

3361 Boyington, Ste. 160
Carrollton, TX 75006

Boz Hot Dogs

770 E. 142nd St.
Dolton, IL 60419

Broadway Bagel Cafe

2133 Royal Windsor Dr., #23
Mississauga, ON L5J 1K5

Buck's Pizza

P.O. Box 405
DuBois, PA 15801

Buddy's Bar-B-Q

5806 Kingston Pike
Knoxville, TN 37919

Buffalo's Cafe

5500 Interstate N. Pkwy., Ste. 545
Atlanta, GA 30328

Bullwinkle's Restaurant & The Family Fun Center

33208 Paseo Cerveza, Ste. D
San Juan Capistrano, CA 92675

Cafe La France

216 Weybosset St.
Providence, RI 02903

Cafe On Main

1621 Washington St.
Blair, NE 68008

Cami's Seafood & Pasta

6272 S. Dixie Hwy.
South Miami, FL 33143

Cap'n Taco

P.O. Box 415
North Olmsted, OH 44070-0415

Carl's Jr. Restaurants

1200 N. Harbor Blvd.
Anaheim, CA 92803

Central Bakery Portuguese Muffins Cafe

711 Pleasant St.
Fall River, MA 02723

Checkers® Drive-In Restaurants Inc.

600 Cleveland St., 8TH Floor
Clearwater, FL 34615

Cheeburger Cheeburger Restaurants Inc.

15951 McGregor Blvd.
Ft. Myers, FL 33908

Chico's 2 In 1 Fried Chicken N' Pizza
584 Voutrait Rd.
Mill Bay, BC V0R 2P0

Chowderhead's Seafood Restaurant
P.O. Box 136
Scarborough, ME 04070-0136

Chubby's Diner
11638 Fair Oaks Blvd., Ste 210
Fair Oaks, CA 95628

Churchs Chicken
6 Concourse Pkwy., Ste. 1700
Atlanta, GA 30328

CJ's Steakloft
369 W. Main St.
Northboro, MA 01532

Coffee Express™ Drive Thrus & Cafes
4 Union Plaza
Bangor, ME 04401

Colter's Bar-B-Q
5910 N. Central Expy., #1355
Dallas, TX 75206

Columbia Steak Express
201 Midland Ave.
Lexington, KY 40508

Columbia Steak House
261 Midland Ave.
Lexington, KY 40508

Coney's "World Famous Hotdogs"
102 Dell St.
Batesville, MS 38606

Congress Rotisserie
10 Columbus Blvd.
Hartford, CT 06106

Corporate Cafe
One Corporate Dr.
Andover, MA 01810

Cucos Mexican Restaurante
110 Veterans Memorial Blvd., Ste. 222
Metairie, LA 70005

Cyber World Cafe
104 Boot Rd.
Downingtown, PA 19335

Daily's Bakery And Cafe
111 W. Olive St.
Glendale, WI 53212

Desi's Famous Pizza Inc.
438 Hazle Ave., Ste. 200
Wilkes-Barre, PA 18702

Dino's Pizza
180 Mine Lake Ct., Ste. 100
Raleigh, NC 27615

Domino's Pizza Inc.
P.O. Box 997
Ann Arbor, MI 48106-0997.

E.B.'s Express
385 Walnut St. Extension
Agawam, MA 01001

East Of Chicago Pizza Company
318 W. Walton
Willard, OH 44890

El Pollo Loco Inc.
3355 Michelson Dr., Ste. 350
Irvine, CA 92612

Empress Chili
10592 Taconic Terr.
Cincinnati, OH 45215

Fat Boys' Bar-B-Q
200 Willard St., Ste. 1-A
Cocoa, FL 32922

Figaro's Italian Kitchen
P.O. Box 12575
Salem, OR 97309-0575

Fire Glazed Ham Store And Cafe
1112 Seventh Ave.
Monroe, WI 53566

Firegrill
1401 17th St., Ste. 800
Denver, CO 80202-1246

Foodee's "A World Of Pizza"
26 S. Main St. #84
Concord, NH 03301-4809

Four Star Pizza
P.O. Box W
Claysville, PA 15323

Frullati Cafe
5720 LBJ Freeway, Ste. 370
Dallas, TX 75240

Giorgio Restaurant
222 St-Laurent Blvd.
Montreal, PQ H2Y 2Y3

Gold Star Chili
5204 Beechmont Ave.
Cincinnati, OH 45230

Grandy's Inc.
997 Grandy's Ln.
Lewisville, TX 75087

Greek's Pizzeria
1600 University Ave.
Muncie, IN 47303

Griddle™ Inc., The
505 Consumers Rd., Ste. 1000
North York, ON M2J 4V8

Happy Joe's Inc.
2705 Commerce Dr.
Bettendorf, IA 52722

Hardee's Food Systems Inc.
1233 Hardee's Blvd.
Rocky Mount, NC 27804-2815

Heid's Of Liverpool
P.O. Box 711
Cohasset, MA 02025

Henning's Fish House
1885 Allison Park Dr.
Richland Center, WI 53581

Hooters Of America Inc.
4501 Circle 75 Pkwy., Ste. E-5110
Atlanta, GA 30339

Hubb's Pub
1535 N. Cogswell St., Ste. A-3
Rockledge, FL 32955

Huddle House Inc.
2969 E. Ponce De Leon Ave.
Decatur, GA 30030

Hudson's Grill Of America Inc.
16970 Dallas Pkwy., Ste. 402
Dallas, TX 75248

Hungry Howie's Pizza And Subs
30300 Stephenson Hwy., Ste. 200
Madison Heights, MI 48071

Italo's Pizza Shop Inc.
3560 Middlebranch Rd., N.E.
Canton, OH 44705

Izzy's Pizza Restaurant
110 3rd Ave. S.E.
Albany, OR 97321

Jason's Deli
2400 Broadway
Beaumont, TX 77702

JB's Restaurants
440 Lawndale Dr.
Salt Lake City, UT 84115

Johnny's "New York Style" Pizza
834 Virginia Ave.
Hapeville, GA 30354

Jolly Pirate Donuts & Coffee Shops
3923 E. Broad St.
Columbus, OH 43213

Jon Smith Subs
3900 Woodlake Blvd., Ste. 206
Lake Worth, FL 33463

La Rosa Mexican Restaurants
246 W. Third St.
Davenport, IA 52801

Larosa's Inc.
2334 Boudinot
Cincinnati, OH 45238

Le Peep Restaurants Inc.
4 W. Dry Creek Cir.
Littleton, CO 80120

Linda's Rotisserie & Kitchen
11 Commerce Dr.
Crawford, NJ 07016

Longbranch Steakhouse And Saloon Inc.
105 Deercreek Rd., Ste. M-204
Deerfield Beach, FL 33442

Magic Wok Inc.
2060 Laskey Rd.
Toledo, OH 43613

Miami Subs Grill
6300 N.W. 31st Ave.
Ft. Lauderdale, FL 33309

Moma's Family Favorite Inc.
5770 Hopkins Rd.
Richmond, VA 23234

Mountain Mike's Pizza
3841 N. Freeway Blvd.
Sacramento, CA 95819

Mr Goodcents Franchise Systems Inc.
16210 W. 110th St.
Lenexa, KS 66219

Mrs. Powell's Bakery Eatery
3380 S. Service Rd.
Burlington, ON L7N 3J5

My Mother's Delicacies Cafe'
501 S. Washington Ave.
Scranton, PA 18505

Naturally Yogurt/ Speedsters Cafe'
P.O. Box 511
San Ramon, CA 94583

Nature's Table Restaurants
800 W. 47th St., Ste. 420
Kansas City, MO 64112

Nature's Way Cafe
800 Lake Ave.
Lake Worth, FL 33460

New Towne Diner & Bakery
200 Broadhollow Rd., Ste. 207
Melville, NY 11747

Noble Roman's Pizza
One Virginia Ave., Ste. 800
Indianapolis, IN 46204

Numero Uno
15414 Cabrito Ave., Ste. A
Van Nuys, CA 91406-1419

Olive's Gourmet Pizza
3249 Scott St.
San Francisco, CA 94123

Original Gino's East Of Chicago, The
205 W. Wacker, Ste. 1800
Chicago, IL 60606

Original Hamburger Stand
4440 Von Karman Ave.
Newport Beach, CA 92660

Pancake Cottage Family Restaurants
P.O. Box 1909
Massapequa, NY 11758

Panchero's Mexican Grill
P.O. Box 1786
Iowa City, IA 52244

Papa Gino's
600 Providence Hwy.
Dedham, MA 02026

Petro's Chili & Chips
5614 Kingston Pike, 2nd Floor
Knoxville, TN 37919

Piccolo's Pizza
421 N. I St.
Madera, CA 93637

Pizza Colore
1550 Larimer St., #312
Denver, CO 80202

Pizza Delight, Rooster's B.B.Q.

P.O. Box 23070
Moncton, NB E1A 6S8

Pizza Forum/Greek's Pizzeria

1600 University Ave.
Muncie, IN 47303

Pizza Inn Inc.

5050 Quorum, Ste. 500
Dallas, TX 75240

Pizza Ranch Inc.

1112 Main St., P.O. Box 823
Hull, IA 51239

Pizzas By Marchelloni

1051 Essington Rd., Ste. 270
Joliet, IL 60435

Pizzeria Uno - Chicago Bar & Grill

100 Charles Park Rd.
West Roxbury, MA 02132

Plus 1 Pizza

P.O. Box 516
Cambridge, OH 43725-0516

Popeyes Chicken & Biscuits

6 Concourse Pkwy., Ste. 1700
Atlanta, GA 30328

Ranch 1

177 Main St.
Fort Lee, NJ 07024

Red Hot & Blue

1600 Wilson Blvd.
Arlington, VA 22209

Renzios

701 W. Hampden Ave., Ste. B109
Englewood, CO 80110

Rising Star Grill

12404 Park Central Dr.
Dallas, TX 75251

Rollo Pollo Rotisserie Chicken

4801 Sherborn Ln., Ste. B-1
Louisville, KY 40207

Ronzio Pizza

194 Waterman St.
Providence, RI 2906

Rosati's Pizza

33 W. Higgins Rd., Ste. 1010
S. Barrington, IL 60010

Round Table Pizza

2175 N. California Blvd., Ste. 400
Walnut Creek, CA 94596

Sam's Place Restaurants

10801 Starkey Rd., Ste. 104-23
Largo, FL 34647

Shooters International Inc.

3033 N.E. 32nd Ave.
Ft. Lauderdale, FL 33308

Spaghetti Jack's Inc.

3151 N. Rock Rd.
Wichita, KS 67226

Spaghetti Shop, The

7301 Ohms Ln., #300
Minneapolis, MN 55439-2336

Steak Escape, America's Favorite Cheesesteak

222 Neilston St.
Columbus, OH 43215

Steak Express

312 Commissioners Rd. W
London, ON N6J 1Y3

Stewart's Restaurants Inc.

114 W. Atlantic Ave.
Clementon, NJ 08021

Strings Italian Cafe

11344 Coloma Rd., Ste. 545
Gold River, CA 95670

Sub & Stuff Sandwich Shops

3151 N. Rock Rd.
Wichita, KS 67226

Sub Station II

P.O. Box 2260
Sumter, SC 29151-2260

Sunshine Cafe Restaurants

7102 Lakeview Pkwy. W. Dr.
Indianapolis, IN 46268

Taco Bell Corp.

17901 Von Karman
Irvine, CA 92714

Taco John's

P.O. Box 1589
Cheyenne, WY 82003-1589

Taco Loco

349-B W. Tremont Ave.
Charlotte, NC 28203

Taco Sam's Chicken Magician

58 Branch Ave.
Oceanport, NJ 07757

Taco Time® International, Inc.

3880 W. 11th Avenue, P.O. Box 2056
Eugene, OR 97402

Taco Villa

3710 Chesswood Dr., Ste. 220
Toronto, ON M3J 2W4

Toarmina's Pizza

673 Barbara
Westland, MI 48185

Tony Maroni's Gourmet Pizza

222 112th Ave. NE, Ste. L-105
Bellevue, WA 98004

Troll's Seafood

14597 Marine Dr.
White Rock, BC V4B 1B7

Tudor's Biscuit World

P.O. Box 3603
Charleston, WV 25536

Villa Pizza Inc.

17 Elm St.
Morristown, NJ 07960

Western Steer Family Steakhouse

P.O. Box 399
Claremont, NC 28610

Z-Techa A Fresh Mexcan Grill
1531 Market St.
Denver, CO 80202

Zoo Pizza
929 E. Hamilton
Milwaukee, WI 53202

Retail Products and Stores

All Nations Flag Co. Inc.
118 W. 5th St.
Kansas City, MO 64105

Area Maps
2090 S. Nova Rd, #B-201
South Daytona, FL 32119

Ashley Avery's Collectables
100 Glenborough, 14th Floor
Houston, TX 77067

Atlantic Mower Parts Supplies, Inc.
13421 S.W. 14 Pl.
Ft. Lauderdale, FL 33325

Building Blocks Toy Stores
6209 Deeside Dr.
Dublin, OH 43017

Butonique The Button Boutique
8971-B Metcalf, Loehmann's Plaza
Overland Park, KS 66212

Can-Do Computer Books
1619 Altadore Ave., S.W.
Calgary, AB T2T 2P8

CD Request
800 W. 47th St., Ste. 420
Kansas City, MO 64112

CD Warehouse
1710 Firman Dr., Ste. 300
Richardson, TX 75081

Dazzler, The
4800 Kingsway, #286
Burnaby, BC V5H 4J2

Dial-A-Gift
2073 Sahara Dr.
Salt Lake City, UT 84124-2722

Dial-A-Rose
12216 US #1
North Palm Beach, FL 33408

Donna Jean's - Unique Country Gifts
1919 S. 40th St., Ste. 202
Lincoln, NE 68506

Easyriders
5055 Chesebro Rd.
Agoura Hills, CA 91301

Elephant House
12741 Research Blvd., Ste. 300
Austin, TX 78759

Elephant Walk; A Gallery Of Life
318 N. Carson St., Ste. 214
Carson City, NV 89701

Express Video Clinic
12508 Summer Tree
Olathe, KS 66062

Field Of Dreams
42-620 Caroline Ct.
Palm Desert, CA 92211-5144

Flag Shop, The
1755 W. 4th Ave.
Vancouver, BC V6J 1M2

Forget Me Knot Gift Baskets
575 Eighth Ave.
New York, NY 10018-3011.

Fotogenix - One Hour Portraits
10450 S. State St., #2204
Sandy, UT 84070

Gendron Gifts
9645 E. Colonial Dr., Ste. 113
Orlando, FL 32817

General Nutrition Centers
921 Penn Ave.
Pittsburgh, PA 15222

Gent's Formal Wear
404 E. Wright St.
Pensacola, FL 32501

Grand Rental Station / Taylor Rental
P.O. Box 1221
Butler, PA 16001

Halloween Express, Inc. Of NC
1860 Georgetown Rd.
Owenton, KY 40359

Hand Me Downs
RR #1
Enniskillen, ON L0B 1J0

Hannoush Jewelers
134 Capital Dr.
West Springfield, MA 01089

Hat Zone Franchising Co. LLC., The
130 Independence Center
Independence, MO 64057

Her Place
301 Mexico Blvd.
Brownsville, TX 78520

Just Legs
935 Richmond Ave.
Victoria, BC V8S-3Z4

Kiddie Kobbler
68 Robertson Rd., Ste. 106
Nepean, ON K2H 8P5

Kids Team
10333 N. Meridian St., Ste. 360
Indianapolis, IN 46290

Kits Cameras
6051 S. 194th St.
Kent, WA 98032

Krug's Big & Tall
16 N. Washington Ave.
Bergenfield, NJ 07621

Learning Express
76 Farmers Row
Groton, MA 01450

Moneysworth & Best Quality Shoe Repair
80 Galaxy Blvd., Unit 11
Toronto, ON M9W 4Y8

Mr. Appliance
P.O. Box 3146
Waco, TX 76707

Music Vending Inc.
4000 Hollywood Blvd., Ste. 730-N
Hollywood, FL 33021

Music-Go-Round
4200 Dahlberg Dr.
Minneapolis, MN 55422

Nation-Wide General Rental Centers Inc.
5510 Hwy. 9 North
Alpharetta, GA 30201

Nature's Reflections Inc.
3375 Buckinghammock Tr.
Vero Beach, FL 32960

Office 1 Superstore
P.O. Box 5093
East Hampton, NY 11937

Original Basket Boutique Ltd., The
4200 Fairway Pl.
N. Vancouver, BC V7G 1Y9

Party City Corporation
1440 Rte. 46
Parsippany, NJ 07054

Photo Drive-Up Franchising Inc.
1900 Camden Ave.
San Jose, CA 95124

Pinch A Penny Inc.
Box 6025
Clearwater, FL 34618

Play It Again Sports
4200 Dahlberg Dr.
Minneapolis, MN 55422

Pool Centers U.S.A. Inc.
4408 Peters Rd.
Ft. Lauderdale, FL 33317

Portrait Masters Inc.
114 High Country Dr.
Cary, NC 27513

President Tuxedo
32185 Hollingsworth
Warren, MI 48092

Raspberry Juncton™
417 Norwich Westerly Rd.
N. Stonington, CT 06359

Roger Dunn Golf Shops
2985 Lasuen St.
Carmel, CA 93923

Sears
3333 Beverly Road D3-234B
Hoffman Estates, IL 60179

Shefield & Sons Tobacconists
P.O. Box 490
Abbotsford, BC V2S 5Z5

Shoe Fixers Franchise Systems Inc.
3550 3 Mile Rd.
Grand Rapids, MI 49504

Shoe Stop Inc.
611 Market St. #1
Kirkland, WA 98033-5422

Sport Shoe Marketing Inc., The
1770 Corporate Dr., Ste. 500
Norcross, GA 30093

Steel Stallions Motorcycles
2500 Military Tr., #200
Boca Raton, FL 33431

Talking Book World
6692 Orchard Lake Rd.
West Bloomfield, MI 48322

Toy Traders Franchise Inc.
4334 Leland St.
Chevy Chase, MD 20815

Verlo Mattress Factory Stores
P.O. Box 298
Whitewater, WI 53190

Weekend Gardener, The
1600 Crossways Blvd., Unit D
Chesapeake, VA 23320

Wicks 'N' Sticks
P.O. Box 4586
Houston, TX 77210-4586

Travel Services

Admiral Of The Fleet Cruise Centers
3202 Meander Ln., Ste. A
Olympia, WA 98502

Cruiseone Inc.
10 Fairway Dr., Ste. 200
Deerfield Beach, FL 33441-1802

Kirby Tours Inc.
2451 S. Telegraph Rd.
Dearborn, MI 48124

Travel Agents International
9887 Fourth St. N.
St. Petersburg, FL 33702

Wildwood Travel Inc.
5218 Yonge St.
Toronto, ON M2N 5P6

Worldhotel
344 W. Main St.
Milford, CT 06460

INDEX OF FRANCHISING
PARTICIPANTS—ALPHABETICAL

Index of Franchising Participants by Category

413

417

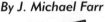

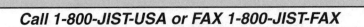

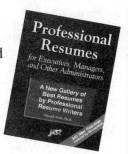

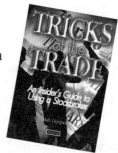

JIST Ordering Information

JIST specializes in publishing the very best results-oriented career and self-directed job search material. Since 1981 we have been a leading publisher in career assessment devices, books, videos, and software. We continue to strive to make our materials the best there are so that people can stay abreast of what's happening in the labor market, and so they can clarify and articulate their skills and experiences for themselves as well as for prospective employers. **Our products are widely available through your local bookstores, wholesalers, and distributors.**

The World Wide Web

For more occupational or book information, get online and see our Web site at **www.jist.com**. Advance information about new products, services, and training events is continually updated.

Quantity Discounts Available!

Quantity discounts are available for businesses, schools, and other organizations.

The JIST Guarantee

We want you to be happy with everything you buy from JIST. If you aren't satisfied with a product, return it to us within 30 days of purchase, along with the reason for the return. Please include a copy of the packing list or invoice to guarantee quick credit to your order.

How to Order

For your convenience, the last page of this book contains an order form.

24-Hour Consumer Order Line:
Call toll free 1-800-JIST-USA
Please have your credit card (VISA, MC, or AMEX) information ready!

Mail: Mail your order to:

JIST Works, Inc.
720 North Park Avenue
Indianapolis, IN 46202-3490
Fax: Toll free 1-800-JIST-FAX

JIST Order Form

Please copy this form if you need more lines for your order.

Purchase Order #: _____

Billing Information

Organization Name: _____

Accounting Contact: _____

Street Address: _____

_____

_____

City, State, Zip: _____

Phone Number: (   ) _____

Shipping Information (if different from above)

Organization Name: _____

Contact: _____

Street Address: (we *cannot* ship to P.O. boxes) _____

_____

_____

City, State, Zip: _____

Phone Number: (   ) _____

```
Phone:
1-800-JIST-USA
Fax: 1-800-JIST-FAX
```

Credit Card Purchases: VISA_____ MC_____ AMEX_____

Card Number: _____

Exp. date: _____

Name as on card: _____

Signature: _____

Quantity	Order Code	Product Title	Unit Price	Total

Subtotal	
+Sales Tax *Indiana Residents add 5% sales tax.*	
+Shipping / Handling *Add $3.00 for the first item and an additional $.50 for each item thereafter.*	
TOTAL	

JIST Works, Inc.
720 North Park Avenue
Indianapolis, IN 46202

JIST thanks you for your order!